# ESSENTIAL ECONOMICS

## Get Ahead of the Curve

**A Student Access Kit for MyEconLab for**
*Essential Economics* **puts this powerful tool at your fingertips.**

### The Power of Practice

MyEconLab puts you in control of your study, providing extensive practice exactly where and when you need it.

MyEconLab gives you unrivalled resources:

- ◆ **Sample Tests** for each chapter to see how much you have learned.
- ◆ A personalized **Study Plan**, which constantly adapts to your strengths and weaknesses.
- ◆ **Help Me Solve This** problem, which breaks the problem into its component steps and guides you through with hints.
- ◆ An advanced **Graphing Tool** integrated into the exercises enables you to make and manipulate graphs to get a better understanding of how concepts, numbers and graphs connect.
- ◆ **Animated Figures** from the textbook.
- ◆ **Pearson e-text**, a searchable electronic version of the textbook, allows you to study anywhere via the Internet.
- ◆ An **Online Glossary** defines key terms and provides examples.
- ◆ **Economics in the News** are questions arising from news items, which are updated weekly during the academic year.
- ◆ **Ask the Authors** enables you to obtain extra help from the authors via email.

See the Guided Tour on page xvi for more details.

If you don't have an access code, you can still access the resources by purchasing access online. Visit **www.myeconlab.com** for details.

# ESSENTIAL ECONOMICS

## PARKIN   POWELL   MATTHEWS

EUROPEAN EDITION

ALWAYS LEARNING

**PEARSON**

**Pearson Education Limited**
Edinburgh Gate
Harlow
Essex CM20 2JE
England

and Associated Companies throughout the world

*Visit us on the World Wide Web at:*
www.pearson.com/uk

**First published 2012**

© Pearson Education Limited 2012

Authorized for sale only in Europe, the Middle East and Africa.

ISBN 978-0-273-71897-0

**British Library Cataloguing-in-Publication Data**
A catalogue record for this book is available from the British Library

10 9 8 7 6 5 4 3 2 1
15 14 13 12

Typeset in 10/12.5pt Times by 35
Printed and bound by Rotolito Lombarda, Italy

# To Our Students

# About the Authors

**Michael Parkin** is Professor Emeritus in the Department of Economics at the University of Western Ontario, Canada, where he teaches the principles course to around 900 students each year. He studied economics at the University of Leicester but received his real training in the subject from an extraordinary group of economists at the University of Essex during the early 1970s. Professor Parkin has held faculty appointments at the Universities of Sheffield, Leicester, Essex and Manchester and visiting appointments at Brown University, Bond University, the Reserve Bank of Australia and the Bank of Japan. He is a past president of the Canadian Economics Association and has served on the editorial boards of the *American Economic Review* and the *Journal of Monetary Economics* and as managing editor of the *Manchester School* and the *Canadian Journal of Economics*. Professor Parkin's economic research has resulted in over 160 publications in journals and edited volumes, including the *American Economic Review*, the *Journal of Political Economy*, the *Review of Economic Studies*, the *Economic Journal*, *Economica*, the *Manchester School*, the *Journal of Monetary Economics* and the *Journal of Money, Credit and Banking*, and edited volumes. He became visible to the public through his work on inflation that discredited the use of prices and incomes policies.

**Melanie Powell** took her first degree at Kingston University and her MSc in economics at Birkbeck College, London University. She has been a research fellow in health economics at York University, a principal lecturer in economics at Leeds Metropolitan University, and the director of economic studies and part-time MBAs at the Leeds University Business School. She is now a Reader at the University of Derby, Derbyshire Business School. Her main interests as a microeconomist are in applied welfare economics, and she has many publications in the area of health economics and decision making. Her current research uses the experimental techniques of psychology applied to economic decision making.

**Kent Matthews** received his training as an economist at the London School of Economics, Birkbeck College University of London and the University of Liverpool. He is currently the Sir Julian Hodge Professor of Banking and Finance at the Cardiff Business School. He has held research appointments at the London School of Economics, the National Institute of Economic and Social Research, the Bank of England and Lombard Street Research Ltd, and faculty positions at the Universities of Liverpool, Western Ontario, Leuven, Liverpool John Moores and Humboldt Berlin. He is the author of eight books and over 60 papers in scholarly journals and edited volumes. His research interest is in applied macroeconomics and the economics of banking.

# Brief Contents

# Pathways through the Chapters

**Flexibility**

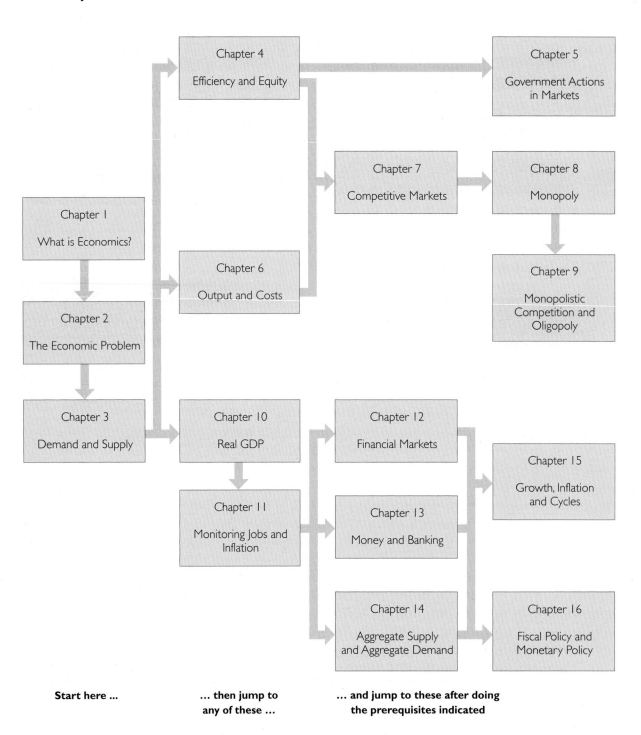

| | | |
|---|---|---|
| Chapter 4 | | Chapter 5 |
| Efficiency and Equity | | Government Actions in Markets |

| Chapter 7 | Chapter 8 |
|---|---|
| Competitive Markets | Monopoly |

| Chapter 1 |
|---|
| What is Economics? |

| Chapter 6 | Chapter 9 |
|---|---|
| Output and Costs | Monopolistic Competition and Oligopoly |

| Chapter 2 |
|---|
| The Economic Problem |

| Chapter 3 | Chapter 10 | Chapter 12 | Chapter 15 |
|---|---|---|---|
| Demand and Supply | Real GDP | Financial Markets | Growth, Inflation and Cycles |

| Chapter 11 | Chapter 13 |
|---|---|
| Monitoring Jobs and Inflation | Money and Banking |

| Chapter 14 | Chapter 16 |
|---|---|
| Aggregate Supply and Aggregate Demand | Fiscal Policy and Monetary Policy |

**Start here ...**          **... then jump to
any of these ...**          **... and jump to these after doing
the prerequisites indicated**

# Contents

### Part 4  Monitoring Business Conditions

# Guided Tour for Students

## Setting the Scene

**Learning Objectives** enable you to see exactly where the chapter is going and to set your goals before you begin the chapter. We link these goals directly to the chapter's major headings.

**Chapter Openers** motivate the topic and set the scene. We carry the introductory story into the main body of the chapter and return to it in the *Reading Between the Lines* or the *Business Case Study* at the end of the chapter.

# Using the Study Tools

Highlighted **Key Terms** within the text simplify your task of learning the vocabulary of economics. Each term appears in a list of **Key Terms** at the end of the chapter and in the **Glossary** at the end of the book. The terms are also highlighted in the index and can be found online in the MyEconLab glossary and Flashcards.

A government regulation that makes it illegal to charge a price higher than a specified level is called a **price ceiling** or **price cap**.

The effects of a price ceiling or crucially on whether the ceiling is that is above or below the equilibriu

**Price cap** A government regulation that sets the maximum price that may legally be charged. (p. 106)

**Price cap regulation** A regulation that specifies the highest price that the firm is permitted to set. (p. 193)

**Price ceiling** A government regulation that sets the maximum price that may

## Key Terms

Black market, 106
Minimum wage, 109
Price cap, 106
Price ceiling, 106
Price floor, 109
Price support, 119
Production quota, 117
Production subsidy, 118
Rent ceiling, 106
Search activity, 106
Tax incidence, 111

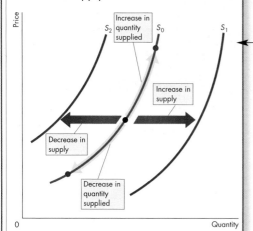

**Figure 3.6** A Change in the Quantity Supplied versus a Change in Supply

When the price of the good changes, there is a movement along the supply curve and a change in the quantity supplied, shown by the blue arrows on supply curve $S_0$.

When any other influence on selling plans changes, there is a shift of the supply curve and a change in supply. An increase in supply shifts the supply curve rightward (from $S_0$ to $S_1$), and a decrease in supply shifts the supply curve leftward (from $S_0$ to $S_2$).

myeconlab Animation

**Diagrams show where the economic action is!** Graphical analysis is the most powerful tool available for teaching and learning economics. We have developed the diagrams with the study and review needs of students in mind. Our diagrams feature:

◆ Original curves consistently shown in blue
◆ Shifted curves consistently shown in red
◆ Colour-blended arrows to suggest movement
◆ Other important features highlighted in red
◆ Graphs often paired with data tables
◆ Graphs labelled with boxed notes
◆ Extended captions that make each diagram and its caption a self-contained object for study and review
◆ Every diagram can be found with a step-by-step animation in MyEconLab.

A **Review Quiz** at the end of every major section is tied to the chapter's learning objectives and enables you to go over the material again to reinforce your understanding of a topic before moving on. More practice on the topics can be found in the **MyEconLab Study Plan**.

## Review Quiz

1 Define the quantity supplied of a good or service.
2 What is the law of supply and how do we illustrate it?
3 What does the supply curve tell us about the price at which firms will supply a given quantity of a good?
4 List all the influences on selling plans and for each influence say whether it changes supply.
5 What happens to the quantity of mobile phones supplied and the supply of mobile phones if the price of a mobile phone falls?

You can work these questions in Study Plan 3.3 and get instant feedback.  myeconlab

# Connecting with Reality

**Economics in Action Boxes** show you the connections between theory and real-world data or events. Tables and figures put the real-world flesh on the bones of the models and help you learn how to apply your newly gained knowledge of economic principles to the economic world around you.

## ECONOMICS IN ACTION

### Global Market for Crude Oil

The demand and supply model provides insights into all competitive markets. Here, we apply what you've learned about the effects of an increase in demand to the global market for crude oil.

Crude oil is like the life-blood of the global economy. It is used to fuel our cars, trucks, aeroplanes, trains and buses, to generate electricity and to produce a wide range of plastics. When the price of crude oil rises, the cost of transport, electricity and materials all increase.

In 2001, the price of a barrel of oil was $20 (using the value of money in 2010). In 2008, before the global financial crisis ended a long period of economic expansion, the price peaked at $127 a barrel. While the price of oil was rising, the quantity of oil produced and consumed also increased. In 2001, the world produced 65 million barrels of oil a day. By 2008, that quantity was 72 million barrels.

Who or what has been raising the price of oil? Oil producers might be greedy, and some of them might be big enough to withhold supply and raise the price. But it wouldn't be in their self-interest to do so for long. The higher price would soon bring forth a greater quantity supplied from other producers and the profit of the producer limiting supply would fall.

Oil producers could try to cooperate and jointly withhold supply. The Organization of Petroleum Exporting Countries, OPEC, is such a group of producers. But OPEC doesn't control the *world* supply and its members' self-interest is to produce the quantities that give them the maximum attainable profit.

constant along supply curve S. The demand for oil in 2001 was $D_{2001}$, so in 2001 the price was $20 a barrel and the quantity was 65 million barrels per day. The demand for oil increased and by 2008 it had reached $D_{2008}$. The price of oil increased to $127 a barrel and the quantity increased to 72 million barrels a day. The increase in the quantity is an *increase in the quantity supplied*, not an increase in supply.

Figure 1 The Global Market for Crude Oil

---

### Reading Between the Lines

#### Demand and Supply: The Price of Coffee

The Financial Times, 30 July 2010

**Coffee Surges on Poor Colombian Harvests**

*Javier Blas*

#### The Essence of the Story

#### Economic Analysis

**Reading Between the Lines** and **Business Case Study**

This Parkin, Powell and Matthews hallmark helps students think like economists by connecting chapter tools and concepts to the world around them. At the end of each chapter in Reading Between the Lines or a Business Case Study, students apply the tools they have just learned by analysing an article from a newspaper or news website or a real-world case. Each article or case sheds additional light on the questions first raised in the Chapter Opener. Questions about the article or case also appear with the end-of-chapter problems and applications.

---

Each chapter closes with a concise **Summary** organized by major topics, a list of **Key Terms** (with page references), **Study Plan Problems and Applications** and **Additional Problems and Applications**. All Study Plan problems are available in MyEconLab with instant feedback. All Additional problems are available in MyEconLab if assigned by your lecturer.

# Using MyEconLab

**MyEconLab** puts you in control of your study. By using MyEconLab, you can *test* your knowledge and *practise* to improve your understanding.

To register, go to **www.myeconlab.com** and follow the instructions on-screen using the code in your Student Access Kit. If you don't have an access code, you can buy one online. See **www.myeconlab.com** for details.

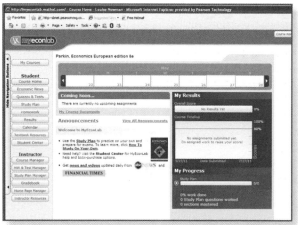

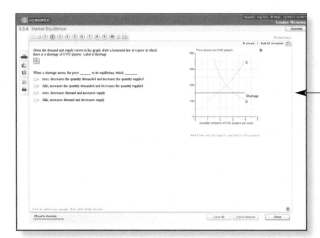

**Sample Tests** (two for each chapter) are preloaded in MyEconLab and enable you to test your understanding and identify the areas in which you need to do further work. Your lecturer might also create custom tests or quizzes.

MyEconLab creates a personal **Study Plan** for you based on your performance on the sample tests. The Study Plan diagnoses weaknesses and consists of a series of additional exercises with detailed feedback and 'Help Me Solve This' explanations for topics in which you need further help. The Study Plan is also linked to other study tools.

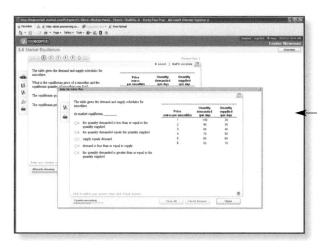

From the Study Plan exercises, you can link to **Help Me Solve This** (step-by-step explanations) and an **electronic version of your textbook** with all the **figures animated**.

# Note on MyEconLab for Lecturers

 ## Why MyEconLab?

If you are using MyEconLab, you, and your students, can access a wealth of resources at **www.myeconlab.com**. MyEconLab also provides you with an effective means of monitoring and testing your students.

 ## Lecturer Support

You can use MyEconLab in a wide variety of ways and spend no time or invest a great deal of time in tailoring it to your personal needs.

Pearson Education offers you personalized support for MyEconLab through its dedicated team of technology specialists. Their job is to support you in your use of all Pearson Education's media products, including MyEconLab.

To contact your technology specialist please go to **www.pearsoned.co.uk/replocator**.

 ## What Do I Need to Do?

Once your students have registered, they automatically have access to MyEconLab. Review the Guided Tour for Students on p. xvi. Students have access to Sample Tests, Study Plan and other resources, but you may choose:

◆ To monitor your students' performance
◆ To set assignments
◆ To create your own self-author exercises

### Monitor Your Students

To monitor your students' activity on MyEconLab you will need to set up a class group. Then MyEconLab's Gradebook automatically records each student's time spent and performance on the Tests and Study Plan and generates reports that you can organize either by student or by chapter. You can easily export data from the Gradebook into your own spreadsheet for combining with your exam and paper test marks.

### Set Assignments

You can use MyEconLab to build your own tests, quizzes or homework assignments from the question base provided. The questions include multiple choice, graph drawing and free response questions. Many of the questions are generated algorithmically so that they present differently each time they are used.

If you set assignments, you need to be aware of the distinction between a Test, Quiz and Homework.

A Test and a Quiz play like an examination with no help and no feedback. Use this format when you want to test your students and give credit for their performance.

Homework plays like the Study Plan exercises. It gives the student detailed feedback and links to Help Me Solve This, e-text and animated figures. Use this format when you want to check that your students have done some practice questions.

### Self-author Exercises

If you want to devote the time, you can create your own exercises by using the Econ Exercise Builder.

 ## Special Versions of MyEconLab

MyEconLab with CourseCompass places the resources inside a course management system. To find out more about the CourseCompass version go to **www.coursecompass.com**.

A MyEconLab Institutional Site licence is also available. Please contact your local Academic Sales Representative at **www.pearsoned.co.uk/replocator** for further details of these options.

# Preface

You know that throughout your life you will make economic decisions and be influenced by economic forces. You want to understand the economic principles that can help you navigate these forces and guide your decisions. *Essential Economics* is our attempt to satisfy this want.

Our goal is to teach you the economic way of thinking. Our focus is on the economic principles and models that enable you to function better in business and in life. The text covers the most important economic topics for a business student or a student just broadly interested in economic issues, but it presents the material with the same rigour you would meet if you were a specialist economics student.

Business is an art. Successful entrepreneurs envision products – goods or services – that people value more than the cost of delivering them. They also possess the skills, ingenuity and energy to convert their ideas into a large sustained positive cash flow.

Some of the skills they employ are technological and are based on engineering and science. Some are personal and based on the psychology of human relations and interactions. Some are financial and use the tools of accounting. And some are economic.

Economics is first and foremost a science. It was born a short 236 years ago in Scotland when Adam Smith first tried to work out what causes some nations to be wealthy and others poor. So from the start, the science of economics has been and remains a science of wealth and its creation.

And that is exactly what the art of business is about – creating wealth. You can think of the place of economics in business as being similar to that of physics in engineering. It is the foundation on which successful businesses are built.

The economics that you will learn in this book won't make you succeed in business. But it will improve your chances of doing so. It won't provide you with a checklist of things to do that will enhance business success, and it won't suggest any quick fixes for the business problems of today. Rather, it is an undiluted presentation of economic principles and models that will serve as a compass as you navigate the unknown future terrain through which your business life will take you.

This text draws on its parent text, *Economics*, now in its eighth edition, and on the many global editions of Parkin texts that are used by students of economics, accounting, business and finance throughout the world. Its teaching and learning features, tools and supplements also benefit from the legacy on which it draws.

We now briefly describe these tools and supplements.

 ## Features to Enhance Teaching and Learning

### Reading Between the Lines and Case Study

This Parkin, Powell and Matthews hallmark helps students think like economists by connecting chapter tools and concepts to the world around them. In *Reading Between the Lines* and *Case Study*, which appears at the end of each chapter, students apply the tools they have just learned by analysing an article from a newspaper or news website or a real-world case. Each article or case sheds additional light on the questions first raised in the Chapter Opener. Questions about the article or case also appear with the end-of-chapter problems and applications.

### Economics in Action Boxes

Each chapter contains carefully placed *Economics in Action* boxes, which address current events and economic data that amplify the topics covered in the chapter.

Instead of simply reporting the current events, the material in the boxes applies the event to an economics lesson, enabling students to see how economics plays a part in the world around them as they read through the chapter.

Some of the many issues covered in these boxes include the global markets for crude oil and wheat, the taxes paid by workers and consumers, how producing more cars can cut cost, Disney World's price discrimination, how the United Nations' Human Development Index measures economic wellbeing, how jobs change in recession and recovery, the size of fiscal stimulus multipliers, and Bank of England decision making.

 **For the Lecturer**

This book enables you to achieve three objectives in your principles course:

◆ Focus on the economic way of thinking
◆ Explain the issues and problems of our time
◆ Choose your own course structure

## Focus on the Economic Way of Thinking

You know how hard it is to encourage a student to think like an economist, but that is your goal. Consistent with this goal, the text focuses on and repeatedly uses the central ideas: choice; trade-off; opportunity cost; the margin; incentives; the gains from voluntary exchange; the forces of demand, supply and equilibrium; the pursuit of economic rent; the tension between self-interest and the social interest; and the scope and limitations of government actions.

## Explain the Issues and Problems of Our Time

Students must *use* the central ideas and tools if they are to begin to *understand* them. There is no better way to motivate students than by using the tools of economics to explain the issues that confront today's world. Issues such as the rising cost of food; how an Iceland volcano disrupted air transport; the emergence of no-frills airlines; Google's near-monopoly on Internet search; competition in tablet computers; the persistent unemployment; the challenges of fiscal policy that face many EU nations; and the challanges of monetary policy that face the Bank of England and the ECB.

## Choose Your Own Course Structure

You want to teach your own course. We have organized this book to enable you to do so. We demonstrate the book's flexibility in the flexibility chart on page viii that shows the alternative pathways through the chapters. By following the arrows through the chart you can select the path that best fits your preference for course structure. Whether you want to teach a traditional course

that blends theory and policy, or one that takes a fast-track through either theory or policy issues, *Essential Economics* gives you the choice.

## Lecturer's Support Tools

This book has the following support tools:

◆ Lecturer's manual
◆ Test banks
◆ PowerPoint resources
◆ MyEconLab

### Lecturer's Manual

Nicola Lynch and Eugen Mihaita of the University of Derby have created a Lecturer's Manual. Each chapter contains an outline, teaching suggestions, a look at where we have been and where we are going, a description of the electronic supplements, and additional discussion questions.

### Test Banks

Robin Bade edited all our Test Bank questions and created many new questions to ensure their clarity and consistency.

An electronic Test Bank provides 2,000 multiple-choice questions. This Test Bank is available in Test Generator Software (TestGen with QuizMaster). Fully networkable, it is available for Windows and Macintosh. TestGen's graphical interface enables lecturers to view, edit and add questions; transfer questions to tests; and print different forms of tests. Tests can be formatted with varying fonts and styles, margins and headers and footers, as in any word-processing document. Search and sort features let the lecturer quickly locate questions and arrange them in a preferred order. QuizMaster, working with your university's computer network, automatically marks the exams, stores the results on disk and allows the lecturer to view or print a variety of reports.

A pdf Test Bank provides a further 750 true-false and numerical questions.

Both Test Banks are available online to download from **www.myeconlab.com**

### PowerPoint Resources

Robin Bade has developed a Microsoft PowerPoint Lecture Presentation for each chapter that includes all the figures from the text, animated graphs, and speaking notes. The lecture notes in the Lecturer's Manual and the slide outlines are correlated, and the speaking notes are based on the Lecturer's Manual Teaching suggestions.

The PowerPoint resources also include a separate set of files that contain large-scale versions of all the text's figures (most of them animated). Use these to make your own presentations.

PowerPoint slides are available for Macintosh and Windows.

### Clicker-Questions in PowerPoint

Andrew Hunt of Durham University has created clicker-ready questions in PowerPoint. These slides are available in both Turning Point and PRS. The slides contain ten multiple-choice questions for each chapter that test the concepts introduced. Lecturers can use these questions as assignments or review quizzes during a lecture. The system also enables student responses to be captured in a gradebook.

### MyEconLab

MyEconLab is an online resource for your economics course. Its central features are a powerful graphing engine and large bank of questions for student study and lecturer testing. Lecturers can create and assign tests, quizzes or homework that incorporate graphing questions. MyEconLab saves lecturers time by automatically marking all questions and tracking results in an online gradebook.

Questions include multiple-choice, free response (usually numerical) and draw-graph. Many questions are generated algorithmically, so there is lots of variety and practice opportunity.

Every week during the academic year, we post a new *Economics in the News* item, with a news headline and a link to a news article. We also provide links to websites where further information about the topic in the article can be found. We also provide a number of questions that can be assigned as topics for essays or as discussion during lectures. These news questions are available in MyEconLab.

The electronic Test Bank is preloaded into MyEconLab, which gives lecturers ample material from which they can create assignments, tests and quizzes.

The Lecturer's Manual and the PowerPoint Resources are available on MyEconLab. 'Ask the Authors' feature gives lecturers the opportunity to communicate with the authors via email.

A Note on MyEconLab for Lecturers on p. xx provides additional information. To request an Instructor Access Code for MyEconLab, visit **www.myeconlab.com**

## For the Student

Two outstanding support tools for the student are:

◆ MyEconLab
◆ PowerPoint Notes

## MyEconLab

Optimize your study time with MyEconLab, our online assessment and tutorial system. When you take a sample test online, MyEconLab gives you targeted feedback and a personalized Study Plan to identify the topics that you need to review.

The Study Plan consists of practice problems taken directly from the end-of-chapter Study Plan Problems and Applications and the Review Quiz in the textbook.

The Study Plan gives you unlimited opportunity to practise. And as you work each exercise, instant feedback helps you understand and apply the concepts. Many Study Plan exercises contain algorithmically generated values to ensure that you get as much practice as you need.

Study Plan exercises link to the following learning resources:

1  Step-by-step *Help Me Solve This* help you to break down a problem much the same way as a lecturer would during a class. These are available for selected problems.

2  Links to the *Pearson e-Text* promote reading of the text when you need to revisit a concept or explanation.

3  *Animated graphs* appeal to a variety of learning styles.

4  A *graphing tool* enables you to build and manipulate graphs to better understand how concepts, numbers and graphs connect.

For more details on how to use MyEconLab, see the Guided Tour for Students on pp. xvi–xix. If you don't have an access code, you can still access the resources by purchasing access online. Visit **www.myeconlab.com** for details.

## PowerPoint Notes

Robin Bade has prepared a set of Microsoft PowerPoint Notes for students. These notes contain an outline of each chapter with the textbook figures animated. Students can download these PowerPoint Notes from MyEconLab, print them, bring them to the lecture and use them to create their own set of study notes.

## Acknowledgements

We extend our gratitude and thanks to the many people who have contributed to this new edition of our text and to all those who made such important contributions to the previous editions on which this one is based. So many people have provided help and encouragement either directly or indirectly that it is impossible to name them all.

We particularly thank our colleagues, present and past, who have helped to shape our understanding of economics and who have provided help in the creation of this new edition. We thank our reviewers who have read and commented on our work and provided countless good ideas that we have eagerly accepted. We also thank our families for their input and patience.

We especially acknowledge and express our deep gratitude to Robin Bade whose innovative work on the most recent Canadian edition has been invaluable to us. We also thank Robin for her meticulous reading of this edition and for the uncountable, some detailed and some major, improvements she has brought to it.

We thank Richard Parkin for his work on the graphics, both in the text and on MyEconLab.

We thank Nicola Lynch and Eugen Mihaita of the University of Derby for their work (with Melanie) on the Lecturer's Manual and Andrew Hunt of Durham University for his work on the Test Banks.

We thank Jeannie Gillmore and Laurel Davies for their work on MyEconLab test questions.

We could not have produced this book without the help of the people for whom it is written, our students. We thank the several thousand students we have been privileged to teach over many years. Their comments on previous editions (and on our teaching) whether in complaint or praise have been invaluable.

Nor could we have produced this book without the help of our publisher. We thank the many outstanding editors, media specialists, and others at Pearson Education who contributed to the concerted publishing effort that brought this edition to completion. They are: Rachel Gear, Editorial Director; Kate Brewin, Publisher; Joe Vella, Managing Editor; Philippa Fiszzon, Senior Editor; Jonathon Price, Copy Editor; Lionel Browne, Proofreader; Kevin Ancient, Design Manager; Nicola Woowat, Designer; Kay Holman, Senior Production Controller; Summa Verbeek, Marketing Manager; and Katie Eyles, Media Development Editor, and Louise Hammond, Media Producer, who managed the development of the online resources.

Finally, we want to thank our reviewers. A good textbook is the distillation of the collective wisdom of a generation of dedicated teachers. We have been privileged to tap into this wisdom. We extend our thanks to Douglas Chalmers, Glasgow Caledonian University; Gary Cook, University of Liverpool; Steve Cook, Swansea University; Adrian Darnell, Durham University; Valerie Dickie, Heriot-Watt University; M. J. McCrostie, University of Buckingham; Maria Gil Molto, Loughborough University; Karen Jackson, University of Bradford; Gorm Jacobsen, Agder University, Norway; Chris Reid, University of Portsmouth; Kevin Reilly, Leeds University; Cillian Ryan, University of Birmingham; Jen Snowball, Rhodes University, South Africa; Phil Tomlinson, University of Bath; Gonzolo Varela, University of Sussex; and Robert Wright, Strathclyde University. We also thank other reviewers who have asked to remain anonymous.

As always, the proof of the pudding is in the eating! The value of this book will be decided by its users and, whether you are a student or a teacher, we encourage you to send us your comments and suggestions.

*Michael Parkin*,
University of Western Ontario,
michael.parkin@uwo.ca

*Melanie Powell*
University of Derby,
m.j.powell@derby.ac.uk

*Kent Matthews*,
Cardiff University,
MatthewsK@Cardiff.ac.uk

# What Is Economics?

**After studying this chapter you will be able to:**

◆ Define economics and distinguish between microeconomics and macroeconomics
◆ Explain the big questions of economics
◆ Explain the key ideas that define the economic way of thinking
◆ Describe how economists go about their work as social scientists and policy advisers

You are studying economics at a time when the world's richest nations are recovering from a deep recession in which incomes shrank and millions of jobs were lost. At the same time some poorer nations, Brazil, China, India and Russia, are growing rapidly and playing ever-greater roles in an expanding global economy. In these turbulent times, new businesses are born and old ones die, new jobs are created and old ones disappear.

To face these challenges and seize new opportunities, you need to understand the powerful forces at play. The economics that you're about to learn will be your most reliable guide. In this chapter you will find out about the questions economists ask, the way they think and the way they search for answers.

## A Definition of Economics

All economic questions arise because we want more than we can get. We want a peaceful and secure world. We want clean air and rivers. We want long and healthy lives. We want good schools and universities. We want space and comfort in our homes. We want a huge range of sports and recreational gear from running shoes to motor bikes. We want the time to enjoy sports and games, read books and magazines, see films, listen to music, travel and so on.

What each one of us can get is limited by time, by the income we earn and by the prices we must pay. Everyone ends up with some unsatisfied wants. As a society, what we can get is limited by our productive resources. These resources include the gifts of nature, human labour and ingenuity and tools and equipment that we have produced.

Our inability to satisfy all our wants is called **scarcity**. The poor and the rich alike face scarcity. A child in Tanzania is hungry and thirsty because her parents can't afford food and the well in her village is dirty and almost empty. The scarcity that she faces is clear and disturbing. But even David Beckham, a multi-millionaire, faces scarcity. He wants to spend the weekend playing football *and* filming an advert, but he can't do both. We face scarcity as a society. We want to provide better healthcare *and* better education *and* a cleaner environment and so on. Scarcity is everywhere. Even parrots face scarcity!

Faced with scarcity, we must *choose* among the available alternatives. The child in Tanzania must *choose* dirty water and scraps of bread or go thirsty and hungry. David Beckham must *choose* the football *or* the filming. As a society, we must *choose* among healthcare, education and the environment.

The choices that we make depend on the incentives that we face. An **incentive** is a reward that encourages or a penalty that discourages an action. If heavy rain fills the well, the child in Tanzania has an *incentive* to choose more water. If the fee received from filming is £1 million, David Beckham has an incentive to skip the football and make the advert. If computer prices tumble, we have an *incentive* as a society to connect more schools to the Internet.

**Economics** is the social science that studies the *choices* that individuals, businesses, governments and entire societies make as they cope with *scarcity* and the *incentives* that influence and reconcile those choices. The subject divides into two main parts:

◆ Microeconomics
◆ Macroeconomics

## Microeconomics

**Microeconomics** is the study of the choices that individuals and businesses make, the way these choices interact in markets and the influence of governments. Some examples of microeconomic questions are: Why are people buying more mobile phones? How would a tax on downloading music affect the sales of CDs?

## Macroeconomics

**Macroeconomics** is the study of the performance of the national economy and the global economy. Some examples of macroeconomic questions are: Why did unemployment increase in 2008 and 2009? Why did Japan's economy stagnate during the 1990s? Can the Bank of England bring prosperity by keeping interest rates low?

***Not only do I want a cracker – we all want a cracker!***

©Frank Modell/The New Yorker Collection/www.cartoonbank.com

### Review Quiz

1   List some examples of scarcity that you face.
2   Find examples of scarcity in today's headlines.
3   Find an illustration of the distinction between microeconomics and macroeconomics in today's headlines.

You can work these questions in Study Plan 1.1 and get instant feedback.

# Two Big Economic Questions

Two big questions summarize the scope of economics:

◆ How do choices end up determining *what*, *how* and *for whom* goods and services get produced?

◆ When do choices made in the pursuit of *self-interest* also promote the *social interest*?

## What, How and For Whom?

**Goods and services** are the objects that people value and produce to satisfy wants. Goods are physical objects such as golf balls. Services are actions performed such as cutting hair and filling teeth. By far the largest part of what people in the rich industrial countries produce today are services such as retail and wholesale services, health services and education. Goods are a small and decreasing part of what we produce.

### What?

What we produce changes over time. Every year, new technologies allow us to build better equipped homes, higher-performance sporting equipment and even deliver a more pleasant experience in the dentist's chair. And technological advance makes us incredibly more productive at producing food and manufacturing goods.

Figure 1.1 shows some trends in what we produce in the UK. It highlights five items that have expanded and three that have shrunk since 2001. What are the forces that bring these changes in what we produce? Why are we producing more construction output and services such as health, education, finance and transport? Why are we producing fewer manufactured goods and doing less mining?

### How?

Goods and services get produced by using productive resources that economists call **factors of production**. Factors of production are grouped into four categories:

◆ Land

◆ Labour

◆ Capital

◆ Entrepreneurship

### Land

The 'gifts of nature' that we use to produce goods and services are called **land**. In economics, land is what in

**Figure 1.1**   Changes in What We Produce

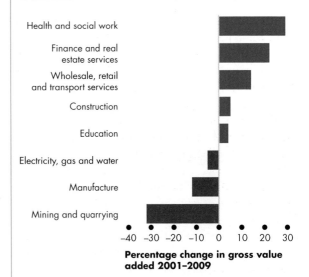

**Percentage change in gross value added 2001–2009**

The production of many services has expanded, while mining and manufacture have shrunk.

Source of data: Office for National Statistics, *Change in Gross Value Added by Industry*.

myeconlab Animation

everyday language we call *natural resources*. It includes land in the everyday sense together with metal ores, oil, gas and coal, water, air, wind and sunshine.

Our land surface and water resources are renewable and some of our mineral resources can be recycled. But the resources that we use to create energy are non-renewable – they can be used only once.

### Labour

The work time and work effort that people devote to producing goods and services is called **labour**. Labour includes the physical and the mental efforts of all the people who work on farms and construction sites and in factories, shops and offices.

The *quality* of labour depends on **human capital**, which is the knowledge and skill that people obtain from education, on-the-job training and work experience. You are building your own human capital today as you work on your economics course, and your human capital will continue to grow as you become better at your job.

Human capital expands over time and varies between countries. Figure 1.2 shows the proportion of young people entering post-secondary education and the growth in this measure since 2000 as a measure of human capital in different countries.

**Figure 1.2    A Measure of Human Capital**

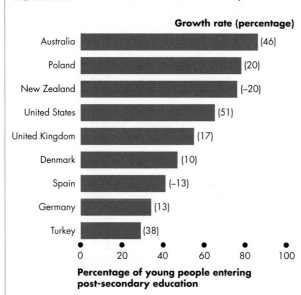

College and university education is a major source of human capital. The figure shows the percentage of young people entering post-secondary education in nine countries in 2007 and its growth rate since 2000. Although Australia has the highest entry rate at 86 per cent and Turkey the lowest at 29 per cent, both countries have a high growth rate of human capital, while New Zealand and Spain have a falling rate.

Source of data: OECD, *Education at a Glance 2009*, Table A2.5.

### Capital

The tools, instruments, machines, buildings and other constructions that businesses now use to produce goods and services are called **capital**.

In everyday language, we talk about money, shares and bonds as being capital. These items are *financial capital*. Financial capital plays an important role in enabling businesses to borrow the funds that they use to buy capital. But financial capital is not used to produce goods and services – it is not a factor of production.

### Entrepreneurship

The human resource that organizes labour, land and capital is called **entrepreneurship**. Entrepreneurs come up with new ideas about what and how to produce, make business decisions and bear the risks that arise from these decisions.

How are the quantities of factors of production that get used to produce the many different goods and services determined?

### For Whom?

Who gets the goods and services that are produced depends on the incomes that people earn. A large income enables a person to buy large quantities of goods and services. A small income leaves a person with few options and small quantities of goods and services.

People earn their incomes by selling the services of the factors of production they own:

1  Land earns **rent**.
2  Labour earns **wages**.
3  Capital earns **interest**.
4  Entrepreneurship earns **profit**.

Which factor of production earns the most income? The answer is labour. Wages and fringe benefits are around 70 per cent of total income. Land, capital and entrepreneurship share the rest. These percentages have been remarkably constant over time.

Knowing how income is shared among the factors of production doesn't tell us how it is shared among individuals. You know of lots of people who earn very large incomes. J. K. Rowling earns more than £20 million a year and David Beckham will make $US250 million over five years.

You know of even more people who earn very small incomes. People who serve fast food earn £5 an hour.

Some differences in income are persistent. On average, men earn more than women and whites earn more than ethnic minorities. Europeans earn more on average than Asians who in turn earn more than Africans. A typical annual income in the poorest countries of the world is just a few hundred pounds, less than the equivalent of a typical weekly wage in the richest countries of the world.

Why is the distribution of income so unequal? Why do women earn less than men? Why do J. K. Rowling and David Beckham earn such huge incomes? Why do university graduates earn more than people with only a few GCSEs? Why do Europeans earn more than Africans? Why are the incomes of Asians rising so rapidly?

Economics provides answers to all these questions about what, how and for whom goods and services get produced. And you will discover these answers as you progress with your study of the subject.

The second big question of economics that we'll now examine is a harder question both to appreciate and to answer.

## When Is the Pursuit of Self-interest in the Social Interest?

Every day, you and 465 million other EU citizens, along with 6.9 billion people in the rest of the world, make economic choices that result in *what*, *how* and *for whom* goods and services get produced.

### Self-interest

A choice is in your **self-interest** if you think that choice is the best one available for you. You make most of your choices in your self-interest. You use your time and other resources in the ways that make the most sense to you, and you don't think too much about how your choices affect other people. Think about when you order a pizza to be delivered to your home. You order the pizza because you are hungry and you don't order it thinking that the delivery person needs an income. When the pizza arrives, the delivery person is not doing you a favour but is working in his or her self-interest.

### Social Interest

A choice is in the **social interest** if it leads to an outcome that is the best for society as a whole. The social interest has two dimensions: efficiency and equity (or fairness). What is best for society is an efficient and fair use of resources.

Economists say that **efficiency** is achieved when the available resources are used to produce goods and services at the lowest possible cost and in the quantities that will give the greatest possible value or benefit. You will study the concept of efficiency in more detail in Chapter 5. For now, just think of efficiency as a situation in which resources are put to their best possible use.

Equity or fairness doesn't have a precise definition. Reasonable people, including economists, have a variety of views about what is fair. There is always room for some disagreement and a need to be careful and clear about which notion of fairness is being used.

### The Big Question

Now let's ask whether we can organize our economic lives so that when each one of us makes a choice in our self-interest, we actually promote the social interest. Can trading in free markets achieve this social interest? Do we need government action to help achieve the social interest? Do we need international cooperation and treaties to help achieve the social interest?

Questions about the social interest are hard ones to answer and they generate a lot of discussion, debate and disagreement. Let's take a closer look at these questions with four examples:

◆ Globalization
◆ The information-age economy
◆ Climate change
◆ Economic stability and financial crisis

### Globalization

The term *globalization* means the expansion of international trade, borrowing and lending and investment.

Globalization is in the self-interest of consumers because they can buy low-cost goods and services produced in other countries. It is also in the self-interest of the multinational firms that produce in low-cost regions and sell in high-price regions. But is globalization in the self-interest of the low-wage workers in India who are sewing the sequins on your low-cost top or in the interest of displaced clothing workers in London? Is it in the social interest?

### ECONOMICS IN ACTION

## Life in a Small and Ever-shrinking World

When high-street fashion shops produce this season's clothes, people in India get low-paid work; and when China Airlines buys new aeroplanes, British workers at Rolls-Royce in Derby build their engines. While globalization brings expanded production and job opportunities for some workers, it also destroys jobs. New jobs in India means workers in Europe's clothing manufacturing industries must learn new skills, take lower-paid service jobs or retire earlier than previously planned.

## The Information-age Economy

The technological change of the past 40 years has been called the *Information Revolution*.

The Information Revolution has clearly served your self-interest: it has provided your mobile phone, laptop, the latest applications and the Internet. It has also served the self-interest of Bill Gates of Microsoft and Gordon Moore of Intel, both of whom have seen their wealth soar.

But did the Information Revolution best serve the social interest? Did Microsoft produce the best possible Windows operating system and sell it at a price that was in the social interest? Did Intel make the right quality of microchips and sell them in the right quantities at the right prices? Was the quality too low and the prices too high? Would the social interest have been better served if Microsoft and Intel had faced competition from other firms?

## Climate Change

Climate change is a huge political issue today. Every serious political leader is acutely aware of the problem and of the popularity of having proposals that might lower carbon emissions to reduce the impact of climate change. Every day you make self-interested choices to use electricity, petrol and diesel, but you also create carbon emissions; you leave your carbon footprint. You can lessen your carbon footprint by walking, riding a bike, taking a cold shower, or planting a tree. But can we rely upon the self-interested decisions of every individual to make decisions that affect the earth's carbon-dioxide concentration in the social interest? Should governments change the incentives we face so that our self-interested choices are also in the social interest? How can governments change incentives? How can we discourage the use of fossil fuels and encourage the use of alternatives such as wind and solar power?

### ECONOMICS IN ACTION

## Microchips and Windows

Gordon Moore, who founded the chip-maker Intel, and Bill Gates, a co-founder of Microsoft, held privileged positions in the *Information Revolution*.

For many years, Intel chips were the only available chips and Windows was the only available operating system for the original IBM PC and its clones. The PC and Apple's Mac competed, but the PC has a huge market share.

An absence of competition gave Intel and Microsoft the power and ability to sell their products at prices far above the cost of production. If the prices of microchips and Windows had been lower, more people would have been able to afford a computer and would have chosen to buy one.

### ECONOMICS IN ACTION

## Greenhouse Gas Emissions

Burning fossil fuels to generate electricity and to power aeroplanes and motor vehicles pours a staggering 28 billion tonnes – 4 tonnes per person – of carbon dioxide into the atmosphere each year.

Two thirds of the world's carbon emissions are produced in the US, China, the EU, Russia and India. The fastest growing emissions are from India and China. The amount of global warming caused by economic activity and its effects are uncertain, but the emissions continue to grow and pose huge risks for climate change and our future.

### Economic Stability and Financial Crisis

The years between 1993 and 2007 were a period of remarkable economic stability, so much so that they've been called the Great Moderation. During those years, European and global economies were booming. Incomes in the US increased by 30 per cent and incomes in China tripled. Even the economic shock waves of 9/11 brought only a small dip in the strong pace of US and global economic growth. But in August 2007, a period of financial stress began. A bank in France was the first to feel the pain that soon would grip the entire global financial system.

## ECONOMICS IN ACTION

## Financial Crisis

Flush with funds and offering record low interest rates, banks went on a lending spree to home buyers. Rapidly rising home prices made home owners feel well off and they were happy to borrow and spend. Banks then bundled their home loans into new assets or securities that were sold and resold to other banks around the world to generate cash for more loans.

In 2006, interest rates began to rise and the rate of rise in home prices slowed and some borrowers defaulted on their loans. What started as a trickle became a flood. As more people defaulted, banks faced losses totalling billions of pounds by mid-2007.

Global credit markets stopped working as banks would not lend to each other or to businesses. Some retail banks faced collapse as depositors raced to withdraw their cash. People began to fear the financial crisis would lead to a prolonged slowdown in economic activity like the Great Depression of the 1930s. Central banks, including the Bank of England, determined to avoid a catastrophe, started lending on a very large scale to the troubled banks.

Banks take in people's deposits and get more funds by borrowing from each other and from other firms. Banks use these funds to make loans. All the banks' choices to borrow and lend and the choices of people and businesses to lend to and borrow from banks are made in self-interest. But does this lending and borrowing serve the social interest? Is there too much borrowing and lending that needs to be reined in, or is there too little and a need to stimulate more?

When the banks got into trouble, the Bank of England and the European Central Bank bailed them out with big loans backed by the taxpayers. Did the Bank of England's bailout of troubled banks like Lloyds TSB serve the social interest? Did the Bank of England's rescue action just allow banks to repeat their dangerous lending in the future?

Banks weren't the only recipients of public funds. Some European governments supported their motor industries with a 'scrappage' scheme to encourage the purchase of new cars. Government support of the motor industry served the European motor industry self-interest. Did the scheme also serve the social interest?

## Review Quiz

1  Describe the broad facts about *what, how* and *for whom* goods and services are produced.
2  Define the four factors of production and give an example of each one. What is the income earned by the people who sell the services of each of these factors of production?
3  Distinguish between self-interest and the social interest.
4  Use headlines from the recent news stories to illustrate the potential for conflict between self-interest and social interest.

You can work these questions in Study Plan 1.2 and get instant feedback.

We've looked at four topics and asked many questions that illustrate the big question: Can choices made in the pursuit of self-interest also promote the social interest? We've asked questions but not answered them because we've not yet explained the economic principles needed to do so.

By working through this book, you will discover the economic principles that help economists figure out when the social interest is being served, when it is not and what might be done when it is not being served.

**The Economic Way of Thinking**

The questions that economics tries to answer tell us about the scope of economics, but they don't tell us how economists think and go about seeking answers to these questions. You're now going to see how economists go about their work.

We're going to look at six key ideas that define the economic way of thinking. These ideas are:

◆ A choice is a *trade-off*.

◆ People make *rational choices* by comparing benefits and costs.

◆ *Benefit* is what you gain from something.

◆ Cost is what you *must give up* to get something.

◆ Most choices are 'how-much' choices made at the *margin*.

◆ Choices respond to *incentives*.

## A Choice Is a Trade-off

Because we face scarcity, we must make choices. And when we make a choice, we select from the available alternatives. For example, you can spend Saturday night studying for your next economics test or having fun with your friends, but you can't do both of these activities at the same time. You must choose how much time to devote to each. Whatever choice you make, you could have chosen something else.

You can think about your choice as a trade-off. A **trade-off** is an exchange – giving up one thing to get something else. When you choose how to spend your Saturday night, you face a trade-off between studying and hanging out with your friends.

## Making a Rational Choice

Economists view the choices that people make as rational. A **rational choice** is one that compares costs and benefits and achieves the greatest benefit over cost for the person making the choice.

Only the wants of the person making a choice are relevant to determine its rationality. For example, you might like your coffee black and strong but your friend prefers his milky and sweet. So it is rational for you to choose espresso and for your friend to choose cappuccino.

The idea of rational choice provides an answer to the first question: What goods and services will be

produced and in what quantities? The answer is those that people rationally choose to buy!

But how do people choose rationally? Why do more people choose an iPod rather than a Creative? Why has the UK government chosen to improve the A1 and M1 motorways joining the North and the South rather than build a new rail track? The answers turn on comparing benefits and costs.

## Benefit: What You Gain

The **benefit** of something is the gain or pleasure that it brings and is determined by **preferences** – by what a person likes and dislikes and the intensity of those feelings. If you get a huge kick out of updating your Facebook page every day, that activity brings you a large benefit. If you have little interest in listening to a news podcast, that activity brings you a small benefit.

Some benefits are large and easy to identify, such as the benefit that you get from being at university. A big piece of that benefit is the goods and services that you will be able to enjoy with the boost to your earning power when you graduate. Some benefits are small, such as the benefit you get from a slice of pizza.

Economists measure benefit as the most that a person is willing to give up to get something. You are willing to give up a lot to be at university but you would give up only an iTunes download for a slice of pizza.

## Cost: What You *Must* Give Up

The **opportunity cost** of something is the highest-valued alternative that must be given up to get it.

To make the idea of opportunity cost clear, think about your opportunity cost of being at university. It has two components: the things you can't afford to buy and the things you can't do with your time.

Start with the things you can't afford to buy. You've spent all your available income on tuition, residence fees, books and a laptop. If you weren't at university, you would have spent this money on going to clubs and films and all the other things that you enjoy. But that's only the start of your opportunity cost. You've also given up the opportunity to get a job. Suppose that the best job you could get if you weren't at university is working at HSBC as a trainee earning £18,000 a year. Another part of your opportunity cost of being at university is all the things that you could buy with the extra £18,000 you would have.

As you well know, being a student eats up many hours in class time, doing homework assignments, preparing for tests and so on. To do all these school activities, you must give up many hours of what would otherwise be leisure time spent with your friends. So the opportunity cost of being at university is all the good things that you can't afford and don't have the spare time to enjoy. You might want to put a value on that cost or you might just list all the items that make up the opportunity cost.

The examples of opportunity cost that we've just considered are all-or-nothing costs – you're either at university or not at university. Most situations are not like this one. They involve choosing *how much* of an activity to do.

## How Much? Choosing at the Margin

You can allocate the next hour between studying and emailing your friends. But the choice is not all or nothing. You must decide how many minutes to allocate to each activity. To make this decision, you compare the benefit of a little bit more study time with its cost – you make your choice at the **margin**.

The benefit that arises from an increase in an activity is called **marginal benefit**. For example, your marginal benefit from one more night of study before a test is the boost it gives to your grade. Your marginal benefit doesn't include the grade you're already achieving without that extra night of work.

The *opportunity cost* of an *increase* in an activity is called **marginal cost**. For you, the marginal cost of studying one more night is the cost of not spending that night on your favourite leisure activity.

To make your decisions, you compare marginal benefit against the marginal cost. If the marginal benefit from an extra night of study exceeds its marginal cost, you study the extra night. If the marginal cost exceeds the marginal benefit, you don't study the extra night.

## Choices Respond to Incentives

Economists take human nature as given and view people as acting in their self-interest. All people – consumers, producers, politicians and civil servants – pursue their self-interest.

Self-interested actions are not necessarily *selfish* actions. You might decide to use your resources in ways that bring pleasure to others as well as to yourself. But a self-interested act gets the most value for *you* based on *your* view about benefit.

The central idea of economics is that we can predict the self-interested choices that people make by looking at the *incentives* they face. People undertake those activities for which marginal benefit exceeds marginal cost and reject those for which marginal cost exceeds marginal benefit.

For example, your economics lecturer gives you a problem set and tells you these problems will be on the next test. Your marginal benefit from working on these problems is large, so you work hard on them. In contrast, your statistics lecturer gives you a problem set on a topic that she says will never be on a test. You get little marginal benefit from working on these problems, so you decide to skip most of them.

Economists see incentives as the key to reconciling self-interest and social interest. When our choices are not in the social interest, it is because of the incentives we face. One of the challenges for economists is to figure out when the incentives that result in self-interested choices are also in the social interest.

Economists emphasize the crucial role that institutions play in influencing the incentives that people face as they pursue their self-interest. Private property protected by a system of laws and markets that enable voluntary exchange are the fundamental institutions. You will learn as you progress with your study of economics that where these institutions exist, self-interest can indeed promote the social interest.

### Review Quiz

1   Explain the idea of a trade-off and think of three trade-offs that you made today.
2   Explain what economists mean by rational choice and think of three choices that you've made today that are rational.
3   Explain why opportunity cost is the best forgone alternative and provide examples of some opportunity costs that you have faced today.
4   Explain what it means to choose at the margin and illustrate with three choices at the margin that you have made today.
5   Explain why choices respond to incentives and think of three incentives to which you have responded today.

You can work these questions in Study Plan 1.3 and get instant feedback.

## Economics as a Social Science and Policy Tool

Economics is a social science and a toolkit for advising on policy decisions.

## Economist as Social Scientist

As social scientists, economists seek to discover how the economic world works. In pursuit of this goal, like all scientists, economists distinguish between positive and normative statements.

### Positive Statements

A *positive* statement is about what is. It says what is currently believed about the way the world operates. A positive statement might be right or wrong, but we can test it by checking it against the facts. 'Our planet is warming because of the amount of coal that we're burning' is a positive statement. We can test whether it is right or wrong.

A central task of economists is to test positive statements about how the economic world works and to weed out those that are wrong. Economics first got off the ground in the late 1700s, so it is a young science compared with, for example, physics, and much remains to be discovered.

### Normative Statements

A normative statement is about *what ought to be*. It depends on values and cannot be tested. Policy goals are normative statements. For example, 'We ought to cut our use of coal by 50 per cent' is a normative policy statement. You may agree or disagree with it, but you can't test it. It doesn't assert a fact that can be checked.

### Unscrambling Cause and Effect

Economists are particularly interested in positive statements about cause and effect. Are computers getting cheaper because people are buying them in greater quantities? Or are people buying computers in greater quantities because they are getting cheaper? Or is some third factor causing both the price of a computer to fall and the quantity of computers bought to increase?

To answer such questions, economists create and test economic models. An **economic model** is a description of some aspect of the economic world that includes only those features that are needed for the purpose at hand.

For example, an economic model of a mobile-phone network might include features such as the prices of calls, the number of mobile phone users and the volume of calls. But the model would ignore mobile-phone colours and ringtones.

A model is tested by comparing its predictions with the facts. However, testing an economic model is difficult because we observe the outcomes of the simultaneous change of many factors. To cope with this problem, economists look for natural experiments (situations in the ordinary course of economic life in which the one factor of interest is different and other things are equal or similar); conduct statistical investigations to find correlations; and perform economic experiments by putting people in decision-making situations and varying the influence of one factor at a time to discover how they respond.

## Economist as Policy Adviser

Economics is useful. It is a toolkit for advising governments and businesses and for making personal decisions. Some of the most famous economists work partly as policy advisers.

For example, Sir Alan Budd, who was Provost of The Queen's College, Oxford University until 2008, was the first Chair of the UK government's new Office for Budget Responsibility in 2010. He has also been an economic adviser to the UK Treasury, Barclays Bank and Credit Suisse First Boston as well as many other economic organizations.

All the policy questions on which economists provide advice involve a blend of the positive and the normative. Economics can't help with the normative part – the policy goal. But for a given goal, economics provides a method of evaluating alternative solutions – comparing marginal benefits and marginal costs and finding the solution that makes the best use of available resources.

 **Review Quiz**

1 Distinguish between a positive statement and a normative statement and provide examples.
2 What is an economic model? Can you think of a model that you might use in your everyday life? Describe it.
3 How do economists try to disentangle cause and effect?
4 How is economics used as a policy tool?

You can work these questions in Study Plan 1.4 and get instant feedback.

## SUMMARY

## Key Points

### A Definition of Economics (p. 2)

◆ All economic questions arise from scarcity – from the fact that wants exceed the resources available to satisfy them.

◆ Economics is the social science that studies the choices people make as they cope with scarcity.

◆ The subject divides into microeconomics and macroeconomics.

Working Problem 1 will give you a better understanding of the definition of economics.

### Two Big Economic Questions (pp. 3–7)

◆ Two big questions summarize the scope of economics:

 1 How do choices end up determining what, how and for whom goods and services get produced?

 2 When do choices made in the pursuit of self-interest also promote the social interest?

Working Problems 2 and 3 will give you a better understanding of the two big questions of economics.

### The Economic Way of Thinking (pp. 8–9)

◆ Every choice is a trade-off – exchanging more of something for less of something else.

◆ People make rational choices by comparing benefit and cost.

◆ Cost – opportunity cost – is what you must give up to get something.

◆ Most choices are 'how much' choices made at the *margin* by comparing marginal benefit and marginal cost.

◆ Choices respond to incentives.

Working Problems 4 and 5 will give you a better understanding of the economic way of thinking.

### Economics as a Social Science and Policy Tool (p. 10)

◆ Economists distinguish between positive statements – what is – and normative statements – what ought to be.

◆ To explain the economic world, economists create and test economic models.

◆ Economics is a tool-kit used to provide advice on government, business and personal economic decisions.

Working Problem 6 will give you a better understanding of economics as a social science and policy tool.

## Key Terms

Benefit, 8
Capital, 4
Economic model, 10
Economics, 2
Efficiency, 5
Entrepreneurship, 4
Factors of production, 3
Goods and services, 3
Human capital, 3
Incentive, 2
Interest, 4
Labour, 3
Land, 3
Macroeconomics, 2
Margin, 9
Marginal benefit, 9
Marginal cost, 9
Microeconomics, 2
Opportunity cost, 8
Preferences, 8
Profit, 4
Rational choice, 8
Rent, 4
Scarcity, 2
Self-interest, 5
Social interest, 5
Trade-off, 8
Wages, 4

## STUDY PLAN PROBLEMS AND APPLICATIONS

 You can work Problems 1 to 6 in MyEconLab Chapter 1 Study Plan and get instant feedback.

### A Definition of Economics (Study Plan 1.1)

1 Apple decides to make iTunes freely available in unlimited quantities.

   a Does Apple's decision change the incentives that people face?

   b Is Apple's decision an example of a microeconomic or a macroeconomic issue?

### Two Big Economic Questions

(Study Plan 1.2)

2 Which of the following pairs does not match?

   a Labour and wages

   b Land and rent

   c Entreprenuership and profit

   d Capital and profit

3 Explain how the following news headlines concern self-interest and the social interest:

   a Tesco Expands in Europe

   b McDonald's Moves into Salads

   c Food Must Be Labelled with Nutrition Data

### The Economic Way of Thinking

(Study Plan 1.3)

4 The night before an economics exam, you go to the cinema instead of working your MyEconLab study plan. You get 50 per cent on your exam compared with the 70 per cent that you normally score.

   a Did you face a trade-off?

   b What was the opportunity cost of your evening at the cinema?

5 **Costs Soar for London Olympics**

   The regeneration of East London, the site of the 2012 Olympic Games, is set to add an extra £1.5 billion to taxpayers' bill.

   Source: *The Times*, 6 July 2006

   Is the cost of regenerating East London an opportunity cost of hosting the 2012 Olympic Games? Explain.

### Economics as a Social Science and Policy Tool (Study Plan 1.4)

6 Which of the following statements is positive, which is normative and which can be tested?

   a The EU should cut its imports.

   b China is the EU's largest trading partner.

   c If the price of antiretroviral drugs increases, HIV/AIDS sufferers will consume fewer of the drugs.

## ADDITIONAL PROBLEMS AND APPLICATIONS

 You can work these problems in MyEconLab if assigned by your lecturer.

### A Definition of Economics

7 **Hundreds Line up for 5p.m. Ticket Giveaway**

   By noon, hundreds of Eminem fans had lined up for a chance to score free tickets to the concert.

   Source: *Detroit Free Press*, 18 May 2009

   When Eminem gave away tickets, what was free and what was scarce? Explain your answer.

### Two Big Economic Questions

8 How does the creation of a successful film influence what, how and for whom goods and services are produced?

9 How does a successful film illustrate self-interested choices that are also in the social interest?

### The Economic Way of Thinking

10 Before starring in *Iron Man*, Robert Downey Jr. had appeared in 45 films that grossed an average of $5 million on the opening weekend. In contrast, *Iron Man* grossed $102 million.

   a How do you expect *Iron Man*'s success to affect the opportunity cost of hiring Robert Downey Jr.?

   b How have the incentives for a film producer to hire Robert Downey Jr. changed?

11 What might be an incentive for you to take an extra university course during the summer break? List some of the benefits and costs involved in your decision. Would your choice be rational?

### Economics as a Social Science and Policy Tool

12 Look at today's *Financial Time*s. What is the leading economic news story? With which big economic questions does it deal? What trade-offs does it discuss?

13 Give two microeconomic and two macroeconomic statements and classify them as positive or normative.

## Chapter 1 Appendix

# Graphs in Economics

**After studying this appendix, you will be able to:**

◆ Make and interpret a scatter diagram

◆ Identify linear and non-linear relationships and relationships that have a maximum and a minimum

◆ Define and calculate the slope of a line

◆ Graph relationships among more than two variables

## Graphing Data

A graph represents a quantity as a distance. Figure A1.1 shows two examples. A distance on the horizontal line represents temperature. A movement from left to right shows an increase in temperature. The point marked 0 represents zero degrees. To the right of 0, the temperature is positive and to the left of 0, it is negative. A distance on the vertical line represents height. The point marked 0 represents sea level. Points above 0 represent metres above sea level. Points below 0 (indicated by a minus sign) represent metres below sea level.

In Figure A1.1, the scale lines are perpendicular to each other and are called *axes*. The vertical line is the *y*-axis, and the horizontal line is the *x*-axis. Each axis has a zero point, which is shared by the two axes. This common zero point is called the *origin*.

To show something in a two-variable graph, we need two pieces of information: the value of the *x* variable and the value of the *y* variable. For example, off the coast of Norway on a winter's day, the temperature is 0 degrees – the value of *x*. A fishing boat is located 0 metres above sea level – the value of *y*. This information appears at the origin at point *A* in Figure A1.1. In the heated cabin of the boat, the temperature is a comfortable 24 degrees. Point *B* represents this information. The same 24 degrees in the cabin of an airliner 9,000 metres above sea level is at point *C*.

Finally, the temperature of the ice cube in the drink of the airline passenger is shown by the point marked *D*. This point represents 9,000 metres above sea level at a temperature of 0 degrees.

We can draw two lines, called *coordinates*, from point *C*. One, called the *y*-coordinate, runs from *C*

**Figure A1.1**    Making a Graph

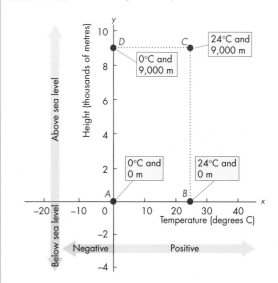

Graphs have axes that measure quantities as distances. Here, the horizontal axis (*x*-axis) measures temperature, and the vertical axis (*y*-axis) measures height.

Point *A* represents a fishing boat at sea level (0 on the *y*-axis) on a day when the temperature is 0°C. Point *B* represents inside the cabin of the boat at a temperature of 24°C.

Point *C* represents inside the cabin of an airliner 9,000 metres above sea level at a temperature of 24°C. Point *D* represents an ice cube in an airliner 9,000 metres above sea level.

myeconlab Animation

to the horizontal axis. Its length is the same as the value marked off on the *y*-axis. The other, called the *x*-coordinate, runs from *C* to the vertical axis. Its length is the same as the value marked off on the *x*-axis. We describe a point in a graph by the values of its *x*-coordinate and its *y*-coordinate. For example, at point *C*, *x* is 24 degrees and *y* is 9,000 metres.

Graphs like that in Figure A1.1 can show any type of quantitative data on two variables. The graph can show just a few points, like Figure A1.1, or many points. Before we look at graphs with many points, let's reinforce what you've just learned by looking at two graphs made with economic data.

Economists measure variables that describe *what*, *how* and *for whom* goods and services are produced. These variables are quantities produced and prices. Figure A1.2 shows two examples of economic graphs.

Figure A1.2(a) is a graph about iTunes song downloads in January 2010. The *x*-axis measures the quantity

**Figure A1.2**   Two Graphs of Economic Data

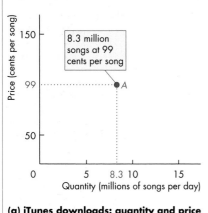

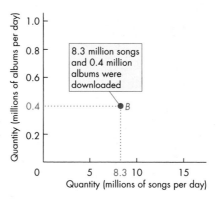

The graph in part (a) tells us that in January 2010, 8.3 million songs per day were downloaded from the iTunes store at a price of 99 cents a song.

The graph in part (b) tells us that in January 2010, 8.3 million songs per day and 0.4 million albums per day were downloaded from the iTunes store.

**(a) iTunes downloads: quantity and price**    **(b) iTunes downloads: songs and albums**

myeconlab Animation

of songs downloaded per day and the *y*-axis measures the price of a song. Point *A* tells us what the quantity and price were. You can 'read' this graph as telling you that in January 2010, 8.3 million songs a day were downloaded at a price of 99¢ per song.

Figure A1.2(b) is a graph about iTunes song and album downloads in January 2010. The *x*-axis measures the quantity of songs downloaded per day and the *y*-axis measures the quantity of albums downloaded per day. Point *B* tells us what these quantities were. You can 'read' this graph as telling you that in January 2010, 8.3 million songs a day and 0.4 million albums a day were downloaded.

The three graphs that you've just seen tell you how to make a graph and how to read a data point on a graph, but they don't improve on the raw data. Graphs become interesting and revealing when they contain a number of data points because then you can visualize the data.

Economists create graphs based on the principles in Figures A1.1 and A1.2 to reveal, describe and visualize the relationships among variables. We're now going to look at some examples. These graphs are called *scatter diagrams*.

## Scatter Diagrams

A **scatter diagram** plots the value of one variable against the value of another variable for a number of different values of each variable. Such a graph reveals whether a relationship exists between two variables and describes their relationship.

The table in Figure A1.3 shows some data on two variables: the number of tickets sold at the box office and the number of DVDs sold for eight of the most popular films in 2009.

What is the relationship between these two variables? Does a big box office success generate a large volume of DVD sales? Or does a box office success mean that fewer DVDs are sold?

We can answer these questions by making a scatter diagram. We do so by graphing the data in the table. Each point in the graph shows the number of box office tickets sold (the *x* variable) and the number of DVDs sold (the *y* variable) of one of the films. With eight films, eight points are 'scattered' within the graph.

The point labelled *A* tells us that Star Trek sold 34 million tickets at the box office and 6 million DVDs.

The points in the graph form a pattern, which reveals that larger box office sales are associated with larger DVD sales. But the points also tell us that this association is weak. You can't predict DVD sales with any confidence by knowing only the number of tickets sold at the box office.

Figure A1.4 shows two scatter diagrams of economic variables. Part (a) shows the relationship between expenditure and income on average. Each dot shows expenditure per person and income per person in a given year from 1999 to 2009. The dots are 'scattered' within the graph. The red dot tells us that in 2007, income per person was £14,000 and expenditure per person was £13,700. The dots in this graph form a pattern, which reveals that as income increases, expenditure increases.

## Figure A1.3   A Scatter Diagram

| Film | Tickets | DVDs |
|------|---------|------|
| | (millions) | |
| *Twilight* | 38 | 10 |
| *Transformers: Revenge of the Fallen* | 54 | 9 |
| *Up* | 39 | 8 |
| *Harry Potter and the Half-Blood Prince* | 40 | 7 |
| **Star Trek** | **34** | **6** |
| *The Hangover* | 37 | 6 |
| *Ice Age: Dawn of the Dinosaurs* | 26 | 5 |
| *The Proposal* | 22 | 5 |

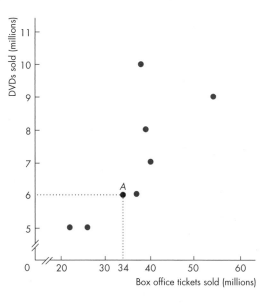

The table lists the number of tickets sold at the box office and the number of DVDs sold for eight popular films. The scatter diagram reveals the relationship between these two variables. Each point shows the values of the two variables for a specific film. For example, point *A* shows the point for *Star Trek*, which sold 34 million tickets at the box office and 6 million DVDs. The pattern formed by the points shows that there is a tendency for large box office sales to bring greater DVD sales. But you couldn't predict how many DVDs a film would sell just by knowing its box office sales.

Figure A1.4(b) shows a scatter diagram of UK unemployment and inflation from 1999 to 2009. The points show no close relationship between the two variables. Movements in the inflation rate are not related to those in the unemployment rate in any simple way.

You can see that a scatter diagram conveys a wealth of information, and it does so in much less space than we have used to describe only some of its features. But you do have to 'read' the graph to obtain all this information.

## Figure A1.4   Scatter Diagrams

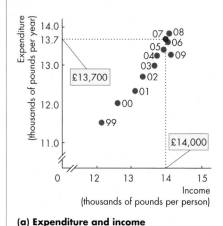

**(a) Expenditure and income**

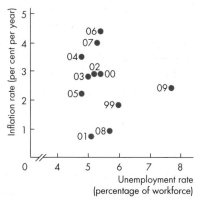

**(b) Unemployment and inflation**

The scatter diagram in part (a) shows the relationship between income and expenditure from 1999 to 2009. The red dot shows that in 2007, income was £14,000 and expenditure was £13,700. The dots form a pattern that shows that as income increases so too does expenditure.

The scatter diagram in part (b) shows a weak relationship between UK unemployment and inflation during most of the 2000s.

## Breaks in the Axes

Figure A1.4(a) and Figure A1.4(b) have breaks in their axes, as shown by the small gaps. The breaks indicate that there are jumps from the origin, 0, to the first values recorded.

In Figure A1.4(a), the breaks are used because the lowest values exceed £11,000. With no breaks in the axes, there would be a lot of empty space, all the points would be crowded into the top right corner and it would be hard to see the relationship between these two variables. By breaking the axes, we bring the relationship into view.

Putting a break in the axes is like using a zoom lens to bring the relationship into the centre of the graph and magnify it so that it fills the graph.

## Misleading Graphs

Breaks can be used to highlight a relationship. But they can also be used to mislead – to make a graph that lies. The most common way of making a graph lie is to use axis breaks and either to stretch or compress a scale. For example, suppose that in Figure A1.4(a), the *y*-axis that measures expenditure ran from zero to £15,000 while the *x*-axis was the same as the one shown, running from £12,000 to £15,000. The graph would now create the impression that despite a huge increase in income, expenditure had barely changed.

To avoid being misled, it is a good idea to get into the habit of looking closely at the values and the labels on the axes of a graph before you start trying to interpret it.

## Correlation and Causation

A scatter diagram that shows a clear relationship between two variables, such as Figure A1.4(a), tells us that the two variables have a high correlation. When a high correlation is present, we can predict the value of one variable from the value of the other variable. But correlation does not imply causation.

Sometimes a high correlation is a coincidence, but sometimes it does arise from a causal relationship. It is likely, for example, that rising income causes rising expenditure (Figure A1.4a).

You've now seen how we can use graphs in economics to show economic data and to reveal relationships between variables. Next, we'll learn how economists use graphs to construct and display economic models.

# Graphs Used in Economic Models

The graphs used in economics are not always designed to show real-world data. Often they are used to show general relationships among the variables in an economic model.

An *economic model* is a stripped down, simplified description of an economy or of a component of an economy such as a business or a household. It consists of statements about economic behaviour that can be expressed as equations or as curves in a graph. Economists use models to explore the effects of different policies or other influences on the economy in ways that are similar to the use of model aeroplanes in wind tunnels and models of the climate.

You will encounter many different kinds of graphs in economic models, but there are some repeating patterns. Once you've learned to recognize these patterns, you will instantly understand the meaning of a graph. Here, we'll look at the different types of curves that are used in economic models, and we'll see some everyday examples of each type of curve. The patterns to look for in graphs are the four cases in which:

◆ Variables move in the same direction

◆ Variables move in opposite directions

◆ Variables have a maximum or a minimum

◆ Variables are unrelated

# Variables That Move in the Same Direction

A relationship in which two variables move in the same direction is called a **positive relationship** or a **direct relationship**. Figure A1.5 shows some examples of positive relationships. Notice that the line that shows such a relationship slopes upward.

Figure A1.5 shows three types of relationships, one that has a straight line and two that have curved lines. But all the lines in these three graphs are called curves. Any line on a graph – no matter whether it is straight or curved – is called a *curve*.

A relationship shown by a straight line is called a **linear relationship**. Figure A1.5(a) shows a linear relationship between the number of kilometres travelled in 5 hours and speed. For example, point *A* shows that if

**Figure A1.5**   Positive (Direct) Relationships

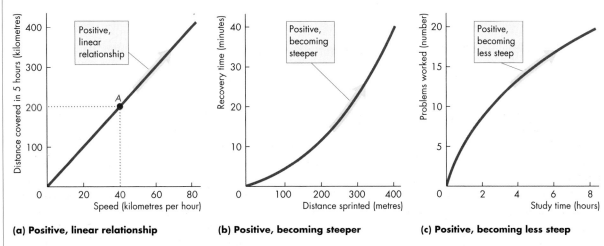

**(a) Positive, linear relationship**   **(b) Positive, becoming steeper**   **(c) Positive, becoming less steep**

Each part of this figure shows a positive (direct) relationship between two variables. That is, as the value of the variable measured on the *x*-axis increases, so does the value of the variable measured on the *y*-axis. Part (a) shows a linear relationship – as the two variables increase together, we move along a straight line.

Part (b) shows a positive relationship such that as the two variables increase together, we move along a curve that becomes steeper.

Part (c) shows a positive relationship such that as the two variables increase together, we move along a curve that becomes less steep.

our speed is 40 kms per hour, we will travel 200 kilometres in 5 hours. If we double our speed to 80 kms per hour, we will travel 400 kilometres in 5 hours.

Figure A1.5(b) shows the relationship between distance sprinted and recovery time (the time it takes the heart rate to return to its normal resting rate). This relationship is an upward-sloping one that starts out quite flat but then becomes steeper as we move along the curve away from the origin. The reason this curve slopes upward and becomes steeper is because the additional recovery time needed from sprinting an additional 100 metres increases. It takes less than 5 minutes to recover from the first 100 metres but more than 10 minutes to recover from the third 100 metres.

Figure A1.5(c) shows the relationship between the number of problems worked by a student and the amount of study time. This relationship is an upward-sloping one that starts out quite steep and becomes flatter as we move away from the origin. Study time becomes less productive as you increase the hours spent studying and become more tired.

## Variables That Move in Opposite Directions

A relationship between variables that move in opposite directions is called a **negative relationship** or an **inverse relationship**. Figure A1.6 shows some examples. Figure A1.6(a) shows the relationship between the number of hours available for playing squash and for playing tennis when the total is 5 hours. One extra hour spent playing tennis means one hour less playing squash and vice versa. This relationship is negative and linear.

Figure A1.6(b) shows the relationship between the cost per kilometre travelled and the length of a journey. The longer the journey, the lower is the cost per kilometre. But as the journey length increases, the cost per kilometre decreases, but the fall in the cost is smaller, the longer the journey. This feature of the relationship is shown by the fact that the curve slopes downward, starting out steep at a short journey length and then becoming flatter as the journey length increases. This relationship arises because some of the costs are fixed.

**Figure A1.6** Negative (Inverse) Relationships

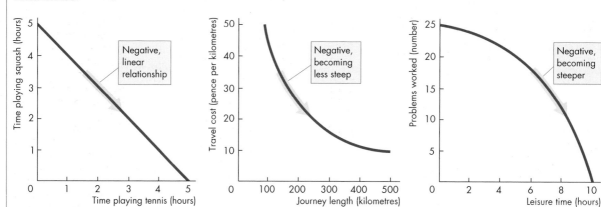

**(a) Negative, linear relationship**   **(b) Negative, becoming less steep**   **(c) Negative, becoming steeper**

Each part of this figure shows a negative (inverse) relationship between two variables. That is, as the value of the variable measured on the *x*-axis increases, the value of the variable measured on the *y*-axis decreases.

 Part (a) shows a linear relationship. The total time spent playing tennis and squash is 5 hours. As the time spent playing tennis increases, the time spent playing squash decreases and we move along a straight line.

 Part (b) shows a negative relationship such that as the journey length increases, the travel cost decreases as we move along a curve that becomes less steep.

 Part (c) shows a negative relationship such that as leisure time increases, the number of problems worked decreases as we move along a curve that becomes steeper.

**myeconlab** Animation

---

Figure A1.6(c) shows the relationship between the amount of leisure time and the number of problems worked by a student. Increasing leisure time produces an increasingly large reduction in the number of problems worked. This relationship is a negative one that starts out with a gentle slope at a small number of leisure hours and becomes steeper as the number of leisure hours increases. This relationship is a different view of the idea shown in Figure A1.5(c).

## Variables That Have a Maximum or a Minimum

Many relationships in economic models have a maximum or a minimum. For example, firms try to make the largest possible profit and to produce at the lowest possible cost. Figure A1.7 shows relationships that have a maximum or a minimum.

 Figure A1.7(a) shows the relationship between rainfall and wheat yield. When there is no rainfall, wheat will not grow, so the yield is zero. As the rainfall increases up to 10 days a month, the wheat yield increases. With 10 rainy days each month, the wheat yield reaches its maximum at 2.0 tonnes per hectare (point *A*). Rain in excess of 10 days a month starts to lower the yield of wheat. If every day is rainy, the wheat suffers from a lack of sunshine and the yield decreases to zero. This relationship is one that starts out sloping upward, reaches a maximum and then slopes downward.

 Figure A1.7(b) shows the reverse case – a relationship that begins sloping downward, falls to a minimum and then slopes upward. Most economic costs are like this relationship. An example is the relationship between the travel cost per kilometre and the speed of a car. At low speeds, the car is creeping in a traffic jam. The number of kilometres per litre is low, so the cost per kilometre is high. At high speeds, the car is travelling faster than its efficient speed, using a large quantity of petrol, and again the number of kilometres per litre is low and the cost per kilometre is high. At a speed of 85 kms per hour, the cost per kilometre is at its minimum (point *B*). This relationship is one that starts out sloping downward, reaches a minimum and then slopes upward.

**Figure A1.7**    Maximum and Minimum Points

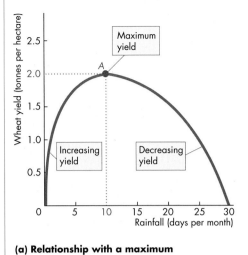

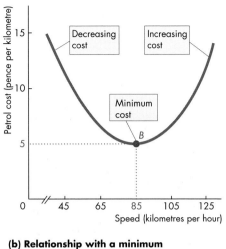

Part (a) shows a relationship that has a maximum point, *A*. The curve slopes upward as it rises to its maximum point, is flat at its maximum and then slopes downward.

Part (b) shows a relationship with a minimum point, *B*. The curve slopes downward as it falls to its minimum point, is flat at its minimum and then slopes upward.

**(a) Relationship with a maximum**

**(b) Relationship with a minimum**

myeconlab Animation

# Variables That Are Unrelated

There are many situations in which no matter what happens to the value of one variable, the other variable remains constant. Sometimes we want to show the independence between two variables in a graph, and Figure A1.8 shows two ways of achieving this.

In describing the graphs in Figures A1.5 to Figure A1.8, we have talked about curves that slope upward or slope downward and curves that become steeper and less steep. Let's spend a little time discussing exactly what we mean by slope and how we measure the slope of a curve.

**Figure A1.8**    Variables That Are Unrelated

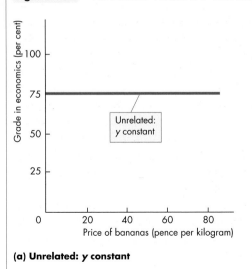

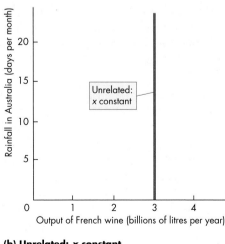

This figure shows how we can graph two variables that are unrelated. In part (a), a student's grade in economics is plotted at 75 per cent on the *y*-axis regardless of the price of bananas on the *x*-axis. The curve is horizontal.

In part (b), the output of the vineyards of France on the *x*-axis does not vary with the rainfall in Australia on the *y*-axis. The curve is vertical.

**(a) Unrelated: *y* constant**

**(b) Unrelated: *x* constant**

myeconlab Animation

## The Slope of a Relationship

We can measure the influence of one variable on another by the slope of the relationship. The **slope** of a relationship is the change in the value of the variable measured on the *y*-axis divided by the change in the value of the variable measured on the *x*-axis. We use the Greek letter $\Delta$ (*delta*) to represent 'change in'. So $\Delta y$ means the change in the value of the variable measured on the *y*-axis, and $\Delta x$ means the change in the value of the variable measured on the *x*-axis. The slope of the relationship is:

$$\frac{\Delta y}{\Delta x}$$

If a large change in the variable measured on the *y*-axis ($\Delta y$) is associated with a small change in the variable measured on the *x*-axis ($\Delta x$), the slope is large and the curve is steep. If a small change in the variable measured on the *y*-axis ($\Delta y$) is associated with a large change in the variable measured on the *x*-axis ($\Delta x$), the slope is small and the curve is flat.

We can make the idea of slope sharper by doing some calculations.

## The Slope of a Straight Line

The slope of a straight line is the same regardless of where on the line you calculate it. The slope of a straight line is constant.

**Figure A1.9**   The Slope of a Straight Line

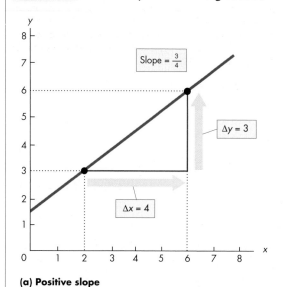

**(a) Positive slope**

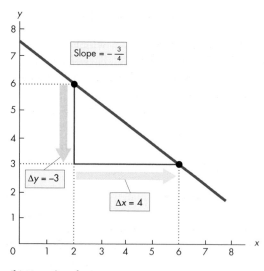

**(b) Negative slope**

To calculate the slope of a straight line, we divide the change in the value of the variable measured on the *y*-axis ($\Delta y$) by the change in the value of the variable measured on the *x*-axis ($\Delta x$), as we move along the curve.

Part (a) shows the calculation of a positive slope. When *x* increases from 2 to 6, $\Delta x$ equals 4. That change in *x* brings about an increase in *y* from 3 to 6, so $\Delta y$ equals 3. The slope ($\Delta y/\Delta x$) equals 3/4.

Part (b) shows the calculation of a negative slope. When *x* increases from 2 to 6, $\Delta x$ equals 4. That increase in *x* brings about a decrease in *y* from 6 to 3, so $\Delta y$ equals –3. The slope ($\Delta y/\Delta x$) equals –3/4.

Let's calculate the slopes of the lines in Figure A1.9. In part (a), when $x$ increases from 2 to 6, $y$ increases from 3 to 6. The change in $x$ is +4: that is, $\Delta x$ is 4. The change in $y$ is +3: that is, $\Delta y$ is 3. The slope of that line is:

$$\frac{\Delta y}{\Delta x} = \frac{3}{4}$$

In part (b), when $x$ increases from 2 to 6, $y$ decreases from 6 to 3. The change in $y$ is *minus* 3: that is, $\Delta y$ is –3. The change in $x$ is *plus* 4: that is, $\Delta x$ is 4. The slope of the curve is:

$$\frac{\Delta y}{\Delta x} = \frac{-3}{4}$$

Notice that the two slopes have the same magnitude (3/4), but the slope of the line in part (a) is positive (3/4), while the slope in part (b) is negative (–3/4). The slope of a positive relationship is positive; the slope of a negative relationship is negative.

## The Slope of a Curved Line

The slope of a curved line is trickier. The slope of a curved line is not constant. Its slope depends on where on the line we calculate it. There are two ways to calculate the slope of a curved line: you can calculate the slope at a point, or you can calculate the slope across an arc of the curve. Let's look at the two alternatives.

### Slope at a Point

To calculate the slope at a point on a curve, you need to construct a straight line that has the same slope as the curve at the point in question. Figure A1.10 shows how this is done. Suppose you want to calculate the slope of the curve at point $A$. Place a ruler on the graph so that it touches point $A$ and no other point on the curve, then draw a straight line along the edge of the ruler. The straight red line is this line, and it is the *tangent* to the curve at point $A$. If the ruler touches the curve only at point $A$, then the slope of the curve at point $A$ must be the same as the slope of the edge of the ruler. If the curve and the ruler do not have the same slope, the line along the edge of the ruler will cut the curve instead of just touching it.

Now that you have found a straight line with the same slope as the curve at point $A$, you can calculate the slope of the curve at point $A$ by calculating the slope of the straight line. Along the straight line, as $x$ increases from

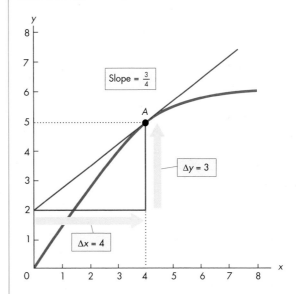

**Figure A1.10**    Slope at a Point

Slope $= \frac{3}{4}$

$A$

$\Delta y = 3$

$\Delta x = 4$

To calculate the slope of the curve at point $A$, draw the red line that just touches the curve at $A$ – the tangent. The slope of this straight line is calculated by dividing the change in $y$ by the change in $x$ along the line. When $x$ increases from 0 to 4, $\Delta x$ equals 4. That change in $x$ is associated with an increase in $y$ from 2 to 5, so $\Delta y$ equals 3. The slope of the red line is 3/4. So the slope of the curve at point $A$ is 3/4.

*myeconlab* Animation

0 to 4 ($\Delta x = 4$) $y$ increases from 2 to 5 ($\Delta y = 3$). The slope of the line is:

$$\frac{\Delta y}{\Delta x} = \frac{3}{4}$$

So the slope of the curve at point $A$ is 3/4.

### Slope Across an Arc

An arc of a curve is a piece of a curve. In Figure A1.11, you are looking at the same curve as in Figure A1.10. But instead of calculating the slope at point $A$, we are going to calculate the slope across the arc from $B$ to $C$. You can see that the slope is greater at $B$ than at $C$. When we calculate the slope across an arc, we are calculating the average slope between two points. As we move along the arc from $B$ to $C$, $x$ increases from 3 to 5 and $y$ increases from 4 to 5.5. The change in $x$ is 2 ($\Delta x = 2$), and the change in $y$ is 1.5 ($\Delta y = 1.5$).

**Figure A1.11    Slope Across an Arc**

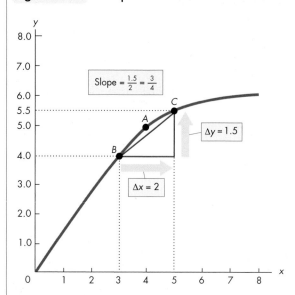

$$\text{Slope} = \frac{1.5}{2} = \frac{3}{4}$$

$\Delta y = 1.5$

$\Delta x = 2$

To calculate the average slope of the curve along the arc *BC*, draw a straight line from point *B* to point *C*. The slope of the line *BC* is calculated by dividing the change in *y* by the change in *x*. In moving from *B* to *C*, $\Delta x$ equals 2 and $\Delta y$ equals 1.5. The slope of the line *BC* is 1.5 divided by 2, or 3/4. So the slope of the curve across the arc *BC* is 3/4.

myeconlab Animation

The slope of the red line *BC* is:

$$\frac{\Delta y}{\Delta x} = \frac{1.5}{2} = \frac{3}{4}$$

So the slope of the curve across the arc *BC* is 3/4.

This calculation gives us the slope of the curve between points *B* and *C*. The actual slope calculated is the slope of the straight line from *B* to *C*. This slope approximates the average slope of the curve along the arc *BC*. In this particular example, the slope across the arc *BC* is identical to the slope of the curve at point *A*. But the calculation of the slope of a curve does not always work out so neatly. You might have some fun constructing some more examples and some counter examples.

You now know how to make and interpret a graph. But so far, we've limited our attention to graphs of two variables. We're now going to learn how to graph more than two variables.

# Graphing Relationships Among More Than Two Variables

We have seen that we can graph the relationship between two variables as a point formed by the *x*- and *y*-coordinates in a two-dimensional graph. You may be thinking that although a two-dimensional graph is informative, most of the things in which you are likely to be interested involve relationships among many variables, not just two. For example, the amount of ice cream consumed depends on the price of ice cream and the temperature. If ice cream is expensive and the temperature is low, people eat a lot less ice cream than when ice cream is inexpensive and the temperature is high. For any given price of ice cream, the quantity consumed varies with the temperature; and for any given temperature, the quantity of ice cream consumed varies with its price.

Figure A1.12 shows a relationship among three variables. The table shows the number of litres of ice cream consumed each day at various temperatures and ice cream prices. How can we graph these numbers?

To graph a relationship that involves more than two variables, we use the *ceteris paribus* assumption.

## Ceteris Paribus

***Ceteris paribus*** (often shortened to *cet. par.*) means 'if all other relevant things remain the same'. To isolate the relationship of interest in a laboratory experiment, a scientist holds everything constant except for the variable whose effect is being studied. Economists use the same method to graph a relationship that has more than two variables.

Figure A1.12(a) shows an example. There, you can see what happens to the quantity of ice cream consumed as the price of ice cream varies when the temperature is held constant.

The curve labelled 20°C shows the relationship between ice cream consumption and the price of a scoop if the temperature remains at 20°C. The numbers used to plot that curve are those in the first two columns of the table. For example, if the temperature is 20°C, 10 litres are consumed when the price is £1.20 a scoop and 6 litres are consumed when the price is £1.60 a scoop.

The curve labelled 25°C shows the relationship between ice cream consumption and the price of a scoop when the temperature remains at 25°C. The numbers used to plot the curve are those in the first and third

**Figure A1.12** Graphing a Relationship Among Three Variables

| Price (pounds per scoop) | Ice cream consumption (litres per day) | |
| --- | --- | --- |
| | 20°C | 25°C |
| 0.40 | 52 | 91 |
| 0.80 | 18 | 32 |
| **1.20** | **10** | **17** |
| 1.60 | 6 | 10 |
| 2.00 | 5 | 8 |
| 2.40 | 4 | 6 |

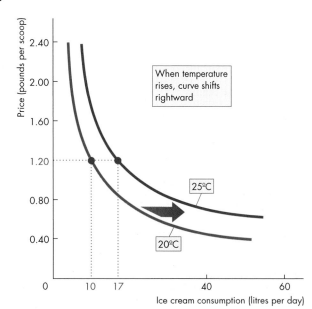

Ice cream consumption depends on its price and the temperature. The table tells us how many litres of ice cream are consumed each day at different prices and two different temperatures. For example, if the price is £1.20 a scoop and the temperature is 20°C, 10 litres of ice cream are consumed.

To graph a relationship among three variables, the value of one variable is held constant. The graph shows the relationship between price and consumption when temperature is held constant. One curve holds temperature at 20°C and the other at 25°C.

A change in the price of ice cream brings a *movement along* one of the curves – along the blue curve at 20°C and along the red curve at 25°C.

When the temperature rises from 20°C to 25°C, the curve that shows the relationship between consumption and price *shifts* rightward from the blue curve to the red curve.

myeconlab Animation

columns of the table. For example, if the temperature is 25°C, 17 litres of ice cream are consumed when the price is £1.20 a scoop and 32 litres when the price is £0.80 a scoop.

When the price of ice cream changes but the temperature is constant, you can think of what happens in the graph as a movement along one of the curves. At 20°C there is a movement along the blue curve and at 25°C there is a movement along the red curve.

## When Other Things Change

The temperature is held constant along each of the curves in Figure A1.12, but in reality the temperature changes. When that event occurs, you can think of what happens in the graph as a shift of the curve.

When the temperature rises from 20°C to 25°C, the curve that shows the relationship between ice cream consumption and the price of ice cream shifts rightward from the blue curve to the red curve.

You will encounter these ideas of movements along and shifts of curves at many points in your study of economics. Think carefully about what you've just learned and make up some examples (with assumed numbers) about other relationships.

With what you have learned about graphs, you can move forward with your study of economics. There are no graphs in this book that are more complicated than those that have been explained in this appendix. Use this appendix as a refresher if you find that you're having difficulty interpreting or making a graph.

# Equations of Straight Lines

If a straight line in a graph describes the relationship between two variables, we call it a *linear relationship*. Figure 1 shows the linear relationship between Cathy's expenditure and income. Cathy spends £100 a week (by borrowing or spending her past savings) when income is zero. And out of each pound earned, Cathy spends 50 pence (and saves 50 pence).

All linear relationships are described by the same general equation. We call the quantity that is measured on the horizontal (or x-axis) $x$ and we call the quantity that is measured on the vertical (or y-axis) $y$. In the case of Figure 1, $x$ is income and $y$ is expenditure.

## A Linear Equation

The equation that describes a linear relationship between $x$ and $y$ is:

$$y = a + bx$$

In this equation, $a$ and $b$ are fixed numbers and they are called constants. The values of $x$ and $y$ vary so these numbers are called variables. Because the equation describes a straight line, it is called a *linear equation*.

The equation tells us that when the value of $x$ is zero, the value of $y$ is $a$. We call the constant $a$ the *y-axis intercept*. The reason is that on the graph the straight line hits the y-axis at a value equal to $a$. Figure 1 illustrates the y-axis intercept.

For positive values of $x$, the value of $y$ exceeds $a$. The constant $b$ tells us by how much $y$ increases above $a$ as $x$ increases. The constant $b$ is the slope of the line.

## Slope of a Line

As we explain on p. 22, the slope of a relationship is the change in the value of $y$ divided by the change in the value of $x$. We use the Greek letter $\Delta$ (delta) to represent 'change in'. So $\Delta y$ means the change in the value of the variable measured on the y-axis, and $\Delta x$ means change in the value of the variable measured on the x-axis. Therefore the slope of the relationship is:

$$\Delta y / \Delta x$$

To see why the slope is $b$, suppose that initially the value of $x$ is $x_1$, or £200 in Figure 2. The corresponding value of $y$ is $y_1$, also £200 in Figure 2. The equation of the line tells us that:

$$y_1 = a + bx_1 \qquad (1)$$

Now the value of $x$ increases by $\Delta x$ to $x_1 + \Delta x$ (or £400 in Figure 2). And the value of $y$ increases by $\Delta y$ to $y_1 + \Delta y$ (or £300 in Figure 2).

The equation of the line now tells us that:

$$y_1 + \Delta y = a + b(x_1 + \Delta x) \qquad (2)$$

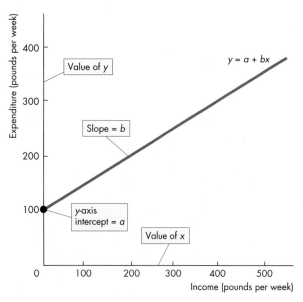

**Figure 1 Linear relationship**

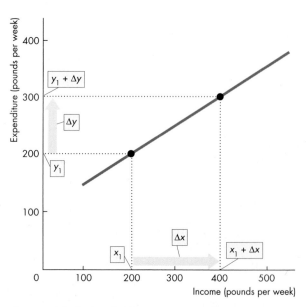

**Figure 2 Calculating slope**

To calculate the slope of the line, subtract equation (1) from equation (2) to obtain:

$$\Delta y = b\Delta x \qquad (3)$$

and now divide equation (3) by $\Delta x$ to obtain:

$$\Delta y / \Delta x = b$$

So the slope of the line is $b$.

We can calculate the slope of the line in Figure 2. When $x$ increases from 200 to 400, $y$ increases from 200 to 300, so $\Delta x$ is 200 and $\Delta y$ is 100. The slope, $b$, equals:

$$\Delta y / \Delta x = 100/200 = 0.5$$

## Position of the Line

The $y$-axis intercept determines the position of the line on the graph. Figure 3 illustrates the relationship between the $y$-axis intercept and the position of the line on the graph. In this graph, the $y$-axis measures saving and the $x$-axis measures income.

When the $y$-axis intercept, $a$, is positive, the line hits the $y$-axis at a positive value of $y$ – as the blue line does. Its $y$-axis intercept is 100.

When the $y$-axis intercept, $a$, is zero, the line hits the $y$-axis at the origin – as the purple line does. Its $y$-axis intercept is 0.

When the $y$-axis intercept, $a$, is negative, the line hits the $y$-axis at a negative value of $y$ – as the red line does. Its $y$-axis intercept is −100.

As the equations of the three lines show, the value of the $y$-axis intercept does *not* influence the slope of the line. All three lines have a slope equal to 0.5.

## Positive Relationships

Figures 1 and 2 show a positive relationship – the two variables $x$ and $y$ move in the same direction. All positive relationships have a slope that is *positive*. In the equation of the line, the constant $b$ is positive.

In the example in Figure 1, the $y$-axis intercept, $a$, is 100. The slope $b$ equals 0.5. The equation of the line is:

$$y = 100 + 0.5x$$

## Negative Relationships

Figure 4 shows a negative relationship – the variables $x$ and $y$ move in opposite directions. All negative relationships have a slope that is *negative*. In the equation of the line, the constant $b$ is negative.

In the example in Figure 4, the $y$-axis intercept, $a$, is 30. The slope, $b$, equals $\Delta y / \Delta x$ as we move along the line. When $x$ increases from 0 to 2, $y$ decreases from 30 to 10, so $\Delta x$ is 2 and $\Delta y$ is −20. The slope equals $\Delta y / \Delta x$, which is −20/2 or −10. The equation of the line is:

$$y = 30 + (-10)x$$

or

$$y = 30 - 10x$$

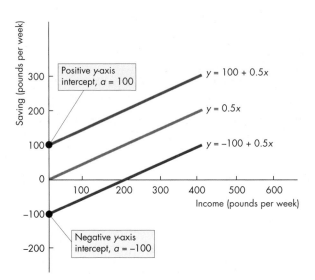

**Figure 3 The y-axis intercept**

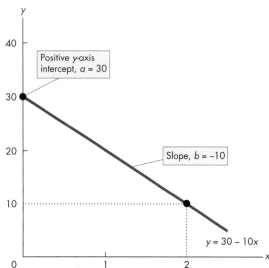

**Figure 4 Negative relationship**

### Review Quiz

1  Explain how we 'read' the three graphs in Figures A1.1 and A1.2.
2  Explain what scatter diagrams show and why we use them.
3  Explain how we 'read' the three scatter diagrams in Figure A1.3 and A1.4.
4  Draw a graph to show the relationship between two variables that move in the same direction.
5  Draw a graph to show the relationship between two variables that move in opposite directions.
6  Draw a graph to show the relationship between two variables that have a maximum and a minimum.

7  Which of the relationships in Questions 4 and 5 is a positive relationship and which is a negative relationship?
8  What are the two ways of calculating the slope of a curved line?
9  How do we graph a relationship among more than two variables?
10  Explain what change will bring a movement along a curve.
11  Explain what change will bring a shift of a curve.

You can work these questions in Study Plan 1.A and get instant feedback.

## SUMMARY

## Key Points

### Graphing Data (pp. 13–16)

◆ A graph is made by plotting the values of two variables $x$ and $y$ at a point that corresponds to their values measured along the $x$-axis and $y$-axis.

◆ A scatter diagram is a graph that plots the values of two variables for a number of different values of each.

◆ A scatter diagram shows the relationship between two variables. It shows whether two variables are positively related, negatively related, or unrelated.

### Graphs Used in Economic Models
(pp. 16–19)

◆ Graphs are used to show relationships among variables in economic models.

◆ Relationships can be positive (an upward-sloping curve), negative (a downward-sloping curve), positive and then negative (have a maximum point), negative and then positive (have a minimum point), or unrelated (a horizontal or vertical curve).

### The Slope of a Relationship (pp. 20–22)

◆ The slope of a relationship is calculated as the change in the value of the variable measured on the $y$-axis divided by the change in the value of the variable measured on the $x$-axis, that is, $\Delta y/\Delta x$.

◆ A straight line has a constant slope.

◆ A curved line has a varying slope. To calculate the slope of a curved line, we calculate the slope at a point or across an arc.

### Graphing Relationships Among More Than Two Variables (pp. 22–23)

◆ To graph a relationship among more than two variables, we hold constant the values of all the variables except two.

◆ We then plot the value of one of the variables against the value of another.

◆ A *cet. par.* change in the value of a variable on an axis of a graph brings a movement along the curve.

◆ A change in the value of a variable held constant along the curve brings a shift of the curve.

## Key Terms

*Ceteris paribus*, 22
Direct relationship, 16
Inverse relationship, 17
Linear relationship, 16
Negative relationship, 17
Positive relationship, 16
Scatter diagram, 14
Slope, 20

**myeconlab**    You can work Problems 1 to 11 in MyEconLab Chapter 1A Study Plan and get instant feedback.

Use this spreadsheet to answer Problems 1 to 3. The spreadsheet gives data on the US economy: column A is the year, column B is the inflation rate, column C is the interest rate, column D is the growth rate and column E is the unemployment rate.

|    | A | B | C | D | E |
|----|------|------|-----|------|-----|
| 1  | 1999 | 2.2 | 4.6 | 4.8 | 4.2 |
| 2  | 2000 | 3.4 | 5.8 | 4.1 | 4.0 |
| 3  | 2001 | 2.8 | 3.4 | 1.1 | 4.7 |
| 4  | 2002 | 1.6 | 1.6 | 1.8 | 5.8 |
| 5  | 2003 | 2.3 | 1.0 | 2.5 | 6.0 |
| 6  | 2004 | 2.7 | 1.4 | 3.6 | 5.5 |
| 7  | 2005 | 3.4 | 3.2 | 3.1 | 5.1 |
| 8  | 2006 | 3.2 | 4.7 | 2.7 | 4.6 |
| 9  | 2007 | 2.8 | 4.4 | 2.1 | 4.6 |
| 10 | 2008 | 3.8 | 1.4 | 0.4 | 5.8 |
| 11 | 2009 | −0.4 | 0.2 | −2.4 | 9.3 |

**1**  Draw a scatter diagram to show the relationship between the inflation rate and the interest rate. Describe the relationship.

**2**  Draw a scatter diagram to show the relationship between the growth rate and the unemployment rate. Describe the relationship.

**3**  Draw a scatter diagram to show the relationship between the interest rate and the unemployment rate. Describe the relationship.

Use the following news clip to work Problems 4 to 6.

***Clash of the Titans* Tops Box Office With Sales of $61.2 million:**

| Film | Cinemas (number) | Revenue (dollars per cinema) |
|------|------|------|
| Clash of the Titans | 3,777 | 16,213 |
| Tyler Perry's Why Did I Get Married | 2,155 | 13,591 |
| How To Train Your Dragon | 4,060 | 7,145 |
| The Last Song | 2,673 | 5,989 |

Source: Bloomberg, 5 April 2010

**4**  Draw a graph of the relationship between the revenue per cinema on the *y*-axis and the number of cinemas on the *x*-axis. Describe the relationship.

**5**  Calculate the slope of the relationship between 4,060 and 2,673 cinemas.

**6**  Calculate the slope of the relationship between 2,155 and 4,060 cinemas.

**7**  Calculate the slope of the following relationship:

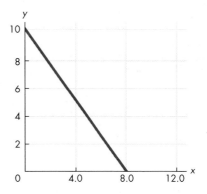

Use the following relationship to work Problems 8 and 9.

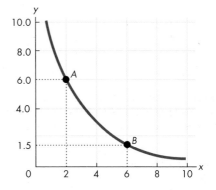

**8**  Calculate the slope of the relationship at point *A* and at point *B*.

**9**  Calculate the slope across the arc *AB*.

Use the following table, which gives the price of a balloon ride, the temperature and the number of rides per day, to work Problems 10 and 11.

| Price (pounds per ride) | Balloon rides (number per day) | | |
|------|------|------|------|
| | **10°C** | **20°C** | **30°C** |
| 5.00 | 32 | 40 | 50 |
| 10.00 | 27 | 32 | 40 |
| 15.00 | 18 | 27 | 32 |
| 20.00 | 10 | 18 | 27 |

**10**  Draw a graph of the relationships between the price and the number of rides, holding the temperature constant at 20°C.

**11**  What happens in the graph in Problem 10 if the temperature rises to 30°C?

### ADDITIONAL PROBLEMS AND APPLICATIONS

Use the following spreadsheet to work Problems 12 to 14. The spreadsheet provides data on oil and petrol: column A is the year, column B is the price of oil (dollars per barrel), column C is the price of petrol (pence per litre), column D is oil production and column E is the quantity of petrol refined (both in millions of barrels per day).

| | A | B | C | D | E |
|---|---|---|---|---|---|
| 1 | 1999 | 24 | 118 | 5.9 | 8.1 |
| 2 | 2000 | 30 | 152 | 5.8 | 8.2 |
| 3 | 2001 | 17 | 146 | 5.8 | 8.3 |
| 4 | 2002 | 24 | 139 | 5.7 | 8.4 |
| 5 | 2003 | 27 | 160 | 5.7 | 8.5 |
| 6 | 2004 | 37 | 190 | 5.4 | 8.7 |
| 7 | 2005 | 49 | 231 | 5.2 | 8.7 |
| 8 | 2006 | 56 | 262 | 5.1 | 8.9 |
| 9 | 2007 | 86 | 284 | 5.1 | 9.0 |
| 10 | 2008 | 43 | 330 | 5.0 | 8.9 |
| 11 | 2009 | 76 | 241 | 4.9 | 8.9 |

**12** Draw a scatter diagram of the price of oil and the quantity of oil produced. Describe the relationship.

**13** Draw a scatter diagram of the price of petrol and the quantity of petrol refined. Describe the relationship.

**14** Draw a scatter diagram of the quantities of oil produced and petrol refined. Describe the relationship.

Use the following data to work Problems 15 to 17.

Draw a graph that shows the relationship between the two variables $x$ and $y$:

| $x$ | 0 | 1 | 2 | 3 | 4 | 5 |
|---|---|---|---|---|---|---|
| $y$ | 25 | 24 | 22 | 18 | 12 | 0 |

**15 a** Is the relationship positive or negative?

**b** Does the slope of the relationship become steeper or flatter as the value of $x$ increases?

**c** Think of some economic relationships that might be similar to this one.

**16** Calculate the slope of the relationship between $x$ and $y$ when $x$ equals 3.

**17** Calculate the slope of the relationship across the arc as $x$ increases from 4 to 5.

**18** In the following graph, calculate the slope of the relationship at point $A$.

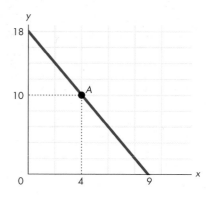

Use the following graph to work Problems 19 and 20.

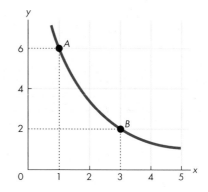

**19** Calculate the slope at points $A$ and $B$.

**20** Calculate the slope across the arc $AB$.

Use the following table, which gives the price of an umbrella, the amount of rainfall and the number of umbrellas purchased, to work Problems 21 to 23.

| Price (pounds per umbrella) | Umbrellas (number purchased per day) | | |
|---|---|---|---|
| | 0 | 200 | 400 |
| | | (mm of rainfall) | |
| 5.00 | 7 | 8 | 12 |
| 10.00 | 4 | 7 | 8 |
| 15.00 | 2 | 4 | 7 |
| 20.00 | 1 | 2 | 4 |

**21** Draw a graph of the relationship between the price and the number of umbrellas purchased, holding the amount of rainfall constant at 200 mm. Describe the relationship.

**22** What happens in the graph in Problem 21 if the price rises and rainfall is constant?

**23** What happens in the graph in Problem 21 if the rainfall increases from 200 mm to 400 mm?

# The Economic Problem

**After studying this chapter you will be able to:**

◆ Define the production possibilities frontier and calculate opportunity cost

◆ Distinguish between production possibilities and preferences and describe an efficient allocation of resources

◆ Explain how current production choices expand future production possibilities

◆ Explain how specialization and trade expand our production possibilities

◆ Describe the economic institutions that coordinate decisions

Why does food cost much more today than it did a few years ago? One reason is that we now use part of our food crop to produce biofuel as a substitute for petrol and diesel. Another reason is that droughts have decreased global grain production.

In this chapter, you will study an economic model – the production possibilities frontier – and you will learn why biofuel production and drought have increased the cost of producing food. You will also learn how to assess whether it is a good idea to increase maize production to produce fuel and how we gain by trading with others.

At the end of the chapter, in *Reading Between the Lines*, we'll apply what you've learned to understanding why biofuel production is raising the cost of food.

## Production Possibilities and Opportunity Cost

Every working day, in mines and factories, shops and offices, on farms and construction sites, 200 million European workers produce a vast variety of goods and services valued at €50 billion. But the quantities of goods and services that we can produce are limited by both our available resources and technology. And if we want to increase our production of one good, we must decrease our production of something else – we face trade-offs.

You are going to learn about the production possibilities frontier, which describes the limit to what we can produce and provides a neat way of thinking about and illustrating the idea of a trade-off.

The **production possibilities frontier** (*PPF*) is the boundary between those combinations of goods and services that can be produced and those that cannot. To illustrate the *PPF*, we focus on two goods at a time and hold the quantities produced of all the other goods and services constant. That is, we look at a *model* economy in which everything remains the same (*ceteris paribus*) except for the production of the two goods we are considering.

Let's look at the production possibilities frontier for CDs and pizza, which stand for *any* pair of goods or services.

## Production Possibilities Frontier

The *production possibilities frontier* for CDs and pizza shows the limits to the production of these two goods, given the total resources available to produce them. Figure 2.1 shows this production possibilities frontier. The table lists some combinations of the quantities of pizzas and CDs that can be produced in a month given the resources available. The figure graphs these combinations. The *x*-axis shows the quantity of pizzas produced and the *y*-axis shows the quantity of CDs produced.

The *PPF* illustrates *scarcity* because we cannot attain the points outside the frontier. They are points that describe wants that can't be satisfied. We can produce at all the points *inside* the *PPF* and *on* the *PPF*. These points are attainable. Suppose that in a typical month, we produce 4 million pizzas and 5 million CDs. Figure 2.1 shows this combination as point *E* and as possibility *E* in the table. The figure also shows other production possibilities.

**Figure 2.1** The Production Possibilities Frontier

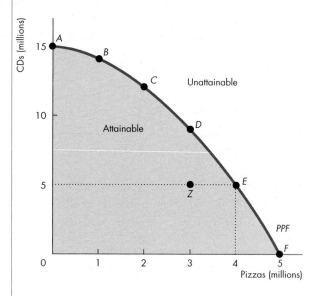

| Possibility | Pizzas (millions) | | CDs (millions) |
|---|---|---|---|
| A | 0 | and | 15 |
| B | 1 | and | 14 |
| C | 2 | and | 12 |
| D | 3 | and | 9 |
| E | 4 | and | 5 |
| F | 5 | and | 0 |

The table lists six points on the production possibilities frontier for CDs and pizza. Row *A* tells us that if we produce no pizza, the maximum quantity of CDs we can produce is 15 million. Points *A*, *B*, *C*, *D*, *E* and *F* in the figure represent the rows of the table. The line passing through these points is the production possibilities frontier (*PPF*).

The *PPF* separates the attainable from the unattainable. Production is possible at any point inside the orange area or on the frontier. Points outside the frontier are unattainable. Points inside the frontier such as point *Z* are inefficient because resources are either wasted or misallocated. At such points, it is possible to use the available resources to produce more of either or both goods.

For example, we might stop producing pizza and move all the people who produce it into producing CDs. Point *A* in Figure 2.1 and possibility *A* in the table show this case. The quantity of CDs produced increases to 15 million, and pizza production dries up. Alternatively, we might close the CD factories and switch all the resources into producing pizza. In this situation, we produce 5 million pizzas. Point *F* in the figure and possibility *F* in the table show this case.

## Production Efficiency

We achieve **production efficiency** if we cannot produce more of one good without producing less of some other good. When production is efficient, we are at a point *on* the *PPF*. If we are at a point *inside* the *PPF*, such as point Z, production is *inefficient* because we have some *unused* resources or we have some *misallocated* resources or both.

Resources are unused when they are idle but could be working. For example, we might leave some of the factories idle or some workers unemployed.

Resources are *misallocated* when they are assigned to tasks for which they are not the best match. For example, we might assign skilled pizza makers to work in a CD factory and skilled CD makers to work in a pizza shop. We could get more pizza *and* more CDs from these same workers if we reassigned them to the tasks that more closely match their skills.

If we produce at a point inside the *PPF* such as Z in Figure 2.1, we can use our resources more efficiently to produce more pizzas, more CDs, or more of *both* pizzas and CDs. But if we produce at a point *on* the *PPF*, we are using our resources efficiently and we can produce more of one good only if we produce less of the other. That is, along the *PPF*, we face a *trade-off*.

## Trade-off Along the *PPF*

Every choice *along* the *PPF* involves a *trade-off* – we must give up something to get something else. On the *PPF* in Figure 2.1, we must give up some CDs to get more pizza or give up some pizza to get more CDs.

Trade-offs arise in every imaginable real-world situation, and you reviewed several of them in Chapter 1. At any given point in time, we have a fixed amount of labour, land, capital and entrepreneurship. By using our available technologies, we can employ these resources to produce goods and services. But we are limited in what we can produce. This limit defines a boundary between what we can attain and what we cannot attain.

This boundary is the real world's production possibilities frontier, and it defines the trade-offs that we must make. On our real-world *PPF*, we can produce more of any one good or service only if we produce less of some other goods or services.

When doctors say that we must spend more on AIDS and cancer research, they are suggesting a trade-off: more medical research for less of some other things. When a politician says that she wants to spend more on education and healthcare, she is suggesting a trade-off: more education and healthcare for less defence expenditure or less private spending (because of higher taxes). When an environmental group argues for less logging in tropical rainforests, it is suggesting a trade-off: greater conservation of endangered wildlife for less hardwood. When your parents say that you should study more, they are suggesting a trade-off: more study time for less leisure or sleep.

All trade-offs involve a cost – an opportunity cost.

## Opportunity Cost

The **opportunity cost** of an action is the highest-valued alternative forgone. The *PPF* helps us to make the concept of opportunity cost precise and enables us to calculate it. Along the *PPF*, there are only two goods, so there is only one alternative forgone: some quantity of the other good. Given our current resources and technology, we can produce more pizzas only if we produce fewer CDs. The opportunity cost of producing an additional pizza is the number of CDs we *must* forgo. Similarly, the opportunity cost of producing an additional CD is the quantity of pizzas we *must* forgo.

For example, at point *C* in Figure 2.1, we produce fewer pizzas and more CDs than at point *D*. If we choose point *D* over point *C*, the additional 1 million pizzas *cost* 3 million CDs. One pizza costs 3 CDs.

We can also work out the opportunity cost of choosing point *C* over point *D* in Figure 2.1. If we move from point *D* to point *C*, the quantity of CDs produced increases by 3 million and the quantity of pizzas produced decreases by 1 million. So if we choose point *C* over point *D*, the additional 3 million CDs *cost* 1 million pizzas. So 1 CD costs 1/3 of a pizza.

### Opportunity Cost Is a Ratio

Opportunity cost is a ratio. It is the decrease in the quantity produced of one good divided by the increase in the quantity produced of another good as we move along the production possibilities frontier.

Because opportunity cost is a ratio, the opportunity cost of producing an additional CD is equal to the *inverse* of the opportunity cost of producing an additional pizza. Check this proposition by returning to the calculations we've just worked through. When we move along the *PPF* from *C* to *D*, the opportunity cost of a pizza is 3 CDs. The inverse of 3 is 1/3, so if we decrease the production of pizzas and increase the production of CDs by moving from *D* to *C*, the opportunity cost of a CD must be 1/3 of a pizza. You can check that this number is correct. If we move from *D* to *C*, we produce 3 million more CDs and 1 million fewer pizzas. Because 3 million CDs cost 1 million pizzas, the opportunity cost of 1 CD is 1/3 of a pizza.

### Increasing Opportunity Cost

The opportunity cost of a pizza increases as the quantity of pizzas produced increases. Also, the opportunity cost of a CD increases as the quantity of CDs produced increases. This phenomenon of increasing opportunity cost is reflected in the shape of the *PPF* – it is bowed outward.

When a large quantity of CDs and a small quantity of pizzas are produced – between points *A* and *B* in Figure 2.1 – the frontier has a gentle slope. A given increase in the quantity of pizzas *costs* a small decrease in the quantity of CDs, so the opportunity cost of a pizza is a small quantity of CDs.

When a large quantity of pizzas and a small quantity of CDs are produced – between points *E* and *F* in Figure 2.1 – the frontier is steep. A given increase in the quatity of pizzas *costs* a large decrease in the quantity of CDs, so the opportunity cost of a pizza is a large quantity of CDs.

The *PPF* is bowed outward because resources are not all equally productive in all activities. People with several years of experience working for Philips are good at producing CDs but not very good at making pizzas. So if we move some of these people from Philips to Domino's, we get a small increase in the quantity of pizzas but a large decrease in the quantity of CDs. Similarly, people who have spent years working at Domino's are good at producing pizzas, but they have no idea how to produce CDs. So if we move some of these people from Domino's to Philips, we get a small increase in the quantity of CDs but a large decrease in the quantity of pizzas. The more of either good we try to produce, the less productive are the additional resources we use to produce that good and the larger is the opportunity cost of a unit of that good.

### Increasing Opportunity Costs Are Everywhere

Just about every activity that you can think of is one with an increasing opportunity cost. We allocate the most skilful farmers and the most fertile land to the production of food. And we allocate the best doctors and the least fertile land to the production of healthcare services. If we shift fertile land and tractors away from farming to hospitals and ambulances and ask farmers to become hospital porters, the production of food drops drastically and the increase in the production of healthcare services is small. The opportunity cost of a unit of healthcare services rises. Similarly, if we shift our resources away from healthcare towards farming, we must use more doctors and nurses as farmers and more hospitals as hydroponic tomato factories. The decrease in the production of healthcare services is large, but the increase in food production is small. The opportunity cost of a unit of food rises. This example is extreme and unlikely, but these same considerations apply to most pairs of goods.

There may be some rare situations in which opportunity cost is constant. Switching resources from bottling ketchup to bottling mayonnaise is a possible example. But in general, when resources are reallocated, they must be assigned to tasks for which they are an increasingly poor match. Increasing opportunity costs are a general fact of life.

### Review Quiz

1   How does the production possibilities frontier illustrate scarcity?
2   How does the production possibilities frontier illustrate production efficiency?
3   How does the production possibilities frontier show that every choice involves a trade-off?
4   How does the production possibilities frontier illustrate opportunity cost?
5   Why is opportunity cost a ratio?
6   Why does the *PPF* for most goods bow outward and what does that imply about the relationship between opportunity cost and the quantity produced?

You can work these questions in Study Plan 2.1 and get instant feedback.

We've seen that what we can produce is limited by the production possibilities frontier. We've also seen that production on the *PPF* is efficient. But we can produce many different quantities on the *PPF*. How do we choose among them? How do we know which point on the *PPF* is the best one?

# Using Resources Efficiently

We achieve *production efficiency* at every point on the *PPF*, but which point is best? The answer is the point on the *PPF* at which goods and services are produced in the quantities that provide the greatest possible benefit. When goods and services are produced at the lowest possible cost and in the quantities that provide the greatest possible benefit, we have achieved **allocative efficiency**.

The questions that we raised when we reviewed the four big issues in Chapter 1 are questions about allocative efficiency. To answer such questions, we must measure and compare costs and benefits.

## The *PPF* and Marginal Cost

**Marginal cost** is the opportunity cost of producing *one more unit*. We can calculate marginal cost from the slope of the *PPF*. As the quantity of pizzas produced increases, the *PPF* gets steeper and marginal cost of a pizza increases. Figure 2.2 illustrates the calculation of the marginal cost of a pizza.

Begin by finding the opportunity cost of pizza in blocks of 1 million pizzas. The first million pizzas cost 1 million CDs, the second million pizzas cost 2 million CDs, the third million pizzas cost 3 million CDs, and so on. The bars in part (a) illustrate these calculations.

The bars in part (b) show the cost of an average pizza in each of the 1 million pizza blocks. Focus on the third million pizzas – the move from *C* to *D* in part (a). Over this range, because the 1 million pizzas cost 3 million CDs, one of these pizzas, on the average, costs 3 CDs – the height of the bar in part (b).

Next, find the opportunity cost of each additional pizza – the marginal cost of a pizza. The marginal cost of a pizza increases as the quantity of pizzas produced increases. The marginal cost at point *C* is less than it is at point *D*. On the average over the range from *C* to *D*, the marginal cost of a pizza is 3 CDs. But it exactly equals 3 CDs only in the middle of the range between *C* and *D*.

The red dot in part (b) indicates that the marginal cost of a pizza is 3 CDs when 2.5 million pizzas are produced. Each black dot in part (b) is interpreted in the same way. The red curve that passes through these dots, labelled *MC*, is the marginal cost curve. It shows the marginal cost of a pizza at each quantity of pizza as we move along the *PPF*.

**Figure 2.2**   The PPF and Marginal Cost

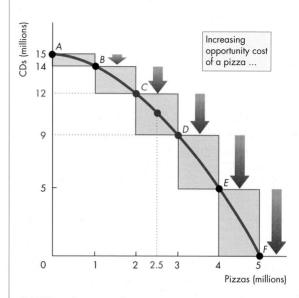

**(a) PPF and opportunity cost**

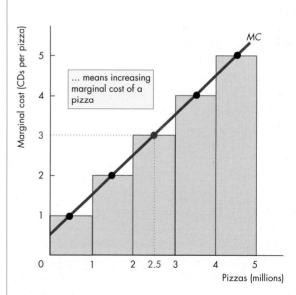

**(b) Marginal cost**

Marginal cost is calculated from the slope of the *PPF* in part (a). As the quantity of pizzas produced increases, the *PPF* gets steeper and the marginal cost of a pizza increases. The bars in part (a) show the opportunity cost of pizza in blocks of 1 million pizzas. The bars in part (b) show the cost of an average pizza in each of these 1 million blocks. The red curve, *MC*, shows the marginal cost of a pizza at each point along the *PPF*. This curve passes through the centre of each of the bars in part (b).

myeconlab Animation

# Preferences and Marginal Benefit

The **marginal benefit** from a good or service is the benefit received from consuming one more unit of it. This benefit is subjective. It depends on people's **preferences** – people's likes and dislikes and the intensity of those feelings.

*Marginal benefit* and *preferences* stand in sharp contrast to *marginal cost* and *production possibilities*. Preferences describe what people like and want and the production possibilities describe the limits or constraints on what is feasible.

We need a concrete way of illustrating preferences that parallels the way we illustrate the limits to production using the *PPF*.

The device that we use to illustrate preferences is the **marginal benefit curve**, which is a curve that shows the relationship between the marginal benefit from a good and the quantity consumed of that good. Note that the *marginal benefit curve* is unrelated to the *PPF* and cannot be derived from it.

We measure the marginal benefit from a good or service by the most that people are willing to pay for an additional unit of it. The idea is that you are willing to pay less for a good than it is worth to you but you are not willing to pay more: the most you are willing to pay for something is its marginal benefit.

It is a general principle that the more we have of any good or service, the smaller is its marginal benefit and the less we are willing to pay for another unit of it. This tendency is so widespread and strong that we call it a principle – the *principle of decreasing marginal benefit*.

The basic reason why the marginal benefit of a good or service decreases as we consume more of it is that we like variety. The more we consume of any one good or service, the more we tire of it and would prefer to switch to something else.

Think about your willingness to pay for pizza (or any other item). If pizza is hard to come by and you can buy only a few slices a year, you might be willing to pay a high price to get an additional slice. But if pizza is all you've eaten for the past few days, you are willing to pay almost nothing for another slice.

You've learned to think about cost as opportunity cost, not pounds or euros. You can think about marginal benefit and willingness to pay in the same terms. The marginal benefit, measured by what you are willing to pay for something, is the quantity of other goods and services that you are willing to forgo. Let's continue with the example of CDs and pizza and illustrate preferences this way.

**Figure 2.3** Preferences and the Marginal Benefit Curve

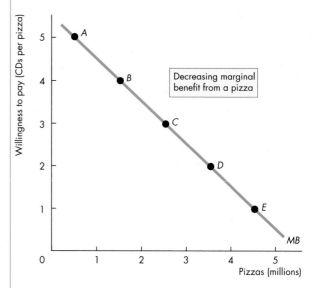

| Possibility | Pizzas (millions) | Willingness to pay (CDs per pizza) |
|---|---|---|
| A | 0.5 | 5 |
| B | 1.5 | 4 |
| C | 2.5 | 3 |
| D | 3.5 | 2 |
| E | 4.5 | 1 |

The smaller the quantity of pizzas produced, the more CDs people are willing to give up for an additional pizza. If pizza production is 0.5 million, people are willing to pay 5 CDs per pizza. But if pizza production is 4.5 million, people are willing to pay only 1 CD per pizza. Willingness to pay measures marginal benefit. A universal feature of people's preferences is that marginal benefit decreases.

myeconlab Animation

Figure 2.3 illustrates preferences as the willingness to pay for pizza in terms of CDs. In row *A*, pizza production is 0.5 million, and at that quantity people are willing to pay 5 CDs per pizza. As the quantity of pizzas produced increases, the amount that people are willing to pay for a pizza falls. When pizza production is 4.5 million, people are willing to pay only 1 CD per pizza.

Let's now use the concepts of marginal cost and marginal benefit to describe the efficient quantity of pizzas to produce.

**Figure 2.4** Efficient Use of Resources

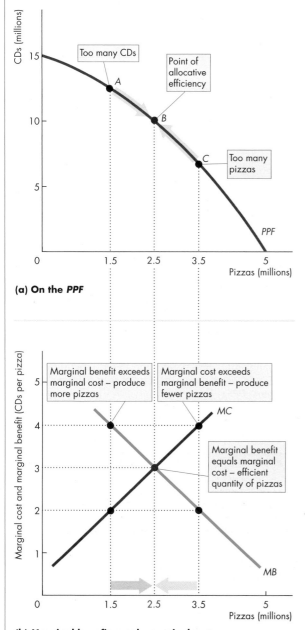

**(a) On the PPF**

**(b) Marginal benefit equals marginal cost**

The greater the quantity of pizzas produced, the smaller is the marginal benefit (*MB*) from pizza – the fewer CDs people are willing to give up to get an additional pizza. But the greater the quantity of pizzas produced, the greater is the marginal cost (*MC*) of pizza – the more CDs people must give up to get an additional pizza. When marginal benefit equals marginal cost, resources are being used efficiently.

myeconlab Animation

# Efficient Use of Resources

At any point on the *PPF*, we cannot produce more of one good without giving up some other good. At the best point on the *PPF*, we cannot produce more of one good without giving up some other good that provides greater benefit. We are producing at the point of allocative efficiency – the point on the *PPF* that we prefer above all other points.

Suppose in Figure 2.4, we produce 1.5 million pizzas. The marginal cost of a pizza is 2 CDs and the marginal benefit from a pizza is 4 CDs. Because someone values an additional pizza more highly than it costs to produce, we can get more value from our resources by moving some of them out of producing CDs and into producing pizzas.

Now suppose we produce 3.5 million pizzas. The marginal cost of a pizza is now 4 CDs, but the marginal benefit from a pizza is only 2 CDs. Because the additional pizza costs more to produce than anyone thinks it is worth, we can get more value from our resources by moving some of them away from producing pizzas and into producing CDs.

But suppose we produce 2.5 million pizzas. Marginal cost and marginal benefit are now equal at 3 CDs. This allocation of resources between pizzas and CDs is efficient. If more pizzas are produced, the forgone CDs are worth more than the additional pizzas. If fewer pizzas are produced, the forgone pizzas are worth more than the additional CDs.

## Review Quiz

1 What is marginal cost? How is it measured?
2 What is marginal benefit? How is it measured?
3 How does the marginal benefit from a good change as the quantity of that good increases?
4 What is allocative efficiency and how does it relate to the production possibilites frontier?
5 What conditions must be satisfied if resources are used efficiently?

You can work these questions in Study Plan 2.2 and get instant feedback.

You now understand the limits to production and the conditions under which resources are used efficiently. Your next task is to study the expansion of production possibilities.

## ◆ Economic Growth

During the past 30 years, production per person in the EU has doubled. An expansion of production possibilities is called **economic growth**. Economic growth increases our *standard of living,* but it does not overcome scarcity and avoid opportunity cost. To make our economy grow, we face a trade-off – the faster we make production grow, the greater is the opportunity cost of economic growth.

## The Cost of Economic Growth

Economic growth comes from technological change and capital accumulation. **Technological change** is the development of new goods and of better ways of producing goods and services. **Capital accumulation** is the growth of capital resources, which includes *human capital.*

Technological change and capital accumulation have vastly expanded our production possibilities. We can produce automobiles that provide us with more transportation than was available when we had only horses and carriages. We can produce satellites that provide global communications on a much larger scale than that available with the earlier cable technology. But if we use our resources to develop new technologies and produce capital, we must decrease our production of consumption goods and services. New technologies and new capital have an opportunity cost. Let's look at this opportunity cost.

Instead of studying the *PPF* of pizzas and CDs, we'll hold the quantity of CDs produced constant and examine the *PPF* for pizzas and pizza ovens. Figure 2.5 shows this *PPF* as the blue curve *ABC*. If we devote no resources to producing pizza ovens, we produce at point *A*. If we produce 3 million pizzas, we can produce 6 pizza ovens at point *B*. If we produce no pizza, we can produce 10 ovens at point *C*.

The amount by which our production possibilities expand depends on the resources we devote to technological change and capital accumulation. If we devote no resources to this activity (point *A*), our *PPF* remains the blue curve $PPF_0$ in Figure 2.5. If we cut the current production of pizza and produce 6 ovens (point *B*), then in the future, we'll have more capital and our *PPF* will rotate outward to the position shown by the red curve $PPF_1$. The fewer resources we devote to producing pizza and the more resources we devote to producing ovens, the greater is the future expansion of our production possibilities.

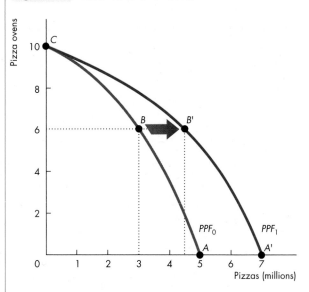

**Figure 2.5** Economic Growth

$PPF_0$ shows the limits to the production of pizza and pizza ovens, with the production of all other goods and services remaining the same. If we allocate no resources to producing pizza ovens and produce 5 million pizzas, our production possibilities will remain the same, $PPF_0$.

But if we decrease pizza production to 3 million and produce 6 ovens, our production possibilities will expand. After one period, the *PPF* rotates outward to $PPF_1$ and we can produce at point *B'*, a point outside the original $PPF_0$.

We can rotate the *PPF* outward, but we cannot avoid opportunity cost. The opportunity cost of producing more pizzas in the future is fewer pizzas today.

myeconlab Animation

Economic growth brings enormous benefit in the form of increased consumption, but it is not free and does not abolish scarcity.

In Figure 2.5, to make economic growth happen we must use some resources to produce new ovens, which leaves fewer resources to produce pizza. To move to *B'* in the future, we must move from *A* to *B* today. The opportunity cost of more pizzas in the future is fewer pizzas today. Also, on the new *PPF*, we continue to face a trade-off and opportunity cost.

The ideas about economic growth that we have explored in the setting of the pizza industry also apply to nations. Hong Kong and the EU provide a striking case study.

## Economic Growth in the EU and Hong Kong

The experience of the EU and Hong Kong is a striking example of the effects of our choices on the rate of economic growth.

Figure 1 shows that, in 1970, the production possibilities per person in the EU were more than double those in Hong Kong. In 1970, the EU was at point *A* on its *PPF* and Hong Kong was at point *A* on its *PPF*. Since 1970, the EU has devoted one-fifth of its resources to accumulating capital and the other four-fifths to consumption. Hong Kong has devoted one-third of its resources to accumulating capital and two-thirds to consumption.

By 2010, the production possibilities per person in Hong Kong had reached a similar level to those in the EU. If Hong Kong continues to devote more resources to accumulating capital than the EU does (at point *B* on its 2010 *PPF*), Hong Kong will continue to grow more rapidly. But if Hong Kong increases consumption and decreases capital accumulation (moving to point *C* on its 2010 *PPF*), then its economic growth rate will slow.

The EU is typical of the rich industrial countries and Hong Kong is typical of the fast-growing Asian economies. Countries like China, India and Taiwan have expanded

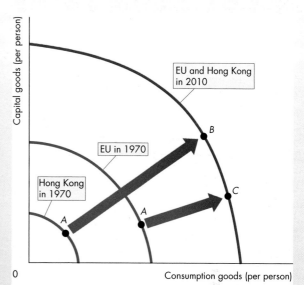

**Figure 1  Economic Growth in the EU and Hong Kong**

their production possibilities by between 5 and 10 per cent a year.

If such high growth rates are maintained, these other Asian countries will continue to close the gap between themselves and the EU, as Hong Kong has done.

## A Nation's Economic Growth

The experiences of the EU and Hong Kong make a striking example of the effects of our choices about consumption and capital goods on the rate of economic growth.

If a nation devotes all its factors of production to producing consumption goods and services and none to advancing technology and accumulating capital, its production possibilities in the future will be the same as they are today.

To expand production possibilities in the future, a nation must devote fewer resources to producing current consumption goods and services and some resources to accumulating capital and developing new technologies. As production possibilities expand, consumption in the future can increase. The decrease in consumption today is the opportunity cost of an increase in consumption in the future.

### Review Quiz

1  What are the two key factors that generate economic growth?
2  How does economic growth influence the *PPF*?
3  What is the opportunity cost of economic growth?
4  Why has Hong Kong experienced faster economic growth than the EU?

You can work these questions in Study Plan 2.3 and get instant feedback.

We have seen that we can increase our production possibilities by accumulating capital and developing new technology. Next, we'll study another way in which we can expand our production possibilities – the amazing fact that *both* buyers and sellers gain from specialization and trade.

**Gains from Trade**

People can produce for themselves all the goods and services that they consume, or they can produce one good or a few goods and trade with others. Producing only one good or a few goods is called *specialization*.

We are going to discover how people gain by specializing in the production of the good in which they have a *comparative advantage* and trading with each other.

## Comparative Advantage and Absolute Advantage

A person has a **comparative advantage** in an activity if that person can perform the activity at a lower opportunity cost than anyone else. Differences in opportunity costs arise from differences in individual abilities and from differences in the characteristics of other resources.

No one excels at everything. One person is an outstanding batter but a poor catcher; another person is a brilliant lawyer but a poor teacher. In almost all human endeavours, what one person does easily, someone else finds difficult. The same applies to land and capital. One plot of land is fertile but has no mineral deposits; another plot of land has outstanding views but is infertile. One machine has great precision but is difficult to operate; another is fast but often breaks down.

Although no one excels at everything, some people excel and can outperform others in many activities – perhaps all activities. A person who is more productive than others has an **absolute advantage**.

Absolute advantage involves comparing productivities – production per hour – whereas comparative advantage involves comparing opportunity cost.

A person who has an absolute advantage does not have a *comparative* advantage in every activity. Maria Sharapova can run faster and play tennis better than most people. She has an absolute advantage in these two activities. But compared with other people, she is a better tennis player than runner, so her *comparative* advantage is in playing tennis.

Because people's abilities and the quality of their resources differ, they have different opportunity costs of producing various goods and services. Such differences give rise to comparative advantage.

To explore the idea of comparative advantage, and its astonishing implications, we'll look at the production process in two smoothie bars: one operated by Erin and the other operated by Jack.

### Erin's Smoothie Bar

Erin produces smoothies and salads. In Erin's high-tech bar, she can turn out either a smoothie or a salad every 2 minutes – see Table 2.1.

If Erin spends all her time making smoothies, she can produce 30 an hour. And if she spends all her time making salads, she can also produce 30 an hour. If she splits her time equally between the two, she can produce 15 smoothies and 15 salads an hour. For each additional smoothie Erin produces, she must decrease her production of salads by one, and for each additional salad she produces, she must decrease her production of smoothies by one. So

> **Erin's opportunity cost of producing 1 smoothie is 1 salad,**

and

> **Erin's opportunity cost of producing 1 salad is 1 smoothie.**

Erin's customers buy smoothies and salads in equal quantities, so she splits her time equally between the items and produces 15 smoothies and 15 salads an hour.

### Jack's Smoothie Bar

Jack also produces both smoothies and salads. But Jack's bar is smaller than Erin's. Also, Jack has only one blender, and it's a slow old machine. Even if Jack uses all his resources to produce smoothies, he can produce only 6 an hour – see Table 2.2. But Jack is good in the salad department, so if he uses all his resources to make salads, he can produce 30 an hour.

Jack's ability to make smoothies and salads is the same regardless of how he splits an hour between the two tasks. He can make a salad in 2 minutes or a smoothie in 10 minutes. For each additional smoothie Jack produces, he must decrease his production of salads by 5. And for each additional salad he produces, he

---

**Table 2.1**

**Erin's Production Possibilities**

| Item | Minutes to produce 1 | Quantity per hour |
|---|---|---|
| Smoothies | 2 | 30 |
| Salads | 2 | 30 |

**Table 2.2**

### Jack's Production Possibilities

| Item | Minutes to produce 1 | Quantity per hour |
|------|---------------------|-------------------|
| Smoothies | 10 | 6 |
| Salads | 2 | 30 |

must decrease his production of smoothies by 1/5 of a smoothie. So

> **Jack's opportunity cost of producing 1 smoothie is 5 salads,**

and

> **Jack's opportunity cost of producing 1 salad is 1/5 of a smoothie.**

Jack's customers, like Erin's, buy smoothies and salads in equal quantities. So Jack spends 50 minutes of each hour making smoothies and 10 minutes of each hour making salads. With this division of his time, Jack produces 5 smoothies and 5 salads an hour.

### Erin's Comparative Advantage

In which of the two activities does Erin have a comparative advantage? Recall that comparative advantage is a situation in which one person's opportunity cost of producing a good is lower than another person's opportunity cost of producing that same good. Erin has a comparative advantage in producing smoothies. Her opportunity cost of a smoothie is 1 salad, whereas Jack's opportunity cost of a smoothie is 5 salads.

### Jack's Comparative Advantage

If Erin has a comparative advantage in producing smoothies, Jack must have a comparative advantage in producing salads. His opportunity cost of a salad is 1/5 of a smoothie, whereas Erin's opportunity cost of a salad is 1 smoothie.

## Achieving the Gains from Trade

Erin and Jack run into each other one evening in a singles bar. After a few minutes of getting acquainted, Erin tells Jack about her amazing smoothie business. Her only problem, she tells Jack, is that she wishes she

could produce more because potential customers leave when the queue gets too long.

Jack is hesitant to risk spoiling his chances by telling Erin about his own struggling business, but he takes the risk. Jack explains to Erin that he spends 50 minutes of every hour making 5 smoothies and 10 minutes making 5 salads. Erin's eyes pop. "Have I got a deal for you!" she exclaims.

Here's the deal that Erin sketches on a serviette. Jack stops making smoothies and allocates all his time to producing salads. Erin stops making salads and allocates all her time to producing smoothies. That is, they both specialize in producing the good in which they have a comparative advantage. Together they produce 30 smoothies and 30 salads – see Table 2.3(b).

They then trade. Erin sells Jack 10 smoothies and Jack sells Erin 20 salads – the price of a smoothie is 2 salads – see Table 2.3(c).

After the trade, Jack has 10 salads – the 30 he produces minus the 20 he sells to Erin. He also has the 10 smoothies that he buys from Erin. So Jack now has increased the quantities of smoothies and salads that he can sell to his customers – see Table 2.3(d).

**Table 2.3**

### Erin and Jack Gain from Trade

| (a) Before trade | Erin | Jack |
|------------------|------|------|
| Smoothies | 15 | 5 |
| Salads | 15 | 5 |

| (b) Production | Erin | Jack |
|----------------|------|------|
| Smoothies | 30 | 0 |
| Salads | 0 | 30 |

| (c) Trade | Erin | Jack |
|-----------|------|------|
| Smoothies | sell 10 | buy 10 |
| Salads | buy 20 | sell 20 |

| (d) After trade | Erin | Jack |
|-----------------|------|------|
| Smoothies | 20 | 10 |
| Salads | 20 | 10 |

| (e) Gains from trade | Erin | Jack |
|----------------------|------|------|
| Smoothies | +5 | +5 |
| Salads | +5 | +5 |

Erin has 20 smoothies – the 30 she produces minus the 10 she sells to Jack. And she has the 20 salads she buys from Jack – see Table 2.3(d). Both Erin and Jack gain 5 smoothies and 5 salads – see Table 2.3(e).

To illustrate her idea, Erin grabs a fresh serviette and draws the graphs in Figure 2.6. The blue *PPF* in part (a) shows Jack's production possibilities. Before trade, he is producing 5 smoothies and 5 salads an hour at point *A*. The blue *PPF* in part (b) shows Erin's production possibilities. Before trade, she is producing 15 smoothies and 15 salads an hour at point *A*.

Erin's proposal is that they each specialize in producing the good in which they have a comparative advantage. Jack produces 30 salads and no smoothies at point *B* on his *PPF*. Erin produces 30 smoothies and no salads at point *B* on her *PPF*.

Erin and Jack then trade smoothies and salads at a price of 2 salads per smoothie or 1/2 of a smoothie per salad. Jack buys smoothies from Erin for 2 salads each, which is less than the 5 salads it costs him to produce a smoothie. Erin buys salads from Jack for 1/2 a smoothie each, which is less than the 1 smoothie that it costs her to produce a salad.

With trade, Jack has 10 smoothies and 10 salads at point *C* – a gain of 5 smoothies and 5 salads. Jack moves to a point *outside* his *PPF*.

With trade, Erin has 20 smoothies and 20 salads at point *C* – a gain of 5 smoothies and 5 salads. Erin moves to a point *outside* her *PPF*.

Despite Erin being more productive than Jack, both Erin and Jack gain from producing more of the good in which they have a comparative advantage and trading.

## Figure 2.6 The Gains from Trade

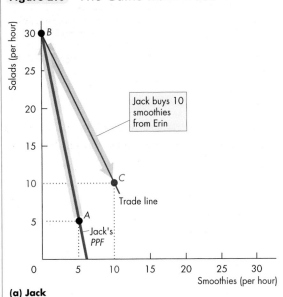

**(a) Jack**

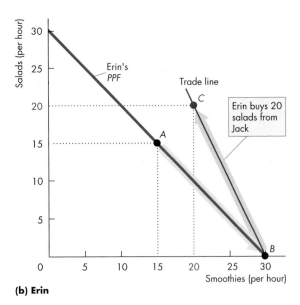

**(b) Erin**

Jack initially produces at point *A* on his *PPF* in part (a), and Erin initially produces at point *A* on her *PPF* in part (b). Jack's opportunity cost of producing a salad is less than Erin's, so Jack has a comparative advantage in producing salads. Erin's opportunity cost of producing a smoothie is less than Jack's, so Erin has a comparative advantage in producing smoothies.

If Jack specializes in salad, he produces 30 salads and no smoothies at point *B* on his *PPF*. If Erin produces

30 smoothies and no salads, she produces at point *B* on her *PPF*.

They exchange salads for smoothies along the red 'Trade line'. Erin buys salads from Jack for less than her opportunity cost of producing them. And Jack buys smoothies from Erin for less than his opportunity cost of producing them. Each goes to point *C* – a point outside his or her *PPF*. Both Jack and Erin increase production by 5 smoothies and 5 salads with no change in resources.

## The EU and China Gain from Trade

In Chapter 1 (see p. 5), we asked whether globalization is in the social interest. What you have just learned about the gains from trade provides a big part of the answer. We gain from specialization and trade.

The gains that we achieve from *international trade* are similar to those achieved by Jack and Erin. When Europeans buy clothes that are manufactured in China and when China buys Airbus aircraft manufactured in the EU, people in both countries gain.

We could slide along our *PPF* producing fewer aircraft and more jackets. Similarly, China could slide along its *PPF* producing more aircraft and fewer jackets. But everyone would lose. The opportunity cost of our jackets and China's opportunity cost of aircraft would rise.

By specializing in aircraft and trading with China, we get our jackets at a lower cost than that at which we can produce them, and China gets its aircraft at a lower cost than that at which it can produce them.

### Review Quiz

1  What gives a person a comparative advantage?
2  Distinguish between comparative advantage and absolute advantage.
3  Why do people specialize and trade?
4  What are the gains from specialization and trade?
5  What is the source of the gains from trade?

You can work these questions in Study Plan 2.4 and get instant feedback.    myeconlab

## Economic Coordination

People gain by specializing in the production of those goods and services in which they have a comparative advantage and trading with each other. Erin and Jack, whose production of salads and smoothies we studied earlier in this chapter, can get together and make a deal that enables them to enjoy the gains from specialization and trade. But for billions of individuals to specialize and produce millions of different goods and services, their choices must somehow be coordinated.

Two competing economic coordination systems have been used: central economic planning and decentralized markets.

Central economic planning might appear to be the best system because it can express national priorities. But when this system was tried, as it was for 60 years in Russia and for 30 years in China, it was a miserable failure. Today, these and most other previously planned economies are adopting a decentralized market system.

Decentralized coordination works best, but for it to do so it needs four complementary social institutions:

◆ Firms
◆ Markets
◆ Property rights
◆ Money

## Firms

A **firm** is an economic unit that employs factors of production and organizes them to produce and sell goods and services. Tesco and Virgin Atlantic are examples of firms.

Firms coordinate a huge amount of economic activity. A Starbucks coffee shop, for example, might buy the machines and labour services of Erin and Jack and start to produce salads and smoothies at all its outlets.

But Tesco would not have become Britian's largest retailer if it had produced all the things that it sells. It became the largest UK retailer by specializing in providing retail services and buying the goods and services it sells from other firms that specialize in their production (just like Erin and Jack did). This trade between Tesco and the producers of the goods and services it sells takes place in markets.

## Markets

In ordinary speech, the word *market* means a place where people buy and sell goods such as fish, meat, fruits and vegetables. In economics, a *market* has a more general meaning. A **market** is any arrangement that enables buyers and sellers to get information and to do business with each other. An example is the market in which oil is bought and sold – the world oil market. The world oil market is not a place. It is the network of oil producers, oil users, wholesalers and brokers who buy and sell oil. In the world oil market, decision makers do not meet physically. They make deals throughout the world by telephone, fax and direct computer link.

Markets have evolved because they facilitate trade. Without organized markets, we would miss out on a substantial part of the potential gains from trade. Enterprising individuals and firms, each pursuing their own self-interest, have profited from making markets – standing ready to buy or sell the items in which they specialize. But markets can work only when property rights exist.

## Property Rights

The social arrangements that govern the ownership, use and disposal of anything that people value are called **property rights**. *Real property* includes land and buildings – the things we call property in ordinary speech – and durable goods such as plant and equipment. *Financial property* includes shares and bonds and money in the bank. *Intellectual property* is the intangible product of creative effort. This type of property includes books, music, computer programs and inventions of all kinds and is protected by copyrights and patents.

Where property rights are enforced, people have the incentive to specialize and produce the goods and services in which they have a comparative advantage. Where people can steal the production of others, resources are devoted not to production but to protecting possessions. Without property rights, we would still be hunting and gathering like our Stone Age ancestors.

## Money

**Money** is any commodity or token that is generally acceptable as a means of payment. Erin and Jack didn't use money; they exchanged salads and smoothies. In principle, trade in markets can exchange any item for any other item. But you can perhaps imagine how complicated life would be if we exchanged goods for other goods. The 'invention' of money makes trading in markets much more efficient.

## Circular Flows Through Markets

Figure 2.7 shows the flows that result from the choices that households and firms make. Households specialize and choose the quantities of labour, land, capital and entrepreneurship to sell or rent to firms. Firms choose the quantities of factors of production to hire. These (red) flows go through the *factor markets*. Households choose the quantities of goods and services to buy, and firms choose the quantities to produce. These (red) flows go through the *goods markets*. Households receive incomes from firms and make expenditures on goods and services (the green flows).

How do markets coordinate all these decisions?

## Coordinating Decisions

Markets coordinate decisions through price adjustments. To see how, think about the market for fresh-baked bread. Suppose that some people who want to buy fresh-baked bread are not able to do so. To make the choices of buyers and sellers compatible, buyers must switch to prepackaged bread or more fresh-baked bread must be offered for sale (or both). A rise in the price of fresh-baked bread produces this outcome. A higher price encourages bakers to offer more fresh-baked bread for sale. It also encourages some people to change the bread they buy. Fewer people buy fresh-baked bread, and more buy prepackaged bread. More fresh-baked bread (and more prepackaged bread) are offered for sale.

Alternatively, suppose that more fresh-baked bread is available than people want to buy. In this case, to make the choices of buyers and sellers compatible, more fresh-baked bread must be bought or less fresh-baked bread must be offered for sale (or both). A fall in the price of fresh-baked bread achieves this outcome. A lower price encourages bakers to produce a smaller quantity of, and encourages people to buy more fresh-baked bread.

**Figure 2.7** Circular Flows in the Market Economy

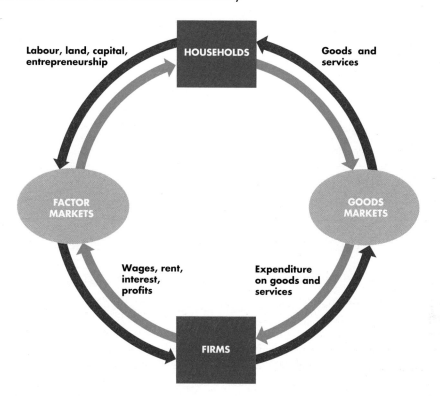

Households and firms make economic choices and markets coordinate these choices.

Households choose the quantities of labour, land, capital and entrepreneurship to sell or rent to firms in exchange for wages, rent, interest and profit. Households also choose how to spend their incomes on the various types of goods and services available.

Firms choose the quantities of factors of production to hire and the quantities of the various goods and services to produce.

Goods markets and factor markets coordinate these choices of households and firms.

The counterclockwise red flows are real flows – the flow of factors of production from households to firms and the flow of goods and services from firms to households.

The clockwise green flows are the payments for the red flows. They are the flow of incomes from firms to households and the flow of expenditure on goods and services from households to firms.

---

## Review Quiz

1  Why are social institutions such as firms, markets, property rights and money necessary?
2  What are the main functions of markets?
3  What are the flows in the market economy that go from firms to households and from households to firms?
4  In the circular flows of the market economy, which flows are real flows? Which flows are money flows?

You can work these questions in Study Plan 2.5 and get instant feedback.    myeconlab

You have now begun to see how economists approach economic questions. Scarcity, choice and divergent opportunity costs explain why we specialize and trade and why firms, markets, property rights and money have developed. You can see all around you the lessons you've learned in this chapter.

*Reading Between the Lines* on pp. 44–45 provides an opportunity to apply the *PPF* model to deepen your understanding of the reasons for the increase in the cost of food associated with the increase in maize production.

# Reading Between the Lines

# The Rising Opportunity Cost of Food

The Guardian, 5 April 2008

## Crop Switch Worsens Global Food Price Crisis

### John Vidal

Two years ago the UN's Food and Agriculture Organization expected biofuels to help eradicate hunger and poverty. . . . Yesterday the UN secretary general, Ban Ki-moon raised real doubt over that policy amid signs that the world was facing its worst food crisis in a generation.

Since . . . 2006 tens of thousands of farmers have switched from food to fuel production. . . . Spurred by generous subsidies and an EU commitment to increase the use of biofuels to counter climate change, at least 8m hectares (20m acres) of maize, wheat, soya and other crops which once provided animal feed and food have been taken out of production in the US. In addition, large areas of Brazil, Argentina, Canada and eastern Europe are diverting . . . crops to biofuels. The result, exacerbated by . . . shortages because of severe weather, has been big increases of all global food commodity prices.

Lester Brown, director of the Earth Policy Institute in Washington, said . . . 'the US has diverted 60m tonnes of food to fuel. On the heels of seven years of consumption of world grains exceeding supply, this has put a great strain on the world's grain supplies'.

Robert Zoellick, president of the World Bank, said this week that prices of all staple food had risen 80% in three years, and that 33 countries faced unrest because of the price rises. . . . In Bangladesh . . . a government source said: 'One reason is that the overall drop in food production because of biofuels has prevented food being exported.' . . .

Last month the UK's chief scientist and food expert, Professor John Beddington, said the prospect of food shortages over the next 20 years was so acute that politicians, scientists and farmers must tackle it immediately.

## The Essence of the Story

◆ In 2006, the UN's Food and Agriculture Organization expected biofuel to reduce poverty and the EU promoted the use of biofuels to counter climate change.

◆ Farmers around the world switched from producing crops for food to crops for biofuel.

◆ World food prices rose 80 per cent in 3 years and policy advisers say the switch to growing crops for biofuels has reduced the amount of food available, adding to the pressure for food price rises.

◆ The UK's chief scientist said the prospect of food shortages must be tackled immediately by politicians, scientists and farmers.

# ◈ Economic Analysis

♦ Biofuel is made from maize (and several other crops), so biofuel and food compete to use the same resources.

♦ To produce more biofuel under UN and EU policy, farmers increased the number of acres devoted to biofuel crop production.

♦ Increasing the production of crops for biofuel means decreasing the production of crops for food and decreasing the production of other crops.

♦ Figure 1 shows the EU production possibilities frontier, *PPF*, for one of the biofuel crops, maize, and other goods and services.

♦ A movement along the *PPF* in Figure 1 from point *A* to point *B* illustrates the increase in the production of maize and decrease in the production of other goods and services.

♦ In moving from point *A* to point *B*, the EU incurs a higher opportunity cost of producing maize, as the greater slope of the *PPF* at point *B* indicates.

♦ In other regions of the world, despite the fact that more land was devoted to maize production, the amount of maize produced didn't change in 2007 and 2008.

♦ The reason is that bad weather lowered the crop yield per hectare in those regions.

♦ Figure 2 shows the rest of the world's *PPF* for maize and other goods and services in 2007 and 2008.

♦ The increase in the amount of land devoted to producing maize is illustrated by a movement along $PPF_{07}$.

♦ With a decrease in the crop yield, production possibilities decreased and the *PPF* rotated inward.

♦ The rotation from $PPF_{07}$ to $PPF_{08}$ illustrates this decrease in production possibilities.

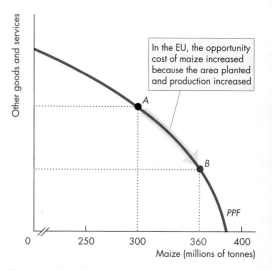

Figure 1  EU *PPF*

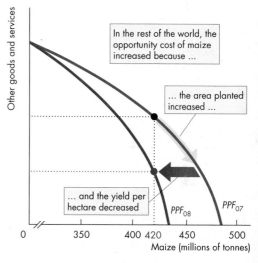

Figure 2  Rest of the world *PPF*

♦ The opportunity cost of producing maize in the rest of the world increased for two reasons: the movement along its *PPF* and the inward rotation of the *PPF*.

♦ With a higher opportunity cost of producing maize, the cost of both biofuel and food increases.

# SUMMARY

## Key Points

### Production Possibilities and Opportunity Cost (pp. 30–32)

◆ The production possibilities frontier is the boundary between production levels that are attainable and those that are unattainable when all available resources are used to their limit.

◆ Production efficiency occurs at points on the production possibilities frontier.

◆ Along the production possibilities frontier, the opportunity cost of producing more of one good is the amount of the other good that must be given up.

◆ The opportunity cost of all goods increases as production of the good increases.

Working Problems 1 to 3 will give you a better understanding of production possibilities and opportunity cost.

### Using Resources Efficiently

(pp. 33–35)

◆ Allocative efficiency occurs when goods and services are produced at the least possible cost and in the quantities that bring the greatest possible benefit.

◆ The marginal cost of a good is the opportunity cost of producing one more unit of it.

◆ The marginal benefit from a good is the benefit received from consuming one more unit of it and is measured by the willingness to pay for it.

◆ The marginal benefit of a good decreases as the amount of the good available increases.

◆ Resources are used efficiently when the marginal cost of each good is equal to its marginal benefit.

Working Problems 4 to 10 will give you a better understanding of using resources efficiently.

### Economic Growth (pp. 36–37)

◆ Economic growth, which is the expansion of production possibilities, results from capital accumulation and technological change.

◆ The opportunity cost of economic growth is forgone current consumption.

◆ The benefit of economic growth is increased future consumption.

Working Problem 11 will give you a better understanding of economic growth.

### Gains from Trade (pp. 38–41)

◆ A person has a comparative advantage in producing a good if that person can produce the good at a lower opportunity cost than everyone else.

◆ People gain by specializing in the activity in which they have a comparative advantage and trading.

Working Problems 12 and 13 will give you a better understanding of the gains from trade.

### Economic Coordination (pp. 41–43)

◆ Firms coordinate a large amount of economic activity, but there is a limit to the efficient size of a firm.

◆ Markets coordinate the economic choices of people and firms.

◆ Markets can work efficiently only when property rights exist and money makes trading in markets more efficient.

Working Problem 14 will give you a better understanding of economic coordination.

## Key Terms

Absolute advantage, 38
Allocative efficiency, 33
Capital accumulation, 36
Comparative advantage, 38
Economic growth, 36
Firm, 41
Marginal benefit, 34
Marginal benefit curve, 34
Marginal cost, 33
Market, 42
Money, 42
Opportunity cost, 31
Preferences, 34
Production efficiency, 31
Production possibilities frontier, 30
Property rights, 42
Technological change, 36

STUDY PLAN PROBLEMS AND APPLICATIONS

**myeconlab**  You can work Problems 1 to 20 in MyEconLab Chapter 2 Study Plan and get instant feedback.

# Production Possibilities and Opportunity Cost (Study Plan 2.1)

Use the following information to work Problems 1 to 3.

Brazil produces ethanol from sugar, and the land used to grow sugar can be used to grow food crops. Suppose that Brazil's production possibilities for ethanol and food crops are as follows:

| Ethanol (barrels per day) | | Food crops (tonnes per day) |
|---|---|---|
| 70 | and | 0 |
| 64 | and | 1 |
| 54 | and | 2 |
| 40 | and | 3 |
| 22 | and | 4 |
| 0 | and | 5 |

**1  a** Draw a graph of Brazil's *PPF* and explain how your graph illustrates scarcity.

  **b** If Brazil produces 40 barrels of ethanol a day, how much food must it produce to achieve production efficiency?

  **c** Why does Brazil face a trade-off on its *PPF*?

**2  a** If Brazil increases its production of ethanol from 40 barrels per day to 54 barrels per day, what is the opportunity cost of the additional ethanol?

  **b** If Brazil increases its production of food crops from 2 tonnes per day to 3 tonnes per day, what is the opportunity cost of the additional food?

  **c** What is the relationship between your answers to parts (a) and (b)?

**3** Does Brazil face an increasing opportunity cost of ethanol? What feature of Brazil's *PPF* illustrates increasing opportunity cost?

# Using Resources Efficiently

## (Study Plan 2.2)

Use the table in Problem 1 to work Problems 4 and 5.

**4** Define marginal cost and calculate Brazil's marginal cost of producing a tonne of food when the quantity produced is 2.5 tonnes per day.

**5** Define marginal benefit, explain how it is measured, and explain why the data in the table does not enable you to calculate Brazil's marginal benefit from food.

**6** Distinguish between production efficiency and allocative efficiency. Explain why many production possibilities achieve production efficiency but only one achieves allocative efficiency.

Use the following graphs to work Problems 7 to 10.

Harry enjoys tennis but wants a high grade in his economics course. The graphs show his *PPF* for these two 'goods' and his *MB* curve for tennis.

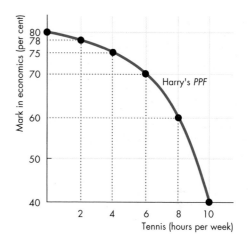

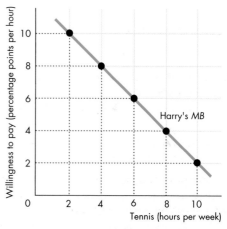

**7** What is Harry's marginal cost of tennis if he plays for (i) 3 hours a week, (ii) 5 hours a week and (iii) 7 hours a week?

**8  a** If Harry uses his time to achieve allocative efficiency, what is his economics mark and how many hours of tennis does he play?

  **b** Explain why Harry would be worse off getting a higher mark than your answer in part (a)?

**9** If Harry becomes a tennis superstar with big earnings from tennis, what happens to his *PPF*, his *MB* curve and his efficient time allocation?

**10** If Harry suddenly finds high marks in economics easier to attain, what happens to his *PPF*, his *MB* curve and his efficient time allocation?

## Economic Growth (Study Plan 2.3)

**11** A farm grows wheat and produces pork. The marginal cost of producing each of these products increases as more of it is produced.

**a** Make a graph that illustrates the farm's *PPF*.

**b** The farm adopts a new technology that allows it to use fewer resources to fatten pigs. On a graph show the impact of the new technology on the farm's *PPF*.

**c** With the farm using the new technology described in part (b), has the opportunity cost of producing a tonne of wheat increased, decreased or remained the same? Explain and illustrate your answer.

**d** Is the farm more efficient with the new technology than it was with the old one? Why?

## Gains from Trade (Study Plan 2.4)

**12** In an hour, Sue can produce 40 caps or 4 jackets and Tessa can produce 80 caps or 4 jackets.

**a** Calculate Sue's opportunity cost of producing a cap.

**b** Calculate Tessa's opportunity cost of producing a cap.

**c** Who has a comparative advantage in producing caps?

**d** If Sue and Tessa specialize in producing the good in which each of them has a comparative advantage, and they trade 1 jacket for 15 caps, who gains from the specialization and trade?

**13** Suppose that Tessa buys a new machine for making jackets that enables her to make 20 jackets an hour. (She can still make only 80 caps per hour.)

**a** Who now has a comparative advantage in producing jackets?

**b** Can Sue and Tessa still gain from trade?

**c** Would Sue and Tessa still be willing to trade 1 jacket for 15 caps? Explain your answer.

## Economic Coordination (Study Plan 2.5)

**14** For 50 years, Cuba has had a centrally planned economy in which the government makes the big decisions on how resources will be allocated.

**a** Why would you expect Cuba's production possibilities (per person) to be smaller than those of the EU?

**b** What are the social institutions that Cuba might lack that help the EU to achieve allocative efficiency?

## Economics in the News (Study Plan 2.N)

Use the following data to work Problems 15 to 17.

Brazil produces ethanol from sugar at a cost of 83 cents per gallon. The US produces ethanol from corn at a cost of $1.14 per gallon. Sugar grown on one acre of land produces twice the quantity of ethanol as the corn grown on an acre. The US imports 5 per cent of the ethanol it uses and produces the rest itself. Since 2003, US ethanol production has more than doubled and US corn production has increased by 45 per cent.

**15** **a** Does Brazil or the US have a comparative advantage in producing ethanol?

**b** Sketch the *PPF* for ethanol and other goods and services for the US.

**c** Sketch the *PPF* for ethanol and other goods and services for Brazil.

**16** **a** Do you expect the opportunity cost of producing ethanol in the US to have increased since 2003? Explain why.

**b** Do you think the US has achieved production efficiency in its manufacture of ethanol? Explain why or why not.

**c** Do you think the US has achieved allocative efficiency in its manufacture of ethanol? Explain why or why not.

**17** Make a graph similar to Figure 2.6 to show how both the US and Brazil gain from specialization and trade.

Use this news clip to work Problems 18 to 20.

**Time For Tea**

Americans are switching to loose-leaf tea for its health benefits. Tea could be grown in the US, but picking tea leaves would be costly because it can only be done by workers and not by machine.

Source: *The Economist*, 8 July 2005

**18** **a** Sketch *PPF*s for the production of tea and other goods and services in India and the US.

**b** Sketch marginal cost curves for the production of tea in India and the US.

**19** **a** Sketch the marginal benefit curves for tea in the US before and after Americans began to appreciate the health benefits of loose tea.

**b** Explain how the quantity of loose tea that achieves allocative efficiency has changed.

**c** Does the change in preferences towards tea affect the opportunity cost of producing tea?

**20** Explain why the US does not produce tea and instead imports it from India.

ADDITIONAL PROBLEMS AND APPLICATIONS

**myeconlab** You can work these problems in MyEconLab if assigned by your lecturer.

## Production Possibilities and Opportunity Cost

Use the following information to work Problems 21 and 22.

Sunland's production possibilities are:

| Food (kilograms per month) | | Sunscreen (litres per month) |
|---|---|---|
| 300 | and | 0 |
| 200 | and | 50 |
| 100 | and | 100 |
| 0 | and | 150 |

**21**  **a** Draw a graph of Sunland's production possibilities frontier.

**b** If Sunland produces 150 kilograms of food how much sunscreen must it produce if it achieves production efficiency?

**c** What is Sunland's opportunity cost of producing 1 kilogram of food?

**d** What is Sunland's opportunity cost of producing 1 litre of sunscreen?

**e** What is the relationship between your answers to parts (c) and (d)?

**22**  What feature of a *PPF* illustrates increasing opportunity cost? Explain why Sunland's opportunity cost does or does not increase.

## Using Resources Efficiently

**23**  In Problem 21, what is the marginal cost of a kilogram of food in Sunland when the quantity produced is 150 kilograms per month? What is special about the marginal cost of food in Sunland?

**24**  The table describes the preferences in Sunland:

| Sunscreen (litres per month) | | Willingness to pay (kilograms per litre) |
|---|---|---|
| 25 | and | 3 |
| 75 | and | 2 |
| 125 | and | 1 |

**a** What is the marginal benefit from sunscreen and how is it measured?

**b** Draw a graph of Sunland's marginal benefit from sunscreen.

## Economic Growth

**25**  Capital accumulation and technological change bring economic growth, which means that the *PPF* keeps shifting outward: production that was unattainable yesterday becomes attainable today; production that is unattainable today will become attainable tomorrow. Why doesn't this process of economic growth mean that scarcity is being defeated and will one day be gone?

## Gains from Trade

Use the following data to work Problems 26 and 27.

Kim can produce 40 pies or 400 cakes an hour. Liam can produce 100 pies or 200 cakes an hour.

**26**  **a** Calculate Kim's opportunity cost of a pie and Liam's opportunity cost of a pie.

**b** If each spends 30 minutes of each hour producing pies and 30 minutes producing cakes, how many pies and cakes does each produce?

**c** Who has a comparative advantage in producing pies? Who has a comparative advantage in producing cakes?

**27**  **a** Draw a graph of Kim's *PPF* and Liam's *PPF*.

**b** On your graph, show a point at which each produces when they spend 30 minutes of each hour producing pies and 30 minutes producing cakes.

**c** On your graph, show what Kim produces and what Liam produces when they specialize.

**d** When they specialize and trade, what are the total gains from trade?

**e** If Kim and Liam share the total gains equally, what trade takes place between them?

## Economic Coordination

**28**  Indicate on a graph of the circular flows in the market economy, the real and money flows in which the following items belong:

**a** You buy an iPad from the Apple Store.

**b** Apple Inc. pays the designers of the iPad.

**c** Apple Inc. decides to expand and rents an adjacent building.

**d** You buy a new e-book from Amazon.

**e** Apple Inc. hires a student as an intern during the summer.

## Economics in the News

**29** After you have studied *Reading Between the Lines* on pp. 44–45 answer the following questions.

   **a** Why might EU climate change policy increase US production of maize?

   **b** Why would you expect an increase in the quantity of US or EU maize production to raise the opportunity cost of maize?

   **c** Why did the cost of producing maize increase in the rest of the world?

   **d** Is it possible that the increased quantity of maize produced, despite the higher cost of production, moves the US closer to allocative efficiency?

**30** **Malaria Eradication Back on the Table**

In response to the Gates Malaria Forum in October 2007, countries are debating the pros and cons of eradication. Dr. Arata Kochi of the World Health Organization believes that with enough money malaria cases could be cut by 90 per cent, but he believes that it would be very expensive to eliminate the remaining10 per cent of cases. He concluded that countries should not strive to eradicate malaria.

        Source: *The New York Times*, 4 March 2008

   **a** Is Dr. Kochi talking about production efficiency or allocative efficiency or both?

   **b** Make a graph with the percentage of malaria cases eliminated on the *x*-axis and the marginal cost and marginal benefit of driving down malaria cases on the *y*-axis. On your graph:

     (i) Draw a marginal cost curve that is consistent with Dr. Kochi's opinion.

     (ii) Draw a marginal benefit curve that is consistent with Dr. Kochi's opinion.

     (iii) Identify the quantity of malaria eradicated that achieves allocative efficiency.

Use the following news clip to work Problem 31.

**31** **Lots of Little Screens**

Inexpensive broadband access has created a generation of television producers for whom the Internet is their native medium. As they redirect the focus from TV to computers, mobile phones, and iPods, the video market is developing into an open digital network.

        Source: *The New York Times*, 2 December 2007

   **a** How has inexpensive broadband changed the production possibilities of video entertainment and other goods and services?

   **b** Sketch a *PPF* for video entertainment and other goods and services before broadband.

   **c** Show how the arrival of inexpensive broadband has changed the *PPF*.

   **d** Sketch a marginal benefit curve for video entertainment.

   **e** Show how the new generation of TV producers for whom the Internet is their native medium might have changed the marginal benefit from video entertainment.

   **f** Explain how the efficient quantity of video entertainment has changed.

Use the following news clip to work Problems 32 to 34.

**Britain's Music Stores Squeezed off the High Street**

The article describes trends in music retailing: Sony Music and Amazon selling online, supermarkets selling at low prices, and traditional high street music retailers HMV, Music Zone, and Virgin Megastores all struggling.

        Source: *The Economist*, 20 January 2007

**32** Draw the *PPF* curves for high street music retailers and online music retailers before and after the Internet became available.

**33** Draw the marginal cost and marginal benefit curves for high street music retailers and online music retailers before and after the Internet became available.

**34** Explain how changes in production possibilities, preferences or both have changed the way in which recorded music is retailed.

Use the following news clip to work Problems 35 and 36.

**He Shoots! He Scores! He Makes Films!**

All-star basketball player Baron Davis and his school friend, Cash Warren, premiered their first film *Made in America* at the Sundance Festival in January 2008. The film, based on gang activity in South Central Los Angeles, received good reviews.

        Source: *The New York Times*, 24 February 2008

**35**  **a** Does Baron Davis have an absolute advantage in basketball and film directing and is this the reason for his success in both activities?

   **b** Does Baron Davis have a comparative advantage in basketball or film directing or both and is this the reason for his success in both activities?

**36**  **a** Sketch a *PPF* between playing basketball and producing other goods and services for Baron Davis and for yourself.

   **b** How do you (and people like you) and Baron Davis (and people like him) gain from specialization and trade?

Guatemala
"Las Nubes"
$8 lb.
Farm:Finca Las Nubes
Varietal:Catuai
Processing:Fully Washed
Altitude:1,500m
Owner:Don Fabio Solis
City: Esquipulas
Region: Chiquimula

# CHAPTER

# 3

# Demand and Supply

**After studying this chapter you will be able to:**

♦ Describe a competitive market and think about a price as an opportunity cost

♦ Explain the influences on demand

♦ Explain the influences on supply

♦ Explain how demand and supply determine prices and quantities bought and sold

♦ Use demand and supply to make predictions about changes in prices and quantities

What makes the price of coffee hit a 12-year high, the price of oil double in a year and the price of wheat nearly double in three months? Will these prices come down? This chapter enables you to answer these and similar questions about why prices rise, fall or just fluctuate.

In this chapter, you will see how people make choices about scarce resources by responding to prices and how prices are determined by demand and supply. The demand and supply model is the main tool of economics. It helps us to answer the big economic question: What, how and for whom goods and services are produced?

At the end of the chapter, in *Reading Between the Lines*, we'll apply the model to the market for coffee and explain why its price increased sharply in 2010.

## Markets and Prices

When you want to buy a new pair of running shoes, or a sandwich, or an energy drink, or a bottle of water, or decide to upgrade your CD player, you must find a place where people sell those items. The place in which you find them is a *market*. You learned in Chapter 2 (p. 42) that a market is any arrangement that enables buyers and sellers to get information and to do business with each other.

A market has two sides: buyers and sellers. There are markets for *goods* such as apples and hiking boots, for *services* such as haircuts and tennis lessons, for *resources* such as computer programmers and earth-movers, and for other manufactured *inputs* such as memory chips and car parts. There are also markets for money, such as the euro and the dollar, and for financial securities such as BP shares and Yahoo! shares. Only our imagination limits what can be traded in markets.

Some markets are physical places where buyers and sellers meet and where an auctioneer or a broker helps to determine the prices. Examples of this type of market are the London Stock Exchange and the Billingsgate fish market.

Some markets are groups of people spread around the world who never meet and know little about each other but are connected through the Internet or by telephone and fax. Examples are the e-commerce markets and currency markets.

But most markets are unorganized collections of buyers and sellers. You do most of your trading in this type of market. An example is the market for football boots. The buyers in this multi-million pound a year market are the several million people who play football (or who want to make an exotic fashion statement). The sellers are the tens of thousands of retail sports equipment and footwear stores. Each buyer can visit several different stores and each seller knows that the buyer has a choice of stores.

## A Competitive Market

Markets vary in the intensity of competition that buyers and sellers face. In this chapter, we're going to study a **competitive market** – a market that has many buyers and many sellers, so no single buyer or seller can influence the price.

Producers offer items for sale only if the price is high enough to cover their opportunity cost. And consumers respond to changing opportunity cost by seeking cheaper alternatives to expensive items.

We are going to study the way people respond to *prices* and the forces that determine prices. But to pursue these tasks, we need to understand the relationship between a price and an opportunity cost.

In everyday life, the *price* of an object is the number of pounds or euros that must be given up in exchange for it. Economists refer to this price as the **money price**.

The *opportunity cost* of an action is the highest-valued alternative forgone. If, when you buy a coffee, the highest-valued thing you forgo is some chocolate, then the opportunity cost of the coffee is the *quantity* of chocolate forgone. We can calculate the quantity of chocolate forgone from the money prices of coffee and chocolate.

If the money price of coffee is £3 a cup and the money price of a chocolate bar is £1, then the opportunity cost of 1 cup of coffee is 3 chocolate bars. To calculate this opportunity cost, we divide the price of a cup of coffee by the price of a chocolate bar and find the *ratio* of one price to the other. The ratio of one price to another is called a **relative price** and a *relative price is an opportunity cost*.

We can express the relative price of coffee in terms of chocolate or any other good. The normal way of expressing a relative price is in terms of a 'basket' of all goods and services. To calculate this relative price, we divide the money price of a good by the money price of a 'basket' of all goods (called a *price index*). The resulting relative price tells us the opportunity cost of the good in terms of how much of the 'basket' we must give up to buy it.

The theory of demand and supply that we are about to study determines *relative prices* and the word 'price' means *relative* price. When we predict that the price of a good or service will fall, we do not mean that its *money* price will fall – although it might. We mean that its *relative* price will fall. That is, its price will fall *relative* to the average price of other goods and services.

 ### Review Quiz

1 What is the distinction between a money price and a relative price?
2 Explain why a relative price is an opportunity cost.
3 Think of examples of goods whose relative price has risen or has fallen by a large amount.

You can work these questions in Study Plan 3.1 and get instant feedback.

Let's begin our study of demand and supply, starting with demand.

## Demand

If you demand something, then you

1   Want it,
2   Can afford it and
3   Plan to buy it.

*Wants* are the unlimited desires or wishes that people have for goods and services. How many times have you thought that you would like something 'if only you could afford it' or 'if it weren't so expensive'? Scarcity guarantees that many – perhaps most – of our wants will never be satisfied. Demand reflects a decision about which wants to satisfy.

The **quantity demanded** of a good or service is the amount that consumers plan to buy during a given time period at a particular price. The quantity demanded is not necessarily the same as the quantity actually bought. Sometimes the quantity demanded exceeds the amount of goods available, so the quantity bought is less than the quantity demanded.

The quantity demanded is measured as an amount per unit of time. For example, suppose that you buy one cup of coffee a day. The quantity of coffee that you demand can be expressed as 1 cup per day, 7 cups per week, or 365 cups per year.

Many factors influence buying plans and one of them is price. We look first at the relationship between the quantity demanded of a good and its price. To study this relationship, we make a *ceteris paribus* assumption. That is, we keep all other influences on buying plans the same and we ask: How, other things remaining the same, does the quantity demanded of a good change as its price changes?

The law of demand provides the answer.

## The Law of Demand

The **law of demand** states:

> Other things remaining the same, the higher the price of a good, the smaller is the quantity demanded; and the lower the price of a good, the greater is the quantity demanded.

Why does a higher price reduce the quantity demanded? For two reasons:

◆   Substitution effect
◆   Income effect

### Substitution Effect

When the price of a good rises, other things remaining the same, its *relative* price – its opportunity cost – rises. Although each good is unique, it has *substitutes* – other goods that can be used in its place. As the opportunity cost of a good rises, people buy less of that good and more of its substitutes.

### Income Effect

When the price of a good rises and other influences on buying plans remain unchanged, the price rises relative to incomes. Faced with a higher price and unchanged income, people cannot afford to buy all the things they previously bought. They must decrease the quantities demanded of at least some goods and services, and normally the good whose price has increased will be one of the goods that people buy less of.

To see the substitution effect and the income effect at work, think about the effects of a change in the price of an energy drink. Many goods are substitutes for an energy drink. For example, an energy bar or an energy gel could be consumed in place of an energy drink.

Suppose that an energy drink initially sells for £3 and then its price falls to £1.50. People now substitute energy drinks for energy bars – the substitution effect. And with a budget that now has some slack from the lower price of an energy drink, people buy more energy drinks – the income effect. The quantity of energy drinks demanded increases for these two reasons.

Now suppose that an energy drink sells for £3 and its price rises to £4. People now substitute energy bars for energy drinks – the substitution effect. Faced with tighter budgets, people buy even fewer energy drinks – the income effect. The quantity of energy drinks demanded decreases for these two reasons.

## Demand Curve and Demand Schedule

You are now about to study one of the two most used curves in economics: the demand curve. And you are going to encounter one of the most critical distinctions: the distinction between *demand* and *quantity demanded*.

The term **demand** refers to the entire relationship between the price of the good and the quantity demanded of the good. Demand is illustrated by the demand curve and the demand schedule. The term *quantity demanded* refers to a point on a demand curve – the quantity demanded at a particular price.

Figure 3.1 shows the demand curve for energy drinks. A **demand curve** shows the relationship between the quantity demanded of a good and its price when all other influences on consumers' planned purchases remain the same.

The table in Figure 3.1 is the *demand schedule*, which lists the quantity demanded at each price when all the other influences on consumers' planned purchases remain the same. For example, if the price of an energy drink is 50 pence, the quantity demanded is 9 million a week. If the price is £2.50, the quantity demanded is 2 million a week. The other rows of the table show the quantities demanded at prices of £1.00, £1.50 and £2.00.

We graph the demand schedule as a demand curve with the quantity demanded on the *x*-axis and the price on the *y*-axis. The points on the demand curve labelled *A* to *E* correspond to the rows of the demand schedule. For example, point *A* on the graph shows a quantity demanded of 9 million energy drinks a week at a price of 50 pence a drink.

## Willingness and Ability to Pay

We can also view a demand curve as a willingness-and-ability-to-pay curve. And the willingness and ability to pay is a measure of *marginal benefit*.

If a small quantity is available, the highest price that someone is willing and able to pay for one more unit is high. As the quantity available increases, the marginal benefit falls and the highest price that someone is willing and able to pay falls along the demand curve.

In Figure 3.1, if only 2 million energy drinks are available each week, the highest price that someone is willing to pay for the 2 millionth drink is £2.50. But if 9 million energy drinks are available each week, someone is willing to pay 50 pence for the last drink bought.

## A Change in Demand

When any factor that influences buying plans other than the price of the good changes, there is a **change in demand**. Figure 3.2 illustrates an increase in demand. When demand increases, the demand curve shifts rightward and the quantity demanded is greater at each and every price. For example, at a price of £2.50, on the original (blue) demand curve, the quantity demanded is 2 million energy drinks a week. On the new (red) demand curve, the quantity demanded is 6 million energy drinks a week. Look closely at the numbers in the table in Figure 3.2 and check that the quantity demanded at each price is greater.

**Figure 3.1** The Demand Curve

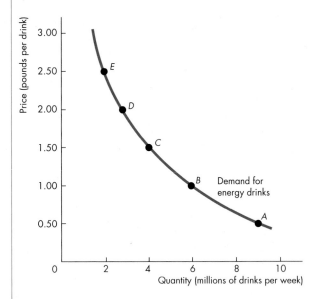

|   | Price (pounds per drink) | Quantity demanded (millions of energy drinks per week) |
|---|---|---|
| A | 0.50 | 9 |
| B | 1.00 | 6 |
| C | 1.50 | 4 |
| D | 2.00 | 3 |
| E | 2.50 | 2 |

The table shows a demand schedule for energy drinks. At a price of 50 pence an energy drink, 9 million a week are demanded; at a price of £1.50 an energy drink, 4 million a week are demanded. The demand curve shows the relationship between quantity demanded and price, everything else remaining the same. The demand curve slopes downward: as price decreases, the quantity demanded increases.

The demand curve can be read in two ways. For a given price, the demand curve tells us the quantity that people plan to buy. For example, at a price of £1.50 an energy drink, the quantity demanded is 4 million energy drinks a week. For a given quantity, the demand curve tells us the maximum price that consumers are willing and able to pay for the last energy drink available. For example, the maximum price that consumers will pay for the 6 millionth drink is £1.00.

## Figure 3.2   An Increase in Demand

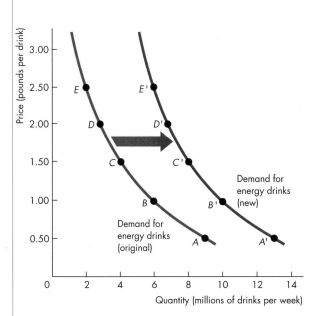

| Original demand schedule<br>Original income | | | New demand schedule<br>New higher income | | |
|---|---|---|---|---|---|
| | **Price**<br>**(pounds**<br>**per drink)** | **Quantity**<br>**demanded**<br>**(millions of**<br>**drinks per week)** | | **Price**<br>**(pounds**<br>**per drink)** | **Quantity**<br>**demanded**<br>**(millions of**<br>**drinks per week)** |
| A | 0.50 | 9 | A' | 0.50 | 13 |
| B | 1.00 | 6 | B' | 1.00 | 10 |
| C | 1.50 | 4 | C' | 1.50 | 8 |
| D | 2.00 | 3 | D' | 2.00 | 7 |
| E | 2.50 | 2 | E' | 2.50 | 6 |

A change in any influence on buyers' plans other than the price of the good itself results in a new demand schedule and a shift of the demand curve. A change in income changes the demand for energy drinks.

At a price of £1.50 an energy drink, 4 million drinks a week are demanded at the original income (row *C* of the table) and 8 million energy drinks a week are demanded at the new higher income. A rise in income increases the demand for energy drinks. The demand curve shifts *rightward*, as shown by the shift arrow and the resulting red curve.

myeconlab Animation

Six main factors bring changes in demand. They are changes in:

◆ Prices of related goods
◆ Expected future prices
◆ Income
◆ Expected future income or credit
◆ Population
◆ Preferences

## Prices of Related Goods

The quantity of energy drinks that consumers plan to buy depends in part on the prices of their substitutes. A **substitute** is a good that can be used in place of another good. For example, a bus ride is a substitute for a train ride and an energy bar is a substitute for an energy drink. If the price of an energy bar rises, people buy fewer energy bars and more energy drinks. The demand for energy drinks increases.

The quantity of a good that people plan to buy also depends on the prices of its complements. A **complement** is a good that is used in conjunction with another good. For example, fish and chips are complements and so are energy drinks and exercise. If the price of an hour at the gym falls, people buy more gym time *and more* energy drinks.

## Expected Future Prices

If the price of a good is expected to rise in the future and if the good can be stored, the opportunity cost of obtaining the good for future use is lower today than it will be when the price has increased. So people retime their purchases – they substitute over time. They buy more of the good now before its price is expected to rise (and less later), so the demand for the good increases.

For example, suppose that Spain is hit by a frost that damages the season's orange crop. You expect the price of orange juice to rise in the future, so you fill your freezer with enough frozen juice to get you through the next six months. Your current demand for frozen orange juice has increased and your future demand has decreased.

Similarly, if the expected future price of a good falls, the opportunity cost of buying the good today is high relative to what it is expected to be in the future. So people retime their purchases. They buy less of the good now before its price is expected to fall, so the demand for the good decreases today and increases in the future.

Computer prices are constantly falling and this fact poses a dilemma. Will you buy a new computer now, in time for the start of the academic year, or will you wait until the price has fallen some more? Because people expect computer prices to keep falling, the current demand for computers is less (the future demand is greater) than it otherwise would be.

## Income

Consumers' income influences demand. When income increases, consumers buy more of most goods; and when income decreases, consumers buy less of most goods. Although an increase in income leads to an increase in the demand for *most* goods, it does not lead to an increase in the demand for *all* goods.

A **normal good** is one for which demand increases as income increases. An **inferior good** is one for which demand decreases as income increases. As income increases, the demand for air travel (a normal good) increases and the demand for long-distance bus trips (an inferior good) decreases.

## Expected Future Income or Credit

When expected future income increases or credit becomes easier to get, demand for the good might increase now. For example, a bank worker gets the news that she will receive a big bonus at the end of the year, so she decides to buy a new car right now.

## Population

Demand also depends on the size and the age structure of the population. The larger the population, the greater is the demand for all goods and services; the smaller the population, the smaller is the demand.

For example, the demand for parking spaces or cinema seats or energy drinks or just about anything that you can imagine is much greater in London than it is in Leeds.

Also, the larger the proportion of the population in a given age group, the greater is the demand for the goods and services used by that age group. For example, the number of older people is increasing relative to the number of babies. As a result, the demand for walking frames is increasing at a faster pace than that at which the demand for prams is increasing.

## Preferences

Demand depends on preferences. *Preferences* are an individual's attitudes towards goods and services.

---

**Table 3.1**

### The Demand for Energy Drinks

**The Law of Demand**

*The quantity of energy drinks demanded*

| *Decreases if*: | *Increases if*: |
|---|---|
| ◆ The price of an energy drink rises | ◆ The price of an energy drink falls |

**Changes in Demand**

*The demand for energy drinks*

| *Decreases if*: | *Increases if*: |
|---|---|
| ◆ The price of a substitute falls | ◆ The price of a substitute rises |
| ◆ The price of a complement rises | ◆ The price of a complement falls |
| ◆ The expected future price of an energy drink falls | ◆ The expected future price of an energy drink rises |
| ◆ Income falls* | ◆ Income rises* |
| ◆ Expected future income falls or credit becomes harder to get* | ◆ Expected future income rises or credit becomes easier to get* |
| ◆ The population decreases | ◆ The population increases |

\* An energy drink is a normal good.

---

Preferences depend on such things as the weather, information and fashion. For example, greater health and fitness awareness has shifted preferences in favour of energy drinks, so the demand for energy drinks has increased.

Table 3.1 summarizes the influences on demand and the direction of those influences.

## A Change in the Quantity Demanded versus a Change in Demand

Changes in the factors that influence buyers' plans cause either a change in the quantity demanded or a change in demand. Equivalently, they cause either a movement along the demand curve or a shift of the demand curve. The distinction between a change in the quantity demanded and a change in demand is the same as that between a movement along the demand curve and a shift of the demand curve.

A point on the demand curve shows the quantity demanded at a given price. So a movement along the demand curve shows a **change in the quantity demanded**. The entire demand curve shows demand. So a shift of the demand curve shows a *change in demand*. Figure 3.3 illustrates and summarizes these distinctions.

## Movement Along the Demand Curve

If the price of the good changes but no other influence on buying plans changes, we illustrate this as a movement along the demand curve.

A fall in the price of a good increases the quantity demanded of it. In Figure 3.3, we illustrate the effect of a fall in price as a movement down along the blue demand curve $D_0$.

A rise in the price of a good decreases the quantity demanded of it. In Figure 3.3, we illustrate the effect of a rise in price as a movement up along the blue demand curve $D_0$.

## A Shift of the Demand Curve

If the price of a good remains constant but some other influence on buyers' plans changes, there is a change in demand for that good. We illustrate a change in demand as a shift of the demand curve. For example, if more people work out at the gym, consumers buy more energy drinks regardless of the price of a drink. That is what a rightward shift of the demand curve shows – more energy drinks are bought at each and every price.

In Figure 3.3, when any influence on buyers' planned purchases changes, other than the price of the good, there is a *change in demand* and the demand curve shifts. Demand *increases* and the demand curve *shifts rightward* (to the red demand curve $D_1$) if income increases (for a normal good), the price of a substitute rises, the price of a complement falls, expected future income increases, the expected future price of the good rises, or the population increases.

Demand *decreases* and the demand curve *shifts leftward* (to the red demand curve $D_2$) if income decreases (for a normal good), the price of a substitute falls, the price of a complement rises, expected future income decreases, the expected future price of the good falls, or the population decreases. (For an inferior good, the effects of changes in income are in the direction opposite to those described above.)

**Figure 3.3    A Change in the Quantity Demanded versus a Change in Demand**

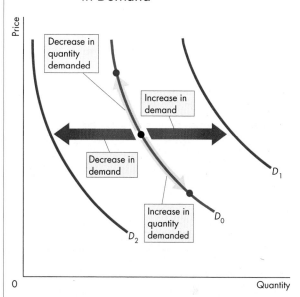

When the price of the good changes, there is a movement along the demand curve and a change in the quantity demanded, shown by the blue arrows on demand curve $D_0$.

When any other influence on buyers' plans changes, there is a shift of the demand curve and a change in demand. An increase in demand shifts the demand curve rightward (from $D_0$ to $D_1$). A decrease in demand shifts the demand curve leftward (from $D_0$ to $D_2$).

myeconlab Animation

### Review Quiz

1   Define the quantity demanded of a good or service.
2   What is the law of demand and how do we illustrate it?
3   What does the demand curve tell us about the price that consumers are willing to pay?
4   List all the influences on buying plans that change demand and for each influence say whether it increases or decreases demand.
5   Distinguish between the quantity demanded of a good and demand for the good.
6   Why does the demand not change when the price of a good changes with no change in the other influences on buying plans?

You can work these questions in Study Plan 3.2 and get instant feedback.

## ◆ Supply

If a firm supplies a good or a service, the firm

1   Has the resources and technology to produce it,
2   Can profit from producing it and
3   Plans to produce it and sell it.

A supply is more than just having the *resources* and the *technology* to produce something. *Resources and technology* are the constraints that limit what is possible.

Many useful things can be produced, but they are not produced unless it is profitable to do so. (No one produces electric bed-making machines, for example!) Supply reflects a decision about which technologically feasible items to produce.

The **quantity supplied** of a good or service is the amount that producers plan to sell during a given time period at a particular price. The quantity supplied is not necessarily the same amount as the quantity actually sold. Sometimes the quantity supplied is greater than the quantity demanded, so the quantity sold is less than the quantity supplied.

Like the quantity demanded, the quantity supplied is measured as an amount per unit of time. For example, suppose that Ford produces 1,000 cars a day. The quantity of cars supplied by Ford can be expressed as 1,000 a day, 7,000 a week, or 365,000 a year. Without the time dimension, we cannot tell whether a particular number is large or small.

Many factors influence selling plans and, again, one of them is price. We look first at the relationship between the quantity supplied of a good and its price. And again, as we did when we studied demand, to isolate this relationship, we keep all other influences on selling plans the same and we ask: How, other things remaining the same, does the quantity supplied of a good change as its price changes?

The law of supply provides the answer.

## The Law of Supply

The **law of supply** states:

> **Other things remaining the same, the higher the price of a good, the greater is the quantity supplied; and the lower the price of a good, the smaller is the quantity supplied.**

Why does a higher price increase the quantity supplied? It is because *marginal cost increases*. As the quantity produced of any good increases, the marginal cost of producing the good increases. (You can refresh your memory of increasing marginal cost in Chapter 2, p. 33.)

It is never worth producing a good if the price received for it does not at least cover the marginal cost of producing it. So when the price of a good rises, other things remaining the same, producers are willing to incur a higher marginal cost and increase production. The higher price brings forth an increase in the quantity supplied.

Let's now illustrate the law of supply with a supply curve and a supply schedule.

## Supply Curve and Supply Schedule

You are now going to study the second of the two most used curves in economics: the supply curve. And you're going to learn about the critical distinction between *supply* and *quantity supplied*.

The term **supply** refers to the entire relationship between the quantity supplied and the price of a good. Supply is illustrated by the supply curve and the supply schedule. The term *quantity supplied* refers to a point on a supply curve – the quantity supplied at a particular price.

Figure 3.4 shows the supply curve of energy drinks. A **supply curve** shows the relationship between the quantity supplied of a good and its price when all other influences on producers' planned sales remain the same. The supply curve is a graph of a supply schedule.

The table in Figure 3.4 sets out the supply schedule for energy drinks. A *supply schedule* lists the quantities supplied at each price when all the other influences on producers' planned sales remain the same. For example, if the price of an energy drink is 50 pence, the quantity supplied is zero – in row *A* of the table. If the price of an energy drink is £1.00, the quantity supplied is 3 million drinks a week – in row *B*. The other rows of the table show the quantities supplied at prices of £1.50, £2.00 and £2.50.

To make a supply curve, we graph the quantity supplied on the *x*-axis and the price on the *y*-axis. The points on the supply curve labelled *A* to *E* correspond to the rows of the supply schedule. For example, point *A* on the graph shows a quantity supplied of zero at a price of 50 pence an energy drink. Point *E* shows a quantity supplied of 6 million drinks at £2.50 an energy drink.

## Figure 3.4    The Supply Curve

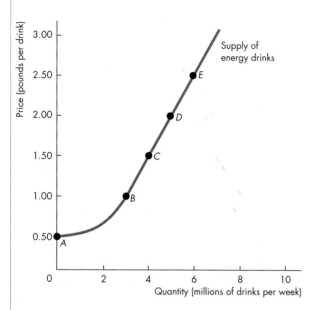

| | Price<br>(pounds per<br>energy drink) | Quantity supplied<br>(millions of energy<br>drinks per week) |
|---|---|---|
| A | 0.50 | 0 |
| B | 1.00 | 3 |
| C | 1.50 | 4 |
| D | 2.00 | 5 |
| E | 2.50 | 6 |

The table shows the supply schedule of energy drinks. For example, at a price of £1.00, 3 million energy drinks a week are supplied; at a price of £2.50, 6 million energy drinks a week are supplied. The supply curve shows the relationship between the quantity supplied and price, other things remaining the same. The supply curve usually slopes upward. As the price of a good increases, the quantity supplied increases.

A supply curve can be read in two ways. For a given price, it tells us the quantity that producers plan to sell at that price. For example, at a price of £1.50 a drink, producers are willing to supply 4 million drinks a week. For a given quantity, the supply curve tells us the minimum price at which producers are willing to sell one more drink. For example, if 6 million drinks are produced each week, the lowest price at which someone is willing to sell the 6 millionth drink is £2.50.

## Minimum Supply Price

The supply curve, like the demand curve, has two interpretations. It is the minimum-supply-price curve. It tells us the lowest price at which someone is willing to sell another unit. This lowest price is *marginal cost*.

If a small quantity is produced, the lowest price at which someone is willing to sell one more unit is low. But as the quantity produced increases, the lowest price at which someone is willing to sell one more unit rises along the supply curve.

In Figure 3.4, if 6 million energy drinks are produced each week, the lowest price that a producer is willing to accept for the 6 millionth drink is £2.50. But if only 4 million energy drinks are produced each week, a producer is willing to accept £1.50 for the last drink sold.

# A Change in Supply

When any factor that influences selling plans other than the price of the good changes, there is a **change in supply**. Six main factors bring changes in supply. They are changes in:

◆ Prices of factors of production
◆ Prices of related goods produced
◆ Expected future prices
◆ Number of suppliers
◆ Technology
◆ The state of nature

## Prices of Factors of Production

The prices of factors of production used to produce a good influence the supply of the good. The easiest way to see this influence is to think about the supply curve as a minimum-supply-price curve. If the price of a factor of production rises, the lowest price a producer is willing to accept rises, so supply decreases. For example, during 2009, as the price of jet fuel increased, the supply of air transportation decreased. Similarly, a rise in the minimum wage decreases the supply of energy drinks.

## Prices of Related Goods Produced

The prices of related goods and services that firms produce influence supply. For example, if the price of soft drinks rises, the supply of energy drinks decreases. Energy drinks and soft drinks are *substitutes in production* – goods that can be produced by using the same resources. If the price of beef rises, the supply of leather increases. Beef and leather are *complements in production* – goods that must be produced together.

## Expected Future Prices

If the expected future price of a good rises, the return from selling it in the future is higher than it is today. So supply decreases today and increases in the future.

## Number of Suppliers

The larger the number of firms that produce a good, the greater is the supply of the good. As firms enter an industry, the supply of the good produced increases. As firms leave an industry, the supply decreases.

## Technology

The term 'technology' is used broadly to mean the way that factors of production are used to produce a good. A technology change occurs when a new method is discovered that lowers the cost of producing a good. For example, new methods used in the factories that produce computer chips have lowered the cost and increased the supply of computer chips.

## The State of Nature

The state of nature includes all the natural forces that influence production, including the state of the weather. Good weather can increase the supply of many crops and bad weather can decrease their supply. Extreme natural events such as insect plagues also influence supply.

Figure 3.5 illustrates an increase in supply. When supply increases, the supply curve shifts *rightward* and the quantity supplied is larger at each and every price. For example, at a price of £1.00, on the original (blue) supply curve, the quantity supplied is 3 million energy drinks a week. On the new (red) supply curve, the quantity supplied is 6 million energy drinks a week. Look closely at the numbers in the table in Figure 3.5 and check that the quantity supplied at each price is larger.

Table 3.2 summarizes the influences on supply and the directions of those influences.

## A Change in the Quantity Supplied versus a Change in Supply

Changes in the influences on selling plans bring either a change in the quantity supplied or a change in supply. Equivalently, they bring either a movement along the supply curve or a shift of the supply curve.

**Figure 3.5** An Increase in Supply

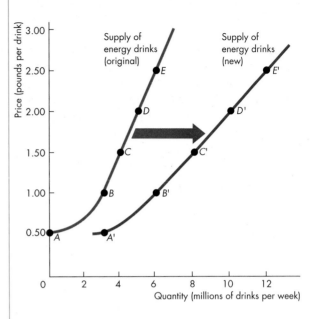

| Original supply schedule Original technology | | | New supply schedule New technology | | |
|---|---|---|---|---|---|
| | **Price (pounds per drink)** | **Quantity supplied (millions of drinks per week)** | | **Price (pounds per drink)** | **Quantity supplied (millions of drinks per week)** |
| A | 0.50 | 0 | A' | 0.50 | 3 |
| B | 1.00 | 3 | B' | 1.00 | 6 |
| C | 1.50 | 4 | C' | 1.50 | 8 |
| D | 2.00 | 5 | D' | 2.00 | 10 |
| E | 2.50 | 6 | E' | 2.50 | 12 |

A change in any influence on sellers' plans other than the price of the good itself results in a new supply schedule and a shift of the supply curve. For example, with a new cost-saving technology for producing energy drinks, the supply of energy drinks changes.

At a price of £1.50 a drink, 4 million energy drinks a week are supplied when producers use the old technology (row *C* of the table) and 8 million energy drinks a week are supplied when producers use the new technology. An advance in technology increases the supply of energy drinks. The supply curve shifts rightward, as shown by the shift arrow and the resulting red curve.

A point on the supply curve shows the quantity supplied at a given price. A movement along the supply curve shows a **change in the quantity supplied**. The entire supply curve shows supply. A shift of the supply curve shows a *change in supply*.

Figure 3.6 illustrates and summarizes these distinctions. If the price of a good changes and other things remain the same, there is a *change in the quantity supplied* of the good. If the price of the good falls, the quantity supplied decreases and there is a movement down the supply curve $S_0$. If the price of a good rises, the quantity supplied increases and there is a movement up the supply curve $S_0$. When any other influence on selling plans changes, the supply curve shifts and there is a *change in supply*. If the supply curve is $S_0$ and if production costs fall, supply increases and the supply curve shifts to the red supply curve $S_1$. If production costs rise, supply decreases and the supply curve shifts to the red supply curve $S_2$.

**Figure 3.6 A Change in the Quantity Supplied versus a Change in Supply**

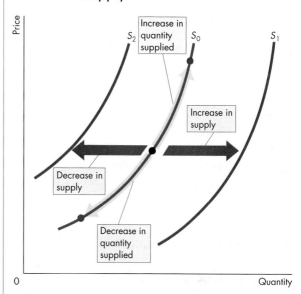

When the price of the good changes, there is a movement along the supply curve and a change in the quantity supplied, shown by the blue arrows on supply curve $S_0$.

When any other influence on selling plans changes, there is a shift of the supply curve and a change in supply. An increase in supply shifts the supply curve rightward (from $S_0$ to $S_1$), and a decrease in supply shifts the supply curve leftward (from $S_0$ to $S_2$).

 Animation

---

### Table 3.2

### The Supply of Energy Drinks

**The Law of Supply**

*The quantity of energy drinks supplied*

| *Decreases if*: | *Increases if*: |
|---|---|
| ◆ The price of an energy drink falls | ◆ The price of an energy drink rises |

**Changes in Supply**

*The supply of energy drinks*

| *Decreases if*: | *Increases if*: |
|---|---|
| ◆ The price of a factor of production used to produce energy drinks rises | ◆ The price of a factor of production used to produce energy drinks falls |
| ◆ The price of a substitute in production rises | ◆ The price of a substitute in production falls |
| ◆ The price of a complement in production falls | ◆ The price of a complement in production rises |
| ◆ The expected future price of an energy drink rises | ◆ The expected future price of an energy drink falls |
| ◆ The number of suppliers of energy drinks decreases | ◆ The number of suppliers of energy drinks increases |
| ◆ A technology change or natural event decreases energy drink production | ◆ A technology change or natural event increases energy drink production |

### Review Quiz

1 Define the quantity supplied of a good or service.
2 What is the law of supply and how do we illustrate it?
3 What does the supply curve tell us about the price at which firms will supply a given quantity of a good?
4 List all the influences on selling plans and for each influence say whether it changes supply.
5 What happens to the quantity of mobile phones supplied and the supply of mobile phones if the price of a mobile phone falls?

You can work these questions in Study Plan 3.3 and get instant feedback. **myeconlab**

Your next task is to use what you've learned about demand and supply and see how prices and quantities are determined.

## Market Equilibrium

We have seen that when the price of a good rises, the quantity demanded *decreases* and the quantity supplied *increases*. We are now going to see how prices coordinate the plans of buyers and sellers and achieve equilibrium.

*Equilibrium* is a situation in which opposing forces balance each other. Equilibrium in a market occurs when the price balances the plans of buyers and sellers. The **equilibrium price** is the price at which the quantity demanded equals the quantity supplied. The **equilibrium quantity** is the quantity bought and sold at the equilibrium price. A market moves towards its equilibrium because:

◆  Price regulates buying and selling plans.

◆  Price adjusts when plans don't match.

## Price as a Regulator

The price of a good regulates the quantities demanded and supplied. If the price is too high, the quantity supplied exceeds the quantity demanded. If the price is too low, the quantity demanded exceeds the quantity supplied. There is one price at which the quantity demanded equals the quantity supplied. Let's work out what that price is.

Figure 3.7 shows the market for energy drinks. The table shows the demand schedule (from Figure 3.1) and the supply schedule (from Figure 3.4). If the price of an energy drink is 50 pence, the quantity demanded is 9 million drinks a week, but no drinks are supplied. There is a shortage of 9 million drinks a week. This shortage is shown in the final column of the table. At a price of £1.00 a drink, there is still a shortage, but only of 3 million drinks a week. If the price is £2.50 a drink, the quantity supplied is 6 million drinks a week, but the quantity demanded is only 2 million. There is a surplus of 4 million drinks a week. The one price at which there is neither a shortage nor a surplus is £1.50 a drink. At that price, the quantity demanded equals the quantity supplied: 4 million drinks a week. The equilibrium price is £1.50 a drink and the equilibrium quantity is 4 million drinks a week.

Figure 3.7 shows that the demand curve and the supply curve intersect at the equilibrium price of £1.50 a drink. At each price *above* £1.50 a drink, there is a surplus. For example, at £2.00 a drink, the surplus is 2 million drinks a week, as shown by the blue arrow. At each price *below* £1.50 a drink, there is a shortage of drinks.

**Figure 3.7**   Equilibrium

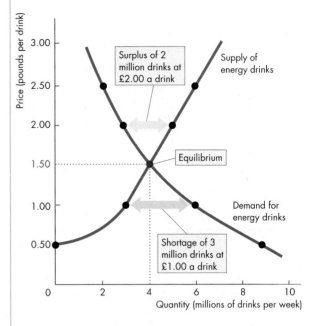

| Price (pounds per drink) | Quantity demanded | Quantity supplied | Shortage (–) or surplus (+) |
|---|---|---|---|
| | (millions of drinks per week) | | |
| 0.50 | 9 | 0 | –9 |
| 1.00 | 6 | 3 | –3 |
| **1.50** | **4** | **4** | **0** |
| 2.00 | 3 | 5 | +2 |
| 2.50 | 2 | 6 | +4 |

The table lists the quantities demanded and quantities supplied as well as the shortage or surplus of drinks at each price. If the price is £1.00 an energy drink, 6 million drinks a week are demanded and 3 million are supplied. There is a shortage of 3 million drinks a week and the price rises.

If the price is £2.00 an energy drink, 3 million drinks a week are demanded and 5 million are supplied. There is a surplus of 2 million drinks a week and the price falls.

If the price is £1.50 an energy drink, 4 million drinks a week are demanded and 4 million are supplied. There is neither a shortage nor a surplus. Neither buyers nor sellers have any incentive to change the price. The price at which the quantity demanded equals the quantity supplied is the equilibrium price. The equilibrium quantity is 4 million drinks a week.

For example, at £1.00 a drink, the shortage is 3 million drinks a week, as shown by the red arrow.

## Price Adjustments

You've seen that if the price is below equilibrium, there is a shortage; and that if the price is above equilibrium, there is a surplus. But can we count on the price to change and eliminate a shortage or surplus? We can, because such price changes are beneficial to both buyers and sellers. Let's see why the price changes when there is a shortage or a surplus.

### A Shortage Forces the Price Up

Suppose the price of an energy drink is £1. Consumers plan to buy 6 million drinks a week and producers plan to sell 3 million drinks a week. Consumers can't force producers to sell more than they plan, so the quantity that is actually offered for sale is 3 million drinks a week. In this situation, powerful forces operate to increase the price and move it towards the equilibrium price. Some producers, noticing many unsatisfied consumers, raise the price. Some producers increase their output. As producers push the price up, the price rises towards its equilibrium. The rising price reduces the shortage because it decreases the quantity demanded and increases the quantity supplied. When the price has increased to the point at which there is no longer a shortage, the forces moving the price stop operating and the price comes to rest at its equilibrium.

### A Surplus Forces the Price Down

Suppose the price is £2 a drink. Producers plan to sell 5 million drinks a week and consumers plan to buy 3 million drinks a week. Producers cannot force consumers to buy more than they plan, so the quantity bought is 3 million drinks a week. In this situation, powerful forces operate to lower the price and move it towards the equilibrium price. Some producers, unable to sell the quantities of drinks they planned to sell, cut their prices. In addition, some producers scale back production. As producers cut the price, the price falls towards its equilibrium. The falling price decreases the surplus because it increases the quantity demanded and decreases the quantity supplied. When the price has fallen to the point at which there is no longer a surplus, the forces moving the price stop operating and the price comes to rest at its equilibrium.

## The Best Deal Available for Buyers and Sellers

When the price is below equilibrium, it is forced up towards the equilibrium. Why don't buyers resist the increase and refuse to buy at the higher price? Because they value the good more highly than the current price and they cannot satisfy all their demands at the current price. In some markets – for example, the auction markets that operate on eBay – the buyers might even be the ones who force the price up by offering to pay higher prices.

When the price is above equilibrium, it is bid down towards the equilibrium. Why don't sellers resist this decrease and refuse to sell at the lower price? Because their minimum supply price is below the current price and they cannot sell all they would like to at the current price. Normally, it is the sellers who force the price down by offering lower prices to gain market share.

At the price at which the quantity demanded equals the quantity supplied neither buyers nor sellers can do business at a better price. Buyers pay the highest price they are willing to pay for the last unit bought and sellers receive the lowest price at which they are willing to supply the last unit sold.

When people freely make offers to buy and sell and when buyers try to buy at the lowest possible price and sellers try to sell at the highest possible price, the price at which trade takes place is the equilibrium price – the price at which the quantity demanded equals the quantity supplied. The price coordinates the plans of buyers and sellers and no one has an incentive to change the price.

### Review Quiz

1   What is the equilibrium price of a good or service?
2   Over what range of prices does a shortage arise? What happens to the price when there is a shortage?
3   Over what range of prices does a surplus arise? What happens to the price when there is a surplus?
4   Why is the price at which the quantity demanded equals the quantity supplied the equilibrium price?
5   Why is the equilibrium price the best deal available for both buyers and sellers?

You can work these questions in Study Plan 3.4 and get instant feedback.

# Predicting Changes in Price and Quantity

The demand and supply theory that we have just studied provides us with a powerful way of analysing influences on prices and the quantities bought and sold. According to the theory, a change in price stems from a change in demand, a change in supply, or a change in both demand and supply. Let's look first at the effects of a change in demand.

## An Increase in Demand

If more people join health clubs, the demand for energy drinks increases. The table in Figure 3.8 shows the original and new demand schedules for energy drinks (the same as those in Figure 3.2) as well as the supply schedule of energy drinks.

The increase in demand creates a shortage at the original price of £1.50 a drink and to eliminate the shortage, the price must rise.

Figure 3.8 shows what happens. The figure shows the original demand for and supply of energy drinks. The original equilibrium price is £1.50 a drink and the quantity is 4 million drinks a week. When demand increases, the demand curve shifts rightward. The equilibrium price rises to £2.50 a drink and the quantity supplied increases to 6 million drinks a week, as highlighted in the figure. There is an *increase in the quantity supplied* but *no change in supply* – a movement along, but no shift of, the supply curve.

## A Decrease in Demand

We can reverse this change in demand. Start at a price of £2.50 a drink with 6 million drinks a week, and then work out what happens if demand decreases to its original level. Such a decrease in demand might arise from a fall in the price of an energy bar (a substitute for energy drinks).

The decrease in demand shifts the demand curve *leftward*. The equilibrium price falls to £1.50 a drink and the equilibrium quantity decreases to 4 million drinks a week.

We can now make our first two predictions:

1 **When demand increases, both the price and the quantity increase.**

2 **When demand decreases, both the price and the quantity decrease.**

**Figure 3.8** The Effects of a Change in Demand

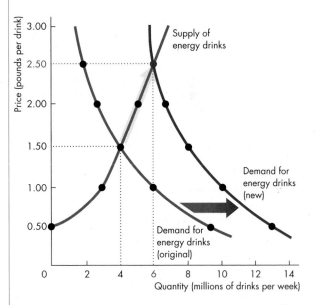

| Price (pounds per drink) | Quantity demanded (millions of drinks per week) | | Quantity supplied (millions of drinks per week) |
| --- | --- | --- | --- |
| | Original | New | |
| 0.50 | 9 | 13 | 0 |
| 1.00 | 6 | 10 | 3 |
| **1.50** | **4** | **8** | **4** |
| 2.00 | 3 | 7 | 5 |
| 2.50 | 2 | 6 | 6 |

Initially, the demand for energy drinks is the blue demand curve. The equilibrium price is £1.50 an energy drink and the equilibrium quantity is 4 million drinks a week. With more health-conscious people doing more exercise, the demand for energy drinks increases and the demand curve shifts rightward to become the red curve.

At £1.50 an energy drink, there is now a shortage of 4 million drinks a week. The price of an energy drink rises to a new equilibrium of £2.50. As the price rises to £2.50, the quantity supplied increases – shown by the blue arrow on the supply curve – to the new equilibrium quantity of 6 million drinks a week. Following an increase in demand, the quantity supplied increases but supply does not change – the supply curve does not shift.

myeconlab Animation

# Global Market for Crude Oil

The demand and supply model provides insights into all competitive markets. Here, we apply what you've learned about the effects of an increase in demand to the global market for crude oil.

Crude oil is like the life blood of the global economy. It is used to fuel our cars, trucks, aeroplanes, trains and buses, to generate electricity and to produce a wide range of plastics. When the price of crude oil rises, the cost of transport, electricity and materials all increase.

In 2001, the price of a barrel of oil was $20 (using the value of money in 2010). In 2008, before the global financial crisis ended a long period of economic expansion, the price peaked at $127 a barrel. While the price of oil was rising, the quantity of oil produced and consumed also increased. In 2001, the world produced 65 million barrels of oil a day. By 2008, that quantity was 72 million barrels.

Who or what has been raising the price of oil? Oil producers might be greedy, and some of them might be big enough to withhold supply and raise the price. But it wouldn't be in their self-interest to do so for long. The higher price would soon bring forth a greater quantity supplied from other producers and the profit of the producer limiting supply would fall.

Oil producers could try to cooperate and jointly withhold supply. The Organization of Petroleum Exporting Countries, OPEC, is such a group of producers. But OPEC doesn't control the *world* supply and its members' self-interest is to produce the quantities that give them the maximum attainable profit.

So even though the global oil market has some big players, they don't fix the price. Instead, the actions of thousands of buyers and sellers and the forces of demand and supply determine the price of oil.

So how have demand and supply changed? Because both the price and the quantity have increased, the demand for oil must have increased. Supply might have changed too, but here we'll suppose that supply has remained the same.

The global demand for oil has increased for one major reason: world income has increased. The increase has been particularly large in the emerging economies of Brazil, China and India. Increased world income has increased the demand for oil-using goods such as electricity, gasoline and plastics, which in turn has increased the demand for oil.

The figure illustrates the effects of the increase in demand on the global oil market. The supply of oil remained

constant along supply curve $S$. The demand for oil in 2001 was $D_{2001}$, so in 2001 the price was $20 a barrel and the quantity was 65 million barrels per day. The demand for oil increased and by 2008 it had reached $D_{2008}$. The price of oil increased to $127 a barrel and the quantity increased to 72 million barrels a day. The increase in the quantity is an *increase in the quantity supplied*, not an increase in supply.

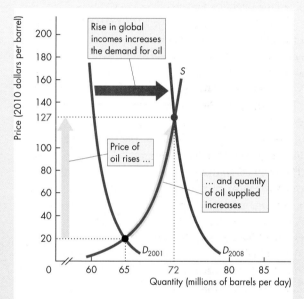

**Figure 1  The Global Market for Crude Oil**

## An Increase in Supply

When the producers of energy drinks switch to new cost-saving technology, the supply of energy drinks increases. The table in Figure 3.9 shows the new supply schedule (the same as that in Figure 3.5). What are the new equilibrium price and quantity? The answer is highlighted in the table: the price falls to £1.00 a drink and the quantity increases to 6 million a week. You can see why by looking at the quantities demanded and supplied at the original price of £1.50 a drink. The quantity supplied at that price is 8 million drinks a week and there is a surplus of drinks. The price falls. Only when the price is £1.00 a drink does the quantity supplied equal the quantity demanded.

Figure 3.9 illustrates the effect of an increase in supply. It shows the demand curve and the original and new supply curves. The initial equilibrium price is £1.50 a drink and the quantity is 4 million drinks a week. When the supply increases, the supply curve shifts rightward. The equilibrium price falls to £1.00 a drink and the quantity demanded increases to 6 million drinks a week, highlighted in the figure. There is an *increase in the quantity demanded* but *no change in demand* – a movement along, but no shift of, the demand curve.

## A Decrease in Supply

Start out at a price of £1.00 a drink with 6 million drinks a week being bought and sold. Then suppose that the cost of labour or raw materials rises and the supply of energy drinks decreases. The decrease in supply shifts the supply curve *leftward*. The equilibrium price rises to £1.50 a drink and the quantity demanded decreases. The equilibrium quantity decreases to 4 million drinks a week.

We can now make two more predictions:

1 **When supply increases, the quantity increases and the price falls.**

2 **When supply decreases, the quantity decreases and the price rises.**

You've now seen what happens to the price and the quantity when either demand or supply changes while the other one remains unchanged. In real markets, both demand and supply can change together. When this happens, to predict the changes in price and quantity, we must combine the effects that you've just seen. That is your final task in this chapter.

**Figure 3.9** The Effects of a Change in Supply

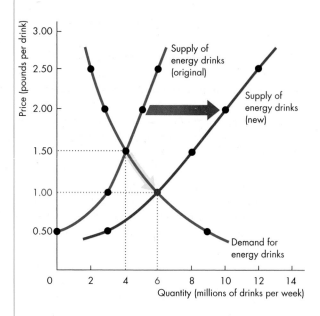

| Price (pounds per drink) | Quantity demanded (millions of drinks per week) | Quantity supplied (millions of drinks per week) | |
|---|---|---|---|
| | | Original | New |
| 0.50 | 9 | 0 | 3 |
| **1.00** | **6** | **3** | **6** |
| **1.50** | **4** | **4** | **8** |
| 2.00 | 3 | 5 | 10 |
| 2.50 | 2 | 6 | 12 |

Initially, the supply of energy drinks is shown by the blue supply curve. The equilibrium price is £1.50 a drink and the equilibrium quantity is 4 million drinks a week. When the new cost-saving technology is adopted, the supply of energy drinks increases and the supply curve shifts rightward to become the red curve.

At £1.50 a drink, there is now a surplus of 4 million drinks a week. The price of an energy drink falls to a new equilibrium of £1.00 a drink. As the price falls to £1.00 a drink, the quantity demanded increases – shown by the blue arrow on the demand curve – to the new equilibrium quantity of 6 million drinks a week. Following an increase in supply, the quantity demanded increases but demand does not change – the demand curve does not shift.

# The World Market for Wheat

We can use the demand and supply model to explain why the price of wheat has rocketed. The global market for wheat is a competitive market. Russia is the fourth largest producer of wheat in the world behind the European Union, China and India. In most years, Russian farmers produce far more wheat than Russia needs so Russia has become one of the world's top three exporters of wheat.

But 2010 was not a normal year. Russia experienced one of the worst droughts in its history in 2010. Temperatures soared to over 35°C in the summer months in western Russia. The extreme heat fanned forest fires, which killed many people and destroyed farms and crops covering an area the size of Portugal.

In August 2010, Russia announced a ban on the export of Russian wheat for the rest of the year. Countries that import a lot of Russian wheat, such as Egypt, suddenly had to find wheat from other exporting countries. There are plentiful stores of wheat from earlier harvests, but Russia is one of the biggest holders of those stores.

Other European wheat producers also suffered drought and Pakistan and Canada produced less wheat because of flooding in 2010. Over the summer, world wheat prices doubled from the year low in June to a year high in July. When Russia announced the export ban, prices jumped again.

The figure shows what was happening in the world market for wheat. Demand, shown by the demand curve, $D$, didn't change in June and July 2010. In June before the fires, wheat stocks were plentiful, fields were full and the price was low at £90 per tonne. The supply curve was $S_{June}$ and the quantity of wheat available was 500 million tonnes.

By July, drought and flooding destroyed crops and decreased world supply to $S_{July}$. With excess demand of 50 million tonnes at the June price, the price began to rise. In July, the price hit £150 per tonne and the quantity of wheat fell to 470 million tonnes. The decrease in supply raised the price and decreased the quantity demanded – a movement along the demand curve – to 470 million tonnes.

When Russia announced the ban on wheat exports in August, the supply of wheat in the global market decreased

further to $S_{August}$. The world price increased to £175 per tonne and the quantity demanded decreased to 460 million tonnes.

The events we've described here in the market for wheat illustrate the effects of a change in supply with no change in demand.

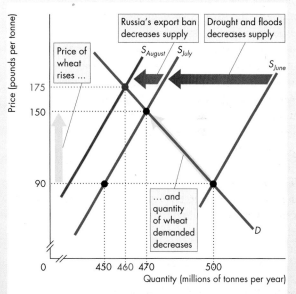

**Figure 1 The World Wheat Market**

## All the Possible Changes in Demand and Supply

Figure 3.10 brings together and summarizes the effects of all the possible changes in demand and supply. With what you've learned about the effects of a change in either demand or supply, you can predict what happens if both demand and supply change together. Let's begin by reviewing what you already know.

### Change in Demand with No Change in Supply

The first row of Figure 3.10, parts (a), (b) and (c), summarizes the effects of a change in demand with no change in supply. In part (a), with no change in either demand or supply, neither the price nor the quantity changes. With an *increase* in demand and no change in supply in part (b), both the price and quantity increase. And with a *decrease* in demand and no change in supply in part (c), both the price and the quantity decrease.

### Change in Supply with No Change in Demand

The first column of Figure 3.10, parts (a), (d) and (g), summarizes the effects of a change in supply with no change in demand. With an *increase* in supply and no change in demand in part (d), the price falls and quantity increases. And with a *decrease* in supply and no change in demand in part (g), the price rises and the quantity decreases.

### Increase in Both Demand and Supply

You've seen that an increase in demand raises the price and increases the quantity. And you've seen that an increase in supply lowers the price and increases the quantity. Figure 3.10(e) combines these two changes. Because either an increase in demand or an increase in supply increases the quantity, the quantity also increases when both demand and supply increase. But the effect on the price is uncertain. An increase in demand raises the price and an increase in supply lowers the price, so we can't say whether the price will rise or fall when both demand and supply increase. We need to know the magnitudes of the changes in demand and supply to predict the effects on price. In the example in Figure 3.10(e), the price does not change. But notice that if demand increases by slightly more than the amount shown in the figure, the price will rise. And if supply increases by slightly more than the amount shown in the figure, the price will fall.

### Decrease in Both Demand and Supply

Figure 3.10(i) shows the case in which demand and supply *both decrease*. For the same reasons as those we've just reviewed, when both demand and supply decrease, the quantity decreases and, again, the direction of the price change is uncertain.

### Decrease in Demand and Increase in Supply

You've seen that a decrease in demand lowers the price and decreases the quantity. You've also seen that an increase in supply lowers the price and increases the quantity. Figure 3.10(f) combines these two changes. Both the decrease in demand and the increase in supply lower the price. So the price falls. But a decrease in demand decreases the quantity and an increase in supply increases the quantity, so we can't predict the direction in which the quantity will change unless we know the magnitudes of the changes in demand and supply. In Figure 3.10(f), the quantity does not change. But notice that if demand decreases by slightly more than the amount shown in the figure, the quantity will decrease. And if supply increases by slightly more than the amount shown in the figure, the quantity will increase.

### Increase in Demand and Decrease in Supply

Figure 3.10(h) shows the case in which demand increases and supply decreases. Now, the price rises and, again, the direction of the quantity change is uncertain.

### Review Quiz

What is the effect on the price and quantity of MP3 players (such as the iPod) if:

1    The price of a PC falls or the price of an MP3 download rises? (Draw the diagrams!)
2    More firms produce MP3 players or electronics workers' wages rise? (Draw the diagrams!)
3    Any two of these events in questions 1 and 2 occur together? (Draw the diagrams!)

You can work these questions in Study Plan 3.5 and get instant feedback.

To complete your study of demand and supply, take a look at *Reading Between the Lines* on pp. 70–71, which explains why the price of coffee increased in 2010 and is expected to rise again. Try to get into the habit of using the demand and supply model to understand movements in prices in your everyday life.

**Figure 3.10   The Effects of All the Possible Changes in Demand and Supply**

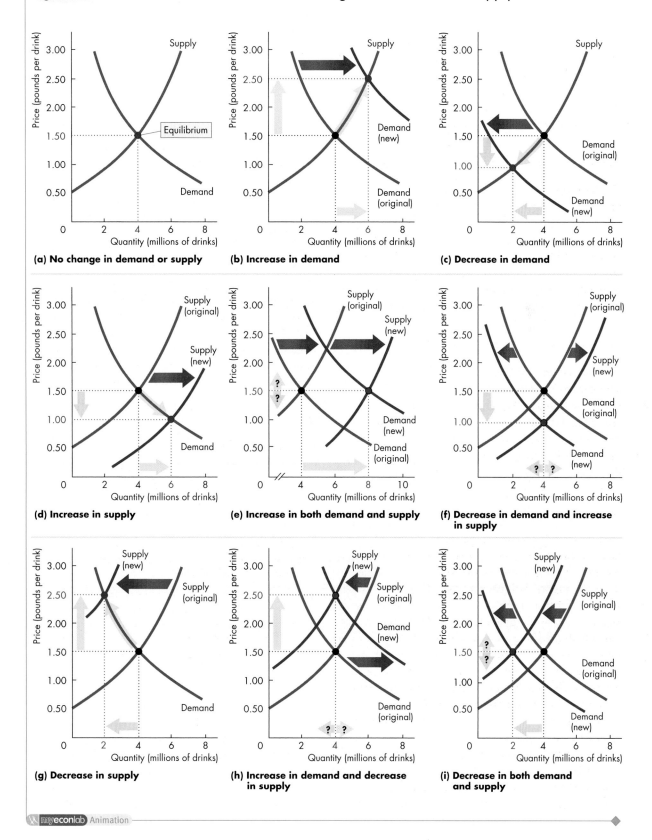

**(a) No change in demand or supply**

**(b) Increase in demand**

**(c) Decrease in demand**

**(d) Increase in supply**

**(e) Increase in both demand and supply**

**(f) Decrease in demand and increase in supply**

**(g) Decrease in supply**

**(h) Increase in demand and decrease in supply**

**(i) Decrease in both demand and supply**

# Reading Between the Lines

# Demand and Supply: The Price of Coffee

The Financial Times, 30 July 2010

## Coffee Surges on Poor Colombian Harvests

FT

Javier Blas

Coffee prices hit a 12-year high on Friday on the back of low supplies of premium Arabica coffee from Colombia after a string of poor crops in the Latin American country.

The strong fundamental picture has also encouraged hedge funds to reverse their previous bearish views on coffee prices.

In New York, ICE September Arabica coffee jumped 3.2 per cent to 178.75 cents per pound, the highest since February 1998. It traded later at 177.25 cents, up 6.8 per cent on the week.

The London-based International Coffee Organisation on Friday warned that the 'current tight demand and supply situation' was 'likely to persist in the near to medium term'.

Coffee industry executives believe prices could rise towards 200 cents per pound in New York before the arrival of the new Brazilian crop later this year.

'Until October it is going to be tight on high quality coffee,' said a senior executive at one of Europe's largest coffee roasters. He said: 'The industry has been surprised by the scarcity of high quality beans'.

Colombia coffee production, key for supplies of premium beans, last year plunged to a 33-year low of 7.8m bags, each of 60kg, down nearly a third from 11.1m bags in 2008, tightening supplies worldwide. . . .

## The Essence of the Story

◆ The price of premium Arabica coffee increased by 3.2 per cent to almost 180 cents per pound in July 2010, the highest price since February 1998.

◆ A sequence of poor crops in Colombia cut the production of premium Arabica coffee to a 33-year low of 7.8 million 60 kilogram bags, down from 11.1 million bags in 2008.

◆ The International Coffee Organisation expects the 'current tight demand and supply' to 'persist in the near to medium term'.

◆ Coffee industry executives say prices might approach 200 cents per pound before the new Brazilian crop arrives later this year.

◆ Hedge funds previously expected the price of coffee to fall but now expect it to rise further.

# Economic Analysis

- This news article reports two sources of changes in supply and demand that changed the price of coffee.

- The first source is the sequence of poor harvests in Colombia. These events decreased the world supply of Arabica coffee.

- Before the reported events, the world production of Arabica was 120 million bags per year and its price was 174 cents per pound.

- The decrease in the Colombian harvest decreased world production to about 116 million bags – a decrease of about 3 per cent of world production.

- Figure 1 shows the situation before the poor Colombian harvests and the effects of those poor Colombian harvests. The demand curve is $D_0$ and initially, the supply curve was $S_0$. The market equilibrium is at 120 million bags per year and a price of 174 cents per pound.

- The poor Colombian harvests decreased supply and the supply curve shifted leftward to $S_1$. The price rose to 180 cents per pound and the quantity decreased to 116 million bags.

- The second source of change influenced both supply and demand. It is a change in the expected future price of coffee.

- The hedge funds are speculators who try to profit from buying at a low price and selling at a high price.

- With the supply of coffee expected to remain low, the price was expected to rise further – a rise in the expected future price of coffee.

- When the expected future price of coffee rises, some people want to buy more coffee (so they can sell it later) – an increase in demand. And some people offer less coffee for sale (so they can sell it later for a higher price) – a decrease in supply.

- Figure 2 shows the effects of these changes in demand and supply. Demand increased from $D_0$ to $D_1$ and supply decreased from $S_0$ to $S_2$.

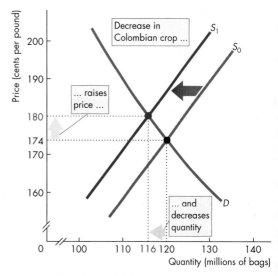

**Figure 1** The effects of the Colombian crop

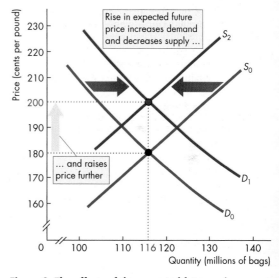

**Figure 2** The effects of the expected future price

- Because demand increases and supply decreases, the price rises. In this example, it rises to 200 cents per pound.

- Also, because demand increases and supply decreases, the change in the equilibrium quantity can go in either direction.

- In this example, the increase in demand equals the decrease in supply, so the equilibrium quantity remains constant at 116 million bags per year.

# Demand, Supply and Equilibrium

## Demand Curve

The law of demand states that as the price of a good or service falls, the quantity demanded of it increases. We illustrate the law of demand by setting out a demand schedule, drawing a graph of the demand curve, or writing down an equation. When the demand curve is a straight line, the following linear equation describes it:

$$P = a - bQ_D$$

where $P$ is the price and $Q_D$ is the quantity demanded. The $a$ and $b$ are positive constants. Figure 1 illustrates this demand curve.

The demand equation tells us three things:

1   The price at which no one is willing to buy the good ($Q_D$ is zero). That is, if the price is $a$, then the quantity demanded is zero. You can see the price $a$ on Figure 1. It is the price at which the demand curve hits the $y$-axis – what we call the demand curve's 'intercept on the $y$-axis'.

2   As the price falls, the quantity demanded increases. If $Q_D$ is a positive number, then the price $P$ must be less than $a$. And as $Q_D$ gets larger, the price $P$ becomes smaller. That is, as the quantity increases, the maximum price that buyers are willing to pay for the good falls.

3   The constant $b$ tells us how fast the maximum price that someone is willing to pay for the good falls as the quantity increases. That is, the constant $b$ tells us about the steepness of the demand curve. The equation tells us that the slope of the demand curve is $-b$.

## Supply Curve

The law of supply states that as the price of a good or service rises, the quantity supplied of it increases. We illustrate the law of supply by setting out a supply schedule, drawing a graph of the supply curve, or writing down an equation. When the supply curve is a straight line, the following linear equation describes it:

$$P = c + dQ_S$$

where $P$ is the price and $Q_S$ the quantity supplied. The $c$ and $d$ are positive constants. Figure 2 illustrates this supply curve.

The supply equation tells us three things:

1   The price at which no one is willing to sell the good ($Q_S$ is zero). If the price is $c$, then the quantity supplied is zero. You can see the price $c$ on Figure 2. It is the price at which the supply curve hits the $y$-axis – what we call the supply curve's 'intercept on the $y$-axis'.

2   As the price rises, the quantity supplied increases. If $Q_S$ is a positive number, then the price $P$ must be greater than $c$. And as $Q_S$ increases, the price $P$ gets larger. That is, as the quantity increases, the minimum price that sellers are willing to accept rises.

3   The constant $d$ tells us how fast the minimum price at which someone is willing to sell the good rises as the quantity increases. That is, the constant $d$ tells us about the steepness of the supply curve. The equation tells us that the slope of the supply curve is $d$.

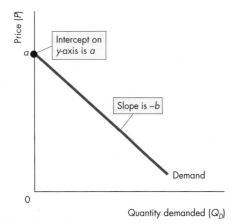

**Figure 1  The demand curve**

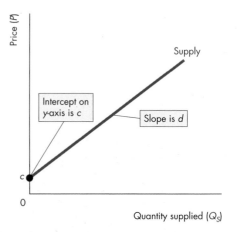

**Figure 2  The supply curve**

# Market Equilibrium

Demand and supply determine market equilibrium. Figure 3 shows the equilibrium price ($P^*$) and equilibrium quantity ($Q^*$) at the intersection of the demand curve and the supply curve.

We can use the equations to find the equilibrium price and equilibrium quantity. The price of a good will adjust until the quantity demanded equals the quantity supplied. That is:

$$Q_D = Q_S$$

So at the equilibrium price ($P^*$) and equilibrium quantity ($Q^*$):

$$Q_D = Q_S = Q^*$$

To find the equilibrium price and equilibrium quantity: first substitute $Q^*$ for $Q_D$ in the demand equation and $Q^*$ for $Q_S$ in the supply equation. Then the price is the equilibrium price ($P^*$), which gives:

$$P^* = a - bQ^*$$

$$P^* = c + dQ^*$$

Notice that:

$$a - bQ^* = c + dQ^*$$

Now solve for $Q^*$:

$$a - c = bQ^* + dQ^*$$

$$a - c = (b + d)Q^*$$

$$Q^* = \frac{a - c}{b + d}$$

To find the equilibrium price ($P^*$) substitute for $Q^*$ in either the demand equation or the supply equation.

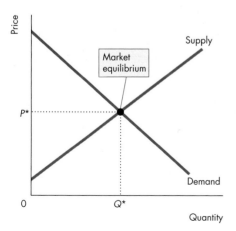

Price

Supply

Market
equilibrium

$P^*$

Demand

0    $Q^*$

Quantity

**Figure 3 Market equilibrium**

Using the demand equation:

$$P^* = a - b\left(\frac{a - c}{b + d}\right)$$

$$P^* = \frac{a(b + d) - b(a - c)}{b + d}$$

$$P^* = \frac{ad + bc}{b + d}$$

Alternatively, using the supply equation:

$$P^* = c + d\left(\frac{a - c}{b + d}\right)$$

$$P^* = \frac{c(b + d) + d(a - c)}{b + d}$$

$$P^* = \frac{ad + bc}{b + d}$$

# An Example

The demand for ice cream is:

$$P = 400 - 2Q_D$$

The supply of ice cream is:

$$P = 100 + 1Q_S$$

The price of an ice cream is expressed in pence and the quantities are expressed in ice creams per day.

To find the equilibrium price ($P^*$) and equilibrium quantity ($Q^*$), substitute $Q^*$ for $Q_D$ and $Q_S$ and substitute $P^*$ for $P$. That is:

$$P^* = 400 - 2Q^*$$

$$P^* = 100 + 1Q^*$$

Now solve for $Q^*$:

$$400 - 2Q^* = 100 + 1Q^*$$

$$300 = 3Q^*$$

$$Q^* = 100$$

And:

$$P^* = 400 - 2(100) = 200$$

The equilibrium price is £2 an ice cream, and the equilibrium quantity is 100 ice creams per day.

SUMMARY

## Key Points

### Markets and Prices (p. 52)

◆ A competitive market is one that has so many buyers and sellers that no one can influence the price.

◆ Opportunity cost is a relative price.

◆ Demand and supply determine relative prices.

Working Problem 1 will give you a better understanding of markets and prices.

### Demand (pp. 53–57)

◆ Demand is the relationship between the quantity demanded of a good and its price when all other influences on buying plans remain the same.

◆ The higher the price of a good, other things remaining the same, the smaller is the quantity demanded – the law of demand.

◆ Demand depends on the prices of related goods (substitutes and complements), expected future prices, income, expected future income and credit, population and preferences.

Working Problems 2 to 5 will give you a better understanding of demand.

### Supply (pp. 58–61)

◆ Supply is the relationship between the quantity supplied of a good and its price when all other influences on selling plans remain the same.

◆ The higher the price of a good, other things remaining the same, the greater is the quantity supplied – the law of supply.

◆ Supply depends on the prices of factors of production used to produce a good, the prices of related goods produced, expected future prices, the number of suppliers, technology and the state of nature.

Working Problems 6 to 9 will give you a better understanding of supply.

### Market Equilibrium (pp. 62–63)

◆ At the equilibrium price, the quantity demanded equals the quantity supplied.

◆ At any price above the equilibrium price, there is a surplus and the price falls.

◆ At any price below the equilibrium price, there is a shortage and the price rises.

Working Problems 10 and 11 will give you a better understanding of market equilibrium.

### Predicting Changes in Price and Quantity (pp. 64–69)

◆ An increase in demand brings a rise in the price and an increase in the quantity supplied. A decrease in demand brings a fall in the price and a decrease in the quantity supplied.

◆ An increase in supply brings a fall in the price and an increase in the quantity demanded. A decrease in supply brings a rise in the price and a decrease in the quantity demanded.

◆ An increase in demand and an increase in supply bring an increased quantity but an uncertain price change. An increase in demand and a decrease in supply bring a higher price but an uncertain change in quantity.

Working Problems 12 and 13 will give you a better understanding of predicting changes in price and quantity.

## Key Terms

Change in demand, 54
Change in supply, 59
Change in the quantity demanded, 57
Change in the quantity supplied, 61
Competitive market, 52
Complement, 55
Demand, 53
Demand curve, 54
Equilibrium price, 62
Equilibrium quantity, 62
Inferior good, 56
Law of demand, 53
Law of supply, 58
Money price, 52
Normal good, 56
Quantity demanded, 53
Quantity supplied, 58
Relative price, 52
Substitute, 55
Supply, 58
Supply curve, 58

## STUDY PLAN PROBLEMS AND APPLICATIONS

myeconlab   You can work Problems 1 to 17 in MyEconLab Chapter 3 Study Plan and get instant feedback.

## Markets and Prices (Study Plan 3.1)

**1** A notice in the *Edgehill Advertiser* in 1862 offered the following exchanges:

1 yard of cloth for 1 pound of bacon
2 yards of cloth for 1 pound of butter
4 yards of cloth for 1 pound of wool
8 yards of cloth for 1 bushel of salt

**a** What is the price of butter in terms of wool?

**b** If the money price of bacon was 20 pence per pound, what do you predict was the money price of butter?

**c** If the money price of bacon was 20 pence per pound and the money price of salt was £2.00 per bushel, do you think anyone would be willing to trade cloth for salt on the terms advertised above?

## Demand (Study Plan 3.2)

**2** The price of food increased during the past year.

**a** Explain why the law of demand applies to food just as it does to all other goods and services.

**b** Explain how the substitution effect influences food purchases and provide some examples of substitutions that people might make when the price of food rises and other things remain the same.

**c** Explain how the income effect influences food purchases and provide some examples of the income effect that might occur when the price of food rises and other things remain the same.

**3** Classify the following goods and services as pairs of likely substitutes and as pairs of likely complements. (You may use an item in more than one pair.) The goods and services are:

coal, oil, natural gas, wheat, maize, rye, pasta, pizza, sausage, skateboard, roller blades, video game, laptop, iPod, mobile phone, text message, e-mail, phone call, voice mail

**4** During 2010, the average income in China increased by 10 per cent. Compared to 2009, how do you expect the following would change:

**a** The demand for beef? Explain your answer.

**b** The demand for rice? Explain your answer.

**5** In January 2010, the price of petrol in the US was $2.70 a gallon. By spring 2010, the price had increased to $3.00 a gallon. Assume that there were no changes in average income, population, or any other influence on buying plans.

Explain how the rise in the price of petrol would affect

**a** The demand for petrol.

**b** The quantity of petrol demanded.

## Supply (Study Plan 3.3)

**6** In 2008, the price of corn increased by 35 per cent and some cotton farmers stopped growing cotton and started to grow corn.

**a** Does this fact illustrate the law of demand or the law of supply? Explain your answer.

**b** Why would a cotton farmer grow corn?

Use the following information to work to Problems 7 to 9.

Dairies make low-fat milk from full-cream milk. In the process of making low-fat milk, the dairies produce cream, which is made into ice cream. In the market for low-fat milk, the following events occur one at a time:

**(i)** The wage rate of dairy workers rises.

**(ii)** The price of cream rises.

**(iii)** The price of low-fat milk rises.

**(iv)** With the period of low rainfall extending, dairies raise their expected price of low-fat milk next year.

**(v)** With advice from healthcare experts, dairy farmers decide to switch from producing full-cream milk to growing vegetables.

**(vi)** A new technology lowers the cost of producing ice cream.

**7** Explain the effect of each event on the supply of low-fat milk.

**8** Use a graph to illustrate the effect of each event.

**9** Does any event (or events) illustrate the law of supply?

## Market Equilibrium (Study Plan 3.4)

**10**  As more people buy computers, the demand for Internet service increases and the price of Internet service decreases. The fall in the price of Internet service decreases the supply of Internet service. Is this statement true or false? Explain your answer.

**11**  The table sets out the demand and supply schedules for chewing gum.

| Price (pence per packet) | Quantity demanded | Quantity supplied |
|---|---|---|
| | (millions of packets a week) | |
| 20 | 180 | 60 |
| 40 | 140 | 100 |
| 60 | 100 | 140 |
| 80 | 60 | 180 |
| 100 | 20 | 220 |

**a**  Draw a graph of the chewing gum market and mark in the equilibrium price and quantity.

**b**  Suppose that chewing gum is 70 pence a packet. Describe the situation in the chewing gum market and explain how the price of chewing gum adjusts.

**c**  Suppose that the price of chewing gum is 30 pence a packet. Describe the situation in the chewing gum market and explain how the price adjusts.

## Predicting Changes in Price and Quantity (Study Plan 3.5)

**12**  The following events occur one at a time:

**(i)**  The price of crude oil rises.

**(ii)**  The price of a car rises.

**(iii)**  All speed limits on motorways are abolished.

**(iv)**  Robots cut car production costs.

Explain which of these events will increase or decrease (and state which occurs).

**a**  The demand for petrol.

**b**  The supply of petrol.

**c**  The quantity of petrol demanded.

**d**  The quantity of petrol supplied.

**13**  In Problem 11, a fire destroys some chewing-gum factories and the quantity of chewing gum supplied decreases by 40 million packets a week at each price.

**a**  Explain what happens in the market for chewing gum and draw a graph to illustrate the changes in the chewing gum market.

**b**  If at the time the fire occurs, there is an increase in the teenage population, which increases the quantity of chewing gum demanded by 40 million packs a week at each price, what are the new equilibrium price and quantity of chewing gum? Illustrate these changes in your graph.

## Economics in the News (Study Plan 3.N)

**14**  **Airline Fares Soar as Oil Cost Bites**

Fuel bills may lead to higher charges. Ryanair increased its airport check-in charges from £5 to £6 per person return and its baggage charges from £20 to £24 per bag return.

Source: Telegraph.co.uk, 9 February 2008

**a**  According to the news clip, what is the influence on the supply of Ryanir flights?

**b**  Explain how supply changes.

**15**  **Of Gambling, Grannies and Good Sense**

Nevada has plenty of jobs for the over 50s and its elderly population is growing faster than that in other states.

Source: The Economist, 26 July 2006

Explain how grannies have influenced:

**a**  The demand in some Las Vegas markets.

**b**  The supply in other Las Vegas markets.

**16**  **Frigid Winter is Bad News for Tomato Lovers**

An unusually cold January in Florida destroyed entire fields of tomatoes and forced many farmers to delay their harvest. Florida's growers are shipping only a quarter of their usual 5 million pounds a week. The price has risen from $6.50 for a 25-pound box a year ago to $30 now.

Source: USA Today, 3 March 2010

**a**  Make a graph to illustrate the market for tomatoes in January 2009 and January 2010.

**b**  On the graph, show how the events in the news clip influence the market for tomatoes.

**c**  Why is the news 'bad for tomato lovers'?

**17**  **Petrol Prices to Top the 2009 High by Weekend**

The cost of filling up the car is rising as the crude oil price soars and petrol prices may exceed the peak price of 2009.

Source: USA Today, 7 January 2010

**a**  Does demand for petrol or the supply of petrol or both change when the price of oil soars?

**b**  Use a demand–supply graph to illustrate what happens to the equilibrium price of petrol and the equilibrium quantity of petrol bought when the price of oil soars.

## ADDITIONAL PROBLEMS AND APPLICATIONS

 **myeconlab**  You can work these problems in MyEconLab if assigned by your lecturer.

## Markets and Prices

**18** What features of the world market for crude oil make it a competitive market?

**19** The money price of a mobile phone is £90 and the money price of the Wii game Super Mario Galaxy is £45.

  **a** What is the opportunity cost of a mobile phone in terms of the Wii game?

  **b** What is the relative price of the Wii game in terms of mobile phones?

## Demand

**20** The price of petrol has increased during the past year.

  **a** Explain why the law of demand applies to petrol just as it does to all other goods and services.

  **b** Explain how the substitution effect influences petrol purchases and provide some examples of substitutions that people might make when the price of petrol rises and other things remain the same.

  **c** Explain how the income effect influences petrol purchases and provide some examples of the income effects that might occur when the price of petrol rises and other things remain the same.

**21** Think about the demand for the three game consoles: Xbox, PS3 and Wii. Explain the effect of the following events on the demand for Xbox games and the quantity of Xbox games demanded, other things remaining the same.

  **a** The price of an Xbox falls.

  **b** The prices of a PS3 and a Wii fall.

  **c** The number of people writing and producing Xbox games increases.

  **d** Consumers' incomes increase.

  **e** Programmers who write code for Xbox games become more costly to hire.

  **f** The expected future price of an Xbox game falls.

  **g** A new game console that is a close substitute for Xbox comes onto the market.

## Supply

**22** Classify the following pairs of goods as substitutes in production, complements in production, or neither.

  **a** Bottled water and health club memberships.

  **b** Potato crisps and baked potatoes.

  **c** Leather purses and leather shoes.

  **d** Hybrids and SUVs.

  **e** Diet coke and regular coke.

**23** As the prices of homes fell across the UK in 2008, the number of homes offered for sale decreased.

  **a** Does this fact illustrate the law of demand or the law of supply? Explain your answer.

  **b** Why would home owners decide not to sell?

**24** **G.M. Cuts Production for Quarter**

General Motors cut its fourth-quarter production schedule by 10 per cent because Ford Motor, Chrysler and Toyota sales declined in August.

  Source: *The New York Times*, 5 September 2007

Explain whether this news clip illustrates a change in the supply of cars or a change in the quantity supplied of cars.

## Market Equilibrium

Use the following figure to work Problems 25 and 26.

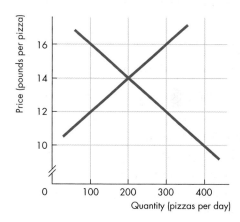

**25** **a** Label the curves. Which curve shows the willingness to pay for pizza?

  **b** If the price is £16 a pizza, is there a shortage or a surplus of pizza and does the price rise or fall?

  **c** Sellers want to receive the highest possible price, so why would they be willing to accept less than £16 a pizza?

**26** **a** If the price of a pizza is £12, is there a shortage or a surplus and does the price rise or fall?

  **b** Buyers want to pay the lowest possible price, so why would they be willing to pay more than £12 for a pizza?

**27** The table sets out demand and supply schedules for crisps.

| Price<br>(pence<br>per bag) | Quantity<br>demanded | Quantity<br>supplied |
|:---:|:---:|:---:|
| | (millions of bags per week) | |
| 50 | 160 | 130 |
| 60 | 150 | 140 |
| 70 | 140 | 150 |
| 80 | 130 | 160 |
| 90 | 120 | 170 |
| 100 | 110 | 180 |

a Draw a graph of the crisps market and mark in the equilibrium price and quantity.

b Describe the situation in the market for crisps and explain how the price adjusts if crisps are 60 pence a bag.

## Predicting Changes in Price and Quantity

**28** In Problem 27, a new dip increases the quantity of crisps demanded by 30 million bags per week at each price.

a How does the demand and/or supply of crisps change?

b How does the price and quantity of crisps change?

**29** If a virus destroys potato crops and the quantity of crisps supplied decreases by 40 million bags a week at each price, how does the equilibrium price and quantity of crisps change?

**30** If the virus in Problem 29 hits just as the new dip comes onto the market, how does the equilibrium price and quantity of crisps change?

## Economics in the News

**31** After you have studied *Reading Between the Lines* on pp. 70–71, answer the following questions.

a What happened to the price of coffee in 2010?

b What substitutions do you expect might have been made to decrease the quantity of coffee demanded?

c What influenced the demand for coffee in 2010 and what influenced the quantity of coffee demanded?

d What influenced the supply of coffee during 2010 and how did supply change?

e How did the combination of the factors you have noted in parts (c) and (d) influence the price and quantity of coffee?

f Was the change in quantity of coffee a change in the quantity demanded or a change in the quantity supplied?

**32** **Eurostar Boosted by *Da Vinci Code***

Eurostar, the train service linking London to Paris, said on Wednesday that first-half year sales rose 6 per cent, boosted by devotees of the blockbuster *Da Vinci Code*.

Source: *CNN*, 26 July 2006

a Explain how *Da Vinci Code* fans helped to raise Eurostar's sales.

b CNN commented on the 'fierce competition from budget airlines'. Explain the effect of this competition on Eurostar's sales.

c What markets in Paris do you think these fans influenced? Explain the influence on three markets.

**33** **'Popcorn Cinema' Experience Gets Pricier**

Cinemas are raising the price of popcorn. Demand for field corn, which is used for animal feed, corn syrup and biofuel, has increased and its price has exploded. That's caused some farmers to shift from growing popcorn to easier-to-grow field corn.

Source: *USA Today*, 24 May 2008

Explain and illustrate graphically the events described in the news clip in the market for

a Popcorn.

b Cinema tickets.

Use the following news clip to work Problems 34 and 35.

**Sony's Blu-Ray Wins High-Definition War**

Toshiba Corp. yesterday withdrew from the race to be the next-generation home movie format, leaving Sony Corp.'s Blu-ray technology the winner. The move could finally jump-start a high-definition home DVD market.

Source: *The Washington Times*, 20 February 2008

**34** a How would you expect the price of a used Toshiba player on eBay to change? Will the price change result from a change in demand, supply or both, and in which directions?

b How would you expect the price of a Blu-ray player to change?

**35** Explain how the market for Blu-ray format films will change.

**36** **Oil Soars to New Record – Over $135 a Barrel**

The price of oil hit a record high, above $135 a barrel, on Thursday – more than twice what it cost a year ago. OPEC has so far blamed price rises on speculators and says there is no shortage of oil.

Source: *BBC News*, 22 May 2008

a Explain how the price of oil can rise even though there is no shortage of oil.

b If a shortage of oil does occur, what does that imply about price adjustments and the role of price as a regulator in the market for oil?

c If OPEC is correct, what factors might have changed demand and/or supply and shifted the demand curve and/or the supply curve to cause the price to rise?

# Chapter 3 Appendix

# Elasticity

**After studying this appendix, you will be able to:**

◆ Define, calculate and explain the factors that influence the price elasticity of demand

◆ Define, calculate and explain the factors that influence the elasticity of supply

## Price Elasticity of Demand

When supply increases, the equilibrium price falls and the equilibrium quantity increases. But does the price fall by a large amount and the quantity increase by a little? Or does the price barely fall and the quantity increase by a large amount?

The answer depends on how responsive the quantity demanded is to a change in price. We describe this responsiveness with the price elasticity of demand.

The **price elasticity of demand** is a units-free measure of the responsiveness of the quantity demanded of a good to a change in its price, when all other influences on buying plans remain the same.

## Calculating Price Elasticity of Demand

We calculate the *price elasticity of demand* by using the formula:

$$\text{Price elasticity of demand} = \frac{\text{Percentage change in quantity demanded}}{\text{Percentage change in price}}$$

Figure A3.1 illustrates the steps in the calculation. Initially, the price of a smoothie is £3.10 and 9 smoothies an hour are sold – the original point in the figure. The price then falls to £2.90 and the quantity demanded increases to 11 smoothies an hour – the new point in the figure. When the price falls by 20 pence a smoothie, the quantity demanded increases by 2 smoothies an hour.

We express the changes in price and quantity as percentages of the *average price* and *average quantity*. The original price is £3.10 and the new price is £2.90, so the average price is £3. Call the percentage change in the price. %$\Delta P$. Then:

$$\%\Delta P = \Delta P/P_{AVE} \times 100 = (\pounds 0.20/\pounds 3.00) \times 100 = 6.67\%$$

**Figure A3.1    Calculating the Elasticity of Demand**

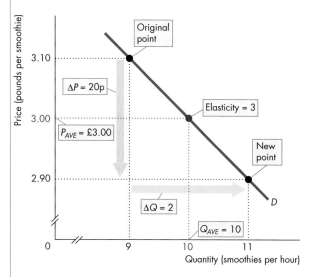

The elasticity of demand is calculated by using the formula:*

$$\text{Price elasticity of demand} = \frac{\text{Percentage change in quantity demanded}}{\text{Percentage change in price}}$$

$$= \frac{\%\Delta Q}{\%\Delta P} = \frac{\Delta Q/Q_{AVE}}{\Delta P/P_{AVE}}$$

$$= \frac{2/10}{0.20/3.00}$$

$$= 3$$

This calculation measures the elasticity at an average price of £3.00 a smoothie and an average quantity of 10 smoothies an hour.

* In the formula, the Greek letter delta (Δ) stands for 'change in' and %Δ stands for 'percentage change in'.

 myeconlab Animation

The original quantity demanded is 9 smoothies and the new quantity demanded is 11 smoothies, so the average quantity demanded is 10 smoothies. Call the percentage change in the quantity demanded. %$\Delta Q$. Then:

$$\%\Delta Q = \Delta Q/Q_{AVE} \times 100 = (2/10) \times 100 = 20\%$$

The price elasticity of demand equals the percentage change in the quantity demanded (20 per cent) divided by the percentage change in price (6.67 per cent), which equals 3. That is:

$$\text{Price elasticity} = \%\Delta Q/\%\Delta P = 20\%/6.67\% = 3.$$

## Average Price and Quantity

We use the *average* price and *average* quantity because it gives the most precise measurement of elasticity – midway between the original and new point.

By using percentages of the *average* price and *average* quantity, we get the same value for the elasticity regardless of whether the price falls from £3.10 to £2.90 or rises from £2.90 to £3.10.

## Percentages and Proportions

When we divide the percentage change in quantity by the percentage change in price, the 100s cancel. A percentage change is a *proportionate* change multiplied by 100. The proportionate change in price is $\Delta P/P_{AVE}$, and the proportionate change in quantity demanded is $\Delta Q/Q_{AVE}$. So if we divide $\Delta Q/Q_{AVE}$ by $\Delta P/P_{AVE}$, we get the same answer as we get by using percentage changes.

## A Units-free Measure

Elasticity is a *units-free measure* because the percentage change in each variable is independent of the units in which the variable is measured. And the ratio of the two percentages is a number without units.

## Minus Sign and Elasticity

When the price of a good *rises*, the quantity demanded *decreases* along the demand curve. Because a *positive* change in price brings a *negative* change in the quantity demanded, the price elasticity of demand is a negative number. But it is the magnitude, or *absolute value*, of the price elasticity of demand that tells us how responsive – how elastic – demand is. To compare price elasticities of demand, we use the magnitude of the elasticity and ignore the minus sign.

## Inelastic and Elastic Demand

If the quantity demanded remains constant when the price changes, then the price elasticity of demand is zero and the good is said to have a **perfectly inelastic demand**.

If the percentage change in the quantity demanded equals the percentage change in price, then the price elasticity equals 1 and the good is said to have a **unit elastic demand**.

If the percentage change in the quantity demanded is less than the percentage change in the price, then the price elasticity of demand is between zero and 1 and the good is said to have an **inelastic demand**.

If the quantity demanded changes by an infinitely large percentage in response to a tiny price change, then the price elasticity of demand is infinity and the good is said to have a **perfectly elastic demand**.

If the percentage change in the quantity demanded exceeds the percentage change in the price, the price elasticity of demand is greater than 1 and the good is said to have an **elastic demand**.

# Factors That Influence the Price Elasticity of Demand

What makes the demand for some goods elastic and the demand for others inelastic? The magnitude of the elasticity of demand depends on:

◆ Closeness of substitutes
◆ Proportion of income spent on the good
◆ Time elapsed since a price change

## Closeness of Substitutes

The closer the substitutes for a good or service, the more elastic is the demand for it. For example, oil has substitutes but none that are currently very close (imagine a steam-driven, coal-fuelled aircraft). So the demand for oil is inelastic.

The degree of substitutability between two goods also depends on how narrowly (or broadly) we define them. For example, a personal computer has no really close substitutes, but a Dell PC is a close substitute for a Gateway PC. So the elasticity of demand for personal computers is smaller than that for a Dell or a Gateway.

In everyday language we call some goods, such as food and housing, *necessities* and other goods, such as exotic vacations, *luxuries*. A necessity is a good that has poor substitutes and that is crucial for our well-being, so the demand for a necessity is inelastic. A luxury is a good that usually has many substitutes, so the demand for a luxury is elastic. *Economics in Action* lists and discusses some UK price elasticities of demand.

## Proportion of Income Spent on the Good

Other things remaining the same, the greater the proportion of income spent on a good, the more elastic is the demand for it.

Think about your own demand for toothpaste and housing. If the price of toothpaste doubles, you consume almost as much as before. Your demand for toothpaste

## Some Real-world Price Elasticities of Demand

The table shows some estimates of price elasticities of demand in the UK. These values range from 1.4 for fresh meat, the most elastic demand in the table, to 0.5 for beer, the least elastic demand in the table. Fresh meat has many substitutes, such as frozen meat and fish, so the demand for fresh meat is elastic. Green vegetables don't have many substitutes, so the demand for green vegetables is inelastic. But a particular green vegetable such as green beans has close substitutes such as green peas and broccoli. The elasticity of demand for green vegetables is smaller than the elasticity of demand for green beans.

You can see that the items with an elastic demand include luxuries (wine and spirits) while items with an inelastic demand include necessities (fruit juice and green vegetables).

The unit elasticity of demand for services is an average of the elasticities for many different services and hides wide variation across them.

### Table 1

#### UK Price Elasticities of Demand

| Good or service | Elasticity |
| --- | --- |
| **Elastic demand** | |
| Fresh meat | 1.4 |
| Spirits | 1.3 |
| Wine | 1.2 |
| **Unit elasticity** | |
| Services | 1.0 |
| Cereals | 1.0 |
| **Inelastic demand** | |
| Durable goods | 0.9 |
| Fruit juice | 0.8 |
| Green vegetables | 0.6 |
| Tobacco | 0.5 |
| Beer | 0.5 |

Sources of data: Ministry of Agriculture, Food and Fisheries, *Household Food Consumption and Expenditure*, 1992, London, HMSO; C. Godfrey, 'Modelling Demand', *Preventing Alcohol and Tobacco Problems*, Vol. 1 (A. Maynard and P. Tether, eds), Avebury, 1990; J. Muellbauer, 'Testing the Barten Model of Household Composition Effects and the Cost of Children', *Economic Journal*, September 1977.

is inelastic. If the rent you pay doubles, you shriek and look for more students to share your accommodation. Your demand for housing is elastic. Why the difference? Housing takes a large proportion of your budget, and toothpaste takes only a tiny proportion. You don't like either price increase, but you hardly notice the higher price of toothpaste, while the higher rent puts your budget under severe strain.

### Time Elapsed Since Price Change

The longer the time that has elapsed since a price change, the more elastic is demand. When the price of oil increased by 400 per cent during the 1970s, people barely changed the quantity of oil and petrol they bought. But gradually, as more efficient car and aeroplane engines were developed, the quantity used decreased. The demand for oil has become more elastic as more time has elapsed since that huge price hike. Similarly, when the price of a PC fell, the quantity of PCs demanded increased only slightly at first. But as more people have become better informed about the variety of ways of using a PC, the quantity of PCs bought has increased sharply. The demand for PCs has become more elastic.

## Elasticity of Supply

You know that when demand increases, the equilibrium price rises and the equilibrium quantity increases. But does the price rise by a large amount and the quantity increase by a little? Or does the price barely rise and the quantity increase by a large amount?

The answer depends on the responsiveness of the quantity supplied to a change in price. And we describe this responsiveness with the elasticity of supply.

The **elasticity of supply** measures the responsiveness of the quantity supplied to a change in the price of a good when all other influences on selling plans remain the same.

## Calculating the Elasticity of Supply

We calculate the elasticity of supply by using the formula:

$$\text{Elasticity of supply} = \frac{\text{Percentage change in quantity supplied}}{\text{Percentage change in price}}$$

We use the same method that you learned when you studied the elasticity of demand to make this calculation.

## Inelastic and Elastic Supply

If the quantity supplied remains constant when the price changes, then the elasticity of supply is zero and the good has a *perfectly inelastic supply*.

If the percentage change in the quantity supplied equals the percentage change in the price, then the elasticity of supply equals 1 and the good has a *unit elastic supply*.

If the percentage change in the quantity supplied is less than the percentage change in the price, then the elasticity of supply is between zero and 1 and the good has an *inelastic supply*.

If the quantity supplied changes by an infinitely large percentage in response to a tiny price change, then the elasticity of supply is infinity and the good has a *perfectly elastic supply*.

If the percentage change in the quantity supplied exceeds the percentage change in the price, the elasticity of supply exceeds 1 and the good has an *elastic supply*.

## Factors That Influence the Elasticity of Supply

The magnitude of the elasticity of supply depends on:

◆ Resource substitution possibilities
◆ Time frame for the supply decision

### Resource Substitution Possibilities

Some goods and services can be produced only by using unique or rare productive resources. These items have a low, even perhaps a zero, elasticity of supply. Other goods and services can be produced by using commonly available resources that could be allocated to a wide variety of alternative tasks. Such items have a high elasticity of supply.

A Van Gogh painting is an example of a good with a vertical supply curve and a zero elasticity of supply. At the other extreme, wheat can be grown on land that is almost equally good for growing corn. So wheat is just as easy to grow as corn, and the opportunity cost of wheat in terms of forgone corn is almost constant. As a result, the supply curve of wheat is almost horizontal and its elasticity of supply is very large. Similarly, when a good is produced in many different countries (for

example, wheat, sugar and beef), the supply of the good is highly elastic.

The supply of most goods and services lies between these two extremes. The quantity produced can be increased but only by incurring a higher cost. If a higher price is offered, the quantity supplied increases. Such goods and services have an elasticity of supply between zero and infinity.

### Time Frame for Supply Decisions

To study the influence of the length of time elapsed since a price change, we distinguish three time frames of supply:

1   Momentary supply
2   Short-run supply
3   Long-run supply

The *momentary supply curve* shows the response of the quantity supplied immediately following a price change. Fruits and vegetables have a perfectly inelastic momentary supply – a vertical supply curve. The momentary supply curve is vertical because, on a given day, no matter what the price of the fruit or vegetable, producers cannot change their output. They have picked, packed and shipped their crop to market, and the quantity available for that day is fixed.

The *short-run supply curve* shows how the quantity supplied responds to a price change when only *some* of the technologically possible adjustments to production have been made. The short-run supply curve slopes upward because producers can take actions quite quickly to change the quantity supplied in response to a price change.

The *long-run supply curve* shows the response of the quantity supplied to a change in the price after all the technologically possible ways of adjusting supply have been exploited. In the case of oranges, the long run is the time it takes new plantings to grow to full maturity – about 15 years.

## Key Terms

Elastic demand, 80
Elasticity of supply, 81
Inelastic demand, 80
Perfectly elastic demand, 80
Perfectly inelastic demand, 80
Price elasticity of demand, 79
Unit elastic demand, 80

# CHAPTER

# 4

# Efficiency and Equity

**After studying this chapter you will be able to:**

◆ Describe the alternative methods of allocating scarce resources

◆ Explain how marginal benefit and marginal cost determine demand and supply

◆ Explain the conditions under which markets are efficient

◆ Explain the main ideas about fairness and evaluate claims that markets result in unfair outcomes

Every time you decide to buy something, whether it's a bunch of roses or an everyday pizza, you express your view about how resources should be used and you make choices in your self-interest. Markets coordinate these choices. But do they allocate resources between roses and pizza and everything else efficiently?

Markets generate huge inequality: is that fair?

Efficiency and fairness (equity) are the two dimensions of the social interest. So our central question is: do markets operate in the social interest?

At the end of the chapter, in *Reading Between the Lines*, we see whether markets coped efficiently with the volcanic ash cloud that shut down Europe's airports in 2010.

## Resource Allocation Methods

The goal of this chapter is to evaluate the ability of markets to allocate resources efficiently and fairly. But to see whether the market does a good job, we must compare it with its alternatives. Resources are scarce, so they must be allocated somehow. And trading in markets is just one of several alternative methods.

Resources might be allocated by

◆ Market price

◆ Command

◆ Majority rule

◆ Contest

◆ First-come, first-served

◆ Lottery

◆ Personal characteristics

◆ Force

Let's briefly examine each method.

## Market Price

When a market price allocates a scarce resource, the people who are willing and able to pay that price get the resource. Two kinds of people decide not to pay the market price: those who can afford to pay but choose not to buy and those who are too poor and simply can't afford to buy.

For many goods and services, distinguishing between those who choose not to buy and those who can't afford to buy does not matter. But for some goods and services, it does matter. For example, poor people can't afford to pay school fees, pay for healthcare, or save to provide a pension when they retire. Because poor people can't afford these items that most people consider to be essential, in most societies they are allocated by one of the other methods.

## Command

A **command system** allocates resources by the order (command) of someone in authority. A command system is used extensively inside firms, public organizations and government departments. For example, if you have a job, most likely someone tells you what to do. Your labour is allocated to specific tasks by a command.

Command systems work well in organizations in which the lines of authority and responsibility are clear and it is easy to monitor the activities being performed. But a command system works badly when the range of activities to be monitored is large and when these activities are difficult to monitor.

A manager might be able to monitor several employees but a government department cannot monitor every firm in the economy. The system works so badly in North Korea, where it is used in place of markets, that it fails even to deliver an adequate supply of food.

## Majority Rule

Majority rule allocates resources in the way that a majority of voters choose. Societies use majority rule to elect representative governments that make some of the biggest decisions. For example, majority rule in each member state of the EU determines the tax rates that eventually allocate scarce resources between private use and public use. Majority rule also determines how tax revenues are allocated among competing uses such as education and healthcare.

Majority rule works well when the decisions being made affect large numbers of people and self-interest must be suppressed to use resources most effectively.

## Contest

A contest allocates resources to a winner (or a group of winners). Sporting events use this method.

Manchester United competes with Chelsea to end up at the top of the Premier League and the winner gets the biggest payoff. Andy Murray competes to win tennis matches and get the biggest prize. But contests are more general than those in a sports arena, though we don't normally call them contests. For example, there is a contest among Nokia, Motorola and Sony Ericsson in the mobile phone market. Managers often create contests inside their firms among employees for special bonuses.

Contests work well when the efforts of the 'players' are hard to monitor and reward directly. If everyone is offered the same wage, there is no incentive for anyone to make a special effort. But if a manager offers everyone in the company the opportunity to win a big prize, people are motivated to work hard and try to become the winner. Only a few people win the prize, but many people work harder in the process of trying to win. So total output produced by the workers of the firm is much greater than it would be without the contest.

## First-come, First-served

A first-come, first-served method allocates resources to those who are first in line. Many restaurants won't accept reservations. They use first-come, first-served to allocate their scarce tables. Scarce space on congested motorways is allocated in this way too: the first to arrive on the slip-road gets the road space. If too many vehicles enter the motorway, the speed slows and people wait on the slip-road for space to become available.

First-come, first-served works best when a scarce resource can serve just one user at a time in a sequence. By serving the user who arrives first, this method minimizes the time spent waiting for the resource to become available.

## Lottery

Lotteries allocate resources to those who pick the winning number, draw the lucky cards, or pick the winning ticket in a gamble. National lotteries throughout Europe reallocate millions of euros' worth of goods and services every year.

But lotteries are more widespread than jackpots and roulette wheels in casinos. Lotteries are used to allocate licensed taxi permits, landing slots to airlines at some airports, fishing rights and the electromagnetic spectrum used by mobile phones.

Lotteries work best when there is no effective way to distinguish among potential users of a scarce resource.

## Personal Characteristics

When resources are allocated on the basis of personal characteristics, people with the 'right' characteristics get the resources. Some of the resources that matter most to you are allocated in this way. For example, you will choose a marriage partner on the basis of personal characteristics. But this method is also used in unfair ways: for example, allocating the best jobs to white, able-bodied males and discriminating against minorities, older people, people with disabilities and females.

## Force

Force plays a crucial role, for both good and ill, in allocating scarce resources. Let's start with the ill.

War, the use of military force by one nation against another, has played an enormous role historically in allocating resources. The economic supremacy of European settlers in the Americas and Australia owes much to the use of this method.

Theft, the taking of the property of others without their consent, also plays a large role. Local crime and international crime throughout Europe allocate billions of euros' worth of resources annually.

But force plays a crucial positive role in allocating resources. It provides the state with an effective method of transferring wealth from the rich to the poor. It also provides the legal framework in which voluntary exchange in markets can take place.

A legal system is the foundation on which our market economy functions. Without courts to enforce contracts, it would not be possible to do business. But the courts could not enforce contracts without the ability to apply force if necessary. The state provides the ultimate force that enables the courts to do their work.

More broadly, the force of the state is essential to uphold the principle of the rule of law. This principle is the bedrock of civilized economic (and social and political) life. With the rule of law upheld, people can go about their daily economic lives with the assurance that their property will be protected – that they can sue for violations against their property (and be sued if they violate the property of others).

Free from the burden of protecting their property and confident in the knowledge that those with whom they trade will honour their agreements, people can get on with focusing on the activity at which they have a comparative advantage and trading for mutual gain.

### Review Quiz

1   Why do we need methods of allocating scarce resources?
2   Describe the alternative methods of allocating scarce resources.
3   Provide an example of each allocation method that illustrates when it works well.
4   Provide an example of each allocation method that illustrates when it works badly.

You can work these questions in Study Plan 4.1 and get instant feedback.

In the next sections, we're going to see how a market can achieve an efficient use of resources and serve the social interest. We will also examine the obstacles to efficiency and see how sometimes an alternative method might improve on the market. After looking at efficiency, we'll turn our attention to the more difficult issue of fairness.

## Benefit, Cost and Surplus

Resources are allocated efficiently and in the *social interest* when they are used in the ways that people value most highly. You saw in Chapter 2 that this outcome occurs when the quantities produced are at the point on the *PPF* at which marginal benefit equals marginal cost (Chapter 2, pp. 33–35). We're now going to see whether competitive markets produce the efficient quantities. We begin on the demand side of a market.

## Demand, Willingness to Pay and Value

In everyday life, we talk about 'getting value for money'. When we use this expression, we are distinguishing between *value* and *price*. Value is what we get and the price is what we pay.

The value of one more unit of a good or service is its marginal benefit. We measure marginal benefit by the maximum price that is willingly paid for another unit of the good or service. But willingness to pay determines demand. *A demand curve is a marginal benefit curve.*

In Figure 4.1(a), Lisa is willing to pay €1 for the 30th slice of pizza and €1 is her marginal benefit from that slice. In Figure 4.1(b), Nick is willing to pay €1 for the 10th slice and €1 is his marginal benefit from that slice. But for what quantity is the economy willing to pay €1? The answer is provided by the market demand curve.

## Individual Demand and Market Demand

The relationship between the price of a good and the quantity demanded by one person is called *individual demand*. And the relationship between the price of a good and the quantity demanded by all buyers is called *market demand*.

> **The market demand curve is the horizontal sum of the individual demand curves and is formed by adding the quantities demanded by all the individuals at each price.**

Figure 4.1(c) illustrates the market demand for pizza if Lisa and Nick are the only people. Lisa's demand curve in part (a) and Nick's demand curve in part (b) sum horizontally to the market demand curve in part (c).

---

**Figure 4.1**    Individual Demand, Market Demand and Marginal Social Benefit

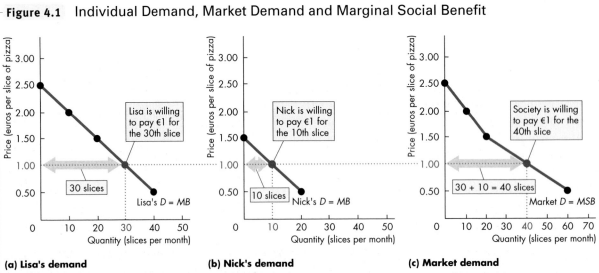

**(a) Lisa's demand**        **(b) Nick's demand**        **(c) Market demand**

At a price of €1 a slice, the quantity demanded by Lisa is 30 slices and the quantity demanded by Nick is 10 slices, so the quantity demanded by the market is 40 slices.

Lisa's demand curve in part (a) and Nick's demand curve in part (b) sum horizontally to the market demand curve in part (c).

The market demand curve is also the marginal social benefit curve (*MSB*).

myeconlab Animation

At a price of €1 a slice, Lisa demands 30 slices and Nick demands 10 slices, so the quantity demanded by the market at €1 a slice is 40 slices.

For Lisa and Nick, their demand curves are their marginal benefit curves. For society, the market demand curve is the marginal benefit curve. We call the marginal benefit to the entire society marginal social benefit. So the market demand curve is also the *marginal social benefit curve (MSB)*.

## Consumer Surplus

We don't always have to pay what we are willing to pay – we get a bargain. When people buy something for less than it is worth to them, they receive a consumer surplus. A **consumer surplus** is the excess of the benefit received from a good over the amount paid for it. We calculate consumer surplus as the marginal benefit (or value) of a good minus its price, summed over the quantity bought.

Figure 4.2(a) shows Lisa's consumer surplus from pizza when the price is €1 a slice. At this price, she buys 30 slices a month because the 30th slice is worth only €1 to her. But Lisa is willing to pay €2 for the 10th slice, so

her marginal benefit from this slice is €1 more than she pays for it – she receives a *consumer surplus* of €1 on the 10th slice.

Lisa's consumer surplus is the sum of the surpluses on *all of the slices she buys*. This sum is the area of the green triangle – the area below the demand curve and above the market price line. The area of this triangle is equal to its base (30 slices) multiplied by its height (€1.50) divided by 2, which is €22.50. The area of the blue rectangle in Figure 4.2(a) shows what Lisa pays for 30 slices of pizza.

Figure 4.2(b) shows Nick's consumer surplus. Part (c) shows the consumer surplus for the economy, which is the sum of the consumer surpluses of Lisa and Nick.

All goods and services, like pizza, have decreasing marginal benefit, so people receive more benefit from consumption than the amount they pay.

## Supply and Marginal Cost

Your next task is to see how market supply reflects marginal cost. The connection between supply and cost closely parallels the related ideas about demand and benefit that you've just studied. Firms are in business to

---

**Figure 4.2** Demand and Consumer Surplus

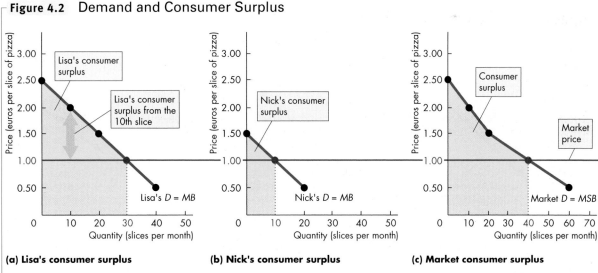

**(a) Lisa's consumer surplus**

**(b) Nick's consumer surplus**

**(c) Market consumer surplus**

Lisa is willing to pay €2 for her 10th slice of pizza (part a). At a market price of €1 a slice, Lisa receives a consumer surplus of €1 on the 10th slice. The green triangle shows her consumer surplus on the 30 slices she buys at €1 a slice.

The green triangle in part (b) shows Nick's consumer surplus on the 10 slices he buys at €1 a slice.

The green area in part (c) shows the consumer surplus for the economy. The blue rectangles show the amounts spent on pizza.

make a profit. To do so, they must sell their output for a price that exceeds the cost of production. Let's investigate the relationship between cost and price.

## Supply, Cost and Minimum Supply-price

Firms make a profit when they receive more from the sale of a good than the cost of producing it. Just as consumers distinguish between value and price, so producers distinguish between *cost* and *price*. Cost is what a producer gives up and price is what a producer receives.

The cost of producing one more unit of a good or service is its marginal cost. Marginal cost is the minimum price that producers must receive to induce them to offer to sell another unit of the good or service. But the minimum supply-price determines supply. *A supply curve is a marginal cost curve.*

In Figure 4.3(a), Maria is willing to produce the 100th pizza for €15, her marginal cost of that pizza. In Figure 4.3(b), Mario is willing to produce the 50th pizza for €15, his marginal cost of that pizza. But what quantity is the economy willing to produce for €15 a pizza? The answer is provided by the *market supply curve*.

## Individual Supply and Market Supply

The relationship between the price of a good and the quantity supplied by one producer is called *individual supply*. And the relationship between the price of a good and the quantity supplied by all producers is called *market supply*.

> **The market supply curve is the horizontal sum of the individual supply curves and is formed by adding the quantities supplied by all the producers at each price.**

Figure 4.3(c) illustrates the market supply if Maria and Mario are the only producers. Maria's supply curve in part (a) and Mario's supply curve in part (b) sum horizontally to the market supply curve in part (c).

At a price of €15 a pizza, Maria supplies 100 pizzas and Mario supplies 50 pizzas, so the quantity supplied by the market at €15 a pizza is 150 pizzas.

For Maria and Mario, their supply curves are their marginal cost curves. For society, the market supply curve is the society's marginal cost curve. We call the society's marginal cost the *marginal social cost*. So the market supply curve is also the *marginal social cost curve (MSC)*.

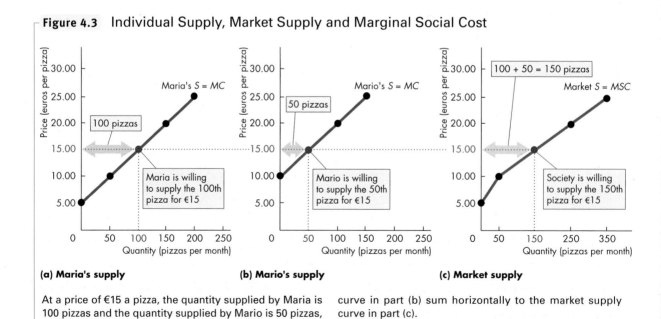

**Figure 4.3** Individual Supply, Market Supply and Marginal Social Cost

**(a) Maria's supply**

**(b) Mario's supply**

**(c) Market supply**

At a price of €15 a pizza, the quantity supplied by Maria is 100 pizzas and the quantity supplied by Mario is 50 pizzas, so the quantity supplied by the market is 150 pizzas.

Maria's supply curve in part (a) and Mario's supply curve in part (b) sum horizontally to the market supply curve in part (c).

The market supply curve is also the marginal social cost curve (*MSC*).

# Producer Surplus

When price exceeds marginal cost, the firm receives a producer surplus. A **producer surplus** is the excess of the amount received from the sale of a good or service over the cost of producing it. Producer surplus is calculated as the price received for a good minus its minimum supply-price (or marginal cost), summed over the quantity sold.

Figure 4.4(a) shows Maria's producer surplus from pizzas when the price is €15 a pizza. At this price, she sells 100 pizzas a month because the 100th pizza costs her €15 to produce. But Maria is willing to produce the 50th pizza for her marginal cost, which is €10. So she receives a *producer surplus* of €5 on this pizza.

Maria's producer surplus is the sum of the surpluses on each pizza she sells. This sum is the area of the blue triangle – the area below the market price and above the supply curve. The area of this triangle is equal to its base (100) multiplied by its height (€10) divided by 2, which is €500. The red area in Figure 4.4(a) below the supply curve shows what it costs Maria to produce 100 pizzas.

The area of the blue triangle in Figure 4.4(b) shows Mario's producer surplus and the blue area in Figure

4.4(c) shows the producer surplus for the market. The producer surplus for the market is the sum of the producer surpluses of Maria and Mario.

Consumer surplus and producer surplus can be used to measure the efficiency of a market. Let's see how we can use these concepts to study the efficiency of a competitive market.

**Review Quiz**

1  What is the relationship between the marginal benefit, value and demand?
2  What is the relationship between individual demand and market demand?
3  What is consumer surplus? How is it measured?
4  What is the relationship between the marginal cost, minimum supply-price and supply?
5  What is the relationship between individual supply and market supply?
6  What is producer surplus? How is it measured?

You can work these questions in Study Plan 4.2 and get instant feedback.

**Figure 4.4   Supply and Producer Surplus**

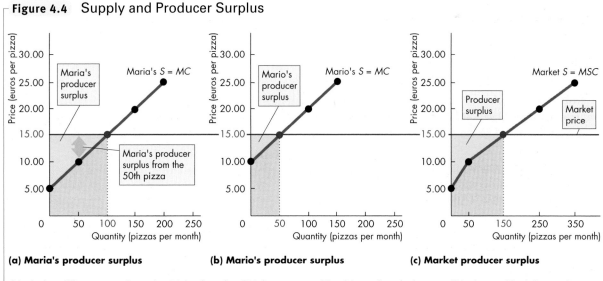

**(a) Maria's producer surplus**   **(b) Mario's producer surplus**   **(c) Market producer surplus**

Maria is willing to produce the 50th pizza for €10 in part (a). At a market price of €15 a pizza, Maria gets a producer surplus of €5 on the 50th pizza. The blue triangle shows her producer surplus on the 100 pizzas that she sells at €15 each.

The blue triangle in part (b) shows Mario's producer surplus on the 50 pizzas that he sells at €15 each.

The blue area in part (c) shows the producer surplus for the market. The red areas show the costs of producing the pizzas sold.

# Is the Competitive Market Efficient?

Figure 4.5(a) shows the market for pizza. The market forces that you studied in Chapter 3 (pp. 62–63) will pull the pizza market to its equilibrium price of €15 a pizza and equilibrium quantity of 10,000 pizzas a day. Buyers enjoy a consumer surplus (green area) and sellers enjoy a producer surplus (blue area). But is this competitive equilibrium efficient?

## Efficiency of Competitive Equilibrium

You've seen that the market demand curve for a good or service tells us the marginal social benefit from it. You've also seen that the market supply of a good or service tells us the marginal social cost of producing it.

Equilibrium in a competitive market occurs when the quantity demanded equals the quantity supplied at the intersection of the demand curve and the supply curve. At this intersection point, marginal social benefit on the demand curve equals marginal social cost on the supply curve. This equality is the condition for allocative efficiency. So in equilibrium, a competitive market achieves allocative efficiency.

Figure 4.5 illustrates the efficiency of the competitive equilibrium. The demand curve and the supply curve intersect in part (a) and marginal social benefit equals marginal social cost in part (b). This condition delivers an efficient use of resources for the society.

If production is less than 10,000 pizzas a day, the marginal pizza is valued more highly than it costs to produce it. If production exceeds 10,000 pizzas a day, it costs more to produce the marginal pizza than the value consumers place on it. Only when 10,000 pizzas a day are produced is the marginal pizza worth what it costs to produce.

The competitive market pushes the quantity of pizzas produced to its efficient level of 10,000 a day. If production is less than 10,000 pizzas a day, a shortage raises the price of a pizza, which increases production. If production exceeds 10,000 pizzas a day, a surplus lowers the price of a pizza, which decreases production. So a competitive pizza market is efficient.

Figure 4.5(a) also shows the consumer surplus and the producer surplus. The sum of consumer surplus and producer surplus is called **total surplus**. When the efficient quantity is produced, total surplus is maximized. Buyers and sellers acting in their self-interest end up promoting the social interest.

**Figure 4.5**    An Efficient Market for Pizza

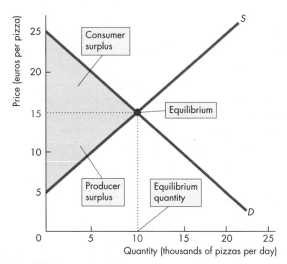

**(a) Equilibrium and surpluses**

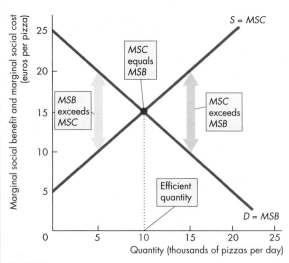

**(b) Efficiency**

Competitive equilibrium in part (a) occurs when the quantity demanded equals the quantity supplied. Resources are used efficiently in part (b) when marginal social benefit, *MSB*, equals marginal social cost, *MSC*. Total surplus, which is the sum of consumer surplus (green triangle) and producer surplus (blue triangle) is maximized.

The efficient quantity in part (b) is the same as the equilibrium quantity in part (a). The competitive pizza market produces the efficient quantity of pizza.

myeconlab  Animation

## The Invisible Hand

Writing in his book, *The Wealth of Nations*, in 1776, Adam Smith was the first to suggest that competitive markets send resources to the uses in which they have the highest value. Smith believed that each participant in a competitive market is 'led by an invisible hand to promote an end [the efficient use of resources] which was no part of his intention'.

You can see the invisible hand at work in the cartoon and in the world today.

### Umbrella for Sale

The cold drinks vendor has both cold drinks and shade and he has a marginal cost and a minimum supply-price of each. The reader on the park bench has a marginal benefit and a willingness to pay for each.

The reader's marginal benefit from shade exceeds the vendor's marginal cost; but the vendor's marginal cost of a cold drink exceeds the reader's marginal benefit. They trade the umbrella. The vendor gets a producer surplus from selling the shade for more than its marginal cost and the reader gets a consumer surplus from buying the shade for less than its marginal benefit. Both are better off and the umbrella has moved to its highest-valued use.

### The Invisible Hand at Work Today

The market economy relentlessly performs the activity illustrated in the cartoon to achieve an efficient allocation of resources.

A European frost cuts the supply of grapes. With fewer grapes available, the marginal social benefit increases. A shortage of grapes raises their price, so the market allocates the smaller quantity available to the people who value them most highly.

A new technology cuts the cost of producing a laptop. With a lower production cost, the supply of laptops increases and the price falls. The lower price encourages

an increase in the quantity demanded. The marginal social benefit from a laptop is brought to equality with its marginal social cost.

© Mike Twohy/The New Yorker Collection/
www.cartoonbank.com

## Market Failure

Markets do not always achieve an efficient outcome. We call a situation in which a market delivers an inefficient outcome one of **market failure**. Market failure can occur because too little of a good or service is produced (underproduction) or too much is produced (overproduction). We'll describe these two market failure outcomes and then see why they arise.

## Underproduction

Figure 4.6(a) shows that the quantity of pizzas produced is 5,000 a day. At this quantity, consumers are willing to pay €20 for a pizza that costs only €10 to produce. The total surplus from pizza is smaller than its maximum possible. The quantity produced is inefficient – there is underproduction.

We measure the scale of inefficiency by **deadweight**

**Figure 4.6**   Underproduction and Overproduction

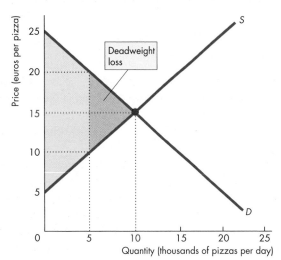

**(a) Underproduction**

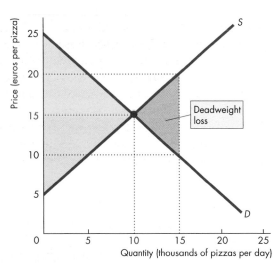

**(b) Overproduction**

If pizza production is cut to only 5,000 a day, a deadweight loss (the grey triangle) arises in part (a). Consumer surplus and producer surplus (the green and blue areas) are reduced. At 5,000 pizzas, the benefit of one more pizza exceeds its cost. The same is true for all levels of production up to 10,000 pizzas a day.

If production increases to 15,000 pizzas a day, a deadweight loss arises in part (b). At 15,000 pizzas a day, the cost of the 15,000th pizza exceeds its benefit. The cost of each pizza above 10,000 exceeds its benefit. Consumer surplus plus producer surplus equals the sum of the green and blue areas minus the deadweight loss triangle.

myeconlab Animation

**loss**, which is the decrease in total surplus that results from an inefficient level of production. The grey triangle in Figure 4.6(a) shows the deadweight loss.

## Overproduction

In Figure 4.6(b), the quantity of pizzas produced is 15,000 a day. At this quantity, consumers are willing to pay only €10 for a pizza that costs €20 to produce. By producing the 15,000th pizza, €10 of resources are wasted. Again, the grey triangle shows the deadweight loss, which reduces the total surplus to less than its maximum.

Inefficient production creates a deadweight loss that is borne by the entire society: it is a *social* loss.

## Sources of Market Failure

Obstacles to efficiency that bring market failure and create deadweight loss are:

◆ Price and quantity regulations
◆ Taxes and subsidies
◆ Externalities
◆ Public goods and common resources
◆ Monopoly
◆ High transactions costs

### Price and Quantity Regulations

*Price regulations* that put a cap on the rent a landlord can charge and laws that require employers to pay a minimum wage sometimes block the price adjustments that balance the quantity demanded and the quantity supplied and lead to underproduction. *Quantity regulations* that limit the amount that a farm is permitted to produce also lead to underproduction.

### Taxes and Subsidies

*Taxes* increase the prices paid by buyers and lower the prices received by sellers. So taxes decrease the quantity produced and lead to underproduction. *Subsidies*, which are payments by the government to producers, decrease the prices paid by buyers and increase the prices received by sellers. So subsidies increase the quantity produced and lead to overproduction.

### Externalities

An *externality* is a cost or a benefit that affects someone other than the seller or the buyer of a good or service.

An electric power utility creates an external cost by burning coal that brings acid rain and crop damage. The utility doesn't consider the cost of pollution when it decides how much power to produce. The result is overproduction. An apartment owner would provide an *external benefit* if she installed a smoke detector. But she doesn't consider her neighbour's marginal benefit when she is deciding whether to install a smoke detector. There is underproduction.

### Public Goods and Common Resources

A *public good* is a good or service that is consumed simultaneously by everyone even if they don't pay for it. Examples are national defence and law enforcement. Competitive markets would underproduce a public good because of the *free-rider problem*: it is in each person's interest to free-ride on everyone else and avoid paying for her or his share of a public good.

A *common resource* is owned by no one but used by everyone. Atlantic cod is an example. It is in everyone's self-interest to ignore the costs of their own use of a common resource that fall on others (called the *tragedy of the commons*), which leads to overproduction.

### Monopoly

A *monopoly* is a firm that is the sole provider of a good or service. Local water supply and cable television are supplied by firms that are monopolies. The self-interest of a monopoly is to maximize its profit. The monopoly has no competitors, so it can set the price to achieve its self-interested goal. To achieve its goal, a monopoly produces too little and charges too high a price. It leads to underproduction.

### High Transactions Costs

Retail markets employ enormous quantities of scarce labour and capital resources. It is costly to operate any market. Economists call the opportunity costs of making trades in a market **transactions costs**.

To use market price to allocate scarce resources, it must be worth bearing the opportunity cost of establishing a market. Some markets are just too costly to operate. For example, when you want to play tennis on your local 'free' court, you don't pay a market price for use of the court. You wait until the court becomes vacant and you 'pay' with your waiting time. When transactions costs are high, the market might underproduce.

You now know the conditions under which resource allocation is efficient. You've seen how a competitive market can be efficient and you've seen some impediments to efficiency.

## Alternatives to the Market

When a market is inefficient, can one of the alternative non-market methods that we described at the beginning of this chapter do a better job? Sometimes it can.

Often, majority rule might be used but majority rule has its own shortcomings. A group that pursues the self-interest of its members can become the majority. For example, a price or quantity regulation that creates a deadweight loss is almost always the result of a self-interested group becoming the majority and imposing costs on the minority. Also, with majority rule, votes must be translated into actions by bureaucrats who have their own agendas based on their self-interest.

Managers in firms issue commands and avoid the transactions costs which would arise if they went to a market every time they needed a job done.

First-come, first-served saves a lot of hassle. A queue could have markets in which people trade their place in the queue – but someone would have to enforce the agreements. Can you imagine the hassle at a busy ATM if you had to buy your spot at the head of the queue?

There is no one efficient mechanism for allocating resources efficiently. But markets, when supplemented by majority rule, command systems inside firms and occasionally by first-come, first-served work well.

> ### Review Quiz
>
> 1  Do competitive markets use resources efficiently? Explain why or why not.
> 2  What is deadweight loss and under what conditions does it occur?
> 3  What are the obstacles to achieving an efficient allocation of resources in the market economy?
>
> You can work these questions in Study Plan 4.3 and get instant feedback.

Is an efficient allocation of resources also a fair allocation? Does the competitive market provide people with fair incomes and do people always pay a fair price? Don't we need the government to step into some competitive markets to prevent the price from falling too low or rising too high? Let's now study these questions.

##  Is the Competitive Market Fair?

When a natural disaster strikes, such as a severe winter storm or a major flood, the prices of many essential items jump. The reason the prices jump is that some people have a greater demand and greater willingness to pay when the items are in limited supply. So the higher prices achieve an efficient allocation of scarce resources. News reports of these price hikes almost never talk about efficiency. Instead, they talk about equity or fairness. The claim often made is that it is unfair for profit-seeking dealers to cheat the victims of natural disaster.

Similarly, when low-skilled people work for a wage that is below what most would regard as a 'living wage', the media and politicians talk of employers taking unfair advantage of their workers.

How do we decide whether something is fair or unfair? You know when *you* think something is unfair. But how do you know? What are the *principles* of fairness?

Philosophers have tried for centuries to answer this question. Economists have offered their answers too. But before we look at the proposed answers, you should know that there is no universally agreed upon answer.

Economists agree about efficiency. That is, they agree that it makes sense to make the economic pie as large as possible and to bake it at the lowest possible cost. But they do not agree about equity. That is, they do not agree about what are fair shares of the economic pie for all the people who make it. The reason is that ideas about fairness are not exclusively economic ideas. They touch on politics, ethics and religion. Nevertheless, economists have thought about these issues and have a contribution to make. So let's examine the views of economists on this topic.

To think about fairness, think of economic life as a game – a serious game. All ideas about fairness can be divided into two broad groups. They are:

◆ It's not fair if the *result* isn't fair.
◆ It's not fair if the *rules* aren't fair.

## It's Not Fair if the *Result* Isn't Fair

The earliest efforts to establish a principle of fairness were based on the view that the result is what matters. The general idea was that it is unfair if people's incomes are too unequal. It is unfair that bank presidents earn millions of pounds a year while bank tellers earn only thousands of pounds a year. It is unfair that a shop owner enjoys a large profit and her customers pay higher prices in the aftermath of a flood.

There was a lot of excitement during the nineteenth century when economists thought they had made the incredible discovery that efficiency requires equality of incomes. To make the economic pie as large as possible, it must be cut into equal pieces, one for each person. This idea turns out to be wrong, but there is a lesson in the reason that it is wrong. So this nineteenth-century idea is worth a closer look.

### Utilitarianism

The nineteenth-century idea that only equality brings efficiency is called *utilitarianism*. **Utilitarianism** is a principle that states that we should strive to achieve 'the greatest happiness for the greatest number'. The people who developed this idea were known as utilitarians. They included some famous thinkers, such as Jeremy Bentham and John Stuart Mill.

Utilitarianism argues that to achieve 'the greatest happiness for the greatest number', income must be transferred from the rich to the poor up to the point of complete equality – to the point that there are no rich and no poor.

They reasoned in the following way: first, everyone has the same basic wants and are similar in their capacity to enjoy life. Second, the greater a person's income, the smaller is the marginal benefit of a pound. The millionth pound spent by a rich person brings a smaller marginal benefit to that person than the marginal benefit of the thousandth pound spent by a poorer person. So by transferring a pound from the millionaire to the poorer person, more is gained than is lost and the two people added together are better off.

Figure 4.7 illustrates this utilitarian idea. Tom and Jerry have the same marginal benefit curve, *MB*. (Marginal benefit is measured on the same scale of 1 to 3 for both Tom and Jerry.) Tom is at point *A*. He earns €5,000 a year and his marginal benefit of a euro is 3. Jerry is at point *B*. He earns €45,000 a year and his marginal benefit of a euro is 1. If a euro is transferred from Jerry to Tom, Jerry loses 1 unit of marginal benefit and Tom gains 3 units. So together, Tom and Jerry are better off. They are sharing the economic pie more efficiently. If a second euro is transferred, the same thing happens: Tom gains more than Jerry loses. And the same is true for every euro transferred until they both reach point *C*. At point *C*, Tom and Jerry have €25,000 each and each has a marginal benefit of 2 units. Now they are sharing the economic pie in the most efficient way. It is bringing the greatest attainable happiness to Tom and Jerry.

**Figure 4.7** Utilitarian Fairness

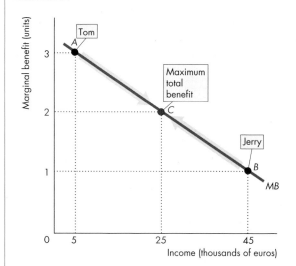

Tom earns €5,000 and has 3 units of marginal benefit at point *A*. Jerry earns €45,000 and has 1 unit of marginal benefit at point *B*. If income is transferred from Jerry to Tom, Jerry's loss is less than Tom's gain. Only when they have €25,000 each and 2 units of marginal benefit (at point *C*) can the sum of their total benefits increase no further.

myeconlab Animation

## The Big Trade-off

One big problem with the utilitarian ideal of complete equality is that it ignores the costs of making income transfers. The economist, Arthur Okun, in his book *Equality and Efficiency: The Big Tradeoff*, says the process of redistributing income is like trying to transfer water from one barrel to another with a leaky bucket. The more we try to increase equity by redistributing income, the more we reduce efficiency. Recognizing the cost of making income transfers leads to what is called the **big trade-off** – a trade-off between efficiency and fairness.

The big trade-off is based on the following facts. Income can be transferred from people with high incomes to people with low incomes only by taxing the high incomes. Taxing people's income from employment makes them work less. It results in the quantity of labour being less than the efficient quantity. Taxing people's income from capital makes them save less. It results in the quantity of capital being less than the efficient quantity. With smaller quantities of both labour and capital, the quantity of goods and services produced is less than the efficient quantity. The economic pie shrinks.

The trade-off is between the size of the economy and the degree of equality with which its produce is shared. The greater the amount of income redistribution through income taxes, the greater the inefficiency – the smaller is the economic pie.

A second source of inefficiency arises because a euro taken from a rich person does not end up as a euro in the hands of a poorer person. Some of it is spent on administration of the tax and transfer system. The cost of the tax-collection agency, HM Revenue & Customs, and the welfare administering agency, the Department for Work and Pensions, must be paid with some of the taxes collected.

Also, taxpayers hire accountants, auditors and lawyers to help ensure that they pay the correct amount of taxes. These activities use skilled labour and capital resources that could otherwise be used to produce goods and services that people value.

You can see that when all these costs are taken into account, taking a euro from a rich person does not give a euro to a poor person. It is even possible that with high taxes, those with low incomes end up being worse off. Suppose, for example, that highly taxed entrepreneurs decide to work less hard and shut down some of their businesses. Low-income workers get fired and must seek other, perhaps even lower-paid, work.

Because of the big trade-off, those who say that fairness is equality propose a modified version of utilitarianism.

## Make the Poorest as Well Off as Possible

A Harvard philosopher, John Rawls, proposed a modified version of utilitarianism in a classic book entitled *A Theory of Justice*, published in 1971. Rawls says that, taking all the costs of income transfers into account, the fair distribution of the economic pie is the one that makes the poorest person as well off as possible.

The incomes of rich people should be taxed and, after paying the costs of administering the tax and transfer system, what is left should be transferred to the poor. But the taxes must not be so high that they make the economic pie shrink to the point that the poorest person ends up with a smaller piece. A bigger share of a smaller pie can be less than a smaller share of a bigger pie. The goal is to make the piece enjoyed by the poorest person as big as possible. Most likely this piece will not be an equal share.

The 'fair results' idea requires a change in the results after the game is over. Some economists say these changes are themselves unfair and they propose a different way of thinking about fairness.

## It's Not Fair if the *Rules* Aren't Fair

The idea that it's not fair if the rules aren't fair is based on a fundamental principle that seems to be hard-wired into the human brain. It is the **symmetry principle**. The symmetry principle is the requirement that people in similar situations be treated similarly. It is the moral principle that lies at the centre of all the big religions. It says, in some form or other, 'behave towards others in the way you expect them to behave towards you'.

In economic life, this principle translates into *equality of opportunity*. But equality of opportunity to do what? This question is answered by the Harvard philosopher, Robert Nozick, in a book entitled *Anarchy, State and Utopia*, published in 1974. Nozick argues that the idea of fairness as an outcome or result cannot work and that fairness must be based on the fairness of the rules. He suggests that fairness obeys two rules:

1   The state must enforce laws that establish and protect private property.

2   Private property may be transferred from one person to another only by voluntary exchange.

The first rule says that everything that is valuable must be owned by individuals and that the state must ensure that theft is prevented. The second rule says that the only legitimate way a person can acquire property is to buy it in exchange for something else that the person owns. If these rules, which are fair rules, are followed, then the result is fair. It doesn't matter how unequally the economic pie is shared, provided that the pie is baked by people, each one of whom voluntarily provides services in exchange for a share of the pie offered in compensation.

These rules satisfy the symmetry principle. And if these rules are not followed, the symmetry principle is broken. You can see these facts by imagining a world in which the laws are not followed.

First, suppose that some resources or goods are not owned. They are common property. Then everyone is free to participate in a grab to use these resources or goods. The strongest will prevail. But when the strongest prevails, the strongest effectively *owns* the resources or goods in question and prevents others from enjoying them.

Second, suppose that we do not insist on voluntary exchange for transferring ownership of resources from one person to another. The alternative is *involuntary* transfer. In simple language, the alternative is theft.

Both of these situations violate the symmetry principle. Only the strong get to acquire what they want.

The weak end up with only the resources and goods that the strong don't want.

In contrast, if the two rules of fairness are followed, everyone, strong and weak, is treated in a similar way. All individuals are free to use their resources and human skills to create things that are valued by themselves and others and to exchange the fruits of their efforts with all others. This is the only set of arrangements that obeys the symmetry principle.

### Fairness and Efficiency

If private property rights are enforced and if voluntary exchange takes place in a competitive market, resources will be allocated efficiently if there are no:

1   Price and quantity regulations

2   Taxes and subsidies

3   Externalities

4   Public goods and common resources

5   Monopolies

6   High transactions costs

And according to the Nozick rules, the resulting distribution of income and wealth will be fair. Let's study a concrete example to examine the claim that if resources are allocated efficiently, they are also allocated fairly.

## Case Study: A Water Shortage in a Natural Disaster

A severe winter storm has broken the pipes that deliver drinking water to a city. Bottled water is available, but there is no tap water. What is the fair way to allocate the bottled water?

### Market Price

Suppose that if the water is allocated by market price, the price jumps to €8 a bottle – five times its normal price. At this price, the people who own water can make a large profit by selling it. People who are willing and able to pay €8 a bottle get the water. And because most people can't afford the €8 price, they end up either without water or consuming just a few drops a day.

You can see that the water is being used efficiently. There is a fixed amount available, some people are willing to pay €8 to get a bottle and the water goes to those people. The people who own and sell water receive a large producer surplus. Total surplus (the sum of consumer surplus and producer surplus) is maximized.

In the rules view, the outcome is also fair. No one is denied the water they are willing to pay for. In the results view, the outcome would most likely be regarded as unfair. The lucky owners of water make a killing and the poorest end up the thirstiest.

## Non-market Methods

Suppose that by a majority vote, the citizens decide that the government will buy all the water, pay for it with a tax and use one of the non-market methods to allocate the water to the citizens. The possibilities now are:

### Command

Someone decides who is the most deserving. Perhaps everyone is given an equal share or perhaps government officials and their families get most of the water.

### Contest

Bottles of water are prizes that go to those who are best at a particular contest.

### First-come, first-served

Water goes to the first off the mark or to those who place the lowest value on their time and can afford to queue for it.

### Lottery

Water goes to those in luck.

### Personal characteristics

Water goes to those with the 'right' characteristics. For example, the old, the young or pregnant women.

These non-market methods deliver an allocation of water that is fair and efficient only by chance. In the rules view they are unfair because the distribution involves involuntary transfers of resources among citizens. In the results view they are unfair because the poorest don't end up being made as well off as possible.

The allocation is inefficient for two reasons. First, resources are used to operate the allocation scheme. Second, some people are willing to pay for more water than they have been allocated and others have been allocated more water than they are willing to pay for.

The second source of inefficiency can be overcome if, after the non-market allocation, people are permitted to trade water at its market price. Those who value water below the market price will sell and those who are willing to pay the market price will buy. Those who value the water most highly are the ones who consume it.

## Market Price with Taxes

Another approach is to allocate the scarce water using the market price but then to alter the redistribution of buying power by taxing the sellers of water and providing benefits to the poor.

Suppose water owners are taxed on each bottle sold and the revenue from these taxes is given to the poorest people. People are then free, starting from this new distribution of buying power, to trade water at the market price. Because the owners of water are taxed on what they sell, they have a weaker incentive to offer water for sale and the supply decreases. The equilibrium price rises to more than €8 a bottle. There is now a deadweight loss in the market for water – similar to the loss that arises from underproduction on p. 91. (We study the effects of a tax and show its inefficiency in Chapter 5 on pp. 111–115.)

So the tax is inefficient. In the rules view, the tax is also unfair because it forces the owners of water to make a transfer to others. In the results view, the outcome might be regarded as being fair.

This brief case study illustrates the complexity of ideas about fairness. Economists have a clear criterion of efficiency but no comparably clear criterion of fairness. Most economists regard Nozick as being too extreme and want a fair tax in the rules. But there is no consensus about what would be a fair tax.

### Review Quiz

1 What are the two big approaches to fairness?
2 Explain the utilitarian idea of fairness and what is wrong with it.
3 Explain the big trade-off and the idea of fairness developed to deal with it.
4 What is the main idea of fairness based on fair rules? Explain your answer.

You can work these questions in Study Plan 4.4 and get instant feedback.

You've now studied efficiency and equity, or fairness, the two biggest issues that run right through the whole of economics. *Reading Between the Lines* on pp. 98–99 looks at an example of an efficient market in our economy today. At many points throughout this book – and in your life – you will return to and use the ideas about efficiency and fairness that you've learned in this chapter. In the next chapter, we study some sources of *in*efficiency and *un*fairness.

# Reading Between the Lines

# Efficiency in Ash Cloud

## Volcano Cloud Hangs Over European Economy

### Tom Odula

The ash cloud from Iceland's volcanic eruption is battering airlines. . . . Each new day of closed airspace is costing jobs or revenues for those dealing in perishables such as roses and mozzarella.

But the volcano disruption is also creating some winners, such as fully booked Scandinavian ferries, hotel owners charging $800 a night and taxi drivers pocketing $5,000 fares. . . .

Some 5,000 workers have been temporarily laid off in Kenya following $12 million in losses in flowers. . . . Still, express delivery services Federal Express and DHL said they have shifted many deliveries onto trucks and rail to limit their losses. . . . And most international commerce remained unaffected, since it is largely routed by sea, said Keith Rockwell, spokesman for the World Trade Organization.

'I wouldn't envision this affecting high-tech or other services trade, but it is terrible for those sectors that are affected,' Rockwell said, citing tourism and exports of fresh produce and flowers.

While travellers managed as best they could within Europe, those waiting for long-haul connections had less options. Rising hotel prices weren't making it easier.

'Yesterday, we had a hotel room at 250 euros. At midday, it was 460 euros, and in the evening, the price was 800 euros for a room – we can't pay that,' said Daniel, a 39-year-old French tourist, as he waited at Hong Kong's airport.

## The Essence of the Story

◆ The ash cloud from an active Icelandic volcano closed airspace and disrupted air transport in Europe.

◆ The volcano disruption created both losers and winners.

◆ Among the winners were Scandinavian ferries, hotel owners and taxi drivers, who sold more and for higher prices.

◆ Among the losers were flower growers in Kenya, Federal Express and DHL and people stranded and facing higher hotel prices.

# Economic Analysis

◆ On a normal day, growers around the world send 20 million flowers for auction in Holland. These flowers are then distributed around the world to their buyers. All this transport is done by air.

◆ When an ash cloud closed Holland's airports, alternative but more costly arrangements were quickly made to fly flowers in and out of Athens and Madrid and transport them by truck to Holland.

◆ Figure 1 illustrates the effects of the ash cloud. The demand curve (marginal benefit curve) shifted leftward from $D_0$ to $D_1$; the supply curve (marginal cost curve) also shifted leftward from $S_0$ to $S_1$; and the flower auction found the new equilibrium and efficient outcome.

◆ In Figure 1, the quantity of flowers traded decreased, but the price did not change. Both demand and supply were influenced by the loss of air transportation and decreased by the same amount.

◆ Consumer surplus (green) and producer surplus (blue) decreased, but total surplus was at its maximum given the situation.

◆ In the market for hotel rooms, there were winners as well as losers.

◆ Figure 2 illustrates the effects of the ash cloud in the market for hotel rooms. The demand curve (marginal benefit curve) shifted rightward from $D_0$ to $D_1$ but the supply curve didn't change. The price and the quantity increased.

◆ Consumer surplus (green) shrank and producer surplus (blue) expanded.

◆ Because at the new quantity and price marginal socal cost equalled marginal social benefit, the outcome was efficient.

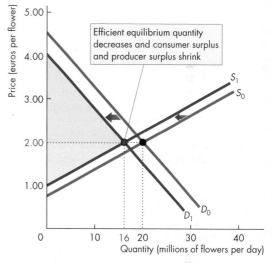

Figure 1  **Dutch flower market: 19 April 2010**

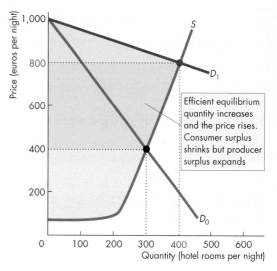

Traders at the daily flower auction in Holland

Figure 2  **Market for hotel rooms: 19 April 2010**

## SUMMARY

## Key Points

### Resource Allocation Methods
(pp. 84–85)

◆ Because resources are scarce, some mechanism must allocate them.

◆ The alternative allocation methods are market price; command; majority rule; contest; first-come, first-served; lottery; personal characteristics; and force.

Working Problems 1 and 2 will give you a better understanding of resource allocation methods.

### Benefit, Cost and Surplus
(pp. 86–89)

◆ The maximum price willingly paid is marginal benefit, so a demand curve is a marginal benefit curve.

◆ The market demand curve is the horizontal sum of the individual demand curves and is the marginal social benefit curve.

◆ Value is what people are *willing to* pay; price is what people *must* pay.

◆ Consumer surplus is the excess of the benefit received from a good or service over the amount paid for it.

◆ The minimum supply-price is the marginal cost, so a supply curve is also a marginal cost curve.

◆ The market supply curve is the horizontal sum of the individual supply curves and is the marginal social cost curve.

◆ Cost is what producers pay; price is what producers receive.

◆ Producer surplus is the excess of the amount received from the sale of a good or service over the cost of producing it.

Working Problems 3 to 10 will give you a better understanding of benefit, cost and surplus.

### Is the Competitive Market Efficient?
(pp. 90–93)

◆ In a competitive equilibrium, marginal social benefit equals marginal social cost and resource allocation is efficient.

◆ Buyers and sellers acting in their self-interest end up promoting the social interest.

◆ The sum of consumer surplus and producer surplus is maximized. Producing less than or more than the efficient quantity creates deadweight loss.

◆ Price and quantity regulations; taxes and subsidies; externalities; public goods and common resources; monopoly; and high transactions costs can create inefficiency and deadweight loss.

Working Problems 11 to 13 will give you a better understanding of the efficiency of competitive markets.

### Is the Competitive Market Fair?
(pp. 94–97)

◆ Ideas about fairness divide into two groups: fair results and fair rules.

◆ Fair-results ideas require income transfers from the rich to the poor.

◆ Fair-rules ideas require property rights and voluntary exchange.

Working Problems 14 and 15 will give you a better understanding of the fairness of competitive markets.

## Key Terms

Big trade-off, 95
Command system, 84
Consumer surplus, 87
Deadweight loss, 91
Market failure, 91
Producer surplus, 89
Symmetry principle, 96
Total surplus, 90
Transactions costs, 93
Utilitarianism, 94

## STUDY PLAN PROBLEMS AND APPLICATIONS

 You can work Problems 1 to 17 in MyEconLab Chapter 4 Study Plan and get instant feedback.

## Resource Allocation Methods

(Study Plan 4.1)

Use the following information to work Problems 1 and 2.

At Fifteen, the Jamie Oliver restaurant in London, reservations are essential. At Square, a restaurant in Leeds, reservations are recommended. At Maddisons, a restaurant in York, reservations are not accepted.

**1 a** Describe the method of allocating scarce table resources at these three restaurants.

   **b** Why do you think restaurants have different reservations policies?

**2** Why do you think restaurants don't use the market price to allocate their tables?

## Benefit, Cost and Surplus (Study Plan 4.2)

Use the following table to work Problems 3 to 5.

The table gives the demand schedules for train travel for the only buyers in the market: Ann, Beth and Cathy.

| Price (euros per kilometre) | Quantity demanded (kilometres) | | |
|---|---|---|---|
| | Ann | Beth | Cathy |
| 3 | 30 | 25 | 20 |
| 4 | 25 | 20 | 15 |
| 5 | 20 | 15 | 10 |
| 6 | 15 | 10 | 5 |
| 7 | 10 | 5 | 0 |
| 8 | 5 | 0 | 0 |
| 9 | 0 | 0 | 0 |

**3** Construct the market demand schedule. What is the maximum price that Ann, Beth and Cathy are willing to pay to travel 20 kilometres? Why?

**4** When the total distance travelled is 60 kilometres,

   **a** What is the marginal social benefit? Why?

   **b** What is the marginal private benefit for each person and how many kilometres does each person travel?

**5** When the price is €4 a kilometre,

   **a** What is each traveller's consumer surplus?

   **b** What is the market consumer surplus?

Use the following news clip to work Problems 6 and 7.

**eBay Saves Billions for Bidders**

If you think you would save money by bidding on eBay auctions, you would probably be right. Two Maryland researchers calculated the difference between the actual purchase price paid for auction items and the top price bidders stated they were willing to pay. They found that the difference averaged at least €4 per auction.

Source: *Information Week*, 28 January 2008

**6** What method is used to allocate goods on eBay? How does the allocation method used by eBay auctions influence consumer surplus?

**7 a** Can an eBay auction give the seller a surplus?

   **b** On a graph show the consumer surplus and producer surplus from an eBay auction.

Use the following table to work Problems 8 to 10.

The table gives the supply schedules of hot air balloon rides for the only sellers in the market: Xavier, Yasmin and Zack.

| Price (euros per ride) | Quantity supplied (rides) | | |
|---|---|---|---|
| | Xavier | Yasmin | Zack |
| 100 | 30 | 25 | 20 |
| 90 | 25 | 20 | 15 |
| 80 | 20 | 15 | 10 |
| 70 | 15 | 10 | 5 |
| 60 | 10 | 5 | 0 |
| 50 | 5 | 0 | 0 |
| 40 | 0 | 0 | 0 |

**8** Construct the market supply schedule. What are the minimum prices that Xavier, Yasmin and Zack are willing to accept to supply 20 rides? Why?

**9** When the total number of rides is 30,

   **a** What is the marginal social cost of a ride?

   **b** What is the marginal cost for each supplier and how many rides does each of the firms supply?

**10** When the price is €70 a ride,

   **a** What is each firm's producer surplus?

   **b** What is the market producer surplus?

## Is the Competitive Market Efficient?
(Study Plan 4.3)

**11** The figure shows the demand for and supply of mobile phones.

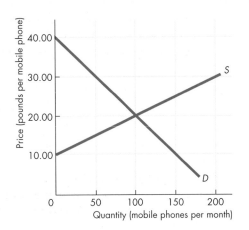

**a** What are the equilibrium price and equilibrium quantity of mobile phones?

**b** Shade in and label the consumer surplus at the competitive equilibrium.

**c** Shade in and label the producer surplus at the competitive equilibrium.

**d** Calculate the total surplus at the competitive equilibrium.

**e** Is the competitive market for mobile phones efficient?

**12** The table gives the demand and supply schedules of sunscreen.

| Price (euros per bottle) | Quantity demanded | Quantity supplied |
|---|---|---|
| | (bottles per day) | |
| 0 | 400 | 0 |
| 5 | 300 | 100 |
| 10 | 200 | 200 |
| 15 | 100 | 300 |
| 20 | 0 | 400 |

Factories producing sunscreen are required to limit production to 100 bottles per day.

**a** What is the maximum price that consumers are willing to pay for the 100th bottle?

**b** What is the minimum price that producers are willing to accept for the 100th bottle?

**c** Describe the situation in the market for sunscreen.

**13** Explain why each restaurant in Problem 1 might be using an efficient allocation method.

## Is the Competitive Market Fair?
(Study Plan 4.4)

**14** Explain why the allocation method used by each restaurant in Problem 1 is fair or not fair.

**15** In Problem 12, how can the 100 bottles available be allocated to beach-goers? Which possible methods would be fair and which would be unfair?

## Economics in the News (Study Plan 4.N)

**16** **The World's Largest Tulip and Flower Market**

Every day 20 million tulips, roses and other cut flowers are auctioned at the Dutch market called the Bloemenveiling. Each day 55,000 Dutch auctions take place, matching buyers and sellers.

Source: Tulip-Bulbs.com

A Dutch auction is one in which the auctioneer starts by announcing the highest price. If no one offers to buy the flowers, the auctioneer lowers the price until a buyer is found.

**a** What method is used to allocate flowers at the Bloemenveiling?

**b** How does a Dutch flower auction influence consumer surplus and producer surplus?

**c** Are the flower auctions at the Bloemenveiling efficient?

**17** **Wii Sells Out Across Japan**

After a two-month TV-ad blitz for Wii in Japan, demand was expected to be much higher than supply. Yodobashi Camera was selling Wii games on a first-come, first-served basis. Eager customers showed up early so as not to miss out on their favourite titles. Those who tried to join the queue after 6 or 7 a.m. were turned away – many could be spotted rushing off to the smaller Akihabara stores that were holding raffles to decide who got a Wii.

Source: *Gamespot News*, 1 December 2006

**a** Why was the quantity demanded of Wii expected to exceed the quantity supplied?

**b** Did Nintendo produce the efficient quantity of Wii? Explain.

**c** Can you think of reasons why Nintendo might want to underproduce and leave the market with fewer Wii than people want to buy?

**d** What are the two methods of resource allocation described in the news clip? Is either method of allocating Wii efficient?

**e** What do you think some of the people who managed to buy a Wii did with it?

**f** Explain which is the fairer method of allocating the Wii: the market price or the two methods described in the news clip.

ADDITIONAL PROBLEMS AND APPLICATIONS

 You can work these problems in MyEconLab if assigned by your lecturer.

## Resource Allocation Methods

**18** At McDonald's, no reservations are accepted; at the Rex Whistler Restaurant at Tate Britain, reservations are accepted; at Zaffrano in Knightsbridge, reservations are essential.

   **a** Describe the method of allocating table resources in these three restaurants.

   **b** Why do you think restaurants have different reservations policies?

## Benefit, Cost and Surplus

Use the following table to work Problems 19 to 22.

The table gives the demand schedules for jet-ski rides by the only suppliers: Rick, Sam and Tom.

| Price (euros per ride) | Quantity demanded (rides per day) | | |
|---|---|---|---|
| | Rick | Sam | Tom |
| 10.00 | 0 | 0 | 0 |
| 12.50 | 5 | 0 | 0 |
| 15.00 | 10 | 5 | 0 |
| 17.50 | 15 | 10 | 5 |
| 20.00 | 20 | 15 | 10 |

**19** What is each owner's minimum supply-price of 10 rides a day?

**20** Which owner has the largest producer surplus when the price of a ride is €17.50? Explain why.

**21** What is the marginal social cost of producing 45 rides a day?

**22** Construct the market supply schedule of jet-ski rides.

Use the following table to work Problems 23 and 24.

The table gives the demand and supply schedules of sandwiches.

| Price (pounds per sandwich) | Quantity demanded | Quantity supplied |
|---|---|---|
| | (sandwiches per hour) | |
| 0 | 300 | 0 |
| 1 | 250 | 50 |
| 2 | 200 | 100 |
| 3 | 150 | 150 |
| 4 | 100 | 200 |
| 5 | 50 | 250 |
| 6 | 0 | 300 |

**23** **a** What is the maximum price that consumers are willing to pay for the 200th sandwich?

   **b** What is the minimum price that producers are willing to accept for the 200th sandwich?

   **c** Are 200 sandwiches a day less than or greater than the efficient quantity?

## Is the Competitive Market Efficient?

**24** **a** If the sandwich market is efficient, what is the consumer surplus, the producer surplus and the total surplus?

   **b** If the demand for sandwiches increases and the sandwich makers continue to produce the efficient quantity, describe the change in producer surplus and the deadweight loss.

Use the following figure, which illlustrates the market for CDs, to work Problems 25 and 26.

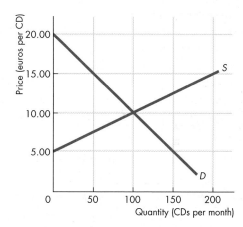

**25** **a** What are the equilibrium price and equilibrium quantity of CDs?

   **b** Calculate the consumer surplus at the competitive equilibrium.

   **c** Calculate the producer surplus at the competitive equilibrium.

   **d** Calculate the total surplus at the competitive equilibrium.

   **e** Is the competitive market for CDs efficient?

**26** If the demand for CDs decreases by 50 per month at each price, but CD producers continue to produce the previously efficient quantity, show on the graph:

   **a** The change in total surplus from CDs.

   **b** The deadweight loss created.

Use the following news clip to work Problems 27 to 29.

**The Right Price for Digital Music**

Apple's $1.29-for-the-latest-songs model isn't perfect and isn't it too much to pay for music that appeals to just a few people? What we need is a system that will be profitable but yet fair to music lovers. The solution: price song downloads according to demand. The more people who download a particular song, the higher will be the price of that song; the fewer people who buy a particular song, the lower will be the price of that song. That is a free-market solution – the market would determine the price.

Source: *Slate*, 5 December 2005

Assume that the marginal social cost of downloading a song from the iTunes Store is zero. (This assumption means that the cost of operating the iTunes Store doesn't change if people download more songs.)

**27  a** Draw a graph of the market for downloadable music with a price of $1.29 for all the latest songs. On your graph, show consumer surplus and producer surplus.

   **b** With a price of $1.29 for all the latest songs, is the market efficient or inefficient? If it is inefficient, show the deadweight loss on your graph.

**28** If the pricing scheme described in the news clip were adopted, how would consumer surplus, producer surplus and the deadweight loss change?

**29  a** If the pricing scheme described in the news clip were adopted, would the market be efficient or inefficient? Explain.

   **b** Is the pricing scheme described in the news clip a 'free-market solution'? Explain.

## Is the Competitive Market Fair?

**30** The winner of the men's and women's tennis singles at the US Open is paid twice as much as the runner-up, but it takes two players to have a singles final. Is the compensation arrangement fair?

Use the following information to work Problems 31 and 32.

A winter storm cuts the power supply and isolates a small town in the mountains. The people rush to buy candles from the town store, which is the only source of candles. The store owner decides to ration the candles to one per family but to keep the price of a candle unchanged.

**31** Who gets to use the candles? Who receives the consumer surplus and who receives the producer surplus on candles?

**32** Is the allocation efficient? Is the allocation fair?

## Economics in the News

**33** After you have studied Reading Between the Lines on pp. 98–99 answer the following questions.

   **a** What is the method used to allocate the world's cut flowers and local hotel rooms?

   **b** Who benefits from this method of resource allocation: buyers, sellers or both? Explain your answer using the ideas of marginal social benefit, marginal social cost, consumer surplus and producer surplus.

   **c** After the ash cloud closed European airports, when the equilibrium quantity of cut flowers decreased, why was the outcome still efficient? Why was there not underproduction and a deadweight loss?

   **d** If the government of Holland placed a limit of 15 million a day on the quantity of flowers traded in the flower market in Holland, would there be underproduction and a deadweight loss created? Explain your answer.

**34  Fight over Water Rates; Escondido Farmers Say Increase would Put Them out of Business**

Agricultural users of water pay less than residential and business users. Since 1993, water rates have increased by more than 90 per cent for residential customers and by only 50 per cent for agricultural users.

Source: *The San Diego Union-Tribune*, 14 June 2006

   **a** Do you think that the allocation of water between agricultural and residential users is likely to be efficient? Explain your answer.

   **b** If agricultural users paid a higher price, would the allocation of resources be more efficient?

   **c** If agricultural users paid a higher price, what would happen to consumer surplus and producer surplus from water?

   **d** Is the difference in price paid by agricultural and residential users fair?

**35  New Zealand's Private Forests**

In the early 1990s, the New Zealand government auctioned half the national forests, converting these forests from public ownership to private ownership. The government's decision was an incentive to get the owners to operate like farmers – that is, take care of the resource and to use it to make a profit.

Source: *Reuters*, 7 September 2007

   **a** When all forests in New Zealand were government owned, was the New Zealand timber industry efficient? Did logging companies operate in the social interest or self-interest?

   **b** Since the early 1990s, has the New Zealand timber industry been efficient? Have logging companies operated in the social interest or self-interest?

   **c** What incentive do private timber companies have to ensure that they take care of the resource?

# Government Actions in Markets

### After studying this chapter you will be able to:

◆ Explain how rent ceilings create housing shortages and inefficiency

◆ Explain how minimum wage laws create unemployment and inefficiency

◆ Explain the effects of a tax

◆ Explain the effects of production quotas and subsidies and price supports on production, costs, prices and inefficiency

◆ Explain how markets for illegal goods work

When people can't afford to buy houses, more people must rent and rental prices shoot up! Should the government cap the rents that landlords charge in difficult times? Perhaps the answer is increasing the minimum wage? Wouldn't that help the low paid?

We all pay taxes and some taxes are rising, so who really pays a tax: buyers or sellers? In the markets for many food items producers receive a subsidy. Who benefits from the subsidy: farmers or consumers? Some goods are illegal, yet they are still traded. How do markets for illegal goods work? This chapter answers these questions. In *Reading Between the Lines* at the end of the chapter, we explore the scale and effect of government support payments to farmers.

## A Housing Market with a Rent Ceiling

We spend more of our income on housing than on any other good or service, so it isn't surprising that rents can be a political issue. When rents are high, or when they jump by a large amount, renters might lobby the government for limits on rents.

A government regulation that makes it illegal to charge a price higher than a specified level is called a **price ceiling** or **price cap**.

The effects of a price ceiling on a market depend crucially on whether the ceiling is imposed at a level that is above or below the equilibrium price.

A price ceiling set *above the equilibrium price* has no effect. The reason is that the price ceiling does not constrain the market forces. The force of the law and the market forces are not in conflict.

But a price ceiling *below the equilibrium price* has powerful effects on a market. The reason is that the price ceiling attempts to prevent the price from regulating the quantities demanded and supplied. The force of the law and the market forces are in conflict.

When a price ceiling is applied to a housing market, it is called a **rent ceiling** – the maximum rent that may be legally charged.

A rent ceiling set below the equilibrium rent creates:

◆ A housing shortage
◆ Increased search activity
◆ A black market

## A Housing Shortage

At the equilibrium price, the quantity demanded equals the quantity supplied. In a housing market, when the rent is at the equilibrium level, the quantity of housing supplied equals the quantity of housing demanded and there is neither a shortage nor a surplus of housing.

But at a rent set below the equilibrium rent, the quantity of housing demanded exceeds the quantity of housing supplied – there is a shortage. So if a rent ceiling is set below the equilibrium rent, there will be a shortage of housing.

When there is a shortage, the quantity available is the quantity supplied and when there is no price ceiling the price would rise. But when there is a price ceiling, the quantity supplied must somehow be allocated among the frustrated demanders. One way in which this allocation occurs is through increased search activity.

## Increased Search Activity

The time spent looking for someone with whom to do business is called **search activity**. We spend some time in search activity almost every time we make a purchase. When you're shopping for the latest hot new mobile phone, and you know four stores that stock it, how do you find which store has the best deal? You spend a few minutes on the Internet, checking out the various prices. In some markets, such as the housing market, people spend a lot of time checking the alternatives available before making a choice.

When a price is regulated and there is a shortage, search activity increases. In the case of a rent-controlled housing market, frustrated would-be renters scan the newspapers, not only for housing adverts but also for death notices! Any information about newly available housing is useful, and apartment seekers race to be first on the scene when news of a possible supplier breaks.

The *opportunity cost* of a good is equal not only to its price but also to the value of the search time spent finding the good. So the opportunity cost of housing is equal to the rent (a regulated price) plus the time and other resources spent searching for the restricted quantity available. Search activity is costly. It uses time and other resources, such as phone calls and car journeys that could have been used in other productive ways.

A rent ceiling controls only the rent portion of the cost of housing. The cost of increased search activity might end up making the full cost of housing higher than it would be without a rent ceiling.

## Black Market

A rent ceiling also encourages illegal trading in a **black market**, an illegal market in which the equilibrium price exceeds the price ceiling. Black markets occur in rent-controlled housing markets. They also occur in the market for tickets to big sporting events and rock concerts, where 'ticket touts' (or 'scalpers') operate.

When a rent ceiling is in force, frustrated renters and landlords constantly seek ways of increasing rents. One common way is for a new tenant to pay a high price for worthless fittings, such as charging €2,000 for threadbare curtains. Another is for the tenant to pay an exorbitant price for new locks and keys called 'key money'.

The level of a black market rent depends on how tightly the rent ceiling is enforced. With loose enforcement, the black market rent is close to the unregulated rent. But with strict enforcement, the black market rent is equal to the maximum price that a renter is willing to pay.

Figure 5.1 illustrates the effects of a rent ceiling. The demand curve for housing is *D* and the supply curve is *S*. A rent ceiling is imposed at €1,000 a month. Rents that exceed €1,000 a month are in the grey-shaded illegal region in the figure. You can see that the equilibrium rent, where the demand and supply curves intersect, is in the illegal region.

At a rent of €1,000 a month, the quantity of housing supplied is 4,400 units and the quantity demanded is 10,000 units. So with a rent of €1,000 a month, there is a shortage of 5,600 units.

To rent the 4,400th unit, someone is willing to pay €1,200 a month. They might pay this amount by incurring search costs that bring the total cost of housing to €1,200 a month, or they might pay a black market price of €1,200 a month. Either way, the renter ends up incurring a cost that exceeds what the equilibrium rent would be in an unregulated market.

## Inefficiency of Rent Ceilings

A rent ceiling set below the equilibrium rent results in an inefficient underproduction of housing services. The *marginal social benefit* of housing exceeds its *marginal social cost* and a deadweight loss shrinks the producer surplus and consumer surplus (see Chapter 4, pp. 87–89).

Figure 5.2 shows this inefficiency. The rent ceiling (€1,000 per month) is below the equilibrium rent (€1,100 per month) and the quantity of housing supplied (4,400 units) is less than the efficient quantity (7,400 units).

Because the quantity of housing supplied (the quantity available) is less than the efficient quantity, there is a deadweight loss, shown by the grey triangle. Producer surplus shrinks to the blue triangle and consumer surplus shrinks to the green triangle. The red rectangle represents the potential loss from increased search activity. This loss is borne by consumers and the full loss from the rent ceiling is the sum of the deadweight loss and the increased cost of search.

**Figure 5.1   A Rent Ceiling**

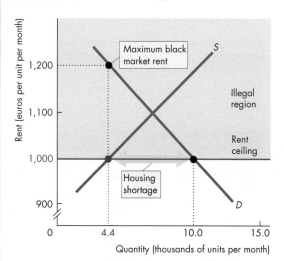

A rent above the rent ceiling of €1,000 a month is illegal (in the grey-shaded region). At a rent of €1,000 a month, the quantity of housing supplied is 4,400 units and the quantity demanded is 10,000 units. There is a housing shortage of 5,600 units.

Frustrated renters spend time searching for housing and they make deals with landlords in a black market. Someone is willing to pay €1,200 a month for the 4,400th unit. This is the maximum black market rent.

**Figure 5.2   The Inefficiency of a Rent Ceiling**

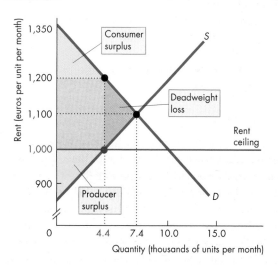

Without a rent ceiling, the market produces an efficient 7,400 units of housing at a rent of €1,100 a month. A rent ceiling of €1,000 a month decreases the quantity of housing supplied to 4,400 units. Producer surplus and consumer surplus shrink and a deadweight loss arises. The red rectangle represents the cost of resources used in increased search activity. The full loss from the rent ceiling equals the sum of the red rectangle and grey triangle.

# Are Rent Ceilings Fair?

Rent ceilings might be inefficient, but don't they achieve a fairer allocation of scarce housing? Let's explore this question.

## The Two Views of Fairness

Chapter 4 (pp. 94–96) reviews two key ideas about fairness. According to the *fair rules* view, anything that blocks voluntary exchange is unfair, so rent ceilings are unfair. But according to the *fair result* view, a fair outcome is one that benefits the less well off. So according to this view, the fairest outcome is the one that allocates scarce housing to the poorest. To see whether rent ceilings help to achieve a fairer outcome in this sense, we need to consider how the market allocates scarce housing resources in the face of a rent ceiling.

## Allocating Housing Among Demanders

Blocking rent adjustments doesn't eliminate scarcity. Rather, because it decreases the quantity of housing available, it creates an even bigger challenge for the housing market. Somehow, the market must ration a smaller quantity of housing and allocate that housing among the people who demand it. When the rent is not permitted to allocate scarce housing, what other mechanisms are available and are they fair? Three possible mechanisms are:

◆ A lottery

◆ First-come, first-served

◆ Discrimination

A lottery allocates housing to those who are lucky, not to those who are poor. First-come, first-served allocated housing in England after the Second World War to those with the foresight to get their names on a list first, not to the poorest. Discrimination allocates scarce housing based on the views and self-interest of owners. Discrimination based on friendship, family ties and criteria such as race, ethnicity or sex is more likely to enter the equation. We might make such discrimination illegal, but we cannot prevent it from occurring.

In principle, self-interested owners and bureaucrats could allocate housing to satisfy some criterion of fairness, but they are not likely to do so. It is hard, then, to make a case for rent ceilings on the basis of fairness. Non-price methods of allocation do not produce a fair outcome.

## Is there a Case for Rent Ceilings?

The economic case against rent ceilings is now widely accepted, so new rent ceiling laws are rare. But when governments try to repeal rent control laws, current renters lobby politicians to maintain the ceilings. Also, other people would be happy if they were lucky enough to find a rent-controlled apartment. So there is usually plenty of political support for rent ceilings.

A Chartered Institute of Housing Report[1] in August 2010 argued that UK housing policy needs to target the lower paid workers who have been priced out of the private home ownership market, who cannot afford private rented property but will not be offered local authority housing. They argue that housing associations should offer below market rent housing (housing with a rent ceiling) to this group.

Because more people support rent ceilings than oppose them, politicians are sometimes willing to support them too. Local authority spending on housing is being cut in the UK and so local and central government politicians are likely to support charitable groups such as housing associations introducing rent ceilings.

The outcome is inefficient because scarce housing resources don't get allocated to the people who value them most highly.

[1] guardian.co.uk/society/2010/aug/15/renting-buying-home

**Review Quiz**

1  What is a rent ceiling and what are its effects if it is set above the equilibrium rent?
2  What are the effects of a rent ceiling that is set below the equilibrium rent?
3  How are scarce housing resources allocated when a rent ceiling is in place?
4  Why does a rent ceiling create an inefficient and unfair outcome in the housing market?

You can work these questions in Study Plan 5.1 and get instant feedback.

You now know how a price ceiling (rent ceiling) works. Next, we'll learn about the effects of a price floor by studying a minimum wage in a labour market.

## A Labour Market with a Minimum Wage

For each of us, the labour market is the market that influences the jobs we get and the wages we earn. Firms decide how much labour to demand, and the lower the wage rate, the greater is the quantity of labour demanded. Households decide how much labour to supply, and the higher the wage rate, the greater is the quantity of labour supplied. The wage rate adjusts to make the quantity of labour demanded equal to the quantity supplied.

When wage rates fail to keep up with rising prices, labour unions might lobby the government for a higher wage rate. A government imposed regulation that makes it illegal to charge a price lower than a specified level is called a **price floor**.

The effects of a price floor on a market depend crucially on whether the floor is imposed at a level that is above or below the equilibrium price.

A price floor set *below the equilibrium price* has no effect. The reason is that the price floor does not constrain the market forces. The force of the law and the market forces are not in conflict. But a price floor *above the equilibrium price* has powerful effects on a market. The reason is that the price floor attempts to prevent the price from regulating the quantities demanded and supplied. The force of the law and the market forces are in conflict.

When a price floor is applied to a labour market, it is called a **minimum wage**. A minimum wage imposed at a level that is above the equilibrium wage creates unemployment. Let's look at the effects of a minimum wage.

## Minimum Wage Brings Unemployment

At the equilibrium price, the quantity demanded equals the quantity supplied. In a labour market, when the wage rate is at the equilibrium level, the quantity of labour supplied equals the quantity of labour demanded. But at a wage rate above the equilibrium wage, the quantity of labour supplied exceeds the quantity of labour demanded – there is a surplus of labour. So when a minimum wage is set above the equilibrium wage, there is a surplus of labour. The demand for labour determines the level of employment, and the surplus of labour is unemployed.

Figure 5.3 illustrates the effect of the minimum wage on unemployment. The demand for labour curve is *D*

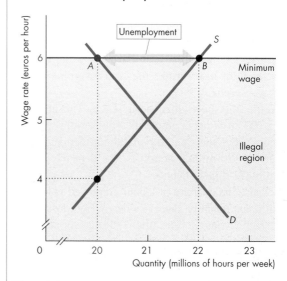

**Figure 5.3**    Minimum Wage and Unemployment

The minimum wage is set at €6 an hour. Any wage below €6 an hour is illegal (in the grey-shaded illegal region). At a minimum wage of €6 an hour, 20 million hours are hired but 22 million hours are available. Unemployment – *AB* – of 2 million hours a week is created. With only 20 million hours demanded, someone is willing to supply the 20 millionth hour for €4.

myeconlab Animation

and the supply of labour curve is *S*. The horizontal red line shows the minimum wage set at €6 an hour. A wage rate below this level is illegal, in the grey-shaded illegal region of the figure. At the minimum wage rate, 20 million hours of labour are demanded (point *A*) and 22 million hours of labour are supplied (point *B*), so 2 million hours of available labour are unemployed.

With only 20 million hours demanded, someone is willing to supply that 20 millionth hour for €4. Frustrated unemployed workers spend time and other resources searching for hard-to-find jobs.

## Inefficiency of a Minimum Wage

In the labour market, the supply curve measures the marginal social cost of labour to workers. This cost is leisure forgone. The demand curve measures the marginal social benefit from labour. This benefit is the value of the goods and services produced. An unregulated labour market allocates the economy's scarce labour resources to the jobs in which they are valued most highly. The market is efficient.

The minimum wage frustrates the market mechanism and results in unemployment and increased job search. At the quantity of labour employed, the marginal social benefit of labour exceeds its marginal social cost and a deadweight loss shrinks the firms' surplus and the workers' surplus.

Figure 5.4 shows this inefficiency. The minimum wage (€6 an hour) is above the equilibrium wage (€5 an hour) and the quantity of labour demanded and employed (20 million hours) is less than the efficient quantity (21 million hours).

Because the quantity of labour employed is less than the efficient quantity, there is a deadweight loss, shown by the grey triangle. The firms' surplus shrinks to the blue triangle and the workers' surplus shrinks to the green triangle. The red rectangle shows the potential loss from increased job search, which is borne by workers. The full loss from the minimum wage is the sum of the deadweight loss and the increased cost of job search.

## Is there a Case for the Minimum Wage?

Minimum wage policies are widespread in Europe. The highest rates are paid in Luxembourg and France and the lowest in Romania and Bulgaria. The UK national minimum wage rate for people over 21 years was raised to £5.93 an hour in October 2010, a 2.2 per cent rise. In contrast to the UK decision to increase the minimum wage, 18 EU countries have frozen or reduced the minimum wage in 2010.

Although the minimum wage is inefficient, not everyone loses from it. The people who find jobs at the minimum wage gain. Supporters of the minimum wage believe that the elasticities of demand and supply in the labour market are low, so not much unemployment results. The consensus is that a 10 per cent rise in the minimum wage decreases teenage employment by between 1 and 3 per cent.

**Figure 5.4** The Inefficiency of a Minimum Wage

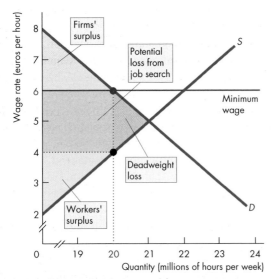

A minimum wage decreases employment. Firms' surplus (blue) and workers' surplus (green) shrink and a deadweight loss (grey area) arises. Job search increases and the red area shows the loss from this activity.

## Is the Minimum Wage Fair?

The minimum wage is unfair on both views of fairness. It delivers an unfair *result* and it imposes unfair *rules*.

The *result* is unfair because only those people who have jobs and keep them benefit from the minimum wage. The unemployed end up worse off than they would be with no minimum wage. Some of them who search for jobs and find them end up worse off because they incur an increased cost of job search. In addition those who find jobs are not always the least well off. When the wage rate doesn't allocate labour, other mechanisms determine who finds a job. One such mechanism is discrimination, another source of unfairness.

The minimum wage imposes an unfair *rule* because it blocks voluntary exchange. Firms looking for workers are willing to hire more labour and people who are looking for work or are willing to work more hours, but they are not permitted by the minimum wage law to do so.

This view is challenged by David Card of the University of California at Berkeley and Alan Krueger of Princeton University, who say that increases in the minimum wage can *increase* teenage employment and actually *decrease* unemployment. They argue that the employment rate of low-income workers *increases* following a wage increase. The higher wage rate makes workers more conscientious and productive and less likely to quit, which lowers unproductive labour turnover. They also argue that a higher wage rate makes managers seek ways to increase labour productivity.

Most economists are sceptical about Card and Krueger's argument. Why, economists ask, don't firms freely pay wage rates above the equilibrium wage to encourage more productive work habits? Also, they point to other explanations for the employment responses. One such explanation is that firms cut employment before the minimum wage is increased in *anticipation* of the increase.

Another effect of the minimum wage is an increase in the quantity of labour supplied. If this effect occurs, it might show up as an increase in the number of people who leave education early to look for work. Some economists say that this response does occur.

### Review Quiz

1  What is a minimum wage and what are its effects if it is set above the equilibrium wage?
2  What are the effects of a minimum wage set below the equilibrium wage?
3  Explain how scarce jobs are allocated when a minimum wage is in place.
4  Explain why a minimum wage creates an inefficient allocation of labour resources.
5  Explain why a minimum wage is unfair.

You can work these questions in Study Plan 5.2 and get instant feedback.    myeconlab

Next we're going to study a more widespread government action in markets: taxes. We'll see how taxes change the prices and quantities of the things taxed. You will discover the surprising fact that while the government can impose a tax, it cannot decide who will pay the tax! You will also see that a tax is inefficient and creates a deadweight loss.

## Taxes

Everything you earn and almost everything you buy is taxed. The income tax and a National Insurance contribution are deducted from your earnings. The prices of most of the things you buy include VAT, and the prices of a few goods such as cigarettes, alcoholic drinks and petrol include a heavy excise tax. Firms also pay some taxes, one of which is a National Insurance contribution for every person they employ.

Who *really* pays these taxes? Because the income tax and National Insurance contribution are deducted from your pay, isn't it obvious that *you* pay these taxes? And isn't it equally obvious that you pay the VAT, that smokers pay the tax on cigarettes and that your employer pays the employer's National Insurance contribution?

You're going to discover that it isn't obvious who *really* pays a tax and that lawmakers don't make that decision. We begin with a definition of tax incidence.

## Tax Incidence

**Tax incidence** is the division of the burden of a tax between buyers and sellers. When the government imposes a tax on the sale of a good,[1] the price paid by buyers might rise by the full amount of the tax, by a lesser amount, or not at all. If the price paid by buyers rises by the full amount of the tax, then the burden of the tax falls entirely on buyers – buyers pay the tax. If the price paid by buyers rises by a lesser amount than the tax, then the burden of the tax falls partly on buyers and partly on sellers. And if the price paid by buyers doesn't change at all, then the burden of the tax falls entirely on sellers.

Tax incidence does not depend on the tax law. The law might impose a tax on sellers or on buyers, but the outcome is the same in either case. To see why, let's look at the tax on cigarettes.

## A Tax on Sellers

During 2003, the government of France increased the tax on the sale of cigarettes three times. We'll assume the tax was €1.50 a pack. To work out the effects of this tax on the sellers of cigarettes, we begin by examining the effects on demand and supply in the market for cigarettes.

---

[1] These propositions also apply to services and factors of production (land, labour and capital).

In Figure 5.5, the demand curve is *D*, and the supply curve is *S*. With no tax, the equilibrium price is €3 per pack and 350 million packs a year are bought and sold.

A tax on sellers is like an increase in cost, so it decreases supply. To determine the position of the new supply curve, we add the tax to the minimum price that sellers are willing to accept for each quantity sold. You can see that without the tax, sellers are willing to offer 350 million packs a year for €3 a pack. So with a €1.50 tax, they will offer 350 million packs a year only if the price is €4.50 a pack. The supply curve shifts to the red curve labelled *S + tax on sellers*.

Equilibrium occurs where the new supply curve intersects the demand curve at 325 million packs a year. The price paid by buyers rises by €1 to €4 a pack. The price received by sellers falls by 50 cents to €2.50 a pack. So buyers pay €1 of the tax and sellers pay the other 50 cents.

## A Tax on Buyers

Suppose that instead of taxing sellers, the French government taxes cigarette buyers €1.50 a pack.

A tax on buyers lowers the amount they are willing to pay sellers, so it decreases demand and shifts the demand curve leftward. To determine the position of this new demand curve, we subtract the tax from the maximum price that buyers are willing to pay for each quantity bought.

You can see in Figure 5.6 that with no tax, buyers are willing to buy 350 million packs a year for €3 a pack. So with a €1.50 tax, they will buy 350 packs a year only if the price including the tax is €3 a pack, which means that they're willing to pay sellers only €1.50 a pack. The demand curve shifts to become the red curve labelled *D − tax on buyers*.

Equilibrium occurs where the new demand curve intersects the supply curve at a quantity of 325 million packs a year. The price received by sellers is €2.50 a pack, and the price paid by buyers is €4.

## Equivalence of Tax on Buyers and Sellers

You can see that the tax on buyers in Figure 5.6 has the same effects as the tax on sellers in Figure 5.5. The quantity decreases to 325 million packs a year, the price paid by buyers rises to €4 a pack and the price received by sellers falls to €2.50 a pack. Buyers pay €1 of the €1.50 tax. Sellers pay the other 50 cents of the tax.

**Figure 5.5**   A Tax on Sellers

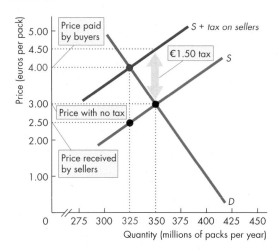

With no tax, 350 million packs a year are bought and sold at €3 a pack. A tax on sellers of €1.50 a pack decreases the supply of cigarettes and shifts the supply curve leftward to *S + tax on sellers*. The equilibrium quantity decreases to 325 million packs a year, the price paid by buyers rises to €4 a pack, and the price received by sellers falls to €2.50 a pack. The tax raises the price paid by buyers by less than the tax and lowers the price received by sellers, so buyers and sellers share the burden of the tax.

myeconlab Animation

## Can We Share the Burden Equally?

Suppose that the government wants the burden of the cigarette tax to fall equally on buyers and sellers and declares that a 75 cents tax be imposed on each. Is the burden of the tax then shared equally?

You can see that it is not. The tax is still €1.50 a pack. You've seen that the tax has the same effect regardless of whether it is imposed on sellers or buyers. So imposing half the tax on one and half on the other is like an average of the two cases you've examined. In this case, the demand curve shifts downward by 75 cents and the supply curve shifts upward by 75 cents. The equilibrium quantity is still 325 million packs. Buyers pay €4 a pack, of which €1 is tax. Sellers receive €2.50 a pack (€3 from buyers minus the 50 cents tax).

When a transaction is taxed, there are two prices: the price paid by buyers, which includes the tax; and the price received by sellers, which excludes the tax. Buyers respond only to the price that includes the tax because

## Figure 5.6    A Tax on Buyers

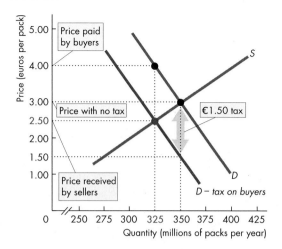

With no tax, 350 million packs a year are bought and sold at €3 a pack. A tax on buyers of €1.50 a pack decreases the demand for cigarettes and shifts the demand curve leftward to D – tax on buyers. The equilibrium quantity decreases to 325 million packs a year. The price paid by buyers rises to €4 a pack and the price received by sellers falls to €2.50 a pack. The tax raises the price paid by buyers by less than the tax and lowers the price received by sellers, so buyers and sellers share the burden of the tax.

myeconlab Animation

that is the price they pay. Sellers respond only to the price that excludes the tax because that is the price they receive.

A tax is like a wedge between the price buyers pay and the price sellers receive. The size of the wedge determines the effects of the tax, not the side of the market – demand side or supply side – on which the government imposes the tax.

## Payroll Taxes

Some governments impose payroll taxes and share the tax equally between both employers (buyers) and workers (sellers). But the principles you've just learned apply to this tax too. The market for labour, not the government, determines how the burden of the tax is divided between firms and workers.

In the cigarette tax example, buyers pay twice as much of the tax as sellers pay. In general, the division of the tax between buyers and sellers depends on the elasticities of demand and supply, as you will now see.

# Tax Incidence and Elasticity of Demand

The division of the tax between buyers and sellers depends partly on the elasticity of demand. There are two extreme cases:

◆ Perfectly inelastic demand – buyers pay
◆ Perfectly elastic demand – sellers pay

## Perfectly Inelastic Demand

Figure 5.7 shows the UK market for insulin. Demand is perfectly inelastic at 100,000 bottles a day, regardless of the price, as shown by the vertical curve D. That is, a diabetic would sacrifice all other goods and services rather than not consume the quantity of insulin that provides good health. The supply curve of insulin is S. With no tax, the price is £2 a bottle and the quantity is 100,000 bottles a day.

If insulin is taxed at 20 pence a bottle, we must add the tax to the minimum price at which drug companies are willing to sell insulin. The result is the new supply curve S + tax. The price rises to £2.20 a bottle, but the quantity does not change. Buyers pay the entire tax of 20 pence a bottle.

## Figure 5.7    Tax with Perfectly Inelastic Demand

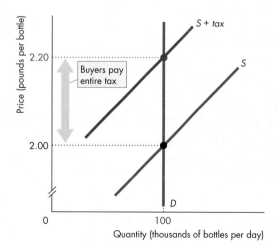

In the market for insulin, demand is perfectly inelastic. With no tax, the price is £2 a bottle and the quantity is 100,000 bottles a day. A tax of 20 pence a bottle decreases supply and shifts the supply curve to S + tax. The price rises to £2.20 a bottle, but the quantity bought does not change. Buyers pay the entire tax.

myeconlab Animation

## Perfectly Elastic Demand

Figure 5.8 shows the market for pink marker pens. Demand is perfectly elastic at £1 a pen, as shown by the horizontal curve *D*. If pink markers are less expensive than the other pens, everyone uses pink. If pink pens are more expensive than the others, no one uses pink. The supply curve is *S*. With no tax, the price of a pink marker pen is £1 and the quantity is 4,000 a week.

Suppose that the government imposes a tax of 20 pence on pink marker pens but not on other colours. The new supply curve is *S* + *tax*. The price remains at £1 a pen and the quantity decreases to 1,000 a week. The tax leaves the price paid by buyers unchanged but lowers the amount received by sellers by the full amount of the tax. Sellers pay the entire tax of 20 pence a pink pen.

We've seen that when demand is perfectly inelastic, buyers pay the entire tax and when demand is perfectly elastic, sellers pay the entire tax. In the usual case, demand is neither perfectly inelastic nor perfectly elastic and the tax is split between buyers and sellers. But the division depends on the elasticity of demand: the more inelastic the demand for a good, the larger is the amount of the tax paid by buyers.

### Figure 5.8   Tax with Perfectly Elastic Demand

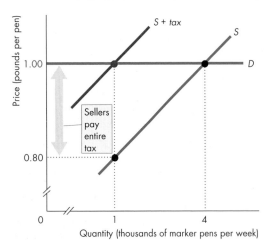

In this market for pink marker pens, demand is perfectly elastic. With no tax, the price of a pen is £1 and the quantity is 4,000 pens a week. A tax of 20 pence a pink pen decreases supply and shifts the supply curve to *S* + *tax*. The price remains at £1 a pen, and the quantity of pink pens sold decreases to 1,000 a week. Sellers pay the entire tax.

## Tax Incidence and Elasticity of Supply

The division of the tax between buyers and sellers depends, in part, on the elasticity of supply. There are two extreme cases:

◆ Perfectly inelastic supply – sellers pay
◆ Perfectly elastic supply – buyers pay

### Perfectly Inelastic Supply

Figure 5.9(a) shows the market for water from a spring which flows at a constant rate that can't be controlled. The quantity supplied is 100,000 bottles a week, as shown by the supply curve *S*. The demand curve for the water from this spring is *D*. With no tax, the price is 50 pence a bottle and the quantity is 100,000 bottles.

Suppose this spring water is taxed at 5 pence a bottle. The supply curve does not change because the spring owners still produce 100,000 bottles a week even though the price has fallen. But buyers are willing to buy the 100,000 bottles only if the price is 50 pence a bottle. So the price remains at 50 pence a bottle. The tax reduces the price received by sellers to 45 pence a bottle and sellers pay the entire tax.

### Perfectly Elastic Supply

Figure 5.9(b) illustrates the market for sand from which computer-chip makers extract silicon. The supply of sand is perfectly elastic at 10 pence a kilogram. The supply curve is *S*. The demand curve is *D*. With no tax, the price is 10 pence a kilogram and 5,000 kilograms a week are bought.

If sand is taxed at 1 penny a kilogram, we add the tax to the minimum supply-price. Sellers are now willing to offer any quantity at 11 pence a kilogram along the curve *S* + *tax*. The price rises to 11 pence a kilogram and 3,000 kilograms a week are bought. The price paid by buyers increases by the full amount of the tax. Buyers pay the entire tax.

We've seen that when supply is perfectly inelastic, sellers pay the entire tax and when supply is perfectly elastic, buyers pay the entire tax. In the usual case, supply is neither perfectly inelastic nor perfectly elastic and the tax is split between sellers and buyers. But how the tax is split depends on the elasticity of supply. The more elastic the supply, the larger is the amount of the tax paid by buyers.

## Figure 5.9 Tax and the Elasticity of Supply

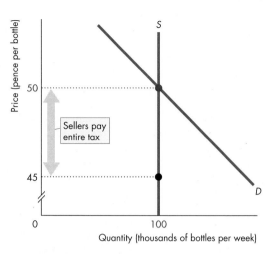

**(a) Inelastic supply**

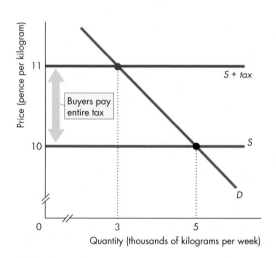

**(b) Elastic supply**

Part (a) shows the market for water from a mineral spring. Supply is perfectly inelastic. With no tax, the price is 50 pence a bottle. With a tax of 5 pence a bottle, the price remains at 50 pence a bottle. The number of bottles bought remains the same, but the price received by sellers decreases to 45 pence a bottle. Sellers pay the entire tax.

Part (b) shows the market for sand. Supply is perfectly elastic. With no tax, the price of sand is 10 pence a kilogram. A tax of 1 penny a kilogram increases the minimum supply-price to 11 pence a kilogram. The supply curve shifts to *S + tax*. The price increases to 11 pence a kilogram. Buyers pay the entire tax.

# Taxes and Efficiency

A tax drives a wedge between the price buyers pay and the price sellers receive and results in inefficient under-production. The price buyers pay is also the buyers' willingness to pay or *marginal social benefit*. The price sellers receive is also the sellers' minimum supply price, which equals *marginal social cost*.

Figure 5.10 shows the inefficiency of a tax on CD players. The demand curve, *D*, shows marginal social benefit, and the supply curve, *S*, shows marginal social cost. With no tax on CD players, the market produces the efficient quantity (5,000 CD players a week).

With a tax, the sellers' minimum supply-price rises by the amount of the tax and the supply curve shifts to *S + tax*. This supply curve does not show marginal social cost. The tax component isn't a social cost of production. It is a transfer of resources to the government.

At the new equilibrium quantity (4,000 CDs a week), both consumer surplus and producer surplus shrink. Part

## Figure 5.10 Taxes and Efficiency

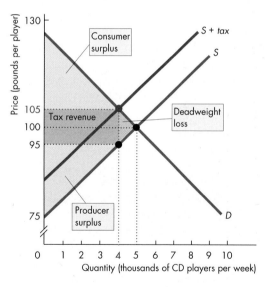

With no tax on CD players, 5,000 CD players are produced. With a tax of £10 a CD player, the buyers' price rises to £105 a player, the sellers' price falls to £95 a player, and the quantity decreases to 4,000 CD players a week. Consumer surplus shrinks to the green area and the producer surplus shrinks to the blue area. Part of the loss of consumer surplus and producer surplus goes to the government as tax revenue (the purple area) and part becomes a deadweight loss (the grey area).

of each surplus goes to the government in tax revenue – the purple area; part becomes a deadweight loss – the grey area.

Only in the extreme cases of perfectly inelastic demand and perfectly inelastic supply does a tax not change the quantity bought and sold so that no deadweight loss arises.

## Taxes and Fairness

We've examined the incidence and the efficiency of taxes, but when political leaders debate tax issues, it is fairness, not incidence and efficiency, that gets the most attention. Some politicians complain that tax cuts are unfair because they give the benefits of lower taxes to the rich. Others say it is fair that the rich get most of the tax cuts because they pay most of the taxes. No easy answers are available to questions about the fairness of taxes.

Economists have proposed two conflicting principles of fairness to apply to a tax system:

◆ The benefits principle
◆ The ability-to-pay principle

### The Benefits Principle

The *benefits principle* is the proposition that people should pay taxes equal to the benefits they receive from the services provided by government. This arrangement is fair because it means that those who benefit most pay most taxes. It makes tax payments and the consumption of government-provided services similar to private consumption expenditures.

The benefits principle can justify high petrol taxes to pay for motorways, high taxes on alcoholic beverages and tobacco products to pay for public healthcare services, and high income tax rates on high incomes to pay for the benefits from law and order and living in a secure environment, from which the rich might benefit more than the poor.

### The Ability-to-Pay Principle

The *ability-to-pay principle* is the proposition that people should pay taxes according to how easily they can bear the burden of the tax. A rich person can more easily bear the burden than a poor person can, so the ability-to-pay principle can reinforce the benefits principle to justify high rates of income tax on high incomes.

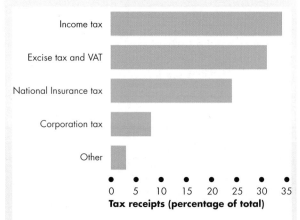

### ECONOMICS IN ACTION

## Workers and Consumers Pay Most Tax

A low elasticity of supply of labour and a high elasticity of demand for labour means that workers pay most of the income taxes and most of the National Insurance taxes. Because the elasticities of demand for alcohol, tobacco and petrol are low and the elasticities of supply are high, the burden of these (excise) taxes falls more on buyers than on sellers.

**Figure 1 UK Taxes**

Source of data: HM Revenue and Customs Annual Tax Receipts Table 1.2.

### Review Quiz

1 How does the elasticity of demand influence the incidence of a tax, the tax revenue and the deadweight loss?
2 How does the elasticity of supply influence the incidence of a tax, the tax revenue and the deadweight loss?
3 Why is a tax inefficient?
4 When would a tax be efficient?
5 What are the two principles of fairness that are applied to a tax system?

You can work these questions in Study Plan 5.3 and get instant feedback.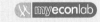

Next, we look at agricultural markets and see how governments intervene in these markets to try to stabilize and boost farm revenues.

# Production Quotas and Subsidies and Price Supports

Fluctuations in the weather bring fluctuations in farm output and prices and sometimes leave farmers with low incomes. To help farmers avoid low prices and low incomes, governments intervene in the markets for farm products. The three main methods of intervention in the markets for farm products are:

◆ Production quotas

◆ Production subsidies

◆ Price supports

## Production Quotas

The markets for sugar beet, milk and cotton (among others) have, from time to time, been regulated with production quotas. A **production quota** is an upper limit to the quantity of a good that may be produced in a specified period. To discover the effects of a production quota, we'll look at the market for sugar beet.

Suppose that the sugar beet growers want to limit total production to get a higher price. They persuade the government to introduce a production quota on sugar beet.

The effect of a production quota depends on whether it is set below or above the equilibrium quantity. If the government introduced a production quota above the equilibrium quantity, nothing would change because sugar beet growers are already producing less than the quota. But a production quota *below the equilibrium quantity* has big effects, which are:

◆ A decrease in supply

◆ A rise in the price

◆ A decrease in marginal cost

◆ Inefficient underproduction

◆ An incentive to cheat and overproduce

Figure 5.11 illustrates these effects.

### A Decrease in Supply

A production quota on sugar beet decreases the supply of sugar beet. Each grower is assigned a production limit that is less than the amount that would be produced – and supplied – without the quota. The total of the growers' limits equals the quota, and any production in excess of the quota is illegal.

The quantity supplied becomes the amount permitted by the production quota, and this quantity is fixed. The

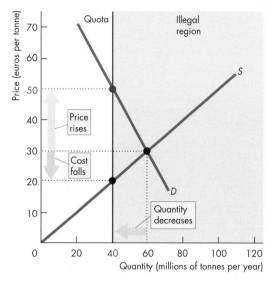

**Figure 5.11**   The Effects of a Production Quota

With no quota, 60 million tonnes a year are produced at €30 a tonne. A quota of 40 million tonnes a year restricts total production to that amount. The equilibrium quantity decreases to 40 million tonnes a year, the price rises to €50 a tonne, and the farmers' marginal cost falls to €20 a tonne. In the new equilibrium, marginal social cost (on the supply curve) is less than marginal social benefit (on the demand curve) and a deadweight loss arises from underproduction.

myeconlab Animation

supply of sugar beet becomes perfectly inelastic at the quantity permitted under the quota.

In Figure 5.11, with no quota, growers would produce 60 million tonnes of sugar beet a year – the market equilibrium quantity. With a production quota set at 40 million tonnes a year, the grey shaded area shows the illegal region. As in the case of price ceilings and price floors, market forces and political forces are in conflict in this illegal region. The vertical red line labelled 'Quota' becomes the supply curve of sugar beet at prices above €20 a tonne.

### A Rise in Price

The production quota raises the price of sugar beet. When the government sets a production quota, it leaves market forces free to determine the price. Because the quota decreases the supply of sugar beet, it raises the price. In Figure 5.11, with no quota, the price is €30 a tonne. With a quota of 40 million tonnes, the price rises to €50 a tonne.

### A Decrease in Marginal Cost

The production quota lowers the marginal cost of growing sugar beet. Marginal cost decreases because growers produce less and stop using the resources with the highest marginal cost. Sugar beet growers slide down their supply (and marginal cost) curves. In Figure 5.11, marginal cost decreases to €20 a tonne.

### Inefficiency

The production quota results in inefficient underproduction. Marginal social benefit at the quantity produced is equal to the market price, which has increased. Marginal social cost at the quantity produced has decreased and is less than the market price. So marginal social benefit exceeds marginal social cost and a deadweight loss arises.

### An Incentive to Cheat and Overproduce

The production quota creates an incentive for growers to cheat and produce more than their individual production limit. With the quota, the price exceeds marginal cost, so the grower can get a larger profit by producing one more unit. But if all growers produce more than their assigned limit, the production quota becomes ineffective, and the price falls to the equilibrium (no quota) price.

To make the production quota effective, growers must set up a monitoring system to ensure that no one cheats and overproduces. But it is costly to set up and operate a monitoring system and it is difficult to detect and punish producers who violate their quotas. Because of the difficulty of operating a quota, producers often lobby governments to establish a quota and provide the monitoring and punishment systems that make it work.

## Production Subsidies

A **production subsidy** is a payment made by the government to a producer for each unit produced. The effects of a production subsidy are opposite to the effects of a tax and they are:

◆  An increase in supply

◆  A fall in the price and an increase in quantity

◆  An increase in marginal cost

◆  Payments by government to farmers

◆  Inefficient *over*production

### An Increase in Supply

In Figure 5.12, with no subsidy, the demand curve *D* and the supply curve *S* determine the price of sugar beet at €40 a tonne and the quantity of sugar beet at 40 million tonnes a year.

Suppose that the government introduces a subsidy of €20 a tonne to sugar beet farmers. A subsidy is like a negative tax or a decrease in cost, so the subsidy brings an increase in supply.

To determine the position of the new supply curve, we subtract the subsidy from the farmers' minimum supply-price. In Figure 5.12, with no subsidy, farmers are willing to offer 40 million tonnes a year at a price of €40 a tonne. With a production subsidy of €20 a tonne, farmers will offer 40 million tonnes a year if the price is as low as €20 a tonne. The supply curve shifts to the red curve labelled *S – subsidy*.

**Figure 5.12**  The Effects of a Production Subsidy

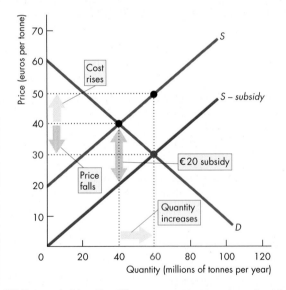

With no subsidy, 40 million tonnes a year are produced at €40 a tonne. A production subsidy of €20 a tonne shifts the supply curve rightward to *S – subsidy*. The equilibrium quantity increases to 60 million tonnes a year, the price falls to €30 a tonne, and the price plus subsidy received by farmers rises to €50 a tonne. In the new equilibrium, marginal social cost (on the blue supply curve) exceeds marginal social benefit (on the demand curve) and a deadweight loss arises from overproduction.

## A Fall in Price and an Increase in Quantity

The subsidy lowers the price of sugar beet and increases the quantity produced. In Figure 5.12, equilibrium occurs where the new supply curve intersects the demand curve at a price of €30 a tonne and a quantity of 60 million tonnes a year.

## An Increase in Marginal Cost

The subsidy lowers the price paid by consumers but increases the marginal cost of producing sugar beet. Marginal cost increases because farmers grow more sugar beet, which means that they must begin to use some resources that are less ideal for growing sugar beet. Farmers slide up their supply (and marginal cost) curves. In Figure 5.12, marginal cost increases to €50 a tonne.

## Payments by Government to Farmers

The government pays a subsidy to sugar beet farmers on each tonne produced. In this example, farmers increase production to 60 million tonnes a year and receive a subsidy of €20 a tonne. So sugar beet farmers receive a subsidy payment from the government that totals €1,200 million a year.

## Inefficient Overproduction

The production subsidy results in inefficient overproduction. At the quantity produced with the subsidy, marginal social benefit is equal to the market price, which has fallen. Marginal social cost has increased and it exceeds the market price. Because marginal social cost exceeds marginal social benefit, the increased production brings inefficiency.

Subsidies spill over to the rest of the world. Because a subsidy lowers the domestic market price, subsidized farmers will offer some of their output for sale on the world market. The increase in supply on the world market lowers the price in the rest of the world. Faced with lower prices, farmers in other countries decrease production and receive smaller revenues.

# Price Supports

A **price support** is a government guaranteed minimum price for a good. The EU Common Agricultural Policy (CAP) is the world's most extensive farm support programme. Every year, the EU sets the target price *above*

*the equilibrium price* for many agricultural products. A price support in an agricultural market operates in a similar way to a price floor in a labour market, but there is a crucial difference between them. The main effects of a price support are:

◆ A rise in the price
◆ An increase in marginal cost
◆ Payments by government to farmers
◆ Inefficient overproduction

Figure 5.13 illustrates the effects of a price support in the market for wheat.

## A Rise in the Price

Without price support, the competitive equilibrium price of wheat is €130 a tonne and 4 million tonnes are produced. If the EU sets a target price of €135 a tonne, the market price increases to €135 a tonne and the quantity demanded decreases to 2 million tonnes.

**Figure 5.13**   The Effects of a Price Support

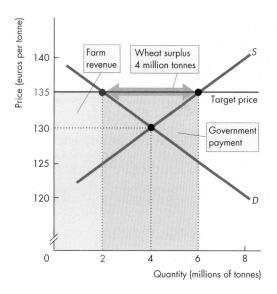

With no price support, 4 million tonnes are produced at €130 a tonne. A price support of €135 a tonne raises the price to €135 a tonne, increases the quantity produced to 6 million tonnes, decreases the quantity sold to 2 million tonnes, and creates a surplus of 4 million tonnes. To maintain the price support, the government buys the surplus for €540 million a year. If the government does not buy the surplus, the price will return to €130 a tonne.

myeconlab Animation

## An Increase in Marginal Cost

A higher price encourages farmers to increase the quantity supplied to 6 million tonnes. But as they grow more wheat, they use more resources that are less suited to growing wheat. The marginal cost of production increases.

## Payments by Government to Farmers

At the guaranteed price, there is a surplus of 4 million tonnes which the EU must buy to avoid the price falling below the target price. In Figure 5.13, this payment to farmers is €540 million a year.

## Inefficient Overproduction

The EU price support system is inefficient because marginal social cost exceeds marginal social benefit. The overproduction or surpluses must be bought and stored at high cost to maintain the target price.

In 2009, the EU spent €55 billion under the CAP to buy and store surplus agricultural produce and more than €120 billion in support payments to farmers.

### Review Quiz

1  Summarize the effects of a production quota on the market price and quantity produced.
2  Explain why a production quota is inefficient.
3  Summarize the effects of a production subsidy on the market price and the quantity produced.
4  Explain why a production subsidy is inefficient.
5  Summarize the effects of a price support on the market price and quantity produced.
6  Explain why a price support is inefficient.

You can work these questions in Study Plan 5.4 and get instant feedback.    **myeconlab**

You've now seen the effects of a wide range of government interventions in markets and how these interventions bring inefficiency.

We're now going to examine markets that the government would like to close down – markets for illegal goods and services. Some examples of illegal goods are drugs, such as cannabis, Ecstasy, cocaine and heroin. Despite the fact that these drugs are illegal, trade in them is a multi-billion pound business. This trade can be understood by using the same economic model and principles that explain trade in legal goods. Let's see how.

## Markets for Illegal Goods

Figure 5.14 shows a market for a drug. With demand curve, $D$, and supply curve, $S$, if drugs are not illegal, the quantity bought and sold is $Q_C$ and the price is $P_C$.

When a good is illegal, the cost of trading in it increases. By how much the cost increases and on whom the cost falls depend on the penalties for breaking the law and the effectiveness with which the law is enforced. The larger the penalties and the more effective the policing, the higher are the costs of trading the drug. Penalties might be imposed on sellers or buyers or both sellers and buyers.

If selling drugs is illegal, sellers will face fines and prison sentences if their activities are detected. Penalties for selling illegal drugs are part of the cost of supplying those drugs. These penalties lead to a decrease in supply and shift the supply curve of the drug leftward. To determine the new supply curve, we add the cost of breaking the law to the minimum price that drug dealers are willing to accept. In Figure 5.14, the cost of breaking the law by selling drugs ($CBL$) is added to the minimum price that dealers will accept and the supply curve shifts leftward to $S + CBL$. If penalties are imposed only on sellers, the market moves from point $E$ to point $F$. The price rises and the quantity bought decreases.

If buying drugs is illegal, buyers face fines and prison sentences if their activities are detected. Penalties for buying the illegal drugs fall on buyers and the cost of breaking the law must be subtracted from the value of the good to determine the maximum price that buyers are willing to pay. Demand decreases and the demand curve shifts leftward. In Figure 5.14, the demand curve shifts to $D - CBL$. If penalties are imposed only on buyers, the market moves from point $E$ to point $G$. The market price falls and the quantity bought decreases.

If penalties are imposed on sellers *and* buyers, both supply and demand decrease. In Figure 5.14, the costs of breaking the law are the same for both buyers and sellers, so the demand and supply curves shift leftward by the same amounts. The market moves to point $H$. The market price remains at the competitive market price, but the quantity bought decreases to $Q_P$. Buyers pay $P_C$ plus the cost of breaking the law, which is $P_B$. And sellers receive $P_C$ minus the cost of breaking the law, which is $P_S$.

The larger the penalty and the greater the degree of law enforcement, the larger is the decrease in demand and/or supply and the greater is the shift of the demand and/or supply curve. If the penalties are heavier on

## Figure 5.14    A Market for an Illegal Good

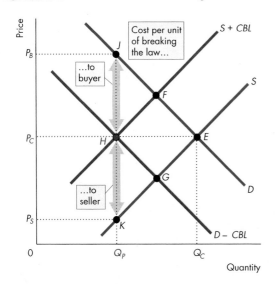

The demand curve for drugs is *D* and the supply curve is *S*. If drugs are not illegal, the quantity bought and sold is $Q_C$ at a price of $P_C$ at point *E*.

If selling drugs is illegal, the cost of breaking the law by selling drugs (*CBL*) is added to the minimum supply-price and supply decreases to *S* + *CBL*. The market moves to point *F*. If buying drugs is illegal, the cost of breaking the law is subtracted from the maximum price that buyers are willing to pay, and demand decreases to *D* – *CBL*. The market moves to point *G*.

With both buying and selling illegal, the supply curve and the demand curve shift and the market moves to point *H*. The market price remains at $P_C$, but the market price plus the penalty for buying rises to $P_B$ (point *J*) and the market price minus the penalty for sellers falls to $P_S$ (point *K*).

 myeconlab Animation

same way that legal drugs such as alcohol are taxed. How would such an arrangement work?

From your study of the effects of taxes, you can see that the quantity of drugs bought would decrease if they were taxed. A sufficiently high tax could be imposed to decrease supply, raise the price and achieve the same decrease in the quantity bought as with a prohibition on drugs. The government would collect tax revenue. Such a debate in the UK concerning cannabis led the government to reduce penalties on the illegal trade in 2003 but not to legalize the trade.

It is likely that a very high tax rate would be needed to cut the quantity of drugs bought to the level prevailing with a prohibition. It is also likely that many drug dealers and consumers would try to cover up their activities to evade the tax. If they did act in this way, they would face the cost of breaking the law – the tax law. If the penalty for tax law violation is as severe and as effectively policed as drug-dealing laws, the analysis we've already conducted applies also to this case. The quantity of drugs bought would depend on the penalties for law breaking and on the way in which the penalties are assigned to buyers and sellers.

Which is more effective: prohibition or taxes? In favour of taxes and against prohibition is the fact that the tax revenue can be used to make law enforcement more effective. It can also be used to run a more effective education campaign against illegal drug use. In favour of prohibition and against taxes is the fact that prohibition sends a signal that might influence preferences, decreasing the demand for illegal drugs. Also, some people intensely dislike the idea of the government profiting from trade in harmful substances.

sellers, the supply curve shifts further than the demand curve and the market price rises above $P_C$. If the penalties are heavier on buyers, the demand curve shifts further than the supply curve and the price falls below $P_C$. In many European countries, the penalties on sellers of illegal drugs are larger than those on buyers. As a result, the decrease in supply is much larger than the decrease in demand. The quantity of drugs traded decreases and the price is higher than in a free market.

With high enough penalties and effective law enforcement, it is possible to reduce the quantity bought to zero. But in reality, such an outcome is unusual as law enforcement is too costly.

Because of this situation, some people suggest that drugs and other illegal goods should be legalized and sold openly but should also be taxed at a high rate in the

### Review Quiz

1   How does a penalty on sellers of an illegal good influence demand, supply, price and the quantity consumed?
2   How does a penalty on buyers of an illegal good influence demand, supply, price and the quantity consumed?
3   How does a penalty on both sellers and buyers of an illegal good influence demand, supply, price and the quantity consumed?
4   What is the case for legalizing drugs?

You can work these questions in Study Plan 5.5 and get instant feedback.    myeconlab

*Reading Between the Lines* on pp. 122–123 looks at why farm subsidies increased in 2009.

# Reading Between the Lines

# Increase in Farm Subsidies

The OECD, 1 July 2010

## Government Support to Farmers Rises Slightly in OECD Countries

The share of farm receipts provided by government programmes rose slightly in OECD countries last year, reversing a declining trend in state support since 2004, according to a new OECD report. . . .

The latest rise in support across the OECD countries was due to the easing back of agricultural commodity prices after they hit record highs in 2008. The falls triggered government programmes aimed at propping up domestic prices or farm income.

The sharpest rises in support to farmers . . . last year occurred in Canada, . . . Korea, . . . Norway, . . . and Switzerland. . . . In each of these countries the main cause was increased price support for dairy products. In the US, support to farmers rose to 10% of total farm receipts from 8% last year while in the EU the rise was to 24% from 22%. . . .

The report . . . says . . . policy makers should reduce subsidies which distort markets and cut the link between government payments and agricultural production.

Compensating farmers for low prices or insulating consumers from price fluctuations through export controls merely contributes to higher volatility in world prices, the report says.

Ken Ash, the OECD's Director of Trade and Agriculture, said: 'More focus should be placed on improving risk management while better functioning and more transparent global markets could reduce price volatility'.

## The Essence of the Story

◆ Governments around the world make income support payments to farmers.

◆ As food prices increased between 2004 and 2008, the percentage of farm incomes from subsidies decreased.

◆ In 2009, a fall in food prices triggered an increase in subsidies as a percentage of farm income.

◆ In the EU, the increase was from 22 per cent of income to 24 per cent of income.

# Economic Analysis

◆ The news article reports an increase in government payments to farmers triggered by lower prices for farm products.

◆ In this chapter, you've seen two ways in which governments support farmers: *production subsidies* and *price supports*.

◆ Figure 1 shows the effect of a production subsidy on wheat. Demand curve is *D*, supply curve is *S* and with no subsidy, the price would be €150 per tonne and the quantity produced would be 15 million tonnes.

◆ With a production subsidy of €20 per tonne, the supply curve is *S − subsidy*. The market price is €140 and the quantity demanded is 20 million tonnes. Farmers receive €2,800 million in the market and €400 million, which is 12.5 per cent of their total revenue, from the government.

◆ If the demand for wheat decreases, the market price falls, the quantity sold decreases, total revenue falls and the total subsidy payment falls. But the subsidy payment *increases as a percentage of total revenue*.

◆ Figure 2 shows the effect of the EU-style price support for wheat. As before, with no intervention the price is €150 a tonne and 15 million tonnes are produced.

◆ With a target price €160, 20 million tonnes are produced but only 10 million tonnes are purchased by consumers for which farmers receive €1,600 million. There is a surplus of 10 million tonnes a year.

◆ To maintain the target price the EU must buy the 10 million tonnes surplus at the target price of €160 a tonne. The government's total payment to farmers is €1,600 million or 50 per cent of their total receipts.

◆ If the target price remains the same and the demand for wheat decreases, the quantity sold decreases, surplus production and the government payment increase and the total government payment to farmers increases.

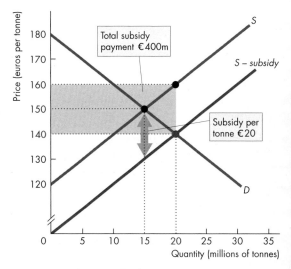

**Figure 1  Production subsidy**

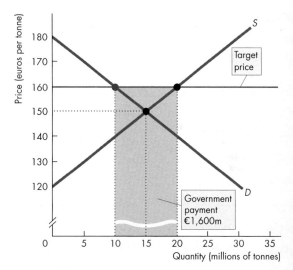

**Figure 2  EU price support payments**

◆ Both systems are inefficient and result in overproduction.

◆ The scale of government support for farmers in the EU is much higher than in most other large countries. (The news article reports the EU at 24 per cent compared to the US at 10 per cent.)

◆ EU farm support is among the most inefficient in the world.

# SUMMARY

## Key Points

### A Housing Market with a Rent Ceiling (pp. 106–108)

◆ A rent ceiling set above the equilibrium rent has no effect.

◆ If a rent ceiling is set below the equilibrium rent it creates a housing shortage, increases search activity and creates a black market.

◆ A rent ceiling that is set below the equilibrium rent is inefficient and unfair.

Working Problems 1 to 6 will give you a better understanding of a housing market with a rent ceiling.

### A Labour Market with a Minimum Wage (pp. 109–111)

◆ A price floor set below the equilibrium price has no effect.

◆ The minimum wage is an example of a price floor.

◆ A minimum wage set above the equilibrium wage rate creates unemployment and increases search activity.

◆ A price floor is inefficient and unfair.

Working Problems 7 to 12 will give you a better understanding of a labour market with a minimum wage.

### Taxes (pp. 111–116)

◆ A tax raises price but usually by less than the tax.

◆ The shares of tax paid by buyers and sellers depend on the elasticity of demand and the elasticity of supply.

◆ The less elastic the demand and more elastic the supply, the greater is the price increase, the smaller is the quantity decrease, and the larger is the portion of the tax paid by buyers.

◆ If demand is perfectly elastic or supply is perfectly inelastic, sellers pay the entire tax. And if demand is perfectly inelastic or supply is perfectly elastic, buyers pay the entire tax.

Working Problems 13 to 15 will give you a better understanding of taxes.

### Production Quotas and Subsidies and Price Supports (pp. 117–120)

◆ A production quota leads to inefficient underproduction, which raises price.

◆ A production subsidy is like a negative tax. It lowers the price and leads to inefficient overproduction.

◆ A price support leads to inefficient overproduction.

◆ The Common Agricultural Policy uses costly price supports.

Working Problems 16 to 18 will give you a better understanding of production quotas, subsidies and price supports.

### Markets for Illegal Goods (pp. 120–121)

◆ Penalties on sellers of an illegal good increase the cost of selling the good and decrease its supply. Penalties on buyers decrease their willingness to pay and decrease demand for the good.

◆ The higher the penalties and the more effective the law enforcement, the smaller is the quantity bought.

◆ A tax that is set at a sufficiently high rate will decrease the quantity of a drug consumed, but there will be a tendency for the tax to be evaded.

Working Problem 19 will give you a better understanding of markets for illegal goods.

## Key Terms

Black market, 106
Minimum wage, 109
Price cap, 106
Price ceiling, 106
Price floor, 109
Price support, 119
Production quota, 117
Production subsidy, 118
Rent ceiling, 106
Search activity, 106
Tax incidence, 111

## STUDY PLAN PROBLEMS AND APPLICATIONS

**myeconlab** You can work Problems 1 to 19 in MyEconlab Study Plan Chapter 5 and get instant feedback.

## A Housing Market with a Rent Ceiling
(Study Plan 5.1)

Use the following graph of the market for rental housing in Townsville to work Problems 1 and 2.

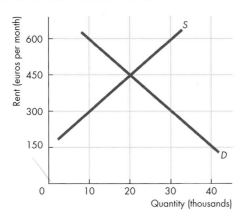

**1 a** What are the equilibrium rent and equilibrium quantity of rented housing?

**b** If a rent ceiling is set at €600 a month, what is the quantity of housing rented and what is the shortage of housing?

**2** If a rent ceiling is set at €300 a month, what is the quantity of housing rented, the shortage of housing and the maximum price that someone is willing to pay for the last unit available?

Use the following news clip to work Problems 3 to 6.

**Capping Petrol Prices**

As petrol prices rise, many people are calling for price caps, but price caps generate a distorted reflection of reality, which leads buyers and suppliers to act in ways inconsistent with the price cap. By masking reality, price caps only make matters worse.

Source: *Pittsburgh Tribune-Review*,
12 September 2005

Suppose that a price ceiling is set below the equilibrium price.

**3** How does the price cap influence the quantity of petrol supplied and the quantity demanded?

**4** How does the price cap influence:

**a** The quantity of petrol sold and the shortage or surplus of petrol?

**b** The maximum price that someone is willing to pay for the last litre of petrol available on a black market?

**5** Draw a graph to illustrate the effects of a price ceiling set below the equilibrium price in the market for petrol.

**6** Explain the various ways in which a price ceiling on petrol that is set below the equilibrium price would make buyers and sellers of petrol better off or worse off. What would happen to total surplus and deadweight loss in this market?

## A Labour Market with a Minimum Wage (Study Plan 5.2)

Use the following data to work Problems 7 to 9.

The table gives the demand and supply schedules of teenage labour.

| Wage rate (pounds per hour) | Quantity demanded | Quantity supplied |
|---|---|---|
| | (hours per month) | |
| 4 | 3,000 | 1,000 |
| 5 | 2,500 | 1,500 |
| 6 | 2,000 | 2,000 |
| 7 | 1,500 | 2,500 |
| 8 | 1,000 | 3,000 |

**7** Calculate the equilibrium wage rate, the number of hours worked and the quantity of unemployment.

**8** If a minimum wage for teenagers is £5 an hour, how many hours do they work and how many hours of teenage labour are unemployed?

**9** If a minimum wage for teenagers is £7 an hour,

**a** How many hours do teenagers work and how many hours are unemployed?

**b** Demand for teenage labour increases by 500 hours a month. What is the wage rate paid to teenagers and how many hours of teenage labour are unemployed?

Use the following news clip to work Problems 10 to 12.

**India Steps Up Pressure for Minimum Wage for Its Workers in the Gulf.**

Oil-rich countries in the Persian Gulf, already confronted by strong labour protests, are facing renewed pressure from India to pay minimum wages for unskilled workers. With five million immigrant workers in the region, India is trying to win better conditions for their citizens.

Source: *International Herald Tribune*,
27 March 2008

Suppose that the Gulf countries paid a minimum wage above the equilibrium wage to Indian workers.

**10** How would the market for labour be affected in the Gulf countries? Draw a supply and demand graph to illustrate your answer.

**11** How would the market for labour be affected in India? Draw a supply and demand graph to illustrate your answer. [Be careful: the minimum wage is in the Gulf countries, not in India.]

**12** Would migrant Indian workers be better off or worse off or unaffected by this minimum wage?

## Taxes (Study Plan 5.3)

**13** The table shows the demand and supply schedules for chocolate brownies in the UK.

| Price (pence per brownie) | Quantity demanded | Quantity supplied |
|---|---|---|
| | (millions per day) | |
| 50 | 5 | 3 |
| 60 | 4 | 4 |
| 70 | 3 | 5 |
| 80 | 2 | 6 |
| 90 | 1 | 7 |

**a** If brownies are not taxed, what is the price of a brownie and how many are consumed?

**b** If sellers are taxed at 20 pence a brownie, what is the price and how many brownies are sold? Who pays the tax?

**c** If buyers are taxed at 20 pence a brownie, what is the price and how many brownies are bought? Who pays the tax?

**14** Imagine the UK government introduces a new tax on luxury items. The government anticipates that the tax will generate £30 million in revenue, but it generated only £16 million in revenue.

**a** Explain whether buyers or sellers of luxury items would pay more of the luxury tax.

**b** Explain why the luxury tax generated less tax revenue than was originally anticipated.

**15** Suppose the tax on petrol is reduced by 18 pence a litre during August. Despite the cut in tax, high petrol prices are predicted to keep UK residents at home this summer.

Would the price of petrol that UK consumers pay fall by 18 pence a litre? How would consumer surplus change? Explain your answers.

## Production Quotas and Subsidies and Price Supports (Study Plan 5.4)

Use the following data to work Problems 16 to 18.

The demand and supply schedules for rice are:

| Price (pounds per box) | Quantity demanded | Quantity supplied |
|---|---|---|
| | (boxes per week) | |
| 1.00 | 3,500 | 500 |
| 1.10 | 3,250 | 1,000 |
| 1.20 | 3,000 | 1,500 |
| 1.30 | 2,750 | 2,000 |
| 1.40 | 2,500 | 2,500 |
| 1.50 | 2,250 | 3,000 |
| 1.60 | 2,000 | 3,500 |

**16** Calculate the price, the marginal cost of producing rice, and the quantity produced if the government sets a production quota of 2,000 boxes a week.

**17** Calculate the price, the marginal cost of producing rice, and the quantity produced if the government introduces a production subsidy of £0.30 a box.

**18** Calculate the price, the marginal cost of producing rice, the quantity produced and the surplus created if the government introduces a price support of £1.50 a box.

## Markets for Illegal Goods (Study Plan 5.5)

**19** The figure shows the market for a banned substance.

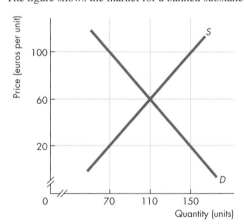

What are the equilibrium price and quantity if a penalty of €20 a unit is imposed on:

**a** Sellers only?

**b** Buyers only?

**c** Both sellers and buyers?

# A Housing Market with a Rent Ceiling

Use the news clip to work Problems 20 and 21.

**Why Rent Control Won't Go Away**

Once in place, rent control usually proves extremely difficult to undo. London and Paris still have rent controls adopted as temporary measures during the First World War. 'Nelson's Third Law' – the contention by the late economist Arthur Nelson that the worse a government regulation is, the more difficult it is to get rid of – seems to apply here.

Source: William Tucker, Heartland Institute, 1 September 1997

**20  a**  Who are the people who gain from rent controls?

  **b**  Why are rent controls inefficient?

**21  a**  Are the rent controls in London that remain from the First World War fair?

  **b**  Explain 'Nelson's Third Law'. Why does it seem to apply to the rental market in London?

# A Labour Market with a Minimum Wage

Use the news clip to work Problems 22 and 23.

**Labour's Manifesto**

The proposal for a 'living wage' of £7.60 an hour for employees in some parts of the public sector also applies to low-skilled workers in the private sector.

Source: *The Financial Times*, 28 September 2010

**22**  On a graph of the market for low-skilled labour, show the effect of the introduction of a living wage on the quantity of labour employed.

**23**  Explain the effects of the high living wage on the workers' surplus and the firms' surplus. Will a living wage make the labour market more efficient or less efficient? Explain.

# Taxes

**24**  The demand and supply schedules for roses are:

| Price (pounds per bunch) | Quantity demanded | Quantity supplied |
|---|---|---|
| | (bunches per week) | |
| 10 | 100 | 40 |
| 12 | 90 | 60 |
| 14 | 80 | 80 |
| 16 | 70 | 100 |
| 18 | 60 | 120 |

**a**  If there is no tax on roses, what is the price and how many bunches of roses are bought?

**b**  If roses are taxed at £6 a bunch, what is the price and quantity bought? Who pays the tax?

Use the following news clip to work Problems 25 to 27.

**Cigarette Smuggling Ring Smashed**

Customs officers have cracked a multimillion-euro cigarette smuggling operation. About 28 million illegally-imported cigarettes – worth 11.8 million euros – were seized. The potential loss to the exchequer is 9.4 million euro.

Source: *Belfast Telegraph*, 23 February 2010

**25**  How has the market for cigarettes in the UK responded to the high tax on cigarettes?

**26**  What effect does the emergence of a black market have on the elasticity of demand in the legal market for cigarettes?

**27**  Why might an increase in the tax rate actually cause a decrease in the tax revenue?

# Production Quotas and Subsidies and Price Supports

Use the following figure to work Problems 28 to 30.

The figure shows the market for tomatoes. The government introduces a price support for tomatoes at €8 per pound.

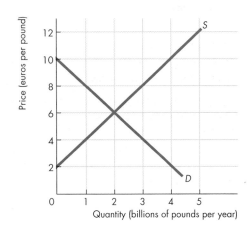

**28**  Before the price support is introduced, what are the equilibrium price and quantity of tomatoes? Is the market for tomatoes efficient?

**29**  After the government introduces a price support, what is the quantity of tomatoes produced, the quantity demanded, and the payment received by tomato farmers?

**30** With the price support, is the market for tomatoes efficient? Who gains and who loses from the price support and is it efficient? Could the price support be regarded as being fair?

**31 French Farmers Man the Blockades in Brussels**

Farmers want the dairy industry to guarantee a minimum milk price of €300 per tonne – against €210 per tonne this month. Max Bottier, a dairy farmer in Normandy, said that he needed €300 per tonne to break even.

Source: *The Times*, 26 May 2009

If a support price for milk is introduced and set at €300 per tonne, how will such a support price change the quantity of milk produced and the quantity bought by consumers? Who buys the excess supply? Will the European milk market be more or less efficient than it is today?

## Markets for Illegal Goods

**32** The table sets out the demand and supply schedules for an illegal drug.

| Price (euros per unit) | Quantity demanded (units per day) | Quantity supplied |
|---|---|---|
| 50 | 500 | 300 |
| 60 | 400 | 400 |
| 70 | 300 | 500 |
| 80 | 200 | 600 |
| 90 | 100 | 700 |

**a** If there are no penalties on buying or selling the drug, what is the price and how many units a day are consumed?

**b** If the penalty on sellers is €20 per unit, what is the price and quantity consumed?

**c** If the penalty on buyers is €20 per unit, what is the price and quantity consumed?

## Economics in the News

**33** After you have studied *Reading Between the Lines* on pp. 122–123 answer the following questions.

**a** Compare and contrast the effects of a production subsidy with a price support system like that of the EU.

**b** Draw a graph to illustrate the effects of an increase in demand with a production subsidy and show why the percentage of farm income received from the government decreases.

**c** Draw a graph to illustrate the effects of an increase in demand with a price support and show why farm income received from the government decreases unless the support price is increased.

**d** Explain why both farm income support schemes are inefficient and why the EU system is even more inefficient than a production subsidy.

Use the following news clip for Problems 34 to 36.

**Coal Shortage at China Plants**

Chinese power plants have run short of coal, an unintended effect of government-mandated price controls designed to shield the public from rising global energy costs. Beijing has also frozen retail prices of petrol and diesel. That helped farmers and the urban poor, but it has spurred sales of big luxury cars and propelled double-digit annual growth in petrol consumption. At the same time, oil refiners are suffering heavy losses and some have begun cutting production, causing fuel shortages.

Source: CNN, 20 May 2008

**34 a** Are China's price controls described in the news clip price floors or price ceilings?

**b** Explain how China's price controls have created shortages or surpluses in the markets for coal, petrol and diesel.

**c** Illustrate your answer to part (b) graphically by using the supply and demand model.

**35** Explain how China's price controls have changed consumer surplus, producer surplus, total surplus, and the deadweight loss in the markets for coal, petrol and diesel.

**36** Show on a graph the change in consumer surplus, producer surplus, total surplus, and the deadweight loss in the markets for coal, petrol and diesel.

**37** On 31 December 1776, Rhode Island established wage controls to limit wages to 70 cents a day for carpenters and 42 cents a day for tailors.

**a** Are these wage controls a price ceiling or a price floor? Why might they have been introduced?

**b** If these wage controls are effective, would you expect to see a surplus or a shortage of carpenters and tailors?

**38 Motorway Protest Over Rising Fuel Prices**

After fuel prices have soared to an all-time high, hundreds of bikers and motorists are expected to stage a go-slow protest along one of the North of England's main motorways. The AA said a two-car family had seen its monthly fuel costs rise from £233.32 to £254.60.

Source: *The Yorkshire Post*, 27 September 2010

Explain to protesting drivers why a price cap on the price of fuel would hurt families more than the high price of fuel.

# CHAPTER 6

# Output and Costs

### After studying this chapter you will be able to:

◆ Distinguish between the short run and the long run

◆ Explain the relationship between a firm's output and labour employed in the short run

◆ Explain the relationship between a firm's output and costs in the short run and derive a firm's short-run cost curves

◆ Explain the relationship between a firm's output and costs in the long run and derive a firm's long-run average cost curve

What do one of the largest European airlines and a small-scale woollen jumper maker have in common? Each firm must decide how much to produce, how many people to employ and how much capital to use. Is being bigger always better for a firm? Why do some firms, such as car makers, have plenty of slack and wish they could sell more whereas others operate flat out all the time? We will answer these questions by looking at the types of decisions firms make and their impact on costs.

In the *Business Case Study* at the end of the chapter, you can see how Europe's second largest airline, easyJet, makes decisions that affect the firm's costs, output and size.

## Time Frames for Decisions

People who operate firms make many decisions. All of these decisions are aimed at one overriding objective: maximum attainable profit. But the decisions are not all equally critical. Some of the decisions are big ones. Once made, they are costly (or impossible) to reverse. If such a decision turns out to be incorrect, it might lead to the failure of the firm. Some of the decisions are small ones. They are easily changed. If one of these decisions turns out to be incorrect, the firm can change its actions and survive.

The biggest decision that any firm makes is what industry to enter. For most entrepreneurs, their background knowledge and interests drive this decision. But the decision also depends on profit prospects. No one sets up a firm without believing it will be profitable. And profit depends on total revenue and total cost.

The firm that we'll study has already chosen the industry in which to operate. It has also chosen its most effective method of organization. But it has not decided the quantity to produce, the quantities of factors of production to hire or the price at which to sell its output.

Decisions about the quantity to produce and the price to charge depend on the type of market in which the firm operates. Perfect competition, monopolistic competition, oligopoly and monopoly all confront the firm with their own special problems. We study these types of markets in Chapters 7, 8 and 9.

But decisions about *how* to produce a given output do not depend on the type of market in which the firm operates. These decisions are similar for *all* types of firms in *all* types of markets.

The actions that a firm can take to influence the relationship between output and cost depend on how soon the firm wants to act. A firm that plans to change its output rate tomorrow has fewer options than one that plans to change its output rate six months from now.

To study the relationship between a firm's output decision and its costs, we distinguish between two decision time frames:

◆ The short run
◆ The long run

## The Short Run

The **short run** is a time frame in which the quantity of at least one factor of production is fixed. For most firms, capital, land and entrepreneurship are fixed factors of production and labour is the variable factor of production.

We call the fixed factors of production the firm's *plant*. So in the short run, a firm's plant is fixed. Fashion First's fixed plant is its factory building and its knitting machines. For an electric power utility, the fixed plant is its buildings, generators, computers and control systems.

To increase output in the short run, a firm must increase the quantity of a variable factor of production, which is usually labour. So to produce more output, Fashion First must hire more labour and operate its knitting machines for more hours per day. Similarly, an electric power utility must hire more labour and operate its generators for more hours per day.

Short-run decisions are easily reversed. The firm can increase or decrease output in the short run by increasing or decreasing the labour it hires.

## The Long Run

The **long run** is a time frame in which the quantities of *all* factors of production can be varied. That is, the long run is a period in which the firm can change its *plant*.

To increase output in the long run, a firm is able to choose whether to change its plant as well as whether to increase the quantity of labour it hires. Fashion First can decide whether to install some additional knitting machines, use a new type of machine, reorganize its management or hire more labour. An electric power utility can decide whether to install more generators. And an airport can decide whether to build more runways, terminals and traffic-control facilities.

Long-run decisions are *not* easily reversed. Once a plant decision is made, the firm must live with it for some time. To emphasize this fact, we call the *past* expenditure on a plant that has no resale value a **sunk cost**. A sunk cost is irrelevant to the firm's current decisions. The only costs that influence its current decisions are the short-run cost of changing the quantity of labour and the long-run cost of changing its plant.

### Review Quiz

1. Distinguish between the short run and the long run.
2. Why is a sunk cost irrelevant to a firm's current decisions?

You can work these questions in Study Plan 6.1 and get instant feedback.

We're going to study costs in the short run and the long run. We begin with the short run and describe the technology constraint the firm faces.

# Short-run Technology Constraint

To increase output in the short run, a firm must increase the quantity of labour employed. We describe the relationship between output and the quantity of labour employed by using three related concepts:

1  Total product
2  Marginal product
3  Average product

These product concepts can be illustrated either by product schedules or by product curves. We'll look first at the product schedules.

## Product Schedules

Table 6.1 shows some data that describe Fashion First's total product, marginal product and average product. The numbers tell us how Fashion First's production changes as more workers are employed, for a fixed level of plant and machines. They also tell us about the productivity of Fashion First's workforce.

Look first at the columns headed 'Labour' and 'Total product'. **Total product** is the maximum output that a given quantity of labour can produce. The table shows how total product increases as Fashion First employs more labour. For example, when Fashion First employs 1 worker, total product is 4 jumpers a day and when Fashion First employs 2 workers, total product is 10 jumpers a day. Each increase in employment brings an increase in total product.

The **marginal product** of labour is the increase in total product resulting from a one-unit increase in the quantity of labour employed with all other inputs remaining the same. For example, in Table 6.1, when Fashion First increases employment from 2 to 3 workers and does not change its capital, the marginal product of the third worker is 3 jumpers – total product increases from 10 to 13 jumpers.

The **average product** tells how productive workers are on the average. The average product of labour is equal to total product divided by the quantity of labour employed. For example, in Table 6.1, 3 workers can knit 13 jumpers a day, so the average product of labour is 13 divided by 3, which is 4.33 jumpers per worker.

If you look closely at the numbers in Table 6.1, you can see some patterns. For example, as Fashion First employs more workers, marginal product at first increases and then begins to decrease. For example, marginal product increases from 4 jumpers a day for the

first worker to 6 jumpers a day for the second worker and then decreases to 3 jumpers a day for the third worker. Also average product at first increases and then decreases. You can see the relationships between the number of workers employed and the three product concepts more clearly by looking at the product curves.

## Product Curves

The product curves are graphs of the relationships between employment and the three product concepts you've just studied. They show how total product, marginal product and average product change as employment changes. They also show the relationships among the three concepts. Let's look at the three product curves.

---

**Table 6.1**

**Total Product, Marginal Product and Average Product**

| | Labour (workers per day) | Total product (jumpers per day) | Marginal product (jumpers per worker) | Average product (jumpers per worker) |
|---|---|---|---|---|
| A | 0 | 0 | | |
| | | | 4 | |
| B | 1 | 4 | | 4.00 |
| | | | 6 | |
| C | 2 | 10 | | 5.00 |
| | | | 3 | |
| D | 3 | 13 | | 4.33 |
| | | | 2 | |
| E | 4 | 15 | | 3.75 |
| | | | 1 | |
| F | 5 | 16 | | 3.20 |

Total product is the total amount produced. Marginal product is the change in total product resulting from a one-unit increase in labour. For example, when labour increases from 2 to 3 workers a day (row C to row D), total product increases from 10 to 13 jumpers a day. The marginal product of going from 2 to 3 workers is 3 jumpers. (Marginal product is shown between the rows because it is the result of a change in the quantity of labour.) Average product of labour is total product divided by the quantity of labour employed. For example, 3 workers produce 13 jumpers a day, so the average product of 3 workers is 4.33 jumpers per worker.

## Total Product Curve

Figure 6.1 shows Fashion First's total product curve, *TP*. As employment increases, so does the number of jumpers knitted. Points *A* to *F* on the curve correspond to the same rows in Table 6.1. These points show total product at various quantities of labour per day. But labour is divisible into hours and even minutes. By varying the amount of labour in the smallest units possible, we can draw the total product curve shown in Figure 6.1.

Look carefully at the shape of the total product curve. As employment increases from zero to 1 worker a day, the curve becomes steeper. Then, as employment continues to increase to 3, 4 and 5 workers per day, the curve becomes less steep.

The total product curve is similar to the *production possibilities frontier* (explained in Chapter 2). It separates the attainable output levels from those that are unattainable. All the points that lie above the curve are unattainable. Points that lie below the curve, in the orange area, are attainable. But they are inefficient – they use more labour than is necessary to produce a given output. Only the points *on* the total product curve are technologically efficient.

**Figure 6.1** Total Product Curve

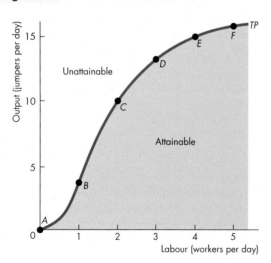

The total product curve (*TP*) is based on the data in Table 6.1. The total product curve shows how the quantity of jumpers changes as the quantity of labour employed changes. For example, using 1 knitting machine, 2 workers can produce 10 jumpers a day (row *C*). Points *A* to *F* on the curve correspond to the rows of Table 6.1. The total product curve separates the attainable output from the unattainable output. Points on the *TP* curve are efficient.

## Marginal Product Curve

Figure 6.2 shows Fashion First's marginal product of labour with 1 knitting machine. Part (a) reproduces the total product curve from Figure 6.1. Part (b) shows the marginal product curve, *MP*.

In Figure 6.2(a), the orange bars illustrate the marginal product of labour. The height of each bar measures marginal product. Marginal product is also measured by the slope of the total product curve. Recall that the slope of a curve is the change in the value of the variable measured on the *y*-axis – output – divided by the change in the variable measured on the *x*-axis – labour – as we move along the curve. A one-unit increase in labour, from 2 to 3 workers, increases output from 10 to 13 jumpers, so the slope from point *C* to point *D* is 3 jumpers per worker, the same as the marginal product that we've just calculated.

By varying the amount of labour in the smallest imaginable units, we can draw the marginal product curve shown in Figure 6.2(b). The *height* of this curve measures the *slope* of the total product curve at a point. The total product curve in part (a) shows that an increase in employment from 2 to 3 workers increases output from 10 to 13 jumpers (an increase of 3). The increase in output of 3 jumpers appears on the *y*-axis of part (b) as the marginal product of going from 2 to 3 workers. We plot that marginal product at the mid-point between 2 and 3 workers. Notice that marginal product in Figure 6.2(b) reaches a peak at 1.5 workers and at that point marginal product is 6 jumpers. The peak occurs at 1.5 workers because the total product curve is steepest when employment increases from 1 to 2 workers.

The total product and marginal product curves differ across firms and types of goods. An airline's product curves are different from those of your local supermarket, which in turn are different from those of Fashion First. But the shapes of the product curves are similar because almost every production process has two features:

◆ Increasing marginal returns initially

◆ Diminishing marginal returns eventually

### Increasing Marginal Returns

Increasing marginal returns occur when the marginal product of an additional worker exceeds the marginal product of the previous worker. Increasing marginal returns arise from increased specialization and division of labour in the production process.

## Figure 6.2  Total Product and Marginal Product

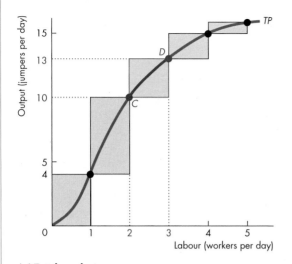

**(a) Total product**

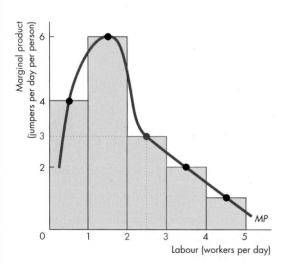

**(b) Marginal product**

Marginal product is illustrated in both parts of the figure by the orange bars. For example, when labour increases from 2 to 3 workers a day, marginal product is the orange bar whose height is 3 jumpers. (Marginal product is shown midway between the quantities of labour to emphasize that it is the result of changing the quantity of labour.)

The steeper the slope of the total product curve (*TP*) in part (a), the larger is marginal product (*MP*) in part (b). Marginal product increases to a maximum (in this example when the second worker is employed) and then declines – diminishing marginal product.

For example, if Fashion First employs just 1 worker, that person has to learn all the different aspects of jumper production: running the knitting machines, fixing breakdowns, packaging and mailing jumpers and buying and checking the type and colour of the wool. All of these tasks have to be done by that one person.

If Fashion First employs a second person, the 2 workers can specialize in different parts of the production process. As a result, 2 workers produce more than twice as much as 1. The marginal product of the second worker is greater than the marginal product of the first worker. Marginal returns are increasing.

### Diminishing Marginal Returns

Most product processes experience increasing marginal returns initially, but all production processes eventually reach a point of diminishing marginal returns. **Diminishing marginal returns** occur when the marginal product of an additional worker is less than the marginal product of the previous worker.

Diminishing marginal returns arise from the fact that more and more workers are using the same capital and working in the same space. As more workers are added, there is less and less for the additional workers to do that is productive. For example, if Fashion First employs a third worker, output increases but not by as much as it did when it added the second worker. In this case, after two workers are employed, all the gains from specialization and the division of labour have been exhausted. By employing a third worker, the factory produces more jumpers, but the equipment is being operated closer to its limits. There are even times when the third worker has nothing to do because the machine is running without the need for further attention. Adding more and more workers continues to increase output but by successively smaller amounts. Marginal returns are diminishing. This phenomenon is such a pervasive one that it is called 'the law of diminishing returns'.

The **law of diminishing returns** states that:

**As a firm uses more of a variable factor of production, with a given quantity of the fixed factor of production, the marginal product of the variable factor eventually diminishes.**

You will return to the law of diminishing returns when we study a firm's costs. But before we do, let's look at average product and the average product curve.

## Average Product Curve

Figure 6.3 illustrates Fashion First's average product of labour, *AP*, and the relationship between the average and marginal product. Points *B* to *F* on the average product curve correspond to those same rows in Table 6.1.

Average product increases from 1 to 2 workers (its maximum value is at point *C*) but then decreases as yet more workers are employed. Also average product is largest when average product and marginal product are equal. That is, the marginal product curve cuts the average product curve at the point of maximum average product. For the number of workers at which the marginal product exceeds average product, average product is *increasing*. For the number of workers at which marginal product is less than average product, average product is *decreasing*.

The relationship between the average product and marginal product curves is a general feature of the relationship between the average and marginal values of any variable. Let's look at a familiar example.

**Figure 6.3** Average Product

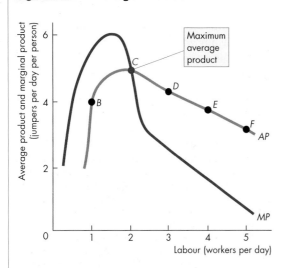

The figure shows the average product of labour and the connection between the average product and marginal product. With 1 worker a day, marginal product exceeds average product, so average product is increasing. With 2 workers a day, marginal product equals average product, so average product is at its maximum. With more than 2 workers a day, marginal product is less than average product, so average product is decreasing.

myeconlab Animation

## How to Pull Up Your Average

Do you want to pull up your average mark? Then make sure that your mark on this test is better than your current average! This test is your marginal test. If your marginal mark exceeds your average mark (like the second test in the graph), your average will rise. If your marginal mark equals your average mark (like the third test in the graph), your average won't change. If your marginal mark is below your average mark (like the fourth test in the figure), your average will fall.

The relationship between your marginal and average grades is exactly the same as that between marginal product and average product.

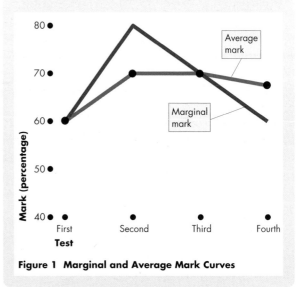

**Figure 1  Marginal and Average Mark Curves**

### Review Quiz

1   Explain how the marginal product and the average product change as the labour employed increases (a) initially and (b) eventually.
2   What is the law of diminishing returns? Why does marginal product eventually diminish?
3   Explain the relationship between marginal product and average product.

You can work these questions in Study Plan 6.2 and get instant feedback.

Norma, the owner of Fashion First, cares about Fashion First's product curves because they influence its costs. Let's look at Fashion First's costs.

# Short-run Cost

To produce more output in the short run, a firm must employ more labour, which means it must increase its costs. We describe the relationship between output and costs by using three concepts:

◆ Total cost
◆ Marginal cost
◆ Average cost

## Total Cost

A firm's **total cost** (*TC*) is the cost of *all* the factors of production it uses. We separate total cost into total *fixed* cost and total *variable* cost.

**Total fixed cost** (*TFC*) is the cost of the firm's fixed factors. For Fashion First, total fixed cost includes the cost of renting knitting machines and *normal profit*, which is the opportunity cost of Norma's entrepreneurship. The quantities of a fixed factor don't change as output changes, so total fixed cost is the same at all outputs.

**Total variable cost** (*TVC*) is the cost of the firm's variable inputs. For Fashion First, labour is the variable factor, so this component of cost is its wage bill. Total variable cost changes as total product changes.

Total cost is the sum of total fixed cost and total variable cost. That is:

$$TC = TFC + TVC$$

The table in Figure 6.4 shows Fashion First's total costs. With one knitting machine that Fashion First rents for £25 a day, *TFC* is £25 a day. To produce jumpers, Fashion First hires labour, which costs £25 a day. *TVC* is the number of workers multiplied by £25. For example, to produce 13 jumpers a day, Fashion First hires 3 workers and its *TVC* is £75. *TC* is the sum of *TFC* and *TVC*, so to produce 13 jumpers a day, Fashion First's total cost, *TC*, is £100. Check the calculation in each row of the table.

Figure 6.4 shows Fashion First's total cost curves, which graph total cost against output. The green total fixed cost curve (*TFC*) is horizontal because total fixed cost is constant at £25. It does not change when output changes. The purple total variable cost curve (*TVC*) and the blue total cost curve (*TC*) both slope upward because total variable cost increases as output increases. The arrows highlight total fixed cost as the vertical distance between the *TVC* and *TC* curves.

**Figure 6.4**   Short-run Total Cost

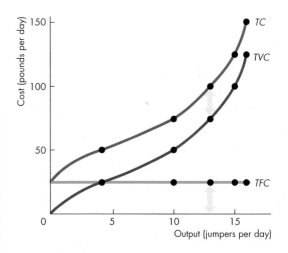

| | Labour (workers per day) | Output (jumpers per day) | Total fixed cost (*TFC*) | Total variable cost (*TVC*) | Total cost (*TC*) |
|---|---|---|---|---|---|
| | | | | (pounds per day) | |
| A | 0 | 0 | 25 | 0 | 25 |
| B | 1 | 4 | 25 | 25 | 50 |
| C | 2 | 10 | 25 | 50 | 75 |
| D | 3 | 13 | 25 | 75 | 100 |
| E | 4 | 15 | 25 | 100 | 125 |
| F | 5 | 16 | 25 | 125 | 150 |

Fashion First rents a knitting machine for £25 a day. This amount is Fashion First's total fixed cost. Fashion First hires workers at a wage rate of £25 a day, and this cost is Fashion First's total variable cost. For example, if Fashion First employs 3 workers, its total variable cost is (3 × £25), which equals £75.

Total cost is the sum of total fixed cost and total variable cost. For example, when Fashion First employs 3 workers, its total cost is £100: total fixed cost of £25 plus total variable cost of £75. The graph shows Fashion First's total cost curves.

Total fixed cost (*TFC*) is constant – it graphs as a horizontal line – and total variable cost (*TVC*) increases as output increases. Total cost (*TC*) also increases as output increases. The vertical distance between the total cost curve and the total variable cost curve is total fixed cost, as illustrated by the two arrows.

 Animation

## Marginal Cost

In Figure 6.4, total variable cost and total cost increase at a decreasing rate at small outputs and begin to increase at an increasing rate as output increases. To understand these patterns in the changes in total cost, we need to use the concept of *marginal cost*.

A firm's **marginal cost** is the change in total cost resulting from a one-unit increase in output. Marginal cost ($MC$) is calculated as the change in total cost ($\Delta TC$) divided by the change in output ($\Delta Q$). That is:

$$MC = \frac{\Delta TC}{\Delta Q}$$

The table in Figure 6.5 shows this calculation. For example, an increase in output from 10 to 13 jumpers increases total cost from £75 to £100. The change in output is 3 jumpers, and the change in total cost is £25. The marginal cost of one of those 3 jumpers is (£25 ÷ 3), which equals £8.33.

Figure 6.5 graphs the marginal cost as the red marginal cost curve, $MC$. This curve is U-shaped because when Fashion First hires a second worker, marginal cost decreases, but when it hires a third, a fourth and a fifth worker, marginal cost successively increases.

Marginal cost decreases at low outputs because of economies from greater specialization. It eventually increases because of *the law of diminishing returns*. The law of diminishing returns means that each additional worker produces a successively smaller addition to output. So to get an additional unit of output, ever more workers are required. Because more workers are required to produce one additional unit of output, the cost of the additional output – marginal cost – must eventually increase.

Marginal cost tells us how total cost changes as output changes. The final cost concept tells us what it costs, on the average, to produce a unit of output. Let's now look at Fashion First's average costs.

## Average Cost

Average cost is cost per unit of output. There are three average costs:

1 Average fixed cost

2 Average variable cost

3 Average total cost

**Average fixed cost** ($AFC$) is total fixed cost per unit of output. **Average variable cost** ($AVC$) is total variable cost per unit of output. **Average total cost** ($ATC$) is total cost per unit of output. The average cost concepts are calculated from the total cost concepts as follows:

$$TC = TFC + TVC$$

Divide each total cost term by the quantity produced, $Q$, to give:

$$\frac{TC}{Q} = \frac{TFC}{Q} + \frac{TVC}{Q}$$

or:

$$ATC = AFC + AVC$$

The table in Figure 6.5 shows the calculation of average total costs. For example, in the third row when output is 10 jumpers, average fixed cost is (£25 ÷ 10), which equals £2.50, average variable cost is (£50 ÷ 10), which equals £5.00, and average total cost is (£75 ÷ 10), which equals £7.50. Note average total cost is equal to average fixed cost (£2.50) plus average variable cost (£5.00).

Figure 6.5 shows the average cost curves. The green average fixed cost curve ($AFC$) slopes downward. As output increases, the same constant fixed cost is spread over a larger output. The blue average total cost curve ($ATC$) and the purple average variable cost curve ($AVC$) are U-shaped. The vertical distance between the average total cost and average variable cost curves is equal to average fixed cost – as indicated by the arrows. That distance between the $ATC$ and $AVC$ curves shrinks as output increases because average fixed cost decreases as output increases.

## Marginal Cost and Average Cost

The red marginal cost curve ($MC$) intersects the average variable cost curve and the average total cost curve *at their minimum point*. When marginal cost is less than average cost, average cost is decreasing, and when marginal cost exceeds average cost, average cost is increasing. This relationship holds for both the $ATC$ and the $AVC$ curves and is another example of the relationship you saw in Figure 6.3 between average product and marginal product and your marginal and average test marks.

## Why the Average Total Cost Curve Is U-shaped

Average total cost, $ATC$, is the sum of average fixed cost, $AFC$, and average variable cost, $AVC$. So the shape

**Figure 6.5** Marginal Cost and Average Costs

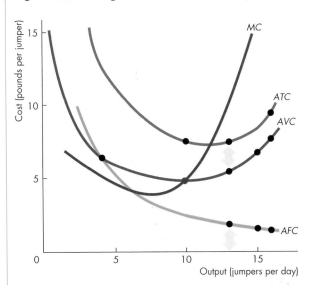

Marginal cost is calculated as the change in total cost divided by the change in output. When output increases from 4 to 10, an increase of 6, total cost increases by £25 and marginal cost is £25 ÷ 6, which equals £4.17. Each average cost concept is calculated by dividing the related total cost by output. When 10 jumpers are produced, *AFC* is £2.50 (£25 ÷ 10), *AVC* is £5 (£50 ÷ 10), and *ATC* is £7.50 (£75 ÷ 10).

The graph shows the marginal cost curve and the average cost curves. The marginal cost curve (*MC*) is U-shaped and intersects the average variable cost curve and the average total cost curve at their minimum points. Average fixed cost (*AFC*) decreases as output increases. The average total cost curve (*ATC*) and average variable cost curve (*AVC*) are U-shaped. The vertical distance between these two curves is equal to average fixed cost, as illustrated by the two arrows.

| Labour (workers per day) | Output (jumpers per day) | Total fixed cost (*TFC*) | Total variable cost (*TVC*) | Total cost (*TC*) | Marginal cost (*MC*) | Average fixed cost (*AFC*) | Average variable cost (*AVC*) | Average total cost (*ATC*) |
|---|---|---|---|---|---|---|---|---|
| | | (pounds per day) | | | | (pounds per jumper) | | |
| 0 | 0 | 25 | | 25 | | | | |
| | | | | | ........ 6.25 | | | |
| 1 | 4 | 25 | 25 | 50 | | 6.25 | 6.25 | 12.50 |
| | | | | | ........ 4.17 | | | |
| 2 | 10 | 25 | 50 | 75 | | 2.50 | 5.00 | 7.50 |
| | | | | | ........ 8.33 | | | |
| 3 | 13 | 25 | 75 | 100 | | 1.92 | 5.77 | 7.69 |
| | | | | | ........ 12.50 | | | |
| 4 | 15 | 25 | 100 | 125 | | 1.67 | 6.67 | 8.33 |
| | | | | | ........ 25.00 | | | |
| 5 | 16 | 25 | 125 | 150 | | 1.56 | 7.81 | 9.38 |

of the *ATC* curve combines the shapes of the *AFC* and *AVC* curves. The U-shape of the average total cost curve arises from the influence of two opposing forces:

1  Spreading fixed cost over a larger output

2  Eventually diminishing returns

When output increases, the firm spreads its total fixed costs over a larger output and its average fixed cost decreases – its *AFC* curve slopes downward.

Diminishing returns means that as output increases, ever-larger amounts of labour are needed to produce an additional unit of output. So as output increases, average variable cost decreases initially but eventually increases and the firm's *AVC* curve eventually slopes upward. The *AVC* curve is U-shaped.

The shape of the *ATC* curve combines these two effects. Initially, as output increases, both average fixed cost and average variable cost decrease, so average total cost decreases and the *ATC* curve slopes downward.

But as output increases further and diminishing returns set in, average variable cost begins to increase. With average fixed cost decreasing more quickly than average variable cost is increasing, the *ATC* curve continues to slope downward. Eventually, average variable cost increases more quickly than average fixed cost decreases, so average total cost increases and the *ATC* curve slopes upward.

# Cost Curves and Product Curves

The technology that a firm uses determines its costs. Figure 6.6 shows the links between the firm's technology constraint (its product curves) and its cost curves. The upper part of the figure shows the average product curve and the marginal product curve – like those in Figure 6.3. The lower part of the figure shows the average variable cost curve and the marginal cost curve – like those in Figure 6.5.

As labour increases up to 1.5 workers a day (upper graph), output increases to 6.5 jumpers a day (lower graph). Marginal product and average product rise and marginal cost and average variable cost fall. At the point of maximum marginal product, marginal cost is at a minimum.

As labour increases from 1.5 workers to 2 workers a day (upper graph), output increases from 6.5 jumpers to 10 jumpers a day (lower graph). Marginal product falls and marginal cost rises, but average product continues to rise and average variable cost continues to fall. At the point of maximum average product, average variable cost is at a minimum. As labour increases further, output increases. Average product diminishes and average variable cost increases.

# Shifts in the Cost Curves

The position of a firm's short-run cost curves depends on two factors:

◆ Technology
◆ Prices of factors of production

### Technology

A technological change that increases productivity shifts the total product curve upward. It also shifts the marginal product curve and the average product curve upward. With better technology, the same factors of production can produce more output. So technological change lowers cost and shifts the cost curves downward.

For example, advances in robotic production techniques have increased productivity in the car industry. As a result, the product curves of BMW, Renault and Volvo have shifted upward and their cost curves have shifted downward. But the relationships between their product curves and cost curves have not changed. The curves are still linked in the way shown in Figure 6.6.

Often, a technological advance results in a firm using more capital (a fixed factor) and less labour (a variable

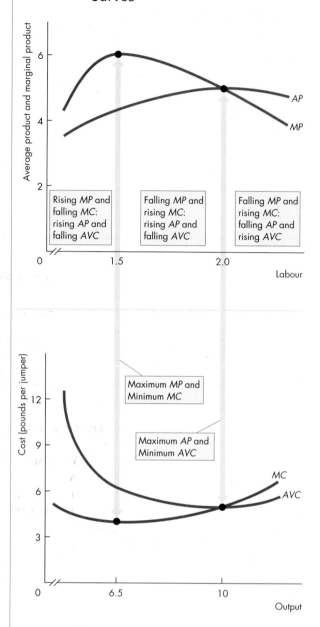

**Figure 6.6** Product Curves and Cost Curves

Rising MP and falling MC: rising AP and falling AVC

Falling MP and rising MC: rising AP and falling AVC

Falling MP and rising MC: falling AP and rising AVC

Maximum MP and Minimum MC

Maximum AP and Minimum AVC

A firm's *MP* curve is linked to its *MC* curve. If, as the firm increases its labour from 0 to 1.5 workers a day, the firm's marginal product rises, its marginal cost falls. If marginal product is at a maximum, marginal cost is at a minimum. If, as the firm hires more labour, its marginal product diminishes, its marginal cost rises.

A firm's *AP* curve is linked to its *AVC* curve. If, as the firm increases its labour to 2 workers a day, its average product rises, its average variable cost falls. If average product is at a maximum, average variable cost is at a minimum. If, as the firm hires more labour, its average product diminishes, its average variable cost rises.

**Table 6.2**

A Compact Glossary of Costs

| Term | Symbol | Definition | Equation |
|------|--------|-----------|----------|
| Fixed cost | | Cost that is independent of the output level; cost of a fixed factor of production | |
| Variable cost | | Cost that varies with the output level; cost of a variable factor of production | |
| Total fixed cost | TFC | Cost of the fixed factors of production (equals their number times their unit price) | |
| Total variable cost | TVC | Cost of the variable factors of production (equals their number times their unit price) | |
| Total cost | TC | Cost of all factors of production | $TC = TFC + TVC$ |
| Total product (output) | TP | Total quantity produced ($Q$) | |
| Marginal cost | MC | Change in total cost resulting from a one-unit increase in total product | $MC = \Delta TC \div \Delta Q$ |
| Average fixed cost | AFC | Total fixed cost per unit of output | $AFC = TFC \div Q$ |
| Average variable cost | AVC | Total variable cost per unit of output | $AVC = TVC \div Q$ |
| Average total cost | ATC | Total cost per unit of output | $ATC = AFC \div AVC$ |

factor). For example, today the telephone companies use computers to provide directory assistance in place of the human operators they used in the 1980s. When such a technological change occurs, total cost decreases, but fixed costs increase and variable costs decrease. This change in the mix of fixed cost and variable cost means that at low output levels, average total cost might increase, while at high output levels, average total cost decreases.

## Prices of Factors of Production

An increase in the price of a factor of production increases costs and shifts the cost curves. But the way the curves shift depends on which factor price changes. An increase in rent or some other component of *fixed* cost shifts the fixed cost curves (*TFC* and *AFC*) upward and the total cost curve (*TC*) upward, but leaves the variable cost curves (*AVC* and *TVC*) and the marginal cost curve (*MC*) unchanged. An increase in the wage rate or some other component of *variable* cost shifts the variable curves (*TVC* and *AVC*) upward, the total cost curve (*TC*) and the marginal cost curve (*MC*) upward, but leaves the fixed cost curves (*AFC* and *TFC*)

unchanged. So for example, if the wage rate of lorry drivers increases, the variable cost and marginal cost of transportation services increase. If the interest expense paid by a trucking company increases, the fixed cost of transportation services increases.

You've now completed your study of short-run costs. All the concepts that you've met are summarized in a compact glossary in Table 6.2.

### Review Quiz

1   What relationships do a firm's short-run cost curves show?
2   How does marginal cost change as output increases (a) initially, and (b) eventually?
3   What does the law of diminishing returns imply for the shape of the marginal cost curve?
4   What is the shape of the *AFC* curve and why?
5   What are the shapes of the *AVC* curve and *ATC* curve and why?

You can work these questions in Study Plan 6.3 and get instant feedback.

## Long-run Cost

In the short run, a firm can vary the quantity of labour but the quantity of capital is fixed. So the firm has variable costs of labour and fixed costs of capital. In the long run, a firm can vary both the quantity of labour and the quantity of capital. So in the long run, all the firm's costs are variable. We are now going to study the firm's costs in the long run, when *all* costs are variable costs and when the quantities of labour and capital vary.

The behaviour of long-run costs depends on the firm's production function. The *production function* is the relationship between the maximum output attainable and the quantities of both labour and capital.

### The Production Function

Table 6.3 shows Fashion First's production function. The table lists the total product for four different quantities of capital. The quantity of capital is defined as the plant size. Plant 1 represents a factory with 1 knitting machine – the case we have just studied. The other three plants have 2, 3 and 4 knitting machines. If Fashion First doubles its plant size from 1 to 2 knitting machines, the various amounts of labour can produce the outputs shown in the column under Plant 2 of the table. The next two columns show the outputs of yet larger plants. Each column in the table could be graphed as a total product curve for each plant size.

### Diminishing Returns

Diminishing returns occur in each of the four plants as the quantity of labour increases. You can check that fact by calculating the marginal product of labour in plants with 2, 3 and 4 knitting machines. At each plant size, as the quantity of labour increases, the marginal product of labour (eventually) decreases.

### Diminishing Marginal Product of Capital

Diminishing returns also occur as the quantity of capital increases. You can check that fact by calculating the marginal product of capital at a given quantity of labour. The *marginal product of capital* is the change in total product divided by the change in capital employed when the amount of labour employed is constant. It is the change in output resulting from a one-unit increase in the quantity of capital employed.

---

**Table 6.3**

### The Production Function

| Labour (workers per day) | Output (jumpers per day) | | | |
|---|---|---|---|---|
| | Plant 1 | Plant 2 | Plant 3 | Plant 4 |
| 1 | 4 | 10 | 13 | 15 |
| 2 | 10 | 15 | 18 | 20 |
| 3 | 13 | 18 | 22 | 24 |
| 4 | 15 | 20 | 24 | 26 |
| 5 | 16 | 21 | 25 | 27 |
| **Knitting machines (number)** | 1 | 2 | 3 | 4 |

The table shows the total product data for four quantities of capital – four plant sizes. The bigger the plant size, the larger is the total product for any given amount of labour employed. But for a given plant size, the marginal product of labour diminishes as more labour is employed. For a given quantity of labour, the marginal product of capital diminishes as the quantity of capital used increases.

---

For example, if Fashion First employs 3 workers and increases its capital from 1 machine to 2 machines, output increases from 13 to 18 jumpers a day. The marginal product of capital is 5 jumpers a day. If with 3 workers, Fashion First increases its capital from 2 machines to 3 machines, output increases from 18 to 22 jumpers a day. The marginal product of the third machine is 4 jumpers a day, down from 5 jumpers a day for the second machine.

We can now see what the production function implies for long-run costs.

## Short-run Cost and Long-run Cost

Continue to assume that labour costs £25 per worker per day and capital costs £25 per machine per day. Using these factor prices and the data in Table 6.3, we can calculate and graph the average total cost curves for factories with 1, 2, 3 and 4 knitting machines. We've already studied the costs of a factory with 1 knitting machine in Figures 6.5 and 6.6. In Figure 6.7, the average total cost curve for that case is $ATC_1$. Figure 6.7 also shows the average total cost curve for a factory with 2 machines, $ATC_2$, with 3 machines, $ATC_3$, and with 4 machines, $ATC_4$.

**Figure 6.7** Short-run Costs of Four Different Plants

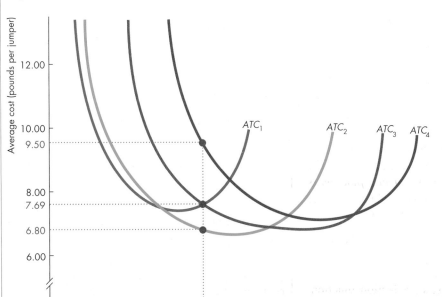

The figure shows short-run average total cost curves for four different quantities of capital.

Fashion First can produce 13 jumpers a day with 1 knitting machine on $ATC_1$, or with 3 knitting machines on $ATC_3$ for an average cost of £7.69 per jumper. Fashion First can produce the same number of jumpers by using 2 knitting machines on $ATC_2$ for £6.80 per jumper or with 4 machines on $ATC_4$ for £9.50 per jumper.

If Fashion First produces 13 jumpers a day, the least-cost method of production (the long-run method) is to use 2 machines on $ATC_2$.

You can see, in Figure 6.7, that plant size has a big effect on the firm's average total cost. Two things stand out.

1  Each short-run *ATC* curve is U-shaped.

2  For each short-run *ATC* curve, the larger the plant, the greater is the output at which average total cost is a minimum.

Each short-run average total cost curve is U-shaped because, as the quantity of labour increases, its marginal product at first increases and then diminishes. This pattern in the marginal product of labour, which we examined in some detail for the plant with 1 knitting machine on pp. 132–133, occurs at all plant sizes.

The minimum average total cost for a larger plant occurs at a greater output than it does for a smaller plant because the larger plant has a higher fixed cost and therefore, for any given output level, a higher average fixed cost.

Which short-run average cost curves Fashion First operates on depends on its plant size. But in the long run, Fashion First chooses its plant size. Its choice of plant size depends on the output that it plans to produce. The reason is that the average total cost of producing a given output depends on the plant size.

To see why, suppose that Fashion First plans to produce 13 jumpers a day. With 1 machine, the average total cost curve is $ATC_1$ (in Figure 6.7) and the average total cost of 13 jumpers a day is £7.69 per jumper. With 2 machines, on $ATC_2$, average total cost is £6.80 per jumper. With 3 machines on $ATC_3$, average total cost is £7.69 per jumper, the same as with 1 machine. Finally, with 4 machines, on $ATC_4$, average total cost is £9.50 per jumper.

The economically efficient plant size for producing a given output is the one that has the lowest average total cost. For Fashion First, the economically efficient plant to use to produce 13 jumpers a day is the one with 2 machines. In the long run, Fashion First chooses the plant size that minimizes average total cost. When a firm is producing a given output at the least possible cost, it is operating on its *long-run average cost curve*.

The **long-run average cost curve** is the relationship between the lowest attainable average total cost and output when both the plant size and labour are varied. The long-run average cost curve is a planning curve. It tells the firm the plant size and the quantity of labour to use at each output to minimize cost. Once the plant size is chosen, the firm operates on the short-run cost curves that apply to that plant size.

# The Long-run Average Cost Curve

Figure 6.8 shows how the long-run average cost curve is derived. The long-run average cost curve *LRAC* consists of pieces of the four short-run *ATC* curves. For output up to 10 jumpers a day, the average total cost is lowest on $ATC_1$. For output rates between 10 and 18 jumpers a day, average total cost is lowest on $ATC_2$. For output rates between 18 and 24 jumpers a day, average total cost is lowest on $ATC_3$. For output rates in excess of 24 jumpers a day, average total cost is lowest on $ATC_4$. The piece of each *ATC* curve with the lowest average total cost is shown as dark blue in Figure 6.8. The dark blue scallop-shaped curve made up of the four pieces is Fashion First's *LRAC* curve.

# Economies and Diseconomies of Scale

**Economies of scale** are features of a firm's technology that make average total cost *fall* as output increases. When economies of scale are present, the *LRAC* curve slopes downward. The *LRAC* in Figure 6.8 shows that Fashion First experiences economies of scale for outputs up to 15 jumpers a day.

Greater specialization of both labour and capital is the main source of economies of scale. For example, if BMW produces only 100 cars a week, each worker must be capable of performing many different tasks and the capital must be general-purpose machines and tools. But if BMW produces 10,000 cars a week, each worker specializes in a small number of tasks, uses task-specific tools and becomes highly proficient.

**Diseconomies of scale** are features of a firm's technology that make average total cost *rise* as output increases. When diseconomies of scale are present, the *LRAC* curve slopes upward. In Figure 6.8, Fashion First experiences diseconomies of scale at outputs greater than 15 jumpers a day.

The challenge of managing a large enterprise is the main source of diseconomies of scale.

**Constant returns to scale** are features of a firm's technology that keep average total costs constant as output increases. When constant returns to scale are present, the *LRAC* curve is horizontal.

The economies of scale and diseconomies of scale at Fashion First arise from the firm's production function in Table 6.3. With 1 worker and 1 machine, the firm produces 4 jumpers a day. With 2 workers and 2 machines, total cost doubles but output more than doubles to 15 jumpers a day, so average total cost decreases and Fashion First experiences economies of scale.

## Figure 6.8 The Long-run Average Cost Curve

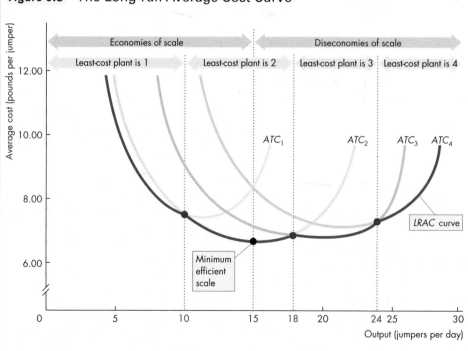

The long-run average cost curve traces the lowest attainable *ATC* when both labour and capital change. The green arrows highlight the output range over which each plant achieves the lowest *ATC*. Within each range, to change the quantity produced, the firm changes the quantity of labour it employs.

Along the *LRAC* curve economies of scale occur if average cost falls as output increases; diseconomies of scale occur if average cost rises as output increases.

Minimum efficient scale is the output at which average cost is lowest, 15 jumpers a day.

## Produce More to Cut Cost

Why do BMW, Citroen and other car makers have expensive equipment lying around that isn't fully used? You can now answer this question with what you have learned in this chapter.

The basic answer is that car production faces economies of scale. A larger output rate brings a lower long-run average cost – the firm's *LRAC* curve slopes downward.

A car producer's average total cost curves look like those in Figure 1. To produce 20 vehicles an hour, the firm installs the plant with the short-run average total cost curve $ATC_1$. The average cost of producing a vehicle is £20,000.

Producing 20 vehicles an hour doesn't use the plant at its lowest possible average total cost. If the firm could sell

enough cars for it to produce 40 vehicles an hour, the firm could use its current plant and produce at an average cost of £15,000 a vehicle.

But if the firm planned to produce 40 vehicles an hour, it would not use its current plant. The firm would install a bigger plant with the short-run average total cost curve $ATC_2$, and produce 40 vehicles an hour for £10,000 a car.

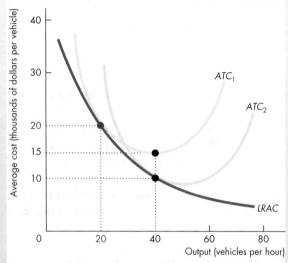

**Figure 1  Car Plant's Average Cost Curves**

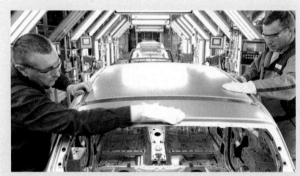

With 4 workers and 4 machines, total cost doubles again, but output less than doubles to 26 jumpers a day, so average total cost increases and Fashion First experiences diseconomies of scale.

## Minimum Efficient Scale

A firm's **minimum efficient scale** is the *smallest* quantity of output at which long-run average cost reaches its lowest level. At Fashion First, the minimum efficient scale is 15 jumpers per day.

The minimum efficient scale plays a role in determining market structure. In a market in which the minimum efficient scale is small relative to the market demand, the market has room for many firms. The market is competitive. In a market in which the minimum efficient scale is large relative to market demand, only a small number of firms, and sometimes only one firm, can make a profit. The market is an oligopoly or monopoly. We will look at these ideas in the next three chapters.

1  What does a firm's production function show and how is it related to a total product curve?
2  Does the law of diminishing returns apply to capital as well as labour? Explain why or why not.
3  What does a firm's *LRAC* curve show? How is it related to the firm's short-run *ATC* curve?
4  What are economies and diseconomies of scale? How do they arise? What do they imply for the shape of the *LRAC* curve?
5  What is a firm's minimum efficient scale?

You can work these questions in Study Plan 6.4 and get instant feedback.

You have now studied how a firm's costs vary as it changes its output. The *Business Case Study* on pp. 144–145 applies what you have learned about a firm's cost curves to Europe's second largest airline, easyJet.

# Business Case Study

# Airline Costs: The No Frills Approach

## EasyJet Cuts Costs in Europe

### EasyJet: The Company, Product and Market

EasyJet is a UK airline and ranks as Europe's second largest behind Ryanair. EasyJet competes with 200 other carriers and provides low cost flights to main airports with frequent services. In 2010, easyJet operated over 400 routes in 27 countries and carried over 48 million passengers. The company has a fleet of 180 aircraft, 6,660 staff, and a UK headquarters. European market demand for flights fell by 5 per cent in 2009 but easyJet passenger numbers grew

### EasyJet's Rapid Growth

EasyJet has grown from an airline with just two aircraft (Boeing 737s) and two routes in 1995 to its current size by buying new aircraft and by acquiring airlines such as Go and GB airways. These buyouts provided second-hand aircraft and additional routes to increase output capacity alongside new planes.

### EasyJet's Rising Costs

EasyJet's total costs increased by 15 per cent from 2008 to 2009. EasyJet's fuel costs increased by £86 million and other costs including airport charges and staff costs also increased. In addition, easyJet bought additional aircraft.

### EasyJet's Costs

| Item | 2008 | 2009 |
|---|---|---|
| Passengers (millions) | 43.7 | 45.2 |
| Seats flown | 51.9 | 52.8 |
| Aircraft | 150.0 | 174.0 |
| Total cost (£ million) | 2,239.7 | 2,623.1 |
| Average total cost (cost per seat) | 43.15 | 49.67 |

Source of data: easyJet PLC, Reports and Accounts 2009, Interim Statement, 2010.

### EasyJet Looks for Cost Cuts

In the past, easyJet has introduced on-line booking, purchase and check-in systems to cut costs alongside charging for baggage and extra services. EasyJet now aims to cut operating costs by £190 million by 2012 – saving £1 per seat. Of this, £20 million will be saved from cutting fuel burn through improved pilot techniques, fuel reporting systems and flight plan systems. £35 million will be saved from crew costs by increased efficiency and new work rostas. Other savings will come from buying new A320 airbus aircraft to replace 737s and other smaller aircraft. A320s are cheaper to own and maintain, have more seats and a cost per seat that is 6 per cent lower than other aircraft.

# Economic Analysis

◆ In 2009, the demand for air travel in Europe fell, but easyJet increased its output (measured by passenger numbers and the number of seats flown) and increased its share of the market.

◆ Other things remaining the same, the expansion of easyJet's output would have lowered its average total cost.

◆ But other things didn't remain the same: the price of fuel increased and easyJet's average total cost increased.

◆ Figures 1 and 2 analyse these two sources of change in total cost by showing what happened to easyJet's *ATC* curve.

◆ Figure 1 shows what would have happened with no change in the price of fuel.

◆ In 2008, easyJet's output was 51.9 million seats flown at an average total cost of £43.45 per seat at point *A* on *ATC* curve $ATC_{08}$.

◆ In 2009, easyJet's output increased to 52.8 million seats flown. With no change in plant size (number of aircraft), the firm would have been able to produce its 2009 output at £40.00 per seat (an assumed value) at point *B* on $ATC_{08}$.

◆ But by buying more aircraft, the firm can lower its costs even more to move to £38.00 per seat (another assumed value) at point *C* on its *LRAC* curve and on $ATC_{09}$.

◆ EasyJet was not able to move to point *C* because the price of fuel increased and Figure 2 shows the consequences.

◆ The higher fuel price shifted the *ATC* curve upward from $ATC_{09}$ to $ATC'_{09}$ and easyJet's average total cost increased to £49.67 per seat at point *D*.

◆ With more (and newer) aircraft, easyJet increased passenger numbers and benefitted from economies of scale.

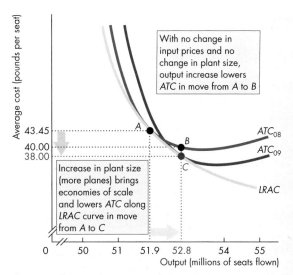

**Figure 1  Changes in output and average cost: constant input prices**

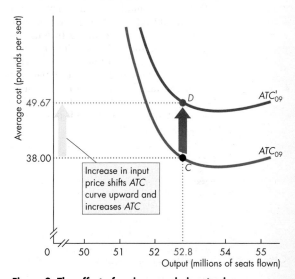

**Figure 2  The effect of an increase in input prices**

◆ By carrying more passengers, easyJet is able to get better deals from fuel suppliers, and from the suppliers of other services.

◆ EasyJet is seeking greater production efficiency by using a new technology to monitor fuel consumption and by introducing a new staff rota system. These changes will shift $ATC'_{09}$ downward.

◆◆◆ **SUMMARY**

## Key Points

### Time Frames for Decisions (p. 130)

◆ In the short run, the quantity of at least one factor of production is fixed and the quantities of the other factors can be varied.

◆ In the long run, the quantities of all factors of production can be varied.

Working Problems 1 and 2 will give you a better understanding of a firm's decision time frames.

### Short-run Technology Constraint (pp. 131–134)

◆ A total product curve shows the quantity of output that a firm can produce using a given quantity of capital and different quantities of labour.

◆ Initially, the marginal product of labour increases as the quantity of labour increases because of increased specialization and the division of labour.

◆ Eventually, marginal product diminishes because an increased quantity of labour must share a fixed quantity of capital – the law of diminishing marginal returns.

◆ Initially, average product increases as the quantity of labour increases, but eventually average product diminishes.

Working Problems 3 to 8 will give you a better understanding of a firm's short-run technology constraint.

### Short-run Cost (pp. 135–139)

◆ As output increases, total fixed cost is constant, and total variable cost and total cost increase.

◆ As output increases, average variable cost, average total cost and marginal cost decrease at small outputs and increase at large outputs. These cost curves are U-shaped.

Working Problems 9 to 14 will give you a better understanding of a firm's short-run cost.

### Long-run Cost (pp. 140–143)

◆ Long-run cost is the cost of production when all factors of production – labour and plant – have been adjusted to their economically efficient levels.

◆ The firm has a set of short-run cost curves for each different plant. For each output, the firm has one least-cost plant. The larger the output, the larger is the plant that will minimize average total cost.

◆ The long-run average cost curve traces the relationship between the lowest attainable average total cost and output when both capital and labour can be varied.

◆ With economies of scale, the long-run average cost curve slopes downward. With diseconomies of scale, the long-run average cost curve slopes upward.

Working Problems 15 to 20 will give you a better understanding of a firm's long-run cost.

## Key Terms

Average fixed cost, 136
Average product, 131
Average total cost, 136
Average variable cost, 136
Constant returns to scale, 142
Diminishing marginal returns, 133
Diseconomies of scale, 142
Economies of scale, 142
Law of diminishing returns, 133
Long run, 130
Long-run average cost curve, 141
Marginal cost, 136
Marginal product, 131
Minimum efficient scale, 143
Short run, 130
Sunk cost, 130
Total cost, 135
Total fixed cost, 135
Total product, 131
Total variable cost, 135

## STUDY PLAN PROBLEMS AND APPLICATIONS

myeconlab  You can work Problems 1 to 21 in MyEconLab Chapter 6 Study Plan and get instant feedback.

### Decision Time Frames (Study Plan 6.1)

**1** Which of the following news items involve a short-run decision and which involve a long-run decision? Explain.

**18 April 2009**: By next March, Tesco plans to open more than 100 shops in the UK, selling mobile and land-line packages in its largest stores.

**6 October 2009**: Tesco said that it would 'mothball' 13 stores in Nevada, Arizona and California – by boarding them up or subletting them, with a plan to reopen them in four to five years once the US economy recovers.

**22 August 2010**: Tesco is lauching its first drive-through supermarket this week. Customers order online and at the supermarket drive-through staff pack the shopping into the boot.

**1 September 2010**: Tesco plans to open 80 vast shopping malls in China by 2016.

**2 Farmers Turn from Tobacco to Flowers**

US tobacco farmers will be subsidized if they switch from growing tobacco to growing crops such as flowers and organic vegetables.

Source: *The New York Times*, 25 February 2001

**a** How does offering farmers a payment to exit tobacco growing influence the opportunity cost of growing tobacco?

**b** What is the opportunity cost of using the equipment owned by a tobacco farmer?

### Short-run Technology Constraint
(Study Plan 6.2)

Use the following table to work Problems 3 to 7.

The table sets out Sue's Snowboards' total product schedule:

| Labour (workers per week) | Output (snowboards per week) |
|---|---|
| 1 | 30 |
| 2 | 70 |
| 3 | 120 |
| 4 | 160 |
| 5 | 190 |
| 6 | 210 |
| 7 | 220 |

**3** Draw the total product curve.

**4** Calculate the average product of labour and draw the average product curve.

**5** Calculate the marginal product of labour and draw the marginal product curve.

**6 a** Over what output range does the firm enjoy the benefits of increased specialization and division of labour?

**b** Over what output range does the firm experience diminishing marginal product of labour?

**c** Over what range of output does the firm experience an increasing average product of labour but a diminishing marginal product of labour?

**7** Explain how it is possible for a firm to experience simultaneously an increasing *average* product but a diminishing *marginal* product.

**8** Sales at a footwear company rose from €160,000 in 2006 to €2.3 million in 2007, but in 2008 sales dipped to €1.5 million. Priscilla, the owner, blames the decline partly on a flood that damaged the firm's office and sapped morale. Assume that the prices of footwear didn't change.

**a** Explain the effect of the flood on the company's total product curve and marginal product curve.

**b** Draw a graph to show the effect of the flood on the company's total product curve and marginal product curve.

### Short-run Cost (Study Plan 6.3)

Use the following data to work Problems 9 to 13.

Sue's Snowboards in Problem 3 employs workers at €500 a week and its total fixed cost is €1,000 a week.

**9** Calculate total cost, total variable cost, and total fixed cost for each output and draw the short-run total cost curves.

**10** Calculate average total cost, average fixed cost, average variable cost, and marginal cost at each output and draw the short-run average and marginal cost curves.

**11** Illustrate the connection between Sue's *AP*, *MP*, *AVC* and *MC* curves like those in Figure 6.6.

**12** Sue's Snowboards rents a factory building. If the rent is increased by €200 a week and other things remain the same, how do Sue's Snowboards' short-run average cost curves and marginal cost curve change?

**13** Workers at Sue's Snowboards negotiate a wage increase of €100 a week for each worker. If other things remain the same, explain how Sue's Snowboards' short-run average cost curves and marginal cost curve change.

**14 Grain Prices Go the Way of the Oil Price**

Every morning millions of Americans confront the latest trend in commodities markets at their kitchen table. Rising prices for crops have begun to drive up the cost of breakfast.

Source: *The Economist*, 21 July 2007

Explain how the rising price of crops affects the average total cost and marginal cost of producing breakfast cereals.

## Long-run Cost (Study Plan 6.4)

Use the table in Problem 3 and the following information to work Problems 15 and 16.

Sue's Snowboards buys a second plant and the output produced by each worker increases by 50 per cent. The total fixed cost of operating each plant is €1,000 a week. Each worker is paid €500 a week.

**15** Calculate the average total cost of producing 180 and 240 snowboards a week when Sue's Snowboards operates two plants. Graph these points and sketch the *ATC* curve.

**16 a** To produce 180 snowboards a week, is it efficient to operate one or two plants?

**b** To produce 160 snowboards a week, is it efficient for Sue's to operate one or two plants?

Use the following table to work Problems 17 to 20.

The table shows the production function of Jackie's Canoe Rides.

| Labour (workers per day) | Output (rides per day) | | | |
|---|---|---|---|---|
| | Plant 1 | Plant 2 | Plant 3 | Plant 4 |
| 10 | 20 | 40 | 55 | 65 |
| 20 | 40 | 60 | 75 | 85 |
| 30 | 65 | 75 | 90 | 100 |
| 40 | 75 | 85 | 100 | 110 |
| Canoes (number) | 10 | 20 | 30 | 40 |

Jackie pays €100 a day for each canoe she rents and €50 a day for each canoe operator she hires.

**17** Graph the *ATC* curves for Plant 1 and Plant 2. Explain why these *ATC* curves differ from each other.

**18** Graph the *ATC* curves for Plant 3 and Plant 4. Explain why these *ATC* curves differ from each other.

**19 a** On Jackie's *LRAC* curve, what is the average cost of producing 40, 75 and 85 rides a week?

**b** What is Jackie's minimum efficient scale?

**20 a** Explain how Jackie's uses her *LRAC* curve to decide how many canoes to rent.

**b** Does Jackie's production function feature economies of scale or diseconomies of scale?

## Economics in the News (Study Plan 6.N)

**21 Airlines Seek Out New Ways to Save on Fuel as Costs Soar**

The financial pain of higher fuel prices is particularly acute for airlines because it is their single biggest expense. Airlines pump about 7,000 gallons into a Boeing 737 and about 60,000 gallons into the bigger 747 jet. Each generation of aircraft is more efficient: an Airbus A330 long-range jet uses 38 per cent less fuel than the DC-10 it replaced, while the Airbus A319 medium-range jet is 27 per cent more efficient than the DC-9 it replaced.

Source: *The New York Times*, 11 June 2008

**a** Is the price of fuel a fixed cost or a variable cost for an airline?

**b** Explain how an increase in the price of fuel changes an airline's total costs, average costs and marginal cost.

**c** Draw a graph to show the effects of an increase in the price of fuel on an airline's *TFC*, *TVC*, *AFC*, *AVC* and *MC* curves.

**d** Explain how a technological advance that makes an airplane engine more fuel efficient changes an airline's total product, marginal product and average product.

**e** Draw a graph to illustrate the effects of a more fuel-efficient aircraft on an airline's *TP*, *MP* and *AP* curves.

**f** Explain how a technological advance that makes an airplane engine more fuel efficient changes an airline's average variable cost, marginal cost and average total cost.

**g** Draw a graph to illustrate how a technological advance that makes an airplane engine more fuel efficient changes an airline's *AVC*, *MC* and *ATC* curves.

# ADDITIONAL PROBLEMS AND APPLICATIONS

 You can work these problems in MyEconLab if assigned by your lecturer.

## Decision Time Frames

**22  A Bakery on the Rise**

Some 500 customers a day line up to buy Avalon's breads, scones, muffins and coffee. Staffing and management are worries. Avalon now employs 35 and plans to hire 15 more. Its payroll will climb by 30 per cent to 40 per cent. The new CEO has executed an ambitious agenda that includes the move to a larger space, which will increase the rent from $3,500 to $10,000 a month.

Source: *CNN*, 24 March 2008

**a** Which of Avalon's decisions described in the news clip is a short-run decision and which is a long-run decision?

**b** Why is Avalon's long-run decision riskier than its short-run decision?

**23  The Sunk-Cost Fallacy**

You have good tickets to a football game an hour's drive away. There's a storm raging outside, and the game is being televised. You can sit warm and safe at home and watch it on TV, or you can bundle up and go to the game. What do you do?

Source: *Slate*, 9 September 2005

**a** What type of cost is your expenditure on tickets?

**b** Why is the cost of the ticket irrelevant to your current decision about whether to stay at home or go to the game?

## Short-run Technology Constraint

**24**  Terri runs a rose farm. One worker produces 1,000 roses a week; hiring a second worker doubles her total product; hiring a third worker doubles her output again; hiring a fourth worker increases her total product but by only 1,000 roses. Construct Terri's marginal product and average product schedules. Over what range of workers do marginal returns increase?

## Short-run Cost

**25**  Use the events described in the news clip in Problem 22. By how much will Avalon's short-run decision increase its total variable cost? By how much will Avalon's long-run decision increase its monthly total fixed cost? Sketch Avalon's short-run *ATC* curve before and after the events described in the news clip.

**26  Coffee King Starbucks Raises Its Prices**

Starbucks is raising its prices because the wholesale price of milk has risen 70 per cent and there's a lot of milk in Starbucks' lattes.

Source: *USA Today*, 24 July 2007

Is milk a fixed factor of production or a variable factor of production? Describe how the increase in the price of milk changes Starbucks' short-run cost curves.

**27**  Bill's Bakery has a fire and Bill loses some of his cost data. The bits of paper that he recovers after the fire provide the data in the following table (all the cost numbers are euros).

| TP | AFC | AVC | ATC | MC |
|----|-----|-----|-----|-----|
| 10 | 120 | 100 | 220 | |
| | | | | 80 |
| 20 | *A* | *B* | 150 | |
| | | | | 90 |
| 30 | 40 | 90 | 130 | |
| | | | | 130 |
| 40 | 30 | *C* | *D* | |
| | | | | *E* |
| 50 | 24 | 108 | 132 | |

Bill asks you to come to his rescue and provide the missing data in the five spaces identified as *A*, *B*, *C*, *D* and *E*.

Use the following table to work Problems 28 and 29.

ProPainters hires students at €250 a week to paint houses. It leases equipment at €500 a week. The table sets out its total product schedule.

| Labour (workers per week) | Output (houses painted per week) |
|:---:|:---:|
| 1 | 2 |
| 2 | 5 |
| 3 | 9 |
| 4 | 12 |
| 5 | 14 |
| 6 | 15 |

**28**  If ProPainters paints 12 houses a week, calculate its total cost, average total cost and marginal cost. At what output is average total cost a minimum?

**29**  Explain why the gap between ProPainters' total cost and total variable cost is the same no matter how many houses are painted.

## Long-run Cost

Use the table in Problem 28 and the following information to work Problems 30 and 31.

If ProPainters doubles the number of students it hires and doubles the amount of equipment it leases, it experiences diseconomies of scale.

**30** Explain how the *ATC* curve with one unit of equipment differs from that when ProPainters uses double the amount of equipment.

**31** Explain what might be the source of the diseconomies of scale that ProPainters experiences.

Use the following information to work Problems 32 and 33.

The table shows the production function of Bonnie's Balloon Rides. Bonnie's pays $500 a day for each balloon it rents and $25 a day for each balloon operator it hires.

| Labour (workers per day) | Output (rides per day) | | | |
|---|---|---|---|---|
| | Plant 1 | Plant 2 | Plant 3 | Plant 4 |
| 1 | 6 | 10 | 13 | 15 |
| 2 | 10 | 15 | 18 | 21 |
| 3 | 13 | 18 | 22 | 24 |
| 4 | 15 | 20 | 24 | 26 |
| 5 | 16 | 21 | 25 | 27 |
| Balloons (number) | 1 | 2 | 3 | 4 |

**32** Graph the *ATC* curves for Plant 1 and Plant 2. Explain why these *ATC* curves differ.

**33** Graph the *ATC* curves for Plant 3 and Plant 4. Explain why these *ATC* curves differ.

**34 a** On Bonnie's *LRAC* curve, what is the average cost of producing 18 rides and 15 rides a day?

   **b** Explain how Bonnie's uses its long-run average cost curve to decide how many balloons to rent.

Use the following news clip to work Problems 35 and 36.

**Gap Will Focus on Smaller Scale Stores**

Gap has too many stores that are 12,500 square feet. The target store size is 6,000 square feet to 10,000 square feet, so Gap plans to combine previously separate concept stores. Some Gap body, adult, maternity, baby and kids stores will be combined in one store.

Source: CNN, 10 June 2008

**35** Thinking of a Gap store as a production plant, explain why Gap is making a decision to reduce the size of its stores. Is Gap's decision a long-run decision or a short-run decision?

**36** How might combining Gap's concept stores into one store help better take advantage of economies of scale?

## Economics in the News

**37** After you have studied the *Business Case Study* on pp. 144–145 answer the following questions.

   **a** For each of the costs described in the news article, explain whether the cost is fixed or variable.

   **b** Explain how introducing the new A320 aircraft is likely to affect *AFC*, *AVC*, *ATC* and *MC* for easyJet. Sketch a graph to illustrate your answer.

   **c** Use the concepts of *AVC*, *MC* and *ATC* to explain why low cost carriers like easyJet can sell some tickets for prices as low as £10.

**38 Self-serve Espresso Bars**

Automated, self-service espresso kiosks are now being introduced in some stores. The machines can grind beans and deliver latte and espresso coffee and take credit and debit cards and cash. The kiosks cost €40,000 per unit, but must be installed and maintained. Self-service kiosks remove the labour costs for service. The kiosks must be refilled by store staff with coffee beans and milk.

Source: MSNBC, 1 June 2008

   **a** What is the total fixed cost of operating one self-service kiosk?

   **b** What are the variable costs of providing coffee at a self-service kiosk?

   **c** Assume that a coffee machine in a traditional service cafe costs less than €40,000. Explain how the fixed costs, variable costs and total costs of traditionally served and self-served coffee differ.

   **d** Sketch the marginal cost and average cost curves implied by your answer to part (c).

**39** The cost of producing electricity using hydro power is about one-third of the cost of using coal, oil or nuclear power plants and is less than one-quarter the cost of using gas turbine plants. Most of the cost differences come from differences in fuel costs. But part of the cost difference comes from differences in plant costs. It costs less to build a hydroelectric plant than a coal, oil or nuclear plant. Gas turbine plants cost the least to build but are the most expensive to operate.

(Based on *Projected Costs of Generating Electricity*, International Energy Agency, 2005)

   **a** Use the above information to sketch the *AFC*, *AVC* and *ATC* curves for electricity production using three technologies: (i) hydro, (ii) coal, oil or nuclear and (iii) gas turbine.

   **b** Use the above information to sketch the marginal cost curves for electricity production using three technologies: (i) hydro, (ii) coal, oil or nuclear and (iii) gas turbine.

   **c** Given the cost differences among the three methods of generating electricity, why do we use more than one?

# CHAPTER
# 7

# Competitive Markets

**After studying this chapter you will be able to:**

◆ Define perfect competition

◆ Explain how a firm makes its output decision and why it sometimes shuts down temporarily

◆ Explain how price and output are determined in a perfectly competitive market

◆ Explain why firms enter and exit a perfectly competitive market and the consequences of entry and exit

◆ Predict the effects of a change in demand and of a technological advance

◆ Explain why perfect competition is efficient

You might be relaxing over a cup of coffee, but coffee shops operate in a fiercely competitive market with lean pickings for most owners. Competition is also fierce in other markets that affect your life, such as personal computers and mobile phones, where prices have tumbled. Agricultural markets, such as the market for tea that you will encounter in *Reading Between the Lines*, are also competitive. What determines prices and profits of firms that operate in a competitive market? Why do firms enter or leave a competitive market? Why do firms sometimes shut down and lay off their workers? Is fierce competition efficient? We answer these questions in this chapter.

**What Is Perfect Competition?**

The firms that you study in this chapter face the force of raw competition. This type of extreme competition is called perfect competition. **Perfect competition** is a market in which:

1 Many firms sell identical products to many buyers.
2 There are no restrictions on entry into the market.
3 Established firms have no advantage over new ones.
4 Sellers and buyers are well informed about prices.

Farming, fishing, paper milling, the manufacture of paper cups, grocery retailing, plumbing and dry cleaning are examples of highly competitive industries.

## How Perfect Competition Arises

Perfect competition arises if the firm's minimum efficient scale is small relative to the market demand for the good. In this situation, there is room for many firms in the industry. A firm's *minimum efficient scale* is the smallest quantity of output at which long-run average cost reaches its lowest level. (See Chapter 6, p. 143.)

In perfect competition, each firm produces a good or service that has no unique characteristics, so consumers don't care which firm's good they buy.

## Price Takers

Firms in perfect competition are price takers. A **price taker** is a firm that cannot influence the market price because its production is an insignificant part of the total market.

Imagine you are a wheat farmer with a hundred hectares under cultivation, which sounds like a lot. But when compared to the millions of hectares in Ukraine, Canada, Australia, Argentina and the US, your hundred hectares is a drop in the ocean. Nothing makes your wheat any better than any other farmer's and all the buyers of wheat know the price at which they can do business.

If the market price of wheat is £85 a tonne and you ask £90 a tonne, no one will buy from you. People can go to the next farmer and the next and the one after that and buy all they need for £85 a tonne. If you set your price at £84 a tonne, you'll have lots of buyers. But you can sell all your output for £85 a tonne, so you're just giving away £1 a tonne. You can do no better than sell for the market price – you are a *price taker*.

## Economic Profit and Revenue

A firm's goal is to maximize **economic profit**, which is equal to total revenue minus total cost. Total cost is the *opportunity cost* of production, which includes **normal profits** – the return to entrepreneurship.

A firm's **total revenue** equals the price of its output multiplied by the quantity sold (price × quantity). **Marginal revenue** is the change in total revenue that results from a one-unit increase in the quantity sold. Marginal revenue is calculated by dividing the change in total revenue by the change in the quantity sold.

Figure 7.1 illustrates these concepts in the market for jumpers. In part (a), the market demand curve, *D*, and the market supply curve, *S*, determine the market price. The market price is £25 a jumper. Fashion First is just one of many producers of jumpers, so the best that it can do is to sell its jumpers for £25 each.

### Total Revenue

Total revenue is equal to the price multiplied by the quantity sold. In the table in Figure 7.1, if Fashion First sells 9 jumpers, the firm's total revenue is 9 × £25, which equals £225.

Figure 7.1(b) shows the firm's total revenue curve (*TR*), which graphs the relationship between total revenue and quantity sold. At point *A* on the *TR* curve, Fashion First sells 9 jumpers and has total revenue of £225. Because each additional jumper sold brings in a constant amount – £25 – the total revenue curve is an upward-sloping straight line.

### Marginal Revenue

Marginal revenue is the change in total revenue that results from a one-unit increase in quantity sold. In the table in Figure 7.1, when the quantity sold increases from 8 to 9 jumpers, total revenue increases from £200 to £225, so marginal revenue is £25 a jumper.

Because the firm in perfect competition is a price taker, the change in total revenue that results from a one-unit increase in the quantity sold equals market price. In *perfect competition, the firm's marginal revenue equals the market price*. Figure 7.1(c) shows Fashion First's marginal revenue curve (*MR*), which is a horizontal line at the market price.

### Demand for the Firm's Product

The firm can sell any quantity it chooses at the market price. So the demand curve for the firm's product is a

**Figure 7.1** Demand, Price and Revenue in Perfect Competition

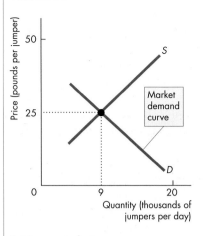

**(a) Jumper industry**

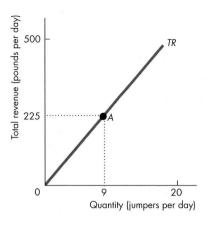

**(b) Fashion First's total revenue**

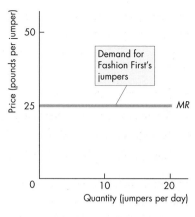

**(c) Fashion First's marginal revenue**

| Quantity sold (Q) (jumpers per day) | Price (P) (pounds per jumper) | Total revenue (TR = P × Q) (pounds) | Marginal revenue (MR = ΔTR/ΔQ) (pounds per jumper) |
|---|---|---|---|
| 8 | 25 | 200 | |
| | | | 25 |
| 9 | 25 | 225 | |
| | | | 25 |
| 10 | 25 | 250 | |

In part (a), market demand and market supply determine the market price (and quantity). Part (b) shows Fashion First's total revenue curve (*TR*). Point *A* corresponds to the second row of the table – Fashion First sells 9 jumpers at £25 a jumper, so total revenue is £225. Part (c) shows Fashion First's marginal revenue curve (*MR*). This curve is the demand curve for jumpers produced by Fashion First. Fashion First faces a perfectly elastic demand for its jumpers at the market price of £25 a jumper.

horizontal line at the market price, the same as the firm's marginal revenue curve.

A horizontal demand curve illustrates a perfectly elastic demand, so the demand for the firm's output is perfectly elastic. One of Fashion First's jumpers is a *perfect substitute* for jumpers from the factory next door or from any other factory. But the *market* demand for jumpers is *not* perfectly elastic. Its elasticity depends on the substitutability of jumpers for other goods and services.

## The Firm's Decisions

The goal of the competitive firm is to maximize economic profit, given the constraints it faces. To achieve its goal, a firm must decide:

1 How to produce at minimum cost

2 What quantity to produce

3 Whether to enter or exit a market

You've already seen how a firm makes the first decision. It does so by operating with the plant that minimizes long-run average cost – by being on its long-run average cost curve. We'll now see how the firm makes the other two decisions. We start by looking at the firm's output decision.

### Review Quiz

1 Why is a firm in perfect competition a price taker?
2 In perfect competition, what is the relationship between the demand for the firm's output and the market demand?
3 In perfect competition, why is a firm's marginal revenue curve also the demand curve for the firm's output?
4 What decisions must a firm make to maximize profit?

You can work these questions in Study Plan 7.1 and get instant feedback.

## The Firm's Output Decision

A firm's cost curves (total cost, average cost, and marginal cost) describe the relationship between its output and costs (see Chapter 6, pp. 135–139). And a firm's revenue curves (total revenue and marginal revenue) describe the relationship between its output and revenue (p. 153). From the firm's cost curves and revenue curves, we can find the output that maximizes the firm's economic profit.

Figure 7.2 shows you how to do this for Fashion First. The table lists Fashion First's total revenue and total cost at different outputs, and part (a) of the figure shows its total revenue curve (*TR*) and total cost curve

(*TC*). These curves are graphs of the numbers shown in the first three columns of the table.

Economic profit equals total revenue minus total cost. The fourth column of the table in Figure 7.2 shows economic profit made by Fashion First and part (b) of the figure graphs these numbers as its economic profit curve (*EP*).

Fashion First maximizes economic profit by producing 9 jumpers a day. Total revenue is £225, total cost is £183 and economic profit is £42. No other output rate achieves a larger profit. At outputs of less than 4 jumpers and more than 12 jumpers a day, Fashion First would incur an economic loss. At either 4 or 12 jumpers a day, Fashion First would make zero economic profit, called a *break-even* point.

**Figure 7.2    Total Revenue, Total Cost and Economic Profit**

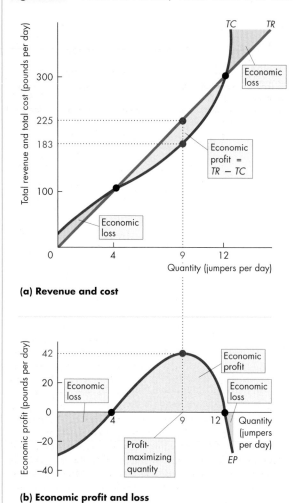

**(a) Revenue and cost**

**(b) Economic profit and loss**

| Quantity (*Q*) (jumpers per day) | Total revenue (*TR*) (pounds) | Total cost (*TC*) (pounds) | Economic profit (*TR* – *TC*) (pounds) |
|---|---|---|---|
| 0 | 0 | 22 | –22 |
| 1 | 25 | 45 | –20 |
| 2 | 50 | 66 | –16 |
| 3 | 75 | 85 | –10 |
| 4 | 100 | 100 | 0 |
| 5 | 125 | 114 | 11 |
| 6 | 150 | 126 | 24 |
| 7 | 175 | 141 | 34 |
| 8 | 200 | 160 | 40 |
| **9** | **225** | **183** | **42** |
| 10 | 250 | 210 | 40 |
| 11 | 275 | 245 | 30 |
| 12 | 300 | 300 | 0 |
| 13 | 325 | 360 | –35 |

The table lists Fashion First's total revenue, total cost and economic profit. Part (a) graphs the total revenue and total cost curves and part (b) graphs economic profit. Fashion First makes maximum economic profit, £42 a day (£225 – £183), when it produces 9 jumpers. At outputs of 4 jumpers a day and 12 jumpers a day, Fashion First makes zero economic profit – these are break-even points. At outputs less than 4 and greater than 12 jumpers a day, Fashion First incurs an economic loss.

 myeconlab Animation

# Marginal Analysis

Another way of finding the profit-maximizing output is to use *marginal analysis*, by comparing marginal revenue, *MR*, with marginal cost, *MC*. As output increases, marginal revenue remains constant but marginal cost changes. At low output levels, marginal cost decreases as output increases but eventually marginal cost increases.

If marginal revenue exceeds marginal cost (if *MR* > *MC*), then the extra revenue from selling one more unit exceeds the extra cost incurred to produce it. The firm makes an economic profit on the marginal unit, so economic profit increases if output *increases*.

If marginal revenue is less than marginal cost (if *MR* < *MC*), then the extra revenue from selling one more unit is less than the extra cost incurred to produce it. The firm incurs an economic loss on the marginal unit, so its economic profit decreases if output increases and its economic profit increases if output *decreases*.

If marginal revenue equals marginal cost (*MR* = *MC*), the firm makes maximum economic profit. The rule *MR* = *MC* is an example of marginal analysis.

Figure 7.3 illustrates these propositions. If Fashion First increases output from 8 jumpers to 9 jumpers, marginal revenue (£25) exceeds marginal cost (£23), so by producing the ninth jumper economic profit increases by £2 from £40 to £42 a day. The blue area in the figure shows the increase in economic profit when the firm increases production from 8 to 9 jumpers a day.

If Fashion First increases output from 9 jumpers to 10 jumpers, marginal revenue (£25) is less than marginal cost (£27), so by producing the tenth jumper, economic profit decreases. The red area in the figure shows the economic loss that arises from increasing production from 9 to 10 jumpers a day.

Fashion First maximizes economic profit by producing 9 jumpers a day, the quantity at which marginal revenue equals marginal cost.

A firm's profit-maximizing output is its quantity supplied at the market price. The quantity supplied at a price of £25 a jumper is 9 jumpers a day. If the price were higher than £25 a jumper, the firm would increase production. If the price were lower than £25 a jumper, the firm would decrease production. These profit-maximizing responses to different market prices are the foundation of the law of supply:

**Other things remaining the same, the higher the market price of a good, the greater is the quantity supplied of that good.**

**Figure 7.3** Profit-maximizing Output

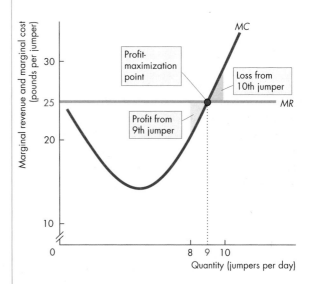

| Quantity (Q) (jumpers per day) | Total revenue (TR) (pounds) | Marginal revenue (MR) (pounds per jumper) | Total cost (TC) (pounds) | Marginal cost (MC) (pounds per jumper) | Economic profit (TR – TC) (pounds) |
|---|---|---|---|---|---|
| 7 | 175 | | 141 | | 34 |
| | | ........ 25 | | ........ 19 | |
| 8 | 200 | | 160 | | 40 |
| | | ........ 25 | | ........ 23 | |
| **9** | **225** | | **183** | | **42** |
| | | ........ 25 | | ........ 27 | |
| 10 | 250 | | 210 | | 40 |
| | | ........ 25 | | ........ 35 | |
| 11 | 275 | | 245 | | 30 |

Another way of finding the profit-maximizing output is to determine the output at which marginal revenue equals marginal cost. The table and figure show that marginal cost and marginal revenue are equal when Fashion First produces 9 jumpers a day. The table shows that if output increases from 8 to 9 jumpers, marginal cost is £23, which is less than the marginal revenue of £25. If output increases from 9 to 10 jumpers, marginal cost is £27, which exceeds the marginal revenue of £25. If marginal revenue exceeds marginal cost, an increase in output increases economic profit. If marginal revenue is less than marginal cost, an increase in output decreases economic profit. If marginal revenue equals marginal cost, economic profit is maximized.

 Animation

## Temporary Shutdown Decision

You've seen that a firm maximizes profit by producing the quantity at which marginal revenue (price) equals marginal cost. But suppose that at this quantity, price is less than average total cost. In this case, the firm incurs an economic loss. Maximum profit is a loss (a minimum loss). What does the firm do?

If the firm expects the loss to be permanent, it goes out of business. But if it expects the loss to be temporary, the firm must decide whether to shut down temporarily and produce no output, or to keep producing. To make this decision, the firm compares the loss from shutting down with the loss from producing and takes the action that minimizes its loss.

### Loss Comparisons

A firm's economic loss equals total fixed cost, *TFC*, plus total variable cost minus total revenue. Total variable cost equals average variable cost, *AVC*, multiplied by the quantity produced, *Q*, and total revenue equals price, *P*, multiplied by the quantity *Q*. So

$$\text{Economic loss} = TFC + (AVC - P) \times Q.$$

If the firm shuts down, it produces no output ($Q = 0$). The firm has no variable costs and no revenue, but it must pay its fixed costs, so its economic loss equals total fixed cost.

If the firm produces, then in addition to its fixed costs, it incurs variable costs. But it also receives revenue. Its economic loss equals total fixed cost – the loss when shut down – plus total variable cost minus total revenue. If total variable cost exceeds total revenue, this loss exceeds total fixed cost and the firm shuts down. Equivalently, if average variable cost *exceeds* price, this loss exceeds total fixed cost and the firm *shuts down*.

### The Shutdown Point

A firm's **shutdown point** is the price and quantity at which it is indifferent between producing and shutting down. The shutdown point occurs at the price and the quantity at which average variable cost is a minimum. At the shutdown point, the firm is minimizing its loss and its loss equals total fixed cost. If the price falls below minimum average variable cost, the firm shuts down temporarily and incurs a loss equal to total fixed cost. At prices above minimum average variable cost but below average total cost, the firm produces the loss-minimizing output and incurs a loss that is less than total fixed cost.

Figure 7.4 illustrates the firm's shutdown decision and the shutdown point that we've just described for Fashion First.

The firm's average variable cost curve is *AVC* and the marginal cost curve is *MC*. Average variable cost has a minimum of £17 a jumper when output is 7 jumpers a day. The *MC* curve intersects the *AVC* curve at its minimum. (We explained this relationship between marginal cost and average cost in Chapter 6; see p. 136.)

The figure shows the marginal revenue curve *MR* when the price is £17 a jumper, a price equal to minimum average variable cost.

Marginal revenue equals marginal cost at 7 jumpers a day, so this quantity maximizes economic profit (minimizes economic loss). The *ATC* curve shows that the firm's average total cost of producing 7 jumpers a day is £20.14 a jumper. The firm incurs a loss equal to £3.14 a jumper on 7 jumpers a day, so its loss is £22 a day, which equals total fixed cost.

**Figure 7.4** The Shutdown Decision

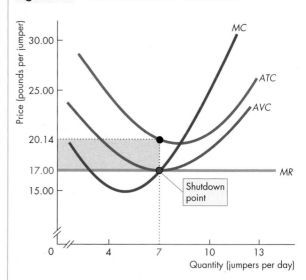

The shutdown point is at minimum average variable cost. At a price below minimum average variable cost, the firm shuts down and produces no output. At a price equal to minimum average variable cost, the firm is indifferent between shutting down and producing no output or producing the output at minimum average variable cost. Either way, the firm minimizes its economic loss. The area of the red rectangle shows that at the shutdown point the economic loss equals total fixed cost.

myeconlab Animation

# The Firm's Short-run Supply Curve

A perfectly competitive firm's supply curve shows how its profit-maximizing output varies as the market price varies, other things remaining the same. The supply curve is derived from the firm's marginal cost curve and average variable cost curves. Figure 7.5 illustrates the derivation of the supply curve.

When the price *exceeds* minimum average variable cost (more than £17), the firm maximizes profit by producing the output at which marginal cost equals price. If the price rises, the firm increases its output – it moves up along its marginal cost curve.

When the price is *less* than minimum average variable cost (less than £17 a jumper), the firm maximizes profit by temporarily shutting down and producing no output. The firm produces zero output at all prices below minimum average variable cost.

When the price *equals* minimum average variable cost, the firm maximizes profit either by temporarily shutting down and producing no output or by producing the output at which average variable cost is a minimum – the shutdown point, $T$. The firm never produces a quantity between zero and the quantity at the shutdown point $T$ (a quantity greater than zero and less than 7 jumpers a day).

The firm's supply curve in Figure 7.5(b) runs along the $y$-axis from a price of zero to a price equal to minimum average variable cost, jumps to point $T$, and then, as the price rises above minimum average variable cost, follows the marginal cost curve.

### Review Quiz

1   Why does a firm in perfect competition produce the quantity at which marginal cost equals price?
2   What is the lowest price at which a firm produces an output? Explain why.
3   What is the relationship between a firm's supply curve, its marginal cost curve, and its average variable cost curve?

You can work these questions in Study Plan 7.2 and get instant feedback.     myeconlab

So far, we've studied a single firm in isolation. We've seen that the firm's profit-maximizing decision depends on the market price, which it takes as given. How is the market price determined? Let's find out.

**Figure 7.5**   A Firm's Supply Curve

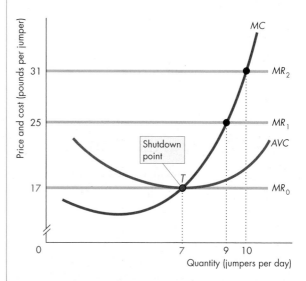

**(a) Marginal cost and average variable cost**

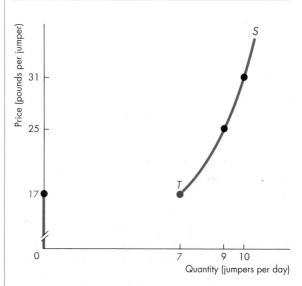

**(b) Fashion First's supply curve**

Part (a) shows Fashion First's profit-maximizing output at each market price. At £25 a jumper, Fashion First produces 9 jumpers. At £17 a jumper, Fashion First produces 7 jumpers. At any price below £17 a jumper, Fashion First produces nothing. Fashion First's shutdown point is $T$.

Part (b) shows Fashion First's supply curve – the quantity of jumpers it will produce at each price. It is made up of the marginal cost curve at all points above minimum average variable cost and the $y$-axis at all prices below minimum average variable cost.

myeconlab Animation

# Output, Price and Profit in the Short Run

To determine the price and quantity in a perfectly competitive market, we need to know how market demand and market supply interact. We start by studying a perfectly competitive market in the short run. The short run is a situation in which the number of firms is fixed.

## Market Supply in the Short Run

The **short-run market supply curve** shows the quantity supplied by all the firms in the market at each price when each firm's plant and the number of firms in the market remain the same.

You've seen how an individual firm's supply curve is determined. The market supply curve is derived from the supply curves of all the individual firms. The quantity supplied by the market at a given price is the sum of the quantities supplied by all the firms in the market at that price.

Figure 7.6 shows the supply curve for the competitive jumper industry. In this example, the industry consists of 1,000 firms exactly like Fashion First. At each price, the quantity supplied by the industry is 1,000 times the quantity supplied by a single firm.

The table in Figure 7.6 shows Fashion First's and the market's supply schedules and how the market supply curve is constructed. At prices below £17 a jumper, every firm in the market shuts down and produces nothing. The quantity supplied by the market is zero. At a price of £17 a jumper, each firm is indifferent between shutting down and producing nothing or producing 7 jumpers a day. Some firms will shut down and others will produce 7 jumpers a day. The quantity supplied by each firm is *either* 0 or 7 jumpers, but the quantity supplied by the market is *between* 0 (all firms shut down) and 7,000 (all firms produce 7 jumpers a day each).

The market supply curve is a graph of the market supply schedule and the points A to D on the supply curve represent the rows of the table.

To construct the market supply curve, we sum the quantities supplied by all firms at each price. Each of the 1,000 firms in the market has a supply schedule like Fashion First's.

At prices below £17 a jumper, the market supply curve runs along the *y*-axis. At a price of £17 a jumper, the market supply curve is horizontal – supply is perfectly elastic. As the price rises above £17 a jumper,

**Figure 7.6** Short-run Market Supply Curve

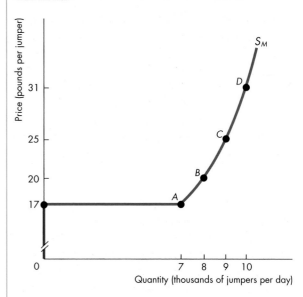

| | Price (pounds per jumper) | Quantity supplied by Fashion First (jumpers per day) | Quantity supplied by market (jumpers per day) |
|---|---|---|---|
| A | 17 | 0 or 7 | 0 to 7,000 |
| B | 20 | 8 | 8,000 |
| C | 25 | 9 | 9,000 |
| D | 31 | 10 | 10,000 |

The market supply schedule is the sum of the supply schedules of all individual firms. A market that consists of 1,000 identical firms has a supply schedule similar to that of the individual firm, but the quantity supplied by the market is 1,000 times as large as that of the individual firm (see the table).

The market supply curve is $S_M$. Points A, B, C and D correspond to the rows of the table. At the shutdown price of £17, each firm produces either 0 or 7 jumpers per day. The market produces between 0 and 7,000 jumpers a day. The market supply is perfectly elastic at the shutdown price.

**myeconlab** Animation

each firm increases its quantity supplied and the quantity supplied by the market increases by 1,000 times that of an individual firm. Figure 7.6 shows the market supply curve $S_M$.

## Short-run Equilibrium

Market demand and market supply determine market price and market output. Figure 7.7 shows the short-run equilibrium. The short-run supply curve, $S$, is the same as $S_M$ in Figure 7.6. If the market demand curve is $D_1$, the equilibrium price is £20 a jumper. Each firm takes this price as given and produces its profit-maximizing output, which is 8 jumpers a day. Because the market has 1,000 firms, the market output is 8,000 jumpers a day.

## A Change in Demand

Changes in market demand bring changes to short-run market equilibrium. Figure 7.7 shows these changes.

If the market demand increases and the demand curve shifts rightward to $D_2$, the price rises to £25 a jumper. At this price, each firm maximizes profit by increasing its output. The new output is 9 jumpers a day for each firm and 9,000 jumpers a day for the industry.

If demand decreases and the demand curve shifts leftward to $D_3$, the price falls to £17. At this price, each firm

maximizes profit by decreasing its output. If each firm produces 7 jumpers a day, the market output decreases to 7,000 jumpers a day.

If the demand curve shifts further leftward than $D_3$, the market price remains constant at £17 because the market supply curve is horizontal at that price. Some firms continue to produce 7 jumpers a day and others temporarily shut down. Firms are indifferent between these two activities, and whichever they choose, they incur an economic loss equal to total fixed cost. The number of firms continuing to produce is just enough to satisfy the market demand at a price of £17 a jumper.

## Profits and Losses in the Short Run

In short-run equilibrium, although the firm produces the profit-maximizing output, it does not necessarily end up making an economic profit. It might do so, but it might alternatively break even (make zero economic profit) or incur an economic loss.

Economic profit (or loss) per jumper is price, $P$, minus average total cost, $ATC$. So the firm's economic profit (loss) is $(P - ATC) \times Q$. If price equals average

**Figure 7.7** Short-run Equilibrium

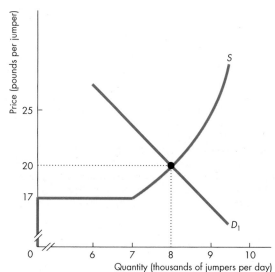

**(a) Equilibrium**

In part (a), the market supply curve is $S$, the market demand curve is $D_1$ and the market price is £20 a jumper. At this price, each firm produces 8 jumpers a day and the market produces 8,000 jumpers a day.

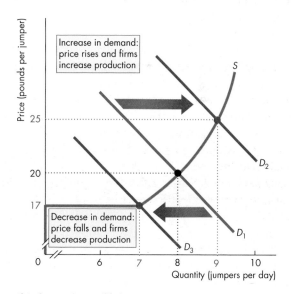

**(b) Change in equilibrium**

In part (b), when the market demand increases to $D_2$, the price rises to £25. Each firm increases its output to 9 jumpers a day and the market output is 9,000 jumpers a day. If demand decreases to $D_3$, the price falls to £17 and each firm decreases its output to 7 jumpers a day. The market output is 7,000 jumpers a day.

total cost, a firm breaks even – makes zero economic profit. The entrepreneur makes normal profit. If price exceeds average total cost, a firm makes an economic profit. If price is less than average total cost, the firm incurs an economic loss. Figure 7.8 shows these three possible short-run profit outcomes for Fashion First. These outcomes correspond to the three levels of market demand that we've just examined.

## Three Possible Short-run Outcomes

Figure 7.8(a) corresponds to the situation in Figure 7.7(b) where the market demand is $D_1$. The equilibrium price of a jumper is £20 and Fashion First produces 8 jumpers a day. Average total cost is £20 a jumper. Price equals average total cost ($ATC$), so Fashion First breaks even (makes zero economic profit).

Figure 7.8(b) corresponds to the situation in Figure 7.7(b) where the market demand is $D_2$. The equilibrium price of a jumper is £25. Fashion First maximizes profit by producing 9 jumpers a day. Here, price exceeds average total cost, so Fashion First makes an economic profit. Economic profit is £42 a day. It is made up of £4.67 a jumper (£25.00 – £20.33), multiplied by 9, the profit-maximizing number of jumpers produced. The

blue rectangle shows this economic profit. The height of the rectangle is profit per jumper, £4.67, and the length is the quantity of jumpers produced, 9 a day, so the area of the rectangle measures Fashion First's economic profit of £42 a day.

Figure 7.8(c) corresponds to the situation in Figure 7.7(b) where the market demand is $D_3$. The equilibrium price of a jumper is £17. Here, price is less than average total cost and Fashion First incurs an economic loss. Price and marginal revenue are £17 a jumper, and the profit-maximizing (in this case, loss-minimizing) output is 7 jumpers a day. Total revenue is £119 a day (7 × £17). Fashion First's average total cost is £20.14 a jumper, so its economic loss per jumper is £3.14 (£20.14 – £17.00). Fashion First's economic loss equals this loss per jumper multiplied by the number of jumpers (£3.14 × 7), which equals £22 a day. The red rectangle shows this economic loss. The height of that rectangle is economic loss per jumper, £3.14, and the length is the quantity of jumpers produced, 7 a day, so the area of the rectangle is Fashion First's economic loss of £22 a day. If the price dips below £17 a jumper, the firm temporarily shuts down and incurs an economic loss equal to total fixed cost.

**Figure 7.8    Three Short-run Outcomes for the Firm**

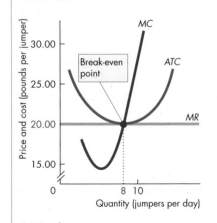    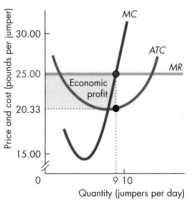    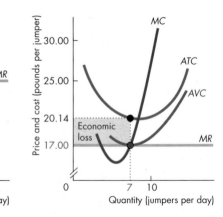

**(a) Break-even**                    **(b) Economic profit**                    **(c) Economic loss**

In the short run, the firm might break even (make zero economic profit), make an economic profit or incur an economic loss. In part (a), the price equals minimum average total cost. At the profit-maximizing output, the firm breaks even and makes zero economic profit. In part (b), the market price is £25 a jumper. At the profit-

maximizing output, the price exceeds the average total cost and the firm makes an economic profit equal to the area of the blue rectangle. In part (c), the market price is £17 a jumper. At the profit-maximizing output, the price is below minimum average total cost and the firm incurs an economic loss equal to the area of the red rectangle.

## Production Cutback and Temporary Shutdown

The high price of petrol and anxiety about unemployment and future incomes brought a decrease in the demand for luxury goods including large luxury cars made by Honda in the UK.

Honda's profit-maximizing response to the decrease in demand was to cut production and lay off workers. Some of the production cuts and layoffs were temporary and some were permanent.

Honda's UK production plant in Swindon was temporarily shut down for four months in 2009 because total revenue was insufficient to cover total variable cost.

The firm also cut its workforce by 1,300 people. This cut was like that at Fashion First when the market demand for jumpers decreased from $D_1$ to $D_3$ in Figure 7.7(b).

### Review Quiz

1  How do we derive the short-run market supply curve in perfect competition?
2  In perfect competition, when market demand increases, explain how the price of the good and the output and profit of each firm change in the short run.
3  In perfect competition, when market demand decreases, explain how the price of the good and the output and profit of each firm change in the short run.

You can work these questions in Study Plan 7.3 and get instant feedback.

## Output, Price and Profit in the Long Run

In short-run equilibrium, a firm might make an economic profit, incur an economic loss or break even. Although each of these three situations is a short-run equilibrium, only one of them is a long-run equilibrium. To see why, we need to examine the forces at work in a competitive market in the long run. The reason is that in the long run, firms can enter or exit the market.

### Entry and Exit

Entry occurs in a market when new firms come into the market and the number of firms increases. Exit occurs when existing firms leave a market and the number of firms decreases.

Firms respond to economic profit and economic loss by either entering or exiting a market. New firms enter a market in which existing firms are making an economic profit. Firms exit a market in which they are incurring an economic loss. Temporary economic profit and temporary economic loss don't trigger entry and exit. It's the prospect of persistent economic profit or loss that triggers entry and exit.

Entry and exit change the market supply, which influences the market price, the quantity produced by each firm, and its economic profit (or loss).

If firms enter a market, supply increases and the market supply curve shifts rightward. The increase in supply lowers the market price and eventually eliminates economic profit. When economic profit reaches zero, entry stops.

If firms exit a market, supply decreases and the market supply curve shifts leftward. The market price rises and economic loss decreases. Eventually, economic loss is eliminated and exit stops.

To summarize:

◆ New firms enter a market in which existing firms are making an economic profit.

◆ As new firms enter a market, the market price falls and the economic profit of each firm decreases.

◆ Firms exit a market in which they are incurring an economic loss.

◆ As firms exit a market, the market price rises and the economic loss incurred by the remaining firms decreases.

◆ Entry and exit stop when firms make zero economic profit.

## A Closer Look at Entry

The jumper market has 800 firms with cost curves like those in Figure 7.9(a). The market demand curve is $D$, the market supply curve is $S_1$, and the price is £25 a jumper in Figure 7.9(b). Each firm produces 9 jumpers a day and makes an economic profit.

This economic profit is a signal for new firms to enter the market. As entry takes place, supply increases and the market supply curve shifts rightward towards $S^*$. As supply increases with no change in demand, the market price gradually falls from £25 to £20 a jumper. At this lower price, each firm makes zero economic profit and entry stops.

Entry results in an increase in market output, but each firm's output decreases. Because the price falls, each firm moves down its supply curve and produces less. Because the number of firms increases, the market produces more.

## A Closer Look at Exit

The jumper market has 1,200 firms with cost curves like those in Figure 7.9(a). The market demand curve is $D$, the market supply curve is $S_2$, and the price is £17 a jumper in Figure 7.9(b). Each firm produces 7 jumpers a day and incurs an economic loss.

This economic loss is a signal for firms to exit the market. As exit takes place, supply decreases and the market supply curve shifts leftward towards $S^*$. As supply decreases with no change in demand, the market price gradually rises from £17 to £20 a jumper. At this higher price, losses are eliminated, each firm makes zero economic profit and exit stops.

Exit results in a decrease in market output, but each firm's output increases. Because the price rises, each firm moves up its supply curve and produces more. Because the number of firms decreases, the market produces less.

---

### Figure 7.9  Entry, Exit and Long-run Equilibrium

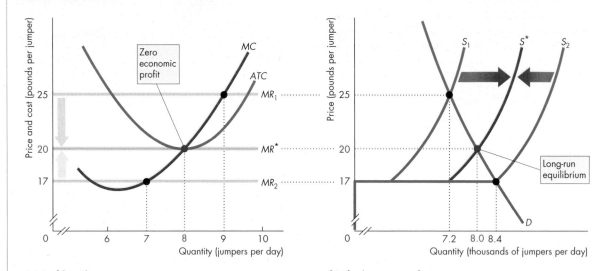

**(a) Fashion First**

**(b) The jumper market**

Each firm has cost curves like those of Fashion First in part (a). The market demand curve is $D$ in part (b).

When the market supply curve in part (b) is $S_1$, the price is £25 a jumper. In part (a), each firm produces 9 jumpers a day and makes an economic profit. Profit triggers the entry of new firms and as new firms enter, the market supply curve shifts rightward, from $S_1$ towards $S^*$. The price falls from £25 to £20 a jumper, and the quantity produced increases from 7,200 to 8,000 jumpers. Each

firm's output decreases to 8 jumpers a day and economic profit falls to zero.

When the market supply curve is $S_2$, the price is £17 a jumper. In part (a), each firm produces 7 jumpers a day and incurs an economic loss. Loss triggers exit and as firms exit, the market supply curve shifts leftward, from $S_2$ towards $S^*$. The price rises from £17 to £20 a jumper, and the quantity produced decreases from 8,400 to 8,000 jumpers. Each firm's output increases from 7 to 8 jumpers a day and economic profit rises to zero.

## Entry and Exit

An example of entry and falling prices occurred during the 1980s and 1990s in the personal computer market. When IBM introduced its first PC in 1981, IBM had little competition. The price was $7,000 (about $16,850 in today's money) and IBM made a large economic profit selling the new machine.

Observing IBM's huge success, new firms such as Gateway, NEC, Dell and a host of others entered the market with machines that were technologically identical to IBM's. In fact, they were so similar that they came to be called 'clones'. The massive wave of entry into the personal computer market increased the market supply and lowered the price. The economic profit for all firms decreased.

Today, a £300 computer is vastly more powerful than its 1981 ancestor that cost 42 times as much. The same PC market that saw entry during the 1980s and 1990s has experienced some exit more recently.

In 2001, IBM, the firm that first launched the PC, announced that it was exiting the market. The intense competition from Gateway, NEC, Dell and others that entered the market following IBM's lead has lowered the price and eliminated the economic profit. So IBM now concentrates on servers and other parts of the computer market.

IBM exited the PC market because it was incurring economic losses. Its exit decreased market supply and made it possible for the remaining firms in the market to make zero economic profit.

Whitbread, which built the first mass brewery in the UK in 1750, is another example of exit. For 250 years, people associated the name Whitbread with brewing beer. But the brewing market became globally competitive, and UK brewing firms suffered economic losses. Whitbread Group plc doesn't make beer any more. After years of shrinking revenues, Whitbread got out of the brewing and pub business in 2001 and is now a profitable hotel and restaurant business with a global coffee brand, Costa Coffee. Whitbread's expansion into its other new business areas increased its profits.

Whitbread exited brewing because it was facing an economic loss. Its exit decreased supply and made it possible for the remaining brewing firms in the market to break even.

## Long-run Equilibrium

You've now seen how economic profit induces entry, which in turn eliminates the profit. You've also seen how economic loss induces exit, which in turn eliminates the loss.

When economic profit and economic loss have been eliminated and entry and exit have stopped, a competitive market is in *long-run equilibrium*.

You've seen how a competitive market adjusts towards its long-run equilibrium. But a competitive market is rarely *in* a state of long-run equilibrium. Instead, it is constantly and restlessly evolving towards long-run equilibrium. The reason is that the market is constantly bombarded with events that change the constraints that firms face.

Markets are constantly adjusting to keep up with changes in tastes, which change demand, and changes in technology, which change costs.

In the next sections, we're going to see how a competitive market reacts to changing tastes and technology and how it guides resources to their highest-valued use.

### Review Quiz

1 What triggers entry in a competitive market? Describe the process that ends further entry.
2 What triggers exit in a competitive market? Describe the process that ends further exit.

You can work these questions in Study Plan 7.4 and get instant feedback.

## Changing Tastes and Advancing Technology

Increased awareness of the health hazard of smoking has decreased the demand for cigarettes. The development of inexpensive cars and air travel has decreased the demand for long-distance trains and buses. Solid-state electronics have decreased the demand for TV and radio repair services. The development of good-quality inexpensive clothing has decreased the demand for sewing machines. What happens in a competitive market when there is a permanent decrease in the market demand for its products?

Advances in video technology have brought a huge increase in the demand for flat panel TV sets. Advances in wireless communication have brought an explosion in the demand for mobile phones. Web services such as MySpace and YouTube have brought a big increase in the demand for broadband Internet service. What happens in a competitive market if the demand for its product increases?

Advances in technology are constantly lowering the costs of production. New biotechnologies have dramatically lowered the costs of producing many food and pharmaceutical products. New electronic technologies have lowered the cost of producing just about every good and service. What happens in a competitive industry when technological change lowers its production costs?

Let's use the theory of perfect competition to answer these questions.

## A Permanent Change in Demand

Figure 7.10(a) shows a market that initially is in long-run competitive equilibrium. The demand curve is $D_0$, the supply curve is $S_0$, the market price is $P_0$ and market output is $Q_0$. Figure 7.10(b) shows a single firm in this initial long-run equilibrium. The firm produces $q_0$ and makes zero economic profit.

Now suppose that demand decreases and the demand curve shifts leftward to $D_1$, as shown in Figure 7.10(a). The market price falls to $P_1$ and the quantity supplied by the market decreases from $Q_0$ to $Q_1$ as the market slides down its short-run supply curve $S_0$.

Figure 7.10(b) shows the situation facing a firm. Price is now below minimum average total cost so the firm incurs an economic loss. But to keep its loss to a minimum, the firm adjusts its output to keep marginal

cost equal to the market price. At a price of $P_1$, each firm produces an output of $q_1$.

The market is now in short-run equilibrium but not long-run equilibrium. It is in short-run equilibrium because each firm is maximizing profit. But it is not in long-run equilibrium because each firm is incurring an economic loss – its average total cost exceeds the market price.

The economic loss is a signal for some firms to exit the market. As they do so, short-run market supply decreases and the supply curve shifts leftward.

As the market supply decreases, the market price rises – as shown by the arrows along the market demand curve $D_1$ in Figure 7.10(a).

At each higher price, a firm's profit-maximizing output is greater, so the firms remaining in the market increase their output as the price rises. Each firm slides up its marginal cost or supply curve in Figure 7.10(b), as shown by the arrows along the $MC$ curve. That is, as some firms exit the market, the output of the market decreases but the output of each firm that remains in the market increases.

Eventually, enough firms exit the market for the market supply curve to have shifted to $S_1$ in Figure 7.10(a). At this time, the price has returned to its original level, $P_0$. At this price, the firms remaining in the market produce $q_0$ in part (b), the same quantity that they produced before the decrease in the market demand. Because firms are now making zero economic profit, no firm wants to enter or exit the market. The market supply curve remains at $S_1$, and the market produces $Q_2$. The market is again in long-run equilibrium.

The difference between the initial long-run equilibrium and the final long-run equilibrium is the number of firms in the market. A permanent decrease in demand has decreased the number of firms. Each remaining firm produces the same output in the new long-run equilibrium as it did initially and makes zero economic profit. In the process of moving from the initial equilibrium to the new one, firms incur economic losses.

We've just worked out how a competitive market responds to a permanent *decrease* in the market demand. A permanent increase in the market demand triggers a similar response, but in the opposite direction. The increase in demand brings a higher market price, increased economic profit and entry. Entry increases the market supply and eventually lowers the price to its original level and economic profit falls to zero.

The demand for Internet services increased permanently during the 1990s and huge profit opportunities

**Figure 7.10  A Decrease in Demand**

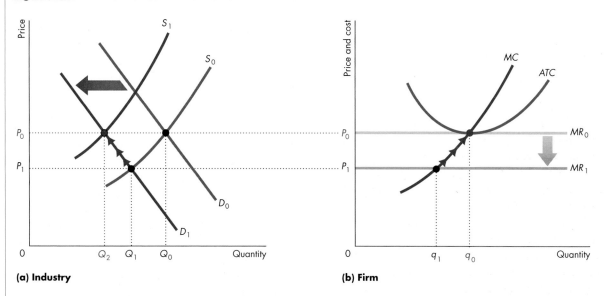

**(a) Industry**

**(b) Firm**

A market starts in long-run competitive equilibrium. Part (a) shows the market demand curve $D_0$, the market supply curve $S_0$, the equilibrium quantity $Q_0$ and the market price $P_0$. Each firm sells at the price $P_0$, so its marginal revenue curve is $MR_0$ in part (b). Each firm produces $q_0$ and makes zero economic profit.

Market demand decreases from $D_0$ to $D_1$ in part (a). The market price falls to $P_1$, each firm decreases its output to $q_1$ in part (b), and the market output decreases to $Q_1$ in part (a).

In this situation, firms incur economic losses. Some firms exit the market, and as they do so, the market supply curve gradually shifts leftward, from $S_0$ to $S_1$. This shift gradually raises the market price from $P_1$ back to $P_0$. While the price is below $P_0$, firms continue to incur economic losses and more firms exit the market. Once the price has returned to $P_0$, each firm makes zero economic profit. Firms have no further incentive to exit the market. Each firm produces $q_0$ and market output is $Q_2$.

myeconlab Animation

arose in this market. The result was a massive rate of entry of Internet service providers. The process of competition and change in the Internet service market is similar to what we have just studied but with an increase in demand rather than a decrease in demand.

We've now studied the effects of a permanent change in demand for a good. In doing so, we began and ended in a long-run equilibrium and examined the process that takes a market from one long-run equilibrium to another. It is this process, not the equilibrium points, that describes the real world.

One feature of the predictions that we have just generated seems odd. In the long run, regardless of whether the change in demand is a permanent increase or a permanent decrease, the market price returns to its original level. Is this outcome inevitable? In fact, it is not. It is possible for the market price in long-run equilibrium to remain the same, rise or fall.

# External Economies and Diseconomies

The change in the long-run equilibrium price depends on external economies and external diseconomies. **External economies** are factors beyond the control of an individual firm that lower its costs as *market* output increases. **External diseconomies** are factors outside the control of a firm that raise its costs as *market* output increases. With no external economies or external diseconomies, a firm's costs remain constant as market output changes.

Figure 7.11 illustrates these three cases and introduces a new supply concept, the long-run market supply curve.

A **long-run market supply curve** shows how the quantity supplied by a market varies as the market price varies, after all the possible adjustments have been made, including changes in plant size and changes in the number of firms in the market.

Figure 7.11(a) shows the case we have just studied – no external economies or external diseconomies. The long-run market supply curve ($LS_A$) is perfectly elastic. In this case, a permanent increase in demand from $D_0$ to $D_1$ has no effect on the price in the long run. The increase in demand brings a temporary increase in price to $P_S$ and a short-run quantity increase from $Q_0$ to $Q_S$. Entry increases short-run supply from $S_0$ to $S_1$, which lowers the price to its original level, $P_0$, and increases the quantity to $Q_1$.

Figure 7.11(b) shows the case of external diseconomies. The long-run market supply curve ($LS_B$) slopes upward. A permanent increase in demand from $D_0$ to $D_1$ increases the price in both the short run and the long run. As in the previous case, the increase in demand brings a temporary increase in price to $P_S$, and a short-run quantity increase from $Q_0$ to $Q_S$. Entry increases short-run supply from $S_0$ to $S_2$, which lowers the price from $P_S$ to $P_2$ and increases the quantity to $Q_2$.

One source of external diseconomies is congestion. The airline market in recent years provides a good illustration. With bigger airline market output, there is more congestion of both airports and airspace, which results in longer delays and extra waiting time for passengers and aircraft. These external diseconomies mean that as the output of air travel services increases (in the absence of technological advances), the airline's average cost increases. As a result, the long-run supply curve is upward-sloping. So a permanent increase in demand brings an increase in quantity and a rise in the price. Technological advances decrease average costs and *shift* the long-run supply curve downward. So even a market that experiences external diseconomies might have falling prices over the long run.

Figure 7.11(c) shows the case of external economies. In this case, the long-run market supply curve ($LS_C$) slopes downward. A permanent increase in demand from $D_0$ to $D_1$ increases the price in the short run and lowers it in the long run. Again, the increase in demand brings a temporary increase in price to $P_S$ and a short-run increase in the quantity from $Q_0$ to $Q_S$. Entry increases short-run supply from $S_0$ to $S_3$, which lowers the price from $P_S$ to $P_3$ and increases the quantity to $Q_3$.

One of the best examples of external economies is the growth of specialist support services for a market as it expands. As farm output increased in the nineteenth

**Figure 7.11** Long-run Changes in Price and Quantity

**(a) Constant-cost industry**

**(b) Increasing-cost industry**

**(c) Decreasing-cost industry**

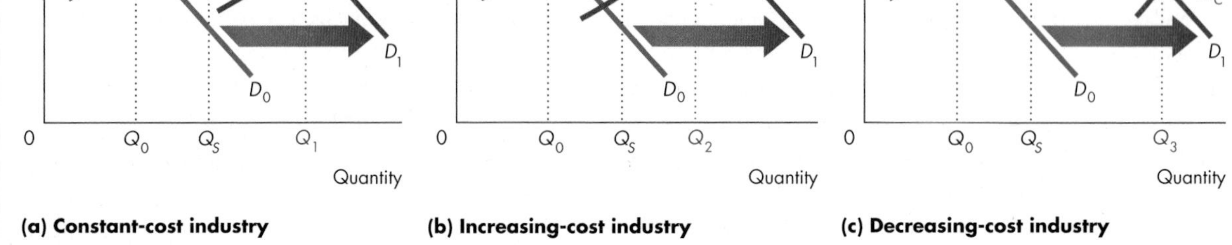

Three possible changes in price and quantity occur in the long run. When demand increases from $D_0$ to $D_1$, entry occurs and the market supply curve shifts rightward.

In part (a), the long-run supply curve $LS_A$ is horizontal. The quantity increases from $Q_0$ to $Q_1$ and the price remains constant at $P_0$.

In part (b), the long-run supply curve is $LS_B$; the price increases to $P_2$ and the quantity increases to $Q_2$. This case occurs in industries with external diseconomies.

In part (c), the long-run supply curve is $LS_C$; the price decreases to $P_3$ and the quantity increases to $Q_3$. This case occurs in a market with external economies.

and early twentieth centuries, the services available to farmers expanded and their costs fell. New firms specialized in the development and marketing of farm machinery and fertilizers. As a result, average farm costs decreased. Farms enjoyed the benefits of external economies. As a consequence, as the demand for farm products increased, the output increased but the price fell.

Over the long term, the prices of many goods and services have fallen, not because of external economies but because of technological change. Let's now study this influence on a competitive market.

## Technological Change

Industries are constantly discovering lower-cost techniques of production. Most cost-saving production techniques cannot be implemented, however, without investing in new plant and equipment. As a consequence, it takes time for a technological advance to spread through a market. Some firms whose plants are on the verge of being replaced will be quick to adopt the new technology, while other firms whose plants have recently been replaced will continue to operate with an old technology until they can no longer cover their average variable cost. Once average variable cost cannot be covered, a firm will scrap even a relatively new plant (embodying an old technology) in favour of a plant with a new technology.

New technology allows firms to produce at a lower cost. As a result, as firms adopt a new technology, their average total cost and marginal cost fall and the *ATC* and *MC* curves shift downward. With lower costs, firms are willing to supply a given quantity at a lower price or, equivalently, they are willing to supply a larger quantity at a given price. In other words, the market supply increases and the market supply curve shifts rightward. With a given demand, the quantity produced increases and the price falls.

Two forces are at work in a market undergoing technological change. Firms that adopt the new technology make an economic profit, so there is entry by new-technology firms. Firms that stick with the old technology incur economic losses; they either exit the market or switch to the new technology.

As old-technology firms disappear and new-technology firms enter, the price falls and the quantity produced increases. Eventually, the market arrives at a long-run equilibrium in which all the firms use the new technology and make zero economic profit. Because in the long run, competition eliminates economic profit,

technological change brings only temporary gains to producers. But the lower prices and better products that technological advances bring are permanent gains for consumers.

The process that we've just described is one in which some firms experience economic profits and others experience economic losses. It is a period of dynamic change for a market. Some firms do well, and others do badly. Often, the process has a geographical dimension – the expanding new-technology firms bring prosperity to what was once a backwater and traditional industrial regions decline. Sometimes, the new-technology firms are in another country, while the old-technology firms are in the domestic economy.

The information revolution of the 1990s produced many examples of changes like these. Commercial banking, which was traditionally concentrated in large cities such as London and Frankfurt, has decentralized with data processing centres in small Yorkshire towns. Scotland's 'silicon glen' has displaced traditional agricultural production.

Technological advances are not confined to the information market. Even in the agricultural sector, bio-technological advances are revolutionizing milk and crop production.

We've seen how a competitive market works in the short run and the long run. But does a competitive market achieve an efficient use of resources?

**Competition and Efficiency**

A competitive market can achieve an efficient use of resources. You first studied efficiency in Chapter 2. Then in Chapter 4, using only the concepts of demand, supply, consumer surplus and producer surplus, you saw how a competitive market achieves efficiency. Now that you have learned what lies behind demand and supply curves in a competitive market, you can gain a deeper understanding of the efficiency of a competitive market.

## Efficient Use of Resources

Resource use is efficient when we produce the goods and services that people value most highly (see Chapter 2, pp. 33–35 and Chapter 4, p. 90). If someone can become better off without anyone else becoming worse off, resources are *not* being used efficiently. For example, suppose we produce a computer that no one wants and no one will ever use and, at the same time, some people are clamouring for more video games. If we produce one less computer and reallocate the unused resources to produce more video games, some people will become better off and no one will be worse off. So the initial resource allocation was inefficient.

In the more technical language that you have learned, resource use is efficient when marginal social benefit equals marginal social cost. In the computer and video games example, the marginal social benefit of a video game exceeds its marginal social cost. And the marginal social cost of a computer exceeds its marginal social benefit. So by producing fewer computers and more video games, we move resources towards a higher-valued use.

## Choices, Equilibrium and Efficiency

We can use what you have learned about the decisions made by consumers and competitive firms and market equilibrium to describe an efficient use of resources.

### Choices

Consumers allocate their budgets to get the most value possible out of them. We derive a consumer's demand curve by finding how the best budget allocation changes as the price of a good changes. So consumers get the most value out of their resources at all points along their demand curves. If the people who consume a good or service are the only ones who benefit from it, then the market demand curve measures the benefit to the entire society and is the marginal social benefit curve.

Competitive firms produce the quantity that maximizes profit. We derive the firm's supply curve by finding the profit-maximizing quantity at each price. So firms get the most value out of their resources at all points along their supply curves. If the firms that produce a good or service bear all the costs of producing it, then the market supply curve measures the marginal cost to the entire society and the market supply curve is the marginal social cost curve.

### Equilibrium and Efficiency

Resources are used efficiently when marginal social benefit equals marginal social cost. Competitive equilibrium achieves this efficient outcome because, with no externalities, price equals marginal social benefit for consumers and price equals marginal social cost for producers.

The gains from trade are the consumer surplus plus the producer surplus. The gains from trade for consumers are measured by *consumer surplus*, which is the area below the demand curve and above the price paid (see Chapter 4, p. 87). The gains from trade for producers are measured by *producer surplus*, which is the area above the supply curve and below the price received (see Chapter 4, p. 89). The total gains from trade are the sum of consumer surplus and producer surplus. When the market for a good or service is in equilibrium, the gains from trade are maximized.

### Illustrating an Efficient Allocation

Figure 7.12 illustrates an efficient allocation in perfect competition in long-run equilibrium. Part (a) shows the situation of an individual firm, and part (b) shows the market. The equilibrium market price is $P^*$. At that price, each firm makes zero economic profit. Each firm has the plant that enables it to produce at the lowest possible average total cost. Consumers are as well off as possible because the good cannot be produced at a lower cost and the price equals that least possible cost.

In part (b), consumers get the most out of their resources at all points on the market demand curve, $D = MSB$. Consumer surplus is the green area. Producers get the most out of their resources at all points on the market supply curve, $S = MSC$. Producer surplus is the blue area. Resources are used efficiently at the quantity $Q^*$ and price $P^*$. At this point, marginal social benefit

**Figure 7.12**   Efficiency of Perfect Competition

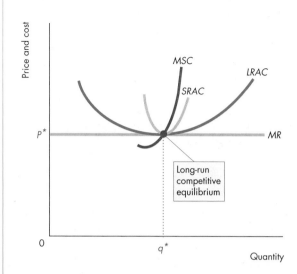

**(a) A single firm**

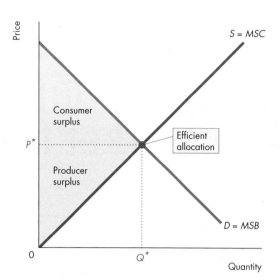

**(b) A market**

Demand, *D*, and supply, *S*, determine the equilibrium price, *P\**. A firm in perfect competition in part (a) produces *q\** at the lowest possible long-run average total cost.

In part (b), consumers have made the best available choices and are on the market demand curve, and firms are producing at least cost and are on the market supply curve. With no externalities, marginal social benefit equals marginal social cost, so resources are used efficiently at the quantity *Q\**.

equals marginal social cost, and total surplus (the sum of producer surplus and consumer surplus) is maximized.

When firms in perfect competition are away from long-run equilibrium, either entry into the market or exit from the market is taking place and the market is moving towards the situation depicted in Figure 7.12. But the competitive market is still efficient. As long as marginal social benefit (on the market demand curve) equals marginal social cost (on the market supply curve), the market is efficient. But it is only in long-run equilibrium that consumers pay the lowest possible price.

You've now completed your study of perfect competition. *Reading Between the Lines* on pp. 170–171 gives you an opportunity to use what you have learned to understand recent events in the competitive market for Kenyan tea.

Although many markets approximate the model of perfect competition, many do not. In Chapter 8, we study markets at the opposite extreme of market power:

monopoly. Then, in Chapter 9, we study markets that lie between perfect competition and monopoly – monopolistic competition and oligopoly. When you have completed this study, you'll have a tool kit that will enable you to understand the variety of real-world markets.

### Review Quiz

1   State the conditions that must be met for resources to be allocated efficiently.
2   Describe the choices that consumers make and explain why consumers are efficient on the market demand curve.
3   Describe the choices that producers make and explain why producers are efficient on the market supply curve.
4   Explain why resources are used efficiently in a competitive market.

You can work these questions in Study Plan 7.6 and get instant feedback.        myeconlab

# Reading Between the Lines

# Perfect Competition: The Market for Kenyan Tea

Reuters, 22 October 2010

## Kenyan Tea Growers Say Strike Has Little Impact

Mark Denge

A week-long strike by some workers in Kenyan tea farms is unlikely to affect auction prices and export volumes. . . .

On Monday . . . workers in the east Africa nation's tea farms went on strike over the use of tea plucking machines which they claimed could cost them their jobs.

Tea Board of Kenya (TBK) Managing Director Sicily Kariuki said . . . 'The smallholder sub-sector, which accounts for about 60 per cent of the total production and is the largest supplier of tea to the auction, is operating without interruptions.'

A bulk of Kenya's tea is produced by Kenya Tea Development Agency (KTDA) that caters for the more than 500,000

smallholder farmers. The agency manages 65 tea factories spread across tea growing zones in the country.

The average price for Kenya's top tea rose slightly to $3.49 per kg at this week's auction from $3.31 per kg last week, while volumes offered were also up.

'The decision of using machines for the picking or not, is purely a business decision motivated by . . . cost-efficiency.' (Kariuki said) . . .

Projected production volumes for 2010 will go beyond the 350 million kg mark . . . output in 2009 was about 315 million kg. . . . Output rose . . . driven by good rains and strong demand from the Indian and Chinese markets.

## The Essence of the Story

◆ Some Kenyan tea farm workers are on strike over the introduction of tea plucking machines.

◆ The machines are being introduced to lower costs.

◆ The strike has not affected the bulk of Kenyan tea picked on 500,000 small farms and so will have little effect.

◆ With good harvests and strong world demand, 2010 will be a good year for Kenyan tea farmers. Both the market price and output are rising.

# Economic Analysis

♦ The market for Kenyan tea is an example of perfect competition. Kenyan tea is sold at auction and growers are price takers.

♦ In 2010, Kenya produced about 350 million kg of tea, of which 210 million kg (60 per cent) was from small farms. So each month, 29 million kg of tea was produced and on average, a small farm produced 35 kg.

♦ Figure 1 shows the market for Kenyan tea in October 2010. Demand is $D_0$ and supply is $S$. The market price is $3.31 per kg and market quantity is 29 million kg.

♦ An increase in world demand shifts the demand curve rightward to $D_1$. The market price rises to $3.49 per kg and the market quantity increases to 31 million kg.

♦ Figure 2 shows the response of a small tea farm where marginal cost is $MC$ and average total cost is $ATC$. At a price of $3.31 per kg, marginal revenue is $MR_0$ and the farm maximizes profit by producing 35 kg. Economic profit is zero in a long-run equilibrium.

♦ The rise in price to $3.49 per kg increases marginal revenue to $MR_1$, so each small farm increases output to 37 kg a month and makes an economic profit.

♦ Figure 3 shows the long-run effects of introducing tea plucking machines. As more and more large tea farms become mechanized, their marginal cost falls and market supply increases.

♦ In the long run, holding demand constant at $D_1$, the expansion of large farms increases supply. The price falls and the quantity demanded increases further. On the small farm in Figure 2, production returns to 35 kg per month and economic profit returns to zero.

♦ If mechanization drives the price below $3.31 per kg, some small farmers go out of business and exit the market.

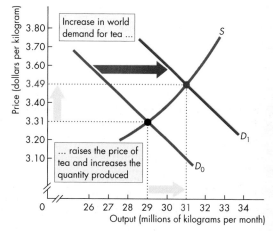

**Figure 1  The global market for Kenyan tea in the short run**

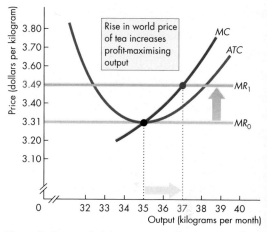

**Figure 2  Output decisions on a small Kenyan tea farm**

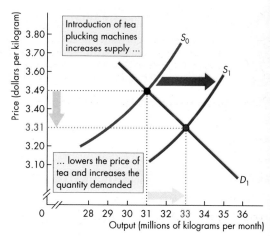

**Figure 3  The global market for Kenyan tea in the long run**

## SUMMARY

## Key Points

### What Is Perfect Competition?
(pp. 152–153)

◆ In perfect competition, many firms sell identical products to many buyers; there are no restrictions on entry; sellers and buyers are well informed about prices.

◆ A perfectly competitive firm is a price taker.

◆ A perfectly competitive firm's marginal revenue always equals the market price.

Working Problems 1 to 3 will give you a better understanding of perfect competition.

### The Firm's Output Decision (pp. 154–157)

◆ The firm produces the output at which marginal revenue (price) equals marginal cost.

◆ In short-run equilibrium, a firm can make an economic profit, incur an economic loss or break even.

◆ If price is less than minimum average variable cost, the firm temporarily shuts down.

◆ At prices below minimum average variable cost, a firm's supply curve runs along the y-axis; at prices above minimum average variable cost, a firm's supply curve is its marginal cost curve.

Working Problems 4 to 7 will give you a better understanding of a firm's output decision.

### Output, Price and Profit in the Short Run (pp. 158–161)

◆ A market supply curve shows the sum of the quantities supplied by each firm at each price.

◆ Market demand and market supply determine price.

Working Problems 8 and 9 will give you a better understanding of output, price and profit in the short run.

### Output, Price and Profit in the Long Run (pp. 161–163)

◆ Economic profit induces entry and economic loss induces exit.

◆ Entry increases supply and lowers the market price and economic profit. Exit decreases supply and raises the market price and economic profit.

◆ In long-run equilibrium, economic profit is zero. There is no entry or exit.

Working Problems 10 and 11 will give you a better understanding of output, price and profit in the long run.

### Changing Tastes and Advancing Technology (pp. 164–167)

◆ A permanent decrease in demand leads to a smaller market output and a smaller number of firms. A permanent increase in the demand leads to a larger market output and a larger number of firms.

◆ The long-run effect of a change in demand on market price depends on whether there are external economies (the price falls), external diseconomies (the price rises) or neither (the price remains constant).

◆ New technologies increase supply and in the long run lower the price and increase the quantity.

Working Problems 12 to 16 will give you a better understanding of changing tastes and advancing technologies.

### Competition and Efficiency
(pp. 168–169)

◆ Resources are used efficiently when we produce goods and services in the quantities that everyone values most highly.

◆ Perfect competition achieves an efficient allocation. In long-run equilibrium, consumers pay the lowest possible price and marginal social benefit equals marginal social cost.

Working Problems 17 and 18 will give you a better understanding of the efficiency of competition.

## Key Terms

Economic profit, 152
External diseconomies, 165
External economies, 165
Long-run market supply curve, 165
Marginal revenue, 152
Normal profit, 152
Perfect competition, 152
Price taker, 152
Short-run market supply curve, 158
Shutdown point, 156
Total revenue, 152

# STUDY PLAN PROBLEMS AND APPLICATIONS

ⓍⓍ myeconlab    You can work Problems 1 to 18 in MyEconLab Chapter 7 Study Plan and get instant feedback.

## What Is Perfect Competition?

(Study Plan 7.1)

Use the following information to work Problems 1 to 3.

Leo's makes amaretto biscuits that are identical to those made by dozens of other firms, and there is free entry in the amaretto biscuit market. Buyers and sellers are well informed about prices.

**1**  In what type of market does Leo's operate? What determines the price of amaretto biscuits and what determines Leo's marginal revenue?

**2  a**  If amaretto biscuits sell for €10 a box and Leo offers his biscuits for sale at €10.50 a box, how many boxes does he sell?

   **b**  If amaretto biscuits sell for €10 a box and Leo offers his biscuit for sale at €9.50 a box, how many boxes does he sell?

**3**  What is the elasticity of demand for Leo's amaretto biscuits and how does it differ from the elasticity of the market demand for amaretto biscuits?

## The Firm's Output Decision

(Study Plan 7.2)

Use the following information to work Problems 4 to 6.

Pat's Pizza Restaurant is a price taker and its costs are:

| Output (pizzas per hour) | Total cost (euros per hour) |
|---|---|
| 0 | 10 |
| 1 | 21 |
| 2 | 30 |
| 3 | 41 |
| 4 | 54 |
| 5 | 69 |

**4**  What is Pat's profit-maximizing output and economic profit if the market price is (i) €14 a pizza, (ii) €12 a pizza and (iii) €10 a pizza?

**5**  What is Pat's shutdown point and what is its economic profit if it shuts down temporarily?

**6**  Derive Pat's supply curve.

**7**  The market for paper is perfectly competitive and there are 1,000 firms that produce paper. The table in the next column sets out the market demand schedule for paper.

| Price (euros per box) | Quantity demanded (thousands of boxes per week) |
|---|---|
| 3.65 | 500 |
| 5.20 | 450 |
| 6.80 | 400 |
| 8.40 | 350 |
| 10.00 | 300 |
| 11.60 | 250 |
| 13.20 | 200 |

Each paper producer has the same costs when it uses its least-cost plant. The following table sets out those costs.

| Output (boxes per week) | Marginal cost | Average variable cost | Average total cost |
|---|---|---|---|
| | | (euros per box) | |
| 200 | 4.60 | 7.80 | 11.80 |
| 250 | 7.00 | 7.00 | 11.00 |
| 300 | 7.65 | 7.10 | 10.43 |
| 350 | 8.40 | 7.20 | 10.06 |
| 400 | 10.00 | 7.50 | 10.00 |
| 450 | 12.40 | 8.00 | 10.22 |
| 500 | 20.70 | 9.00 | 11.00 |

**a**  What is the market price?

**b**  What is the market's output?

**c**  What is the output produced by each firm?

**d**  What is the economic profit made or economic loss incurred by each firm?

## Output, Price and Profit in the Short Run (Study Plan 7.3)

**8**  In Problem 7, as more and more computer users read documents online rather than print them out, the market demand for paper decreases and in the short run the demand schedule becomes:

| Price (euros per box) | Quantity demanded (thousands of boxes per week) |
|---|---|
| 2.95 | 500 |
| 4.13 | 450 |
| 5.30 | 400 |
| 6.48 | 350 |
| 7.65 | 300 |
| 8.83 | 250 |
| 10.00 | 200 |
| 11.18 | 150 |

If each paper producer has the costs set out in Problem 7, what is the market price and the economic profit or loss of each firm in the short run?

**9 British Airways Ups Fuel Surcharges**

British Airways announced it would increase the fuel surcharge on all its flights starting on June 3, the third hike since the start of the year. On long-haul flights of more than 9 hours the fuel surcharge will rise by £30 to £109 per flight, whereas on short haul flights it will increase by £3 to £16.

Source: Forbes.com, 29 May 2008

**a** Explain how an increase in fuel prices might cause an airline to change its output (number of flights) in the short run.

**b** Draw a graph to show the increase in fuel prices on an airline's output in the short run.

**c** Explain why an airline might incur an economic loss in the short run as fuel prices rise.

## Output, Price and Profit in the Long Run (Study Plan 7.4)

**10** The pizza market is perfectly competitive, and all pizza producers have the same costs as Pat's Pizza Restaurant in Problem 4.

**a** At what price will some firms exit the pizza market in the long run?

**b** At what price will firms enter the pizza market in the long run?

**11** In Problem 7, in the long run,

**a** Do firms have an incentive to enter or exit the paper market?

**b** If firms do enter or exit the market, explain how the economic profit or loss of the remaining paper producers will change.

**c** What is the long-run equilibrium market price and the quantity of paper produced? What is the number of firms in the market?

## Changing Tastes and Advancing Technology (Study Plan 7.5)

**12** If in the long run, the market demand for paper remains the same as in Problem 8,

**a** What is the long-run equilibrium price of paper, the market output, and the economic profit or loss of each firm?

**b** Does this market experience external economies, external diseconomies, or constant cost? Illustrate by drawing the long-run supply curve.

Use the following news clip to work Problems 13 and 14.

**Coors Brewing Expanding Plant**

Coors Brewing Company will expand its Virginia packaging plant at a cost of $24 million. The addition will accommodate a new production line, which will bottle beer faster. Coors Brewing employs 470 people at its Virginia plant. The expanded packaging line will add another eight jobs.

Source: Denver Business Journal, 6 January 2006

**13 a** How will Coors' expansion change its marginal cost curve and short-run supply curve?

**b** What does this expansion decision imply about the point on Coors' *LRAC* curve at which the firm was before the expansion?

**14 a** If other breweries follow the lead of Coors, what will happen to the market price of beer?

**b** How will the adjustment that you have described in part (a) influence the economic profit of Coors and other beer producers?

**15** Explain and illustrate graphically how the growing world population is influencing the world market for wheat and a representative individual wheat farmer.

**16** Explain and illustrate graphically how the nappy service market has been affected by the decrease in the birth rate and the development of disposable nappies.

## Competition and Effiency (Study Plan 7.6)

**17** In a perfectly competitive market in long-run equilibrium, can consumer surplus be increased? Can producer surplus be increased? Can a consumer become better off by making a substitution away from this market?

**18 Never Pay Retail Again**

Not only has scouring the Web for the best possible price become standard protocol before buying a big-ticket item, but more consumers are employing creative strategies for scoring hot deals. Comparison shopping and haggling are all becoming mainstream marks of savvy shoppers. Online shoppers can check a comparison service like Price Grabber before making a purchase.

Source: CNN, 30 May 2008

**a** Explain the effect of the Internet on the degree of competition in the market.

**b** Explain how the Internet influences market efficiency.

ADDITIONAL PROBLEMS AND APPLICATIONS

 myeconlab You can work these problems in MyEconLab if assigned by your lecturer.

## What Is Perfect Competition?

Use the following information to work Problems 19 to 21.

Two service stations stand on opposite sides of the road: Rutter's and Sheetz's. Rutter's doesn't even have to look across the road to know when Sheetz's changes its petrol price. When Sheetz's raises the price, Rutter's pumps are busy. When Sheetz's lowers prices, there's not a car in sight. Both service stations survive but each has no control over the price.

**19** In what type of market do these service stations operate? What determines the price of petrol and what determines the marginal revenue from petrol?

**20** Describe the elasticity of demand for petrol that each of these service stations faces.

**21** Why does each of these service stations have so little control over the price of the petrol it sells?

## The Firm's Output Decision

**22** The figure shows the costs of Quick Copy, one of the many copy shops in London.

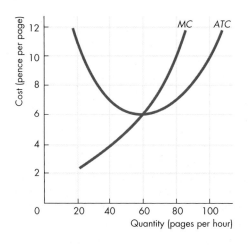

If the market price of copying one page is 10 pence, calculate Quick Copy's

**a** Profit-maximizing output.

**b** Economic profit.

**23** The market for smoothies is perfectly competitive and the table in the next column sets out the market demand for smoothies.

| Price (euros per smoothie) | Quantity demanded (smoothies per hour) |
|---|---|
| 1.90 | 1,000 |
| 2.00 | 950 |
| 2.20 | 800 |
| 2.91 | 700 |
| 4.25 | 550 |
| 5.25 | 400 |
| 5.50 | 300 |

Each of the 100 producers of smoothies has the following costs when it uses its least-cost plant.

| Output (smoothies per hour) | Marginal cost | Average variable cost | Average total cost |
|---|---|---|---|
| | | (euros per smoothie) | |
| 3 | 2.50 | 4.00 | 7.33 |
| 4 | 2.20 | 3.53 | 6.03 |
| 5 | 1.90 | 3.24 | 5.24 |
| 6 | 2.00 | 3.00 | 4.67 |
| 7 | 2.91 | 2.91 | 4.34 |
| 8 | 4.25 | 3.00 | 4.25 |
| 9 | 8.00 | 3.33 | 4.44 |

**a** What is the market price of a smoothie?

**b** What is the market output?

**c** How many smoothies does each firm sell?

**d** What is the economic profit made or economic loss incurred by each firm?

**24 Honda Workers Return after Four Month Shutdown**

Honda shut down its UK Swindon car plant for four months in 2009, cutting annual production by 50 per cent to 11,300 vehicles and shedding 1,300 workers through voluntary redundancies. Workers were paid 2 months full pay and 2 months on 60 per cent of pay during the shutdown.

Source: Independent online, 17 February 2009

**a** Explain how the shutdown decision will affect the company's *TFC*, *TVC* and *TC*.

**b** Under what conditions would this shutdown decision maximize the company's economic profit (or minimize its loss)?

**c** Under what conditions did Honda start producing again?

**25 Mini Announces 850 Lay-offs**

Mini announced 850 redundancies at the Cowley car plant in Oxfordshire. The company is blaming 'volatile market conditions' for the need to change from three shifts a day to two shifts a day, which means closing production altogether at weekends.

Source: *The Independent*, 17 February 2009

Explain why 'volatile market conditions' created a situation in which Mini's profit-maximizing decision was to switch from three to two shifts.

## Output, Price and Profit in the Short Run

**26 Wheat Prices Down 40 per cent from Peak**

Wheat prices in April have fallen more than 40 per cent from their peak in February. Farmers planted more wheat as prices increased and this year's harvest may be a record crop.

Source: BBC online, 25 April 2008

Why did wheat prices fall in 2008? Draw a graph to show the short-run effect on an individual farmer's economic profit.

## Output, Price and Profit in the Long Run

**27** In Problem 23, do firms enter or exit the market in the long run? What is the market price and the equilibrium quantity in the long run?

**28** In Problem 24, under what conditions will Honda exit the car market?

## Changing Tastes and Advancing Technology

**29 Another DVD Format, but It's Cheaper**

New Medium Enterprises claims the quality of its new system, HD VMD, is equal to Blu-ray's but it costs only $199 – cheaper than the $300 cost of a Blu-ray player. Chairman of the Blu-ray Disc Association says New Medium will fail because it believes that Blu-ray technology will always be more expensive. But mass production will cut the cost of a Blu-ray player to $90.

Source: *The New York Times*, 10 March 2008

**a** Explain how technological change in Blu-ray production might lead to lower prices in the long run. Illustrate your explanation with a graph.

**b** Even if Blu-ray prices do drop to $90 in the long run, why might the HD VMD still end up being less expensive at that time?

## Competition and Efficiency

**30** In a perfectly competitive market, each firm maximizes its profit by choosing only the quantity to produce. Regardless of whether the firm makes an economic profit or incurs an economic loss, the short-run equilibrium is efficient. Is the statement true? Explain why or why not.

## Economics in the News

**31** After you have studied *Reading Between the Lines* on pp. 170–171 answer the following questions.

**a** What are the features of the global market for Kenyan tea that make it competitive?

**b** Given that the strike was not expected to affect price or quantity to any great extent, why did the market price and quantity of Kenyan tea rise?

**c** If the market price were to fall below $3 a kilogram, what would happen to an individual small tea farmer's marginal revenue, marginal cost, average total cost, and economic profit?

**d** If large tea farms are successful in introducing mechanized picking, what is likely to happen to the marginal cost, average total cost and economic profit of a large tea farm?

**32 Mobile Phone Sales Hit 1 Billion Mark**

More than 1.15 billion mobile phones were sold worldwide in 2007, a 16 per cent increase in a year. Emerging markets, especially China and India, provided much of the growth as many people bought their first phone. In mature markets, such as Japan and Western Europe, consumers' appetite for feature-laden phones was met with new models packed with TV tuners, touch screens and cameras.

Source: CNET News, 27 February 2008

**a** Explain the effects of the increase in global demand for mobile phones on the market for mobile phones and on an individual mobile phone producer in the short run.

**b** Draw a graph to illustrate your answer in part (a).

**c** Explain the long-run effects of the increase in global demand for mobile phones on the market for mobile phones.

**d** What factors will determine whether the price of a mobile phone will rise, fall, or stay the same in the new long-run equilibrium?

# Monopoly

After studying this chapter you will be able to:

◆ Explain how monopoly arises and distinguish between single-price and price-discriminating monopolies

◆ Explain how a single-price monopoly determines its output and price

◆ Compare the performance and efficiency of single-price monopoly and competition

◆ Explain how a price-discriminating monopoly increases profit

◆ Explain the effects of monopoly regulation

Google, Microsoft and eBay are dominant players in the markets they serve. They are obviously not like firms in perfect competition. How do firms like these behave? How do they choose the quantities to produce and the prices to charge? How does their behaviour compare with perfectly competitive firms? Do they charge too much and produce too little? Would more competition among search engines or satellite broadcasters bring greater efficiency? Find out in this chapter.

*Reading Between the Lines*, at the end of the chapter, looks at whether Google may have abused its market power in Europe.

## ◆ Monopoly and How It Arises

A **monopoly** is a market with a single firm that produces a good or service for which no close substitute exists and which is protected by a barrier that prevents other firms from selling that good or service.

## How Monopoly Arises

Monopoly has two key features:

◆ No close substitute
◆ Barriers to entry

### No Close Substitute

If a good has a close substitute, even though only one firm produces it, that firm effectively faces competition from the producer of the substitute. A monopoly sells a good or service that has no good close substitute. Water supplied by a local water board and bottled spring water are close substitutes for drinking, but not for showering or washing a car. A local water board is a monopoly.

### Barriers to Entry

A constraint that protects a firm from potential competitors is called a **barrier to entry**. Three types of barrier to entry are

◆ Natural
◆ Ownership
◆ Legal

**Natural Barriers to Entry**
Natural barriers to entry create **natural monopoly**, a market in which economies of scale enable one firm to supply the entire market at the lowest possible cost.

In Figure 8.1, the market demand curve for electric power is *D*, and the long-run average cost curve is *LRAC*. Economies of scale prevail over the entire length of the *LRAC* curve.

One firm can produce 4 million kilowatt-hours at 5 pence a kilowatt-hour. At this price, the quantity demanded is 4 million kilowatt-hours. So if the price were 5 pence, one firm could supply the entire market. If two firms shared the market, it would cost each of them 10 pence a kilowatt-hour to produce a total of 4 million kilowatt-hours. In conditions like those shown in Figure 8.1, one firm can supply the entire market at

**Figure 8.1** Natural Monopoly

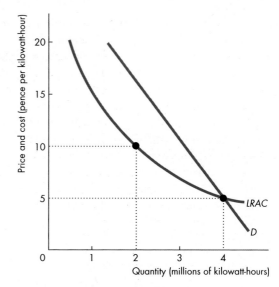

The market demand curve for electric power is *D*, and the long-run average cost curve is *LRAC*. Economies of scale exist over the entire *LRAC* curve. One firm can distribute 4 million kilowatt-hours at a cost of 5 pence a kilowatt-hour. This same total output costs 10 pence a kilowatt-hour with two firms. So one firm can meet the market demand at a lower cost than two or more firms can, and the market is a natural monopoly.

 Animation

a lower cost than two or more firms can. The market is a natural monopoly.

**Ownership Barriers to Entry**
An ownership barrier to entry occurs if one firm owns a significant portion of a resource. An example of this type of monopoly occurred during the last century when De Beers controlled up to 90 per cent of the world's supply of diamonds. (Today, its share is only 65 per cent.)

**Legal Barriers to Entry**
Legal barriers to entry create legal monopoly. A **legal monopoly** is a market in which competition and entry are restricted by the granting of a monopoly franchise, a government licence, a patent or a copyright.

A *monopoly franchise* is an exclusive right granted to a firm to supply a good or service. An example in the UK is the Post Office, which has the exclusive right to carry first-class mail.

A *government licence* controls entry into particular occupations and professions. This type of barrier to entry occurs in medicine, law, dentistry and many other professional services. A government licence doesn't always create a monopoly, but it does restrict competition.

A *patent* is an exclusive right granted to the inventor of a product or service. A *copyright* is an exclusive right granted to the author or composer of a literary, musical, dramatic or artistic work. Patents and copyrights are valid for a limited time period. In the UK, a patent is valid for 16 years. Patents encourage the *invention* of new products and production methods. Patents also stimulate *innovation* – the use of new inventions – by encouraging inventors to publicize their discoveries and offer them for use under licence. Patents have stimulated innovations in areas as diverse as tomato seeds, pharmaceuticals, memory chips and video games.

## ECONOMICS IN ACTION

### Information-age Monopolies

Information-age technologies have created four big natural monopolies. These firms have large plant costs but almost zero marginal cost, so they experience economies of scale.

Microsoft has captured 90 per cent of the personal computer operating system market with Windows and 73 per cent of the Web browser market with Internet Explorer. eBay has captured 85 per cent of the consumer-to-consumer Internet auction market and Google has 78 per cent of the search engine market.

New technologies also destroy monopoly. Firms can now gain access to free software and Linux systems via the Internet from innovations in Cloud computing, weakening Microsoft's monopoly. FedEx and e-mail have weakened the monopoly of the Post Office.

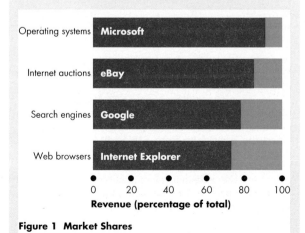

**Figure 1  Market Shares**

## Monopoly Price-setting Strategies

A major difference between monopoly and competition is that a monopoly sets its own price. In doing so, the monopoly faces a market constraint: to sell a larger quantity, the monopoly must charge a lower price. But there are two monopoly situations that create two pricing strategies:

◆ Single price
◆ Price discrimination

### Single Price

A **single-price monopoly** is a monopoly that must sell each unit of its output for the same price to all its customers. De Beers sells diamonds (of a given size and quality) for the same price to all its customers. If it tried to sell at a low price to some customers and at a higher price to others, only the low-price customers would buy from De Beers. Others would buy from De Beers' low-price customers. De Beers is a *single-price* monopoly.

### Price Discrimination

When a firm practises **price discrimination**, it sells different units of a good or service for different prices. Many firms price discriminate. Microsoft sells Windows and Office software at different prices to different buyers. Computer manufacturers who install the software on new machines, students, teachers, governments and businesses all pay different prices. Airlines offer a dizzying array of different prices for the same trip. Pizza producers often charge one price for a single pizza and almost give away a second pizza. These are all examples of *price discrimination*.

When a firm price discriminates, it looks as though it is doing its customers a favour. In fact, it is charging the highest possible price for each unit that it sells and making the largest possible profit.

### Review Quiz

1  How does monopoly arise?
2  How does a natural monopoly differ from a legal monopoly?
3  Distinguish between a price-discriminating monopoly and a single-price monopoly.

You can work these questions in Study Plan 8.1 and get instant feedback.

## A Single-price Monopoly's Output and Price Decision

To understand how a single-price monopoly makes its output and price decision, we must first study the link between price and marginal revenue.

## Price and Marginal Revenue

Because in a monopoly there is only one firm, the demand curve facing the firm is the market demand curve. Let's look at Gina's Cut and Dry, the only hairdressing salon within a 15 mile radius of a North Yorkshire town. The table in Figure 8.2 shows the market demand schedule. At a price of £20, she sells no haircuts. The lower the price, the more haircuts per hour Gina can sell. For example, at £12, consumers demand 4 haircuts per hour (row *E*).

*Total revenue* (*TR*) is the price (*P*) multiplied by the quantity sold (*Q*). For example, in row *D*, Gina sells 3 haircuts at £14 each, so total revenue is £42. *Marginal revenue* (*MR*) is the change in total revenue (*ΔTR*) resulting from a one-unit increase in the quantity sold. For example, if the price falls from £16 (row *C*) to £14 (row *D*), the quantity sold increases from 2 to 3 haircuts. Total revenue rises from £32 to £42, so the change in total revenue is £10. Because the quantity sold increases by 1 haircut, marginal revenue equals the change in total revenue and is £10. Marginal revenue is placed between the two rows to emphasize that marginal revenue relates to the *change* in the quantity sold.

Figure 8.2 shows the market demand curve and marginal revenue curve (*MR*) and also illustrates the calculation we've just made. Notice that at each level of output, marginal revenue is less than price – the marginal revenue curve lies below the demand curve.

Why is marginal revenue *less* than price? It is because when the price is lowered to sell one more unit, two opposing forces affect total revenue. The lower price results in a revenue loss and the increased quantity sold results in a revenue gain. For example, at a price of £16, Gina sells 2 haircuts (point *C*). If she lowers the price to £14, she sells 3 haircuts and has a revenue gain of £14 on the third haircut. But she now receives only £14 on the first two – £2 less than before. She loses £4 of revenue on the first 2 haircuts. To calculate marginal revenue, she must deduct this amount from the revenue gain of £14. So her marginal revenue is £10, which is less than the price.

**Figure 8.2**   Demand and Marginal Revenue

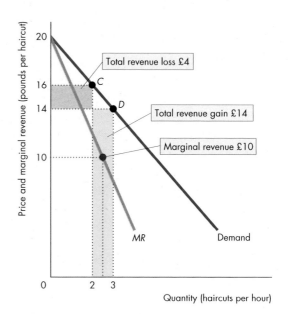

The table shows the demand schedule. Total revenue (*TR*) is price multiplied by quantity sold. For example, in row *C*, the price is £16 a haircut. Cut and Dry sells 2 haircuts and its total revenue is £32. Marginal revenue (*MR*) is the change in total revenue that results from a one-unit increase in the quantity sold. For example, when the price falls from £16 to £14 a haircut, the quantity sold increases by 1 haircut and total revenue increases by £10. Marginal revenue is £10. The demand curve and the marginal revenue curve, *MR*, are based on the numbers in the table and illustrate the calculation of marginal revenue when the price falls from £16 to £14 a haircut.

| | Price (P) (pounds per haircut) | Quantity demanded (Q) (haircuts per hour) | Total revenue (TR = P × Q) (pounds) | Marginal revenue (MR = ΔTR/ΔQ) (pounds per haircut) |
|---|---|---|---|---|
| A | 20 | 0 | 0 | |
| | | | | 18 |
| B | 18 | 1 | 18 | |
| | | | | 14 |
| C | **16** | **2** | **32** | |
| | | | | **10** |
| D | 14 | 3 | 42 | |
| | | | | 6 |
| E | 12 | 4 | 48 | |
| | | | | 2 |
| F | 10 | 5 | 50 | |

# Marginal Revenue and Elasticity

A single-price monopoly's marginal revenue is related to the *elasticity of demand* for its good. The demand for a good can be *elastic* (the elasticity of demand is greater than 1), *inelastic* (the elasticity of demand is less than 1), or *unit elastic* (the elasticity of demand is equal to 1). Demand is *elastic* if a 1 per cent fall in the price brings a greater than 1 per cent increase in the quantity demanded. Demand is *inelastic* if a 1 per cent fall in the price brings a less than 1 per cent increase in the quantity demanded. And demand is *unit elastic* if a 1 per cent fall in the price brings a 1 per cent increase in the quantity demanded. (See Appendix to Chapter 3, pp. 79–82.)

If demand is elastic, a fall in price brings an increase in total revenue – the increase in revenue from the increase in quantity sold outweighs the decrease in revenue from the lower price – and marginal revenue is *positive*. If demand is inelastic, a fall in the price brings a decrease in total revenue – the increase in revenue from the increase in quantity sold is outweighed by the decrease in revenue from the lower price – and marginal revenue is *negative*. If demand is unit elastic, total revenue does not change – the increase in revenue from the increase in quantity sold offsets the decrease in revenue from the lower price – and marginal revenue is *zero*.

Figure 8.3 illustrates the relationship between marginal revenue, total revenue and elasticity. As the price of a haircut gradually falls from £20 to £10, the quantity of haircuts demanded increases from 0 to 5 an hour, marginal revenue is positive in part (a), total revenue increases in part (b) and the demand for haircuts is elastic. As the price falls from £10 to £0, the quantity of haircuts demanded increases from 5 to 10 an hour, marginal revenue is negative in part (a), total revenue decreases in part (b) and the demand for haircuts is inelastic. When the price is £10 a haircut, marginal revenue is zero in part (a), total revenue is a maximum in part (b) and the demand for haircuts is unit elastic.

## In Monopoly, Demand Is Always Elastic

The relationship between marginal revenue and elasticity that you've just discovered implies that a profit-maximizing monopoly never produces an output in the inelastic range of its demand curve. If it did so, it could produce a smaller quantity, charge a higher price and increase its economic profit. Let's now look at a monopoly's price and output decision.

**Figure 8.3** Marginal Revenue and Elasticity

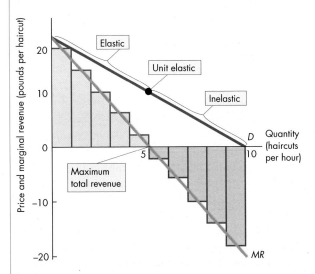

**(a) Demand and marginal revenue curves**

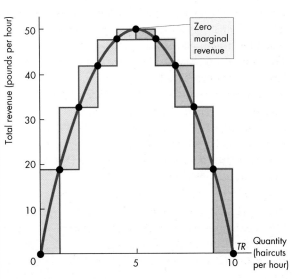

**(b) Total revenue curve**

In part (a), the demand curve is *D* and the marginal revenue curve is *MR*. In part (b), the total revenue curve is *TR*. Over the range from 0 to 5 haircuts an hour, a price cut increases total revenue, so marginal revenue is positive – as shown by the blue bars. Demand is elastic. Over the range from 5 to 10 haircuts an hour, a price cut decreases total revenue, so marginal revenue is negative – as shown by the red bars. Demand is inelastic. At 5 haircuts an hour, total revenue is maximized and marginal revenue is zero. Demand is unit elastic.

myeconlab Animation

# Price and Output Decision

A monopoly sets its price and output at the levels that maximize economic profit. To determine this price and output level, we need to study the behaviour of both cost and revenue as output varies. A monopoly faces the same types of technology and cost constraints as a competitive firm, so its costs (total cost, average cost and marginal cost) behave just like those of a firm in perfect competition. And a monopoly's revenues (total revenue, price and marginal revenue) behave in the way we've just described.

Let's see how Cut and Dry maximizes its profit.

## Maximizing Economic Profit

You can see in Table 8.1 and Figure 8.4(a) that total cost (*TC*) and total revenue (*TR*) both rise as output increases, but *TC* rises at an increasing rate and *TR* rises at a decreasing rate.

Economic profit, which equals *TR* minus *TC*, increases at small output levels, reaches a maximum and then decreases. The maximum profit (£12) occurs when Cut and Dry sells 3 haircuts for £14 each. If it sells 2 haircuts for £16 each or 4 haircuts for £12 each, Cut and Dry's economic profit will be only £8.

## Marginal Revenue Equals Marginal Cost

You can see Cut and Dry's marginal revenue (*MR*) and marginal cost (*MC*) in Table 8.1 and Figure 8.4(b). When Cut and Dry increases output from 2 to 3 haircuts, *MR* is £10 and *MC* is £6. *MR* exceeds *MC* by £4 and Cut and Dry's profit increases by that amount. If Cut and Dry increases output yet further, from 3 to 4 haircuts, *MR* is £6 and *MC* is £10. In this case, *MC* exceeds *MR* by £4, so Cut and Dry's profit decreases by that amount.

When *MR* exceeds *MC*, profit increases if output increases. When *MC* exceeds *MR*, profit increases if output *decreases*. When *MC* equals *MR*, profit is maximized.

Figure 8.4(b) shows the maximum profit as price (on the demand curve *D*) minus average total cost (on the *ATC* curve) multiplied by the quantity produced – the blue rectangle.

## Maximum Price the Market Will Bear

Unlike a firm in perfect competition, a monopoly influences the price of what it sells. But a monopoly doesn't set the price at the maximum *possible* price. At the maximum possible price, the firm would be able to sell only one unit of output, which in general is less than the profit-maximizing quantity. Rather, a monopoly

---

**Table 8.1**

## A Monopoly's Output and Price Decision

| Price (P) (pounds per haircut) | Quantity demanded (Q) (haircuts per hour) | Total revenue (TR = P × Q) (pounds) | Marginal revenue (MR = ΔTR/ΔQ) (pounds per haircut) | Total cost (TC) (pounds) | Marginal cost (MC = ΔTC/ΔQ) (pounds per haircut) | Profit (TR − TC) (pounds) |
|---|---|---|---|---|---|---|
| 20 | 0 | 0 | | 20 | | −20 |
| | | | 18 | | 1 | |
| 18 | 1 | 18 | | 21 | | −3 |
| | | | 14 | | 3 | |
| 16 | 2 | 32 | | 24 | | 8 |
| | | | 10 | | 6 | |
| **14** | **3** | **42** | | **30** | | **+12** |
| | | | 6 | | 10 | |
| 12 | 4 | 48 | | 40 | | +8 |
| | | | 2 | | 15 | |
| 10 | 5 | 50 | | 55 | | −5 |

Total revenue (*TR*) equals price (*P*) multiplied by the quantity sold (*Q*). Profit equals total revenue minus total cost (*TC*). Profit is maximized when the price is £14 a haircut and 3 haircuts are sold. Total revenue is £42 an hour, total cost is £30 an hour and economic profit is £12 an hour.

**Figure 8.4** A Monopoly's Output and Price

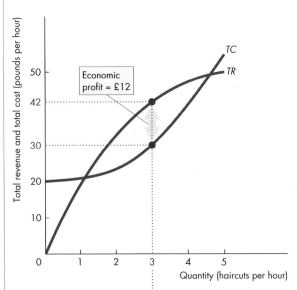

**(a) Total revenue and total cost curves**

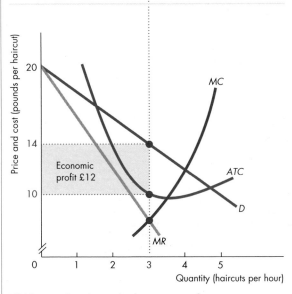

**(b) Demand and marginal revenue and cost curves**

In part (a), economic profit is the vertical distance equal to total revenue (*TR*) minus total cost (*TC*) and it is maximized at 3 haircuts an hour.

In part (b), economic profit is maximized when marginal cost (*MC*) equals marginal revenue (*MR*). The profit-maximizing output is 3 haircuts an hour. The price is determined by the demand curve (*D*) and is £14 a haircut. The average total cost is £10 a haircut, so economic profit, the blue rectangle, is £12, which equals the profit per haircut (£4) multiplied by 3 haircuts.

myeconlab Animation

produces the profit-maximizing quantity and sells that quantity for the highest price it can get.

All firms maximize profit by producing the output at which marginal revenue equals marginal cost. For a competitive firm, price equals marginal revenue, so price also equals marginal cost. For a monopoly, price exceeds marginal revenue, so price also exceeds marginal cost.

A monopoly charges a price that exceeds marginal cost, but does it always make an economic profit? In Figure 8.4(b), Cut and Dry produces 3 haircuts an hour. Its average total cost is £10 (read from the *ATC* curve) and its price is £14 (read from the *D* curve). It makes a profit of £4 a haircut (£14 minus £10). Cut and Dry's economic profit is shown by the blue rectangle, which equals the profit per haircut (£4) multiplied by the number of haircuts (3), for a total of £12 an hour.

If firms in a perfectly competitive market make a positive economic profit, new firms enter. That does *not* happen in monopoly. Barriers to entry prevent new firms from entering a market in which there is a monopoly. So a monopoly can make a positive economic profit and might continue to do so indefinitely. Sometimes that profit is large, as in the international diamond business.

Cut and Dry makes a positive economic profit. But suppose that the owner of the shop that Gina rents increases Cut and Dry's rent. If Cut and Dry pays an additional £12 an hour, its fixed cost increases by £12 an hour. Its marginal cost and marginal revenue don't change, so its profit-maximizing output remains at 3 haircuts an hour. Economic profit decreases by £12 an hour to zero. If Cut and Dry pays more than an additional £12 an hour for its shop rent, it incurs an economic loss. If this situation were permanent, Cut and Dry would go out of business.

## Review Quiz

1  What is the relationship between marginal cost and marginal revenue when a single-price monopoly maximizes profit?
2  How does a single-price monopoly determine the price it will charge its customers?
3  What is the relationship between price, marginal revenue and marginal cost when a single-price monopoly is maximizing profit?
4  Why can a monopoly make a positive economic profit even in the long run?

You can work these questions in Study Plan 8.2 and get instant feedback.

## Single-price Monopoly and Competition Compared

Imagine a market that is made up of many small firms operating in perfect competition. Then imagine that a single firm buys out all these small firms and creates a monopoly.

What will happen in this market? Will the price rise or fall? Will the quantity produced increase or decrease? Will economic profit increase or decrease? Will either the original competitive situation or the new monopoly situation be efficient?

These are the questions we're now going to answer. First, we look at the effects of monopoly on the price and quantity produced. Then we turn to the questions about efficiency.

## Comparing Price and Output

Figure 8.5 shows the market we'll study. The market demand curve is $D$. The demand curve is the same regardless of how the market is organized. But the supply side and the equilibrium are different in monopoly and competition. First, let's look at the case of perfect competition.

### Perfect Competition

Initially, with many small, perfectly competitive firms in the market, the market supply curve is $S$. This supply curve is obtained by summing the supply curves of all the individual firms in the market.

In perfect competition, equilibrium occurs where the market supply curve and market demand curve intersect. The quantity produced is $Q_C$ and the price is $P_C$. Each firm takes the price $P_C$ and maximizes its profit by producing the output at which its own marginal cost equals the price. Because each firm is a small part of the total market, there is no incentive for any firm to try to manipulate the price by varying its output.

### Monopoly

Now suppose that this market is taken over by a single firm. Consumers do not change, so the market demand curve remains the same as in the case of perfect competition. But now the monopoly recognizes this demand curve as a constraint on the price at which it can sell its output. The monopoly's marginal revenue curve is $MR$.

The monopoly maximizes profit by producing the quantity at which marginal revenue equals marginal cost. To find the monopoly's marginal cost curve, first recall that in perfect competition the market supply curve is the sum of the supply curves of the firms in the market. Also recall that each firm's supply curve is its marginal cost curve (see Chapter 7, p. 157). So when the market is taken over by a single firm, the competitive market's supply curve becomes the monopoly's marginal cost curve. To remind you of this fact, the supply curve is also labelled $MC$.

The output at which marginal revenue equals marginal cost is $Q_M$. This output is smaller than the competitive output $Q_C$. And the monopoly charges the price $P_M$, which is higher than $P_C$. We have established that:

> **Compared with a perfectly competitive market, a single-price monopoly produces a smaller output and charges a higher price.**

We've seen how the output and price of a monopoly compare with those in a competitive market. Let's now compare the efficiency of the two types of market.

**Figure 8.5** Monopoly's Smaller Output and Higher Price

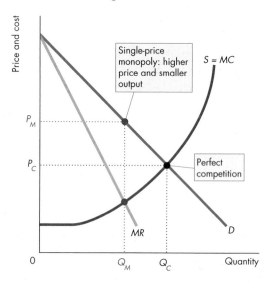

A competitive market produces the quantity $Q_C$ at price $P_C$. A single-price monopoly produces the quantity $Q_M$ at which marginal revenue equals marginal cost and sells that quantity for the price $P_M$. Compared with perfect competition, a single-price monopoly produces a smaller output and charges a higher price.

myeconlab Animation

# Efficiency Comparison

You saw in Chapter 7 (pp. 168–169) that perfect competition (with no external costs and benefits) is efficient. Figure 8.6(a) illustrates the efficiency of perfect competition and serves as a benchmark against which to measure the inefficiency of monopoly.

Along the demand curve and marginal social benefit curve ($D = MSB$), consumers are efficient. Along the supply curve and marginal social cost curve ($S = MSC$), producers are efficient. In competitive equilibrium, the price is $P_C$, the quantity is $Q_C$ and marginal social benefit equals marginal social cost.

*Consumer surplus* is the green triangle under the demand curve and above the equilibrium price (see Chapter 4, p. 87). *Producer surplus* is the blue area above the supply curve and below the equilibrium price (see Chapter 4, p. 89). Total surplus (the sum of the consumer surplus and producer surplus) is maximized.

Also, in long-run competitive equilibrium, entry and exit ensure that each firm produces its output at the minimum possible long-run average cost.

To summarize: at the competitive equilibrium, marginal social benefit equals marginal social cost; total surplus is maximized; firms produce at the lowest possible long-run average cost; and resource use is efficient.

Figure 8.6(b) illustrates the inefficiency of monopoly and the sources of that inefficiency. A monopoly produces $Q_M$ and charges $P_M$. The smaller output and higher price drive a wedge between marginal social benefit and marginal social cost and create a *deadweight loss*. The grey area shows the deadweight loss and its magnitude is a measure of the inefficiency of monopoly.

Consumer surplus shrinks for two reasons. First, consumers lose by having to pay more for the good. This loss to consumers is a gain for the producer and increases the producer surplus. Second, consumers lose by getting less of the good, and this loss is part of the deadweight loss.

Although the monopoly gains from a higher price, it loses some of the original producer surplus because it produces a smaller output. That loss is another part of the deadweight loss.

Because a monopoly restricts output below the market quantity of perfect competition and faces no competitive threat, it does not produce at the lowest possible long-run average cost. As a result, monopoly damages the consumer interest in three ways: it produces less, it increases the cost of production, and it raises the price to above the increased cost of production.

**Figure 8.6**    Inefficiency of Monopoly

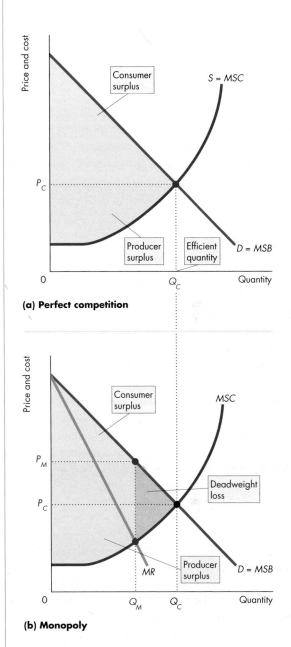

**(a) Perfect competition**

**(b) Monopoly**

In perfect competition in part (a), output is $Q_C$ and the price is $P_C$. Marginal social benefit (*MSB*) equals marginal social cost (*MSC*); total surplus, the sum of consumer surplus (the green triangle) and producer surplus (the blue area), is maximized; and in the long run, firms produce at the lowest possible average cost.

A monopoly in part (b) restricts output to $Q_M$ and raises the price to $P_M$. Consumer surplus shrinks, the monopoly gains and a deadweight loss (the grey area) arises.

## Redistribution of Surpluses

You've seen that monopoly is inefficient because marginal social benefit exceeds marginal social cost and there is deadweight loss – a social loss. But monopoly also brings a *redistribution* of surpluses.

Some of the lost consumer surplus goes to the monopoly. In Figure 8.6(b), the monopoly gets the difference between the higher price, $P_M$, and the competitive price, $P_C$, on the quantity sold, $Q_M$. So the monopoly takes part of the consumer surplus. This portion of the loss of consumer surplus is not a loss to society. It is a redistribution from consumers to the monopoly producer.

## Rent Seeking

You've seen that monopoly creates a deadweight loss and is inefficient. But the social cost of monopoly can exceed the deadweight loss because of an activity called rent seeking. Any surplus – consumer surplus, producer surplus or economic profit – is called **economic rent**. And **rent seeking** is the pursuit of wealth by capturing economic rent.

You've seen that a monopoly makes its economic profit by diverting part of consumer surplus to itself – by converting consumer surplus into economic profit. So the pursuit of economic profit by a monopoly is rent seeking. It is the attempt to capture consumer surplus.

Rent seekers pursue their goals in two main ways. They might:

◆ Buy a monopoly
◆ Create a monopoly

### Buy a Monopoly

To rent seek by buying a monopoly, a person searches for a monopoly that is for sale at a lower price than the monopoly's economic profit. Trading of taxi licences is an example of this type of rent seeking. In some cities, taxis are regulated. The city restricts both the fares and the number of taxis that can operate so that operating a taxi results in economic profit or rent. A person who wants to operate a taxi must buy a licence from someone who already has one. People rationally devote time and effort to seeking out profitable monopoly businesses to buy. In the process, they use up scarce resources that could otherwise have been used to produce goods and services. The value of this lost production is part of the social cost of monopoly. The amount paid for a monopoly is not a social cost because the payment is just a transfer of an existing producer surplus from the buyer to the seller.

### Create a Monopoly

Rent seeking by creating a monopoly is mainly a political activity. It takes the form of lobbying and seeking to influence the political process. Such influence is sometimes sought by making political contributions in exchange for legislative support or by indirectly seeking to influence political outcomes through publicity in the media or via more direct contacts with politicians and bureaucrats. An example of this type of rent seeking would be the donations that alcohol and tobacco companies make to political parties in an attempt to avoid a tightening of legislation on activities such as advertising and licensing, which might affect their profits.

This type of rent seeking is a costly activity that uses up scarce resources. In aggregate, firms spend millions of pounds lobbying Parliament in the pursuit of licences and laws that create barriers to entry and establish a monopoly. Everyone has an incentive to rent seek, and because there are no barriers to entry into rent seeking, there is a great deal of competition in this activity. The winners of the competition become monopolies.

## Rent-seeking Equilibrium

How much will a person be willing to give up to acquire a monopoly right? The answer is the entire value of a monopoly's economic profit. Barriers to entry create monopoly. But there is no barrier to entry into rent seeking. Rent seeking is like perfect competition. If an economic profit is available, a new rent seeker will try to get some of it. And competition among rent seekers pushes up the price that must be paid for a monopoly to the point at which the rent seeker makes zero economic profit by operating the monopoly.

Figure 8.7 shows a rent-seeking equilibrium. The cost of rent seeking is a fixed cost that must be added to a monopoly's other costs. Rent seeking and rent-seeking costs increase to the point at which no economic profit is made. The average total cost curve, which includes the fixed cost of rent seeking, shifts upward until it just touches the demand curve. Economic profit is zero. It has been lost in rent seeking.

Consumer surplus is unaffected. But the deadweight loss of monopoly now includes the original deadweight loss plus the lost producer surplus, shown by the enlarged grey area in Figure 8.7.

**Figure 8.7**    Rent-seeking Equilibrium

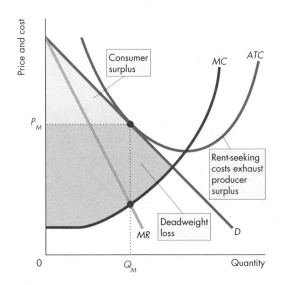

With competitive rent seeking, a monopoly uses all its economic profit to prevent another firm from taking its economic rent. The firm's rent-seeking costs are fixed costs. They add to total fixed cost and to average total cost and the *ATC* curve shifts upward. Rent seeking will continue until the *ATC* curve has shifted up by so much that at the profit-maximizing price, the firm breaks even. The grey area shows the deadweight loss.

myeconlab Animation

**Review Quiz**

1   Why does a single-price monopoly produce a smaller output and charge a higher price than what would prevail if the market were perfectly competitive?
2   How does a monopoly transfer consumer surplus to itself?
3   Why is a single-price monopoly inefficient?
4   What is rent seeking and how does it influence the inefficiency of monopoly?

You can work these questions in Study Plan 8.3 and get instant feedback.

So far, we've considered only a single-price monopoly. But many monopolies do not operate with a single price. Instead, they price discriminate. Let's now see how price-discriminating monopoly works.

# Price Discrimination

You encounter *price discrimination* – selling a good or service at a number of different prices – when you travel, go to the cinema, go shopping or go out to eat. Many firms that price discriminate are not monopolies, but monopolies price discriminate when they can do so.

To be able to price discriminate, a monopoly must be able to identify and separate different buyer types and sell a product that cannot be resold.

Not all price *differences* are price *discrimination*. Some goods that are similar but not identical have different prices because they have different production costs. For example, the cost of producing electricity depends on the time of day. If an electric power company charges a higher price during the peak consumption periods from 7:00 to 9:00 in the morning and from 4:00 to 7:00 in the evening than it does at other times of the day, it is not price discriminating.

At first sight, price discrimination appears to be inconsistent with profit maximization. Why would a railway company give a student discount? Why would a hairdresser charge students and senior citizens less? Aren't these firms losing profit by being so generous to their customers?

## Capturing Consumer Surplus

Price discrimination captures consumer surplus and converts it into economic profit. It does so by getting buyers to pay a price as close as possible to the maximum willingness to pay.

Firms price discriminate in two broad ways:

◆  Among groups of buyers
◆  Among units of a good

### Discriminating Among Groups of Buyers

People differ in the value they place on a good – their marginal benefit and willingness to pay. Some of these differences are correlated with features such as age, employment status, and other easily distinguished characteristics. When such a correlation is present, firms can profit by price discriminating among the different groups of buyers.

For example, a face-to-face sales meeting with a customer might bring a large and profitable order. So for salespeople and other business travellers, the marginal benefit from a trip is large and the price that such a traveller is willing to pay for a trip is high. In contrast, for a holiday traveller, any of several different trips and even no holiday trip are options. So for holiday travellers, the marginal benefit of a trip is small and the price that such a traveller is willing to pay for a trip is low. Because business travellers are willing to pay more than holiday travellers are, it is possible for an airline to profit by price discriminating between these two groups.

### Discriminating Among Units of a Good

Everyone experiences diminishing marginal benefit and has a downward-sloping demand curve. For this reason, if all the units of the good are sold for a single price, buyers end up with a consumer surplus equal to the value they get from each unit of the good minus the price paid for it.

A firm that price discriminates by charging a buyer one price for a single item and a lower price for a second or third item can capture some of the consumer surplus. Buy one pizza and get a second one free (or for a low price) is an example of this type of price discrimination.

(Note that some discounts for bulk arise from lower costs of production for greater bulk. In these cases, such discounts are not price discrimination.)

Let's see how price discriminating increases economic profit.

## Profiting by Price Discriminating

Global Air has a monopoly on an exotic route. Figure 8.8 shows the demand curve (*D*) and the marginal revenue curve (*MR*) for travel on this route. It also shows Global Air's marginal cost curve (*MC*) and average total cost curve (*ATC*).

Initially, Global is a single-price monopoly and maximizes its profit by producing 8,000 trips a year (the quantity at which *MR* equals *MC*). The price is €1,200 per trip. The average total cost of producing a trip is €600, so economic profit is €600 a trip. On 8,000 trips, Global's economic profit is €4.8 million a year, shown by the blue rectangle. Global's customers enjoy a consumer surplus shown by the green triangle.

Global is struck by the fact that many of its customers are business travellers and it suspects they are willing to pay more than €1,200 a trip. So Global does some market research, which reveals that some business travellers are willing to pay as much as €1,800 a trip. Also, these customers frequently change their travel plans at the last moment. Another group of business travellers is willing to pay €1,600. These customers

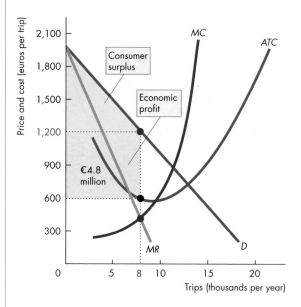

**Figure 8.8**   A Single Price of Air Travel

Global Air has a monopoly on an air route. The market demand curve is *D* and marginal revenue curve is *MR*. Global Air's marginal cost curve is *MC* and its average total cost curve is *ATC*. As a single-price monopoly, Global maximizes profit by selling 8,000 trips a year at €1,200 a trip. Its profit is €4.8 million a year – the blue rectangle. Global's customers enjoy a consumer surplus – the green triangle.

know a week ahead when they will travel and they never want to stay over a weekend. Yet another group would pay up to €1,400. These travellers know two weeks ahead when they will travel and also don't want to stay over a weekend.

So Global announces a new fare schedule:

No restrictions, €1,800

7-day advance purchase, non-refundable, €1,600

14-day advance purchase, non-refundable, €1,400

14-day advance purchase, must stay over a weekend, €1,200.

Figure 8.9 shows the outcome with this new fare structure and also shows why Global is pleased with its new fares. Global sells 2,000 seats at each of its four prices. Global's economic profit increases by the dark blue steps in Figure 8.9. Its economic profit is now its original €4.8 million a year plus an additional €2.4 million from its new higher fares. Consumer surplus has shrunk to the total of the four green triangles.

**Figure 8.9** Price Discrimination

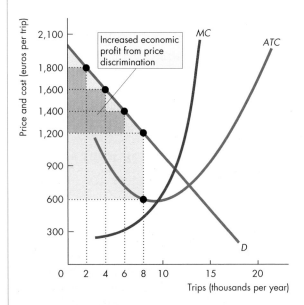

Global revises its fare structure: no restrictions at €1,800, 7-day advance purchase at €1,600, 14-day advance purchase at €1,400, and must stay over a weekend at €1,200. Global sells 2,000 trips at each of its four new fares. Its economic profit increases by €2.4 million a year to €7.2 million a year, which is shown by the original blue rectangle plus the blue steps. Global's customers' consumer surplus (total green area) shrinks.

# Perfect Price Discrimination

**Perfect price discrimination** occurs if a firm is able to sell each unit of output for the highest price anyone is willing to pay for it. In such a case, the entire consumer surplus is eliminated and captured by the producer. To practise perfect price discrimination, a firm must be creative and come up with a host of prices and special conditions, each one of which appeals to a tiny segment of the market.

With perfect price discrimination, something special happens to marginal revenue. For the perfect price discriminator, the market demand curve becomes the firm's marginal revenue curve. The reason is that when the price is cut to sell a larger quantity, the firm sells only the marginal unit at the lower price. All the other units continue to be sold for the highest price that each buyer is willing to pay. So for the perfect price discriminator, marginal revenue *equals* price and the demand curve becomes the firm's marginal revenue curve.

With marginal revenue equal to price, Global can obtain even greater profit by increasing output up to the point at which price (and marginal revenue) is equal to marginal cost.

So Global now seeks additional travellers who will not pay as much as €1,200 a trip but who will pay more than marginal cost. Global offers a variety of holiday specials at different low fares that appeal only to new travellers. Existing customers continue to pay the higher fares. With all these fares and specials, Global increases sales, extracts the entire consumer surplus and maximizes economic profit.

Figure 8.10 shows the outcome with perfect price discrimination. The fares paid by the original 8,000 travellers extract the entire consumer surplus from this group. The new fares between €900 and €1,200 have attracted 3,000 additional travellers and taken their entire consumer surplus also. Global now makes an economic profit of more than €9 million.

**Figure 8.10** Perfect Price Discrimination

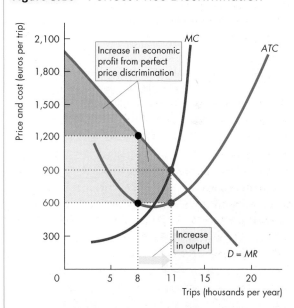

Dozens of fares discriminate among many different types of business travellers and many new low fares with restrictions appeal to holiday travellers. With perfect price discrimination, the market demand curve becomes Global's marginal revenue curve. Economic profit is maximized when the lowest price equals marginal cost. Here, Global sells 11,000 trips and makes an economic profit of more than €9 million a year.

## Efficiency and Rent Seeking with Price Discrimination

With perfect price discrimination, output increases to the point at which price equals marginal cost – where the marginal cost curve intersects the market demand curve. This output is identical to that of perfect competition. Perfect price discrimination pushes consumer surplus to zero but increases producer surplus to equal the sum of consumer surplus and producer surplus in perfect competition. Deadweight loss with perfect price discrimination is zero. So perfect price discrimination achieves efficiency.

> **The more perfectly the monopoly can price discriminate, the closer its output gets to the competitive output and the more efficient is the outcome.**

But there are two differences between perfect competition and perfect price discrimination. First, the distribution of the total surplus is different. It is shared by consumers and producers in perfect competition, whereas the producer gets it all with perfect price discrimination. Second, because the producer grabs the entire total surplus, rent seeking becomes profitable.

People use resources in pursuit of economic rent, and the bigger the rents, the more resources get used in pursuing them. With free entry into rent seeking, the long-run equilibrium outcome is that rent seekers use up the entire producer surplus.

Real-world airlines are just as creative as Global, as you can see in the cartoon!

*Would it bother you to hear how little I paid for this flight?*

From William Hamilton, *Voodoo Economics*, 1992, Chronicle Books, p. 3. Reprinted with permission from William Hamilton.

---

**ECONOMICS IN ACTION**

## Attempting Perfect Price Discrimination

If you want to spend a day at Disney World Paris (2 parks), it will cost you £61. The figure shows the prices for a second, third, fourth, and fifth day. The Disney Corporation hopes that it has read your willingness to pay correctly and not left you with too much consumer surplus. But notice that the fourth day costs more than the third. It seems that Disney has forgotten that your marginal benefit diminishes!

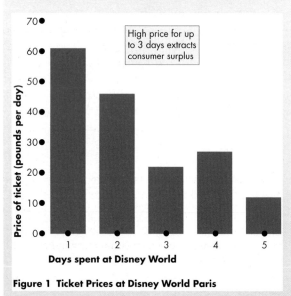

**Figure 1 Ticket Prices at Disney World Paris**

---

**Review Quiz**

1 What is price discrimination and how is it used to increase a monopoly's profit?
2 Explain how consumer surplus changes when a monopoly price discriminates.
3 Explain how consumer surplus, economic profit and output change when a monopoly perfectly price discriminates.
4 What are some of the ways that real-world airlines use to price discriminate?

You can work these questions in Study Plan 8.4 and get instant feedback.

You've seen that monopoly is profitable, but costly for consumers. Monopoly results in inefficiency. Because of these features of monopoly, it is subject to policy debate and regulation. We'll now study key monopoly policy issues.

## Monopoly Regulation

Natural monopoly presents a dilemma. With economies of scale, it produces at the lowest possible cost. But with market power, it has an incentive to raise the price above the competitive price and produce too little – to operate in the self-interest of the monopoly and not in the social interest.

**Regulation** – rules administered by a government agency to influence prices, quantities, entry, and other aspects of economic activity in a firm or industry – is a possible solution to this dilemma.

To implement regulation, the government establishes agencies to oversee and enforce the rules. For example, in the UK, OFGEN regulates prices for electricity and gas supply, and OFWAT regulates water prices. By the 1970s, almost a quarter of the nation's output was produced by regulated industries (far more than just natural monopolies) and a process of deregulation began.

**Deregulation** is the process of removing regulation of prices, quantities, entry and other aspects of economic activity in a firm or industry. During the past 30 years, deregulation has occurred in UK domestic airlines, telephone service, electricity, water and gas supply, national rail services, and banking and financial services among other things. While deregulation is progressing in other EU countries, it is not as widespread as in the UK.

Regulation is a possible solution to the dilemma presented by natural monopoly but not a guaranteed solution. There are two theories about how regulation actually works:

1   Social interest theory

2   Capture theory

The **social interest theory** is that the political and regulatory process relentlessly seeks out inefficiency and introduces regulation that eliminates deadweight loss and allocates resources efficiently.

The **capture theory** is that regulation serves the self-interest of the producer, who captures the regulator and maximizes economic profit. Regulation that benefits the producer but creates a deadweight loss gets adopted because the producer's gain is large and visible while each individual consumer's loss is small and invisible. No individual consumer has an incentive to oppose the regulation but the producer has a big incentive to lobby for it.

We're going to examine efficient regulation that serves the social interest and see why it is not a simple matter to design and implement such regulation.

## Efficient Regulation of a Natural Monopoly

A gas distribution company is a natural monopoly – it can supply the entire market at a lower price than two or more competing firms can. Centrica is the current name for a private gas supplier that was a UK government monopoly called British Gas. The firm has invested heavily in household meters, pipes, regional storage facilities and other equipment. These fixed costs are part of the firm's average total cost. Its average total cost decreases as the number of customers supplied increases because the fixed cost is spread over a larger number of households.

Unregulated and acting as a monopoly after privatization, Centrica produces the quantity that maximizes profit. Like all single-price monopolies, the profit-maximizing quantity is less than the efficient quantity, and underproduction results in a deadweight loss.

How can Centrica be regulated to produce the efficient quantity of gas? The answer is by being regulated to set its price equal to marginal cost, known as the **marginal cost pricing rule**. The quantity demanded at a price equal to marginal cost is the efficient quantity – the quantity at which marginal social benefit equals marginal social cost.

Figure 8.11 illustrates the marginal cost pricing rule. The demand curve for gas is *D*. Centrica's marginal cost curve is *MC*, which is assumed to be constant at 10 pence per cubic metre. That is, the cost of supplying each additional household with gas is 10 pence per cubic metre. The efficient outcome occurs if the price is regulated at 10 pence per cubic metre with 4 million cubic metres a day produced.

But there is a problem: at the efficient output, because price equals marginal cost, the price is below average total cost. Average total cost minus the price is the loss per unit produced. It's pretty obvious that if Centrica is required to use a marginal cost pricing rule it will not stay in business for long. How can a company cover its costs and, at the same time, obey a marginal cost pricing rule?

There are two possible ways of enabling the firm to cover its costs: price discrimination and a two-part price (called a *two-part tariff*). For example, a mobile phone company offers plans at a fixed monthly price that give access to the phone network and unlimited free calls. The price of a call (zero) equals the marginal cost of a call. Similarly, a gas supplier can charge a one-time connection fee that covers its fixed cost and then charge a monthly fee equal to marginal cost.

**Figure 8.11**   Regulating a Natural Monopoly

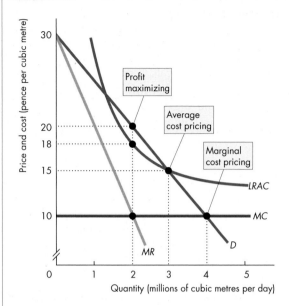

A natural monopoly gas producer faces the market demand curve *D*. The firm's marginal cost is constant at 10 pence per cubic metre, as shown by the curve labelled *MC*. The long-run average cost curve is *LRAC*.

Unregulated, as a profit-maximizer, the firm produces 2 million cubic metres a day and charges a price of 20 pence per cubic metre. An efficient marginal cost pricing rule sets the price at 10 pence per cubic metre. The monopoly produces 4 million cubic metres per day and incurs an economic loss. A second-best average cost pricing rule sets the price at 15 pence per cubic metre. The monopoly produces 3 million cubic metres per day and makes zero economic profit.

myeconlab Animation

# Second-best Regulation of a Natural Monopoly

A natural monopoly cannot always be regulated to achieve an efficient outcome. Two possible ways of enabling a regulated monopoly to avoid an economic loss are:

◆ Average cost pricing
◆ Government subsidy

## Average Cost Pricing

An **average cost pricing rule** sets the price equal to average total cost. With this rule the firm produces the quantity at which the long-run average cost curve cuts the demand curve. This rule results in the firm making zero economic profit – breaking even. But because for a natural monopoly average cost exceeds marginal cost, the quantity produced is less than the efficient quantity and a deadweight loss arises.

Figure 8.11 illustrates the average cost pricing rule. The price is 15 pence a cubic metre and 3 million cubic metres a day are produced.

## Government Subsidy

A government subsidy is a direct payment to the firm equal to its economic loss. To pay a subsidy, the government must raise the revenue by taxing some other activity. You saw in Chapter 5 that taxes themselves generate deadweight loss.

## And the Second-Best Is . . .

Which is the better option, average cost pricing or marginal cost pricing with a government subsidy? The answer depends on the relative magnitudes of the two deadweight losses. Average cost pricing generates a deadweight loss in the market served by the natural monopoly. A subsidy generates deadweight losses in the markets for the items that are taxed to pay for the subsidy. The smaller deadweight loss is the second-best solution to regulating a natural monopoly. Making this calculation in practice is too difficult and average cost pricing is generally preferred to a subsidy.

Implementing average cost pricing presents the regulator with a challenge because it is not possible to be sure what a firm's costs are. So regulators use one of two practical rules:

◆ Rate of return regulation
◆ Price cap regulation

### Rate of Return Regulation

Under **rate of return regulation**, a firm must justify its price by showing that its return on capital doesn't exceed a specified target rate. This type of regulation can end up serving the self-interest of the firm rather than the social interest. The firm's managers have an incentive to inflate costs by spending on items such as private jets, free football tickets (disguised as public relations expenses), and lavish entertainment. Managers also have an incentive to use more capital than the efficient amount. The rate of return on capital is regulated but not the total return on capital, and the greater the amount of capital, the greater is the total return.

## Price Cap Regulation

For the reason that we've just examined, rate of return regulation is increasingly being replaced by price cap regulation. **Price cap regulation** is a price ceiling – a rule that specifies the highest price the firm is permitted to set. This type of regulation gives a firm an incentive to operate efficiently and keep costs under control. Price cap regulation has become common for the electricity and telecommunications industries and is replacing rate of return regulation.

To see how a price cap works, let's suppose that the gas distribution company is subject to this type of regulation. Figure 8.12 shows that without regulation, the firm maximizes profit by producing 2 million cubic metres a day and charging a price of 20 pence a cubic metre. If a price cap is set at 15 pence a cubic metre, the firm is permitted to sell any quantity it chooses at that price or at a lower price.

At 2 million cubic metres a day, the firm now incurs an economic loss. It can decrease the loss by increasing output to 3 million cubic metres a day. To increase output above 3 million cubic metres a day, the firm would have to lower the price and again it would incur an economic loss. So the profit-maximizing quantity is 3 million cubic metres a day – the same as with average cost pricing.

Notice that a price cap lowers the price and increases output. This outcome is in sharp contrast to the effect of a price ceiling in a competitive market that you studied in Chapter 5 (pp. 106–108). The reason is that in a monopoly, the unregulated equilibrium output is less than the competitive equilibrium output, and the price cap regulation replicates the conditions of a competitive market.

In Figure 8.12, the price cap delivers average cost pricing. In practice, the regulator might set the cap too high. For this reason, price cap regulation is often combined with *earnings sharing regulation* – a regulation that requires firms to make refunds to customers when profits rise above a target level.

### Figure 8.12 Price Cap Regulation

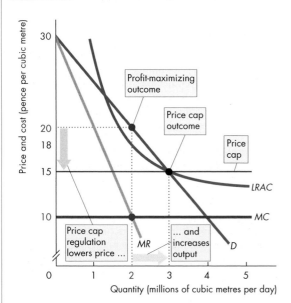

A natural monopoly gas producer faces the market demand curve D. The firm's marginal cost is constant at 10 pence per cubic metre – shown by the curve labelled MC. The long-run average total cost curve is LRAC. Unregulated, the firm produces 2 million cubic metres a day and charges a price of 20 pence per cubic metre.

A price cap is set at 15 pence a cubic metre. The maximum price that the firm can charge is 15 pence a cubic metre, so the firm has an incentive to minimize cost and produce the quantity demanded at the price cap. The price cap regulation lowers the price to 15 pence a cubic metre and the firm increases the quantity to 3 million cubic metres a day.

myeconlab Animation ◆

You've now completed your study of monopoly. *Reading Between the Lines* on pp. 194–195 looks at Google's dominant position in the market for Internet search advertising.

In the next chapter, we study markets that lie between the extremes of perfect competition and monopoly and that blend elements of the two.

# Reading Between the Lines

# Google Accused of Anti-competitive Practice

The Telegraph, 24 February 2010

## Google under Investigation for Alleged Breach of EU Competition Rule

The European Commission has launched an antitrust investigation against Google. . . . The investigation comes under the Lisbon Treaty's 'abuse of dominant position' powers and is the first time that Google has been targeted by the European Union. . . .

The Commission has written to Google with a series of questions over how its search functions operate and also questioned the way it sells advertising. It acted after complaints from the UK search site Foundem, a price comparison site, Ciao, an online shopping site owned by Microsoft, and ejustice.fr, a French site which details legal cases and solicitor services.

Foundem claims that Google, which has a 90pc share of the search market in the UK, has penalized the site with a 'search penalty' on its business. . . . Foundem said: "Google has always used various penalty filters to remove certain sites entirely from its search results or place them so far down the rankings that they will never be found."

Google has dismissed the claims, saying that its search algorithms are aimed at pointing people to the best sites and that it does not pick and choose favourites. Google said: "We've always worked hard to ensure that our success is earned the right way, through technological innovation and great products, rather than by locking in our users or advertisers or creating artificial barriers to entry."

## The Essence of the Story

◆ The EU has started an investigation into claims that Google abuses its market position.

◆ Some companies claim Google uses advertising and penalty filters in its search function to limit access to competitors.

◆ Google has a 90 per cent share of the UK search market.

◆ Google dismisses the claims saying it did not have favourites or create barriers to entry and its success arises from innovation and good products which get people to the best sites.

# Economic Analysis

◆ Google gained its dominant position in the search market by selling advertisements associated with search keywords within its innovative search engine.

◆ Google sells keywords based on a combination of willingness-to-pay and the number of clicks an advertisement receives.

◆ Google has steadily improved its search engine and its interface with both searchers and advertisers to make searches more powerful and advertising more effective.

◆ Figure 1 shows Google's extraordinary success in terms of its revenue, cost and profit.

◆ Google could have provided a basic search engine without innovation.

◆ If Google had followed this strategy, people would use competitor search engines and advertisers would have been willing to pay low prices for Google ads.

◆ Google would have faced the market described in Figure 2 and made a small economic profit.

◆ Instead, Google improved its search engine and the effectiveness of advertising. The demand for Google search and ads increased.

◆ Google's innovation is not a barrier to entry but by selling keywords to the highest bidder it achieves perfect price discrimination.

◆ Figure 3 shows how, with perfect price discrimination, Google's producer surplus is maximized. Google produces the efficient quantity of search and advertising by accepting ads as long as price exceeds marginal cost.

◆ Google has a dominant position but doesn't appear to be acting against the EU social interest: there is no anti-competition case to answer.

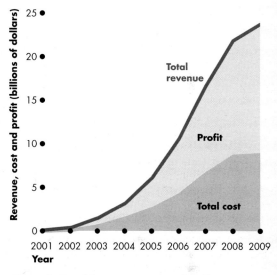

Figure 1   Google's revenue, cost and profit

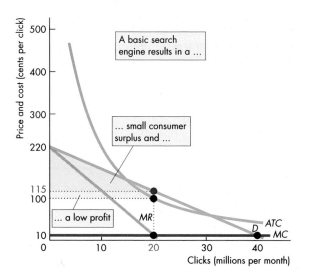

**Figure 2  Basic search engine**

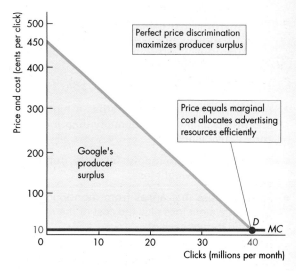

**Figure 3  Google with keywords and other features**

> SUMMARY

## Key Points

### Monopoly and How It Arises
(pp. 178–179)

◆ A monopoly is a market with a single supplier of a good or service that has no close substitutes and in which barriers to entry prevent competition.

◆ Barriers to entry may be legal (monopoly franchise, licence, patent or copyright), ownership of a resource, or natural (created by economies of scale).

◆ A monopoly might be able to price discriminate when there is no resale possibility.

◆ Where resale is possible, a firm charges one price.

Working Problems 1 to 4 will give you a better understanding of monopoly and how it arises.

### A Single-price Monopoly's Output and Price Decision (pp. 180–183)

◆ A monopoly's demand curve is the market demand curve and a single-price monopoly's marginal revenue is less than price.

◆ A monopoly maximizes profit by producing the output at which marginal revenue equals marginal cost and by charging the maximum price that consumers are willing to pay for that output.

Working Problems 5 to 9 will give you a better understanding of a single-price monopoly's output and price.

### Single-price Monopoly and Competition Compared (pp. 184–187)

◆ A single-price monopoly charges a higher price and produces a smaller quantity than a perfectly competitive market.

◆ A single-price monopoly restricts output and creates a deadweight loss.

◆ The total loss that arises from monopoly equals the deadweight loss plus the cost of the resources devoted to rent seeking.

Working Problems 10 to 12 will give you a better understanding of the comparison of single-price monopoly and perfect competition.

### Price Discrimination (pp. 187–190)

◆ Price discrimination is an attempt by the monopoly to convert consumer surplus into economic profit.

◆ Perfect price discrimination extracts the entire consumer surplus; each unit is sold for the maximum price that each customer is willing to pay; the quantity produced is efficient.

◆ Rent seeking with perfect price discrimination might eliminate the entire consumer surplus and producer surplus.

Working Problems 13 to 16 will give you a better understanding of price discrimination.

### Monopoly Regulation (pp. 191–193)

◆ Monopoly regulation might serve the social interest or the interest of the monopoly (monopoly captures the regulator).

◆ Price equal to marginal cost achieves efficiency but results in economic loss.

◆ Price equal to average cost enables the firm to cover its costs but is inefficient.

◆ Rate of return regulation creates incentives for inefficient production and inflated cost.

◆ Price cap regulation with earnings sharing regulation can achieve a more efficient outcome than rate of return regulation.

Working Problems 17 to 19 will give you a better understanding of monopoly regulation.

## Key Terms

Average cost pricing rule, 192
Barrier to entry, 178
Capture theory, 191
Deregulation, 191
Economic rent, 186
Legal monopoly, 178
Marginal cost pricing rule, 191
Monopoly, 178
Natural monopoly, 178
Perfect price discrimination, 189
Price cap regulation, 193
Price discrimination, 179
Rate of return regulation, 192
Regulation, 191
Rent seeking, 186
Single-price monopoly, 179
Social interest theory, 191

# STUDY PLAN PROBLEMS AND APPLICATIONS

 **myeconlab** You can work Problems 1 to 19 in MyEconLab Chapter 8 Study Plan and get instant feedback.

## Monopoly and How It Arises
(Study Plan 8.1)

Use the following information to work Problems 1 to 3.

The Post Office has a monopoly on first class mail and the exclusive right to put mail in private mailboxes. Pfizer Inc. makes LIPITOR, a prescription drug that lowers cholesterol. Yorkshire Water is the sole supplier of drinking water in parts of northern England.

**1  a** What are the substitutes, if any, for the goods and services described above?

   **b** What are the barriers to entry, if any, that protect these three firms from competition?

**2** Which of these three firms, if any, is a natural monopoly? Explain your answer and illustrate it by drawing an appropriate figure.

**3  a** Which of these three firms, if any, is a legal monopoly? Explain your answer.

   **b** Which of these three firms is most likely to be able to profit from price discrimination and which is most likely to sell its good or service for a single price?

**4  Barbie's Revenge: Brawl over Doll Is Heading to Trial**

Four years ago, Mattel Inc. exhorted its executives to help save Barbie from a new doll clique called the Bratz. With its market share dropping at a 'chilling rate,' Barbie needed to be more 'aggressive, revolutionary, and ruthless.' Mattel has gone to court and is trying to seize ownership of the Bratz line, which Mattel accuses of stealing the idea for the pouty-lipped dolls with the big heads.

Source: The Wall Street Journal, 23 May 2008

**a** Before Bratz entered the market, what type of monopoly did Mattel Inc. possess in the market for 'the pouty-lipped dolls with the big heads'?

**b** What is the barrier to entry that Mattel might argue should protect it from competition in the market for Barbie dolls?

**c** Explain how the entry of Bratz dolls might be expected to change the demand for Barbie dolls.

## A Single-price Monopoly's Output and Price Decision (Study Plan 8.2)

Use the following table to work Problems 5 to 8.

Minnie's Mineral Springs, a single-price monopoly, faces the market demand schedule:

| Price (euros per bottle) | Quantity demanded (bottles) |
|---|---|
| 10 | 0 |
| 8 | 1 |
| 6 | 2 |
| 4 | 3 |
| 2 | 4 |
| 0 | 5 |

**5  a** Calculate the total revenue schedule for Minnie's Mineral Springs.

   **b** Calculate the marginal revenue schedule.

**6  a** Draw a graph of the market demand curve and Minnie's marginal revenue curve.

   **b** Why is Minnie's marginal revenue less than the price?

**7  a** At what price is Minnie's total revenue maximized?

   **b** Over what range of prices is the demand for water from Minnie's Mineral Springs elastic?

**8** Why will Minnie not produce a quantity at which the market demand for water is inelastic?

**9** Minnie's Mineral Springs faces the demand schedule in Problem 5 and has the following total cost schedule:

| Quantity produced (bottles) | Total cost (euros) |
|---|---|
| 0 | 1 |
| 1 | 3 |
| 2 | 7 |
| 3 | 13 |
| 4 | 21 |
| 5 | 31 |

**a** Calculate Minnie's profit-maximizing output and price.

**b** Calculate economic profit.

## Single-price Monopoly and Competition Compared (Study Plan 8.3)

Use the following news clip to work Problems 10 to 12.

**Zoloft Faces Patent Expiration**

Pfizer's antidepressant Zoloft, with $3.3 billion in 2005 sales, loses patent protection on June 30. When a brand name drug loses its patent, both the price of the drug and the dollar value of its sales each tend to drop 80 per cent over the next year, as competition opens to a host of generic drugmakers. The real winners are the patients and the insurers, who pay much lower prices. The Food and Drug Administration insists that generics work identically to brand-names.

Source: CNN, 15 June 2006

**10 a** Assume that Pfizer has a monopoly in the antidepressant market and that Pfizer cannot price discriminate. Use a graph to illustrate the market price and quantity of Zoloft sold.

**b** On your graph, identify consumer surplus, producer surplus, and deadweight loss.

**11** How might you justify protecting Pfizer from competition with a legal barrier to entry?

**12 a** Explain how the market for an antidepressant drug changes when a patent expires.

**b** Draw a graph to illustrate how the expiration of the Zoloft patent will change the price and quantity in the market for antidepressants.

**c** Explain how consumer surplus, producer surplus, and deadweight loss change with the expiration of the Zoloft patent.

## Price Discrimination (Study Plan 8.4)

Use the following news clip to work Problems 13 and 14.

**The Saturday-Night Stay Requirement Is on Its Final Approach**

The Saturday-night stay – the requirement that airlines instituted to ensure that business travellers pay an outrageous airfare if he or she wants to go home for the weekend – has gone the way of the dodo bird. Experts agree that low-fare carriers, such as Southwest, are the primary reason major airlines are adopting more consumer-friendly fare structures, which include the elimination of the Saturday-night stay, the introduction of one-way and walk-up fares, and the general restructuring of fares.

Source: *Los Angeles Times*, 15 August 2004

**13** Explain why the opportunity for price discrimination exists for air travel. How does an airline profit from price discrimination?

**14** Describe the change in price discrimination in the market for air travel when discount airlines entered the market and explain the effect of discount airlines on the price and the quantity of air travel.

Use the following information to work Problems 15 and 16.

La Bella Pizza can produce a pizza for a marginal cost of €2. Its standard price is €15 per pizza. It offers a second pizza for €5. It also distributes coupons that give a €5 rebate on a standard price pizza.

**15** How can La Bella Pizza make a larger economic profit with this range of prices than it could if it sold every pizza for €14.99? Draw a figure that illustrates your answer.

**16** How might La Bella Pizza make even more economic profit? Would La Bella Pizza then be more efficient than if it charged €15 for each pizza?

## Monopoly Regulation (Study Plan 8.5)

Use the following information to work Problems 17 to 19.

The figure shows a situation similar to that facing Milford Haven pipelines owned by National Grid, a firm that operates a natural gas distribution system in the UK. The gas distributor is a natural monopoly that cannot price discriminate.

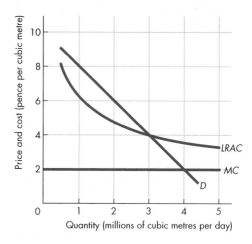

What quantity will the gas distributor produce, what price will it charge, what is total surplus and what is the deadweight loss if it is:

**17** An unregulated profit-maximizing firm?

**18** Regulated to make zero economic profit?

**19** Regulated to be efficient?

ADDITIONAL PROBLEMS AND APPLICATIONS

 You can work these problems in MyEconLab if assigned by your lecturer.

## Monopoly and How It Arises

Use the following list, which gives some information about seven firms, to answer Problems 20 and 21.

- ◆ Coca-Cola cuts its price below that of Pepsi-Cola in an attempt to increase its market share.
- ◆ A single firm, protected by a barrier to entry, produces a personal service that has no close substitutes.
- ◆ A barrier to entry exists, but the good has some close substitutes.
- ◆ A firm offers discounts to students and seniors.
- ◆ A firm can sell any quantity it chooses at the going price.
- ◆ The government issues Nike an exclusive licence to produce footballs.
- ◆ A firm experiences economies of scale even when it produces the quantity that meets the entire market demand.

**20** In which of the seven cases might monopoly arise?

**21** Which of the seven cases are natural monopolies and which are legal monopolies? Which can price discriminate, which cannot, and why?

## A Single-price Monopoly's Output and Price Decision

Use the following information to work Problems 22 to 26.

Hot Air Balloon Rides is a single-price monopoly. Columns 1 and 2 of the table set out the market demand schedule and columns 2 and 3 set out the total cost schedule:

| Price (pounds per ride) | Quantity demanded (rides per month) | Total cost (pounds per month) |
|---|---|---|
| 220 | 0 | 80 |
| 200 | 1 | 160 |
| 180 | 2 | 260 |
| 160 | 3 | 380 |
| 140 | 4 | 520 |
| 120 | 5 | 680 |

**22** Construct Hot Air's total revenue and marginal revenue schedules.

**23** Draw a graph of the market demand curve and Hot Air's marginal revenue curve.

**24** Find Hot Air's profit-maximizing output and price and calculate the firm's economic profit.

**25** If the government imposes a tax on Hot Air's profit, how do its output and price change?

**26** If instead of taxing Hot Air's profit, the government imposes a sales tax on balloon rides of £30 a ride, what are the new profit-maximizing quantity, price and economic profit?

**27** The figure illustrates the situation facing the publisher of the only newspaper containing local news in an isolated community.

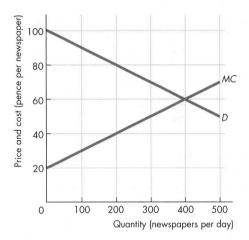

**a** On the graph, mark the profit-maximizing quantity and price.

**b** What is the publisher's daily total revenue?

## Single-price Monopoly and Competition Compared

**28** Show on the graph in Problem 27 the consumer surplus and the deadweight loss created by the monopoly. Explain why this market might encourage rent seeking.

**29** If the newspaper market in Problem 27 were perfectly competitive, what would be the quantity, price, consumer surplus and producer surplus? Mark each on the graph.

**30** **Telecoms Look to Grow by Acquisition**

Multibillion-dollar telecommunications mergers show how global cellular powerhouses are scouting for growth in emerging economies while consolidating in their own, crowded backyards. France Télécom offered to buy TeliaSonera, a Swedish–Finnish telecommunications operator, but within hours, TeliaSonera rejected the offer as too low. Analysts said higher bids – either from France Télécom or others – could persuade TeliaSonera to accept a deal. In the United States, Verizon Wireless agreed to buy Alltel for $28.1 billion – a deal that would make the company the biggest mobile phone operator in the United States. A combination of France Télécom and TeliaSonera would create the world's fourth-largest mobile operator, smaller only than China Mobile, Vodafone and Telefónica of Spain.

Source: *International Herald Tribune*, 5 June 2008

**a** Explain the rent-seeking behaviour of global telecommunications companies.

**b** Explain how mergers may affect the efficiency of the telecommunications market.

## Price Discrimination

**31** **AT&T Moves Away from Unlimited-Data Pricing**

AT&T said it will eliminate its $30 unlimited data plan as the crush of data use from the iPhone has hurt call quality. AT&T is introducing new plans costing $15 a month for 200 megabytes of data traffic or $25 a month for 2 gigabytes. AT&T says those who exceed 2 gigabytes of usage will pay $10 a month for each additional gigabyte. AT&T hopes that these plans will attract more customers.

Source: *The Wall Street Journal*, 2 June 2010

**a** Explain why AT&T's new plans might be price discrimination.

**b** Draw a graph to illustrate the original plan and the new plans.

## Monopoly Regulation

**32** **Sky High Prices**

Ofcom may force Sky to put a cap on its wholesale prices to rivals like BT Vision. Ofcom said that a cap on the prices Sky charged rivals to show sports and film channels was the 'most appropriate way to ensure fair and effective competition'. BT is ready to undercut Sky's prices for sports channels if prices are capped.

Source: BBC News, 30 March 2010

**a** What is the effect of Sky's monopoly of UK satellite television provision on the prices charged to access the satellite network?

**b** Explain why Ofcom thinks a price cap is the 'most appropriate way to ensure fair and effective competition'.

Use the following news clip to work Problems 33 and 34.

**Google vs eBay**

Google is the most popular search engine and 75 per cent of referrals to websites originate from its searches. Some bankers estimate Google's value at $15 billion or more. It is almost impossible for Google to stay permanently ahead of other search-engine technologies because it takes only a bright idea by another set of programmers to lose its lead. Google does not have the natural-monopoly advantages that have made eBay dominant – network effect of buyers and sellers knowing they do best by all trading in one place.

Source: *The Economist*, 30 October 2002

**33** **a** Why is eBay a monopoly but Google not a monopoly?

**b** Under what circumstances would eBay's monopoly be illegal? Explain why.

**34** **a** How would you regulate the Internet auction business to ensure that resources are used efficiently?

**b** 'Anyone is free to buy shares in eBay, so everyone could benefit from eBay's economic profit, and the bigger that economic profit, the better for all.' Evaluate this statement.

## Economics in the News

**35** After you have studied *Reading Between the Lines* on pp. 194–195 answer the following questions.

**a** Why do the companies that complained about Google say that it needs to be investigated? Do you agree? Explain why or why not.

**b** Explain why it would be inefficient to regulate Google to make it charge the same price per keyword click to all advertisers.

**c** Explain why selling keywords to the highest bidder can lead to an efficient allocation of advertising resources.

# CHAPTER
# 9

# Monopolistic Competition and Oligopoly

**After studying this chapter you will be able to:**

◆ Define and identify monopolistic competition

◆ Explain how price and output are determined in monopolistic competition

◆ Explain why advertising and branding costs are high

◆ Define and identify oligopoly

◆ Use game theory to explain how price and output are determined in oligopoly

You enjoy a huge variety of choice created by the globalized trade in brand name products such as Adidas and Nike. In the markets for computer chips, batteries, and big aeroplanes, only two producers compete for market share in the pursuit of profit. Do these firms operate like those in perfect competition or do they restrict output to increase profit like a monopoly?

Find out in this chapter. And in *Reading Between the Lines* at the end of the chapter, see how Apple hopes its iPad will fight off the new wave of competition in the tablet computer market.

## What Is Monopolistic Competition?

You have studied perfect competition in which a large number of firms produce at the lowest possible cost, make zero economic profit and are efficient. You've also studied monopoly, in which a single firm restricts output, produces at a higher cost and price than in perfect competition and is inefficient.

Most real-world markets are competitive but not perfectly competitive because firms in these markets have some power to set their prices as monopolies do. We call this type of market *monopolistic competition*.

**Monopolistic competition** is a market structure in which:

◆ A large number of firms compete.

◆ Each firm produces a differentiated product.

◆ Firms compete on product quality, price and marketing.

◆ Firms are free to enter and exit.

## Large Number of Firms

In monopolistic competition, as in perfect competition, the industry consists of a large number of firms. The presence of a large number of firms has three implications for the firms in the industry.

### Small Market Share

In monopolistic competition, each firm supplies a small part of the total industry output. Consequently, each firm has only limited market power to influence the price of its product. Each firm's price can deviate from the average market price by a relatively small amount.

### Ignore Other Firms

A firm in monopolistic competition must be sensitive to the average market price of the product, but each firm does not pay attention to any one individual competitor. Because all the firms are relatively small and each firm has only a small share of the total market, no one firm can dictate market conditions. So no one firm's actions directly affect the actions of the other firms.

### Collusion Impossible

Firms in monopolistic competition would like to be able to conspire to fix a higher price – called collusion. But because there are many firms, collusion is not possible.

## Product Differentiation

A firm practises **product differentiation** if it makes a product that is slightly different from the products of competing firms. A differentiated product is one that is a close substitute but not a perfect substitute for the products of the other firms. Some people are willing to pay more for one variety of the product, so when its price rises, the quantity demanded decreases but it does not (necessarily) fall to zero. For example, Adidas, Asics, Diadora, Etonic, Fila, New Balance, Nike, Puma and Reebok all make differentiated running shoes. Other things remaining the same, if the price of Adidas running shoes rises and the prices of the other shoes remain constant, Adidas sells fewer shoes and the other producers sell more. But Adidas shoes don't disappear unless the price rises by a large enough amount.

## Competing on Quality, Price and Marketing

Product differentiation enables a firm to compete with other firms in three areas: product quality, price and marketing.

### Quality

The quality of a product is the physical attributes that make it different from the products of other firms. Quality includes design, reliability, the service provided to the buyer and the buyer's ease of access to the product. Quality lies on a spectrum that runs from high to low. Some firms – such as Dell Computer Corp. – offer high-quality products. They are well designed and reliable, and the customer receives quick and efficient service. Other firms offer a lower-quality product that is less well designed, that might not work perfectly and that the buyer must travel some distance to obtain.

### Price

Because of product differentiation, a firm in monopolistic competition faces a downward-sloping demand curve. So, like a monopoly, the firm can set both its price and its output. But there is a trade-off between the product's quality and price. A firm that makes a high-quality product can charge a higher price than a firm that makes a low-quality product.

## Marketing

Because of product differentiation, a firm in monopolistic competition must market its product. Marketing takes two main forms: advertising and packaging. A firm that produces a high-quality product wants to sell it for a suitably high price. To be able to sell a high-quality product for a high price, a firm must advertise and package its product in a way that convinces buyers that they are getting the higher quality for which they are paying. For example, pharmaceutical companies advertise and package their brand-name drugs to persuade buyers that these items are superior to lower-priced generic alternatives. Similarly, a low-quality producer uses advertising and packaging to persuade buyers that although the quality is low, the low price more than compensates for this fact.

## Entry and Exit

In monopolistic competition, there is free entry and free exit. Consequently, a firm cannot make an economic profit in the long run. When existing firms make economic profits, new firms enter the industry. This entry lowers prices and eventually eliminates economic profit. When firms incur economic losses, firms leave the industry. This exit increases prices and eventually eliminates economic loss. In long-run equilibrium, firms neither enter nor leave the industry and the firms in the industry make zero economic profit.

## Examples of Monopolistic Competition

Figure 1 in *Economics in Action* shows 10 examples of industries in the UK which are monopolistically competitive. These industries have a large number of firms, they produce differentiated products and they compete on quality, price and marketing. In the most concentrated of these industries, dairy products, the largest 5 firms produce 32 per cent of industry output and the largest 15 firms produce 57 per cent of industry output. In the least concentrated of these industries, furniture, the largest 5 firms produce only 5 per cent of industry output and the largest 15 firms produce 13 per cent of industry output.

### Review Quiz

1   What are the distinguishing characteristics of monopolistic competition?
2   How do firms in monopolistic competition compete?
3   Provide some examples of industries near your university that operate in monopolistic competition (excluding those in the figure below).

You can work these questions in Study Plan 9.1 and get instant feedback.

## ECONOMICS IN ACTION

### Monopolistic Competition Today

These 10 industries operate in monopolistic competition. The red bar shows the percentage of industry output produced by the 5 largest firms and the blue bar shows the percentage of industry output produced by the next 10 largest firms. So the entire length of the bar shows the percentage of industry output produced by the largest 15 firms.

The industries shown have many firms that produce differentiated products and compete on quality, price and marketing.

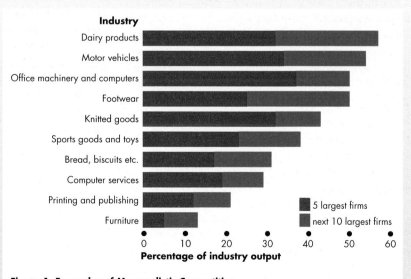

**Figure 1 Examples of Monopolistic Competition**

## Price and Output in Monopolistic Competition

Suppose you've been employed by French Connection to manage the production and marketing of jackets. Think about the decisions that you must make at French Connection. First, you must decide on the design and quality of jackets and on your marketing plan. Second, you must decide on the quantity of jackets to produce and the price at which to sell them.

We'll suppose that French Connection has already made its decisions about design, quality and marketing, and now we'll concentrate on the output and pricing decision. We'll study quality and marketing decisions in the next section.

For a given quality of jackets and marketing activity, French Connection faces given costs and market conditions. How, given its costs and the demand for its jackets, does French Connection decide the quantity of jackets to produce and the price at which to sell them?

## The Firm's Short-run Output and Price Decision

In the short run, a firm in monopolistic competition makes its output and price decision just like a monopoly firm does. Figure 9.1 illustrates this decision for French Connection jackets.

The demand curve for French Connection jackets is *D*. This demand curve tells us the quantity of French Connection jackets demanded at each price, given the prices of other jackets. It is not the demand curve for jackets in general.

The *MR* curve shows the marginal revenue curve associated with the demand curve for French Connection jackets. It is derived just like the marginal revenue curve of a single-price monopoly that you studied in Chapter 8.

The *ATC* curve and the *MC* curve show the average total cost and the marginal cost of producing French Connection jackets.

French Connection's goal is to maximize its economic profit. To do so, it will produce the output at which marginal revenue equals marginal cost. In Figure 9.1, this output is 125 jackets a day. French Connection charges the price that buyers are willing to pay for this quantity, which is determined by the demand curve. This price is £75 per jacket. When it produces 125 jackets a day, French Connection's average total cost is £25 per jacket and it makes an economic

**Figure 9.1** Economic Profit in the Short Run

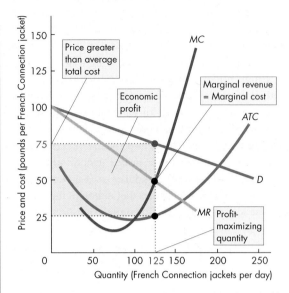

Profit is maximized where marginal revenue equals marginal cost. The profit-maximizing quantity is 125 jackets a day. The price of £75 a jacket exceeds the average total cost of £25 a jacket, so the firm makes an economic profit of £50 a jacket. The blue rectangle illustrates economic profit, which equals £6,250 a day (£50 a jacket multiplied by 125 jackets a day).

 Animation

profit of £6,250 a day (£50 per jacket multiplied by 125 jackets a day). The blue rectangle shows French Connection's economic profit.

## Profit Maximizing Might Be Loss Minimizing

Figure 9.1 shows that French Connection is making a healthy economic profit. But such an outcome is not inevitable. A firm might face a level of demand for its product that is too low for it to make an economic profit.

Excite@Home was such a firm. Offering high-speed Internet service, Excite@Home hoped to capture a large share of the Internet portal market in competition with AOL, MSN, Yahoo! and a host of other providers.

Figure 9.2 illustrates the situation facing Excite@Home in 2001. The demand curve for its portal service is *D*, the marginal revenue curve is *MR*, the average total cost curve is *ATC* and the marginal

## Figure 9.2 Economic Loss in the Short Run

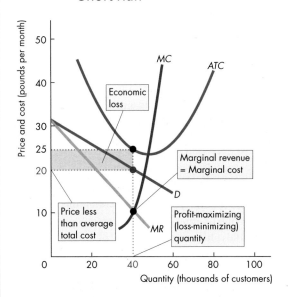

Profit is maximized where marginal revenue equals marginal cost. The loss-minimizing quantity is 40,000 customers. The price of £20 a month is less than the average total cost of £25 a month, so the firm incurs an economic loss of £5 a customer. The red rectangle illustrates economic loss, which equals £200,000 a month (£5 a customer multiplied by 40,000 customers).

myeconlab Animation ──────────────────◆

cost curve is *MC*. Excite@Home maximized profit – equivalently, it minimized its loss – by producing the output at which marginal revenue equals marginal cost. In Figure 9.2, this output is 40,000 customers.

Excite@Home charged the price that buyers were willing to pay for this quantity, which was determined by the demand curve and which was £20 a month. With 40,000 customers, Excite@Home's average total cost was £25 per customer, so it incurred an economic loss of £200,000 a month (£5 a customer multiplied by 40,000 customers). The red rectangle shows Excite@Home's economic loss.

So far, the firm in monopolistic competition looks like a single-price monopoly. It produces the quantity at which marginal revenue equals marginal cost and then charges the price that buyers are willing to pay for that quantity, determined by the demand curve. The key difference between monopoly and monopolistic competition lies in what happens next when firms either make an economic profit or incur an economic loss.

## Long Run: Zero Economic Profit

A firm like Excite@Home is not going to incur an economic loss for long. Eventually, it goes out of business. Also, there is no restriction on entry in monopolistic competition, so if firms in an industry are making an economic profit, other firms have an incentive to enter that industry.

As Burberry, Gap and other firms start to make jackets similar to those made by French Connection, the demand for French Connection jackets decreases. The demand curve for French Connection jackets and the marginal revenue curve shift leftward. And as these curves shift leftward, the profit-maximizing quantity and price fall.

Figure 9.3 shows the long-run equilibrium. The demand curve for French Connection jackets and the marginal revenue curve have shifted leftward. The firm produces 75 jackets a day and sells them for £50 each. At this output level, average total cost is also £50 per jacket.

## Figure 9.3 Output and Price in the Long Run

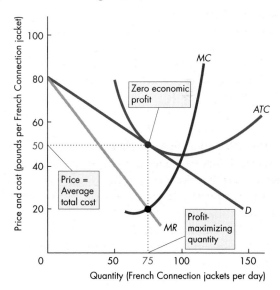

Economic profit encourages entry, which decreases the demand for each firm's product. When the demand curve touches the *ATC* curve at the quantity at which *MR* equals *MC*, the market is in long-run equilibrium. The output that maximizes profit is 75 jackets a day and the price is £50 per jacket. Average total cost is also £50 per jacket, so economic profit is zero.

myeconlab Animation ──────────────────◆

So French Connection is making zero economic profit on its jackets. When all the firms in the industry are making zero economic profit, there is no incentive for new firms to enter.

If demand is so low relative to costs that firms incur economic losses, exit will occur. As firms leave an industry, the demand for the products of the remaining firms increases and their demand curves shift rightward. The exit process ends when all the firms in the industry are making zero economic profit.

## Monopolistic Competition and Perfect Competition

Figure 9.4 compares monopolistic competition and perfect competition and highlights two key differences between them:

◆ Excess capacity

◆ Markup

### Excess Capacity

A firm has **excess capacity** if it produces below its **efficient scale**, which is the quantity at which average total cost is a minimum – the quantity at the bottom of the U-shaped *ATC* curve. In Figure 9.4, the efficient scale is 100 jackets a day. French Connection in part (a) produces 75 French Connection jackets a day and has *excess capacity* of 25 jackets a day. But if all jackets are alike and are produced by firms in perfect competition, each firm in part (b) produces 100 jackets a day, which is the efficient scale. Average total cost is the lowest possible only in *perfect* competition.

You can see the excess capacity in monopolistic competition all around you. Family restaurants (except for the truly outstanding ones) almost always have some empty tables. It is rare that every pump at a petrol station is in use with customers queuing up to be served. There is always an abundance of estate agents ready to help find or sell a home. These industries are examples

---

**Figure 9.4** Excess Capacity and Markup

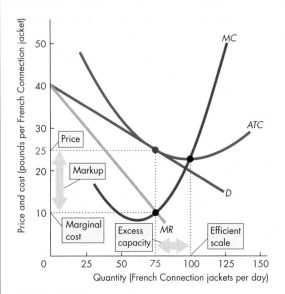

**(a) Monopolistic competition**

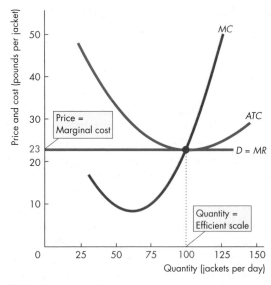

**(b) Perfect competition**

The efficient scale is 100 jackets a day. In monopolistic competition in the long run, because the demand curve for the firm's product is downward sloping, the quantity produced is less than the efficient scale and the firm has excess capacity. Price exceeds marginal cost and this gap is the firm's markup.

In contrast, because in perfect competition the demand for each firm's product is perfectly elastic, the quantity produced in the long run equals the efficient scale and price equals marginal cost. The perfectly competitive firm produces at the least possible cost and there is no markup.

myeconlab Animation

of monopolistic competition. The firms have excess capacity. They could sell more by cutting their prices, but they would then incur economic losses.

### Markup

A firm's **markup** is the amount by which the price exceeds marginal cost. Figure 9.4(a) shows French Connection's markup. In perfect competition, price always equals marginal cost and there is no markup. Figure 9.4(b) shows this case. In monopolistic competition, buyers pay a higher price than in perfect competition and also pay more than marginal cost.

## Is Monopolistic Competition Efficient?

Resources are used efficiently when marginal social benefit equals marginal social cost. Price measures marginal social benefit and the firm's marginal cost equals marginal social cost (assuming there are no external benefits or costs). So if the price of a French Connection jacket exceeds the marginal cost of producing it, the quantity of French Connection jackets produced is less than the efficient quantity. And you've just seen that in long-run equilibrium in monopolistic competition, price *does* exceed marginal cost. So is the quantity produced in monopolistic competition less than the efficient quantity?

### Making the Relevant Comparison

Two economists meet in the street, and one asks the other how her husband is. 'Compared to what?' is the quick reply. This bit of economic wit illustrates a key point: before we can conclude that something needs fixing, we must check out the available alternatives.

The markup that drives a gap between price and marginal cost in monopolistic competition arises from product differentiation. It is because French Connection jackets are not quite the same as jackets from Banana Republic, Diesel, DKNY, Earl Jackets, Gap or any of the other dozens of producers of jackets that the demand for French Connection jackets is not perfectly elastic. The only way in which the demand for jackets from French Connection might be perfectly elastic is if there is only one kind of jacket and all firms make it. In this situation, French Connection jackets are indistinguishable from all other jackets. They don't even have labels.

If there was only one kind of jacket, the total benefit from jackets would almost certainly be less than it is

with variety. People value variety – not only because it enables each person to select what he or she likes best but also because it provides an external benefit. Most of us enjoy seeing variety in the choices of others. Contrast a scene from the China of the 1960s, when everyone wore a Mao tunic, with the China of today, where everyone wears the clothes of their own choosing. Or contrast a scene from the Germany of the 1930s, when almost everyone who could afford a car owned a first-generation Volkswagen Beetle, with the world of today with its enormous variety of styles and types of cars.

If people value variety, why don't we see infinite variety? The answer is that variety is costly. Each different variety of any product must be designed, and then customers must be informed about it. These initial costs of design and marketing – called setup costs – mean that some varieties that are too close to others already available are just not worth creating.

### The Bottom Line

Product variety is both valued and costly. The efficient degree of product variety is the one for which the marginal social benefit from product variety equals its marginal social cost. The loss that arises because the quantity produced is less than the efficient quantity is offset by a gain that arises from having a greater degree of product variety. So compared to the alternative – complete product uniformity – monopolistic competition is probably efficient.

### Review Quiz

1   How does a firm in monopolistic competition decide how much to produce and at what price to offer its product for sale?
2   Why can a firm in monopolistic competition make an economic profit only in the short run?
3   Why do firms in monopolistic competition operate with excess capacity?
4   Why is there a price markup over marginal cost in monopolistic competition?
5   Is monopolistic competition efficient?

You can work these questions in Study Plan 9.2 and get instant feedback.

You've seen how the firm in monopolistic competition determines its output and price when it produces a given product and undertakes a *given* marketing effort. But how does the firm choose its product quality and marketing effort? We'll now study these decisions.

## Product Development and Marketing

When we studied French Connection's price and output decision, we assumed that it had already made its product quality and marketing decisions. We're now going to study these decisions and the impact they have on the firm's output, price and economic profit.

## Innovation and Product Development

The prospect of new firms entering the industry keeps firms in monopolistic competition on their toes!

To enjoy economic profits, firms in monopolistic competition must be continually seeking ways of keeping one step ahead of imitators – other firms that imitate the success of the economically profitable firms.

One major way of trying to maintain economic profit is for a firm to seek out new products that will provide it with a competitive edge, even if only temporarily. A firm that introduces a new and differentiated product faces a less elastic demand for its product and so the firm is able to increase its price and make an economic profit. But economic profit is an incentive for new firms to enter the market. So eventually imitators will enter the market and make close substitutes for the innovative product and compete away the economic profit arising from an initial advantage. So to restore economic profit, the firm must again innovate.

### Profit-maximizing Product Innovation

The decision to innovate and develop a new or improved product is based on the same type of profit-maximizing calculation that you've already studied.

Innovation and product development are costly activities, but they also bring in additional revenues. The firm must balance the marginal cost and marginal revenue. The marginal pound spent on developing a new or improved product is the marginal cost of product development. The marginal pound that the new or improved product earns for the firm is the marginal revenue of product development.

At a low level of product development, the marginal revenue from a better product exceeds the marginal cost. At a high level of product development, the marginal cost of a better product exceeds the marginal revenue. When the marginal cost and the marginal revenue of product development are equal, the firm is undertaking the profit-maximizing amount of product development.

### Efficiency and Product Innovation

Is the profit-maximizing amount of product innovation also the efficient amount? Efficiency is achieved if the marginal social benefit from a new and improved product equals its marginal social cost.

The marginal social benefit from an innovation is the increase in the price that consumers are willing to pay for it. The marginal social cost is the amount that the firm must pay to make the innovation. Profit is maximized when marginal *revenue* equals marginal cost. But in monopolistic competition, marginal revenue is less than the price, so product innovation is probably not pushed to its efficient level.

Monopolistic competition brings many product innovations that cost little to implement and are purely cosmetic, such as new and improved packaging or a new scent in laundry powder. And even when there is a genuine improved product, the innovation is never as good as what the consumer would like. For example, 'The Legend of Zelda: Twilight Princess' is regarded as an almost perfect, and an incredibly cool video game, but reviewers complain that it isn't quite perfect. It is a game with features whose marginal revenue equals the marginal cost of creating them.

## Advertising

A firm with a differentiated product needs to ensure that its customers know how its product is different from the competition. A firm also might attempt to create a consumer perception that its product is different from its competitors, even when that difference is small. Firms use advertising and packaging to achieve this goal.

### Advertising Expenditures

Firms in monopolistic competition incur huge costs to ensure that buyers appreciate and value the differences between their own products and those of their competitors. So a large proportion of the price that we pay for a good covers the cost of selling it. Advertising in newspapers and magazines and on radio, television and the Internet is the main selling cost. But it is not the only one. Selling costs include the cost of shopping centres, glossy catalogues and brochures and the salaries, airfares and hotel bills of sales staff.

Advertising costs are only a part and often a small part of the total selling costs. The biggest part of the selling costs is the retailing services. The retailer's selling costs (and economic profit) are often as much as 50 per cent of the price you pay.

Advertising expenditures and other selling costs affect the profits of firms in two ways: they increase costs and they change demand. Let's look at these effects.

## ECONOMICS IN ACTION

## Advertising Expenditures

The total scale of advertising costs is hard to estimate, but, on average, probably 15 per cent of the price of an item is spent on advertising. The figure shows estimated UK advertising expenditure in different media.

Most UK advertising expenditure occurs on television and in the press, newspapers and magazines. The Internet has recently overtaken direct mail as the third most important medium for advertising.

Of the price that customers pay for a good, the cost of selling it is a large and rising component. Real advertising expenditure in the UK increased by 36 per cent between 1995 and 2005 and by 57 per cent between 1990 and 2005. With the downturn, advertising expenditure fell by 2.5 per cent in 2008 and 13 per cent in 2009 to £14.5 billion. In 2010 it was expected to rise by 3.4 per cent.

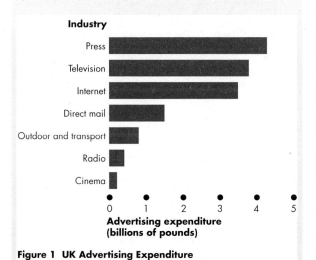

**Figure 1  UK Advertising Expenditure**

Source of data: Advertising Association,
http://www.adassoc.org.uk.

## Selling Costs and Total Costs

Selling costs are fixed costs and they increase the firm's total cost. So, just like fixed production costs, advertising costs per unit decrease as production increases.

Figure 9.5 shows how selling costs change a firm's average total cost. The blue curve shows the average total cost of production. The red curve shows the firm's average total cost of production with advertising. The height of the shaded area between the two curves shows the average fixed cost of advertising. The *total* cost of advertising is fixed. But the *average* cost of advertising decreases as output increases.

Figure 9.5 shows that if advertising increases the quantity sold by a large enough amount, it can lower average total cost. For example, if the quantity sold increases from 25 jackets a day with no advertising to 100 jackets a day with advertising, average total cost falls from £60 to £40 a jacket. The reason is that although the *total* fixed cost has increased, the greater fixed cost is spread over a greater output, so average total cost decreases.

**Figure 9.5   Selling Costs and Total Cost**

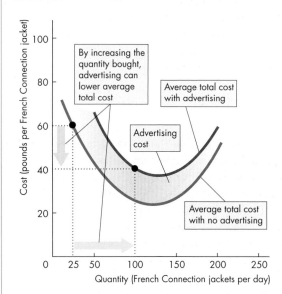

Selling costs such as the cost of advertising are fixed costs. When added to the average total cost of production, selling costs increase average total cost by a greater amount at small outputs than at large outputs. If advertising enables sales to increase from 25 jackets a day to 100 jackets a day, average total cost falls from £60 to £40 a jacket.

myeconlab Animation

## Selling Costs and Demand

Advertising and other selling efforts change the demand for a firm's product. But how? Does demand increase or does it decrease? The most natural answer is that advertising increases demand. By informing people about the quality of its products or by persuading people to switch from the products of other firms, a firm might expect to increase the demand for its own products.

But all firms in monopolistic competition advertise. And all seek to persuade customers that they have the best deal. If advertising enables a firm to survive, it might increase the number of firms in the market. And to the extent that the number of firms does increase, advertising *decreases* the demand faced by any one firm. Advertising by all the firms might also make the demand for any one firm's product more elastic. In this case, advertising ends up not only lowering average total cost but also lowering the markup and the price.

Figure 9.6 illustrates this possible effect of advertising. In part (a), with no advertising, the demand for French Connection jackets is not very elastic. Profit is maximized at 75 jackets per day and the markup is large. In part (b), advertising, which is a fixed cost, increases average total cost from $ATC_0$ to $ATC_1$ but leaves marginal cost unchanged at $MC$. Demand for the firm's product becomes much more elastic, the profit-maximizing quantity increases and the markup shrinks.

## Using Advertising to Signal Quality

Some advertising, like the David Beckham Gillette ads on television and in glossy magazines or the huge amounts that Coke and Pepsi spend, seems hard to understand. There doesn't seem to be any concrete information about a shaver in the smiling face of a footballer. And surely everyone knows about Coke and Pepsi. What is the gain from pouring millions of pounds a month into advertising these well-known colas?

One answer is that advertising is a signal to the consumer of a high-quality product. A **signal** is an action taken by an informed person (or firm) to send a message to uninformed people. Think about two shavers: Gillette

---

**Figure 9.6** Advertising and the Markup

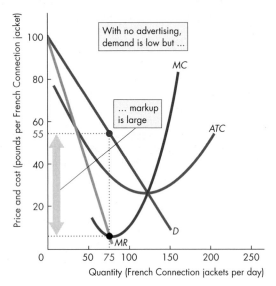

**(a) No firms advertise**

With no firms advertising, demand is low and not very elastic. The profit-maximizing output is small, the markup is large and the price is high.

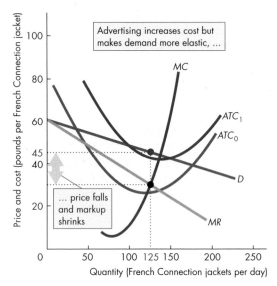

**(b) All firms advertise**

Advertising increases average total cost and shifts the *ATC* curve upward from $ATC_0$ to $ATC_1$. With all firms advertising, the demand for each firm's product becomes more elastic. Output increases, the markup shrinks and the price falls.

Fusion and Bland. Bland knows that its blades are poor and of variable quality that depends on which cheap batch of unsold blades it happens to buy each week. So Bland knows that while it could get a lot of people to try Bland by advertising, they would all quickly discover what a poor product it is and switch back to the shaver they bought before. Gillette, in contrast, knows that its blade gives a high-quality consistent shave and that once consumers have tried it, there is a good chance they'll never use anything else. On the basis of this reasoning, Bland doesn't advertise but Gillette does.

And Gillette spends a lot of money to make a big splash. Fusion users who know that Gillette has done a $10 million deal with Beckham know that the firm would not spend so much money advertising if its product were not truly good. So consumers reason that a Gillette shaver is indeed a really good product. The flashy expensive ad has signalled that a Fusion shaver is really good without saying anything about the shaver.

Notice that if advertising is a signal, it doesn't need any specific product information. It just needs to be expensive and hard to miss. That's what a lot of advertising looks like. So the signalling theory of advertising predicts much of the advertising that we see.

## Brand Names

Many firms create and spend a lot of money promoting a brand name. Why? What benefit does a brand name bring to justify the sometimes high cost of establishing it?

The basic answer is that a brand name provides information about the quality of a product to consumers and an incentive to the producer to achieve a high and consistent quality standard.

To see how a brand name helps the consumer, think about how you use brand names to get information about quality. You've decided to take a holiday in the sun and you're trying to decide where to go. You see advertisements for Club Med and Sheraton Resorts and for Joe's Beachside Shack and Annie's Dive. You know about Club Med and Sheraton Resorts because you've stayed in them before. You've also seen their advertisements and know what to expect from them.

You have no information at all about Joe's and Annie's. They might be better than the places you do know about, but without that knowledge, you're not going to chance them. You use the brand name as information and choose Club Med.

This same story explains why a brand name provides an incentive to achieve high and consistent quality.

Because no one would know whether Joe's and Annie's were offering a high standard of service, they have no incentive to do so. But equally, because everyone expects a given standard of service from Club Med, a failure to meet a customer's expectation would almost certainly lose that customer to a competitor. So Club Med has a strong incentive to deliver what it promises in the advertising that creates its brand name.

## Efficiency of Advertising and Brand Names

To the extent that advertising and brand names provide consumers with information about the precise nature of product differences and product quality, they benefit the consumer and enable a better product choice to be made. But the opportunity cost of the additional information must be weighed against the gain to the consumer.

The final verdict on the efficiency of monopolistic competition is ambiguous. In some cases, the gains from extra product variety unquestionably offset the selling costs and the extra cost arising from excess capacity. The tremendous varieties of books and magazines, clothing, food and drinks are examples of such gains. It is less easy to see the gains from being able to buy a brand-name drug that has a chemical composition identical to that of a generic alternative. But many people do willingly pay more for the brand-name alternative.

### Review Quiz

1  How, other than by adjusting price, do firms in monopolistic competition compete?
2  Why might product innovation and development be efficient and why might it be inefficient?
3  How do selling costs influence a firm's cost curves and its average total cost?
4  How does a firm's advertising influence demand?
5  Are advertising and brand names efficient?

You can work these questions in Study Plan 9.3 and get instant feedback.

Monopolistic competition is one of the most common market structures that you encounter in your daily life. But there is another commonly found market structure, oligopoly, and that is what we now turn to.

## What Is Oligopoly?

Oligopoly, like monopolistic competition, lies between perfect competition and monopoly. The firms in oligopoly might produce an identical product and compete only on price, or they might produce a differentiated product and compete on price, product quality and marketing. **Oligopoly** is a market structure in which:

◆ Natural or legal barriers prevent the entry of new firms

◆ A small number of firms compete

## Barriers to Entry

Either natural or legal barriers to entry can create oligopoly. You saw in Chapter 8 how economies of scale and demand form a natural barrier to entry that can create a *natural monopoly*. These same factors can create a *natural oligopoly*.

Figure 9.7 illustrates two natural oligopolies. The demand curve, *D* (in both parts of the figure), shows the market demand for taxi rides in a town. If the average total cost curve of a taxi company is $ATC_1$ in part (a), the market is a natural **duopoly** – an oligopoly with two firms. You can probably see some examples of duopoly where you live. Some cities have only two suppliers of milk, two local newspapers, two taxi companies, two car rental firms, two copy centres or two bookshops.

The lowest price at which the firm would remain in business is £10 a ride. At that price, the quantity of rides demanded is 60 a day, the quantity that can be provided by just two firms. There is no room in this market for three firms. But if there were only one firm, it would make an economic profit and a second firm would enter to take some of the business and economic profit.

If the average total cost curve of a taxi company is $ATC_2$ in part (b), the efficient scale of one firm is 20 rides a day. This market is large enough for three firms.

A legal oligopoly arises when a legal barrier to entry protects the small number of firms in a market. A city might license two taxi firms or two bus companies, for example, even though the combination of market demand and economies of scale leaves room for more than two firms.

**Figure 9.7** Natural Oligoply

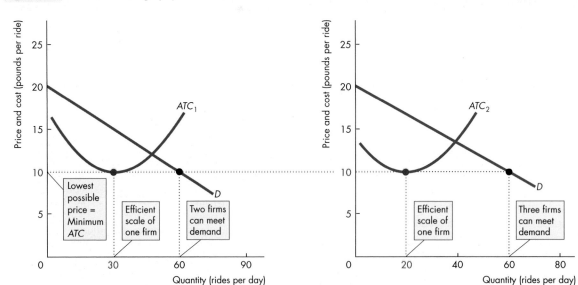

**(a) Natural duopoly**

**(b) Natural oligopoly with three firms**

The lowest possible price is £10 a ride, which is the minimum average total cost. When a firm produces 30 rides a day, the efficient scale, two firms can satisfy the market demand. This natural oligopoly has two firms – a natural duopoly.

When the efficient scale of one firm is 20 rides per day, three firms can satisfy the market demand at the lowest possible price. This natural oligopoly has three firms.

## Small Number of Firms

Because barriers to entry exist, oligopoly consists of a small number of firms, each of which has a large share of the market. Such firms are interdependent and they face a temptation to cooperate to increase their joint economic profit.

### Interdependence

With a small number of firms in a market, each firm's actions influence the profits of all the other firms. When Starbucks opened in Meadowhall Shopping Centre all the other coffee shops took a hit. Within days, Café Moda began to attract Starbucks' customers with enticing offers and lower prices. Eventually, Café Moda survived but others went out of business. The coffee shops in Meadowhall are interdependent.

### Temptation to Cooperate

When a small number of firms share a market, they can increase their profits by forming a cartel and acting like a monopoly. A **cartel** is a group of firms acting together – colluding – to limit output, raise price and increase economic profit. Cartels are illegal, but they do operate in some markets. But for reasons you'll discover in this chapter, cartels tend to break down.

## Examples of Oligopoly

The *Economics in Action* shows some examples of oligopoly. The dividing line between oligopoly and monopolistic competition is hard to pin down. As a practical matter, we try to identify oligopoly by looking at the five-firm concentration ratio along with other information about the geographical scope of the market and barriers to entry. A concentration ratio that divides oligopoly from monopolistic competition is generally taken to be 60 per cent. A market in which the concentration ratio exceeds 60 per cent is usually an example of oligopoly and a market in which the concentration ratio is below 60 per cent is monopolistic competition.

### Review Quiz

1   What are the two distinguishing characteristics of oligopoly?
2   Why are firms in oligopoly interdependent?
3   Why do firms in oligopoly face the temptation to collude?
4   Give some examples of oligopolies that you buy from.

You can work these questions in Study Plan 9.4 and get instant feedback.

## ECONOMICS IN ACTION

### Oligopoly in the UK

These 10 markets are oligopolies. The red bar shows the percentage of industry output produced by the five largest firms and the blue bar shows the percentage of industry output produced by the next 10 largest firms. So the entire length of the bar shows the percentage of industry output produced by the largest 15 firms.

These UK markets have a few interdependent firms and the most concentrated are those with a five-firm concentration ratio above 60 per cent.

Source of data: UK Census of Production 2005.

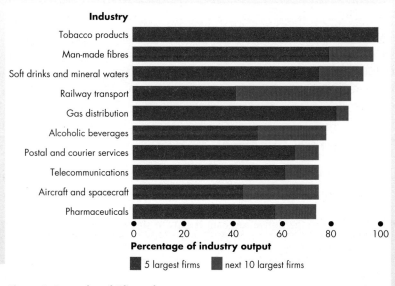

**Figure 1   Examples of Oligopoly**

**Oligopoly Games**

Economists think about oligopoly as a game and to study oligopoly markets they use a set of tools called game theory. **Game theory** is a set of tools for studying *strategic behaviour* – behaviour that takes into account the expected behaviour of others and the recognition of mutual interdependence. Game theory was invented by John von Neumann in 1937 and extended by von Neumann and Oskar Morgenstern in 1944. Today, it is one of the major research fields in economics.

Game theory seeks to understand oligopoly as well as all other forms of economic, political, social and even biological rivalries, by using a method of analysis specifically designed to understand games of all types, including the familiar games of everyday life. We will begin our study of game theory and its application to the behaviour of firms by thinking about familiar games.

## What Is a Game?

What is a game? At first thought, the question seems silly. After all, there are many different games – ball games and parlour games, games of chance and games of skill. But what is it about all these different activities that make them games? What do they have in common? All games share four features:

◆ Rules
◆ Strategies
◆ Payoffs
◆ Outcome

We're going to look at these features of a game by playing 'the prisoners' dilemma' game. This game captures some of the essential features of many games, including oligopoly, and it gives a good illustration of how game theory works and generates predictions.

## The Prisoners' Dilemma

Art and Bob have been caught red-handed, stealing a car. Facing airtight cases, they will receive a 2-year sentence each for their crime. During his interviews with the two prisoners, the police sergeant begins to suspect that he has stumbled on the two people who were responsible for a multimillion-pound bank robbery some months earlier. But this is just a suspicion. The police sergeant has no evidence on which he can convict them of the greater crime unless he can get them to confess. But how can he extract a confession? He makes the prisoners play a game, which we now describe.

### Rules

Each prisoner (player) is placed in a separate room and cannot communicate with the other prisoner. Each is told that he is suspected of having carried out the bank robbery and that:

> **If both of them confess to the larger crime, each will receive a sentence of 3 years for both crimes.**

> **If he alone confesses and his accomplice does not, he will receive an even shorter sentence of 1 year whereas his accomplice will receive a 10-year sentence.**

### Strategies

In game theory, **strategies** are all the possible actions of each player. Art and Bob each have two possible actions:

1  Confess to the bank robbery
2  Deny having committed the bank robbery

Because there are two players, each with two strategies, there are four possible outcomes:

1  Both confess
2  Both deny
3  Art confesses and Bob denies
4  Bob confesses and Art denies

### Payoffs

Each prisoner can work out his *payoff* in each of these four situations. We can tabulate the four possible payoffs for each of the prisoners in what is called a payoff matrix for the game. A **payoff matrix** is a table that shows the payoffs for every possible action by each player for every possible action by each other player.

Table 9.1 shows a payoff matrix for Art and Bob. The squares show the payoffs for each prisoner – the red triangle in each square shows Art's and the blue triangle shows Bob's. If both confess (top left), each gets a 3-year sentence. If Bob confesses but Art denies (top right), Art gets a 10-year sentence and Bob gets a 1-year sentence. If Art confesses and Bob denies (bottom left), Art gets a 1-year sentence and Bob gets a 10-year sentence. Finally, if both of them deny (bottom right), neither can be convicted of the bank robbery charge but both are sentenced for the car theft – a 2-year sentence.

## Outcome

The choices of both players determine the outcome of the game. To predict that outcome, we use an equilibrium idea proposed by John Nash of Princeton University (who received the Nobel Prize for Economic Science in 1994 and was the subject of the 2001 film *A Beautiful Mind*). In a **Nash equilibrium**, player A takes the best possible action given the action of player B and player B takes the best possible action given the action of player A.

In the case of the prisoners' dilemma, the Nash equilibrium occurs when Art makes his best choice given Bob's choice and when Bob makes his best choice given Art's choice.

To find the Nash equilibrium, we compare all the possible outcomes associated with each choice and eliminate those that are dominated – that are not as good as some other choice. Let's find the Nash equilibrium for the prisoners' dilemma game.

### Finding the Nash Equilibrium

Look at the situation from Art's point of view. If Bob confesses, Art's best action is to confess because in that case, he is sentenced to 3 years rather than 10 years. If Bob does not confess, Art's best action is still to confess because in that case he receives 1 year rather than 2 years. So Art's best action is to confess.

Now look at the situation from Bob's point of view. If Art confesses, Bob's best action is to confess because in that case, he is sentenced to 3 years rather than 10 years. If Art does not confess, Bob's best action is still to confess because in that case, he receives 1 year rather than 2 years. So Bob's best action is to confess.

Because each player's best action is to confess, each does confess, each gets a 3-year prison term, and the police sergeant has solved the bank robbery. This is the Nash equilibrium of the game.

The Nash equilibrium for the prisoners' dilemma is called a **dominant-strategy equilibrium**, which is an equilibrium in which the best strategy for each player is to confess *regardless of the strategy of the other player*.

### The Dilemma

The dilemma arises as each prisoner contemplates the consequences of denying. Each prisoner knows that if both of them deny, they will receive only a 2-year sentence for stealing the car. But neither has any way of knowing that his accomplice will deny. But each also knows that if he denies it is in the best interest of the

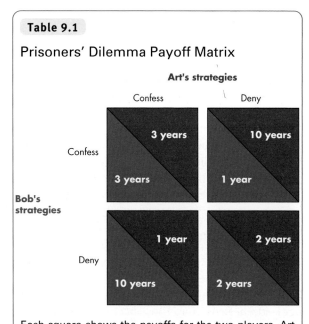

**Table 9.1**

## Prisoners' Dilemma Payoff Matrix

**Art's strategies**

|  | Confess | Deny |
|---|---|---|
| **Confess** | 3 years / 3 years | 10 years / 1 year |
| **Deny** | 1 year / 10 years | 2 years / 2 years |

**Bob's strategies**

Each square shows the payoffs for the two players, Art and Bob, for each possible pair of actions. In each square, the red triangle shows Art's payoff and the blue triangle shows Bob's. For example, if both confess, the payoffs are in the top left square. The equilibrium of the game is for both players to confess and each gets a 3-year sentence.

other to confess. So each considers whether to deny and rely on his accomplice to deny or to confess hoping that his accomplice denies but expecting him to confess. The dilemma leads to the equilibrium of the game.

### A Bad Outcome

For the prisoners, the equilibrium of the game, with each confessing, is not the best outcome. If neither of them confesses, each gets only 2 years for the lesser crime. Isn't there some way in which this better outcome can be achieved? It seems that there is not, because the players cannot communicate with each other. Each player can put himself in the other player's place, and so each player can figure out that there is a best strategy for each of them. The prisoners are indeed in a dilemma. Each knows that he can serve 2 years *only* if he can trust the other to deny. But each prisoner also knows that it is *not* in the best interest of the other to deny. So each prisoner knows that he must confess, thereby delivering a bad outcome for both.

The firms in an oligopoly are in a similar situation to Art and Bob in the prisoners' dilemma game. Let's see how we can use this game to understand oligopoly.

# An Oligopoly Price-fixing Game

We can use game theory and a game like the prisoners' dilemma to understand price fixing, price wars and other aspects of the behaviour of firms in oligopoly.

We'll begin with a price-fixing game. To understand price fixing, we're going to study the special case of duopoly – an oligopoly with two firms. Duopoly is easier to study than oligopoly with three or more firms, and it captures the essence of all oligopoly situations. Somehow, the two firms must share the market. And how they share it depends on the actions of each.

## Cost and Demand Conditions

Two firms, Trick and Gear, produce identical switchgears, so one firm's product is a perfect substitute for the other's and the market price of each firm's product is identical. The quantity demanded depends on that price – the higher the price, the smaller is the quantity demanded.

The market is a natural duopoly like the one in Figure 9.7(a). The two firms can produce this good at a lower cost than either one firm or three firms can. And when price equals minimum average total cost, the two firms share the market equally and economic profit is zero as in perfect competition.

## Collusion

Trick and Gear enter into a **collusive agreement** – an agreement to form a cartel to restrict output, raise the price and increase profit to the maximum possible monopoly level. Because such an agreement is illegal in the EU, it is undertaken in secret.

The strategies that firms in a cartel can pursue are to:

1   Comply
2   Cheat

A firm that complies carries out the agreement and restricts its output to the agreed monopoly level. A firm that cheats breaks the agreement and produces more than the agreed amount to its own benefit and to the cost of the firm that complies.

Each firm has an incentive to cheat because the monopoly price exceeds marginal cost, so an increase in output increases profit. But the increase in output also lowers the price, and inflicts a loss on the firm that complies with the agreement.

Because each firm has two strategies, there are four possible combinations of actions for the firms:

1   Both firms comply
2   Both firms cheat
3   Trick complies and Gear cheats
4   Gear complies and Trick cheats

## The Payoff Matrix

Table 9.2 sets out the payoff matrix for this game. It is constructed in the same way as the payoff matrix for the prisoners' dilemma in Table 9.1. The squares show the payoffs for the two firms – Gear and Trick. In this case, the payoffs are profits. (For the prisoners' dilemma, the payoffs were losses.)

The table shows that if both firms cheat (top left), they achieve the perfectly competitive outcome – zero economic profit for both firms. If both firms comply (bottom right), they make the monopoly profit and each firm has an economic profit of £2 million. The top right and bottom left squares show what happens if one firm cheats while the other complies. The firm that cheats makes an economic profit of £4.5 million, and the one that complies incurs a loss of £1 million.

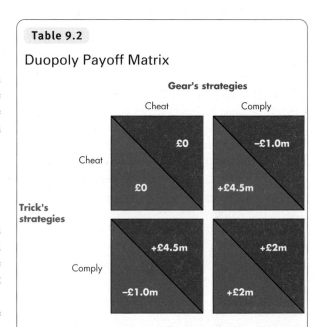

**Table 9.2**

## Duopoly Payoff Matrix

Each square shows the payoffs from a pair of actions. For example, if both firms comply with the collusive agreement, the payoffs are recorded in the bottom right square. The red triangle shows Gear's payoff, and the blue triangle shows Trick's. In the Nash equilibrium, both firms cheat.

### Nash Equilibrium in the Duopolists' Dilemma

The duopolists have a dilemma like the prisoners' dilemma. Do they comply or cheat? To answer this question, we must find the Nash equilibrium.

Look at things from Gear's point of view. Gear reasons as follows. Suppose that Trick cheats. If I comply, I will incur an economic loss of £1 million. If I also cheat, I will make zero economic profit. Zero is better than *minus* £1 million, so I'm better off if I cheat. Now suppose Trick complies. If I cheat, I will make an economic profit of £4.5 million, and if I comply, I will make an economic profit of £2 million. A £4.5 million profit is better than a £2 million profit, so I'm better off if I cheat.

So regardless of whether Trick cheats or complies, it pays Gear to cheat. Cheating is Gear's best strategy.

Trick comes to the same conclusion as Gear because the two firms face an identical situation. So both firms cheat. The Nash equilibrium of the duopoly game is that both firms cheat. And, although the industry has only two firms, they charge the same price and produce the same quantity as those in a competitive industry. Also, as in perfect competition, each firm makes zero economic profit.

This conclusion is not general and does not always arise. But many games are like the prisoners' dilemma and we'll look at another one that is commonly played in oligopoly markets.

## An R&D Game

Firms in oligopoly must decide whether to mount expensive advertising campaigns; whether to modify their product; whether to make their product more reliable and more durable; whether to price discriminate and, if so, among which groups of customers and to what degree; whether to undertake a large research and development (R&D) effort aimed at lowering production costs; and whether to enter or leave an industry.

All of these choices can be analysed as games that are similar to the one that we've just studied. Let's look at one example: an R&D game.

For example, in a duopoly R&D game, the success of the firm depends on its ability to create a product that people value highly relative to the cost of producing it. The firm that creates the most highly valued product at least cost can undercut the rest of the market, increase its market share and increase its profit. But the R&D that achieves product improvements and cost reductions is costly. So the cost of R&D must be deducted from the profit resulting from the increased market share. If neither firm undertakes R&D, both firms might be better off, but if one firm does R&D, the other must follow.

Another game is the retail strategic game that is playing out in the UK supermarket sector. This industry is dominated by three companies – Tesco, Asda and Sainsbury's – that share 63 per cent of the market. Morrisons has the next largest share at 11 per cent and the remainder is taken by small independent chains. In 1997, Sainsbury's was the market leader and Tesco was in second position. In 2006, Tesco was market leader and Sainsbury's was in third position behind Asda. *Economics in Action* overleaf looks at this retail strategic game.

## A Repeated Duopoly Game

If two firms play a game repeatedly, one firm has the opportunity to penalize the other for previous 'bad' behaviour. If Gear cheats this week, perhaps Trick will cheat next week. Before Gear cheats this week, won't it consider the possibility that Trick will cheat next week? What is the equilibrium of this game?

Actually, there is more than one possibility. One is the Nash equilibrium that we have just analysed. Both players cheat, and each makes zero economic profit for ever. In such a situation, it will never pay one of the players to start complying unilaterally because to do so would result in a loss for that player and a profit for the other. But a **cooperative equilibrium** in which the players make and share the monopoly profit is possible.

A cooperative equilibrium might occur if cheating is punished. There are two extremes of punishment. The smallest penalty is called 'tit for tat'. A *tit-for-tat strategy* is one in which a player cooperates in the current period if the other player cooperated in the previous period but cheats in the current period if the other player cheated in the previous period. The most severe form of punishment is called a *trigger strategy*. A *trigger strategy* is one in which a player cooperates if the other player cooperates but plays the Nash equilibrium strategy for ever thereafter if the other player cheats.

In the duopoly game between Gear and Trick, a tit-for-tat strategy keeps both players cooperating and making monopoly profits. Let's see why with an example.

Table 9.3 shows the economic profit that Trick and Gear will make over a number of periods under two alternative sequences of events: colluding and cheating with a tit-for-tat response by the other firm.

# A Prisoners' Dilemma in Supermarket Strategy

Tesco and Asda have expanded rapidly and Sainsbury's has stagnated. Table 1 shows sales data and Figure 1 shows market shares in recent years.

The battle for market share was fought and won on strategic marketing decisions. Three main strategies were used: loyalty cards to encourage repeat buying, expanding non-food retailing, and overseas expansion to capture new markets and economies of scale.

Tesco introduced its customer loyalty card in 1997 but Sainsbury's did not follow immediately. Tesco increased floor space and expanded into non-food retailing in 2000. Asda followed Tesco, but Sainsbury's did not. Tesco

### Table 1

## UK Supermarket Sales

| Supermarket | Annual revenue (billions of pounds) | | | |
| --- | --- | --- | --- | --- |
| | 2000 | 2005 | 2006 | 2009 |
| Tesco | 18.5 | 33.9 | 39.5 | 54.3 |
| Sainsbury's | 16.2 | 16.6 | 16.1 | 20.0 |
| Asda | 8.9 | 9.7 | 15.2 | 18.6 |

expanded overseas trading and floor space for computers in 2006, but Sainsbury's did not follow.

Tesco's marketing strategies were designed to increase sales and market share at the expense of its competitors, and they worked. With each strategy, Tesco increased market share and annual revenue.

## The Game the Supermarkets Play

Table 2 represents the competition between Tesco and Sainsbury's as a strategic game. The payoffs in the table are changes in profit. If neither supermarket expands the floor space for computer retailing, both save marketing and development costs, market shares are similar and profits increase for both companies by 8 per cent (bottom right). Marketing and product development costs will cut profits, so if both companies expand computer retailing, market shares are similar and economic profits rise by only 4 per cent (top left).

The Nash equilibrium is for both firms to expand computer retailing. But Sainsbury's did not play its Nash equilibrium strategy. Profit increased by 16 per cent for Tesco and fell by 3 per cent for Sainsbury's (bottom left of table).

Sainsbury's paid a high price for not following Tesco's marketing lead in 1997, 2000 and 2006. It slipped to third place in market share behind the fast-growing Asda.

Today, Tesco and Asda are locked in a similar strategic game to that played previously by Tesco and Sainsbury's. So far, Tesco and Asda have matched each others' moves, but Tesco has the first mover advantage and will be hard to catch.

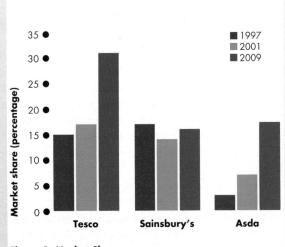

**Figure 1  Market Share**

Source of data: TNS (www.tns-global.com) Worldpanel grocery market press reports.

### Table 2

A Strategic Game

**Table 9.3**

Cheating with Punishment

| Period of play | Collude Trick's profit (millions of pounds) | Gear's profit | Cheat with tit-for-tat Trick's profit (millions of pounds) | Gear's profit |
|---|---|---|---|---|
| 1 | 2 | 2 | 4.5 | −1.0 |
| 2 | 2 | 2 | −1.0 | 4.5 |
| 3 | 2 | 2 | 2.0 | 2.0 |
| 4 | • | • | • | • |

If duopolists repeatedly collude, each makes an economic profit of £2 million per period of play. If one player cheats in period 1, the other player plays a tit-for-tat strategy and cheats in period 2. The profit from cheating can be made for only one period and must be paid for in the next period by incurring a loss. Over two periods of play, the best that a duopolist can achieve by cheating is an economic profit of £3.5 million, compared to an economic profit of £4 million by colluding.

If both firms stick to the collusive agreement in period 1, each makes an economic profit of £2 million. Suppose that Trick contemplates cheating in period 1. The cheating produces a quick £4.5 million economic profit and inflicts a £1 million economic loss on Gear.

But a cheat by Trick in period 1 produces a response from Gear in period 2. If Trick wants to get back into a profit-making situation, it must return to the agreement in period 2 even though it knows that Gear will punish it for cheating in period 1. So in period 2, Gear punishes Trick and Trick cooperates. Gear now makes an economic profit of £4.5 million, and Trick incurs an economic loss of £1 million.

Adding up the profits over two periods of play, Trick would have made more profit by cooperating: £4 million compared with £3.5 million.

What is true for Trick is also true for Gear. Because each firm makes a larger profit by sticking with the collusive agreement, both firms do so and the monopoly price, quantity and profit prevail.

In reality, whether a cartel works like a one-play game or a repeated game depends primarily on the number of players and the ease of detecting and punishing cheating. The larger the number of players, the harder it is to maintain a cartel.

A repeated duopoly game can help us understand real-world behaviour and, in particular, price wars.

Some price wars can be interpreted as the implementation of a tit-for-tat strategy. But the game is a bit more complicated than the one we've looked at because the players are uncertain about the demand for the product.

Playing a tit-for-tat strategy, firms have an incentive to stick to the monopoly price. But fluctuations in demand lead to fluctuations in the monopoly price, and sometimes, when the price changes, it might seem to one of the firms that the price has fallen because the other has cheated. In this case, a price war will break out. The price war will end only when each firm is satisfied that the other is ready to cooperate again. There will be cycles of price wars and the restoration of collusive agreements. Fluctuations in the world price of oil might be interpreted in this way.

### A Computer Chip Price War

The prices of computer chips during 1995 and 1996 can be explained by the game you've just examined. Until 1995, the market for chips for IBM-compatible computers was dominated by Intel Corporation. Intel was able to make maximum economic profit by producing the quantity of chips at which marginal cost equalled marginal revenue. The price of Intel's chips was set to ensure that the quantity demanded equalled the quantity produced. Then in 1995 and 1996, with the entry of a small number of new firms, the industry became an oligopoly. If the firms had maintained Intel's price and shared the market, together they could have made economic profits equal to Intel's profit. But the firms were in a prisoners' dilemma, so prices fell towards the competitive level.

# Reading Between the Lines

# Product Differentiation in the Tablet Computer Market

---

The Telegraph online, 21 October 2010

## The Tablet Computer Has Gone Mainstream

Claudine Beaumont, Technology Editor

Apple's Steve Jobs believes his company is in an almost unassailable position and has the 'tiger by the tail' in this new market. But that isn't stopping everyone from BlackBerry to Next trying to emulate the iPad's success.

There's an avalanche of tablet computers, with some proving more successful than others.

Apple is bullish about the iPad's sales figures. . . . In the past three months, the company has recorded $20 billion (£12.6 billion) in sales, representing a tidy profit of $4.31 billion (£2.71 billion) over that period. Much of that success has been down to its latest gadget, the iPad . . . with around eight million sold to date. . . .

But, once again, Apple has managed to exploit the latent potential in a new segment of the market – just as it did with MP3 players and smartphones. . . .

Dozens of consumer electronics companies are now building their own tablet computers, with mixed results. Google's Android operating system . . . is proving particularly popular with manufacturers. Samsung's . . . Galaxy Tab . . . has earned rave reviews. . . . Research in Motion, the company behind the popular BlackBerry smartphone range, is also launching its own tablet.

In the six months since Apple's iPad went on sale, tablet computers have gone from niche products to mass-market devices. Even high street retailer Next has started selling one, at the almost pocket money price of £180. . . . Expect the avalanche of tablets to snowball in the next few months, with devices from HP, Microsoft and Asus set to hit the shelves.

These devices will have to be faultless . . . and . . . cost substantially less than Apple's £429 . . . to turn shoppers' heads.

---

## ◈ The Essence of the Story

- ◆ Six months after launching the iPad, Apple says it has an unassailable position in the tablet computer market.

- ◆ Apple has sold 8 million iPads since the launch and earned $4.31 billion in profits over the last three months.

- ◆ Google, Samsung and other new competitors have flooded into the market. Next offers a tablet at only £180.

- ◆ Other makers, such as HP and Microsoft, are close behind but will have to price competitively and match Apple's quality.

# ◈ Economic Analysis

- By creating a substantially differentiated product with its iPad, Apple attracted many new customers and sold 8 million units worldwide in the first six months.

- But within three months of the launch, many competing but differentiated tablet computers came onto the market.

- The monopolistic competition model explains what is happening in the tablet computer market.

- Figure 1 shows the market for Apple's iPad in its first three months, before competitors entered the market.

- Because the Apple iPad is different from other handheld devices and has features that users value, the demand curve, $D$, and marginal revenue curve, $MR$, create a large short-run profit opportunity.

- The marginal cost curve is $MC$ and the average total cost curve is $ATC$. Apple maximizes its economic profit by producing the quantity at which $MR$ equals $MC$, which is 4 million iPads per quarter.

- This quantity of iPads can be sold for the equivalent of £429 each.

- The blue rectangle shows Apple's economic profit.

- Apple thinks it will maintain its profit from the iPad but this is unlikely because this market is profitable and new firms will enter.

- Within three months of the iPad launch, many competitors had entered the market.

- Figure 2 shows how entry will affect Apple in the long run.

- The demand for the iPad will decrease as the market is shared with the new entrants.

- Apple's profit-maximizing price for the iPad will decrease as more firms enter the market for tablet computers.

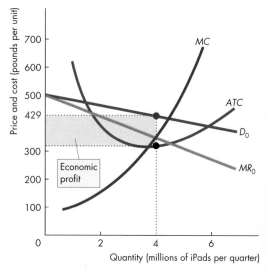

**Figure 1   Before entry**

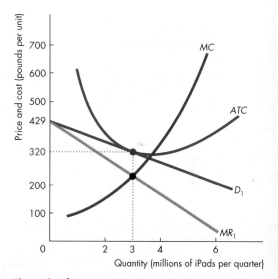

**Figure 2   After entry**

- Apple's profit-maximizing price will decrease and in the long run its economic profit will be eliminated.

- With zero economic profit, Apple will have an incentive to develop another new differentiated product and again start the cycle of innovation and short-run profit described here.

## SUMMARY

## Key Points

### What Is Monopolistic Competition?
(pp. 202–203)

◆ In monopolistic competition, a large number of firms compete on product quality, price and marketing.

Working Problems 1 and 2 will give you a better understanding of what monopolistic competition is.

### Price and Output in Monopolistic Competition (pp. 204–207)

◆ Each firm in monopolistic competition faces a downward-sloping demand curve and produces the profit-maximizing quantity.

◆ Entry and exit result in zero economic profit and excess capacity in long-run equilibrium.

Working Problems 3 to 10 will give you a better understanding of price and output in monopolistic competition.

### Product Development and Marketing
(pp. 208–211)

◆ Firms innovate and develop new products.

◆ Advertising expenditures increase total cost, but average total cost might fall if the quantity sold increases by enough.

◆ Advertising expenditures might increase or decrease the demand for a firm's product.

◆ Whether monopolistic competition is inefficient depends on the value we place on product variety.

Working Problems 11 to 16 will give you a better understanding of product development and marketing.

### What Is Oligopoly? (pp. 212–213)

◆ Oligopoly is a market in which a small number of firms compete.

Working Problems 17 and 18 will give you a better understanding of what oligopoly is.

### Oligopoly Games (pp. 214–219)

◆ Oligopoly is studied by using game theory, which is a method of analysing strategic behaviour.

◆ In a prisoners' dilemma game, two prisoners acting in their own self-interest harm their joint interest.

◆ An oligopoly (duopoly) price-fixing game is a prisoners' dilemma in which the firms might collude or cheat.

◆ In Nash equilibrium, both firms cheat and output and price are the same as in perfect competition.

◆ Firms' decisions about advertising and R&D can be studied by using game theory.

◆ In a repeated game, a punishment strategy can produce a cooperative equilibrium in which price and output are the same as in monopoly.

Working Problems 19 to 21 will give you a better understanding of oligopoly games.

## Key Terms

Cartel, 213
Collusive agreement, 216
Cooperative equilibrium, 217
Dominant-strategy equilibrium, 215
Duopoly, 212
Efficient scale, 206
Excess capacity, 206
Game theory, 214
Markup, 207
Monopolistic competition, 202
Nash equilibrium, 215
Oligopoly, 212
Payoff matrix, 214
Product differentiation, 202
Signal, 210
Strategies, 214

 You can work Problems 1 to 22 in MyEconLab Chapter 9 Study Plan and get instant feedback.

# What Is Monopolistic Competition?

(Study Plan 9.1)

**1** Which of the following items are sold by firms in monopolistic competition? Explain your selections.

Satellite television service; Wheat; Athletic shoes; Fizzy drinks; Toothbrushes; Ready-mix concrete

**2** The five-firm concentration ratio for audio equipment makers is 30 and for electric lamp makers it is 89. Which of these markets is an example of monopolistic competition?

# Price and Output in Monopolistic Competition (Study Plan 9.2)

Use the following information to work Problems 3 and 4.

Sara is a dot.com entrepreneur who has established a website at which people can design and buy sweatshirts. Sara pays £1,000 a week for her Web server and Internet connection. The sweatshirts that her customers design are made to order by another firm, and Sara pays this firm £20 a sweatshirt. Sara has no other costs. The table sets out the demand schedule for Sara's sweatshirts.

| Price (pounds per sweatshirt) | Quantity demanded (sweatshirts per week) |
|---|---|
| 0 | 100 |
| 20 | 80 |
| 40 | 60 |
| 60 | 40 |
| 80 | 20 |
| 100 | 0 |

**3** Calculate Sara's profit-maximizing output, price and economic profit.

**4 a** Do you expect other firms to enter the Web sweatshirt business and compete with Sara?

   **b** What happens to the demand for Sara's sweatshirts in the long run? What happens to Sara's economic profit in the long run?

Use the figure in the next column, which shows the situation facing a producer of running shoes, to work Problems 5 to 10.

**5** What quantity does the firm produce, what price does it charge and what is its economic profit or economic loss?

**6** In the long run, how does the number of firms producing running shoes change?

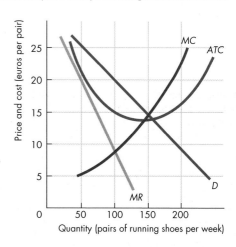

**7** In the long run, how does the price of running shoes and the quantity the firm produces change? What happens to the market output?

**8** Does the firm have excess capacity in the long run? If the firm has excess capacity in the long run, why doesn't it decrease its capacity?

**9** In the long run, compare the price of a pair of running shoes and the marginal cost of producing the pair.

**10** Is the market for running shoes efficient or inefficient in the long run?

# Product Development and Marketing

(Study Plan 9.3)

Use the following information to work Problems 11 to 14.

Suppose that Tommy Hilfiger's marginal cost of a jacket is a constant £100 and the total fixed cost at one of its stores is £2,000 a day. This store sells 20 jackets a day, which is its profit-maximizing number of jackets. Then, the stores nearby start to advertise their jackets. The Tommy Hilfiger store now spends £2,000 a day advertising its jackets and its profit-maximizing number of jackets sold jumps to 50 a day.

**11 a** What is this store's average total cost of a jacket sold before the advertising begins?

   **b** What is this store's average total cost of a jacket sold after the advertising begins?

**12 a** Can you say what happens to the price of a Tommy Hilfiger jacket? Why or why not?

   **b** Can you say what happens to Tommy's markup? Why or why not?

   **c** Can you say what happens to Tommy's economic profit? Why or why not?

**13** How might Tommy Hilfiger use advertising as a signal? How is a signal sent and how does it work?

**14** How does having a brand name help Tommy Hilfiger to increase its economic profit?

Use the following news clip to work Problems 17 and 18.

**Food's Next Billion-dollar Brand?**

While it's not the biggest brand in margarine, Smart Balance has an edge on its rivals in that it's made with a patented blend of vegetable and fruit oils that has been shown to help improve consumers' cholesterol levels. Smart Balance sales have sky-rocketed while overall sales for margarine have stagnated. It remains to be seen if Smart Balance's healthy message and high price will resound with consumers.

Source: *Fortune*, 4 June 2008

**15** How do you expect advertising and the Smart Balance brand name will affect Smart Balance's ability to make a positive economic profit?

**16** Are long-run economic profits a possibility for Smart Balance? In long-run equilibrium, will Smart Balance have excess capacity or a markup?

## What is Oligopoly? (Study Plan 9.4)

**17** Two firms make most of the chips that power a PC: Intel and Advanced Micro Devices. What makes the market for PC chips a duopoly? Sketch the market demand curve and cost curves that describe the situation in this market and that prevent other firms from entering.

**18** **Sparks Fly for Energizer**

Energizer is gaining market share against competitor Duracell and its profit is rising despite the sharp rise in the price of zinc, a key battery ingredient.

Source: www.businessweek.com, August 2007

In what type of market are batteries sold? Explain your answer.

## Oligopoly Games (Study Plan 9.5)

**19** Consider a game with two players and in which each player is asked a question. The players can answer the question honestly or lie. If both answer honestly, each receives €100. If one answers honestly and the other lies, the liar receives €500 and the honest player gets nothing. If both lie, then each receives €50.

   **a** Describe strategies and payoffs of this game.

   **b** Construct the payoff matrix.

   **c** What is the equilibrium of this game?

   **d** Compare this game to the prisoners' dilemma. Are the two games similar or different? Explain your answer.

Use the following information to work Problems 5 and 6.

Two firms, Soapy plc and Suddsies plc, are the only producers of soap powder. They collude and agree to share the market equally. If neither firm cheats on the agreement, each makes €1 million economic profit. If either firm cheats, the cheat makes an economic profit of €1.5 million while the complier incurs an economic loss of €0.5 million. If both cheat, they break even. Neither firm can monitor the other's actions.

**20** **a** What are the strategies in this game?

   **b** Construct the payoff matrix.

**21** **a** What is the equilibrium if the game is played only once?

   **b** Is the equilibrium a dominant-strategy equilibrium? Explain your answer.

## Economics in the News
### (Study Plan 9.N)

**22** **Computer Makers Prepare to Stake Bigger Claim in Phones**

Emboldened by Apple's success with its iPhone, many PC makers and chip companies are charging into the mobile phone business, promising new devices that can pack the horsepower of standard computers into palm-size packages – devices that handle the full glory of the Internet, power two-way video conferences and stream high-definition movies to your TV. It is a development that spells serious competition for established mobile phone makers and phone companies.

Source: *The New York Times*, 15 March 2009

   **a** Draw a graph of the cost curves and revenue curves of a mobile phone company that makes a positive economic profit in the short run.

   **b** If mobile phone companies start to include the popular features introduced by PC makers, explain how this decision will affect their profit in the short run.

   **c** What do you expect to happen to the mobile phone company's economic profit in the long run, given the information in the news clip?

   **d** Draw a graph to illustrate your answer to part (c).

**ADDITIONAL PROBLEMS AND APPLICATIONS**

 myeconlab  You can work these problems in MyEconLab if assigned by your lecturer.

## What Is Monopolistic Competition?

**23**  Which of the following items are sold by firms in monopolistic competition? Explain your selections.

Orange juice; Canned soup; PCs; Chewing gum; Breakfast cereals; Corn

**24**  The five-firm concentration ratio for man-made fibre makers is 79 and for knitted goods makers it is 45. Which of these markets is an example of monopolistic competition?

## Price and Output in Monopolistic Competition

Use the following information to work Problems 25 and 26.

Lorie teaches singing. Her fixed costs are £1,000 a month and it costs her £50 of labour to give one class. The table shows the demand schedule for Lorie's singing lessons.

| Price (pounds per lesson) | Quantity demanded (lessons per week) |
|---|---|
| 0 | 250 |
| 50 | 200 |
| 100 | 150 |
| 150 | 100 |
| 200 | 50 |
| 250 | 0 |

**25**  Calculate Lorie's profit-maximizing output, price and economic profit.

**26**  **a**  Do you expect other firms to enter the singing lesson business and compete with Lorie?

   **b**  What happens to the demand for Lorie's lessons in the long run? What happens to Lorie's economic profit in the long run?

Use the figure in the next column, which shows the situation facing Mike's Bikes, a producer of mountain bikes, to work Problems 27 to 31. The demand and costs of other bike producers are similar to those of Mike's Bikes.

**27**  What quantity does the firm produce and what price does it charge? Calculate the firm's economic profit or economic loss.

**28**  What will happen to the number of firms producing mountain bikes in the long run?

**29**  How will the price of a mountain bike and the number of bikes produced by Mike's Bikes change in the long run?

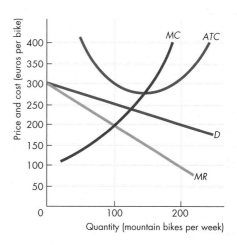

**30**  Is there any way for Mike's Bikes to avoid having excess capacity in the long run?

**31**  Is the market for mountain bikes efficient or inefficient in the long run? Explain your answer.

## Product Development and Marketing

Use the following information to work Problems 32 to 34.

Bianca bakes delicious cookies. Her total fixed cost is £40 a day and her average variable cost is £1 a bag. Few people know about Bianca's Cookies and she is maximizing her profit by selling 10 bags a day for £5 a bag. Bianca thinks that if she spends £50 a day on advertising, she can increase her market share and sell 25 bags a day for £5 a bag.

**32**  If Bianca's advertising works as she expects, can she increase her economic profit by advertising?

**33**  If Bianca advertises, will her average total cost increase or decrease at the quantity produced?

**34**  If Bianca advertises, will she continue to sell her cookies for £5 a bag or will she change her price?

Use the following news clip to work Problems 35 and 36.

**A Thirst for More Champagne**

Champagne exports have tripled in the past 20 years. That poses a problem for northern France, where the bubbly hails from – not enough grapes. So French authorities have unveiled a plan to extend the official Champagne grape-growing zone to cover 40 new villages. This revision has provoked debate. The change will take several years to become effective. In the meantime the vineyard owners whose land values will jump markedly if the changes are finalized certainly have reason to raise a glass.

Source: *Fortune*, 12 May 2008

**35** **a** Why is France so strict about designating the vineyards that can use the Champagne label?

**b** Explain who most likely opposes this plan.

**36** Assuming that vineyards in these 40 villages are producing the same quality of grapes with or without this plan, why will their land values 'jump markedly' if this plan is approved?

**37** **Under Armour's Big Step Up**

Under Armour, the red-hot brand of athletic apparel, has joined Nike, Adidas and New Balance as a major player in the market for athletic footwear. Under Armour plans to revive the long-dead cross-training category. But will young athletes really spend $100 for a cross-training shoe to lift weights in?

Source: *Time*, 26 May 2008

What factors influence Under Armour's ability to make an economic profit in the cross-training shoe market?

## What is Oligopoly?

**38** **An Energy Drink with a Monster of a Stock**

The $5.7 billion energy-drink category, in which Monster holds the No. 2 position behind industry leader Red Bull, has slowed down as copycat brands jostle for shelf space. Over the past five years Red Bull's market share in dollar terms has gone from 91 per cent to well under 50 per cent and much of that loss has been Monster's gain.

Source: *Fortune*, 25 December 2006

**a** Describe the structure of the energy-drink market. How has that structure changed over the past few years?

**b** If Monster and Red Bull formed a cartel, how would the price of energy drinks and profits change?

## Oligopoly Games

Use the following information to work Problems 39 and 40.

Black and Green are the only two producers of aniseed beer, a New Age product designed to displace ginger beer. Black and Green are trying to figure out how much of this new beer to produce. They know the following:

(i) If they both limit production to 10,000 litres a day, they will make the maximum attainable joint profit of £200,000 a day – £100,000 a day each.

(ii) If either firm produces 20,000 litres a day while the other produces 10,000 a day, the one that produces 20,000 litres will make an economic profit of £150,000 and the other one will incur an economic loss of £50,000.

(iii) If both increase production to 20,000 litres a day, each firm will make zero economic profit.

**39** Construct a payoff matrix for the game that Black and Green must play.

**40** Find the Nash equilibrium of the game that Black and Green play.

**41** Why do Coca-Cola and PepsiCo spend huge amounts on advertising? Do they benefit? Does the consumer benefit? Explain your answer by constructing a game to illustrate the choices Coca-Cola and PepsiCo make.

Use the following information to work Problems 19 and 20.

Microsoft with Xbox 360, Nintendo with Wii, and Sony with PlayStation 3 are slugging it out in the market for the latest generation of video game consoles. Xbox 360 was the first to market; Wii has the lowest price; PS3 uses the most advanced technology and has the highest price.

**42** **a** Thinking of the competition among these firms in the market for consoles as a game, describe the firms' strategies concerning design, marketing and price.

**b** What, based on the information provided, turned out to be the equilibrium of the game?

**43** Can you think of reasons why the three consoles are so different?

## Economics in the News

**44** After you have studied *Reading Between the Lines* on pp. 220–221 answer the following questions.

**a** Describe the cost curves (*MC* and *ATC*) and the marginal revenue and demand curves for the iPad when Apple first introduced it.

**b** How do you think the creation of the iPad influenced the demand for laptop computers?

**c** Explain the effects of the introduction of the iPad on other firms in the market for hand-held computers.

**d** Draw a graph to illustrate your answer to part (c).

**e** Explain the effect on Apple of the decisions by HP and Samsung to bring their own tablet computers to market.

**f** Draw a graph to illustrate your answer to part (e).

**g** Do you think the tablet computer market is efficient? Explain your answer.

# CHAPTER
# 10

# Real GDP

The recent recession in the UK has been described as the worst since the 1930s. To assess the state of the economy, economists, commentators and politicians turn to the measure of GDP and the growth of GDP. What exactly is GDP and what does it tell us about the state of the economy? And how can we compare economic growth in the 2000s with that in the 1930s?

This chapter explains how the economic statisticians at the Office for National Statistics measure GDP. *Reading Between the Lines* at the end of the chapter looks at the recession of 2008–2009 and compares it with the recession during the 1930s.

**After studying this chapter you will be able to:**

◆ Define GDP and explain why it equals aggregate expenditure and aggregate income

◆ Explain how the Office for National Statistics measures UK GDP

◆ Describe how GDP is used and explain its limitations

**Gross Domestic Product**

What exactly is GDP, how is it calculated, what does it mean and why do we care about it? You are going to discover the answers to these questions in this chapter. First, what is GDP?

# GDP Defined

**GDP** or **gross domestic product** is the market value of all the final goods and services produced within a country in a given time period – usually a year. This definition has four parts:

◆ Market value

◆ Final goods and services

◆ Produced within a country

◆ In a given time period

We examine each in turn.

## Market Value

To measure total production, we must add together the production of apples and oranges, computers and popcorn. Just counting the items doesn't get us very far. For example, which is the greater total production: 100 apples and 50 oranges, or 50 apples and 100 oranges?

GDP answers this question by valuing items at their *market values* – the prices at which items are traded in markets. If the price of an apple is 10 pence, the market value of 50 apples is £5. If the price of an orange is 20 pence, the market value of 100 oranges is £20. By valuing production at market prices, we can add the apples and oranges together. The market value of 50 apples and 100 oranges is £5 plus £20, or £25.

## Final Goods and Services

To calculate GDP, we value the *final goods and services* produced. A **final good** (or service) is an item that is bought by its final user during a specified time period. It contrasts with an **intermediate good** (or service), which is an item that is produced by one firm, bought by another firm and used as a component of a final good or service.

For example, a Ford Focus is a final good, but a tyre on the Ford Focus is an intermediate good. A Dell computer is a final good, but an Intel Pentium chip inside it is an intermediate good.

If we were to add the value of intermediate goods and services produced to the value of final goods and services, we would count the same thing many times – a problem called *double counting*. The value of a Ford Focus already includes the value of the tyres, and the value of a Dell PC already includes the value of the Pentium chip inside it.

Some goods can be an intermediate good in some situations and a final good in other situations. For example, the ice cream that you buy on a hot summer day is a final good, but the ice cream that a café buys and uses to make sundaes is an intermediate good. The sundae is the final good. So whether a good is an intermediate good or a final good depends on what it is used for, not on what it is.

Some items that people buy are neither final goods nor intermediate goods and they are not part of GDP. Examples of such items include financial assets – stocks and bonds – and secondhand goods – used cars or existing homes. A secondhand good was part of GDP in the year in which it was produced, but not in GDP this year.

## Produced Within a Country

Only goods and services that are produced *within a country* count as part of that country's GDP. When James Dyson, a British entrepreneur who makes vacuum cleaners, produces them in Malaysia, the market value of those cleaners is part of Malaysia's GDP, not part of the UK's GDP. Toyota, a Japanese firm, produces cars in Deeside, Wales, and the value of this production is part of UK GDP, not part of Japan's GDP.

## In a Given Time Period

GDP measures the value of production *in a given time period* – normally either a quarter of a year (called the quarterly GDP data) or a year (called the annual GDP data).

GDP measures not only the value of total production but also total income and total expenditure. The equality between the value of total production and total income is important because it shows the direct link between productivity and living standards. Our standard of living rises when our incomes rise and we can afford to buy more goods and services. But we must produce more goods and services if we are to be able to buy more goods and services.

Rising incomes and a rising value of production go together. They are two aspects of the same phenomenon: increasing production. To see why, we study the circular flow of expenditure and income.

# GDP and the Circular Flow of Expenditure and Income

Figure 10.1 illustrates the circular flow of expenditure and income. The economy consists of households, firms, governments and the rest of the world (the rectangles), which trade in factor markets and goods (and services) markets. Let's focus first on households and firms.

## Households and Firms

Households sell and firms buy the services of labour, capital and land in factor markets. For these factor services, firms pay income to households: wages for labour services, interest for the use of capital and rent for the use of land. A fourth factor of production, entrepreneurship, receives profit.

Firms' retained earnings – profits that are not distributed to households – are also part of the household sector's income. You can think of retained earnings as being income that households save and lend back to

firms. Figure 10.1 shows the *aggregate income* received by all households, including retained earnings, as the blue flow labelled Y.

Households buy and firms sell consumption goods and services – such as beer, pizzas and dry cleaning services – in goods markets. Total payment for these goods and services is **consumption expenditure**, shown by the red flow labelled C.

Firms buy and sell new capital equipment – such as computer systems, aeroplanes, trucks, trains and assembly line equipment – in goods markets.

Some of what firms produce is not sold but is added to their stocks (or inventories). For example, if Ford produces 1,000 cars and sells 950 of them, the other 50 cars remain unsold and the firm's stock of cars increases by 50. When a firm adds unsold output to its stocks, we can think of the firm as buying goods from itself. The purchase of new plant, equipment and buildings, and the additions to stocks, are **investment**, shown by the red flow labelled I.

**Figure 10.1**   The Circular Flow of Expenditure and Income

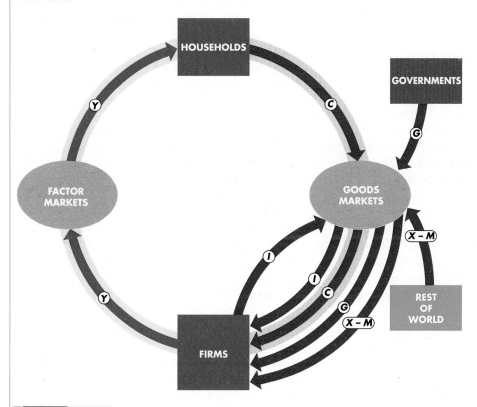

Households make consumption expenditures (*C*); firms make investments (*I*); the government purchases goods and services (*G*); the rest of the world buys net exports (*X* – *M*). Firms pay incomes (*Y*) to households.

Aggregate income (blue flow) equals aggregate expenditure (red flows).

**Billions of pounds in 2010**

| | |
|---|---:|
| *C* = | 948 |
| *I* = | 208 |
| *G* = | 338 |
| *X* – *M* = | –46 |
| *Y* = | 1,448 |

myeconlab Animation

## Governments

Governments buy goods and services from firms and their expenditure on goods and services is called **government expenditure**. In Figure 10.1, government expenditure on goods and services is shown as the red flow $G$.

Governments finance their expenditure with taxes, but taxes are not part of the circular flow of expenditure and income. Governments also make financial transfers to households, such as unemployment benefits and subsidies to firms. These financial transfers, like taxes, are not part of the circular flow of expenditure and income. Financial transfers and taxes are neither expenditures on goods and services nor income from the services of factors of production.

## Rest of World

Firms in the UK sell goods and services to the rest of the world, **exports**, and buy goods and services from the rest of the world, **imports**. The value of exports $(X)$ minus the value of imports $(M)$ is called **net exports**. Figure 10.1 shows net exports by the red flow $X - M$.

If net exports are positive, the net flow of goods and services is from the rest of the world to UK firms. If net exports are negative, the net flow of goods and services is from UK firms to the rest of the world.

## GDP Equals Expenditure Equals Income

GDP can be measured in two ways: by the total expenditure on goods and services (called the expenditure approach) or by the total income earned by producing goods and services (called the income approach).

The total expenditure – *aggregate expenditure* – is the sum of the red flows in Figure 10.1. Aggregate expenditure equals consumption expenditure plus investment plus government expenditure plus net exports.

Aggregate income earned by producing goods and services is equal to the total amount paid for the factors used – wages, interest, rent and profit. The blue flow in Figure 10.1 shows aggregate income. Because firms pay out as incomes (including retained profits) everything they receive from the sale of their output, aggregate income (the blue flow) equals aggregate expenditure (the sum of the red flows). That is:

$$Y = C + I + G + X - M$$

The table in Figure 10.1 shows the UK numbers for 2010. You can see that the sum of the expenditures is £1,448 billion, which also equals aggregate income.

Because aggregate expenditure equals aggregate income, these two methods of valuing GDP give the same answer. So:

**GDP equals aggregate expenditure and equals aggregate income.**

The circular flow model is the foundation on which the national economic accounts are built.

## Why Is Domestic Product 'Gross'?

What does the 'gross' in GDP mean? *Gross* means before deducting the depreciation of capital. The opposite of 'gross' is net, which means after deducting the depreciation of capital.

**Depreciation** is the decrease in the value of a firm's capital that results from wear and tear and obsolescence. The total amount spent on purchases of new capital and on replacing depreciated capital is called **gross investment**. The amount by which the value of the firm's capital increases is called **net investment**.

Net investment = Gross investment − Depreciation

For example, if easyJet buys 5 new aeroplanes and retires 2 old aeroplanes from service, its gross investment is the value of the 5 new aeroplanes, depreciation is the value of the 2 old aeroplanes retired, and net investment is the value of 3 new aeroplanes.

*Gross investment* is one of the expenditures included in the expenditure approach to measuring GDP. So the resulting value of total product is a gross measure.

*Gross profit*, which is a firm's profit before subtracting depreciation, is one of the incomes included in the income approach to measuring GDP. So again, the resulting value of total product is a gross measure.

### Review Quiz

1  Define GDP and distinguish between a final good and an intermediate good. Provide examples.
2  Why does GDP equal aggregate income and also equal aggregate expenditure?
3  What is the distinction between gross and net?

You can work these questions in Study Plan 10.1 and get instant feedback.

Let's now see how the ideas that you have just studied can be used in practice. We'll see how GDP and its components are measured in the UK today.

# Measuring UK GDP

The Office for National Statistics uses the concepts that you met in the circular flow model to measure GDP and its components, which it publishes in the *United Kingdom National Accounts – The Blue Book*.

Because the value of aggregate output equals aggregate expenditure and aggregate income, there are two approaches available for measuring GDP, and both are used. They are:

◆ The expenditure approach

◆ The income approach

## The Expenditure Approach

The *expenditure approach* measures GDP as the sum of consumption expenditure ($C$), investment ($I$), government expenditure on goods and services ($G$) and net exports of goods and services ($X - M$), corresponding to the red flows in the circular flow model in Figure 10.2. Table 10.1 shows the results of this approach for 2010. The table also shows the terms used in the *United Kingdom National Accounts – The Blue Book*.

*Consumption expenditure* is the expenditure by households on goods and services produced in the UK and the rest of the world. It includes goods such as beer, CDs, books and magazines; and services such as insurance, banking and legal advice. It includes the purchases of consumer durable goods such as cars and washing

---

### Table 10.1

## GDP: The Expenditure Approach

| Item | Symbol | Amount in 2010 (billions of pounds) | Percentage of GDP |
|---|---|---|---|
| Consumption expenditure (Final consumption expenditure: personal) | $C$ | 948 | 65.5 |
| Investment (Gross capital formation) | $I$ | 208 | 14.4 |
| Government expenditure (Final consumption expenditure: governments) | $G$ | 338 | 23.3 |
| Net exports (External balance of goods and services) | $X - M$ | −46 | −3.2 |
| Gross domestic product | $Y$ | 1,448 | 100.0 |

The expenditure approach measures GDP as the sum of consumption expenditure ($C$), investment ($I$) government expenditure ($G$) and net exports ($X - M$). In 2010, GDP as measured by the expenditure approach was £1,448 billion. Almost two-thirds of aggregate expenditure is consump-tion expenditure.

Source of data: Office for National Statistics, *Statistical Bulletin*, 28 September 2010.

---

machines, but it does *not* include the purchase of new houses, which is counted as part of investment.

*Investment* is expenditure on capital equipment and buildings by firms and expenditure on new residential houses by households. It also includes the change in firms' stocks or inventories.

*Government expenditure* is the expenditure on goods and services by all levels of government – from Westminster to the local town hall. This item includes expenditure on national defence, law and order, street lighting and refuse collection. It does *not* include unemployment benefits because they are not purchases of goods and services.

*Net exports* are the value of UK exports minus the value of UK imports. When a UK company sells a car to a buyer in the US, the value of that car is part of UK exports. When your local Skoda dealer stocks up on the latest model, its expenditure is part of UK imports.

Table 10.1 shows the relative magnitudes of the four items of aggregate expenditure.

---

**Figure 10.2    Aggregate Expenditure**

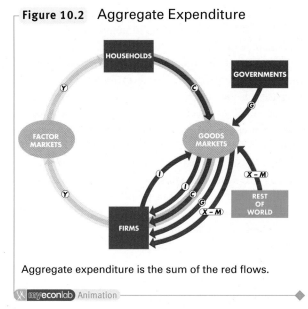

Aggregate expenditure is the sum of the red flows.

myeconlab Animation

# The Income Approach

The *income approach* measures GDP by summing the incomes paid by firms to households for the services of the factors of production they hire – wages for labour, interest for capital, rent for land and profit for entrepreneurship. Let's see how the income approach works.

In the *United Kingdom National Accounts – The Blue Book*, incomes are grouped into three components:

1  Compensation of employees

2  Gross operating surplus

3  Mixed income

*Compensation of employees* is the total payments by firms for labour services. This item includes gross wages and benefits, such as pension contributions and is shown by the blue flow *W* in Figure 10.3.

*Gross operating surplus* is the total profit made by companies and the surpluses generated by publicly owned enterprises. Some of the profits are paid to households in the form of dividends, and some are retained by companies as undistributed profits. The surpluses from publicly owned enterprises are either retained by the enterprises or paid to the government as part of its general revenue. They are all income and are shown by the blue flow *P* in Figure 10.3.

*Mixed income* is a combination of rental income and income from self-employment. Rental income is the payment for the use of land and other rented inputs. It includes payments for rented housing and imputed rent for owner-occupied housing. (Imputed rent is an

---

**Table 10.2**

## GDP: The Income Approach

| Item | Amount in 2010 (billions of pounds) | Percentage of GDP |
|---|---|---|
| Compensation of employees | 788 | 54.4 |
| Gross operating surplus | 308 | 21.3 |
| Mixed income | 170 | 11.7 |
| Gross domestic income at factor cost | 1,266 | 87.4 |
| Indirect taxes less subsidies | 182 | 12.6 |
| Gross domestic product | 1,448 | 100.0 |

The sum of all factor incomes equals gross domestic income at factor cost. GDP equals net domestic income at factor cost plus indirect taxes less subsidies. In 2010, GDP measured by the factor incomes approach was £1,448 billion. Compensation of employees was by far the largest part of total factor income.

Source of data: Office for National Statistics, *Statistical Bulletin*, 28 September 2010.

---

estimate of what homeowners would pay to rent the housing they own and use themselves. By including this item in the national accounts, we measure the total value of housing services, whether they are owned or rented.) Income from self-employment is a mixture of the factor incomes that we have just reviewed. The proprietor of an owner-operated business supplies labour, capital and perhaps land and buildings to the business.

Table 10.2 shows these three components of aggregate income and their relative magnitudes.

The sum of the incomes is called *gross domestic income at factor cost*. The term *factor cost* is used because it is the cost of the *factors of production* used to produce final goods and services. When we sum all the expenditures on final goods and services, we arrive at a total called *domestic product at market prices*. Market prices and factor cost would be the same except for indirect taxes and subsidies.

An *indirect tax* is a tax paid by consumers when they buy goods and services, such as VAT. An indirect tax makes the market price exceed the factor cost. A *subsidy* is a payment by the government to a producer. With a subsidy, the factor cost exceeds the market price. To get from factor cost to market price, we add indirect taxes and subtract subsidies.

---

**Figure 10.3**   Aggregate Income

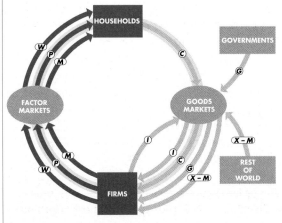

Aggregate income is the sum of the components of the blue flows.

myeconlab Animation

## Nominal GDP and Real GDP

Often, we want to compare GDP in two periods, say 2000 and 2010. In 2000, GDP was £977 billion and in 2010 it was £1,448 billion – 48 per cent higher than in 2000. This increase in GDP is a combination of an increase in production and a rise in prices. To isolate the increase in production from the rise in prices, we distinguish between *real* GDP and *nominal* GDP.

**Real GDP** is the value of final goods and services produced in a given year when valued at the *prices of a reference base year*. By comparing the value of production in the two years at the same prices, we reveal the change in production.

Currently, the reference base year is 2006 and we describe real GDP as measured in 2006 pounds – in terms of what the pound would buy in 2006.

**Nominal GDP** is the value of final goods and services produced in a given year when valued at the prices of that year. Nominal GDP is just a more precise name for GDP.

Economic statisticians at the Office for National Statistics calculate real GDP using the method described in the Mathematical Note on pp. 244–245. Here, we'll explain the basic idea but not the technical details.

## Calculating Real GDP

We'll calculate real GDP for an economy that produces one consumption good, one capital good and one government service. Net exports are zero.

Table 10.3 shows the quantities produced and the prices in 2006 (the base year) and in 2010. In part (a), we calculate nominal GDP in 2006. For each item, we multiply the quantity produced in 2006 by its price in 2006 to find the total expenditure on the item. We sum the expenditures to find nominal GDP, which in 2006 is £100 million. Because 2006 is the base year, both real GDP and nominal GDP equal £100 million.

In Table 10.3(b), we calculate nominal GDP in 2010, which is £300 million. Nominal GDP in 2010 is three times its value in 2006. But by how much has production increased? Real GDP will tell us.

In Table 10.3(c), we calculate real GDP in 2010. The quantities of the goods and services produced are those of 2010, as in part (b). The prices are those in the reference base year – 2006, as in part (a).

For each item, we multiply the quantity produced in 2010 by its price in 2006. We then sum these expenditures to find real GDP in 2010, which is £160 million. This number is what total expenditure would have been in 2010 if prices had remained the same as they were in 2006.

Nominal GDP in 2010 is three times its value in 2006, but real GDP in 2010 is only 1.6 times its 2006 value – a 60 per cent increase in production.

---

**Table 10.3**

### Calculating Nominal GDP and Real GDP

| Item | Quantity (millions) | Price (pounds) | Expenditure (millions of pounds) |
|---|---|---|---|
| **(a) In 2006** | | | |
| C  Shirts | 10 | 5 | 50 |
| I  Computer chips | 3 | 10 | 30 |
| G  Security services | 1 | 20 | 20 |
| Y  Real and Nominal GDP in 2006 | | | 100 |
| **(b) In 2010** | | | |
| C  Shirts | 4 | 5 | 20 |
| I  Computer chips | 2 | 20 | 40 |
| G  Security services | 6 | 40 | 240 |
| Y  Nominal GDP in 2010 | | | 300 |
| **(c) Quantities of 2010 valued at prices of 2006** | | | |
| C  Shirts | 4 | 5 | 20 |
| I  Computer chips | 2 | 10 | 20 |
| G  Security services | 6 | 20 | 120 |
| Y  Real GDP in 2010 | | | 160 |

In 2006, the reference base year, real GDP equals nominal GDP and was £100 million. In 2010, nominal GDP increased to £300 million. But real GDP in 2010 in part (c), which is calculated by using the quantities of 2010 in part (b) and the prices of 2006 in part (a), was only £160 million – a 60 per cent increase from 2006.

---

### Review Quiz

1. What is the expenditure approach to measuring GDP?
2. What is the income approach to measuring GDP?
3. What adjustment must be made to total income to make it equal to GDP?
4. What is the distinction between nominal GDP and real GDP?
5. How is real GDP calculated?

You can work these questions in Study Plan 10.2 and get instant feedback.

## The Uses and Limitations of Real GDP

We use estimates of real GDP for two main purposes. They are:

◆ To compare the standard of living over time
◆ To compare the standard of living across countries

## The Standard of Living Over Time

One method of comparing the standard of living over time is to calculate real GDP per person in different years. **Real GDP per person** is real GDP divided by the population. Real GDP per person tells us the value of goods and services that the average person can enjoy. By using *real* GDP, we remove any influence that rising prices and a rising cost of living might have had on our comparison.

We're interested in both the long-term trends and the shorter-term cycles in the standard of living.

### Long-term Trend

A handy way of comparing real GDP per person over time is to express it as a ratio of some reference year. For example, in 1960 real GDP per person was £8,070 and in 2010 it was £21,216. So real GDP per person in 2010 was 2.6 times its 1960 level – that is, £21,216 divided by £8,070. To the extent that real GDP per person measures the standard of living, people were 2.6 times as well off in 2010 as their grandparents had been in 1960.

Figure 10.4 shows the path of UK real GDP per person for the 50 years from 1960 to 2010 and highlights two features of our expanding living standard:

◆ The growth of potential GDP per person
◆ Fluctuations of real GDP per person

#### The Growth of Potential GDP
**Potential GDP** is the value of production when all the economy's labour, capital, land and entrepreneurial ability are fully employed. Potential GDP per person, the smoother black line in Figure 10.4, grows at a steady pace because the quantities of the factors of production and their productivities grow at a steady pace.

But potential GDP per person doesn't grow at a constant pace. During the 1960s, it grew at 2.8 per cent per year but slowed to only 2.1 per cent per year during the

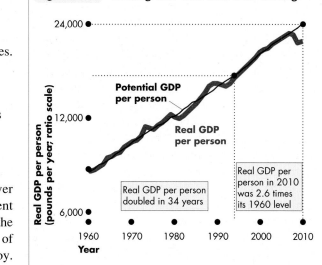

**Figure 10.4** Rising UK Standard of Living

Real GDP per person in the UK doubled between 1960 and 1994. In 2010, real GDP per person was 2.6 times its 1960 level. Real GDP per person, the red line, fluctuates around potential GDP per person, the black line. (The y-axis is a ratio scale – see the Appendix, pp. 242–243.)

Source of data: Office for National Statistics, *Statistical Bulletin*. 28 September 2010.

myeconlab Animation

1970s. This slowdown might seem small, but it had big consequences, as you'll soon see.

#### Fluctuations of Real GDP
You can see that real GDP per person, shown by the red line in Figure 10.4, fluctuates around potential GDP per person, and sometimes real GDP per person shrinks.

Let's take a closer look at the two features of our expanding living standard that we've just outlined.

### Productivity Growth Slowdown

How costly was the slowdown in productivity growth after 1970? The answer is provided by the *Lucas wedge*, which is the pound value of the accumulated gap between what real GDP per person would have been if the 1960s growth rate had persisted and what real GDP per person turned out to be. (Nobel Laureate Robert E. Lucas Jr. drew attention to this gap.)

Figure 10.5 illustrates the Lucas wedge. The wedge started out small during the 1970s, but by 2010 real GDP per person was £5,962 per year lower than it would have been with no growth slowdown and the accumulated gap was £88,000 per person.

## Figure 10.5   The Cost of Slower Growth

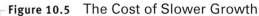

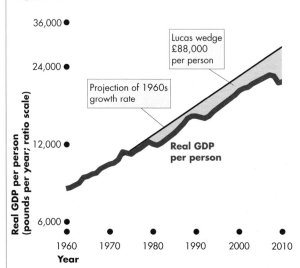

The black line projects the 1960s growth rate of real GDP per person to 2010. The Lucas wedge arises from the slowdown of productivity growth that began during the 1970s. The cost of the slowdown is £88,000 per person.

Source of data: Office for National Statistics, *Statistical Bulletin*. 28 September 2010.

myeconlab Animation

## Real GDP Fluctuations – The Business Cycle

We call the fluctuations in the pace of expansion of real GDP the business cycle. The **business cycle** is a periodic but irregular up-and-down movement of total production and other measures of economic activity. The business cycle isn't a regular predictable cycle like the phases of the moon, but every cycle has two phases:

1  Expansion
2  Recession

and two turning points:

1  Peak
2  Trough

Figure 10.6 shows these features of the most recent UK business cycle.

An **expansion** is a period during which real GDP increases. In the early stage of an expansion real GDP returns to potential GDP and as the expansion progresses, potential GDP grows and real GDP eventually exceeds potential GDP.

A common definition of **recession** is a period during which real GDP decreases – its growth rate is negative – for at least two successive quarters. The definition used by the National Bureau of Economic Research, which dates the US business cycle phases and turning points, is 'a period of significant decline in total output, income, employment and trade, usually lasting from six months to a year, and marked by contractions in many sectors of the economy'.

An expansion ends and a recession begins at a business cycle peak, which is the highest level that real GDP has attained up to that time. A recession ends at a trough, when real GDP reaches a temporary low point and from which the next expansion begins.

In the second quarter of 2008 the UK economy went into recession. From a long way below potential GDP, a recovery began at the end of 2009. The recovery looked strong in the first half of 2010, but doubts are beginning to emerge about whether the pace of the recovery will be sustained. *Reading Between the Lines* on pp. 240–241 discusses why.

## Figure 10.6   The Most Recent UK Business Cycle

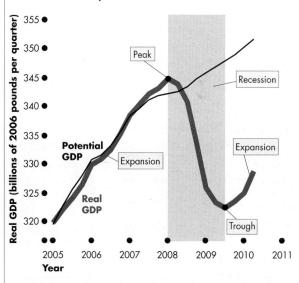

A business cycle expansion, which began in the fourth quarter of 2001, ended at a peak in the second quarter of 2008. A deep and long recession followed the 2008 peak and ended in a trough at the end of 2009 when an expansion began.

Source of data: Office for National Statistics, *Statistical Bulletin*. 28 September 2010.

 myeconlab Animation

# The Standard of Living Across Countries

Two problems arise in using real GDP to compare living standards across countries. First, the real GDP of one country must be converted into the same currency units as the real GDP of the other country. Second, the goods and services in both countries must be valued at the same prices. Comparing the US and China provides a striking example of these two problems.

## China and the US in US Dollars

In 2010, real GDP per person in the US was $42,800 and in China it was 23,400 yuan. The yuan is the currency of China and the price at which the dollar and the yuan exchanged, the market exchange rate, was 8.2 yuan per US$1. Using this exchange rate, 23,400 yuan converts to $2,850. These numbers tell us that real GDP per person in the US was 15 times that in China.

The red line in Figure 10.7 shows real GDP per person in China from 1980 to 2010 when the market exchange rate is used to convert yuan to US dollars.

## China and the US at PPP

Figure 10.7 shows a second estimate of China's real GDP per person that values China's production on the same terms as US production. It uses *purchasing power parity* or *PPP* prices, which are the *same prices* for both countries.

**Figure 10.7** Two Views of Real GDP in China

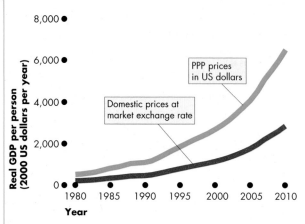

Real GDP per person in China has grown rapidly. But how rapidly it has grown and to what level depends on how real GDP is valued. When GDP in 2010 is valued at the market exchange rate, US income per person is 15 times that in China. China looks like a poor developing country. But the comparison is misleading. When GDP is valued at purchasing power parity prices, US income per person is only 6.5 times that in China.

Source of data: International Monetary Fund, World Economic Outlook database, April 2010.

 myeconlab Animation

The price of a Big Mac is $3.75 in Chicago and 13.25 yuan or $1.62 in Shanghai. To compare real GDP in China and the US, we must value China's Big Macs at the $3.75 US price – the PPP price.

The prices of some goods are higher in the US than in China, so these items get a smaller weight in China's real GDP than they get in US real GDP. An example is a Big Mac that costs $3.75 in Chicago. In Shanghai, a Big Mac costs 13.25 yuan which is the equivalent of $1.62. So in China's real GDP, a Big Mac gets less than half the weight that it gets in US real GDP.

Some prices in China are higher than in the US but more prices are lower, so Chinese prices put a lower value on China's production than do US prices.

According to the PPP comparisons, real GDP per person in the US in 2010 was 6.5 times that of China, not 15 times.

You've seen how real GDP is used to make standard of living comparisons over time and across countries. But real GDP isn't a perfect measure of the standard of living and we'll now examine its limitations.

# Limitations of Real GDP

Real GDP measures the value of goods and services that are bought in markets. Some of the factors that influence the standard of living and that are not part of GDP are:

◆ Household production
◆ Underground economic activity
◆ Health and life expectancy
◆ Leisure time
◆ Environmental quality
◆ Political freedom and social justice

## Household Production

An enormous amount of production takes place every day in our homes. Changing a light bulb, cutting the grass, washing the car and growing vegetables are all examples of household production. Because these productive activities are not traded in markets, they are not included in GDP.

The omission of household production from GDP means that GDP *underestimates* total production. But it also means that the growth rate of GDP *overestimates* the growth rate of total production. The reason is that some of the growth rate of market production (included in GDP) is a replacement for home production. So part of the increase in GDP arises from a decrease in home production.

Two trends point in this direction. One is the trend in the number of women who have jobs, which increased from 52.7 per cent of the female population of working age in 1971 to 56.7 per cent in 2010. The other is the trend in the purchase of traditionally home-produced goods and services in the market. For example, more households now buy takeaways, eat in restaurants and use childcare services. This trend means that increasing proportions of food preparation and childcare that used to be part of household production are now measured as part of GDP. So real GDP grows more rapidly than does real GDP plus home production.

## Underground Economic Activity

The *underground economy* is the part of the economy purposely hidden from view by the people operating in it to avoid taxes and regulations or because the goods and services they are producing are illegal. Because underground economic activity is unreported, it is omitted from GDP.

The underground economy is easy to describe, even if it is hard to measure. It includes the production and distribution of illegal drugs, prostitution, production that uses illegal labour that is paid less than the minimum wage, and jobs done for cash to avoid paying income taxes. This last category might be quite large and includes tips earned by taxi drivers, hairdressers and hotel and restaurant workers.

Estimates of the scale of the underground economy range between 3.5 and 13.5 per cent of GDP (£51 billion to £195 billion) in the UK and much more in some countries, particularly in Eastern European countries that are making the transition from centrally planned economies to market economies.

If the underground economy is a constant proportion of the total economy, the growth rate of real GDP provides a useful estimate of *changes* in economic welfare and the standard of living. But sometimes production shifts from the underground economy to the rest of the economy, and sometimes it shifts the other way. The underground economy expands relative to the rest of the economy if taxes rise sharply or if regulations become especially restrictive. And the underground economy shrinks relative to the rest of the economy if the burdens of taxes and regulations ease.

Whose production is more valuable: the chef's whose work gets counted in GDP . . .

. . . or the busy mother's whose dinner preparations and child minding don't get counted?

During the 1980s, when tax rates were cut, there was an increase in the reporting of previously hidden income and tax revenues increased. So some part (but probably a very small part) of the expansion of real GDP during the 1980s represented a shift from the underground economy rather than an increase in production.

## Health and Life Expectancy

Good health and a long life – the hopes of everyone – do not show up in real GDP, at least not directly. A higher real GDP does enable us to spend more on medical research, healthcare, healthy food and exercise equipment. As real GDP has increased, our life expectancy has lengthened – from 70 years at the end of the Second World War to approaching 80 years today.

But we face new health and life expectancy problems every year. AIDS, drug abuse, suicide and murder are taking young lives at a rate that causes serious concern. When we take these negative influences into account, we see that real GDP growth overstates the improvements in the standard of living.

## Leisure Time

Leisure time is an economic good that adds to our standard of living. Other things remaining the same, the more leisure we have, the better off we are. Our time spent working is valued as part of GDP, but our leisure time is not. Yet that leisure time must be at least as valuable to us as the wage that we earn for the last hour worked. If it were not, we would work instead of taking the leisure. Over the years, leisure time has steadily increased. The working week has become shorter and the number and length of holidays have increased. These improvements in economic well-being are not reflected in GDP.

## Environmental Quality

Economic activity directly influences the quality of the environment. The burning of hydrocarbon fuels is the most visible activity that damages our environment. But it is not the only example. The depletion of non-renewable resources, the mass clearing of forests, and the pollution of lakes and rivers are other major environmental consequences of industrial production.

Resources used to protect the environment are valued as part of GDP. For example, the value of catalytic converters that help to protect the atmosphere from vehicle emissions is part of GDP. But if we did not use such pieces of equipment and instead polluted the atmosphere, we would not count the deteriorating air that we were breathing as a negative part of GDP.

An industrial society possibly produces more atmospheric pollution than does an agricultural society. But pollution does not always increase as we become wealthier. Wealthy people value a clean environment and are willing to pay for one. Compare the pollution in China today with pollution in the UK. China, a poor country, pollutes its rivers, lakes and atmosphere in a way that is unimaginable in the UK.

## Political Freedom and Social Justice

Most people value political freedoms such as those provided by the western democracies. They also value social justice or fairness – equality of opportunity and of access to social security safety nets that protect people from the extremes of misfortune.

A country might have a very large real GDP per person but have limited political freedom and equity. For example, a small elite might enjoy political liberty and extreme wealth, while the vast majority are effectively enslaved and live in abject poverty. Such an economy would generally be regarded as having less economic welfare than one that had the same amount of real GDP but in which political freedoms were enjoyed by everyone. Today, China is the world's fastest-growing economy but the Chinese people have limited political freedoms. India's economy is growing less quickly than China's but the people of India enjoy a democratic political system. Economists have no easy way to determine which of these two countries is better off.

## The Bottom Line

Do we get the wrong message about the growth in economic welfare by looking at the growth of real GDP? The influences that are omitted from real GDP are probably important and could be large.

Developing countries have more household production and a larger underground economy than do developed countries, so the gap between their living standards is exaggerated. Also, as real GDP grows, part of the measured growth might reflect a switch from home production to market production and from underground to regular production. This measurement error overstates the growth in economic well-being and the improvement in the standard of living.

## A Broader Indicator of Economic Well-being

The limitations of real GDP reviewed in this chapter affect the standard of living and general well-being of every country. So to make international comparisons of the general state of economic well-being, we must look at real GDP and other indicators.

The United Nations has constructed a broader measure called the Human Development Index (HDI), which combines real GDP, life expectancy and health and education. Real GDP per person (measured on the PPP basis) is a major component of the HDI.

The dots in the figure show the relationship between real GDP per person and the HDI. The United Arab Emirates (UAE) has one of the highest real GDP per person, but it ranks 35th on the HDI. Norway has the highest HDI, and the UK, Australia and Japan have a higher HDI than the UAE. The HDI of the UAE is lower than that of 34 other countries because the people of those countries live longer and have better access to healthcare and education than do citizens of the UAE.

African nations have the lowest levels of economic well-being. The Democratic Republic of Congo has the lowest real GDP per person and Niger has the lowest HDI. But real

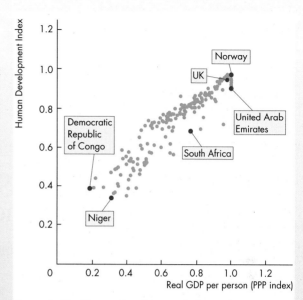

**Figure 1   The Human Development Index**

Source of data: United Nations, hdr.undp.org/en/statistics/data

GDP per person in South Africa is in the middle of the range and its HDI is also in the middle of the range.

---

Other influences on the standard of living include the amount of leisure time available, the quality of the environment, the security of jobs and homes and the safety of city streets.

It is possible to construct broader measures that combine the many influences that contribute to human happiness. Real GDP will be one element in those broader measures, but it will by no means be the whole of those measures. The United Nations' Human Development Index (HDI) is one example of attempts to provide broader measures of economic well-being and the standard of living. This measure places a good deal of weight on real GDP. Dozens of other measures have been proposed. One includes resource depletion and emissions in a Green GDP measure. Another emphasizes the enjoyment of life rather than the production of goods in a 'genuine progress index' or GPI.

Despite all the alternatives, real GDP per person remains the most widely used indicator of economic well-being and the standard of living.

1   Distinguish between real GDP and potential GDP and describe how each grows over time.
2   How does the growth rate of real GDP contribute to an improved standard of living?
3   What is a business cycle and what are its phases and turning points?
4   What is PPP and how does it help us to make valid international comparisons of real GDP?
5   Explain why real GDP might be an unreliable indicator of the standard of living.

You can work these questions in Study Plan 10.3 and get instant feedback.

You now know how economists measure GDP and what the GDP data tell us. In *Reading Between the Lines* on pp. 240–241, we examine the path of GDP as we emerge from recession during 2010. Your task in the next chapter is to learn how we monitor employment and unemployment and retail prices.

## Reading Between the Lines

# The Fragile UK Recovery

The Financial Times, 6 October 2010

## Employers Fear Recovery is in Peril from Spending Cuts

Daniel Pimlotte

The economy grew at a reasonable pace in the third quarter but businesses are increasingly alarmed about the prospects for another recession or much weaker growth, according to a closely watched survey. Growth between July and September looks likely to have been 0.4 to 0.5 per cent, according to polling company Markit, an estimate based on its surveys of purchasing managers in the service, manufacturing and building sectors.

That is not far from the 0.6 per cent long-run average pace at which the UK has grown but much slower than the 1.2 per cent growth in the second quarter. Markit warned that

many companies were worried about spending cuts, with greater detail on the austerity measures due this month in the government's spending review.

'Orders are not coming through at anything like the pace before the public sector contracts are being cut. Businesses believe these cuts are arriving at the wrong time.'

The evidence of business fears came as Markit published its combined index of activity in services, manufacturing and construction.

Services sector data published on Tuesday showed weak business confidence and new orders rising at the slowest pace in 15 months.

## The Essence of the Story

◆ A poll of purchasing managers suggest that growth in the third quarter of 2010 could be between 0.4 and 0.5 per cent.

◆ This quarterly growth rate translates into an annual growth rate of 2 per cent, which is not far from the UK long-term growth rate of 2.4 to 2.5 per cent a year.

◆ Many businesses are worried about cuts in government spending that might depress demand and stall the recovery.

◆ The fragility of demand and the growth of GDP have raised the prospect that the economy may recover very slowly or even turn down into a double-dip recession.

# Economic Analysis

◆ The 2008–2009 recession was an unusually deep one and although the second quarter of 2010 showed a strong recovery, predictions for subsequent quarters were for weak growth.

◆ Figure 1 illustrates the severity of the 2008–2009 recession using the concepts of potential GDP and real GDP that you learned about in this chapter.

◆ At the trough in the third quarter of 2009, real GDP was about £25 billion below potential GDP or 7 per cent of potential GDP.

◆ To put the magnitude of the gap between potential GDP and real GDP into perspective, each person's share (your share) of the lost production for the whole of 2009 was about £1,667.

◆ The prediction from the Markit survey is that the economy will grow by only 0.5 per cent in the third quarter of 2010, which shows the fragility of the recovery and possibly a second downturn.

◆ However, a slowdown in the growth rate does not necessarily mean that the economy will slip back into recession.

◆ The 2008–2009 recession has been described as the worst recession since the 1930s. Figure 2 shows the quarterly profile of the 1930s recession plotted alongside the 2008–2009 recession.

◆ The similarity of the downturn and the recovery between the two periods is striking. It is also the case that just when the economy came out of deep recession in 1931 the economy slipped back into recession in 1932.

◆ While the recession and recovery during the 1930s looks similar to the quarterly profile of 2008–2009 there are many differences in policy that do not make it obvious that the economy will turn downwards in 2011, as it did in 1932.

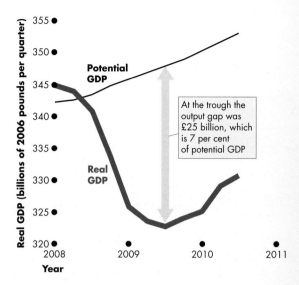

Figure 1  The deep 2008–2009 recession

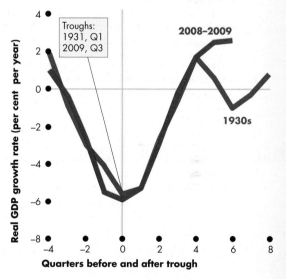

Figure 2  The 1930s versus 2008–2009

◆ *The Economist* magazine publishes the results of a weekly poll of forecasters and on 9 October 2010 the range of forecasts for UK GDP growth in 2011 was from a low of 0.6 per cent a year to a high of 2.4 per cent a year.

# Chapter 10 Appendix

# Graphs in Macroeconomics

## After studying this appendix, you will be able to:

◆ Make and interpret a time-series graph

◆ Make and interpret a graph that uses a ratio scale

## The Time-series Graph

In macroeconomics we study the fluctuations and trends in the key variables that describe macroeconomic performance and policy. These variables include GDP and its expenditure and income components that you've learned about in this chapter. They also include variables that describe the labour market and consumer prices that you study in Chapter 11.

Regardless of the variable of interest, we want to be able to compare its value today with that in the past; and we want to describe how the variable has changed over time. The most effective way to do these things is to make a time-series graph.

## Making a Time-series Graph

A **time-series graph** measures time (for example, years, quarters or months) on the *x*-axis and the variable or variables in which we are interested on the *y*-axis. Figure A10.1 is an example of a time-series graph. It provides some information about unemployment in the UK since 1980. In this figure, we measure time in years starting in 1980. We measure the unemployment rate (the variable that we are interested in) on the *y*-axis.

A time-series graph enables us to visualize how a variable has changed over time and how its value in one period relates to its value in another period. It conveys an enormous amount of information quickly and easily.

Let's see how to 'read' a time-series graph.

## Reading a Time-series Graph

To practise reading a time-series graph, take a close look at Figure A10.1. The graph shows the level, change and speed of change of the variable.

**Figure A10.1**    A Time-series Graph

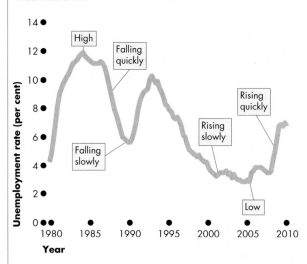

A time-series graph plots the level of a variable on the *y*-axis against time (here measured in years) on the *x*-axis. This graph shows the unemployment rate each year from 1980 to 2010. It shows when unemployment was high, when it was low, when it increased, when it decreased and when it changed quickly and changed slowly.

myeconlab Animation

◆ The *level* of the variable: it tells us when unemployment is high and low. When the line is a long distance above the *x*-axis, the unemployment rate is high, as it was, for example, in 1983 and again in 2009. When the line is close to the *x*-axis, the unemployment rate is low, as it was, for example, in 2001.

◆ The *change* in the variable: it tells us how unemployment changes – whether it increases or decreases. When the line slopes upward, as it did in 2008 and 2009, the unemployment rate is rising. When the line slopes downward, as it did in 1984 and 1997, the unemployment rate is falling.

◆ The *speed* of change in the variable: it tells us whether the unemployment rate is rising or falling quickly or slowly. If the line is very steep, then the unemployment rate increases or decreases quickly. If the line is not steep, the unemployment rate increases or decreases slowly. For example, the unemployment rate rose quickly in 2008 and slowly in 2003 and it fell quickly in 1987 and slowly in 1989.

## Ratio Scale Reveals Trend

A time-series graph also reveals whether a variable has a **cycle**, which is a tendency for a variable to alternate between upward and downward movements, or a **trend**, which is a tendency for a variable to move in one general direction.

The unemployment rate in Figure A10.1 has a cycle but no strongly visible trend. When a trend is present, a special kind of time-series graph, one that uses a ratio scale on the *y*-axis, reveals the trend.

## A Time-series with a Trend

Many macroeconomics variables, among them GDP and the average level of prices, have an upward trend. Figure A10.2 shows an example of such a variable: the average prices paid by consumers.

In Figure A10.2(a), consumer prices since 1970 are graphed on a normal scale. In 1970 the level is 100. In other years, the average level of prices is measured as a percentage of the 1970 level.

The graph clearly shows the upward trend of prices. But it doesn't tell us when prices were rising fastest or whether there was any change in the trend. Just looking at the upward-sloping line in Figure A10.2(a) gives the impression that the pace of growth of consumer prices was constant.

## Using a Ratio Scale

On a graph axis with a normal scale, the gap between 1 and 2 is the same as that between 3 and 4. On a graph axis with a ratio scale, the gap between 1 and 2 is the same as that between 2 and 4. The ratio 2 to 1 equals the ratio 4 to 2. By using a ratio scale, we can 'see' when the growth rate (the percentage change per unit of time) changes.

Figure A10.2(b) shows an example of a ratio scale. Notice that the values on the *y*-axis get closer together but the gap between 400 and 200 equals the gap between 200 and 100. The ratio gaps are equal.

Graphing the data on a ratio scale reveals the trends. In the case of consumer prices, the trend is much steeper during the 1970s and early 1980s than in the later years. The steeper the line in the ratio-scale graph in part (b), the faster are prices rising. Prices rose rapidly during the 1970s and early 1980s and more slowly in the later 1980s and 1990s. The ratio-scale graph reveals this fact. We use ratio-scale graphs extensively in macroeconomics.

**Figure A10.2    Ratio Scale Reveals Trend**

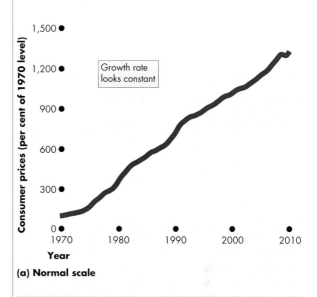

**(a) Normal scale**

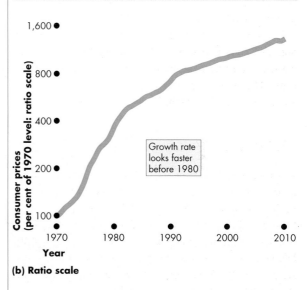

**(b) Ratio scale**

The graph shows the average of consumer prices from 1970 to 2010. The level is 100 in 1970 and the value in other years is a percentage of the 1970 level. Consumer prices normally rise each year so the line slopes upward. In part (a), where the *y*-axis scale is normal, the rate of increase appears to be constant.

In part (b), where the *y*-axis is a ratio scale (the ratio of 400 to 200 equals the ratio 200 to 100), prices rose faster in the 1970s and early 1980s and slower in the later years. The ratio scale reveals this trend.

 myeconlab Animation

# Chain Volume Measure of Real GDP

In the real GDP calculation on p. 233, real GDP in 2010 is 1.6 times its value in 2006. But suppose that we use 2010 as the reference base year and value real GDP in 2006 at 2010 prices. If you do the mathematics, you will see that real GDP in 2006 is £150 million at 2010 prices. GDP in 2010 is £300 million (in 2010 prices), so now the numbers say that real GDP has doubled. Which is correct? Did real GDP increase 1.6 times or double? Should we use the prices of 2006 or 2010? The answer is that we need to use both sets of prices.

The Office for National Statistics uses a measure of real GDP called the **chain volume measure** of real GDP. Three steps are needed to calculate this measure:

♦ Value production in the prices of adjacent years

♦ Find the average of two percentage changes

♦ Link (chain) back to the reference base year

## Value Production in Prices of Adjacent Years

The first step is to value production in adjacent years at the prices of both years. We'll make these calculations for 2010 and its preceding year, 2009.

Table 1 shows the quantities produced and prices in the two years. Part (a) shows the nominal GDP calculation for 2009 – the quantities produced in 2009 valued at the prices of 2009. Nominal GDP in 2009 is £145 million. Part (b) shows the nominal GDP calculation for 2010 – the quantities produced in 2010 valued at the prices of 2010. Nominal GDP in 2010 is £300 million. Part (c) shows the value of the quantities produced in 2010 at the prices of 2009 – a total of £160 million. And part (d) shows the value of the quantities produced in 2009 at the prices of 2010 – a total of £275 million.

## Find the Average of Two Percentage Changes

The second step is to find the percentage change in the value of production based on the prices in the two adjacent years. Table 2 summarizes these calculations.

Part (a) shows that, valued at the prices of 2009, production increased from £145 million in 2009 to £160 million in 2010, an increase of 10.3 per cent.

---

| **Table 1** |
| :-- |

**Real GDP Calculation Step 1: Value Production in Adjacent Years at Prices in Both Years**

| Item | Quantity (millions) | Price (pounds) | Expenditure (millions of pounds) |
| :-- | :--: | :--: | :--: |
| **(a) In 2009** | | | |
| C  Shirts | 3 | 5 | 15 |
| I   Computer chips | 3 | 10 | 30 |
| G  Security services | 5 | 20 | 100 |
| Y  Real and Nominal GDP in 2009 | | | **145** |
| **(b) In 2010** | | | |
| C  Shirts | 4 | 5 | 20 |
| I   Computer chips | 2 | 20 | 40 |
| G  Security services | 6 | 40 | 240 |
| Y  Nominal GDP in 2010 | | | **300** |
| **(c) Quantities of 2010 valued at prices of 2009** | | | |
| C  Shirts | 4 | 5 | 20 |
| I   Computer chips | 2 | 10 | 20 |
| G  Security services | 6 | 20 | 120 |
| Y  2010 production at 2009 prices | | | **160** |
| **(d) Quantities of 2009 valued at prices of 2010** | | | |
| C  Shirts | 3 | 5 | 15 |
| I   Computer chips | 3 | 20 | 60 |
| G  Security services | 5 | 40 | 200 |
| Y  2009 production at 2010 prices | | | **275** |

Step 1 is to value the production of adjacent years at the prices of both years. Here, we value the production of 2009 and 2010 at the prices of both 2009 and 2010. The value of 2009 production at 2009 prices, in part (a), is nominal GDP in 2009. The value of 2010 production at 2010 prices, in part (b), is nominal GDP in 2010. Part (c) calculates the value of 2010 production at 2009 prices, and part (d) calculates the value of 2009 production at 2010 prices. We use these numbers in Step 2.

---

Part (b) shows that, valued at the prices of 2010, production increased from £275 million in 2009 to £300 million in 2010, an increase of 9.1 per cent. Part (c) shows that the average of these two percentage changes in the value of production is 9.7. That is, $(10.3 + 9.1) \div 2 = 9.7$.

By applying this average percentage change to real GDP, we can find the value of real GDP in 2010. Real GDP in 2009 is £145 million, so a 9.7 per cent increase

## Table 2

**Real GDP Calculation Step 2:**
**Find Average of Two Percentage Changes**

| Value of Production | Millions of pounds | |
| --- | --- | --- |
| **(a) At 2009 prices** | | |
| Nominal GDP in 2009 | 145 | |
| 2010 production at 2009 prices | 160 | |
| Percentage change in production at 2009 prices | | **10.3** |
| **(b) At 2010 prices** | | |
| 2009 production at 2010 prices | 275 | |
| Nominal GDP in 2010 | 300 | |
| Percentage change in production at 2010 prices | | **9.1** |
| **(c) Average percentage change in 2010** | | **9.7** |

Using the numbers in Step 1, the percentage change in production from 2009 to 2010 valued at 2009 prices is 10.3 per cent, in part (a). The percentage change in production from 2009 to 2010 valued at 2010 prices is 9.1 per cent, in part (b). The average of these two percentage changes is 9.7 per cent, in part (c).

## Table 3

**Real GDP Calculation Step 3:**
**Repeat Growth Rate Calculations**

| Year | **2006** | 2007 | 2008 | 2009 | **2010** |
| --- | --- | --- | --- | --- | --- |
| Growth rate | 8.0 | 6.0 | 7.0 | 8.0 | **9.7** |

is £14 million. Then real GDP in 2010 is £145 million plus £14 million, which equals £159 million. Because real GDP in 2009 is in 2009 pounds, real GDP in 2010 is also in 2009 pounds.

Although the real GDP of £159 million is expressed in 2009 pounds, the calculation uses the average of the prices of the final goods and services that make up GDP in 2009 and 2010.

## Link (Chain) Back to the Base Year

The third step is to express GDP in the prices of the reference base year. To do this, the Office for National Statistics performs calculations like the ones that you've just worked through to find the percentage change in real GDP in each pair of years. It then selects a base year (currently 2006) in which, by definition, real GDP equals nominal GDP. Finally, it uses the percentage changes to calculate real GDP in 2006 prices starting from real GDP in 2006.

To illustrate this third step, we'll assume that the Office for National Statistics has calculated the growth rates since 2006 shown in Table 3. The 2010 growth rate that we've just calculated is highlighted in the table. The other (assumed) growth rates are calculated in exactly the same way as that for 2010.

Figure 1 illustrates the chain link calculations. In the reference base year, 2006, real GDP equals nominal GDP, which we'll assume is £135 million. Table 3 tells us that the growth rate in 2006 was 8 per cent, so real GDP in 2006 is 8 per cent higher than it was in 2005, which means that real GDP in 2005 is £125 million ($125 \times 1.08 = 135$).

Table 3 also tells us that the growth rate in 2007 was 6 per cent, so real GDP in 2007 is 6 per cent higher than it was in 2006, which means that real GDP in 2007 is £143 million ($135 \times 1.06 = 143$).

By repeating these calculations for each year, we obtain the chain volume measure of real GDP in 2006 pounds for each year. In 2009, chain volume measure of real GDP in 2006 pounds is £165 million. So the 9.7 per cent growth rate in 2010 that we calculated in Table 2 means that real GDP in 2010 is £181 million.

Notice that the growth rates are independent of the reference base year, so changing the reference base year does not change the growth rates.

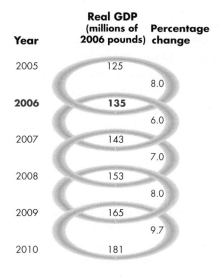

**Figure 1 Real GDP calculation step 3:**
**link (chain) back to base year**

# SUMMARY

## Key Points

### Gross Domestic Product (pp. 228–230)

◆ GDP, or gross domestic product, is the market value of all the final goods and services produced in a country during a given period.

◆ A final good is an item that is bought by its final user and it contrasts with an intermediate good, which is a component of a final good.

◆ GDP is calculated by using the expenditure or income totals in the circular flow model of expenditure and income.

◆ Aggregate expenditure on goods and services equals aggregate income and GDP.

Working Problems 1 to 7 will give you a better understanding of gross domestic product.

### Measuring UK GDP (pp. 231–233)

◆ Because aggregate expenditure, aggregate income and the value of aggregate output are equal, we can measure GDP by either the expenditure approach or the income approach.

◆ The expenditure approach adds together consumption expenditure, investment, government expenditure on goods and services and net exports.

◆ The income approach adds together the incomes paid to the factors of production – wages, interest, rent and profit – and indirect taxes less subsidies.

◆ Real GDP is measured using a common set of prices to remove the effects of inflation from GDP.

Working Problems 8 to 15 will give you a better understanding of measuring UK GDP.

## The Uses and Limitations of Real GDP (pp. 234–239)

◆ Real GDP is used to compare the standard of living over time and across countries.

◆ Real GDP per person grows and fluctuates around the more smoothly growing potential GDP.

◆ A slowing of the growth rate of real GDP per person during the 1970s has lowered incomes by a large amount.

◆ International real GDP comparisons use PPP prices.

◆ Real GDP is not a perfect measure of economic welfare because it excludes household production, the underground economy, health and life expectancy, leisure time, environmental quality and political freedom and social justice.

Working Problem 16 will give you a better understanding of the uses and limitations of real GDP.

## Key Terms

Business cycle, 235
Chain volume measure, 244
Consumption expenditure, 229
Cycle, 243
Depreciation, 230
Expansion, 235
Exports, 230
Final good, 228
Government expenditure, 230
Gross domestic product (GDP), 228
Gross investment, 230
Imports, 230
Intermediate good, 228
Investment, 229
Net exports, 230
Net investment, 230
Nominal GDP, 233
Potential GDP, 234
Real GDP, 233
Real GDP per person, 234
Recession, 235
Time-series graph, 242
Trend, 243

## STUDY PLAN PROBLEMS AND APPLICATIONS

 myeconlab   You can work Problems 1 to 17 in MyEconLab Chapter 10 Study Plan and get instant feedback.

## Gross Domestic Product (Study Plan 10.1)

**1** Classify each of the following items as a final good or service or an intermediate good or service and identify which is a component of consumption expenditure, investment, or government expenditure on goods and services:

- ◆ Banking services bought by a student.
- ◆ New cars bought by Hertz, the car rental firm.
- ◆ Newsprint bought by *The Times* newspaper.
- ◆ The purchase of a new limo for the prime minister.
- ◆ New house bought by Wayne Rooney.

**2** The firm that printed this textbook bought the paper from XYZ Paper Mills. Was this purchase of paper part of GDP? If not, how does the value of the paper get counted in GDP?

Use the following figure, which illustrates the circular flow model, to work Problems 3 and 4.

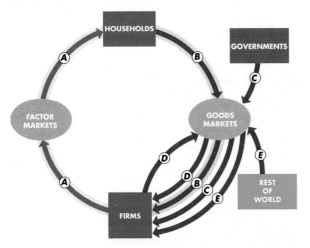

**3** During 2008, in an economy:

- ◆ Flow *B* was £90 billion.
- ◆ Flow *C* was £20 billion.
- ◆ Flow *D* was £30 billion.
- ◆ Flow *E* was –£7 billion.

Name the flows and calculate the value of:

**a** Aggregate income.

**b** GDP.

**4** During 2009, flow A was £130 billion, flow B was £91 billion, flow D was £33 billion, and flow E was –£8 billion.

Calculate the 2009 values of

**a** GDP.

**b** Government expenditure.

**5** Use the following data to calculate aggregate expenditure and imports of goods and services.

- ◆ Government expenditure: £20 billion.
- ◆ Aggregate income: £100 billion.
- ◆ Consumption expenditure: £67 billion.
- ◆ Investment: £21 billion.
- ◆ Exports of goods and services: £30 billion.

**6 US Economy Shrinks Modestly**

GDP fell 1 per cent as businesses cut investment by 8.9 per cent, consumers cut spending by 1.2 per cent, purchases of new houses fell 38 per cent, and exports fell 29.9 per cent.

Source: Reuters, 31 July 2009

Use the letters on the figure in Problem 3 to indicate the flow in which each item in the news clip occurs. How can GDP have fallen by only 1.0 per cent with the big expenditure cuts reported?

**7** A market research firm deconstructed an Apple iPod and studied the manufacturers' costs and profits of each of the parts and components. The final results are:

- ◆ An Apple iPod sells in the US for $299.
- ◆ A Japanese firm, Toshiba, makes the hard disk and display screen, which cost $93.
- ◆ Other components produced in South Korea cost $25.
- ◆ Other components produced in the US cost $21.
- ◆ The iPod is assembled in China at a cost of $5.
- ◆ The costs and profits of retailers, advertisers and transportation firms in the US are $75.

**a** What is Apple's profit?

**b** Where in the national accounts of the US, Japan, South Korea and China are these transactions recorded?

**c** What contribution does one iPod make to world GDP?

## Measuring UK GDP (Study Plan 10.2)

Use the following table, which lists some macroeconomic data for the UK, to work Problems 8 and 9.

| Item | Billions of pounds |
|---|---|
| Compensation of employees | 750 |
| Consumption expenditure | 900 |
| Gross operating surplus | 300 |
| Investment | 250 |
| Government expenditure | 300 |
| Net exports | −40 |
| Mixed income | 150 |

**8**  Calculate UK GDP.

**9**  Given the data supplied, which approach (expenditure or income) to measuring GDP can you use to calculate UK GDP? Explain your answer.

Use the following data to work Problems 10 and 11.

The national accounts of Parchment Paradise are kept on (you guessed it) parchment. A fire destroys the statistics office. The accounts are now incomplete but they contain the following data:

◆ Consumption expenditure: £2,000.

◆ Indirect taxes less subsidies: £100.

◆ Gross operating surplus: £500.

◆ Investment: £800.

◆ Government expenditure: £400.

◆ Compensation of employees: £2,000.

◆ Net exports: –£200.

**10**  Calculate GDP.

**11**  Calculate gross domestic income at factor cost.

Use the following data to work Problems 12 and 13.

Tropical Republic produces only bananas and coconuts. The base year is 2009. The table gives the quantities produced and the prices.

| Quantities | 2009 | 2010 |
|---|---|---|
| Bananas | 800 kilograms | 900 kilograms |
| Coconuts | 400 | 500 |
| **Prices** | **2008** | **2009** |
| Bananas | £2 per kilogram | £4 per kilogram |
| Coconuts | £10 each | £5 each |

**12**  Calculate nominal GDP in 2009 and 2010.

**13**  Calculate real GDP in 2010 expressed in base-year prices.

Use the following news clip to work Problems 14 and 15.

**Toyota to Shift US Manufacturing Efforts**

Toyota plans to adjust its US manufacturing operations to meet customer demands for smaller, more fuel-efficient vehicles. In 2008, Toyota started building a plant to produce the 2010 Prius for the US market in Blue Springs, Mississippi. Earlier models of the Prius were produced in Asia.

Source: CNN, 10 July 2008

**14**  Explain how this change by Toyota will influence US GDP and the components of aggregate expenditure.

**15**  Explain how this change by Toyota will influence the factor incomes that make up US GDP.

## The Uses and Limitations of Real GDP (Study Plan 10.3)

**16**  Based on the following data, in which year did the US standard of living (i) increase and (ii) decrease? Explain your answer.

| Year | Real GDP | Population |
|---|---|---|
| 2006 | $13.0 trillion | 300 million |
| 2007 | $13.2 trillion | 302 million |
| 2008 | $13.2 trillion | 304 million |
| 2009 | $12.8 trillion | 307 million |

## Mathematical Note (Study Plan 10.MN)

**17**  The table provides data on the economy of Maritime Republic that produces only fish and crabs.

| Quantities | 2009 | 2010 |
|---|---|---|
| Fish | 1,000 tonnes | 1,100 tonnes |
| Crabs | 500 tonnes | 525 tonnes |
| **Prices** | **2009** | **2010** |
| Fish | £20 per tonne | £30 per tonne |
| Crabs | £10 per tonne | £8 per tonne |

**a**  Calculate Maritime Republic's nominal GDP in 2009 and 2010.

**b**  Calculate Maritime Republic's chain volume measure of real GDP in 2010 expressed in 2009 pounds.

## Data Graphing

Use the Data Grapher in MyEconLab to work Problems 18 and 19.

**18**  In which country in 2009 was the growth rate of real GDP per person highest: Canada, Japan or the US?

**19**  In which country in 2009 was the growth rate of real GDP per person lowest: France, China or the US?

## ADDITIONAL PROBLEMS AND APPLICATIONS

 myeconlab  You can work these problems in MyEconLab if assigned by your lecturer.

## Gross Domestic Product

**20** Classify each of the following items as a final good or service or an intermediate good or service and identify which is a component of consumption expenditure, investment, or government expenditure on goods and services:

◆ Banking services bought Google.

◆ Security system bought by Barclays.

◆ Coffee beans bought by Starbucks.

◆ New coffee grinders bought by Starbucks.

◆ Starbucks grande mocha frappuccino bought by a student.

◆ An aircraft carrier bought by the Royal Navy.

Use the figure in Problem 3 on p. 247 to work Problems 21 and 22.

**21** In 2009, flow $A$ was £1,000 billion, flow $C$ was £250 billion, flow $B$ was £650 billion, and flow $E$ was £50 billion. Calculate investment.

**22** In 2010, flow $D$ was £2 trillion, flow $E$ was –£1 trillion, flow $A$ was £10 trillion, and flow $C$ was £4 trillion. Calculate consumption expenditure.

Use the following information to work Problems 23 and 24.

Mitsubishi Heavy Industries makes the wings of the new Boeing 787 Dreamliner in Japan. Toyota assembles cars for the US market in Kentucky.

**23** Explain where these activities appear in the US national accounts.

**24** Explain where these activities appear in Japan's national accounts.

Use the following news clip to work Problems 25 and 26, and use the circular flow model to illustrate your answers.

**Boeing Bets the House**

Boeing is producing some components of its new 787 Dreamliner in Japan and is assembling it in the US. Much of the first year's production will be sold to ANA (All Nippon Airways), a Japanese airline.

Source: *The New York Times*, 7 May 2006

**25** Explain how Boeing's activities and its transactions affect US and Japanese GDP.

**26** Explain how ANA's activities and its transactions affect US and Japanese GDP.

## Measuring UK GDP

Use the following data to work Problems 27 and 28.

The table lists some macroeconomic data for the UK.

| Item | Billions of pounds |
| --- | --- |
| Compensation of employees | 770 |
| Consumption expenditure | 900 |
| Gross operating surplus | 300 |
| Investment | 200 |
| Government expenditure | 2,900 |
| Net exports | –30 |

**27** Calculate UK GDP.

**28** Given the data supplied, which approach (expenditure or income) to measuring GDP can you use to calculate UK GDP? Explain your answer.

Use the following data to work Problems 29 to 31.

An economy produces only apples and oranges. The base year is 2009, and the table gives the quantities produced and the prices.

| Quantities | 2009 | 2010 |
| --- | --- | --- |
| Apples | 60 | 160 |
| Oranges | 80 | 220 |

| Prices | 2009 | 2010 |
| --- | --- | --- |
| Apples | £0.50 each | £1 each |
| Oranges | £0.25 each | £2 each |

**29** Calculate nominal GDP in 2009 and 2010.

**30** Calculate real GDP in 2009 and 2010 expressed in base-year prices.

**31** **GDP Expands 11.4 per cent, Fastest in 13 Years**

China's gross domestic product grew 11.4 per cent last year and marked a fifth year of double-digit growth. The increase was especially remarkable given that the US is experiencing a slowdown due to the sub-prime crisis and housing slump. Citigroup estimates that each 1 per cent drop in the US economy will shave 1.3 per cent off China's growth, because Americans are heavy users of Chinese products. In spite of the uncertainties, China is expected to post its sixth year of double-digit growth next year.

Source: *The China Daily*, 24 January 2008

Use the expenditure approach for measuring China's GDP to explain why 'each 1 per cent drop in the US economy will shave 1.3 per cent off China's growth'.

## The Uses and Limitations of Real GDP

**32** The United Nations' Human Development Index (HDI) is based on real GDP per person, life expectancy at birth, and indicators of the quality and quantity of education.

   **a** Explain why the HDI might be better than real GDP as a measure of economic welfare.

   **b** Which items in the HDI are part of real GDP and which items are not in real GDP?

   **c** Do you think the HDI should be expanded to include items such as pollution, resource depletion, and political freedom? Explain.

   **d** What other influences on economic welfare should be included in a comprehensive measure?

**33** **UK Living Standards Outstrip US**

Oxford analysts report that living standards in Britain are set to rise above those in America for the first time since the nineteenth century. Real GDP per person in Britain will be £23,500 this year, compared with £23,250 in America, reflecting not only the strength of the pound against the dollar but also the UK economy's record run of growth since 2001. But the Oxford analysts also point out that Americans benefit from lower prices than those in Britain.

Source: The Sunday Times, 6 January 2008

If real GDP per person is more in the UK than in the US but Americans benefit from lower prices, does this comparison of real GDP per person really tell us which country has the higher standard of living?

**34** Use the news clip in Problem 31.

   **a** Why might China's recent GDP growth rates overstate the actual increase in the level of production taking place in China?

   **b** Explain the complications involved with attempting to compare economic welfare in China and the US by using the GDP for each country.

**35** **Poor India Makes Millionaires at Fastest Pace**

India, with the world's largest population of poor people created millionaires at the fastest pace in the world in 2007. India added another 23,000 more millionaires in 2007 to its 2006 tally of 100,000 millionaires measured in euros. That is 1 millionaire for about 7,000 people living on less than €2 a day.

Source: The Times of India, 25 June 2008

   **a** Why might real GDP per person misrepresent the standard of living of the average Indian?

   **b** Why might €2 a day underestimate the standard of living of the poorest Indians?

## Economics in the News

**36** After you have studied *Reading Between the Lines* on pp. 240–241 answer the following questions.

   **a** Which measure of GDP would you use to describe the shape of the recovery from recession: real GDP or nominal GDP? Explain your answer.

   **b** Which measure of GDP would you use to describe the rate of growth of the standard of living: real GDP or nominal GDP? Explain your answer.

   **c** If the growth rate of potential GDP is 2.5 per cent a year, how fast must the UK economy grow to close the gap between actual GDP and potential GDP: less than 2.5 per cent a year, more than 2.5 per cent a year or 2.5 per cent a year?

   **d** Why might the news article be wrong about the economy sliding into a double-dip recession?

**37** **Totally Gross**

GDP has proved useful in tracking both short-term fluctuations and long-run growth. Which isn't to say GDP doesn't miss some things. Amartya Sen, at Harvard, helped create the UN Human Development Index, which combines health and education data with per capita GDP to give a better measure of the wealth of nations. Joseph Stiglitz, at Columbia, advocates a 'green net national product' that takes into account the depletion of natural resources. Others want to include happiness in the measure. These alternative benchmarks have merit but can they be measured with anything like the frequency, reliability and impartiality of GDP?

Source: Time, 21 April 2008

   **a** Explain the factors that the news clip identifies as limiting the usefulness of GDP as a measure of economic welfare.

   **b** What are the challenges involved in trying to incorporate measurements of those factors in an effort to better measure economic welfare?

   **c** What does the ranking of the UK in the Human Development Index imply about the levels of health and education relative to other nations?

## Mathematical Note

**38** Use the information in Problem 29 to calculate the chain volume measure of real GDP in 2010 expressed in 2009 pounds.

## Data Graphing

Use the Data Grapher in MyEconLab to work Problems 39 and 40.

**39** In which country in 2009 was the growth rate of real GDP per person highest: UK, Japan or France?

**40** In which country in 2009 was the growth rate of real GDP per person lowest: China, the US or Australia?

# CHAPTER 11

# Monitoring Jobs and Inflation

**After studying this chapter you will be able to:**

◆ Explain why unemployment is a problem and describe the trends and cycles in labour market indicators

◆ Explain why unemployment is an imperfect measure of underutilized labour and why it is present even at full employment

◆ Explain why inflation is a problem, how we measure it and why the official measures might be biased

Each month, we track the course of employment and unemployment as measures of economic health. How do we measure the unemployment rate? Is it a reliable vital sign for the economy?

Having a good job that pays a decent wage is only one half of the equation that translates into a good standard of living. The other half is the cost of living. We track the cost of the items we buy with two other numbers that are published every month: the CPI and RPI. How are these numbers calculated and do they provide a good guide to the changes in our cost of living?

These are the questions we study in this chapter. In *Reading Between the Lines* at the end of the chapter, we put the spotlight on the CPI and RPI.

## Employment and Unemployment

The state of the labour market has a big impact on our incomes and our lives. In a few years you will be entering the labour market. What kind of market will you enter? Will there be plenty of good jobs to choose among, or will jobs be so hard to find that you end up taking one that doesn't use your education and pays a low wage? The answer depends, to a large degree, on the total number of jobs available and on the number of people competing for them.

Those leaving university in 2010 had an unusually tough time in the jobs market. As recession deepened, the number of unemployed steadily increased until, in May 2009, it passed the 2.4 million mark. Unemployment remained above that level for the rest of 2009 and the whole of 2010. In a normal year, unemployment is less than half that level. And in normal times, the UK economy is an incredible job-creating machine. Even in 2009, 26 million people had jobs. But in recent years, population growth has outstripped jobs growth, so unemployment has become a major problem.

## Why Unemployment is a Problem

Unemployment is a serious personal, social and economic problem for two main reasons. It results in:

◆ Lost incomes and production
◆ Lost human capital

### Lost Incomes and Production

The loss of a job brings with it a loss of income and lost production. These losses are devastating for the people who have to bear them. Unemployment benefits create a safety net and cushion the blow of loss of earnings, but they do not replace lost earnings.

Lost production means lower income and lower consumption. It also means lower investment in capital, which lowers the standard of living both in the present and the future.

### Lost Human Capital

Prolonged unemployment permanently damages a person's job prospects by destroying human capital.

## ECONOMICS IN ACTION

## What Kept John Maynard Keynes Awake at Night

In 1921, the UK unemployment rate shot up to 15 per cent. It remained between 10 and 15 per cent until the early 1930s when it jumped yet higher to almost 25 per cent. Unemployment wouldn't return to below 5 per cent until the first years of the Second World War in the 1940s.

Puzzled by persistently high unemployment, economist John Maynard Keynes set to work trying to understand how it could happen and what might be done about it. He published his answers in 1936 in the *General Theory of Employment, Interest, and Money*, a book that created what we now call macroeconomics.

Many economists have studied this period of economic history and a shorter yet equally severe Great Depression that occurred in the US and many other economies. Among them are the current chairman of the US Federal Reserve System, Ben Bernanke.

A key reason why the Federal Reserve and the Bank of England were so aggressive in cutting interest rates and injecting money to save banks like Bear Stearns in the US and Northern Rock and the Royal Bank of Scotland in the

UK during the recent recession is that economists today are keenly aware of the horrors of total economic collapse. Both the Federal Reserve and the Bank of England were determined to avoid what they see as the mistakes of the 1920s and 1930s that brought Britain's interwar depression and the Great Depression in the US.

Think about a manager who loses his job when his employer downsizes. He takes work as a taxi driver. After a year he finds out that he can't compete with fresh graduates. Eventually he gets a management job but in a small firm at a lower salary than he was earning before. He has lost some of his human capital.

The cost of unemployment is spread unequally and is one of the most important causes of poverty and social deprivation.

Governments try to measure unemployment accurately and adopt policies to ease its pain. Let's see how the UK government measures unemployment.

## Labour Force Survey

Every working day, interviewers of the Social and Vital Statistics Division of the Office for National Statistics (the ONS) contact close to 1,000 households (60,000 in a three-month period) and ask them questions about the age and labour market status of the household's members. This survey is called the Labour Force Survey (or LFS). The ONS uses the information obtained to describe the changing anatomy of the labour market.

Figure 11.1 shows the population categories used by the ONS and the relationships among them. The population divides into two groups: the working-age population and others. The **working-age population** is the total number of men aged 16 to 64 and women aged 16 to 59 who are not in prison, hospital or some other form of institutional care.

Members of the working-age population are either economically active or economically inactive. The **economically active** – also called the **workforce** – are people who have a job or are willing and able to take a job. The **economically inactive** are people who don't want a job. Most of the economically inactive are in full-time education or have retired.

The economically active are either employed or unemployed. To be counted as employed, a person must have either a full-time job or a part-time job. A student who does part-time work is counted as employed. To be counted as *un*employed, people must be available for work within the two weeks following their interview and must be in one of three categories:

1  Without work, but having made specific efforts to find a job within the previous four weeks.

2  Waiting to be called back to a job from which they have been laid off.

3  Waiting to start a new job within 30 days.

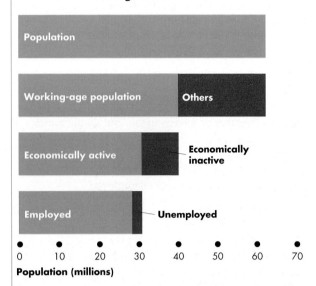

**Figure 11.1**    Population Workforce Categories

The population is divided into the working-age population and others (the young, the retired and institutionalized). The working-age population is divided into those who are economically active (in the workforce) and those who are economically inactive. The economically active are either employed or unemployed.

Source of data: Office for National Statistics.

myeconlab Animation

People in the working-age population who are neither employed nor unemployed are classified as economically inactive.

In 2010, the population of the UK was 62.1 million. There were 22.1 million below or above working age or living in institutions. So the working-age population in 2010 was 40 million. Of this number, 9.3 million were economically inactive (not in the workforce). The remaining 30.7 million were economically active. Of the economically active, 28.3 million were employed and 2.4 million were unemployed.

## Three Labour Market Indicators

The Office for National Statistics calculates three indicators of the state of the labour market. They are:

◆  The unemployment rate

◆  The employment rate

◆  The economic activity rate

## The Unemployment Rate

The amount of unemployment is an indicator of the extent to which people who want jobs can't find them. The **unemployment rate** is the percentage of economically active people who are unemployed.

$$\text{Unemployment rate} = \frac{\text{Number of people unemployed}}{\text{Workforce}} \times 100$$

and

$$\text{Workforce} = \text{Number employed} + \text{Number unemployed}$$

In the UK in 2010, the number of people employed was 28.3 million and the number unemployed was 2.4 million. By using the above equations, the workforce was 30.7 million (28.3 million plus 2.4 million) and the unemployment rate was 7.8 per cent (2.4 million divided by 30.7 million, multiplied by 100).

Figure 11.2 shows the unemployment rate between 1980 and 2010. The average unemployment rate was 10 per cent during the decade of the 1980s and 8.3 per cent during the 1990s, but during the 2000s it was 5.5 per cent. The unemployment rate fluctuates and reached

peak values at the end of recessions in 1980–1982 and 1990–1992. In 2010, it was not possible to say if the unemployment rate had reached a peak.

## The Employment Rate

The number of people of working age who have jobs is an indicator of the availability of jobs and the degree of match between people's skills and jobs. The **employment rate** is the percentage of the people of working age who have jobs. That is:

$$\text{Employment rate} = \frac{\text{Number of people employed}}{\text{Working-age population}} \times 100$$

In 2010, the number of people employed in the UK was 28.3 million and the working-age population was 40 million. By using the above equation, you can calculate the employment rate. It was 70.8 per cent (28.3 million divided by 40 million, multiplied by 100).

Figure 11.3 shows the UK employment rate. It has followed a gently rising trend through the period since 1980. This upward trend means that the economy has created jobs at a faster rate than the working-age population has grown.

**Figure 11.2** The Unemployment Rate: 1980–2010

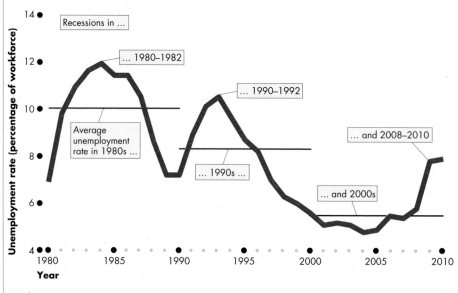

The average unemployment rate was 10 per cent during the 1980s, 8.3 per cent during the 1990s and 5.5 per cent during the 2000s.
The unemployment rate increases in recessions and decreases in expansions.
In 2010, it was unclear whether the unemployment rate had peaked.

Source of data: Office for National Statistics.

**Figure 11.3** Economic Activity Rate and Employment Rate: 1980–2010

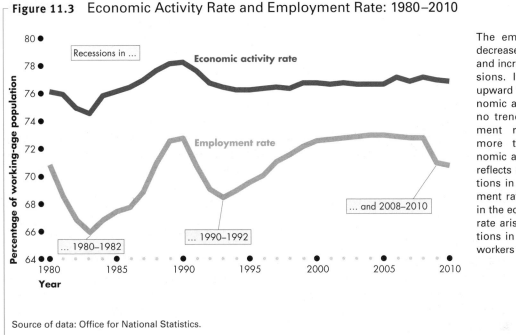

The employment rate decreases in recessions and increases in expansions. It has a slight upward trend. The economic activity rate has no trend The employment rate fluctuates more than the economic activity rate and reflects cyclical fluctuations in the unemployment rate. Fluctuations in the economic activity rate arise from fluctuations in the number of workers who want a job.

Source of data: Office for National Statistics.

myeconlab Animation

---

This labour market indicator also fluctuates over the business cycle. It reached a trough of 65.9 per cent in 1983, and its fluctuations coincide with, but are opposite to, those in the unemployment rate.

### The Economic Activity Rate

The number of people in the workforce is an indicator of the willingness of the people of working age to take jobs. The **economic activity rate** is the percentage of the working-age population who are economically active. They are the members of the workforce.

$$\text{Economic activity rate} = \frac{\text{Workforce}}{\text{Working-age population}} \times 100$$

In 2010, the workforce was 30.7 million and the working-age population was 40 million. By using the above equation, you can calculate the economic activity rate. It was 76.8 per cent (30.7 million divided by 40 million, multiplied by 100).

Figure 11.3 shows the economic activity rate. It rose slightly from 76.1 per cent in 1980 to 76.8 per cent in 2010. It also had some mild fluctuations, which result from unsuccessful job seekers leaving the workforce during a recession and re-entering during an expansion.

## Other Definitions of Economic Inactivity and Unemployment

Do fluctuations in the economic activity rate over the business cycle mean that people who leave the workforce during a recession should be counted as unemployed? Or are they correctly counted as economically inactive?

The ONS believes that the official unemployment definition gives the correct measure of the unemployment rate. But the ONS provides data on the reasons for economic inactivity. These data provide information on two relevant groups of people:

◆ Discouraged workers
◆ Others who want a job

### Discouraged Workers

A **discouraged worker** is someone who is available and willing to work but who has stopped actively looking for a job because he or she believes that no jobs are available. These workers often temporarily leave the workforce during a recession and re-enter during an expansion.

The distinction between an unemployed person and a discouraged worker turns on whether there has been recent job search activity. Both are available for work and want work but the unemployed person has looked for a job while the discouraged worker has given up looking.

Figure 11.4 shows the percentage of economically inactive people who are discouraged workers from 1993 (when the ONS started measuring this number) to 2010.

You can see that discouraged workers are a tiny percentage of the economically inactive and have become less important during the 2000s. The number did, though, increase during the recent recession.

## Others Who Want a Job

Others who want a job are people who are economically inactive and are willing to work but who have stopped actively looking for a job and who are not available to start a job in the next two weeks.

Like the discouraged workers, many of these people temporarily leave the workforce during a recession and re-enter during an expansion.

Figure 11.4 shows the percentage of economically inactive people who say they want a job (excluding discouraged workers) from 1993 to 2010.

You can see that this category of people is large. On average, about 25 per cent of the economically inactive say they want a job. This percentage fluctuates between a low of 22 per cent and a high of more than 27 per cent. The correlation between these fluctuations and the business cycle is not strong.

The official unemployment measure excludes economically inactive people because they haven't made specific efforts to find a job within the past four weeks and they are not available for work in the next two weeks. In other respects, they are unemployed.

## Most Costly Unemployment

All unemployment is costly, but the most costly is long-term unemployment that results from job loss. People who are unemployed for a few weeks and then find another job bear some costs of unemployment. But these costs are low compared to the costs borne by people who remain unemployed for many weeks.

Also, people who are unemployed because they voluntarily leave their jobs to find better ones or because they have just entered or re-entered the labour market bear some costs of unemployment. But these costs are lower than those borne by people who lose their job and are forced back into the job market.

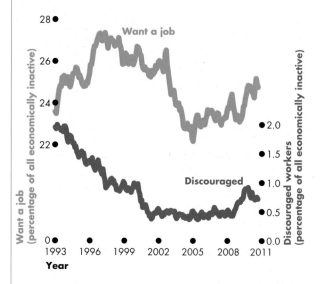

**Figure 11.4**   Discouraged Workers and Others Who Want a Job: 1993–2010

Discouraged workers make up a very small percentage of the economically inactive. They fell from 2 per cent in 1993 to about 0.5 per cent during most of the 2000s. In the 2009 recession, they increased to almost 1 per cent. Others who want a job average about 25 per cent of the economically inactive and this percentage fluctuates but does not correlate closely with the business cycle.

Source of data: Office for National Statistics.

*myeconlab* Animation

### Review Quiz

1   What determines if a person is economically active?
2   What distinguishes an unemployed person from one who is economically inactive?
3   Describe the trends and fluctuations in the UK unemployment rate from 1980 to 2010.
4   Describe the trends and fluctuations in the UK employment rate and economic activity rate from 1980 to 2010.
5   Describe the types of economic inactivity that might be considered to be underutilized labour resources.

You can work these questions in Study Plan 11.1 and get instant feedback.

You've now seen how we measure employment and unemployment. Your next task is to see what we mean by full employment and how unemployment and real GDP fluctuate over the business cycle.

## Unemployment and Full Employment

There is always someone without a job who is searching for one, so there is always some unemployment. The key reason is that the economy is a complex mechanism that is always changing – it experiences frictions, structural change and cycles.

## Frictional Unemployment

There is an unending flow of people into and out of the workforce as people move through the stages of life – from being in school to finding a job, to working, perhaps to becoming unhappy with a job and looking for a new one and, finally, to retiring from full-time work.

There is also an unending process of job creation and job destruction as new firms are born, firms expand or contract and some firms fail and go out of business.

The flows into and out of the workforce and the processes of job creation and job destruction create the need for people to search for jobs and for businesses to search for workers. Businesses don't usually hire the first person who applies for a job, and unemployed people don't usually take the first job that comes their way. Instead, both firms and workers spend time searching for what they believe will be the best available match. By this process of search, people can match their own skills and interests with the available jobs and find a satisfying job and a good income.

The unemployment that arises from the normal labour turnover we've just described – from people entering and leaving the workforce and from the ongoing creation and destruction of jobs – is called **frictional unemployment**. Frictional unemployment is a permanent and healthy phenomenon in a dynamic growing economy.

## Structural Unemployment

The unemployment that arises when changes in technology or international competition change the skills needed to perform jobs or change the location of jobs is called **structural unemployment**. Structural unemployment usually lasts longer than frictional unemployment because workers must usually retrain and possibly relocate to find a job. For example, on the day the shipyards in the Upper Clyde announced the loss of 600 jobs, a computer chip company in Gwent announced the creation of 750 new jobs. The unemployed former shipyard workers remained unemployed for several months until they moved home, retrained and got one of the new jobs created in other parts of the country.

Structural unemployment is painful, especially for older workers for whom the best available option might be to retire early or to take a lower-skilled, lower-paid job.

## Cyclical Unemployment

The higher than normal unemployment at a business cycle trough and the lower than normal unemployment at a business cycle peak is called **cyclical unemployment**. A worker who is laid off because the economy is in a recession and who gets rehired some months later when the expansion begins has experienced cyclical unemployment.

## 'Natural' Unemployment

Natural unemployment is the unemployment that arises from frictions and structural change when there is no cyclical unemployment – when all the unemployment is frictional and structural. Natural unemployment as a percentage of the workforce is called the **natural unemployment rate**.

**Full employment** is defined as a situation in which the unemployment rate equals the natural unemployment rate.

What determines the natural unemployment rate? Is it constant or does it change over time?

The natural unemployment rate is influenced by many factors but the most important ones are:

◆ The age distribution of the population
◆ The scale of structural change
◆ The real wage rate
◆ Unemployment benefits

### The Age Distribution of the Population

An economy with a young population has a large number of new job seekers every year and has a high level of frictional unemployment. An economy with an ageing population has fewer new job seekers and a low level of frictional unemployment.

### The Scale of Structual Change

The scale of structural change is sometimes small. The same jobs using the same machines remain in place for many years. But sometimes there is a technological upheaval. The old ways are swept aside: millions of jobs are lost and the skill to perform them loses value. The amount of structural unemployment fluctuates with the pace and volume of technological change and the change driven by fierce international competition, especially from fast-changing Asian economies. A high level of structural unemployment is present in many parts of the UK today.

## The Real Wage Rate

The natural unemployment rate is influenced by the level of the real wage rate. Real wage rates that bring unemployment are a minimum wage and an efficiency wage. Chapter 5 (see pp. 109–110) explains how the minimum wage creates unemployment. An *efficiency wage* is a wage set above the going market wage to enable firms to attract the most productive workers, get them to work hard and discourage them from leaving.

## Unemployment Benefits

Unemployment benefits increase the natural unemployment rate by lowering the opportunity cost of job search. European countries have more generous unemployment benefits and higher natural unemployment rates than the US. Extending unemployment benefits increases the natural unemployment rate.

There is no controversy about the existence of a natural unemployment rate. Nor is there disagreement that the natural unemployment rate changes. But economists don't know its exact size or the extent to which it fluctuates.

There is no official estimate of the natural unemployment rate for the UK. The one in Figure 11.5 is our own estimate. In 2010 our estimate of the natural unemployment rate was 4.8 per cent – about a half of the unemployment in that year.

## Real GDP and Unemployment Over the Business Cycle

The quantity of real GDP at full employment is potential GDP (p. 234). Over the business cycle, real GDP fluctuates around potential GDP. The gap between real GDP and potential GDP is called the **output gap**. As the output gap fluctuates over the business cycle, the unemployment rate fluctuates around the natural unemployment rate.

**Figure 11.5** The Output Gap and the Unemployment Rate

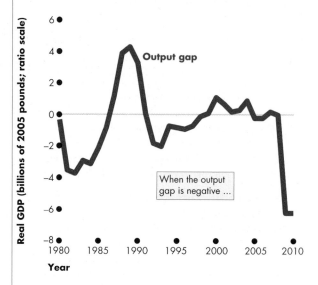

**(a) Output gap**

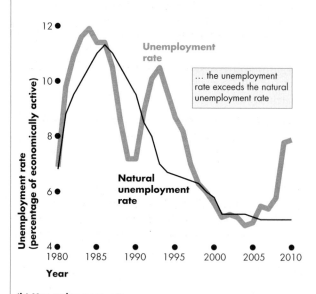

**(b) Unemployment rate**

As real GDP fluctuates around potential GDP in part (a), the unemployment rate fluctuates around the natural unemployment rate in part (b). During the recession in the early 1990s, the output gap became negative and the unemployment rate increased to 10 per cent. During the 1980s the natural unemployment rate fell. The graph shows our estimate of how far it fell.

Sources of data: Office for National Statistics; and authors' assumptions and calculations.

myeconlab Animation

## Jobs in Recession and Recovery

You've seen in Figure 11.5 how fluctuations in the output gap line up with fluctuations in the unemployment rate around the natural unemployment rate.

Here, we are looking at the relationship between real GDP and employment. When real GDP falls during a recession, employment falls too; when real GDP rises in an expansion, employment rises. But there is a delay in the response of employment that is visible in high frequency quarterly data.

The figure shows the changes in real GDP and employment during the recession and expansion during 2008 to 2010. Real GDP shrank until the third quarter of 2009 and then started to expand. Total employment shrank with real GDP, but kept on shrinking until the first quarter of 2010. Only in the second quarter of 2010 did total employment begin to increase.

There is an interesting difference in the way that part-time and full-time employment change during recession and expansion. Part-time employment increases right through the recession. Full-time employment falls until the expansion has been running for six months.

In a recession firms are reluctant to take on new full-time workers. Hiring part-time workers gives them greater flexibility to respond in either direction to changes in production.

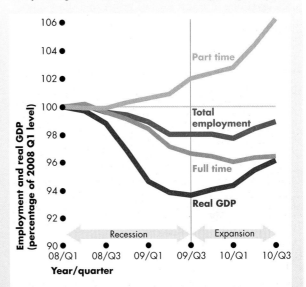

**Figure 1  Real GDP and Employment in Recession and Recovery**

Source of data: Office for National Statistics.

Figure 11.5 illustrates these fluctuations in the UK between 1980 and 2010 – the output gap in part (a) and the unemployment rate and natural unemployment rate in part (b).

When the economy is at full employment, the unemployment rate equals the natural unemployment rate and real GDP equals potential GDP so the output gap is zero. When the unemployment rate is less than the natural unemployment rate, real GDP is greater than potential GDP and the output gap is positive. And when the unemployment rate is greater than the natural unemployment rate, real GDP is less than potential GDP and the output gap is negative.

Figure 11.5(b) shows an estimate of the natural unemployment rate that is consistent with the estimate of the output gap in part (a). While we have a good estimate of real GDP and unemployment, we must use assumptions to estimate potential GDP, the output gap and the natural unemployment rate. So the picture presented in the figure is just one estimate. In the figure, the natural unemployment rate is high during the 1980s but falls steadily through the 1980s and 1990s to 5 per cent by

2006. This estimate of the natural unemployment rate in the UK is one that many, but not all, economists would accept.

### Review Quiz

1  Define frictional, structural and cyclical unemployment and provide an example of each type of unemployment.
2  What is the natural unemployment rate?
3  What factors might make the natural unemployment rate change?
4  How does the unemployment rate fluctuate over the business cycle?

You can work these questions in Study Plan 11.2 and get instant feedback.

Your final task in this chapter is to learn about another vital sign that gets monitored every month, the Retail Prices Index (RPI) and the Consumer Prices Index (CPI). What are the RPI and CPI, how do we measure them and what do they mean?

## The Price Level, Inflation and Deflation

What will it *really* cost you to pay off your student loan? What will your parents' life savings buy when they retire? The answers depend on what happens to the **price level**, the average level of prices and the value of money. A persistently rising price level is called **inflation**; a persistently falling price level is called **deflation**.

We are interested in the price level, inflation and deflation for two main reasons. First, we want to measure the price level and the inflation rate or deflation rate. Second, we want to distinguish between the money values and real values of economic variables such as your student loan and your parents' savings.

We begin by explaining why inflation and deflation are problems, then we look at how we measure the price level and the inflation rate, and finally we return to the task of distinguishing real values from money values.

## Why Inflation and Deflation are Problems

Low, steady and anticipated inflation or deflation isn't a problem, but an unexpected burst of inflation or period of deflation brings four big problems and costs:

◆ Redistributes income
◆ Redistributes wealth
◆ Lowers real GDP and employment
◆ Diverts resources from production

### Redistributes Income

Workers and employers sign wage contracts that last for a year or more. An unexpected burst of inflation raises prices but doesn't immediately raise wages. Workers are worse off because their wages buy less than they bargained for and employers are better off because their profits rise.

An unexpected deflation has the opposite effect. With a fall in prices, workers are better off because their fixed wages buy more than they bargained for and employers are worse off with lower profits.

### Redistributes Wealth

People enter into loan contracts that are fixed in money terms and that pay an interest rate agreed as a percentage of the money borrowed and lent. With an unexpected burst of inflation, the money that the borrower repays to the lender buys less than the money originally loaned. The borrower wins and the lender loses. The interest paid on the loan doesn't compensate the lender for the loss in the value of the money loaned. With an unexpected deflation, the money that the borrower repays to the lender buys more than the money originally loaned. The borrower loses and the lender wins.

### Lowers Real GDP and Employment

Unexpected inflation that raises firms' profits brings a rise in investment and a boom in production and employment. Real GDP rises above potential GDP and the unemployment rate falls below the natural rate. But this situation is temporary. Profitable investment dries up, spending falls, real GDP falls below potential GDP and the unemployment rate rises. Avoiding these swings in production and jobs means avoiding unexpected swings in the inflation rate.

An unexpected deflation has even greater consequences for real GDP and jobs. Businesses and households that are in debt (borrowers) are worse off and they cut their spending. A fall in total spending brings a recession and rising unemployment.

### Diverts Resources from Production

Unpredictable inflation or deflation turns the economy into a casino and diverts resources from productive activities to forecasting inflation. It can become more profitable to forecast the inflation rate or deflation rate correctly than to invent a new product. Doctors, lawyers, accountants, farmers – just about everyone – can make themselves better off, not by specializing in the profession for which they have been trained but by spending more of their time dabbling as amateur economists and inflation forecasters and managing their investments.

From a social perspective, the diversion of talent that results from unpredictable inflation is like throwing scarce resources into a landfill. This waste of resources is a cost of inflation.

At its worst, inflation becomes **hyperinflation** – an inflation rate of 50 per cent a month or higher that grinds the economy to a halt and society to a collapse. Hyperinflation is rare, but Zimbabwe has experienced it in recent years.

The ONS monitors the price level every month and devotes considerable resources to measuring it accurately. You're now going to see how the ONS does this.

# The Price Indexes

The ONS calculates two price indexes every month. They are the **Retail Prices Index (RPI)** and the **Consumer Prices Index (CPI)** and both measure an average of the prices paid by consumers for a fixed 'basket' of goods and services. What you learn in this section will help you to interpret the RPI and the CPI and see how they tell you what has happened to the value of your money.

## Reading the RPI and CPI

The RPI is defined to equal 100 for a period called the **reference base period**. Currently, the reference base period is January 1987. That is, for January 1987, the RPI equals 100. In January 2010, the RPI was 217.9. This number tells us that the average of the prices paid by households for a particular basket of consumer goods and services was 117.9 per cent higher in January 2010 than it was in January 1987.

The reference base period for the CPI is June 2005 and in June 2010, the CPI was 114.6. We read the CPI and calculate the percentage change since the base period in the same way as you've just seen for the RPI. The CPI in June 2010 was 14.6 per cent higher than in June 2005.

## Constructing the RPI and CPI

Constructing the RPI and the CPI is a huge operation that costs millions of pounds and involves three stages:

◆ Selecting the basket
◆ Conducting a monthly price survey
◆ Calculating the price index

### Selecting the Basket

The first stage in constructing a price index is to select the 'basket' of goods and services that the index will cover. The RPI basket contains the goods and services bought by an average household in the UK. The idea is to make the relative importance of the items in the RPI basket the same as that in the budget of an average household. For example, because people spend more on housing than on bus rides, the RPI places more weight on the price of housing than on the price of a bus ride.

The CPI basket is a bit different from the RPI basket and covers *all* expenditure on consumer goods and services made in the UK by private households, residents of institutions and tourists.

To determine the spending patterns of households and to select the RPI and CPI baskets, the ONS conducts periodic expenditure surveys. These surveys are costly and so are undertaken infrequently. Figure 11.6 shows the RPI and CPI baskets in 2010.

**Figure 11.6** The RPI and CPI Baskets

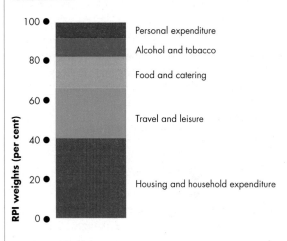

**(a) The RPI basket**

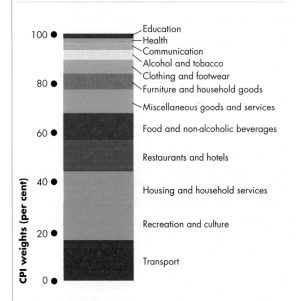

**(b) The CPI basket**

The RPI basket contains items that a typical household buys. The CPI basket is broader and contains all the goods and services bought by households in the UK.

Source of data: Office for National Statistics.

 myeconlab Animation

For the RPI, there are five major categories of which by far the largest is housing and household expenditure. Travel and leisure comes next and is larger than food, alcoholic drinks and tobacco combined.

The ONS breaks down each of these categories into ever smaller ones, right down to distinguishing between packaged and loose new potatoes!

The CPI basket contains 12 major categories of which transport and recreation and culture are the largest.

As you look at the relative importance of the items in the RPI and CPI baskets, remember that they apply to an *average* household. *Individual* households are spread around the average. Think about your own expenditure and compare the basket of goods and services you buy with the RPI and CPI baskets.

### Conducting a Monthly Price Survey

Each month, ONS employees check 110,000 prices of more than 550 types of goods and services. They visit shops in about 150 places throughout the UK to see the goods and the prices to ensure accuracy. Because the RPI and CPI aim to measure price *changes*, it is important that the prices recorded each month refer to exactly the same item. For example, suppose the price of a packet of biscuits has decreased but a packet now contains fewer biscuits. Has the price of biscuits decreased, remained the same or increased? The ONS price checker must record the details of changes in quality or packaging so that price changes can be isolated from other changes.

### Calculating the Price Index

The RPI and CPI calculations have three steps:

1  Find the cost of the basket at base-period prices.

2  Find the cost of the basket at current-period prices.

3  Calculate the index for the base period and the current period.

We'll work through these three steps for a simple example of an RPI calculation. Suppose the RPI basket contains only two goods and services: oranges and haircuts. We'll construct an annual price index rather than a monthly index with the reference base period 2010 and the current period 2011.

Table 11.1 shows the quantities in the RPI basket and the prices in the base period and current period. Part (a) contains the data for the base period. In that period, consumers bought 10 oranges at £1 each and 5 haircuts at

---

**Table 11.1**

### The RPI: A Simplified Calculation

**(a) The cost of the RPI basket at base-period prices: 2010**

RPI basket

| Item | Quantity | Price | Cost of basket |
|------|----------|-------|----------------|
| Oranges | 10 | £1 | £10 |
| Haircuts | 5 | £8 | £40 |
| Cost of the RPI basket at base-period prices | | | £50 |

**(b) The cost of the RPI basket at current-period prices: 2011**

RPI basket

| Item | Quantity | Price | Cost of basket |
|------|----------|-------|----------------|
| Oranges | 10 | £2 | £20 |
| Haircuts | 5 | £10 | £50 |
| Cost of the RPI basket at current-period prices | | | £70 |

---

£8 each. To find the cost of the RPI basket in the base-period prices, multiply the quantities in the basket by the base-period prices. The cost of oranges is £10 (10 at £1 each), and the cost of haircuts is £40 (5 at £8 each). So total cost of the RPI basket in the base period is £50 (£10 + £40).

Part (b) contains the price data for the current period. The price of an orange increased from £1 to £2, which is a 100 per cent increase (£1 ÷ £1 × 100 = 100). The price of a haircut increased from £8 to £10, which is a 25 per cent increase (£2 ÷ £8 × 100 = 25).

A price index provides a way of averaging these price increases by comparing the cost of the basket rather than the price of each item. To find the cost of the RPI basket in the current period, 2011, multiply the quantities in the basket by their 2011 prices. The cost of oranges is £20 (10 at £2 each), and the cost of haircuts is £50 (5 at £10 each). So total cost of the basket at current-period prices is £70 (£20 + £50).

You've now taken the first two steps towards calculating a RPI: calculating the cost of the RPI basket in the base period and the current period. The third step uses the numbers you've just calculated to find the value of the RPI in 2010 and 2011.

To calculate the RPI, we use the formula:

$$\text{RPI} = \frac{\text{Cost of basket at current-period prices}}{\text{Cost of basket at base-period prices}} \times 100$$

'chained' back to the reference base year. This procedure means that the weights in the GDP deflator are current weights so they avoid some of the sources of bias that we described above.

The main disadvantage of the GDP deflator is that it is calculated only every quarter and with a time lag and is subject to ongoing revisions. These features make it unsuitable for timely and firm estimation of the inflation rate. But it is a good measure for macroeconomic analysis and our efforts to understand economic performance.

## The Alternatives Compared

No matter whether we calculate the inflation rate using the RPI, the CPI or the GDP deflator, the number bounces around a good deal from quarter to quarter. How do the alternative measures compare? How different are the inflation stories they tell?

The three measures give different average inflation rates and different inflation fluctuations. Since 2000, the RPI has increased at an average rate of 2.7 per cent per year, the CPI at an average rate of 1.9 per cent per year and the GDP deflator at 2.5 per cent per year.

Figure 11.8 shows the path of each measure of inflation since 2000. You can see that the RPI is much more variable than the other two measures and it is the only one to show deflation in 2009. The CPI has a mild upward trend and the GDP deflator has no trend.

The key conclusion is that there is no unique measure of inflation and we must carefully determine which measure is most useful for the purpose at hand.

## Real Variables in Macroeconomics

One major purpose of price index numbers is to measure and distinguish nominal variables and real variables. You saw in Chapter 10 how we measure real GDP. And you've seen in this chapter how we can use nominal GDP and real GDP to calculate the GDP deflator measure of the price level.

Viewing real GDP as nominal GDP deflated, opens up the idea of other real variables. By using the GDP deflator, we can deflate other nominal variables such as the nominal wage rate to find their real values.

There is one variable that is a bit different – an interest rate. A real interest rate is not a nominal interest rate divided by the price level. You'll learn how to adjust the nominal interest rate for inflation to find the real interest rate in Chapter 12. But all the other real variables of macroeconomics are calculated by dividing a nominal variable by the price level.

**Figure 11.8** Comparing Three Measures of Inflation

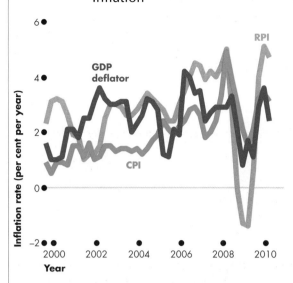

The three measures of the inflation rate give different average rates and different fluctuations. The RPI and CPI measures tend to increase and decrease together, but the RPI measure fluctuates more. The GDP deflator measure is the least volatile.

Source of data: Office for National Statistics.

 Animation

### Review Quiz

1 What is the price level?
2 What are the RPI and CPI and how are they calculated?
3 How do we calculate the inflation rate and what is the relationship between the price index and the inflation rate?
4 How might a price index be biased?
5 What problems arise from the biased RPI and CPI?
6 What is the GDP deflator and what are its advantages and disadvantages?

You can work these questions in Study Plan 11.3 and get instant feedback. **myeconlab**

You've now completed your study of the measurement of macroeconomic performance. Your task in the following chapters is to learn what determines that performance. But first, take a look at the differences in the CPI and the RPI in the period 2008 to 2010 in *Reading Between the Lines* on pp. 266–267.

# Reading Between the Lines

# Measuring Inflation

The Financial Times, 14 September 2010

## Measuring up with a Tale of Two Indices

Chris Giles

What measure of inflation should trade unionists, meeting in Manchester this week, use for pay bargaining this autumn? The answer is likely to lead to much dispute.

Inflation, according to the retail prices index, was 4.6 per cent in August, while it was 3.1 per cent if measured by the newer consumer price index.

These debates are both unfortunate and bogus, argues Stephen Nickell, Warden of Nuffield College, Oxford, and a former member of the monetary policy committee.

The average British household faces only one inflation rate, and . . . [w]hat matters is that there is a reliable, single inflation statistic that measures the changing cost of consumption.

Some of the differences between the RPI and CPI are well known, such as the historic inclusion of mortgage interest payments in the RPI and the exclusion of owner-occupied housing costs in the CPI. . . . In August these housing differences contributed 0.72 per-

centage points of the difference between the indices. . . .

Much less well-known, however, is that another important discrepancy between the two inflation measures has emerged this year. . . . This relates to different techniques for averaging prices in shops.

In August, clothing and footwear inflation measured by the RPI stood at 6.3 per cent, while the CPI inflation for the same goods was –1.7 per cent – a total difference of 8 percentage points. . . .

The upshot for union wage bargainers is that, unless they are sure their members need to wear Nicole Farhi, the RPI is probably overstating the inflation rate they experience. 'Put simply, the CPI is the better guide,' says Allan Monks of JP Morgan.

The measure of inflation most used for wage settlements is the Retail Price Index, . . . which . . . climbed in the 12 months to November by 3.9 per cent, . . . the highest reading since May 1998.

## The Essence of the Story

◆ In August 2010, the annual inflation rate was 4.6 per cent according to the RPI and 3.1 per cent according to the CPI.

◆ Among many differences in coverage of the two indexes, the RPI includes mortgage interest payments but the CPI excludes them.

◆ The two indexes use different price sampling methods.

◆ A consequence of these differences is that the RPI said clothing and footwear prices increased 6.3 per cent in August while the CPI said they *decreased* 1.7 per cent.

# Economic Analysis

- The CPI and the RPI give conflicting accounts of UK inflation.

- Figure 1 shows the CPI inflation rate minus the RPI inflation rate for each month from January 2009 to September 2010. The CPI inflation rate was higher in 2009 and the RPI inflation rate was higher in 2010.

- The actual items included in the baskets of the two price indexes are different even when the category has the same name.

- For example, clothing and footwear, noted in the news article, includes different items in the two baskets.

- Even for goods that are common, such as alcohol and tobacco, the two inflation measures differ.

- Figure 2 shows the inflation rate of alcohol and tobacco measured by the CPI and the RPI. Sampling bias makes the CPI alcohol and tobacco inflation rate higher than the RPI inflation rate.

- Trades unions may want to use the RPI rate of inflation as the basis for wage bargaining because the RPI measure of inflation is higher than the CPI measure. But Figure 3 shows that earnings growth has followed neither measure of inflation.

- Real wage rates are determined in the market for labour. To translate real wage rates into money wage rates, unions and employers need a good measure of inflation.

- While the ONS tries to measure inflation so that there is a minimum of bias, both the CPI and the RPI remain imperfect measures of inflation.

- Unions and employers find it necessary to look at both measures of inflation in seeking what Stephen Nickell calls a 'reliable, single inflation statistic that measures the changing cost of consumption'.

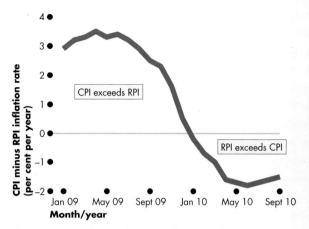

Figure 1  The difference between the CPI and RPI inflation rates

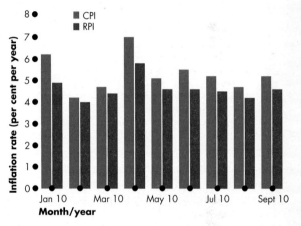

Figure 2  Inflation rates of alcohol and tobacco in two indexes

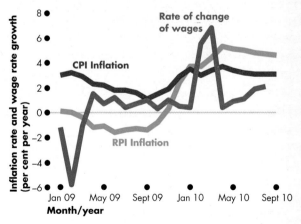

Figure 3  Inflation and wage rate

## SUMMARY

## Key Points

### Employment and Unemployment
(pp. 252–256)

◆ Unemployment is a serious personal, social and economic problem because it results in lost output and income and human capital.

◆ The unemployment rate averaged 10 per cent during the 1980s, 8.3 per cent during the 1990s and 5.5 per cent during the 2000s.

◆ The unemployment rate, the economic activity rate and the employment rate fluctuate with the business cycle.

Working Problems 1 to 7 will give you a better understanding of employment and unemployment.

### Unemployment and Full Employment
(pp. 257–259)

◆ People are constantly entering and leaving the state of unemployment.

◆ Three types of unemployment are frictional, structural and cyclical.

◆ When all the unemployment is frictional and structural, the unemployment rate equals the natural unemployment rate, the economy is at full employment and real GDP equals potential GDP.

◆ Over the business cycle, real GDP fluctuates around potential GDP and the unemployment rate fluctuates around the natural unemployment rate.

Working Problems 8 to 13 will give you a better understanding of unemployment and full employment.

### The Price Level, Inflation and Deflation (pp. 260–265)

◆ Inflation and deflation that are unexpected redistribute income and wealth and divert resources from production.

◆ The Retail Prices Index (RPI) and the Consumer Prices Index (CPI) measure the average prices paid by consumers for a specified basket of goods and services.

◆ The inflation rate is the percentage change in the RPI (or CPI) from one year to the next.

◆ The RPI and CPI probably overstate the inflation rate because of the bias that arises from new goods, quality changes and substitutions between goods and services.

◆ The RPI bias increases government outlays and the CPI bias might lead to inappropriate interest rate policy.

Working Problems 14 to 27 will give you a better understanding of the price level, inflation and deflation.

## Key Terms

Consumer Prices Index (CPI), 261
Cyclical unemployment, 257
Deflation, 260
Discouraged worker, 255
Economic activity rate, 255
Economically active, 253
Economically inactive, 253
Employment rate, 254
Frictional unemployment, 257
Full employment, 257
GDP deflator, 264
Hyperinflation, 260
Inflation, 260
Inflation rate, 263
Natural unemployment rate, 257
Output gap, 258
Price level, 260
Reference base period, 261
Retail Prices Index (RPI), 261
Structural unemployment, 257
Unemployment rate, 254
Workforce, 253
Working-age population, 253

# STUDY PLAN PROBLEMS AND APPLICATIONS

**myeconlab**  You can work Problems 1 to 27 in MyEconLab Chapter 11 Study Plan and get instant feedback.

## Employment and Unemployment

### (Study Plan 11.1)

**1** In 2008, the Labour Force Survey measured the economically active at 30,512,000, employment at 28,771,000 and the working-age population at 39,575,000. Calculate for 2008:

  **a** The unemployment rate.

  **b** The economic activity rate.

  **c** The employment rate.

**2** During 2009, the working-age population increased by 230,000, employment fell by 549,000 and the number of economically active people increased by 98,000. Use this information along with the data in Problem 1 to calculate the change in unemployment during 2009.

Use the following information to work Problems 3 and 4.

In July 2009, in the economy of Sandy Island, 10,000 people were employed, 1,000 were unemployed and 5,000 were economically inactive.

**3** Calculate the unemployment rate and the employment rate in July 2009.

**4** During August 2009, 80 people lost their jobs and didn't look for new ones, 20 people quit their jobs and retired, 150 unemployed people were hired, 50 people quit the workforce and became economically inactive and 40 people entered the workforce to look for work.

  Calculate the number of people unemployed, the number of people employed and the unemployment rate at the end of August 2009.

Use the following information to work Problems 5 and 6.

The UK unemployment rate was 6.9 per cent in January 2009 and 8.1 per cent in January 2010.

**5** Predict what happened to unemployment between January 2009 and January 2010 if the economically active population remained the same.

**6** Predict what happened to the economically active population if the number of people unemployed remained the same.

**7** **Shrinking US Workforce Keeps Unemployment Rate From Rising**

  An exodus of discouraged workers from the US job market has kept the unemployment rate from climbing to 10 per cent. Had the workforce not decreased by 661,000, the unemployment rate would have been 10.4 per cent. The number of discouraged workers rose to 929,000 last month.

  Source: Bloomberg, 9 January 2010

  What is a discouraged worker? Explain how an increase in discouraged workers influences the official unemployment rate.

## Unemployment and Full Employment

### (Study Plan 11.2)

Use the following news clip to work Problems 8 to 10.

**Jobs Market is on the 'Road to Recovery'**

A new study suggests the job market is on the 'road to recovery', despite 2.5 million people unemployed. With a strong rise in demand for permanent staff in the past four months and with the rise in demand for temporary staff in December the biggest in six months, the recovery looks strong. But KPMG warns the future of the recovery is uncertain, as the government's austerity measures take effect.

Source: BBC News, 12 January 2011

**8** With the demand for permanent and temporary workers rising strongly, explain which type of unemployment is most likely to fall if the recovery continues.

**9** As the government's austerity measures take effect, explain which type of unemployment might increase.

**10** Why might the government's cutbacks in the public service (part of the austerity measures) change the natural unemployment rate in the UK?

Use the following news clip to work Problems 11 to 13.

**US Economic Pain Deepens**

A spike in the unemployment rate – the biggest in more than two decades – raised new concerns that the US economy is heading into a recession. The unemployment rate soared to 5.5 per cent in May from 5 per cent in April – much higher than forecasted. The surge marked the biggest one-month jump in unemployment since February 1986, and the 5.5 per cent rate is the highest seen since October 2004.

Source: CNN, 6 June 2008

**11** Based on information in the news clip, how does the US unemployment rate in May 2008 compare to that in earlier recessions?

**12** Why might the unemployment rate tend to actually underestimate the unemployment problem, especially during a recession?

**13** Given the information in the news clip, does the jump in the US unemployment rate in May 2008 look like an increase in the natural unemployment rate or an increase in the cyclical unemployment rate? What information would you need on the output gap to confirm your answer?

# The Price Level, Inflation and Deflation (Study Plan 11.3)

Use the following information to work Problems 14 and 15.

The people on Coral Island buy only juice and cloth. The RPI basket contains the quantities bought in 2009. The average household spent €60 on juice and €30 on cloth in 2009 when the price of juice was €2 a bottle and the price of cloth was €5 a metre. In the current year, 2010, juice is €4 a bottle and cloth is €6 a metre.

**14** Calculate the RPI basket and the percentage of the household's budget spent on juice in 2009.

**15** Calculate the RPI and the inflation rate in 2010.

Use the following data to work Problems 16 to 18.

The Office for National Statistics reported the following RPI data:

June 2008: 216.8

June 2009: 213.4

June 2010: 221.1

**16** Calculate the inflation rates for the years ended June 2009 and June 2010. How did the inflation rate change in 2010?

**17** Why might these RPI numbers be biased?

**18** Does the GDP deflator help to avoid some of the bias in the RPI numbers?

**19** **Inflation Can Act as a Safety Valve**

Workers will more readily accept a real wage cut that arises from an increase in the price level than a cut in their nominal wage rate.

Source: FT.com, 28 May 2009

How does inflation influence the real wage rate?

**20** The IMF *World Economic Outlook* reports the following price level data (2000 = 100):

| Region | 2006 | 2007 | 2008 |
|--------|------|------|------|
| US | 117.1 | 120.4 | 124.0 |
| Eurozone | 113.6 | 117.1 | 119.6 |
| Japan | 98.1 | 98.1 | 98.8 |

**a** In which region was inflation the highest in 2007 and 2008?

**b** Describe the path of the price level in Japan.

**21** **We are Heading Back to Massive Inflation**

Inflation is an arbitrary tax that falls hardest on those who have done the right thing: it penalises thrift, disadvantages businesses and weakens competitiveness.

Source: *The Telegraph*, 13 January 2011

**a** Explain why unexpected inflation 'penalizes thrift'.

**b** Explain why unexpected inflation 'disadvantages businesses'.

**c** Explain why unexpected inflation 'weakens competitiveness'.

Use the following data to work Problems 22 to 24.

The Office for National Statistics reported that the annual CPI inflation rate in November 2010 was 3.3 per cent and the annual RPI inflation rate was 4.7 per cent.

Food and non-alcoholic drink prices rose by 1.6 per cent, compared to a 0.6 per cent rise a year earlier. Bread and cereal prices rose by 1.9 per cent and meat prices rose by 1.0 per cent.

Clothing and footwear prices rose by 2.0 per cent, compared with 0.6 per cent a year earlier, while furniture and household equipment rose 1.6 per cent.

Air transport fares fell by 6.4 per cent, compared with a fall of 2.6 per cent a year earlier. Fuel and lubricant prices rose by 1.6 per cent, compared with 2.8 per cent a year earlier. Recreation and culture prices fell by 0.2 per cent this year but rose by 0.2 per cent a year earlier.

**22** Which components of the CPI basket experienced price increases (i) faster than the average and (ii) slower than the average?

**23** The change in which price contributed most to the 3.3 per cent increase in the CPI?

**24** Distinguish between the CPI and RPI. Why might the RPI inflation rate be higher than the CPI inflation rate?

**25** What is the GDP deflator and what are the main differences between it and the RPI and CPI?

**26** Why might the GDP deflator provide a more reliable indicator of the inflation rate than the CPI and RPI?

**27** If the GDP deflator does provide a more reliable indicator of the inflation rate than the CPI and RPI, why might we nevertheless use the CPI and RPI?

## ADDITIONAL PROBLEMS AND APPLICATIONS

**myeconlab** You can work these problems in MyEconLab if assigned by your lecturer.

## Employment and Unemployment

**28** What is the unemployment rate supposed to measure and why is it an imperfect measure?

**29** The Office for National Statistics reported the following data for 2010:

Economic activity rate: 76.6 per cent

Working-age population: 40.01 million

Employment rate: 70.7 per cent

Calculate the

**a** Workforce.

**b** Number of people employed

**c** Unemployment rate.

**30** In 2009, the Labour Force Survey measured the economically active at 30.6 million, employment at 28.2 million and the working-age population at 39.8 million. Calculate for 2009:

**a** The unemployment rate.

**b** The economic activity rate.

**c** The employment rate.

**31** The ONS reported the following reasons for economic inactivity in August to October 2010 (the numbers are thousands):

| | |
|---|---|
| Students | 2,209 |
| Looking after family at home | 2,265 |
| Temporarily sick | 175 |
| Long-term sick | 2,216 |
| Discouraged workers | 67 |
| Retired | 1,530 |
| Other | 823 |
| Do not want a job | 6,969 |
| Want a job | 2,367 |

**a** Which of the above categories were counted in the official unemployment rate? Explain your answer.

**b** Which of the above categories of reasons for economic inactivity would you expect to fluctuate with real GDP over the business cycle?

**c** What are the implications of your answer to part (b) for the mismeasurement of the unemployment rate?

**32** A high unemployment rate tells us that a large percentage of the workforce is unemployed, but it doesn't tell us why the unemployment rate is high. What other information would be useful to tell us why the unemployment rate is high?

**33** Why might the official unemployment rate underestimate the underutilisation of labour resources?

**34** **Some Firms Struggle to Hire Despite High Unemployment**

With about 15 million Americans looking for work, some employers are swamped with job applicants, but many employers can't hire enough workers. During the recession, millions of middle-skill, middle-wage jobs disappeared. Now with the recovery, these people can't find the skilled jobs that they seek and have a hard time adjusting to lower-skilled work with less pay.

Source: *The Wall Street Journal*, 9 August 2010

**a** What has changed in the jobs market?

**b** If the government decided to extend the period over which a worker can claim unemployment benefits, how will the cost of unemployment change?

## Unemployment and Full Employment

Use the following data to work Problems 35 to 37.

The IMF *World Economic Outlook* reports the following unemployment rates:

| Region | 2007 | 2008 |
|---|---|---|
| US | 4.6 | 5.4 |
| Eurozone | 7.4 | 7.3 |
| Japan | 3.9 | 3.9 |

**35** What do these numbers tell you about the phase of the business cycle in the three regions in 2008?

**36** What do these numbers tell us about the relative size of the natural unemployment rates in the three regions?

**37** Do these numbers tell us anything about the relative size of the economic activity rate and the employment rate in the three regions?

**38** **A Half-Year of Job Losses**

Employers trimmed jobs in June for the sixth straight month, with the total for the first six months at 438,000 jobs lost by the US economy.

The job losses in June were concentrated in manufacturing and construction, two sectors that have been badly battered in the recession.

Source: CNN, 3 July 2008

**a** Based on the news clip, what might be the main source of increased unemployment?

**b** Based on the news clip, what might be the main type of unemployment that increased?

# The Price Level, Inflation and Deflation

**39** A typical family on Sandy Island consumes only juice and cloth. Last year, which was the reference base year, the family spent €40 on juice and €25 on cloth. Last year, juice was €4 a bottle and cloth was €5 a metre. This year, juice is €4 a bottle and cloth is €6 a metre. Calculate:

   **a** The RPI basket.

   **b** The RPI in the current year.

   **c** The inflation rate in the current year.

**40** Amazon.com agreed to pay its workers $20 an hour in 1999 and $22 an hour in 2001. The price level for these years was 166 in 1999 and 180 in 2001. Calculate the real wage rate in each year. Did these workers really get a pay raise between 1999 and 2001?

**41** In the third quarter of 2010, UK real GDP was £331.2 billion and nominal GDP was £365.9 billion. In the third quarter of 2009, real GDP was £322.7 billion and nominal GDP was £348.1 billion. Calculate the GDP deflator in these two quarters and the inflation rate over the year.

# Economics in the News

**42** After you have studied *Reading Between the Lines* on pp. 266–267 answer the following questions.

   **a** What was the inflation rate as measured by the CPI and the RPI in August 2010?

   **b** Explain why the two measures of inflation deliver different inflation rates.

   **c** If you were the wage negotiator for your local union, explain which of these two measures of inflation you would use as your basis of negotiation.

   **d** If you were an entrepreneur and your workers asked for an increase in their wage to keep their real wage constant, which measure of inflation would you use to calculate the increase in the real wage? Explain.

**43** **Out of a Job and Out of Luck at 54**

Too young to retire, too old to get a new job. That's how many older workers feel after getting the sack and spending time on the unemployment line. Many lack the skills to craft resumes and search online, experts say. Older workers took an average of 21.1 weeks to get a new job in 2007, about 5 weeks longer than younger people. 'Older workers will be more adversely affected because of the time it takes to transition into another job', said Deborah Russell, AARP's director of workforce issues.

Source: CNN, 21 May 2008

   **a** What type of unemployment might older workers be more prone to experience?

   **b** Explain how the unemployment rate of older workers is influenced by the business cycle.

   **c** Why might older unemployed workers become discouraged workers during a recession?

**44** **Land Rover Jaguar Job Applications 'Overwhelm' Halewood**

More than 14,000 people applied for 1,500 new jobs at a new Jaguar Land Rover car plant at Halewood on Merseyside. The jobs have been created by the decision to produce a new Range Rover at this plant.

Source: BBC, 15 January 2010

   **a** What does this news clip suggest about unemployment on Merseyside?

   **b** How will this new car plant change the economic activity rate, the employment rate and the working age population on Merseyside?

   **c** How will this new car plant change the natural unemployment rate and the cyclical unemployment rate on Merseyside?

# Data Graphing

Use the Data Grapher in MyEconLab to work Problems 45 to 47.

**45** In which country in 2009 was the unemployment rate highest and in which was it lowest: Canada, Japan, France or the UK?

**46** In which country in 2009 was the inflation rate highest and in which was it lowest: Australia, the UK, France or the US?

**47** Make a scatter diagram of UK inflation and unemployment. Describe the relationship.

# Financial Markets

After studying this chapter you will be able to:

◆ Describe the flows of funds through financial markets and institutions

◆ Explain how investment and saving along with borrowing and lending decisions are made and interact in the loanable funds market

◆ Explain how a government deficit (or surplus) influences the real interest rate, saving and investment

◆ Explain how international borrowing and lending influence the real interest rate, saving and investment

On 17 September 2007, long queues of depositors wanting to withdraw their funds formed outside the branches of the mortgage lender Northern Rock. On that same day in Detroit, Michigan, a distraught family loaded its pick-up truck, locked the door of its mortgaged home and drove away from its debt. How are these two events connected? They are connected through the global financial market that you study in this chapter. You will learn how financial markets work – mostly very well but sometimes badly.

In *Reading Between the Lines* at the end of the chapter, you will apply what you've learned to understand the influence on financial markets of large government budget deficits in the UK, Portugal, Ireland, Greece and Spain.

**Financial Institutions and Financial Markets**

The financial institutions and markets that we study in this chapter play a crucial role in the economy. They provide the channels through which saving flows to finance the investment in new capital that makes the economy grow. In studying the economics of financial institutions and markets, we distinguish between:

◆ Finance and money
◆ Physical capital and financial capital

## Finance and Money

In economics, we use the term *finance* to describe the activity of borrowing and lending. Borrowing and lending provides the funds that finance expenditures on capital that make productivity grow.

The study of finance examines how households, firms and governments obtain and use financial resources and how they cope with the risks that arise in this activity.

We use the term *money* to describe the stuff that we use to make payments for goods and services, for factors of production including expenditures on new capital and to make financial transactions – to receive and repay loans.

The study of money looks at how households and firms use it, how much of it they hold, how banks create and manage it, and how its quantity influences the economy.

In the economic lives of individuals, businesses and governments, finance and money are closely interrelated. Money is what you get when you borrow from a bank. Money is what you use when you finance the purchase of a new car. And banks and other financial institutions provide both financial services and monetary services. Nevertheless, by distinguishing between *finance* and *money* and studying them separately, we will better understand our financial and monetary markets and institutions.

For the rest of this chapter, we study finance. Money is the topic of the next chapter.

## Physical Capital and Financial Capital

Economists distinguish between physical capital and financial capital. *Physical capital* is the tools, instruments, machines, buildings and other items that have been produced in the past and that are used today to produce goods and services. Inventories of raw materials, semifinished goods, and components are part of physical capital. When economists use the term capital, they mean physical capital. The funds that firms use to buy physical capital are called **financial capital**.

Along the *production possibilities frontier (PPF)* in Chapter 2 (see pp. 30–36), the quantity of capital is fixed. An increase in the quantity of capital increases production possibilities and shifts the *PPF* outward. You're going to see, in this chapter, how investment, saving, borrowing and lending decisions influence the quantity of capital and make it grow, and, as a consequence, make real GDP grow. We begin by describing the links between capital and investment and between wealth and saving.

## Capital and Investment

The quantity of capital changes because of investment and depreciation. *Investment* increases the quantity of capital and *depreciation* decreases it (see Chapter 10, p. 230). The total amount spent on new capital is called **gross investment**. The change in the value of capital is called **net investment**. Net investment equals gross investment minus depreciation. Figure 12.1 illustrates these terms. On 1 January 2011, Ace Bottling Inc. had machines worth €30,000 – Ace's initial capital. During 2011, the market value of Ace's machines fell by 67 per cent – €20,000. After this depreciation, Ace's machines were valued at €10,000. During 2011, Ace spent €30,000 on new machines. This amount is Ace's gross investment. By 31 December 2011, Ace Bottling had capital valued at €40,000, so its capital had increased by €10,000. This amount is Ace's net investment. Ace's net investment equals its gross investment of €30,000 minus depreciation of its initial capital of €20,000.

## Wealth and Saving

**Wealth** is the value of all the things that people own. What people own is related to what they earn, but it is not the same thing. People earn an income, which is the amount they receive during a given time period from supplying the services of the resources they own. **Saving** is the amount of income that is not paid in taxes or spent on consumption goods and services.

Saving increases wealth. Wealth also increases when the market value of assets rises – called capital gains – and decreases when the market value of assets falls – called capital losses.

**Figure 12.1** Capital and Investment

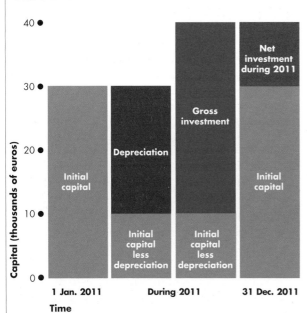

On 1 January 2011, Ace Bottling had capital worth €30,000. During the year, the value of Ace's capital fell by €20,000 – depreciation – and it spent €30,000 on new capital – gross investment. Ace's net investment was €10,000 (€30,000 gross investment minus €20,000 depreciation) so that at the end of 2011, Ace had capital worth €40,000.

 Animation

For example, at the end of term you have €250 in the bank and a coin collection worth €300, so your wealth is €550. During the summer, you earn €5,000 (net of taxes) and spend €1,000 on consumption goods and services, so your saving is €4,000. Your bank account increases to €4,250 and your wealth becomes €4,550. The €4,000 increase in wealth equals saving. If coins rise in value and your coin collection is now worth €500, you have a capital gain of €200, which is also added to your wealth.

National wealth and national saving work like this personal example. The wealth of a nation at the end of a year equals its wealth at the start of the year plus its saving during the year, which equals income minus consumption expenditure.

To make real GDP grow, saving and wealth must be transformed into investment and capital. This transformation takes place in the markets for financial capital and through the activities of financial institutions. We're now going to describe these markets and institutions.

# Financial Capital Markets

Saving is the source of the funds that are used to finance investment, and these funds are supplied and demanded in three types of financial markets:

◆ Loan markets
◆ Bond markets
◆ Stock markets

## Loan Markets

Businesses often want short-term finance to buy inventories or to extend credit to their customers. Sometimes they get this finance in the form of a loan from a bank. Households often want finance to purchase a high expenditure item, such as a car or household furnishings and appliances. They get this finance as bank loans, often in the form of outstanding credit card balances. Households also get finance to buy new homes. (Expenditure on new homes is counted as part of investment.) These funds are usually obtained as a loan that is secured by a **mortgage** – a legal contract that gives ownership of a home to the lender in the event that the borrower fails to meet the agreed loan payments (repayments and interest). Mortgage loans were at the centre of the sub-prime loans crisis of 2007–2008. All of these types of financing take place in loan markets.

## Bond Markets

When Wal-Mart (the largest retailer in the world) expands its business into China, it gets the finance it needs by selling bonds. National and local governments also raise finance by issuing bonds.

A **bond** is a promise to make specified payments on specified dates. For example, you can buy a Wal-Mart bond that promises to pay $5.00 every year until 2024 and then to make a final payment of $100 in 2025.

The buyer of a bond from Wal-Mart makes a loan to the company and is entitled to the payments promised by the bond. When a person buys a newly issued bond, he or she may hold the bond until the borrower has repaid the amount borrowed or sell it to someone else. Bonds issued by firms and governments are traded in the **bond market**.

The term of a bond might be long (decades) or short (just a month or two). Firms often issue very short-term bonds as a way of getting paid for their sales before the buyer is able to pay. These short-term bonds are called commercial paper. For example, when Rolls-Royce sells

£100 million of aero engines to Qantas, Rolls-Royce wants to be paid when the items are shipped. But Qantas doesn't want to pay until the engines are installed and the engines are earning an income. In this situation, Qantas might promise to pay GM £101 million three months in the future. A bank would be willing to buy this promise for (say) £100 million. Rolls-Royce gets £100 million immediately and the bank gets £101 million in three months when Qantas honours its promise. The UK Treasury issues promises of this type, called Treasury bills.

Another type of bond is a **mortgage-backed security**, which entitles its holder to the income from a package of mortgages. Mortgage lenders create mortgage-backed securities. They make mortgage loans to homebuyers and then create securities that they sell to obtain more funds to make more mortgage loans. The holder of a mortgage-backed security is entitled to receive payments that derive from the payments received by the mortgage lender from the homebuyer–borrower.

Mortgage-backed securities were at the centre of the storm in the financial markets in 2007–2008.

## Stock Markets

When Boeing wants finance to expand its aeroplane building business, it issues stock. A **stock** is a certificate of ownership and claim to the firm's profits. Boeing has issued about 900 million shares of its stock. So if you owned 900 Boeing shares, you would own one millionth of Boeing and be entitled to receive one millionth of its profits. Unlike a stockholder, a bondholder does not own part of the firm that issued the bond.

A **stock market** is a financial market in which shares of stocks of corporations are traded. The London Stock Exchange, the Frankfurt Stock Exchange, the New York Stock Exchange and the Tokyo Stock Exchange are all examples of stock markets.

# Financial Institutions

Financial markets are highly competitive because of the role played by financial institutions in those markets. A **financial institution** is a firm that operates on both sides of the markets for financial capital. The financial institution is a borrower in one market and a lender in another.

Financial institutions also stand ready to trade so that households with funds to lend and firms or households seeking funds can always find someone on the other side of the market with whom to trade.

The key financial institutions are:

◆ Commercial banks
◆ Mortgage companies (building societies)
◆ Pension funds
◆ Insurance companies

## Commercial Banks

Commercial banks are financial institutions that accept deposits, provide payment services and make loans to firms and households. The bank that you use for your own banking services and that issues your debit card is a commercial bank. These institutions play a central role in the monetary system and we study them in detail in Chapter 13.

## Mortgage Companies (Building Societies)

Mortgage companies are financial institutions that specialise in making loans for property purchases. In the UK these companies are called building societies. Traditionally building societies took deposits and made loans from the deposit funds they held. Since the 1990s, the building societies began to borrow funds from other financial institutions to make mortgage loans. Many building societies became banks so that they could fund their mortgage business by borrowing from the global interbank market.

In the US, two large financial institutions that specialize in mortgages, the Federal National Mortgage Association, or Fannie Mae, and the Federal Home Loan Mortgage Corporation, or Freddie Mac, were at the epicentre of the global financial crisis (see *Economics in Action* opposite). These financial institutions bought mortgages from banks, packaged them into mortgage-backed securities, and sold them to financial institutions all over the world.

In September 2008, Fannie and Freddie owned or guaranteed $6 trillion worth of mortgages (half of the US$12 trillion of mortgages) and were taken over by the US federal government.

Many former UK building societies followed the model of Fannie Mae and Freddie Mac. They borrowed funds in the global interbank loans market and loaned them to house buyers. They then packaged the mortgage loans into mortgage-backed securities and sold them to other financial institutions. Often the buyers of these securities would be the lenders of the funds that were used to make the loans to house buyers.

## Pension Funds

Pension funds are financial institutions that use the pension contributions of firms and workers to buy bonds and stocks. The mortgage-backed securities of Fannie Mae and Freddie Mac and specialized mortgage lenders in the UK are among the assets of pension funds. Some pension funds are very large and play an active role in the firms whose stock they hold.

## Insurance Companies

Insurance companies enable households and firms to cope with risks such as accident, theft, fire, ill-health and a host of other misfortunes. They receive premiums from their customers and pay claims. Insurance companies use the funds they have received but not paid out as claims to buy bonds and stocks on which they earn interest income.

In normal times, insurance companies have a steady inflow of funds from premiums and interest and a steady, but smaller, outflow of funds paying claims. Their profit is the gap between the two flows.

In unusual times, when large and widespread losses are being incurred, insurance companies can run into difficulty in meeting their obligations.

## Insolvency and Illiquidity

A financial institution's **net worth** is the market value of what it has lent minus the market value of what it has borrowed. If net worth is positive, the institution is solvent. But if net worth is negative, the institution is insolvent and must go out of business. The owners of an insolvent financial institution – usually its stockholders – bear the loss.

A financial institution both borrows and lends, so it is exposed to the risk that its net worth might become negative. To limit that risk, financial institutions are regulated and a minimum amount of their lending must be backed by their net worth.

Sometimes, a financial institution is solvent but illiquid. A firm is *illiquid* if it has made long-term loans with borrowed funds and is faced with a sudden demand to repay more of what it has borrowed than its available cash.

In normal times, a financial institution that is illiquid can borrow from another institution. But if all the financial institutions are short of cash, the market for loans among financial institutions dries up. In such a situation, the central bank can provide funds.

Insolvency and illiquidity were at the core of the financial meltdown of 2007–2008.

## ECONOMICS IN ACTION

### The 2008 Financial Crisis

Bear Stearns: absorbed by JPMorgan Chase with help from the US Federal Reserve. Lehman Brothers: gone. Fannie Mae and Freddie Mac: taken into government oversight. Merrill Lynch: absorbed by Bank of America. AIG: given an $85 billion lifeline by the Federal Reserve and sold off in parcels to financial institutions around the world. Wachovia: taken over by Wells Fargo. Washington Mutual: taken over by JPMorgan Chase. Morgan Stanley: 20 per cent bought by Mitsubishi, a large Japanese bank. These are some of the events in the financial crisis of 2008. What was going on?

Between 2002 and 2005, mortgage lending exploded and home prices rocketed. Mortgage lenders bundled their loans into mortgage-backed securities and sold them to eager buyers around the world. When interest rates began to rise in 2006 and asset prices fell, financial institutions took big losses. Some losses were too big to bear and big-name institutions failed.

## Interest Rates and Asset Prices

Stocks, bonds, short-term securities and loans are collectively called financial assets. The interest rate on a financial asset is the interest received expressed as a percentage of the price of the asset.

Because the interest rate is a percentage of the price of an asset, if the asset price rises, other things remaining the same, the interest rate falls. Conversely, if the asset price falls, other things remaining the same, the interest rate rises.

To see this inverse relationship between an asset price and the interest rate, let's look at an example. We'll consider a bond that promises to pay its holder €5 a year forever. What is the rate of return – the interest rate – on this bond? The answer depends on the price of the bond. If you could buy this bond for €50, the interest rate would be 10 per cent per year:

Interest rate = (€5 ÷ €50) × 100 = 10 per cent.

But if the price of this bond increased to €200, its rate of return or interest rate would be only 2.5 per cent per year. That is,

Interest rate = (€5 ÷ €200) × 100 = 2.5 per cent.

This relationship means that the price of an asset and the interest rate on that asset are determined simultaneously – one implies the other.

This relationship also means that if the interest rate on the asset rises, the price of the asset falls, debts become harder to pay and the net worth of the financial institution falls. Insolvency can arise from a previously unexpected large rise in the interest rate. In the next part of this chapter, we learn how interest rates and asset prices are determined in the financial markets.

**Review Quiz**

1   Distinguish between physical capital and financial capital and give two examples of each.
2   What is the distinction between gross investment and net investment?
3   What are the three main types of markets for financial capital and what makes them different?
4   What are the main types of financial institutions and how do they differ?
5   Explain the connection between the price of a financial asset and its interest rate.

You can work these questions in Study Plan 12.1 and get instant feedback.

## The Loanable Funds Market

In macroeconomics, we group all the financial markets that we described in the previous section into a single loanable funds market. The **loanable funds market** is the aggregate of all the individual financial markets.

The circular flow model of Chapter 10 (see p. 229) can be extended to include flows in the loanable funds market that finance investment.

## Funds that Finance Investment

Figure 12.2 shows the flows of funds that finance investment. They come from three sources:

1   Household saving
2   Government budget surplus
3   Borrowing from the rest of the world

Households' income, $Y$, is spent on consumption goods and services, $C$, saved, $S$, or paid in net taxes, $T$. **Net taxes** are the taxes paid to governments minus the cash transfers received from governments (such as social security and unemployment benefits). So income is equal to the sum of consumption expenditure, saving and net taxes:

$$Y = C + S + T$$

You saw in Chapter 10 (p. 230) that $Y$ also equals the sum of the items of aggregate expenditure: consumption expenditure, $C$, investment, $I$, government expenditure, $G$, and exports, $X$, minus imports, $M$. That is:

$$Y = C + I + G + X - M$$

By using these two equations, you can see that

$$I + G + X = M + S + T$$

Subtract $G$ and $X$ from both sides of the last equation to obtain

$$I = S + (T - G) + (M - X)$$

This equation tells us that investment, $I$, is financed by household saving, $S$, the government budget surplus, $(T - G)$, and borrowing from the rest of the world, $(M - X)$.

A government budget surplus $(T > G)$ contributes funds to finance investment, but a government budget deficit $(T < G)$ competes with investment for funds and decreases the amount available to invest.

**Figure 12.2    Financial Flows and the Circular Flow of Expenditure and Income**

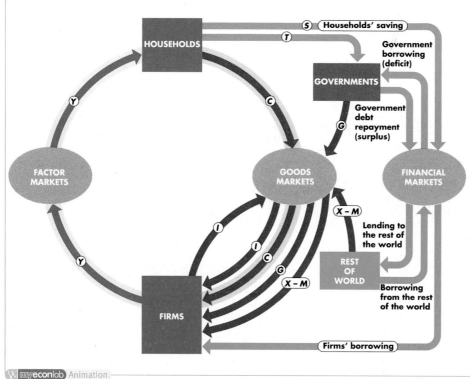

Households use their income for consumption expenditure (*C*), saving (*S*) and net taxes (*T*). Firms borrow to finance their investment expenditure.

Governments borrow to finance a budget deficit or repay debt if they have a budget surplus. The rest of the world borrows to finance its deficit or lends its surplus.

If we export less than we import, we borrow ($M - X$) from the rest of the world to finance some of our investment. If we export more than we import, we lend ($X - M$) to the rest of the world and part of UK saving finances investment in other countries.

The sum of private saving, *S*, and government saving, ($T - G$), is called **national saving**. National saving and foreign borrowing finance investment.

In 2010, total investment in the UK was £208 billion. The government (national and local combined) had a deficit of £144 billion. This total of £352 billion was financed by private saving of £306 billion and borrowing from the rest of the world (negative net exports) of £46 billion.

You're going to see how investment and saving and the flows of loanable funds – all measured in constant 2005 euros – are determined. The price in the loanable funds market that achieves equilibrium is an interest rate, which we also measure in real terms as the real interest rate. In the loanable funds market, there is just one interest rate, which is an average of the interest rates on all the different types of financial securities that we described earlier. Let's see what we mean by the real interest rate.

## The Real Interest Rate

The **nominal interest rate** is the number of pounds or euros that a borrower pays and a lender receives in interest in a year expressed as a percentage of the number of pounds or euros borrowed and lent. For example, if the annual interest paid on a €500 loan is €25, the nominal interest rate is 5 per cent per year: €25 ÷ €500 × 100 or 5 per cent.

The **real interest rate** is the additional goods and services that the lender can buy with the interest received. It is the nominal interest rate adjusted to remove the effects of inflation on the buying power of money. The real interest rate is approximately equal to the nominal interest rate minus the inflation rate.

You can see why if you suppose that you have put €500 in a savings account that earns 5 per cent a year. At the end of a year, you have €525 in your savings account. Suppose that the inflation rate is 2 per cent per year – during the year, all prices increased by 2 per cent. Now, at the end of the year, it costs €510 to buy what €500 would have bought one year ago. Your money in the bank has really only increased by €15, from €510 to €525. That €15 is equivalent to a real interest rate of

3 per cent a year on your original €500. So the real interest rate is the 5 per cent nominal interest rate minus the 2 per cent inflation rate.[1]

The real interest rate is the opportunity cost of loanable funds. The real interest paid on borrowed funds is the opportunity cost of borrowing. And the real interest rate forgone when funds are used either to buy consumption goods and services or to invest in new capital goods is the opportunity cost of not saving or not lending those funds.

We're now going to see how the loanable funds market determines the real interest rate, the quantity of funds loaned, saving and investment. In the rest of this section, we will ignore the government and the rest of the world and focus on households and firms in the loanable funds market. We will study:

◆ The demand for loanable funds

◆ The supply of loanable funds

◆ Equilibrium in the loanable funds market

## The Demand for Loanable Funds

The *quantity of loanable funds demanded* is the total quantity of funds demanded to finance investment, the government budget deficit and international investment or lending during a given period. Our focus here is on investment. We'll bring the other two items into the picture in later sections of this chapter.

What determines investment and the demand for loanable funds to finance it? Many details influence this decision, but we can summarize them in two factors:

1  The real interest rate

2  Expected profit

Firms invest in capital only if they expect to earn a profit and fewer projects are profitable at a high real interest rate than at a low real interest rate, so:

**Other things remaining the same, the higher the real interest rate, the smaller is the quantity of loanable funds demanded; and the lower the real interest rate, the greater is the quantity of loanable funds demanded.**

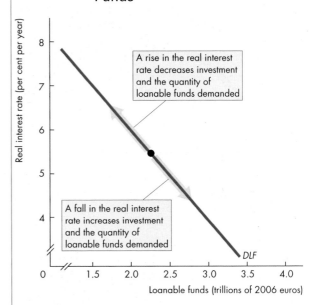

**Figure 12.3**   The Demand for Loanable Funds

A change in the real interest rate changes the quantity of loanable funds demanded and brings a movement along the demand for loanable funds curve.

myeconlab Animation

### Demand for Loanable Funds Curve

The **demand for loanable funds** is the relationship between the quantity of loanable funds demanded and the real interest rate, when all other influences on borrowing plans remain the same. The demand curve *DLF* in Figure 12.3 is a demand for loanable funds curve.

To understand the demand for loanable funds, think about Amazon.com's decision to borrow €100 million to build a new warehouse. If Amazon expects a return of €5 million a year from this investment before paying interest costs and the interest rate is less than 5 per cent a year, Amazon would make a profit, so it builds the warehouses. But if the interest rate is more than 5 per cent a year, Amazon would incur a loss, so it doesn't build the warehouses. The quantity of loanable funds demanded is greater the lower is the real interest rate.

### Changes in the Demand for Loanable Funds

When the expected profit changes, the demand for loanable funds changes. Other things remaining the same, the greater the expected profit from new capital, the greater is the amount of investment and the greater the demand for loanable funds.

---

[1] The exact real interest rate formula, which allows for the change in the purchasing power of both the interest and the loan is:
Real interest rate = (Nominal interest rate − Inflation rate) ÷ (1 + Inflation rate/100). If the nominal interest rate is 5 per cent a year and the inflation rate is 2 per cent a year, the real interest rate is: (5 − 2) ÷ (1 + 0.02) = 2.94 per cent a year.

Expected profit rises during a business cycle expansion and falls during a recession; rises when technological change creates profitable new products; rises as a growing population brings increased demand for goods and services; and fluctuates with contagious swings of optimism and pessimism, called 'animal spirits' by Keynes and 'irrational exuberance' by Alan Greenspan.

When expected profit changes, the demand for loanable funds curve shifts.

## The Supply of Loanable Funds

The *quantity of loanable funds supplied* is the total funds available from private saving, the government budget surplus and international borrowing during a given period. Our focus here is on saving. We'll bring the other two items into the picture later.

How do you decide how much of your income to save and supply in the loanable funds market? Your decision is influenced by many factors, but chief among them are:

1 The real interest rate

2 Disposable income

3 Expected future income

4 Wealth

5 Default risk

We begin by focusing on the real interest rate.

**Other things remaining the same, the higher the real interest rate, the greater is the quantity of loanable funds supplied; and the lower the real interest rate, the smaller is the quantity of loanable funds supplied.**

### The Supply of Loanable Funds Curve

The **supply of loanable funds** is the relationship between the quantity of loanable funds supplied and the real interest rate when all other influences on lending plans remain the same. The curve *SLF* in Figure 12.4 is a supply of loanable funds curve.

Think about a student's decision to save some of what she earns from her summer job. With a real interest rate of 2 per cent a year, she decides that it is not worth saving much – better to spend the income and take a student loan if funds run out during the semester. But if the real interest rate jumped to 10 per cent a year, the payoff from saving would be high enough to encourage her to cut back on spending and increase the amount she saves.

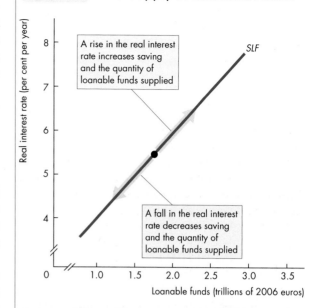

**Figure 12.4  The Supply of Loanable Funds**

A rise in the real interest rate increases saving and the quantity of loanable funds supplied

A fall in the real interest rate decreases saving and the quantity of loanable funds supplied

A change in the real interest rate changes the quantity of loanable funds supplied and brings a movement along the supply of loanable funds curve.

myeconlab Animation

### Changes in the Supply of Loanable Funds

The supply of loanable funds changes if disposable income, expected future income, wealth or default risk changes.

**Disposable Income**
A household's *disposable income* is the income minus net taxes. When disposable income increases, both saving and consumption expenditure increase. So the greater a household's disposable income, other things remaining the same, the greater is its saving.

**Expected Future Income**
The higher a household's expected future income, the smaller is its saving today.

**Wealth**
The higher a household's wealth, other things remaining the same, the smaller is its saving. If a person's wealth increases because of a capital gain, the person sees less need to save.

For example, during 2007 when house prices were still rising, wealth increased despite the fact that personal saving dropped close to zero.

**Default Risk**

Default risk is the risk that a loan will not be repaid. The greater that risk, the higher is the interest rate needed to induce a person to lend and the smaller is the supply of loanable funds.

## Shifts of the Supply of Loanable Funds Curve

When any of the four influences on the supply of loanable funds changes, the supply of loanable funds changes and the supply curve shifts. An increase in disposable income, a decrease in expected future income, a decrease in wealth, or a fall in default risk increases saving and increases the supply of loanable funds.

# Equilibrium in the Loanable Funds Market

You've seen that other things remaining the same, the higher the real interest rate, the greater is the quantity of loanable funds supplied and the smaller is the quantity of loanable funds demanded. There is one real interest rate at which the quantities of loanable funds demanded and supplied are equal, and that interest rate is the equilibrium real interest rate.

Figure 12.5 shows how the demand for and supply of loanable funds determine the real interest rate. The *DLF* curve is the demand curve and the *SLF* curve is the supply curve. If the real interest rate exceeds 6 per cent a year, the quantity of loanable funds supplied exceeds the quantity demanded – a surplus of funds. Borrowers find it easy to get funds, but lenders are unable to lend all their funds. The real interest rate falls until the quantity of funds supplied equals the quantity demanded.

If the real interest rate is less than 6 per cent a year, the quantity of loanable funds supplied is less than the quantity demanded – a shortage of funds. Borrowers can't get the funds they want, but lenders are able to lend all the funds they have available. So the real interest rate rises and continues to rise until the quantity of funds supplied equals the quantity demanded.

Regardless of whether there is a surplus or a shortage of loanable funds, the real interest rate changes and is pulled towards an equilibrium level. In Figure 12.5, the equilibrium real interest rate is 6 per cent a year. At this interest rate there is neither a surplus nor a shortage of loanable funds. Borrowers can get the funds they want, and lenders can lend all the funds they have available. The investment plans of borrowers and the saving plans of lenders are consistent with each other.

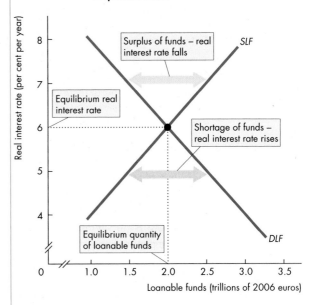

**Figure 12.5**  Loanable Funds Market Equilibrium

A surplus of funds lowers the real interest rate and a shortage of funds raises it. At an interest rate of 6 per cent a year, the quantity of funds demanded equals the quantity supplied and the market is in equilibrium.

myeconlab Animation

# Changes in Demand and Supply

Financial markets are highly volatile in the short run but remarkably stable in the long run. Volatility in the market comes from fluctuations in either the demand for loanable funds or the supply of loanable funds. These fluctuations bring fluctuations in the real interest rate and in the equilibrium quantity of funds lent and borrowed. They also bring fluctuations in asset prices.

Here we'll illustrate the effects of increases in demand and supply in the loanable funds market.

## An Increase in Demand

If the profits that firms expect to earn increase, they increase their planned investment and increase their demand for loanable funds to finance that investment. With an increase in the demand for loanable funds, but no change in the supply of loanable funds, there is a shortage of funds. As borrowers compete for funds, the interest rate rises and lenders increase the quantity of funds supplied.

Figure 12.6(a) illustrates these changes. An increase in the demand for loanable funds shifts the demand curve rightward from $DLF_0$ to $DLF_1$. With no change in

## Figure 12.6    Changes in Demand and Supply

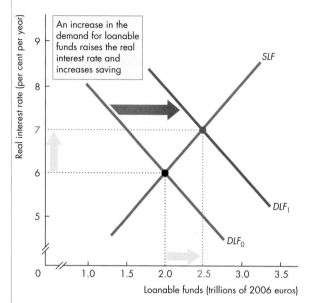

**(a) An increase in demand**

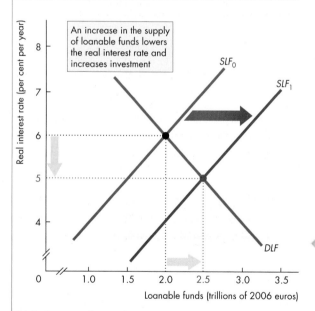

**(b) An increase in supply**

In part (a), the demand for loanable funds increases and supply doesn't change. The real interest rate rises (financial asset prices fall) and the quantity of funds increases.

In part (b), the supply of loanable funds increases and demand doesn't change. The real interest rate falls (financial asset prices rise) and the quantity of funds increases.

 Animation

the supply of loanable funds, there is a shortage of funds at a real interest rate of 6 per cent a year. The real interest rate rises until it is 7 per cent a year. Equilibrium is restored and the equilibrium quantity of funds has increased.

### An Increase in Supply

If one of the influences on saving plans changes and increases saving, the supply of loanable funds increases. With no change in the demand for loanable funds, the market is flush with loanable funds. Borrowers find bargains and lenders find themselves accepting a lower interest rate. At the lower interest rate, borrowers find additional investment projects profitable and increase the quantity of loanable funds that they borrow.

Figure 12.6(b) illustrates these changes. An increase in supply shifts the supply curve rightward from $SLF_0$ to $SLF_1$. With no change in demand, there is a surplus of funds at a real interest rate of 6 per cent a year. The real interest rate falls until it is 5 per cent a year. Equilibrium is restored and the equilibrium quantity of funds has increased.

### Long-run Growth of Demand and Supply

Over time, both demand and supply in the loanable funds market fluctuate and the real interest rate rises and falls. Both the supply of loanable funds and the demand for loanable funds tend to increase over time. On the average, they increase at a similar pace, so although demand and supply trend upward, the real interest rate has no trend. It fluctuates around a constant average level.

### Review Quiz

1  What is the loanable funds market?
2  Why is the real interest rate the opportunity cost of loanable funds?
3  How do firms make investment decisions?
4  What determines the demand for loanable funds and what makes it change?
5  How do households make saving decisions?
6  What determines the supply of loanable funds and what makes it change?
7  How do changes in the demand for and supply of loanable funds change the real interest rate and quantity of loanable funds?

You can work these questions in Study Plan 12.2 and get instant feedback.    **myeconlab**

## Loanable Funds Fuel the US Home Price Bubble

The financial crisis that gripped the US and global economies in 2007 and cascaded through the financial markets in 2008 had its origins much earlier in events taking place in the loanable funds market.

Between 2001 and 2005, a massive injection of loanable funds occurred. Some funds came from the rest of the world, but that source of supply has been stable. The Federal Reserve (the US central bank) provided funds to keep interest rates low and that was a major source of the increase in the supply of funds. (The next chapter explains how a central bank does this.)

Figure 1 illustrates the loanable funds market starting in 2001. In that year, the demand for loanable funds was $DLF_{01}$ and the supply of loanable funds was $SLF_{01}$. The equilibrium real interest rate was 4 per cent a year and the equilibrium quantity of loanable funds was $29 trillion (in 2005 dollars).

During the ensuing four years, a massive increase in the supply of loanable funds shifted the supply curve rightward to $SLF_{05}$. A smaller increase in demand shifted the demand for loanable funds curve to $DLF_{05}$. The real interest rate fell to 1 per cent a year and the quantity of loanable funds increased to $36 trillion – a 24 per cent increase in just four years.

With this large increase in available funds, much of it in the form of mortgage loans to home buyers, the demand for

homes increased by more than the increase in the supply of homes. Home prices rose and the expectation of further increases fuelled the demand for loanable funds.

By 2006, the expectation of continued rapidly rising home prices brought a very large increase in the demand for loanable funds. At the same time, the Federal Reserve began to tighten credit. The result of the Fed's tighter credit policy was a slowdown in the pace of increase in the supply of loanable funds.

Figure 2 illustrates these events. In 2006, the demand for loanable funds increased from $DLF_{05}$ to $DLF_{06}$ and the supply of loanable funds increased by a smaller amount from $SLF_{05}$ to $SLF_{06}$. The real interest rate increased to 3 per cent a year.

The rise in the real interest rate (and a much higher rise in the nominal interest rate) put many home owners in financial difficulty. Mortgage repayments increased and some borrowers stopped repaying their loans.

By August 2007, the damage from mortgage default and foreclosure was so large that the credit market began to dry up. A large decrease in both demand and supply kept interest rates roughly constant but decreased the quantity of new business.

The total quantity of loanable funds didn't decrease, but the rate of increase slowed to a snail's pace and financial institutions most exposed to the bad mortgage debts and the securities that they backed (described on p. 276) began to fail.

These events illustrate the crucial role played by the loanable funds market.

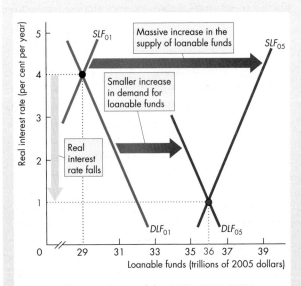

**Figure 1  The Foundation of the Crisis: 2001–2005**

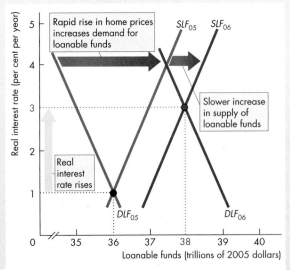

**Figure 2  The Start of the Crisis: 2005–2006**

## TABLE 8–1: Basicranial Ossification Centers

| Bone | Site and Number of Ossification Centers | | Initial Appearance (weeks) |
|---|---|---|---|
| | Intramembranous | Endochondral | |
| Occipital | Supranuchal squamous (2) | — | 8 |
| | | Infranuchal squamous (2) | 10 |
| | | Basilar (1) | 11 |
| | | Exoccipital (2) | 12 |
| Temporal | Squamous (1) | — | 8 |
| | Tympanic ring (4) | — | 12 |
| | — | Petrosal (14) | 16 |
| | — | Styloid (2) | Perinatal |
| Ethmoid | — | Lateral labyrinths (2) | 16 |
| | — | Perpendicular plate; crista (1) | 36 |
| Vomer | Alae (2) | — | 8 |
| Sphenoid | — | Presphenoid (3) | 16 |
| | — | Postsphenoid (4) | 16 |
| | — | Orbitosphenoids (2) | 9 |
| | — | Alisphenoids (2) | 8 |
| | — | Pterygoid hamuli (2) | 12 |
| | Medial pterygoid plates (2) | — | 8 |
| | Lateral pterygoid plates (2) | — | 8 |
| | — | Sphenoidal conchae (2) | 20 |
| Inferior nasal concha | — | Lamina (1) | 20 |

(IX), vagus (X) and spinal accessory (XI) nerves and the internal jugular vein passing between the otic capsule and the parachordal cartilage account for the large *jugular foramen*. The hypoglossal nerve (XII) passing between the occipital sclerotomes accounts for the *hypoglossal* or *anterior condylar canal*. The spinal cord determines the *foramen magnum* (see Fig. 8–1).

### Chondrocranial Ossification

Approximately 110 ossification centers appear in the embryonic human skull (Table 8–1). Many of these centers fuse to produce 45 bones in the neonatal skull. In the young adult, 22 skull bones are recognized.

Centers of ossification within the basal plate, commencing with the alisphenoids in the eighth week pc, lay the basis for the endochondral bone portions of the occipital, sphenoid and temporal bones (all of which also have intramembranous bone components), and for the wholly endochondral ethmoid and inferior nasal concha bones (Fig. 8–5).

Unossified chondrocranial remnants persist at birth as the alae and septum of the nose, the spheno-occipital and sphenopetrous junctions, the apex of the petrous bone, between the separate parts of the occipital bone, and in the foramen lacerum.

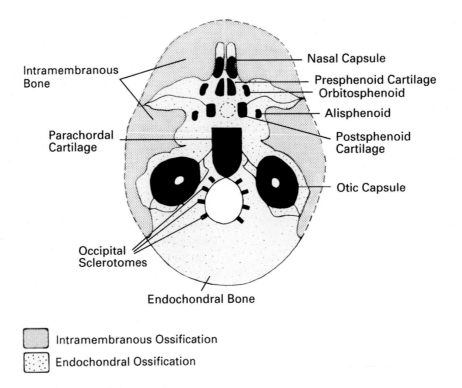

**Figure 8–5** Schema of adult cranial base indicating sites of primordial cartilages of chondrocranium (in black) and extent of endochondral (light stipple) and intramembranous (heavy stipple) ossification.

### Occipital Bone

Derived from both the basicranial cartilage—contributed by the occipital sclerotomes—and the desmocranial membrane, the occipital bone ossifies from seven centers (two intramembranous, five endochondral) around the medulla oblongata, which determines the foramen magnum (Fig. 8–6; see Fig. 8–5). The occipital bone develops in a modified vertebral pattern, with components representing the centrum, traverse processes, and neural arches of several successive occipital vertebrae. The basioccipital cartilage, like the vertebral bodies, is traversed by the notochord, vestiges of which persist until birth. The squamous portion above the superior nuchal line ossifies from a pair of intramembranous ossification centers in the 8th week pc, and infranuchally from a pair of endochondral ossification centers in the 10th week pc. The paired infranuchal chondral segments fuse, and a median wedge of cartilage (Kerckring's center) usually develops posterior to the foramen magnum, but the median intramembranous suture remains unfused at its dorsal margin. The transverse nuchal suture between the cartilaginous and membranous portions of the occipital squama may persist, but in most cases it normally fuses by the 12th week pc.

The single median basicranial endochondral ossification center appearing at the 11th week forms the basioccipital bone anterior to the foramen magnum and the anterior one-third of the occipital condyles. A pair of endochondral ossification centers appearing at the 12th week form the

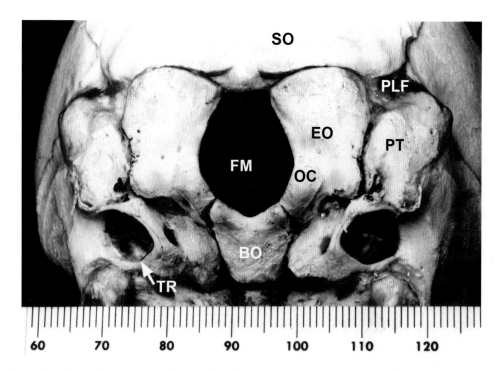

**Figure 8–6** Base of neonatal skull depicting forming occipital bone surrounding the foramen magnum. Note the synchondroses in the occipital condyles between the exoccipital and basioccipital and absence of the mastoid processes. BO, basioccipital; EO, exoccipital; FM, foramen magnum; OC occipital condyle; PLF, posterolateral fontanelle; PT, petrous temporal; SO, squamous occipital; TR, tympanic ring.

exoccipital bones, lateral to the foramen magnum, including the posterior two-thirds of the occipital condyles; these surround the hypoglossal nerves to form the hypoglossal canals. The occipital squama starts to fuse with the exoccipitals at the posterior intraoccipital synchondroses during the second or third year postnatally. The exoccipitals join the basioccipital at the anterior intraoccipital synchrondroses, which lie within the condyles. During the third or fourth year, these anterior synchondroses start to disappear; by the age of 7, the squamous, exoccipital and basilar portions have united into a single occipital bone. A pharyngeal tubercle appears on the ventral aspect of the basioccipital to provide attachment for the median pharyngeal raphe. The nuchal lines and the occipital protuberance enlarge postnatally with nuchal muscular usage.

Postnatally, the endocranial surfaces of the occipital bone are predominantly resorptive and the ectocranial surfaces are depositary, resulting in downward displacement of the floor of the posterior cranial fossa to accommodate the enlarging brain. The squamous and basilar portions have independent rates of growth.

### Temporal Bone

The squamous and tympanic components of this bone ossify in membrane, whereas the petrosal and styloid elements ossify endochondrally from some 21 ossification centers. The squamous portion ossifies intramembranously from a single center appearing in the eighth week pc; the zygomatic process extends from this ossification center. The tympanic ring surrounding the external acoustic meatus ossifies from four intramembranous centers, starting in the third month pc. The inner-ear otocyst induces chondrogenesis in the periotic mesenchyme, of both neural crest and mesodermal origin, to form the otic capsule; local repression of chondrogenesis accounts for the perilymphatic space within the capsule. The petrosal part ossifies endochondrally in the otic capsule from about 14 centers; the centers first appear in the 16th week around the nerves of the inner ear and fuse during the 6th month pc, when the contained inner-ear labyrinth has reached its final size. The otic capsule is initially continuous with the basioccipital cartilage, but the synchondrosis converts to the foramen lacerum and jugular foramen.

The middle ear within the petrosal bone contains derivatives of the first and second pharyngeal arches that form the malleus, incus and stapes bones (see p. 65).

The petrosal bone forming the adult otic capsule consists of three layers: the inner endosteal and outer periosteal layers contain haversian canals, whereas the middle layer consists of highly mineralized endochondral fetus-type bone that, uniquely, is retained throughout life and not replaced by canalicular haversian bone. The osseous labyrinth remains unaltered throughout life as an inner woven bone capsule protecting the membranous labyrinth. By contrast, the petrosal outer periosteal layer remodels to lamellar bone and adapts to functional stresses. The styloid process ossifies from two centers in the hyoid (second) pharyngeal arch cartilage (see p. 68); the upper center appears just before birth and the lower center just after birth.

At 22 weeks pc, the petrous part and tympanic ring fuse incompletely, leaving the petrotympanic fissure through which the chorda tympani nerve and remnants of the diskomalleolar ligament pass. At birth, the tympanic ring fuses incompletely with the squamous part of the temporal bone, forming the persisting squamotympanic fissure. Later, the ring grows laterally to form the tympanic plate. The petrous, squamous and proximal styloid process portions fuse during the first year of life, and the distal and proximal styloid processes fuse at about puberty.

The mandibular (glenoid) fossa is only a shallow depression at birth, deepening with development of the articular eminence (see Chapter 13). The mastoid process develops after the second year, when it is invaded by extensions of the tympanic antrum to form mastoid air cells.

### Ethmoid Bone

This wholly endochondral bone, which forms the median floor of the anterior cranial fossa and parts of the roof, lateral walls, and median septum of the nasal cavity, ossifies from three centers: a single median center in the mesethmoid cartilage forms the perpendicular plate and crista galli just before birth; a pair of centers for the lateral labyrinths appears in the nasal capsular cartilages at the fourth month pc; and a secondary ossification center appears between the cribriform plates and crista galli at birth (see Fig. 8–4). At 2 years of age, the perpendicular plate unites with the labyrinths, through fusion of the cribriform plate, to form a single ethmoid bone.

Resorption of the endocranial surface of the cribriform plates, with deposition on the opposite nasal surface, results in downward movement of the anterior cranial floor. Postnatal growth of the cribriform plate is slight and is complete by 4 years. Postnatal growth of the other nasal elements is a potent factor in the enlargement of the middle third of the face.

### Inferior Nasal Concha

This endochondral bone ossifies in the cartilage of the lateral part of the nasal capsule (the ectethmoid) from a single center that appears in the fifth month pc (see Fig. 8–4). Peripheral ossification of the cartilaginous scroll creates a double bony lamella when the cartilage resorbs. The inferior concha detaches from the ectethmoid to become an independent bone.

### Sphenoid Bone

This multicomposite bone has up to 19 intramembranous and endochondral ossification centers. Its central body, the basisphenoid, derives from the basicranial cartilage, whereas its wings and pterygoid plates have both cartilaginous and intramembranous ossification centers.

The sphenoid body is derived from presphenoid and postsphenoid (basisphenoid) centers. A single median and two paired presphenoid ossification centers arise in the fourth month pc in the mesethmoid portion of the tuberculum sellae. The postsphenoid bone, arising from two sets of paired centers in the basisphenoid cartilage on either side of the upwardly projecting hypophyseal (Rathke's) pouch during the fourth month pc, forms the sella turcica, the dorsum sellae and basisphenoid (in which the notochord terminates). Coalescence of the ossification centers obliterates the orohypophyseal track; persistence of the track as a craniopharyngeal canal in the sphenoid body gives rise to craniopharyngeal tumors.

Endochondral ossification centers for the greater wings of the sphenoid appear in the alisphenoid cartilages, and for the lesser wings in the orbitosphenoid cartilages. Also, intramembranous ossification centers appear in the eighth week pc for parts of the greater wings and for the medial and lateral pterygoid plates.

The medial pterygoid plates ossify endochondrally from secondary cartilages in their hamular processes. In many fetuses, the pterygoid hamulus is a distinct, fully ossified bone at birth; it is, with the alisphenoid, the first sphenoidal elements to ossify (early in the eighth week). The hamulus is initially demarcated by a suture from the medial pterygoid plate.

Adjacent to the projecting cranial end of the basisphenoid are the paired, initially separate, sphenoidal conchae (bones of Bertin), which are incorporated into the sphenoid body postnatally and into which the sphenoidal sinuses later invaginate.

The midsphenoidal synchondrosis between the presphenoid and postsphenoid fuses shortly before birth. In most mammals other than humans, this synchondrosis fuses late postnatally or not at all. The basisphenoid and alisphenoids are still separated at birth by mixed cartilaginous/ligamentous articulations. The basisphenoid articulates chondrally with the basioccipital and ligamentously with the petrosal bone. Normally, the spheno-occipital synchondrosis fuses in adolescence (see p. 112); its premature fusion in infancy results in a depressed nasal bridge and the "dished" face that characterizes many craniofacial anomalies.

## CRANIAL BASE

The chondrocranium is important as a shared junction between the neurocranial and facial skeletons: its endocranial surface relates to the brain, whereas its ectocranial aspect responds to the pharynx and facial complex and their muscles. The cranial base is relatively stable during growth compared with the calvaria and face, providing some basis against which the growth of the latter skull elements can be compared. The extremely rapid growth of the neurocranium, particularly the calvaria, contrasts with the slower, more prolonged growth of the facial skeleton. The chondrocranial base of the newborn skull is smaller than the calvarial desmocranial part, which extends beyond the base laterally and posteriorly. The relative stability of the chondrocranium maintains the early established relationships of the blood vessels, cranial nerves and spinal cord running through it from their sources to their destinations.

## CRANIAL BASE ANGULATION

The central region of the cranial base is composed of prechordal (located rostrally) and chordal parts which meet at an angle at the hypophyseal fossa (sella turcica). The lower angle, formed by lines from nasion to sella to basion in the sagittal plane (Fig. 8–7), is initially highly obtuse: approximately 150° in the 4-week-old embryo (precartilage stage); it flexes to approximately 130° in the 7- to 8-week-old embryo (cartilage stage) and becomes more acute (115° to 120°) at 10 weeks (preossification stage). Between 6 and 10 weeks, the whole head is raised by extension of the neck, lifting the face from the thorax (see Fig. 10–4). This head extension is concomitant with palatal fusion. At the time of ossification of the cranial base, between 10 to 20 weeks, the cranial base angle widens to between 125° and 130°, and maintains this angulation postnatally. The flattening of the cranial base is probably caused by rapid growth of the brain during the fetal period, as the chondrocranium retains its preossification acute flexure in anencephaly.

Growth of the cranial base is highly uneven, in keeping with the highly irregular shape it develops to accommodate the undulating ventral surface of the brain. The uneven growth of the parts of the brain is reflected

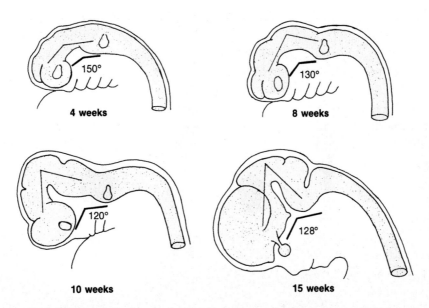

**Figure 8–7** The mesencephalic flexure angles within the brain and the cranial base angles (indicated by heavy angulated lines) at various ages.

in the adaption of related parts of the cranial base as compartments or cranial fossae. The diencephalon is the most precocious in growth, the telencephalon next, and the rhombencephalon (with cerebellum) the least advanced. The anterior and posterior parts of the cranial base, demarcated at the sella turcica, grow at different rates. Between the 10th and 40th weeks pc, the anterior cranial base increases its length and width sevenfold, but the posterior cranial base grows only fivefold. Growth of the central ventral axis of the brain (the brainstem), and of the related body of the sphenoid and basioccipital bones is slow, providing a comparatively stable base. Around this base, the anterior, middle and posterior fossae of the cranial floor, related to the frontal and temporal lobes of the cerebrum and the cerebellum respectively, expand enormously, in keeping with the exuberant efflorescence of these parts of the brain (Figs. 8–8 and 8–9).

Expansion of the cranial base takes place as a result of (1) growth of the cartilage remnants of the chondrocranium that persist between the bones, and (2) expansive forces emanating from the growing brain (a capsular functional matrix) displacing the bones at the suture lines (Fig. 8–10).

By their interstitial growth, the interposed cartilages, known as synchondroses, can separate the adjacent bones as appositional bone growth adds to their sutural edges. Thus, growth of the bones within the ventral midline, the cribriform plate of the ethmoid, the presphenoid and basisphenoid and the basioccipital bones contribute to growth of the cranial base. The cartilages between these bones contribute variably to cranial elongation and lateral expansion. Growth in anteroposterior length of the anterior cranial fossa depends on growth at the sphenofrontal, frontoethmoidal and sphenoethmoidal sutures. The last two sutures cease

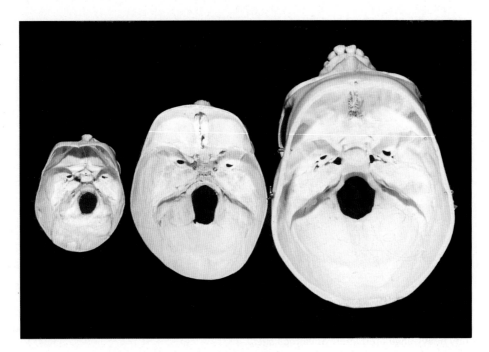

**Figure 8–8** The cranial bases of a neonate (left), a 1-year-old child (center) and an adult (right) demonstrating the relatively small amount of growth in the brainstem area (sella turcica, clivus and foramen magnum) compared with enormous expansion of the surrounding parts. Note also the thickening of the calvarial bones from infancy to adulthood, and the beginning of development of diploë in the 1-year-old skull.

contributing to sagittal plane growth after the age of 7 years. The internal surfaces of the frontal bone and cribriform plate cease remodeling at about 4 years, thereby becoming stable from about 6 to 7 years of age. Further growth of the anterior cranial base (anterior to the foramen cecum) is associated with expansion of the developing frontal air sinuses.

Postnatal growth in the spheno-occipital synchondrosis* is the major contributor to growth of the cranial base, persisting into early adulthood. This prolonged growth period allows for continued posterior expansion of the maxilla to accommodate later erupting molar teeth and provides space for the growing nasopharynx. The spheno-occipital synchondrosis is the last of the synchondroses to fuse, beginning on its cerebral surface at 12 to 13 years in girls and 14 to 15 years in boys and completing ossification of the external aspect by 20 years of age.

In addition to proliferative synchondrosal growth, the cranial base undergoes selective remodelling by resorption and deposition. The clivus, while resorbing on its cerebral surface, shows apposition on the nasopha-

---

*Prenatally, this synchondrosis is not a major growth site. Postnatally, greater bone deposition occurs on the occipital than on the sphenoidal side of the synchondrosis which proliferates interstitially in its midzone. Continued growth of the inferior aspect of the synchondrosis after fusion of its superior (cerebral) surface would result in upward, backward displacement of the basiocciput relative to the sphenoid, tending to flatten the spheno-occipital angle and thus the cranial base. This tendency is counteracted by internal resorption of the clivus, thereby maintaining a fairly constant spheno-occipital angle during growth.

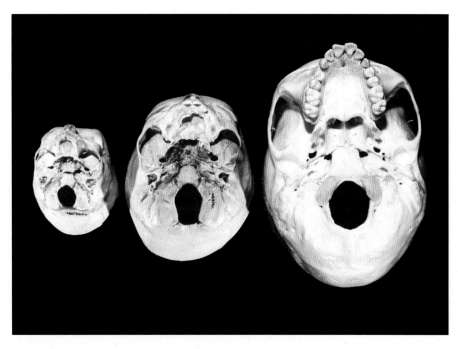

**Figure 8–9** The skull bases of a neonate (left), a 1-year-old child (center) and an adult (right), demonstrating the extent of anterior facial growth.

ryngeal (inferior) surface of the basioccipital bone and the anterior margin of the foramen magnum; thus it can continue to lengthen after closure of the spheno-occipital synchondrosis. To maintain the size of the foramen magnum, resorption occurs at its posterior margin. The separate squamous, condylar and basilar parts of the occipital bone fuse together only after birth. The temporal bone is composed of separate petrous, squamous, styloid and tympanic ring parts at birth, when their union begins. At birth, the temporal mandibular fossa is flat and lacks an articular tubercle; the occipital condyles also are flat and will become prominent only during childhood.

During growth, marked resorption in the floors of the cranial fossae deepens these endocranial compartments, a process aided by displacement of the floors of the fossae by sutural expansion of the lateral walls of the neurocranium. Enlargement of the sella turcica is due to remodeling of its inner contour; although its anterior wall is stable by 5 to 6 years of age, its posterior wall, and to a varying extent its floor, is resorbing until 16 to 17 years of age.* Parts of the petrous portion of the temporal bone do not resorb, and are sites of some bone deposition.

Phylogenetically, the oldest portion of the skull, the cranial base, is also the most conservative in growth of the main elements of the skull. The differing areas of sutural accretion, surface deposition and resorption of bone, and the displacement, flexing and readjustments of the bones of

*Owing to the variable remodeling that occurs in the sella turcica, the reference point sella (the center of the sella turcica) cannot be regarded as stable until well after puberty.

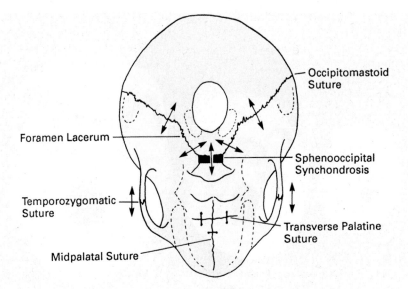

**Figure 8–10** Directions of growth of cranial base bones at suture sites, accounting for multidirectional expansion of the cranial base.

the cranial base to each other, provide an extremely complicated pattern of overall growth. The dependence of the juxtaposed calvaria and facial skeleton upon the cranial base confers considerable significance upon the latter's growth behavior in determining the final shape and size of the cranium, and, ultimately, the morphology of the entire skull, including the occlusion of the dentition. Inadequate chondrocranial growth precludes allocation of sufficient space for full eruption of all the teeth, particularly if the maxilla is small. This leads to impacted eruption of the last teeth to emerge, namely, the third molars.

## ANOMALIES OF DEVELOPMENT

In anencephaly, absence of the calvaria results in cranioschisis, characterized by a short, narrow, lordotic chondrocranium, in many cases with notochordal anomalies (see Fig. 3–18).

Afflictions of cartilage growth produce a reduced cranial base with increased angulation, due to loss of the flattening effects of growth of the spheno-occipital synchondrosis. This results in a "dished" deformity of the middle third of the facial skeleton, accentuated by a bulging of the neurocranium. Such diverse conditions as achondroplasia, cretinism and Down syndrome (trisomy 21) all produce a similar characteristic facial deformity by their inhibiting effect on chondrocranial growth. Anencephalics retain the acute cranial base flexure typical of early fetuses; this suggests that brain growth contributes to flattening of the cranial base.

Certain forms of dental malocclusion may be related to defects of the chondrocranium that minimize the space available for the maxillary dentition.

# SELECTED BIBLIOGRAPHY

Declau F, Jacob W, Dorrine W, et al. Early ossification within the human fetal otic capsule: morphological and microanalytical findings. J Laryng Otol 1989; 103:1113–1121.

Declau F, Jacob W, Dorrine W, Marquet J. Early bone formation in the human fetal otic capsule. A methodological approach. Acta Otolaryngol Suppl 1990; 470:56–60.

Dimitriadis AS, Haritani-Kouridou A, Antoniadis K, Ekonomou L. The human skull base angle during the second trimester of gestation. Neuroradiology 1995; 37:68–71.

Hallgrimson B, Lieberman DE, Liu W et al. Epigenetic interactions and the structure of phenotypic variations in the cranium. Evol Dev 2007; 9:76–91.

Jeffrey N, Spoor F. Ossification and midline shape changes of the human fetal cranial base. Am J Phys Anthrop 2004; 123:78–90

Jeffery N. A high resolution MRI study of linear growth of the human fetal skull base. Neuroradiology 2002; 44:358–366.

Kjaer I, Becktor KB, Nolting D, Fischer-Hansen B. The association between prenatal sella turcica morphology and notochordal remnants in the dorsum sellae. J Craniofac Genet Dev Biol 1997; 17:105–111.

Kjaer I, Fischer-Hansen B. The adenohypophysis and the cranial base in early human development. J Craniofac Genet Dev Biol 1995; 15:157–161.

Kjaer I, Keeling JW, Fischer-Hansen B. The prenatal human cranium—normal and pathologic development. Copenhagen: Munksgaard, 1999.

Kjaer I, Keeling JW, Graem N. Cranial base and vertebral column in human anencephalic fetuses. J Craniofac Genet Dev Biol 1994; 14:235–244.

Kjaer I, Keeling JW, Graem N. Midline maxillofacial skeleton in human anencephalic fetuses. Cleft Palate-Craniofac J 1994; 31:250–256.

Kjaer I, Keeling JW, Reintoft I, et al. Pituitary gland and sella turcica in human trisomy 21 fetuses related to axial skeletal development. Am J Med Genet 1998; 80:494–500.

Krmpotic-Nemanic J, Padovan I, Vinter I, Jalsovec D. Development of the cribriform plate and of the lamina mediana. Anat Anz 1998; 180:555–559.

Krmpotic Nemanic J, Vinter I, Kelovic Z. Ossicula Bertini in human adults. Anat Anz 1998; 180:55–57.

Lee SK, Kim YS, Jo YA, et al. Prenatal development of cranial base in normal Korean fetuses. Anat Rec 1996; 246:524–534.

Marin-Padilla M. Cephalic axial skeletal-neural dysraphic disorders: embryology and pathology. Can J of Neurol Sci 1991; 18:153–169.

McBratney-Owen B, Iseki S, Bamforth SD, et al. Development and tissue origins of the mammalian cranial base. Dev Biol 2008; 322: 121–132.

Molsted K, Kjaer I, Dahl E. Cranial base in newborns with complete cleft lip and palate: radiographic study [see comments]. Cleft Palate-Craniofac J 1995; 32:199–205.

Morimoto N, Ogihara N, Katayama K, Shiota K. Three-dimensional ontogenetic shape changes in the human cranium during the fetal period. J Anat 2008; 212:627–635.

Ricciardelli FJ. Embryology and anatomy of the cranial base. Clin Plast Surg 1995; 22:361–372.

Ronning O. Basicranial synchondroses and the mandibular condyle in craniofacial growth. Acta Odontol Scand 1995; 53:162–166.

Seirsen B, Jakobsen J, Skovgaard LT, Kjaer I. Growth in the external cranial base evaluated on human dry skulls, using nerve canal openings as references. Acta Odontol Scand 1997; 55:356–364.

# 9 Facial Skeleton

The face may be conveniently, if somewhat arbitrarily, divided into thirds—the upper, middle and lower—their boundaries being approximately the horizontal planes passing through the pupils of the eyes and the rima oris. The three parts correspond generally to the embryonic frontonasal, maxillary and mandibular prominences, respectively (see p. 39). The upper third of the face is predominantly of neurocranial composition, with the frontal bone of the calvaria being primarily responsible for the forehead. The middle third is skeletally the most complex, composed in part of the cranial base and incorporating both the nasal extension of the upper third and part of the masticatory apparatus (including the maxillary dentition). The lower third of the face completes the masticatory apparatus, being composed skeletally of the mandible and its dentition.

The upper third of the face initially grows the most rapidly, in keeping with its neurocranial association and the precocious development of the frontal lobes of the brain. It is also the first to achieve its ultimate growth potential, ceasing to grow significantly after 12 years of age. In contrast, the middle and lower thirds grow more slowly over a prolonged period, not ceasing growth until late adolescence (Fig. 9–1). Completion of the masticatory apparatus by eruption of the third molars (18 to 25 years of age) marks the cessation of growth of the lower two-thirds of the face (Fig. 9–2).

The facial bones develop intramembranously from ossification centers in the neural crest mesenchyme of the embryonic facial prominences (Fig. 9–3 and Table 9–1). An epithelial-mesenchymal interaction between the

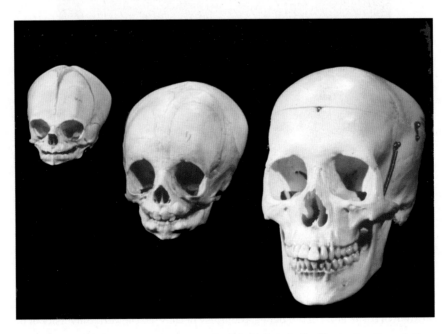

Figure 9–1 Neonatal (left), 1-year (center) and adult (right) skulls, illustrating the relative growth of the face and neurocranium. Note the enormous expansion of the face in the adult relative to the neonate. Note the midmandibular and frontal sutures in the neonate.

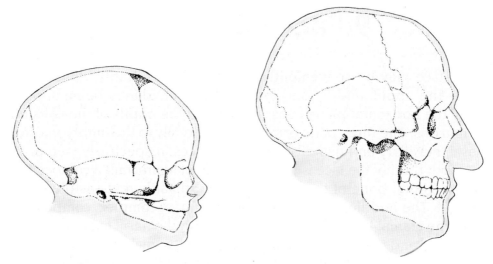

**Figure 9–2** Lateral aspects of the skulls of a neonate and adult illustrating the relative growth of the face and the neurocranium.

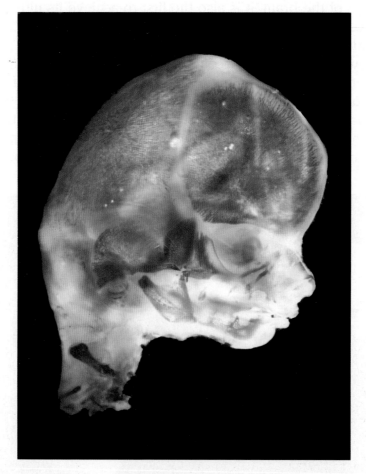

**Figure 9–3** Head of a 16-week-old fetus stained with alizarin red and alcian blue and cleared to show the extent of ossification of the bones. (Courtesy of Dr. V. H. Diewert, University of British Columbia.)

**TABLE 9–1: Intramembranous Ossification Centers**

| Bone | Site and Number of Ossification Oenters | | Initial Appearance |
|---|---|---|---|
| | Primary centers | Secondary centers | |
| Frontal | Superciliary arch (2) | | 8 weeks |
| | | Trochlear fossa (2) | 8.5 weeks |
| | | Zygomatic process (2) | 9 weeks |
| | | Nasal spine (2) | 10–12 years |
| Parietal | Eminence (2) | | 8 weeks |
| Occipital (interparietal) | Supranuchal squamous (medial) (2) | | 8 weeks |
| | | Supranuchal squamous (lateral) (2) | 12 weeks |
| Temporal (desmocranial portion) | Squamous/ zygomatic (1) | | 8 weeks |
| | Tympanic ring (4) | | 12 weeks |
| Nasal | Central (1) | | 8 weeks |
| Lacrimal | Central (1) | | 8–12 weeks |
| Maxilla | Body (1) | | 7 weeks |
| | | Zygomatic (1) | 8 weeks |
| | | Orbitonasal (1) | 8 weeks |
| | | Nasopalatine (1) | 8 weeks |
| Premaxilla | Intermaxillary (2) | | 7 weeks |
| Palatine | Jnctn. horiz./perp. plates (1) | | 8 weeks |
| Vomer | Alae (2) | | 8 weeks |
| Mandible | Body (1) | | 6–7 weeks |
| | | Coronoid, condylar | 10–14 weeks |
| | | Mental ossicles | 7 months pc |
| Zygomatic | Body (1) | | 8 weeks |

ectomesenchyme of the facial prominences and the overlying ectodermal epithelium is essential for the differentiation of the facial bones.

The ossification centers for the upper third of the face are those of the frontal bone, which contributes also to the anterior part of the neurocranium. As the *frontal bone* is also a component of the calvaria, details of its ossification are given in Chapter 7 (see p.96).

In the frontonasal prominence, intramembranous single ossification centers appear in the eighth week for each of the *nasal* and *lacrimal* bones in the membrane covering the cartilaginous nasal capsule. The embryonic facial maxillary prominences develop numerous intramembranous ossification centers. The first centers to appear, early in the eighth week post-conception (pc), are those for the *medial pterygoid plates* of the *sphenoid* bone and for the *vomer*. The ossification center for the medial pterygoid plate first appears in a nodule of secondary cartilage that forms the *pterygoid hamulus*, but subsequent ossification of this plate is intramembranous. Further intramembranous centers develop for the *greater wing of the sphenoid* (in addition to its endochondral alisphenoidal center) and the *lateral pterygoid plate*. Bony fusion of the medial and lateral pterygoid plates takes place in the fifth month pc. For other details of sphenoid bone development, see Chapter 8 (p. 113). Single ossification centers appear for each of the palatine bones, and two bilaterally for the vomer in the maxillary mesenchyme surrounding the cartilaginous nasal septum in the eighth week pc. For further details of vomer development, see Chapter 8 (p. 106).

A primary intramembranous ossification center appears for each maxilla in the seventh week at the termination of the infraorbital nerve just above the canine tooth dental lamina. Secondary zygomatic, orbitonasal, nasopalatine and intermaxillary ossification centers appear and fuse rapidly with the primary centers.

The two intermaxillary ossification centers generate the alveolar ridge and primary palate region that is homologous with the premaxilla in other mammals. In humans, this area encloses the four maxillary incisor teeth; in the neonate, it is demarcated by a lateral fissure from the incisive foramen to between the lateral incisor and canine teeth, forming the so-called *os incisivum*. This bone disappears as a separate entity by fusion of the fissure in the first postnatal year.

Single ossification centers appear for each of the *zygomatic bones* and the *squamous portions of the temporal bones* in the eighth week pc. In the lower third of the face, the mandibular prominences develop bilateral single intramembranous centers for the *mandible* and four minute centers for the *tympanic ring* of the temporal bone.

The attachment of the facial skeleton anteroinferiorly to the calvarial base determines the chondrocranial influence on facial growth. The sites of attachment are clearly defined by the pterygomaxillary fissure and pterygopalatine fossa between the sphenoid bone of the calvarial base and the maxillary and palatine bones of the posterior aspect of the face. The zygomatic bone is attached to the calvarial skeleton at the temporozygomatic and frontozygomatic sutures. The maxillary and nasal bones of the anterior aspect are attached to the calvaria at the frontomaxillary and frontonasal sutures. The interposition of three sets of space-occupying sense organs between the neural and facial skeletons complicates the attachments of these two skull components to each other, and influences the growth of the facial skeleton in particular. The eye, the nasal cavity, and its septum, and the external ear, situated along the approximate boundaries of the upper and middle thirds of the face, act to some extent as functional matrices in determining certain aspects of the growth pattern of the face. The tongue, teeth and oromasticatory musculature are similarly interposed between the middle and lower thirds of the face, and their functioning also influences facial skeletal growth.

Growth of the eyes provides an expanding force separating the neural and facial skeletons, particularly at the frontomaxillary and frontozygomatic sutures, thereby contributing to skull height. The eyes appear to migrate medially from their initially lateral situation in the primitive face as a result of the enormous expansion of the frontal and temporal lobes of the brain in early cranial development. The forward-directed eyes of humans (and higher primates) confer a capability for stereoscopic vision and depth perception.

The eyeballs initially grow rapidly, following the neural pattern of growth and contributing to rapid widening of the fetal face. The orbits complete half their postnatal growth during the first 2 years after birth, and thus appear disproportionately large in the child's face. The brain and eyeball, growing concomitantly in a similarly rapid pattern, "compete" for space; the final form of the intervening orbital wall reflects mutual adjustment between these competing functional matrices. The orbital cavities attain their adult dimensions at about 7 years of age.

The nasal cavity, and in particular the nasal septum, have considerable influence in determining facial form. In the fetus, a septomaxillary ligament arising from the sides and anteroinferior border of the nasal septum, and inserting into the anterior nasal spine, transmits septal growth "pull" upon the maxilla. Facial growth is directed downward and forward by the septal cartilage which, between the 10th and 40th weeks pc, expands its vertical length sevenfold. At birth, the nasal cavity lies almost entirely between the orbits; growth of the nasal septal cartilage continues, but at a decreasing rate, until the age of 6, lowering the nasal cavity floor below the orbits.

The thrust and pull created by nasal septal growth separate to varying degrees the frontomaxillary, frontonasal, frontozygomatic and zygomaticomaxillary sutures. The growth potential of the nasal septal cartilage is clearly demonstrated in cases of bilateral cleft lip and palate: the tip of the nose, columella, philtrum, prolabium and primary palate form a "proboscis," which, freed from its lateral attachments to the maxillae, protrudes conspicuously on the face as a result of vomerine and nasal septal growth (see Fig. 3–23). This growth thrust normally dissipates into adjacent facial structures, indicating some resistance to its growth thrust. It is of interest that the nasal septum deflects from the midline during late childhood, indicating some resistance to septal growth thrust. The expansion of the eyeballs, the brain, and the spheno-occipital synchondrosal cartilage also acts variously in separating the facial sutures. Furthermore, the situation of these sutures later subjects them to forces exerted by the masticatory muscles, in having to buttress against masticatory pressures transmitted through adjacent bones.

Growth of the maxilla depends upon the influence of several functional matrices that act upon different areas of the bone, thus theoretically allowing its subdivision into "skeletal units" (Fig. 9–4). The "basal body" develops beneath the infraorbital nerve, later surrounding it to form the infraorbital canal. The "orbital unit" responds to the growth of the eyeball; the "nasal unit" depends upon the septal cartilage for its growth; and the teeth provide the functional matrix for the "alveolar unit." The "pneumatic unit" reflects maxillary sinus expansion, which is more a responder than a determiner of this skeletal unit. Development of the maxillary sinus is further described in Chapter 11 (see p. 145).

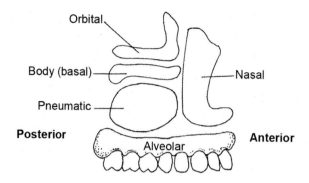

Figure 9–4 Schema of "skeletal units" of the maxilla.

The complexity of action of these functional forces on the facial bones results in different effects on different sutures (Fig. 9–5). Thus, the temporozygomatic suture in the zygomatic arch grows predominantly in an anteroposterior horizontal direction, largely due to the longitudinal growth of the brain and the spheno-occipital synchondrosal cartilage. The anteroposterior growth at the nasomaxillary sutures, creating the elevated bridge of the nose, results from anteroposterior nasal septal expansion. The frontomaxillary, frontozygomatic, frontonasal, ethmoidomaxillary and frontoethmoidal sutures are the sites of bone growth in a largely vertical direction as a result of eyeball and nasal septal expansion. If growth of the nasal septum is defective, the height of the middle third of the face is less affected than its anteroposterior dimension, resulting in concavity of the face. Lateral expansion of the zygomaticomaxillary sutures by the eyes

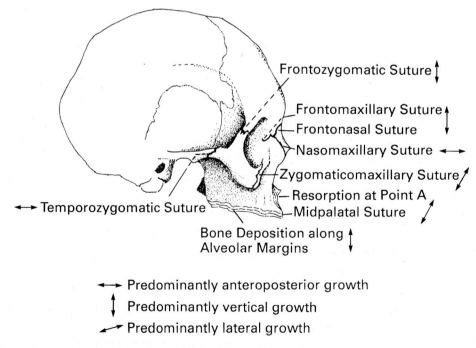

Figure 9–5 Directions of growth and resorption of the facial bones at various sites. The overall effect of the combination of these growth sites is a downward and forward displacement of the face vis-à-vis the cranial base.

and growth at the intermaxillary suture contribute to the widening of the face. Facial width is relatively less in proportion to the neurocranium in the neonate than in the adult. The face of the newborn is twice as broad in comparison with its height than in the adult, and adjusts to adult proportions during the childhood years.

The overall effect of these diverse directions of growth is osseous accretion predominantly on the posterior and superior surfaces of the facial bones. Encapsulated fatty tissue, interposed between the posterosuperior surfaces of the maxilla and the cranial base (sphenoid bone), provides a compression-resisting structure. Bone deposition on the posterosuperior maxillary surface and in the region of the maxillary alveolar tuberosity displaces the maxilla away from this retromaxillary fat pad. With fat pads and the chondrocranium acting as a base against which facial bone growth takes place, the middle (and, as will be seen later, the lower) third of the face moves in a marked downward and slightly forward direction vis-à-vis the cranial base. Growth at these sutures sites is greatest until the age of 4 years. Thereafter, these sutures function mainly as sites of fibrous union of the skull bones, allowing for adjustments brought by surface apposition and remodeling.

Remodeling takes place on all bone surfaces to adjust the bones to their new positions after displacement. Of particular interest is the deposition of bone along the alveolar margins of the maxillae (and mandible), forming incipient alveolar processes in which tooth germs are developing. When tooth germs are congenitally absent, these processes fail to develop. The growth of the alveolar processes adds considerably to the vertical height of the face and the depth of the palate, and allows concomitant expansion of the maxillary sinuses. Bone deposition on the posterior surface of the maxillary tuberosity induces corresponding anterior displacement of the entire maxilla. Eruption of teeth initially located immediately subjacent to the orbit accentuates both vertical and posterior growth of the maxillae. The growth pattern of the dental alveolar arch differs from that of the facial skeleton, being related to the sequence of tooth eruption. Resorption along the anterior surface of the bodies of the maxillae creates the supraalveolar concavity (Point A in orthodontic parlance), thus emphasizing the projection of the anterior nasal spine of the maxilla.

The empty space of the nasal cavity may also influence facial growth and form. Inadequate use of the nasal cavity by mouth breathing has been associated with the narrow pinched face and high-vaulted palatal arch of the "adenoidal facies," so-called because of a postulated association with hypertrophied pharyngeal tonsils or adenoids. The cause-and-effect relationship of this particular (inherited?) facial form with mouth-breathing, if any, has not been substantiated.

The role of the ear, as a space-occupying sense organ in determining facial form, is somewhat ambiguous, and is probably minimal. The otic capsule that houses the vestibulocochlear apparatus completes its ossification from 14 centers to form the petrous temporal bone at the time that the internal ear approaches its adult size in the latter part of the fifth and early in the sixth month of fetal life. The inner ear is the only organ that approaches adult size by this age. This early completion minimizes any influence on subsequent growth of the cranial skeleton. However, the location of the inner and middle ears in the floor of the cranial cavity necessarily results in encroachment of the vestibulocochlear organ on the brain space between the middle and posterior endocranial fossae. Together with the deposition of osseous tissue on the endocranial surface of the petrous temporal bone, this infringement on brain space may cause compensatory increases of the cranial cavity in other directions.

## ANOMALIES OF DEVELOPMENT

Maldevelopment of the face may arise from aberrations of morphogenesis at many levels of development and may be genetically or environmentally determined. Many congenital abnormalities originate in maldevelopment of neural crest tissue (neurocristopathy) that gives rise to much of the skeletal and connective tissue primordia of the face. Neural crest cells may be deficient in number, may not complete migration to their destination or fail in their inductive capacity or cytodifferentiation. Also, a failure of ectoderm or endoderm matrix to respond to neural crest induction may give rise to facial defects.

Absence or insufficiency of neural crest ectomesenchyme in the frontonasal prominence may result in cleft lips. Deficiencies of maxillary prominence and pharyngeal arch ectomesenchyme (possibly because of the long path of neural crest migration) may result in absent facial bones. The clinical syndrome of mandibulofacial dysostosis (Treacher Collins syndrome), with its sunken cheeks, is due to severe hypoplasia or absence of the zygomatic bones. Deficient facial bone development in anhidrotic ectodermal dysplasia, with its "dished" face, may reflect defective mechanisms of ectodermal induction by neural crest tissue. Down syndrome (trisomy 21) features less proclined and shortened or even absent nasal bones, accounting for the characteristic "saddle nose" and a maxilla of subnormal size. Deficient maxillary development may also be associated with clefts of the upper lip and palate (Fig. 9–6).

Incomplete brain development (holoprosencephaly) greatly influences facial formation. An extreme defect arising from holoprosencephaly is a median eye (cyclopia) (see Fig. 3–19). In normal development, the distance separating the eyes greatly influences the character of the face. A narrow interocular distance (*hypotelorism*) confers a sharp "foxy" appearance to the face; ocular *hypertelorism*, characterized by an abnormally wide interorbital distance, confers a "wide-eyed" appearance. This latter mild developmental defect is due to an embryological morphokinetic arrest that leaves the orbits in a fetal position: the nasal bones and cribriform plate of the ethmoid remain especially widened and the sphenoid bone is enlarged. A more severe form of hypertelorism results in a bifid nose.

The ectomesenchymal and mesodermal deficiencies that produce these abnormalities are occasionally due to chromosomal anomalies and

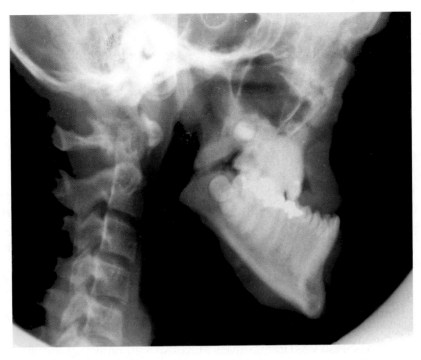

**Figure 9–6** Radiograph of deficient maxillary development in a 16-year-old boy who also manifested a right-sided cleft of the lip and palate. The mandible is overgrown.

mutant genes, but environmental factors are involved in most cases. Facial clefts, including those afflicting the lips and palate, are components of over 250 named syndromes, many of which are of single gene inheritance.

Unilateral defective facial development (hemifacial microsomia) produces an asymmetrical face. The underdeveloped structures on the affected side are the ear, including the ear ossicles (microtia), zygomatic bone, and mandible. In addition, the parotid gland, tongue and facial muscles are unilaterally defective. This condition results from a destructive hematoma emanating from the primitive stapedial artery at about the 32nd day of development.

Congenital excrescences of abnormal facial growth may occur as midline frontal or nasal masses; they include encephaloceles, gliomas and dermoid cysts. Congenital invaginations of the face constitute dermal sinuses and fistulae. There is intracranial communication in many of these facial anomalies through defects of the cranial bones. Herniation of the intracranial contents through the frontonasal, fronto-ethmoidal or frontosphenoidal complexes occurs if the foramen cecum of the ethmoid-frontal bone fails to close (see Fig. 7–3).

Other defects of facial development have been dealt with on p. 55.

## SELECTED BIBLIOGRAPHY

Arnold WH, Sperber GH, Machin GA. Cranio-facial skeletal development in three human synophthalmic holoprosencephalic fetuses. Anat Anz 1998; 180: 45–53.

Cussenot O, Zouaoui A, Hidden G. Growth of the facial bones of the fetus. Surg Radiol Anat 1990; 12:230–231.

Flugel C, Schram K, Rohen JW. Postnatal development of skull base, neuro- and viscerocranium in man and monkey: morphometric evaluation of CT scans and radiograms. Acta Anat 1993; 146:71–80.

Gill PP, VanHook J, FitzSimmons J, et al. Upper face morphology of second-trimester fetuses. Early Human Dev 1994; 37:99–106.

Guis F, Ville Y, Vincent Y, et al. Ultrasound evaluation of the length of the fetal nasal bones throughout gestation. Ultrasound Obstet Gynecol 1995; 5:304–307.

Kimes KR, Mooney MP, Siegel MI, Todhunter JS. Growth rate of the vomer in normal and cleft lip and palate human fetal specimens. Cleft Palate-Craniofac J 1992; 29:38–42.

Kjaer I. Prenatal skeletal maturation of the human maxilla. J Craniofac Genet Dev Biol 1989; 9:257–264.

Kjaer I. Correlated appearance of ossification and nerve tissue in human fetal jaws. J Craniofac Genet Dev Biol 1990; 10:329–336.

Lee SK, Kim YS, Lim CY, Chi JG. Prenatal growth pattern of the human maxilla. Acta Anat 1992; 145:1–10.

Mandarim-de-Lacerda CA, Urania-Alves M. Growth allometry of the human face: analysis of the osseous component of the mid and lower face in Brazilian fetuses. Anat Anz 1993; 175:475–479.

Nemzek WR, Brodie HA, Chong BW, et al. Imaging findings of the developing temporal bone in fetal specimens. AJNR: Am J Neuroradiol 1996; 17:1467–1477.

Niida S, Yamanoto S, Kodama H. Variations in the running pattern of trabeculae in growing human nasal bones. J Anat 1991; 179:39–41.

Piza JE, Northrop CC, Eavey RD. Neonatal mesenchyme temporal bone study: typical receding pattern versus increase in Potter's sequence. Laryngoscope 1996; 107:856–864.

Sandikcioglu M, Molsted K, Kjaer I. The prenatal development of the human nasal and vomeral bones. J Craniofac Genet Dev Biol 1994; 14:124–134.

Siegel MI, Mooney MP, Kimes KR, Todhunter J. Developmental correlates of mid-facial components in a normal and cleft lip and palate human fetal sample. Cleft Palate-Craniofac J 1991; 28:408–412.

# 10 Palate

In its embryological development, the human palate passes through stages representing divisions of the oronasal chamber found in primitive crossopterygian fish, reptiles and early mammals. Development of internal nares, or choanae, marks the adoption of air breathing by establishing a connection between the olfactory sacs and the stomodeum. The separation of a continuous respiratory channel (the nostrils) from an intermittently required food ingestion channel (the mouth) enabled the development of leisurely mastication without respiratory interference. This separation occurs only anteriorly, since the nasopharynx and oropharynx share a common channel posteriorly, accounting for momentary asphyxiation during swallowing. However, in the neonate and infant until 6 months of age, concomitant breathing and swallowing occurs as a result of the epiglottis and soft palate being in contact, maintaining a continuous airway between the nasopharynx and laryngopharynx. Milk passes on either side of this airway channel into the esophagus. An oropharynx only develops upon descent of the larynx, thus separating the soft palate from the epiglottis.

The existence of an intact palate has enabled sophisticated masticatory movements and epicurian enjoyment to evolve by virtue of the taste and texture senses embedded in the palate, accounting for the popular concept of the palate being the seat of taste, hence "palatable." Moreover, an intact palate is quintessential for the production of normal speech. Deficiencies of palatal development will result in food and salivary spillage into the nostrils and impaired speech articulation.

The three elements that make up the secondary definitive palate—the two lateral maxillary palatal shelves and the primary palate of the frontonasal prominence—initially are widely separated because of the vertical orientation of the lateral shelves on either side of the tongue (see Figs. 3–12, 3–14 and 3–16). During the eighth week pc, a remarkable transformation in position of the lateral shelves takes place, when they alter from vertical to horizontal as a prelude to their fusion and partitioning the oronasal chamber (Figs. 10–1 to 10–3).

The transition from vertical to horizontal position is completed within hours.* Several mechanisms have been proposed for this rapid elevation of the palatal shelves, including biochemical transformations in the physical consistency of the connective tissue matrix of the shelves; variations in vasculature and blood flow to these structures; a sudden increase in their tissue turgor; rapid differential mitotic growth; an "intrinsic shelf force"; and muscular movements. The intrinsic shelf-elevating force is chiefly generated by accumulation and hydration of hyaluronic acid. The alignment

---

*There is a considerable sex difference in the timing of human palatal closure. Shelf elevation and fusion begin a few days earlier in male than in female embryos, possibly accounting for sex differences in the incidence of cleft palates.

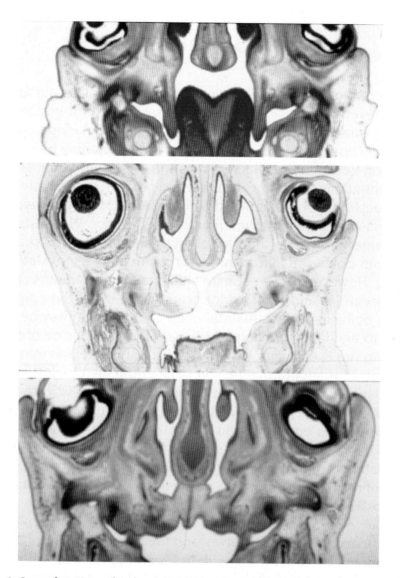

**Figure 10–1** Coronal sections of embryos at 7.5 (top) 8 (middle), and 9 (bottom) weeks depicting palatal shelf elevation and fusion. (Figure courtesy of Dr. Virginia Diewert and Carnegie Embryo Collection.)

of mesenchymal cells within the palatal shelves may serve to direct the elevating forces while palatal mesenchymal cells are themselves contractile. The withdrawal of the fetus's face from against the heart prominence by uprighting of the head facilitates jaw opening (Fig. 10–4). Mouth-opening reflexes have been implicated in the withdrawal of the tongue from between the vertical shelves, and pressure differences between the nasal and oral regions due to tongue muscle contraction may account for palatal shelf elevation.

During palate closure, the mandible becomes more prognathic, the vertical dimension of the stomodeal chamber increases, but maxillary width remains stable, allowing shelf contact to occur. Also, forward growth of Meckel's cartilage relocates the tongue more anteriorly, concomitant with upper facial elevation.

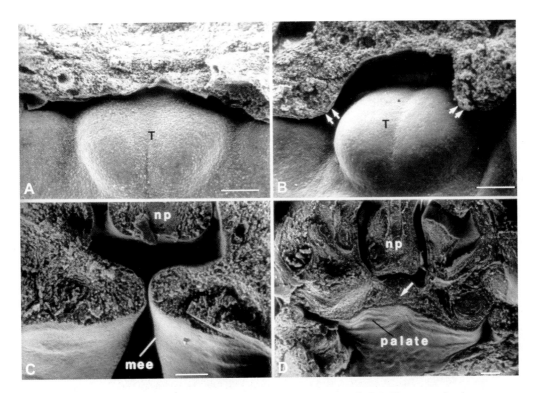

**Figure 10–2**  Coronal scanning electron micrographs of mouse embryos at stages of palatogenesis corresponding to human embryos at A: 40 days; B: 50 days; C: 56 days; D: 60 days; T: tongue; np: nasal prominence (septum); mee: medial edge epithelium. (Courtesy of Dr. H. C. Slavkin.)

The palatal shelves are not homogeneous along their dorsoventral length. They exhibit heterogeneous patterns that divide the fetal palate into several discrete molecular and morphological regions. These regional distinctions account for variations in the morphogenetic mechanisms of palatal fusion along the length of the palate, and different causes and degrees of palatoschisis (palatal clefting).

The epithelium overlying the edges of the palatal shelves is of special significance. The dorsal surface epithelium differentiates into pseudostratified ciliated respiratory-type epithelium to line the nasal cavity; the

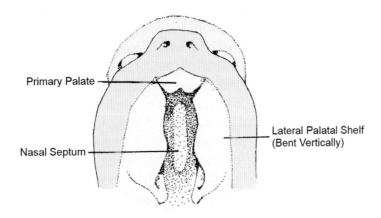

**Figure 10–3**  Schematic view of the three primordia of the palate in a 7.5-week-old embryo.

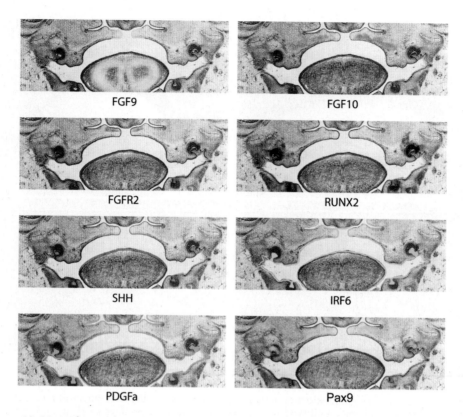

**Figure 10–3A** Midcoronal sections of an 8-week-old human embryo upon which are depicted the gene expression patterns derived from mouse embryos. Gene expression patterns are as follows: FGF9 (yellow) is expressed in the ectoderm of the palatal shelves, enamel knot, and myoblasts of the tongue; FGF 10 (purple) is initially expressed in the anterior palatal mesenchyme beneath the medial edge epithelium (MEE) on the oral side and gradually displaced ventrolaterally, the tongue, and floor of the mouth; FGFR2 (red) is expressed in the oral epithelium and the medial nasal palatal mesenchyme; RUNX2 (blue) is expressed in the MEE and the chondrogenic condensations; SHH (green) is expressed in the MEE and oral side of the palatal epithelium and tongue dorsal epithelium. IRF6 (cyan) is expressed in the tooth germs, and initially in the tips of the palatal shelves and then in the oral epithelium, and the base of the nasal septum; PDGFa (orange) is expressed in the epithelium of the pharynx; Pax9 (light green) is expressed in the palatal shelf, tooth mesenchyme, and medial nasal mesenchyme, and myoblasts of the tongue. (SEMs from Hinrichsen: Human-Embryologie. By kind permission of Springer Verlag.)

ventral surface epithelium differentiates into stratified keratinized epithelium to line the oral cavity and the medial edge epithelium undergoes a transition into mesenchyme (epithelial-mesenchymal transition). All these differential events are influenced by a whole host of genes, amongst which are CD44, PDGFC, IRF6, TGFβ3, TWIST, MSX1, PVRL1 (encodes nectin-1), TBX22, FGFR1, SATB2 and RUNX1 that are responsible for fusion of the palatal shelves upon mutual contact of the medial edge epithelia (Figs. 10–3A, 10–3B). The transcription factor HAND2 functions through SHH signaling and is an intrinsic regulator of medial edge epithelium transition into mesenchyme. Further, forward signaling by EphB2 and EphB3 and integration of IRF6 and Jagged2 signaling is required for intact palate development. Deficiencies in any of these factors accounts for failure of fusion leading to clefting of the palate. Fusion also occurs between the dorsal surfaces of the fusing palatal shelves and the lower edge of

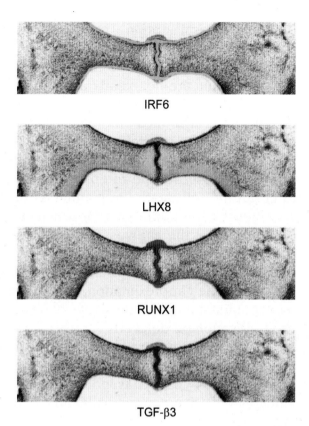

IRF6

LHX8

RUNX1

TGF-β3

**Figure 10–3B** Midpalatal fusion gene expression patterns derived from mouse embryos. Gene expression patterns of IRF6 (cyan) in the medial edge epithelium; LHX8 (green) expression is restricted to the oral palatal mesenchyme; RUNX1 (blue) is expressed in the epithelial tips of the palatal shelves; TGF-β3 (red) is expressed in the medial edge epithelium. (SEMs from Hinrichsen: Human-Embryologie. By kind permisssion by Springer Verlag.)

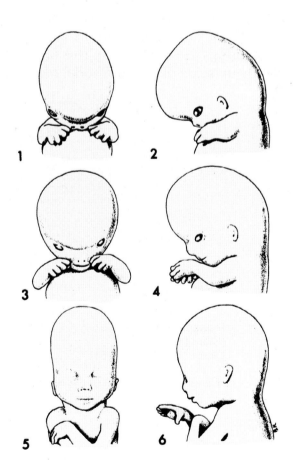

**Figure 10–4** Depiction of head lifting at 8 weeks allowing jaw opening and palatal shelf elevation. 1,2, 6 weeks; 3,4, 7 weeks; 5,6, 8 weeks. (Courtesy of Dr. V. Diewert. University of British Columbia.)

the midline nasal septum. The fusion seam initially forms anteriorly in the hard palate region, with subsequent merging of the soft palate region. The mechanisms of adhesive contact, fusion and subsequent degeneration of the epithelium are not clearly understood. A combination of degenerating epithelial cells and a surface coat accumulation of glycoproteins and desmosomes facilitates epithelial adherence between contacting palatal shelves. Only the medial edge epithelium of the palatal shelves (in contrast to their oral and nasal surface epithelia) undergoes cytodifferentiation involving a decline of epidermal growth factor receptors that lead to apoptotic cell death. Programmed cell death of the fusing epithelia, specified by the underlying mesenchyme, is essential to mesenchymal coalescence of the shelves. Some epithelial cells also migrate into the palatal mesenchyme, contributing to seam disruption. The epithelium at their leading edges may contribute to failure of fusion by not breaking down after shelf approximation, leading to "epithelial pearl" formation, or by not maintaining an adhesiveness beyond a critical time should palatal shelf-elevation be delayed.

Fusion of the three palatal components initially produces a flat, un-arched roof to the mouth. The fusing lateral palatal shelves overlap the anterior primary palate, as indicated later by the sloping pathways of the junctional incisive neurovascular canals that carry the previously formed incisive nerves and blood vessels. The site of junction of the three palatal components is marked by the incisive papilla overlying the incisive canal. The line of fusion of the lateral palatal shelves is traced in the adult by the midpalatal suture,* and on the surface by the midline raphe of the hard palate (Figs. 10–5 and 10–6). This fusion seam is minimized in the soft palate by invasion of extraterritorial mesenchyme.

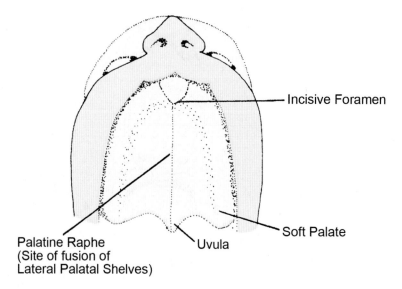

Figure 10–5  Lines of fusion of the embryological primordia of the palate.

---

*Inclusive of the palatal portion of the intermaxillary suture and the median palatine suture between the two palatine bones.

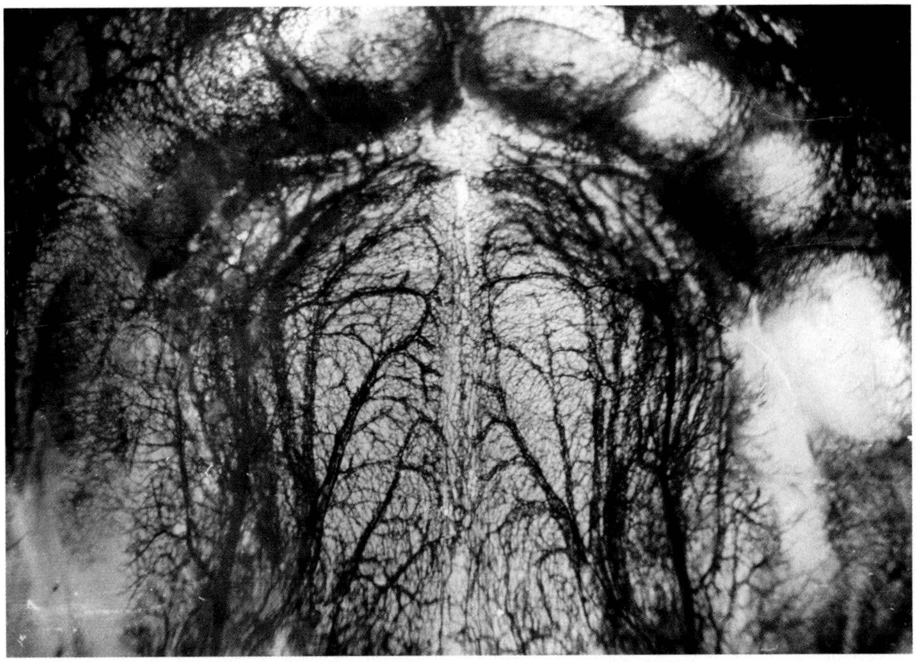

**Figure 10–6** Photomicrograph of the palate of a human 6-month-old fetus. Bone removed by microdissection and the arteries and capillaries injected with India ink. Note the midline raphe and the arterial anastomotic arcades, with only capillaries crossing over the midline. The tooth buds in the dental arch are outlined by the surrounding vascular networks. (Courtesy of Dr. William P. Maher.)

Ossification of the palate proceeds during the eighth week pc from the spread of bone into the mesenchyme of the fused lateral palatal shelves and from trabeculae appearing in the primary palate as "premaxillary centers," all derived from the single primary ossification centers of the maxillae. Posteriorly, the hard palate is ossified by trabeculae spreading from the single primary ossification centers of each of the palatine bones.

Midpalatal sutural structure is first evident at 10.5 weeks, when an upper layer of fiber bundles develops across the midline. In infancy, the midpalatal suture in coronal section has a Y shape, and it binds the vomer with the palatal shelves. In childhood, the junction between the three bones rises into a T shape, with the interpalatal section taking a serpentine course. In adolescence, the suture becomes so interdigitated that mechanical interlocking and interstitial islets of bone are formed. The palatine bone elements of the palate remain separated from the maxillary elements by the transverse palatomaxillary sutures into adulthood.

Ossification does not occur in the most posterior part of the palate, giving rise to the region of the soft palate. Myogenic mesenchymal tissue of the first and fourth pharyngeal arches migrates into this faucial region, supplying the musculature of the soft palate and fauces. The tensor veli palatini is derived from the first arch, and the levator palatini, uvular and faucial pillar muscles from the fourth arch, accounting for the innervation by the first arch trigeminal nerve of the tensor veli palatini muscle, and by the fourth arch pharyngeal plexus and vagus nerve for all the other muscles.

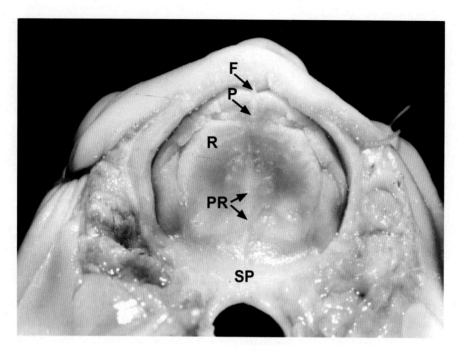

**Figure 10–7**  Palate and upper lip of a 22-week-old fetus. Note the midline frenulum (F), the papilla (P) overlying the incisive foramen, and the grooved alveolar arch divided into segments containing the developing tooth buds. The palatine raphe (PR) marks the site of palatal shelf fusion. The rugae (R) become more prominent toward birth. The soft palate (SP) is extensive.

The tensor veli palatini is the earliest of the five palatal muscles to develop, forming myoblasts at 40 days. It is followed by palatopharyngeus (45 days), levator veli palatini (eighth week), palatoglossus and the uvular muscle at the ninth week pc. Palatoglossus, derived from the tongue musculature, attaches to the soft palate during the 11th week pc. The hard palate grows in length, breadth and height, becoming an arched roof for the mouth (Fig. 10–7). The fetal palate increases in length more rapidly than in width between 7 and 18 weeks pc, after which the width increases faster than the length. In early prenatal life, the palate is relatively long, but from the fourth month pc, it widens as a result of midpalatal sutural growth and appositional growth along the lateral alveolar margins. At birth, the length and breadth of the hard palate are almost equal. The postnatal increase in palatal length is due to appositional growth in the maxillary tuberosity region and, to some extent, at the transverse maxillopalatine suture.

Growth at the midpalatal suture ceases between 1 and 2 years of age, but no synostosis occurs to signify its cessation.* Growth in width of the midpalatal suture is larger in its posterior than in its anterior part, so that the posterior part of the nasal cavity widens more than its anterior part. Obliteration of the midpalatal suture may start in adolescence, but

---

*The retention of a syndesmosis in the midpalatal suture into adulthood, even after growth has normally ceased at this site, permits the application of expansion. Forceful separation of the suture by an orthodontic appliance reinstitutes compensatory bone growth at this site, expanding palatal width.

complete fusion is rarely found before 30 years of age. The timing and degree of fusion of this suture varies greatly.

Lateral appositional growth continues until 7 years of age, by which time the palate achieves its ultimate anterior width. Posterior appositional growth continues after lateral growth has ceased, so that the palate becomes longer than wider during late childhood. During infancy and childhood, bone apposition also occurs on the entire inferior surface of the palate, accompanied by concomitant resorption from its superior (nasal) surface. This bone remodeling results in descent of the palate and enlargement of the nasal cavity. Nasal capacity must increase to keep pace with the increasing respiratory requirements engendered by general body growth. A fundamental drive in facial growth is provision of an adequate nasal capacity; if the need is not met, it is diverted to the mouth for maintenance of respiration.

The appositional growth of the alveolar processes contributes to deepening, as well as widening, of the vault of the bony palate, at the same time adding to the height and breadth of the maxillae (Fig. 10–8). The cortical and trabecular bone of the palate responds to masticatory loads with greater cortical bone thickness along the dental lamina, indicating mechanical loading influences palatal morphology. The lateral alveolar processes help to form an anteroposterior palatal furrow, which, together with a concave floor produced by a tongue curled from side to side, results in a palatal tunnel ideally suited to receive a nipple. A variable number of transverse palatal rugae develop in the mucosa covering the hard palate. They appear even before palatal fusion, which occurs at 56 days pc. The rugae, which are most prominent in the infant, hold the nipple while it is being milked by the tongue. The anterior palatal furrow is well marked during the first year of life (i.e., the active suckling period), and normally flattens out into the palatal arch after 3 or 4 years of age when suckling has been discontinued. Persistence of thumb-sucking or finger-sucking may retain the accentuated palatal furrow into childhood.

At Birth

1 Year

Figure 10–8 Cross-sectional views of the palate at various ages. Note the increasing depth of the palatal arch concomitant with tooth eruption.  Adult

# ANOMALIES OF PALATAL DEVELOPMENT

Successful fusion of the three embryonic components of the palate involves complicated synchronization of shelf movements with growth and withdrawal of the tongue and growth of the mandible and head. Mistiming of any of these critical events, by environmental agents or due to genetic predisposition, results in failure of fusion, leading to clefts of the palate. The incidence of cleft palate with or without cleft lip has been estimated at approximately 1 per 1000 births.

The entrapment of epithelial "rests" or "pearls" in the line of fusion of the palatal shelves, particularly the midline raphe of the hard palate, may give rise later to median palatal "rest" cysts. A common superficial expression of these epithelial entrapments is development of epithelial cysts or nodules, known as Epstein's pearls, along the median raphe of the hard palate and at the junction of the hard and soft palates. Small mucosal gland retention cysts (Bohn's nodules) may occur on the buccal and lingual aspects of the alveolar ridges, and dental lamina cysts composed of epithelial remnants of this lamina may develop on the crests of the alveolar ridges. All these superficial cysts of the palate in the newborn usually disappear by the third postnatal month. An anterior midline maxillary cyst developing in the region of the primary palate cannot be of fissural origin, but is a nasopalatine duct cyst encroaching anteriorly into the palate. Cysts are rare in the soft palate because of the mesenchymal merging of the shelves in this region, although submucous clefts may occur.

Delay in elevation of the palatal shelves from the vertical to the horizontal (see p. 50) while the head is growing continuously results in a widening gap between the shelves so that they cannot meet, and therefore cannot fuse. When eventually they do become horizontal, this leads to clefting of the palate. Other causes of cleft palate are defective shelf fusion, failure of medial edge epithelial cell death, possible postfusion rupture and failure of mesenchymal consolidation and differentiation.

The least severe form of cleft palate is the bifid uvula, of relatively common occurrence. Increasingly severe clefts always incur posterior involvement, the cleft advancing anteriorly in contradistinction to the direction of normal fusion. The lines of fusion of the lateral palatal shelves with the primary palate dictate the diversion from the midline of a severe palatal cleft anteriorly to either right or left, or in rare instances to both. If the cleft involves the alveolar arch, it usually passes between the lateral incisor and canine teeth. Such severe clefting of the palate may or may not be associated with unilateral or bilateral cleft upper lip; the two conditions are determined independently. The vertical nasal septum may fuse with the left or right palatal shelf, or neither, in cases of severe cleft palate (Figs. 10–9 and 10–10).

Clefts of the soft palate alone incur varying degrees of speech difficulty and minor swallowing problems because of the inability to close off the oropharynx completely from the nasopharynx during these pharyngeal functions (Figs. 10–11 and 10–12). Clefts of the hard palate, which almost

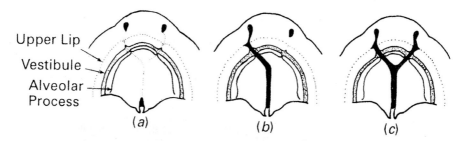

Figure 10–9  Variations in palatal clefting: (a) bifid uvula; (b) unilateral cleft palate and lip; (c) bilateral cleft palate and lip.

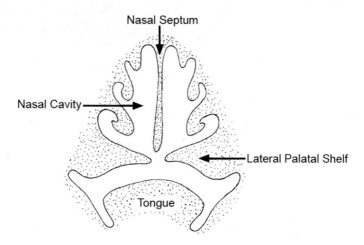

Figure 10–10  Schematic coronal section through a bilaterally cleft palate with an oral opening into both nasal cavities.

invariably include soft-palate clefts, give rise to feeding problems, particularly in infants, in whom the vacuum-producing sucking processes demand an intact hard palate. Spillage of food into the nasal fossa(e) is symptomatic of feeding difficulties. Such infants require early reparative surgery and/or obturator fitting to maintain good nutrition and aid development

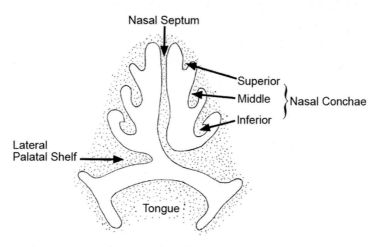

Figure 10–11  Schematic coronal section through a unilateral cleft palate with an oral opening into one nasal cavity only.

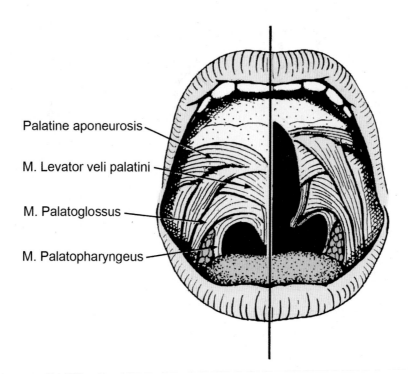

Palatine aponeurosis

M. Levator veli palatini

M. Palatoglossus

M. Palatopharyngeus

**Figure 10–12** Muscle disposition in cleft palate. Left half normal palate. Right half cleft palate.

of correct enunciation. Cleft palate is a feature of a number of congenital defect syndromes among which are mandibulofacial dysostosis (Treacher Collins syndrome), micrognathia (Pierre Robin sequence), orodigitofacial dysostosis syndrome, and Stickler syndrome. The palate is narrower, shorter and lower than normal in Down syndrome (trisomy 21), although it is often described as having a high midline elevation, but horizontally flattened laterally along the alveolar ridges, creating a "steeple palate." A highly arched palate is also characteristic of Marfan syndrome, an inherited disorder manifesting skeletal and cardiovascular anomalies, in which hyperchondroplasia is a feature, but with paradoxically a short nasal septal cartilage. Cleidocranial dysostosis, a congenital defect of intramembranous bones, also manifests a highly arched palate, with or without a cleft. Other congenital conditions displaying a high arched palate are craniofacial dysostosis (Crouzon syndrome, FGFR2), acrocephalosyndactyly (Apert syndrome, FGFR2), progeria, Stickler syndrome (COL2A1, COL11A1/2), Turner syndrome (45,X sex chromosome complement, previous notated as "XO"), and oculodentodigital dysplasia (connexin-43 gene/GJA1).

A fairly common genetic anomaly of the palate is a localized midpalatal overgrowth of bone of varying size, known as *torus palatinus*. This may enlarge in adulthood, and although it does not directly influence dental occlusion, if prominent, it may interfere with the seating of a removable orthodontic appliance or upper denture.

# SELECTED BIBLIOGRAPHY

Arnold WH, Rezwani T, Baric I. Location and distribution of epithelial pearls and tooth buds in human fetuses with cleft lip and palate. Cleft Palate-Craniofac J 1998; 35:359–365.

Barrow JR, Capecchi MR. Compensatory defects associated with mutations in Hoxa1 restore normal palatogenesis to Hoxa2 mutants. Development 1999; 126:5011–5026.

Behrents RG, Harris EF. The premaxillary-maxillary suture and orthodontic mechanotherapy [see comments]. Am J Orthod Dent Orthop 1991; 99:1–6.

Charoenchaikorn K, Yokomizo T, Rice DP, et al. Runx1 is involved in the fusion of the primary and secondary palatal shelves. Dev Biol 2009; 326: 392–402.

Citterio HL, Gaillard DA. Expression of transforming growth factor alpha (TGF alpha), epidermal growth factor receptor (EGF-R) and cell proliferation during human palatogenesis: an immunohistochemical study. Int J Dev Biol 1994; 38:499–505.

Cohen SR, Chen L, Trotman CA, Burdi AR. Soft-palate myogenesis: a developmental field paradigm. Cleft Palate-Craniofac J 1993; 30:441–446.

Del Santo M Jr, Minarelli AM, Liberti EA. Morphological aspects of the mid-palatal suture in the human foetus: a light and scanning electron microscopy study. Eur J Orthod 1998; 20:93–99.

Diewert VM. Craniofacial growth during human secondary palate formation and potential relevance of experimental cleft palate observations. J Craniofac Genet Develop Biol Supp 1986; 2:267–276.

Dudas M, Kim J, Nagy A, et al. Epithelial and ectomesenchymal role of type I Tgf-beta receptor Alk5 during facial morphogenesis and palatal fusion. Dev Biol 2006; 296: 298–314.

Gorsky M, Bukai A, Shohat M. Genetic influences on the prevalence of torus palatinus. Am J Med Genet 1998; 75:138–140.

Greene RM, Linask KK, Pisano MM, et al. Transmembrane and intracellular signal tranduction during palatal ontogeny. J Craniofac Genet Dev Biol 1991; 11:262–276.

Gritli-Linde A. Molecular control of secondary palate development. Dev Biol 2007; 301:309–326.

Harris MJ, Juriloff DM, Peters CE. Disruption of pattern formation in palatal rugae in fetal mice heterozygous for First arch (Far). J Craniofac Genet Dev Biol 1990; 10:363–371.

Han J, Mayo J, Xu X et al. Indirect modulation of Shh signaling by Dlx5 affects the oral-nasal patterning of palate and rescues cleft palate in Msx1-null mice. Development 2009; 136:4225–4233.

Kimes KR, Mooney MP, Siegel MI, Todhunter JS. Size and growth rate of the tongue in normal and cleft lip and palate human fetal specimens. Cleft Palate-Craniofac J 1991; 28:212–216.

Kjaer I. Human prenatal palatal closure related to skeletal maturity of the jaws. J Craniofac Genet Dev Biol 1989; 9:265–270.

Kjaer I. Human prenatal palatal shelf elevation related to craniofacial skeletal maturation. Eur J Orthod 1992; 14:26–30.

Kjaer I. Mandibular movements during elevation and fusion of palatal shelves evaluated from the course of Meckel's cartilage. J Craniofac Genet Dev Biol 1997; 17:80–85.

Kjaer I, Bach-Petersen S, Graem N, Kjaer T. Changes in human palatine bone location and tongue position during prenatal palatal closure. J Craniofac Genet Dev Biol 1993; 13:18–23.

Kjaer I, Keeling J, Russell B, et al. Palate structure in human holoprosencephaly correlates with the facial malformation and demonstrates a new palatal developmental field. Am J Med Genet 1997; 73:387–392.

Lisson JA, Kjaer I. Location of alveolar clefts relative to the incisive fissure. Cleft Palate-Craniofac J 1997; 34:292–296.

Menegaz RA, Sublett SV, Gigueroa SD, et al. Phenotypic plasticity and function of the hard palate in growing rabbits. Anat Rec 2009; 292:277–284.

Meng L, Bian Z, Torensma R, Von deb Hof JW. Biological mechanisms in palatogenesis and cleft palate. J Dent Res 2009.; 88: 22–33.

Millard DR Jr. Embryonic rationale for the primary correction of classical congenital clefts of the lip and palate. Ann R Coll Surg Engl 1994; 76:150–160.

Moreno LM, Mansilla MA, Bullard SA et al. FOXE1 association with both isolated cleft lip with or without cleft palate, and isolated cleft palate. Hum Mol Genet 2009; 18:4879–4896.

Nawshad A. Palatal seam disintegration: to die or not to die? That is no longer the question. Dev Dyn 2008; 237:2643–2656.

Nijo BJ, Kjaer I. The development and morphology of the incisive fissure and the transverse palatine suture in the human fetal palate. J Craniofac Genet Dev Biol 1993; 13:24–34.

Revelo B, Fishman LS. Maturational evaluation of ossification of the midpalatal suture. Am J Orthod Dent Orthop 1994; 105:282–292.

Richardson RJ, Dixon J, Jiang R, Dixon MJ. Integration of IRF6 and Jagged 2 signalling is essential for controlling palatal adhesion and fusion competence. Hum Mol Genet 2009; 18: 2632–2642.

Risely M, Garrod D, Henkemeyer M, McLean W. EphB2 and EphB3 forward *signaling* are required for palate development. Mech Dev 2009; 126:230–239.

Rude FP, Anderson L, Conley D, Gasser RF. Three-dimensional reconstructions of the primary palate region in normal human embryos. Anat Rec 1994; 238: 108–113.

Shaw WC, Simpson JP. Oral adhesions associated with cleft lip and palate and lip fistulae. Cleft Palate J; 1980; 17:127–131.

Silau AM, Njio B, Solow B, Kjaer I. Prenatal sagittal growth of the osseous components of the human palate. J Craniofac Genet Dev Biol 1994; 14:252–256.

Welsh IC, O'Brien TP. Signaling integration in the rugae growth zone directs sequential SHH signaling center formation during the rostral outgrowth of the palate. Dev Biol 2009; 336:53–57.

Wu M, Li J, Engleka KA, et al. Persistent expression of Pax3 in neural crest causes cleft palate and defective osteogenesis. Dev Biol 2008; 319:500–501.

Xiong W, He F, Morikawa Y, et al. Hand2 is required in the epithelium for palatogenesis in mice. Dev Biol 2009; 330:131–141.

Yu W, Kamara H, Svoboda KKH. The role of twist during palate development. Dev Dyn 2008; 237:2716–2725.

# 11 Paranasal Sinuses

The four sets of paranasal sinuses—maxillary, sphenoidal, frontal and ethmoidal—begin their development at the end of the third month post-conception (pc) as outpouchings of the mucous membranes of the middle and superior nasal meatus and the sphenoethmoidal recesses. The early paranasal sinuses expand into the cartilage walls and roof of the nasal fossae by growth of mucous membrane sacs (primary pneumatization) into the maxillary, sphenoid, frontal and ethmoid bones. The sinuses enlarge into bone (secondary pneumatization) from their initial small outpocketings, always retaining communication with the nasal fossae through *ostia* (Fig. 11–1).

Pneumatization of the paranasal bones occurs at different rates, and even varies between the sides. The maxillary sinus is the first to develop, at 10 weeks, from the middle meatus by primary pneumatization into the ectethmoid cartilage. Secondary pneumatization into the ossifying maxilla starts in the fifth month pc in this most precocious of the sinuses, which at birth* is large enough to be clinically important and radiographically identifiable. The maxillary sinus enlarges by bone resorption of the maxilla's internal walls (except medially) slightly faster than overall maxillary growth. Sinus expansion causes resorption of cancellous bone except on the medial wall, where internal bone resorption is constrained by opposing nasal surface resorption, thereby enlarging the nasal cavity. The rapid and continuous downward growth of this sinus after birth brings its

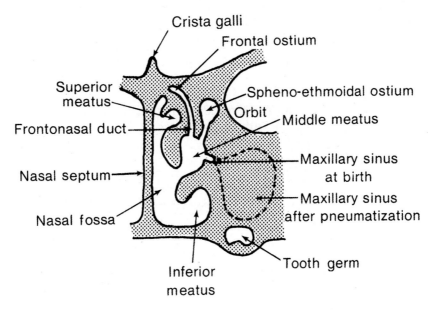

Figure 11–1 Coronal sectional schema of paranasal sinuses.

---

*The maxillary sinus averages 7 mm in length and 4 mm in height and width at birth, and expands approximately 2 mm vertically and 3 mm anteroposteriorly each year.

walls in close proximity to the roots of the maxillary cheek teeth, and its floor below its osteal opening. As each tooth erupts, the vacated bone becomes pneumatized by the expanding maxillary sinus, whose floor descends from its prenatal level above the nasal floor to its adult level below the nasal floor. In adulthood, the roots of the molar teeth commonly project into the sinus lumen.

The sphenoidal sinuses start developing at 4 months pc by constricting the posterosuperior portion of the sphenoethmoid recess and thus bypassing primary pneumatization. The recess is between the sphenoidal conchae (bones of Bertin) and the sphenoid body. Secondary pneumatization occurs at 6 to 7 years into the sphenoid and later the basisphenoid bones. It continues growing in early adulthood, and may invade the wings and, rarely, the pterygoid plates of the sphenoid bone.

Ethmoid air cells from the middle and superior meatus and sphenoethmoid recess invade the ectethmoid nasal capsule (primary pneumatization) from the fourth month pc. Secondary pneumatization occurs between birth and 2 years as groups of 3 to 15 air cells grow irregularly to form the ethmoid labyrinth (Fig. 11–2). The most anterior ethmoidal cells grow upward into the frontal bone; they may form the frontal sinuses, retaining their origin from the middle meatus of the nose as the frontonasal duct. The ethmoidal air cells may also expand into the sphenoid, lacrimal or even maxillary bones (extramural sphenoidal, lacrimal and maxillary sinuses).

The frontal sinuses start as mucosal invaginations (primary pneumatization) in the frontal recess of the middle meatus of the nasal fossa at 3 to 4 months pc but do not invade the frontal bone (secondary pneumatization) until between 6 months and 2 years postnatally and are not visible radiographically before 6 years. They grow upward at an extremely variable rate until puberty. All the paranasal sinuses appear to continue increasing their size into old age.

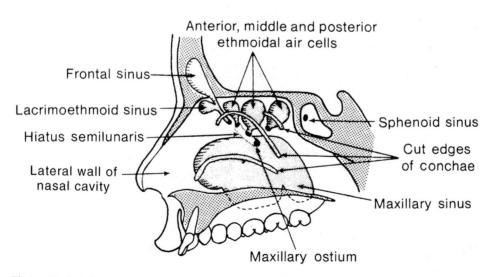

**Figure 11–2** Schematic view of paranasal sinuses in the adult and their communications (ostia) with the nasal fossa.

## ANOMALIES OF DEVELOPMENT

Absence of development of the frontal and sphenoidal sinuses is characteristic of Down syndrome (trisomy 21). Diminution or absence of sinuses is also found in Apert syndrome (acrocephalosyndactyly). If an interfrontal (metopic) suture persists, the frontal sinuses are small, or even absent.

## SELECTED BIBLIOGRAPHY

Arredondo de Arreola G, Lopez Serna N, de Hoyos Parra R, Arreola Salinas MA. Morphogenesis of the lateral nasal wall from 6 to 36 weeks. Otolaryngol Head Neck Surg 1996; 114:54–60.

Bingham B, Wang RG, Hawke M, Kwok P. The embryonic development of the lateral nasal wall from 8 to 24 weeks. Laryngoscope 1991; 101:992–997.

Gulisano M, Montella A, Orlandini SZ, Pacini P. Morphological study of fetal nasopharyngeal epithelium in man. Acta Anat 1992; 144:152–159.

Helfferich F, Viragh S. Histological investigations of the nasal mucosa in human fetuses. Eur Arch Otorhinolaryngol Suppl 1997; 1:S39–S42.

Koppe T, Yamamoto T, Tanaka O, Nagai H. Investigations on the growth pattern of the maxillary sinus in Japanese human fetuses. Okajimas Folia Anat Japonica 1994; 71:311–318.

Kubal WS. Sinonasal anatomy. Neuroimaging Clin North Am 1998; 8:143–156.

Marquez S, Tessema B, Clement PA, Schaefer SD. Development of the ethmoid sinus and extramural migration: the anatomical basis of this paranasal sinus. Anat Rec 2008; 291: 1535–1553.

Monteiro VJ, Dias MP. Morphogenic mechanisms in the development of ethmoidal sinuses. Anat Rec 1997; 249:96–102.

Sato I, Sunohara M, Mikami A, et al. Immunocytochemical study of the maxilla and maxillary sinus during human fetal development. Okajimas Folia Anat Jpn 1998; 75:205–216.

Skladzien J, Litwin JA, Nowogrodzky-Zagorska N, Miodonski AJ. Corrosion casting study on the vasculature of nasal mucosa in the human fetus. Anat Rec 1995; 242:411–416.

Smith TD, Siegel MI, Mooney MP, et al. Formation and enlargement of the paranasal sinuses in normal and cleft lip and palate human fetuses. Cleft Palate Craniofac J 1997; 34:483–489.

Wake M, Takeno S, Hawke M. The early development of sino-nasal mucosa. Laryngoscope 1994; 104:850–855.

Wang RG, Jiang SC. The embryonic development of the human ethmoid labyrinth from 8–40 weeks. Acta Otolaryngol 1997; 117:118–122.

Wang RG, Jiang SC, Gu R. The cartilaginous nasal capsule and embryonic development of human paranasal sinuses. J Otolaryngol 1994; 23:239–243.

# 12 Mandible

*The human mandible has no one design for life. Rather, it adapts and remodels through the seven stages of life, from the slim arbiter of things to come in the infant, through a powerful dentate machine and even weapon in the full flesh of maturity, to the pencil-thin, porcelain-like problem that we struggle to repair in the adversity of old age.*

D. E. Poswillo (1988)

The cartilages and bones of the mandibular skeleton form from embryonic neural crest cells (see p. 25) that originated in the mid- and hindbrain regions of the neural folds. These cells migrate ventrally to form the mandibular (and maxillary) facial prominences, where they differentiate into bones and connective tissues.

The first structure to develop in the region of the lower jaw is the mandibular division of the trigeminal nerve that precedes the ectomesenchymal condensation forming the first (mandibular) pharyngeal arch. The prior presence of the nerve has been postulated as requisite for inducing osteogenesis by the production of neurotrophic factors. The mandible is derived from ossification of an osteogenic membrane formed from ectomesenchymal condensation at 36 to 38 days of development. Transforming growth factor (TGF)–β signaling is required in the mandibular primordium where intramembranous ossification is to take place. The levels and timing of bone morphogenetic protein (BMP) signaling is tightly regulated by extracellular antagonists and intracellular cofactors to ensure adequate differentiation of both cartilage and bone.

The mandibular ectomesenchyme must interact initially with the epithelium of the mandibular arch before primary ossification can occur; the resulting intramembranous bone lies lateral to Meckel's cartilage of the first (mandibular) pharyngeal arch (see p. 65) (Fig. 12–1). A single ossification center for each half of the mandible arises in the sixth week postconception (pc)* in the region of the bifurcation of the inferior alveolar nerve and artery into mental and incisive branches. The ossifying membrane is lateral to Meckel's cartilage and its accompanying neurovascular bundle. Ossification spreads from the primary center below and around the inferior alveolar nerve and its incisive branch, and upward to form a trough for the developing teeth. Spread of the intramembranous ossification dorsally and ventrally forms the body and ramus of the mandible. Meckel's cartilage becomes surrounded and invaded by bone. Ossification stops dorsally at the site that will become the mandibular lingula, from where Meckel's cartilage continues into the middle ear. The prior presence of the neurovascular bundle ensures formation of the mandibular foramen and canal and the mental foramen.

---

*The mandible and the clavicle are the first bones to begin to ossify.

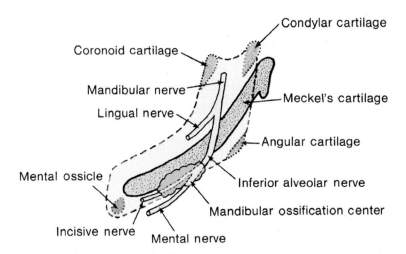

**Figure 12–1** Schema of the origins of the mandible. The center of ossification is lateral to Meckel's cartilage at the bifurcation of the inferior alveolar nerve.

The first pharyngeal arch core of Meckel's cartilage almost meets its fellow of the opposite side ventrally. It diverges dorsally to end in the tympanic cavity of each middle ear, which is derived from the first pharyngeal pouch, and is surrounded by the forming petrous portion of the temporal bone. The dorsal end of Meckel's cartilage ossifies to form the basis of two of the auditory ossicles, namely, the malleus and incus. The third ossicle, the stapes, is derived primarily from the cartilage of the second pharyngeal arch (Reichert's cartilage, see p. 67).

Almost all of Meckel's cartilage disappears.* Parts transform into the sphenomandibular and anterior malleolar ligaments. A small part of its ventral end (from the mental foramen ventrally to the symphysis) forms accessory endochondral ossicles that are incorporated into the chin region of the mandible. Meckel's cartilage dorsal to the mental foramen undergoes resorption on its lateral surface at the same time as intramembranous bony trabeculae are forming immediately lateral to the resorbing cartilage. Thus, the cartilage from the mental foramen to the lingula is not incorporated into ossification of the mandible.

The initial woven bone formed along Meckel's cartilage is soon replaced by lamellar bone, and typical haversian systems are already present at the fifth month pc. This earlier remodeling than other bones is attributed as a response to the early intense sucking and swallowing that stress the mandible.

Secondary accessory cartilages appear between the 10th and 14th weeks pc to form the head of the condyle, part of the coronoid process and the mental protuberance (see Fig. 12–1). The appearance of these secondary mandibular cartilages is dissociated from the primary pharyngeal (Meckel's) and chondrocranial cartilages. The secondary cartilage of

---

*Meckel's cartilage lacks the enzyme phosphatase found in ossifying cartilages, thus precluding its ossification, and disappears by the 24th week pc.

the coronoid process develops within the temporalis muscle as its predecessor. The coronoid accessory cartilage becomes incorporated into the expanding intramembranous bone of the ramus and disappears before birth. In the mental region, on either side of the symphysis, one or two small cartilages appear and ossify in the seventh month pc to form a variable number of *mental ossicles* in the fibrous tissue of the symphysis. The ossicles become incorporated into the intramembranous bone when the symphysis menti is converted from a syndesmosis into a synostosis during the first postnatal year.

The condylar secondary cartilage appears during the 10th week pc as a cone-shaped structure in the ramal region. This condylar cartilage is the primordium of the future condyle. Cartilage cells differentiate from its center, and the cartilage condylar head increases by interstitial and appositional growth. By the 14th week, the first evidence of endochondral bone appears in the condyle region. The condylar cartilage serves as an important center of growth* for the ramus and body of the mandible. Much of the cone-shaped cartilage is replaced with bone by the middle of fetal life, but its upper end persists into adulthood, acting as both a growth cartilage and an articular cartilage. Changes in mandibular position and form are related to the direction and amount of condylar growth. The condylar growth rate increases at puberty, peaks between 12.5 and 14 years of age, and normally ceases at about 20 years. However, the continuing presence of the cartilage provides a potential for continued growth, which is realized in conditions of abnormal growth such as acromegaly.

The shape and size of the diminutive fetal mandible undergo considerable transformation during its growth and development. The ascending ramus of the neonatal mandible is low and wide; the coronoid process is relatively large and projects well above the condyle; the body is merely an open shell containing the buds and partial crowns of the deciduous teeth; the mandibular canal runs low in the body. The initial separation of the right and left bodies of the mandible at the midline symphysis menti is gradually eliminated between the 4th and 12th months postnatally, when ossification converts the syndesmosis into a synostosis, uniting the two halves.

Although the mandible appears in the adult as a single bone, it is developmentally and functionally divisible into several skeletal subunits (Fig. 12–2). The "basal bone" of the body forms one unit, to which are attached the alveolar, coronoid, angular and condylar processes and the chin. Each of these skeletal subunits is influenced in its growth pattern by a functional matrix that acts upon the bone: the teeth act as a functional matrix for the alveolar unit; the action of the temporalis muscle influences the coronoid process; the masseter and medial pterygoid muscles act upon

---

* The nature of this growth, as primary (an initial source of morphogenesis) or secondary (compensating for functional stimulation), is controversial, but experimental evidence indicates the need for mechanical stimuli for normal growth.

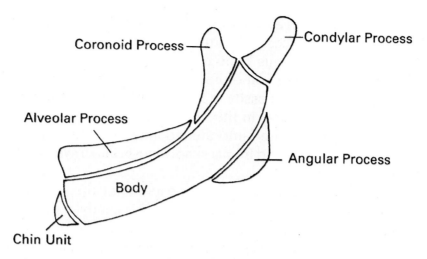

**Figure 12–2** Schema of "skeletal units" of the mandible.

the angle and ramus of the mandible; and the lateral pterygoid has some influence on the condylar process. The functioning of the related tongue and perioral muscles, and the expansion of the oral and pharyngeal cavities, provide stimuli for mandibular growth to reach its full potential. Of all the facial bones, the mandible undergoes the most growth postnatally and evidences the greatest variation in morphology.

Limited growth takes place at the symphysis menti until fusion occurs. The main sites of postnatal mandibular growth are at the condylar cartilages, the posterior borders of the rami, and the alveolar ridges. These areas of bone deposition account grossly for increases in the height, length and width of the mandible. However, superimposed upon this basic incremental growth are numerous regional remodeling changes, subjected to the local functional influences that involve selective resorption and displacement of individual mandibular elements (Fig. 12–3).

The condylar cartilage of the mandible serves the uniquely dual roles of an articular cartilage in the temporomandibular joint, characterized by a fibrocartilage surface layer, and as a growth cartilage analogous to the epiphyseal plate in a long bone, characterized by a deeper hypertrophying cartilage layer. The subarticular appositional proliferation of cartilage within the condylar head provides the basis for growth of a medullary core of endochondral bone, on whose outer surface a cortex of intramembranous bone is laid. The growth cartilage may act as a "functional matrix" to stretch the periosteum, inducing the lengthened periosteum to form intramembranous bone beneath it. The diverse histological origins of the medulla and cortex are effaced by their fusion. The formation of bone within the condylar heads causes the mandibular rami to grow upward and backward, displacing the entire mandible in an opposite downward, forward direction. Bone resorption subjacent to the condylar head accounts for the narrowed condylar neck. The attachment of the lateral pterygoid muscle to this neck and the growth and action of the tongue and masticatory muscles are functional forces implicated in this phase of mandibular growth.

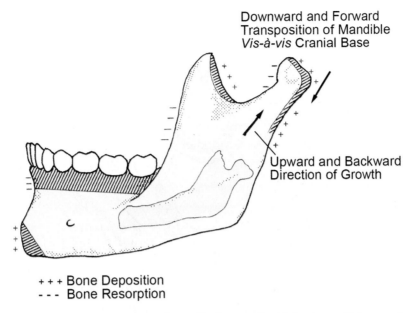

Downward and Forward
Transposition of Mandible
*Vis-à-vis* Cranial Base

Upward and Backward
Direction of Growth

+ + + Bone Deposition
- - - Bone Resorption

**Figure 12–3** Schematic representation of mandibular growth with fetal mandible superimposed upon adult mandible.

Any damage to the condylar cartilages restricts the growth potential and normal downward and forward displacement of the mandible, unilaterally or bilaterally, according to the side(s) damaged. Lateral deviations of the mandible and varying degrees of micrognathia and accompanying malocclusion result.

In the infant, the condyles of the mandible are inclined almost horizontally, so that condylar growth leads to an increase in the length of the mandible rather than increase in height. Owing to the posterior divergence of the two halves of the body of the mandible (in a V shape), growth in the condylar heads of the increasingly more widely displaced rami results in overall widening of the mandibular body, which, with remodeling, keeps pace with the widening cranial base (Fig 12–4). No interstitial widening of the mandible can take place at the fused symphysis menti after the first year apart from some widening by surface apposition.

Bone deposition occurs on the posterior border of the ramus, while concomitant resorption on the anterior border maintains the proportions of the ramus, and, in effect, moves it backward in relation to the body of the mandible. This deposition: resorption extends up to the coronoid process, involving the mandibular notch, and progressively repositions the mandibular foramen posteriorly, accounting for the anterior overlying plate of the lingula. The attachment of the elevating muscles of mastication to the buccal and lingual aspects of the ramus and to the mandibular angle and coronoid process influences the ultimate size and proportions of these mandibular elements.

The posterior displacement of the ramus converts former ramal bone into the posterior part of the body of the mandible. In this manner, the body of the mandible lengthens, the posterior molar region relocating

Direction of Condylar Growth

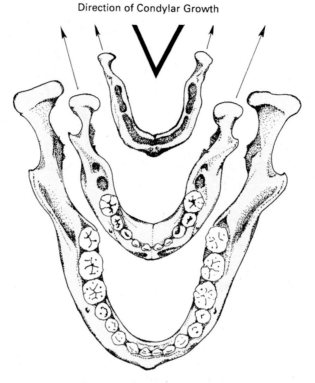

**Figure 12–4** Mandibles of a neonate (top), 4-year-old child (middle), and adult (below), illustrating the constant width of the anterior body of the mandible but lateral expansion of the rami with growth.

anteriorly into the premolar and canine regions. This is one means by which additional space is provided for eruption of the molar teeth, all three of which originate in the ramus-body junction. Their forward migration and posterior ramal displacement lengthen the molar region of the mandible.

The forward shift of the growing mandibular body changes the direction of the mental foramen during infancy and childhood. The mental neurovascular bundle emanates from the mandible at right angles or even a slightly forward direction at birth. In adulthood, the mental foramen (and its neurovascular content) is characteristically directed backward. This change may be ascribed to forward growth in the body of the mandible, while the neurovascular bundle "drags along" (Fig. 12–5). A contributory factor may be the differential rates of bone and periosteal growth. The latter, by its firm attachment to the condyle and comparatively loose attachment to the mandibular body, grows more slowly than the body, which slides forward beneath the periosteum. The changing direction of the foramen has clinical implications in the administration of local anesthetic to the mental nerve: in infancy and childhood, the syringe needle may be applied at right angles to the body of the mandible to enter the mental foramen, whereas in the adult, the needle has to be applied obliquely from behind to achieve entry.

The location of the mental foramen also alters its vertical relationship within the body of the mandible from infancy to old age. When teeth are

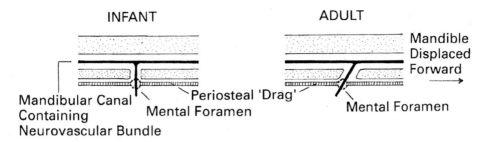

INFANT          ADULT

Mandible
Displaced
Forward
→

Mandibular Canal          Periosteal 'Drag'          Mental Foramen
Containing          Mental Foramen
Neurovascular Bundle

**Figure 12–5** Schematic expansion of the alteration of direction of the mental foramen from lateral in the infant to posterior in the adult as a result of forward displacement of the mandible and "dragging" of the mental neurovascular bundle.

present, the mental foramen is located midway between the upper and lower borders of the mandible. In the edentulous mandible, lacking an alveolar ridge, the mental foramen appears near the upper margin of the thinned mandible (Fig. 12–6).

The alveolar process develops as a protective trough in response to the tooth buds, and becomes superimposed upon the basal bone of the mandibular body. It adds to the height and thickness of the body of the

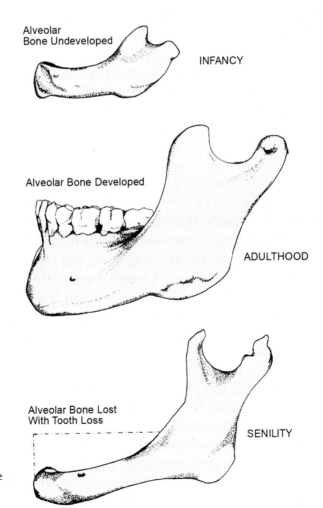

Alveolar
Bone Undeveloped

INFANCY

Alveolar Bone Developed

ADULTHOOD

Alveolar Bone Lost
With Tooth Loss

SENILITY

**Figure 12–6** Lateral view of the mandible in infancy, adulthood and senility, illustrating the influence of alveolar bone on the contour of the mandibular body. Note the altering obliquity of the angle of the mandible. Note the location of the mental foramen that varies in relation to the upper border of the body of the mandible.

mandible, and is particularly manifest as a ledge extending lingually to the ramus to accommodate the third molars. The alveolar bone fails to develop if teeth are absent, and resorbs in response to tooth extraction. The orthodontic movement of teeth takes place in the labile alveolar bone of both maxilla and mandible, and fails to involve the underlying basal bone.

The chin, formed in part of the mental ossicles from accessory cartilages and the ventral end of Meckel's cartilage, is very poorly developed in the infant. It develops almost as an independent subunit of the mandible, influenced by sexual as well as specific genetic factors. Sex differences in the symphyseal region of the mandible are not significant until other secondary sex characteristics develop. Thus, the chin becomes significant only at adolescence from development of the mental protuberance and tubercles. Whereas small chins are found in adults of both sexes, very large chins are characteristically masculine. The skeletal "unit" of the chin may be an expression of the functional forces exerted by the lateral pterygoid muscles that, in pulling the mandible forward, indirectly stress the mental symphyseal region by their concomitant inward pull. Bone buttressing to resist muscle stressing, which is more powerful in the male, is expressed in the more prominent male chin. The protrusive chin is a uniquely human trait; it is lacking in all other primates and hominid ancestors.

The mental protuberance forms by osseous deposition during childhood. Its prominence is accentuated by bone resorption in the alveolar region above it, creating the supramental concavity known as Point B in orthodontic terminology. Underdevelopment of the chin is known as *microgenia*.

A genetically determined exostosis on the lingual aspect of the body of the mandible, the *torus mandibularis*, develops, usually bilaterally, in the canine-premolar region. These tori are unrelated to any muscle attachments or known functional matrices.

During fetal life, the relative sizes of the maxilla and mandible vary widely. Initially, the mandible is considerably larger than the maxilla, a predominance lessened later by the relatively greater development of the maxilla; by about 8 weeks pc, the maxilla overlaps the mandible. The subsequent relatively greater growth of the mandible results in approximately equal size of the upper and lower jaws by the 11th week. Mandibular growth lags behind maxillary between the 13th and 20th weeks pc owing to a changeover from Meckel's cartilage to condylar secondary cartilage as the main growth determinant of the lower jaw. At birth, the mandible tends to be retrognathic to the maxilla, although the two jaws may be of equal size. This retrognathic condition is normally corrected early in postnatal life by rapid mandibular growth and forward displacement to establish orthognathia, or an Angle Class I maxillomandibular relationship. Inadequate mandibular growth results in an Angle Class II relation, and overgrowth of the mandible produces a Class III relation. The mandible can grow for much longer than the maxilla.

## ANOMALIES OF DEVELOPMENT

The mandible may be grossly deficient or absent in the condition of agnathia, which reflects a deficiency of neural crest tissue in the lower part of the face. Aplasia of the mandible and hyoid bone (*first- and second-arch syndrome*) is a rare lethal condition with multiple defects of the orbit and maxilla. Well-developed, albeit low-set, ears and auditory ossicles in this syndrome suggest ischemic necrosis of the mandible and hyoid bone occurs after formation of the ear.

*Micrognathia*, a diminutive mandible (Fig. 12–7), is characteristic of several syndromes, including Pierre Robin and the cat-cry (*cri du chat*) syndromes, mandibulofacial dysostosis (Treacher Collins syndrome), progeria, Down syndrome (trisomy 21), oculomandibulodyscephaly (Hallerman-Streiff syndrome) and Turner syndrome (45,X sex-chromosome complement, previously referred to as XO).

A central dysmorphogenic mechanism of defective neural crest production, migration or destruction may be responsible for the hypoplastic mandible common to these conditions. Absent or deficient neural crest

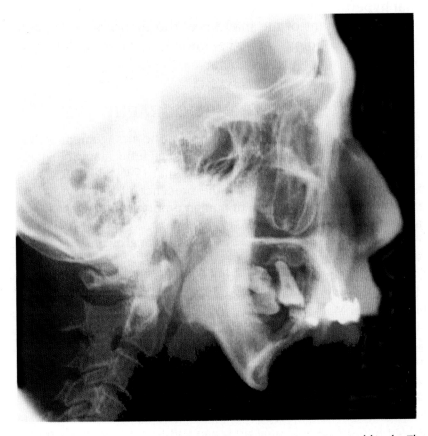

**Figure 12–7** Radiograph of deficient mandibular development in a 45-year-old male. The severe micrognathia is due to mandibular condyle degeneration consequent to bilateral condylar fractures at age 4 years, with reduction by wires still present in condyles. The temporomandibular joints are ankylosed, with dental malocclusion present. Compare and contrast with Figure 9-6. (Courtesy of Dr. G. W. Raborn.)

tissue around the optic cup causes a "vacuum" so that the developing otic pit, normally adjacent to the second pharyngeal arch, moves cranially into first arch territory and the ear becomes located over the angle of the mandible. Derivatives of the deficient ectomesenchyme, specifically the zygomatic, maxillary and mandibular bones, are hypoplastic, accounting for the typical facies common to these syndromes.

In the Pierre Robin sequence, the underdeveloped mandible usually demonstrates catch-up growth in the child; in mandibulofacial dysostosis, deficiency of the mandible is maintained throughout growth; in unilateral agenesis of the mandibular ramus, the malformation increases with age. Hemifacial microsomia (Goldenhar syndrome, oculoauriculovertebral spectrum, facioauricolovertebral syndrome) also becomes more severe with retarded growth.

Variations in condylar form may occur, among them the rare *bifid*, or *double, condyle* that results from the persistence of septa dividing the fetal condylar cartilage.

Macrognathia, producing prognathism, is usually an inherited condition, but abnormal growth phenomena such as hyperpituitarism may produce mandibular overgrowth of increasing severity with age. Congenital hemifacial hypertrophy, evident at birth, tends to accentuate at puberty. Unilateral enlargement of the mandible, the mandibular fossa, and the teeth is of obscure etiology. More common is isolated unilateral condylar hyperplasia.

## SELECTED BIBLIOGRAPHY

Azeredo RA, Watanabe I, Liberti EA, Semprini M. The arrangement of the trabecular bone in the vestibular surface of the human fetus mandible. I. A scanning electron microscopy study (1). Bull Assoc Anat 1996; 80:7–12.

Bareggi R, Narducci P, Grill V, et al. On the presence of a secondary cartilage in the mental symphyseal region of human embryos and fetuses. Surg Radiol Anat 1994; 16:379–384.

Bareggi R, Sandrucci MA, Baldini G, et al. Mandibular growth rates in human fetal development. Arch Oral Biol 1995; 40:119–125.

Barni T, Maggi M, Fantoni G, et al. Identification and localization of endothelin-1 and its receptors in human fetal jaws. Develop Biol 1995; 169:373–377.

Ben-Ami Y, von der Mark K, Franzen A, et al. Immunohistochemical studies of the extracellular matrix in the condylar cartilage of the human fetal mandible: collagens and noncollagenous proteins. Am J Anat 1991; 190:157–166.

Ben-Ami Y, Lewinson D, Silbermann M. Structural characterization of the mandibular condyle in human fetuses: light and electron microscopy studies. Acta Anat 1992; 145:79–87.

Ben-Ami Y, von der Mark K, Franzen A, et al. Transformation of fetal secondary cartilage into embryonic bone in organ cultures of human mandibular condyles. Cell Tissue Res 1993; 271:317–322.

Berraquero R, Palacios J, Gamallo C, et al. Prenatal growth of the human mandibular condylar cartilage. Am J Orthod Dentofacial Orthop 1995; 108:194–200.

Cesarani A, Tombolini A, Fagnani E, et al. The anterior ligament of the human malleus. Acta Anat 1991; 142:313–316.

Chavez-Lomeli ME, Mansilla Lory J, Pompa JA, Kjaer I. The human mandibular canal arises from three separate canals innervating different tooth groups. J Dent Res 1996; 75:1540–1544.

Chitty LS, Campbell S, Altman DG. Measurement of the fetal mandible—feasibility and construction of a centile chart. Prenatal Diag 1993; 13: 749–756.

Czerwinski F, Mahaczek-Kordowska A. Microangiographic studies on vascularization of the human fetal corpus of the mandible. Folia Morpholol (Warsz) 1992; 51:43–48.

Eames BF, Schneider RA. The genesis of cartilage size and shape during development and evolution. Development 2008; 135: 3947–3958.

Hu D, Colnot C, Marcucio RS. Effect of bone morphogenetic protein signaling on development of the jaw skeleton. Dev Dyn 2008; 237: 3727–3737.

Kjaer I. Formation and early prenatal location of the human mental foramen. Scand J Dent Res 1989; 97:1–7.

Kjaer I, Bagheri A. Prenatal development of the alveolar bone of human deciduous incisors and canines. J Dent Res 1999; 78:667–672.

Mandarim-de Lacerda CA, Alves MU. Human mandibular prenatal growth: bivariate and multivariate growth allometry comparing different mandibular dimensions. Anat Embryol 1992; 186:537–541.

Merida-Velasco JA, Sanchez-Montesinos I, Espin-Ferra J, et al. Developmental differences in the ossification process of the human corpus and ramus mandibulae. Anat Rec 1993; 235:319–324.

Oka K, Oka S, Hosokawa R, et al. TGF-beta mediated Dlx5 signaling plays a crucial role in osteochondroprogenitor cell lineage determination during mandible development. Dev Biol 2008; 321:303–309.

Orliaguet T, Darcha C, Dechelotte P, Vanneuville G. Meckel's cartilage in the human embryo and fetus. Anat Rec 1994; 238:491–497.

Orliaguet T, Dechelotte P, Scheye T, Vanneuville G. Relations between Meckel's cartilage and the morphogenesis of the mandible in the human embryo. Surg Radiol Anat 1993; 15:41–46.

Orliaguet T, Dechelotte P, Scheye T, Vanneuville G. The relationship between Meckel's cartilage and the development of the human fetal mandible. Surg Radiol Anat 1993; 15:113–118.

Ouchi Y, Abe S, Sun-Ki R, et al. Attachment of the sphenomandibular ligament to bone during intrauterine embryo development for the control of mandibular movement. Bull Tokyo Dent Coll 1998; 39:91–94.

Rodriguez-Vazquez JF, Merida-Velasco JR, Arraez-Aybar LA, Jimenez-Collado J. A duplicated Meckel's cartilage in a human fetus. Anat Embryol 1997; 195: 497–502.

Rodriguez-Vazquez JF, Merida-Velasco JR, Jimenez Collado J. A study of the os goniale in man. Acta Anat 1991; 142:188–192.

Rodriguez-Vazquez JF, Merida-Velasco JR, Jimenez Collado J. Development of the human sphenomandibular ligament. Anat Rec 1992; 233:453–460.

Rodriguez-Vazquez JF, Merida-Velasco JR, Merida-Velasco JA, et al. Development of Meckel's cartilage in the symphyseal region in man. Anat Rec 1997; 249:249–254.

Sherer DM, Metlay LA, Woods JR Jr. Lack of mandibular movement manifested by absent fetal swallowing: a possible factor in the pathogenesis of micrognathia. Am J Perinatol 1995; 12:30–33.

Uchida Y, Akiyoshi T, Goto M, Katsuki T. Morphological changes of human mandibular bone during fetal periods. Okajimas Folia Anat Jpn 1994; 71:227–247.

Watson WJ, Katz VL. Sonographic measurement of the fetal mandible: standards for normal pregnancy. Am J Perinatol 1993; 10:226–228.

# 13 Temporomandibular Joint

## GENETICS

The expression of many genes that play critical roles in cartilage differentiation and growth include BMP4, FGF2, IHH, CBFA1 (RUNX2/OSF2), TGFβ2, VEGF, SOX9, AGGRECAN, COL2A1 and COLXA1, and a crucial role for SHOX genes. The combined ontogeny of intramembranous and endochondral bone in temporomandibular joint development presents a very complex genetic milieu in determining the precise roles and timing of expression and repression of this cocktail of genes.

## MORPHOGENESIS

The temporomandibular joint is a secondary development, both in its evolutionary (phylogenetic) and embryological (ontogenetic) history. The joint between the malleus and incus that develops at the dorsal end of Meckel's cartilage is phylogenetically the primary jaw joint, and is homologous with the jaw joint of reptiles. With the development, both in evolution and embryologically, of the middle-ear chamber, this primary Meckel's joint loses its association with the mandible, reflecting adaption of the bones of the primitive jaw joint to sound conduction (see Chapter 18). The mammalian temporomandibular joint develops as an entirely new and separate jaw joint mechanism.

In the human fetus, the primitive joint within Meckel's cartilage, before the malleus and incus form, functions briefly as a jaw joint, mouth-opening movements having started at 8 weeks postconception (pc)—well before development of the definitive temporomandibular joint. When the temporomandibular joint forms at 10 weeks pc, both the malleoincudal and definitive jaw joints move in synchrony for about 8 weeks in fetal life. They are both moved by muscles supplied by the same mandibular division of the trigeminal nerve, that is, the tensor tympani to the malleus and the masticatory muscles to the mandible.

The embryonic development of the temporomandibular joint differs considerably from that of other synovial joints, reflecting its complicated evolutionary history. Most synovial joints complete the development of their initial cavity by the seventh week pc, but the temporomandibular joint does not start to appear until this time. Whereas limb joints develop directly into their adult form by cavity formation within the single blastema from which both adjoining endochondral bones develop (Fig. 13–1), the temporomandibular joint develops from initially widely separated temporal and condylar blastemata that grow toward each other (Fig. 13–2). The temporal blastema arises from the otic capsule, a component of the basicranium that forms the petrous temporal bone. The condylar blastema arises from the secondary condylar cartilage of the mandible. In contrast to

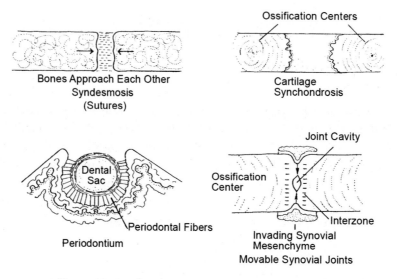

Figure 13–1 Embryonic origins of various types of joints.

other synovial joints, fibrous cartilage, rather than hyaline cartilage, forms on the articular facets of the temporal mandibular fossa and mandibular condyle. In the latter site, the underlying secondary cartilage acts as a growth center.

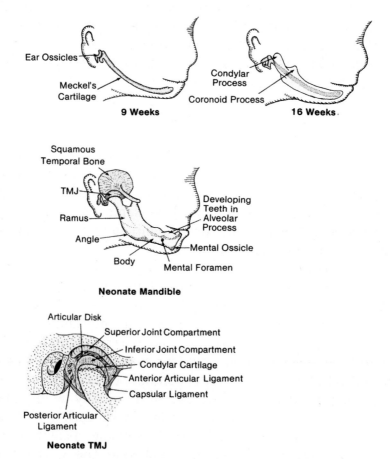

Figure 13–2 Development of the mandible and temporomandibular joint.

Because Meckel's cartilage plays no part in development of the mandibular condyle, it does not contribute to formation of the definitive temporomandibular joint. Membranous bone forming lateral to Meckel's cartilage, first appearing at 6 weeks pc, forms the initial mandibular body and ramus. Concomitantly, the lateral pterygoid muscle develops medial to the future condylar area and initiates movement of Meckel's cartilage by its contractions at 8 weeks pc, functioning through the primary meckelian joint.

Between the 10th and 12th weeks pc, the accessory mandibular condylar cartilage develops as the first blastema, growing toward the later-developing temporal blastema. The temporal articular fossa is initially convex, but progressively assumes its definitive concave shape. The initially wide intervening mesenchyme is narrowed by condylar growth and differentiates into layers of fibrous tissue. During the 10th week pc, two clefts develop in the interposed vascular fibrous connective tissue, forming the two joint cavities and thereby defining the intervening articular disk. The inferior compartment forms first (at 10 weeks), separating the future disk from the developing condyle, and the upper compartment starts to appear at about 11.5 weeks. Cavitation occurs by degradation rather than by enzymic liquefaction or cell death. Synovial membrane invasion may be necessary for cavitation. Synovial fluid production by this method lubricates movements in the joint.

Muscle movement is requisite to joint cavitation: the connective tissues separating the initially discrete, small spaces have to be ruptured for the spaces to coalesce into functional cavities. Early immobilization of developing joints results in absence of joint cavities and fusion of the articulations, with consequent skeletal distortions.

Early functional activity of the temporomandibular joint provides biomechanical stresses that produce ischemia in the differentiating tissues of the joint, facilitating chondrogenesis in the condyle and articular fossa. Functional pressures contribute to contouring of the articulating surfaces.

The articular disk, appearing at 7.5 weeks, is biconcave ab initio, suggesting genetic determination and not functional shaping. It gains thickness and density, subdividing into superior, intermediate and inferior laminae. The disk is continuous ventrally with the tendon of the lateral pterygoid muscle. The dorsal aspect subdivides its attachments: the superior lamina, following the contour of the squamous temporal bone, inserts in the region of the petrosquamous fissure; the intermediate lamina continues into the middle ear through the petrotympanic fissure, inserting into the malleus and anterior ligament of the malleus (diskomalleolar ligament); the inferior lamina curves caudally and inserts into the dorsal aspect of the mandibular condyle.

A condensation of mesenchyme forms the anlage of the joint capsule, progressively isolating the joint with its synovial membrane from the surrounding tissues. The joint capsule composed of fibrous tissue, recognizable by the 11th week pc, forms lateral ligaments.

The temporomandibular joint of the newborn child is a comparatively lax structure, with stability solely dependent upon the capsule surrounding the joint; it is more mobile than at any time later. At birth, the mandibular fossa is almost flat and bears no articular tubercle: only after eruption of the permanent dentition, at 7 years, does the articular tubercle begin to become prominent; its development accelerates until the 12th year of life. When the condyle is absent, there is no well-defined fossa or tubercle.

The joint structures grow laterally, concomitant with widening of the neurocranium. The temporal element, rather than the condyles, is critical in establishing this lateral growth. The articular surface of the fossa and tubercle becomes more fibrous and less vascular with age. In postnatal life, as the articular tubercle grows, the disk changes shape and becomes more compact, less cellular and more collagenous. The mature disk is avascular and aneural in its central portion, but is filled with vessels, nerves and elastic fibers posteriorly, attaching it to the squamotympanic suture.

## ANOMALIES OF DEVELOPMENT

Defective development of the joint results in ankylosis, producing immobilization and impaired mandibular formation. Absence of all elements of the joint is exceedingly rare. Failure of cavitation of one or both joint compartments results in ankylosis that may be unilateral or bilateral. The functionless joint results in mandibular maldevelopment together with masticatory distress of varying severity. Whereas absence of the articular disk is exceedingly rare, its perforation, resulting in intercompartmental communication, is fairly common, and not necessarily debilitating.

## SELECTED BIBLIOGRAPHY

Ashworth GJ. The attachments of the temporomandibular joint meniscus in the human fetus. Br J Oral Maxillofac Surg 1990; 28:246–250.

Bach-Petersen S, Kjaer I, Fischer-Hansen B. Prenatal development of the human osseous temporomandibular region. J Craniofac Genet Dev Biol 1994; 14:135–143.

Berraquero R, Palacios J, Gamallo C, et al. Prenatal growth of the human mandibular condylar cartilage. Am J Orthod Dentofacial Orthop 1995; 108:194–200.

Gu S, Wei N, Yu L, et al. Shox2 –deficiency leads to dysplasia and ankylosis of the temporomandiblar joint in mice. Mech Dev 2008; 125:729–742.

Merida-Velasco JR, Rodriguez-Vazquez JF, Merida-Velasco JA, et al. Development of the human temporomandibular joint. Anat Rec 1999; 255:20–33.

Merida-Velasco JR, Rodriguez-Vazquez JF, Merida-Velasco JA, Jimenez-Collado J. The vascular relationship between the temporomandibular joint and the middle ear in the human fetus. J Oral Maxillofac Surg 1999; 57:146–153.

Ogutcen-Toller M. The morphogenesis of the human discomalleolar and sphenomandibular ligaments. J Cranio-Maxillofac Surg 1995; 23:42–46.

Ogutcen-Toller M, Juniper RP. The embryologic development of the human lateral pterygoid muscle and its relationships with the temporomandibular joint disc and Meckel's cartilage. J Oral Maxillofac Surg 1993; 51:772–778; discussion 778–779.

Ogutcen-Toller M, Juniper RP. The development of the human lateral pterygoid muscle and the temporomandibular joint and related structures: a three-dimensional approach. Early Hum Dev 1994; 39:57–68.

Radlanski RJ, Lieck S, Bontschev NE. Development of the human temporomandibular joint. Computer-aided 3D-reconstructions. Eur J Oral Sci 1999; 107: 25–34.

Ramieri G, Bonardi G, Morani V, et al. Development of nerve fibres in the temporomandibular joint of the human fetus. Anat Embryol 1996; 194;57–64.

Razook SJ, Gotcher JE Jr, Bays RA. Temporomandibular joint noises in infants: review of the literature and report of cases. Oral Surg Oral Med Oral Pathol 1989; 67:658–664.

Rodriguez-Vazquez JF, Merida-Velasco JR, Jimenez-Collado J. Relationships between the temporomandibular joint and the middle ear in human fetuses. J Dent Res 1993; 72:62–66.

Sato I, Ishikawa H, Shimada K, et al. Morphology and analysis of the development of the human temporomandibular joint and masticatory muscle. Acta Anat 1994; 149:55–62.

Valenza V, Farina E, Carini F. The prenatal morphology of the articular disk of the human temporomandibular joint. Ital J Anat Embryol 1993; 98:221–230.

# 14 Skull Growth: Sutures and Cephalometrics

*In cranial development, the contents induce the container...*

J. Schowing (1974)

The hard unyielding nature of the bones of the skull that are studied postmortem belie the plasticity of bone tissue in the living. It is this plasticity, responsive to the influences of the surrounding soft tissues and the metabolism of the individual, that allows bone growth and, incidentally, bone distortions to occur.

The mechanisms of bone growth are described in Chapter 6; it is the purpose of this chapter to collate the growth of all the disparate components of the skull (detailed in Chapters 7 to 13), to provide a basis for clinical analysis of the growing skull. Little attention has been paid to *prenatal growth* of the skull, compared with its prenatal *development*; further, most studies have been directed toward *postnatal* skull growth because of its clinical significance and the possibilities of therapeutic intervention in the event of abnormalities.

Skull growth is studied at both the macroscopic and microscopic levels. Polycystin-1 is required for proliferation of osteochondroprogenitor cells of both mesodermal and neural crest origin for skull growth. Anatomically, one can calculate changes from measurements of shape, size and structure of postmortem material and with cephalometric radiographic techniques in the living. Comparison of distances between radiological landmarks on skull radiographs provides a basis for assessing facial growth patterns. The measurement of distances between landmarks and the angles between skull planes constitute cephalometrics, a science employed in diagnostic orthodontics. Microscopically, examination of bone growth involves study of osteoblastic and osteoclastic activity, vascular alterations and correlation of patterns of lamellar organization with surface remodeling. Microradiography reveals the progress of mineralization in bone trabeculae, and labeling with radioactive isotopes and intravital dyes provides information about sites of bone deposition and resorption. Intravital bone-labeling dyes will show the contour of bone growth by three-dimensional reconstruction of serial sections of bone tissue.

Skull growth results from a combination of (1) bone remodeling (deposition and resorption) (see p. 85), (2) apposition of bone at sutures and synchondroses and (3) transposition-displacement of enlarged and remodeled bones.

## SYNCHONDROSES

Endochondral bone-junction sites are known as *synchondroses*, where cartilage is interposed between contiguous bones. Skull growth may occur by intrinsic cartilage growth or by endochondral bone apposition. Most of the synchondroses that exist prenatally disappear soon after birth. The most persistent, of significance in postnatal skull growth, is the spheno-occipital synchondrosis (see p. 113). The rostral half of the spheno-occipital synchondrosis is of dual neural crest-mesodermal origin, whereas the caudal half is of wholly mesodermal origin. The sphenoethmoidal junction may persist postnatally as a synchondrosis, although desmo-lytic degeneration of the cartilage produces a suture that is of minimal significance in postnatal growth even though fusing occurs only late in adolescence.

The synchondroses within the condylar areas of the occipital bones may contribute slightly to skull growth; they start to fuse between 3 and 4 years of age (see p. 111). The three synchondroses between the four parts of the prenatal sphenoid bone (the midsphenoidal synchondrosis between the presphenoid and postsphenoid, and the bilateral synchondroses between the body and greater wings of the sphenoid) fuse at birth and thus do not contribute to postnatal skull growth.

## SUTURES

Sutures are one of a variety of immovable bone joints (synarthroses) that, by definition, are limited to the skull. Their locations are genetically determined, but environmental stresses influence their form. Cranial suture fusion and maintenance of patency depend on an array of transcription factors, growth factor receptors, cytokines and extracellular matrix molecules (Fig. 14–1). Heterozygous loss of TWIST1 function and a reduction in expression of ephrin (EphA4) causes coronal synostosis. Sutures play a significant role in skull growth. Although they form a firm bond between adjacent bones, they allow slight movement and thus absorb mechanical stress. Intramembranous skull bones are separated by a zone of connective tissue, the sutural ligament or membrane, made up of several layers (Fig. 14–2). The sutural ligament is part of the initial membrane in which the bones ossify. The suture sites appear to inhibit osteogenesis by a cellular degeneration mechanism (apoptosis) that differs from necrosis in that the cells participate in this process, which determines the site's location between encroaching adjacent bones. The sutures of the calvaria differ from those of the facial skeleton, reflecting the slightly different mechanisms of intramembranous osteogenesis in the two areas. The calvarial bones develop in the ectomeninx and their intervening sutures are composed of parallel fibers continuous with the pericranium and dura mater. By contrast, the facial bones ossify in relatively unstructured mesenchyme, each forming a separate periosteal fibrous covering whose fibers are tangential to the bone, with no fibers uniting adjacent bones until sutural junction is near. Secondary cartilage is a component of some sutures, predominantly in the sagittal and midpalatal sutures. This intra-membranous cartilage may indicate mechanical stress, as it also appears in fracture-healing sites. The possible contribution of sutural cartilages to skull growth has not been assessed.

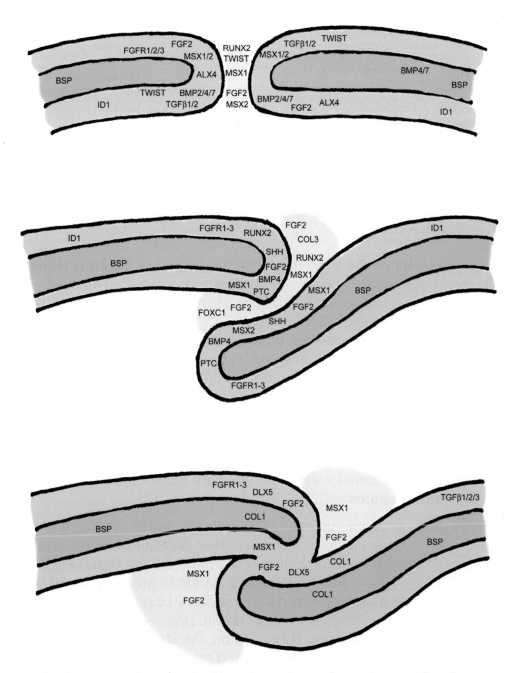

**Figure 14–1** Genes and transcription factors acting on sites of suture formation, based on mouse models. Schematic of suture patterning progression. Representative factors illustrated include transcription factors ALX4, DLX5, FOXC1, ID1 (Inhibitor of DNA binding 1), MSX1, -2, RUNX2 and TWIST. Participatory signaling factors include FGF1, -2, -3, and their receptors (FGFR1-3), TGFβ-1, -2, BMP2, -4, -7, and SHH (and its receptor PTC [patched]). Structural factors found in the suture include COL1 (collagen type I), and bone sialoprotein (BSP). (Courtesy of Dr. Yingli Wang, Mount Sinai School of Medicine, N.Y.)

The skull contains several types of suture:

1. *Serrate suture*—the bone edges are saw-like or notched. Examples are the sagittal and coronal sutures, that, together with the convex shape of the articulating parietal and frontal bones, enable the cranium to withstand blows of considerable force.

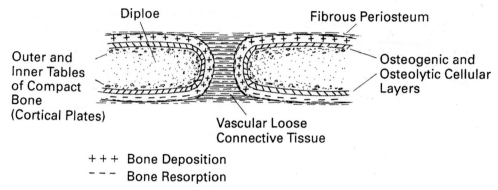

+ + + Bone Deposition

‾ ‾ ‾ Bone Resorption

Figure 14–2 Schematic diagram of suture between calvarial bones.

2. *Denticulate suture*—the small tooth-like projections of the articulating bones widen toward their free ends. This union provides an even more effective interlocking than does a serrate suture. An example is the lambdoid suture.

3. *Squamous or beveled suture*—one bone overlaps another, as at the squamous suture between the temporal and parietal bones. The articulating bones are reciprocally beveled, one internally, one externally. The beveled surfaces may be mutually ridged or serrated.

4. *Plane or butt-end suture*—the flat-end contiguous bone surfaces are usually roughened and irregular in a complementary manner. An example is the midpalatal suture.

Other types of fibrous joints in the skull are more specialized and are not classified as sutures.

1. *Schindylesis*—a "tongue-in-groove" type of articulation in which a thin plate of one bone fits into a cleft in another. An example is the articulation of the perpendicular plate of the ethmoid bone with the vomer.

2. *Gomphosis*—a "peg-in-hole" type of articulation in which a conical process of one bone is inserted into a socket-like portion of another. An example is the initial (prefusion) styloid process articulation with the petrous temporal bone. By extension, the attachment of teeth into the dental alveoli of the maxilla and mandible are described as gomphoses. The coronal and sagittal sutures, by interdigitation of the projections from the frontal and parietal bones, assume a multi-gomphosis joint structure to resist mechanical forces exerted at the sutures.

## Growth at Suture Sites

Sutures are the sites of cellular proliferation and fiber formation where appositional osteogenesis contributes to growth of the adjacent bones. Experimental evidence indicates that sutural bone growth is compensatory to separating forces that are the primary determinants of skull growth. Bone separation is not a pure translatory movement, but rather an alternating oscillatory separation. It responds to functional matrices operating

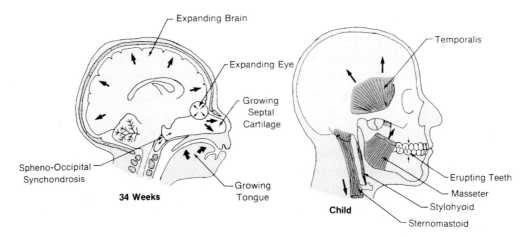

Figure 14–3 Functional matrices operating on skull growth.

by pressure or tension on the bones arising from growth of organs or muscle pull (Fig. 14–3).

Changes in head shape are also subject to external factors, such as molding at birth and increasing nasopharyngeal capacity with increasing body size (Fig. 14–4).

For further discussion of this topic, see pp. 83 and 96.

### Sutural Fusion

Closure or fusion of sutures, by intramembranous ossification, converts syndesmoses into synostoses. The majority of craniosynostosis syndromes are the result of mutations in genes encoding fibroblast growth factor receptor (FGFR)–1, FGFR-2, FGFR-3 and the transcription factors TWIST and MSX2. Such fusion effectively closes off further growth potential at a suture site. Sutures begin to fuse on both the outer and inner tables of skull bones simultaneously, but closure on the outer table is slower, more variable and less complete. There is great variation in the timing of sutural closures, making this phenomenon an unreliable criterion of age. However, some sutures consistently close before others.

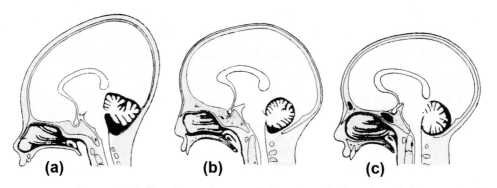

Figure 14–4 Changes in skull and nasopharyngeal shape in sagittal sections of: (a) neonate; (b) 6-year-old; (c) 13-year-old. Note distended neurocranium at birth and enlarging nasopharyngeal capacity with increasing age. (Not drawn to scale)

The interfrontal or metopic suture* starts closing after the first year and is usually obliterated by 7 years of age, thereby converting the paired frontal bones into a single bone. The sagittal, coronal and lambdoidal sutures fuse between 20 and 40 years of age. The occipitomastoid, sphenotemporal and squamous sutures may not be completely fused even at 70 years.

### Craniosynostosis

Premature fusion of sutures (synostosis) results in premature cessation of sutural growth. Abnormal intrauterine compression of the cranium is a factor in causing premature fusion by altering the immature sutural tissue and initiating mineralization of the sutural ligament. Synostosis is largely confined to the calvaria; it is far less common in the face because of early structural differences in facial and calvarial sutures: the former are composed of periosteal capsules, whereas the latter are layered in the directions of bone growth.

Arrested bone growth occurs at right angles to the fused suture, with consequent abnormal compensatory growth in other directions that results in distortions of skull shape. The effects of premature synostosis on skull shape depend upon the location of the sutures and timing of the fusion, and may be part of certain malformation syndromes; for example, Apert syndrome (acrocephalosyndactyly) and Crouzon syndrome (craniofacial dysostosis).

Suture closure is also sensitive to brain growth; for example, sutures and fontanelles close prematurely in microcephaly, and fusion of sutures is delayed in hydrocephaly.

Isolated premature synostoses produce characteristic skull distortions as a result of redirection of continued neural growth toward the patent sutures. Synostosis of the sagittal suture limits lateral skull growth, redirecting growth anteroposteriorly. Bilateral synostosis of the coronal sutures limits anteroposterior growth of the calvaria, producing a pointed (oxycephaly), short (brachycephaly) skull; premature synostosis of one side of the coronal or lambdoidal suture causes obliquity of the skull (plagiocephaly). The degree of skull deformity depends upon the number of sutures involved and the time of onset of the premature fusion—the earlier the synostosis, the greater the deformity.

Premature fusion of the synchondroses of the skull base causes underdevelopment of the middle third of the face (see p. 126), with a reduced cranial base and excessive vaulting of the calvaria, and in some cases, anomalies such as exophthalmia, midfacial hypoplasia and dental malocclusion.

## CRANIOFACIAL GROWTH

The rapid directional growth of the basicranial cartilages and Meckel's cartilage between 7 and 10 weeks postconception (pc) accounts

---

*Persistence of the metopic suture into adulthood occurs in approximately 15% of individuals.

for the typical facial changes and appearances before ossification. Because growth movements of the cartilages are important to spatial relocation of the developing facial bones, alterations in cartilage growth at this time may have significant irreversible consequences for later craniofacial morphology.

Craniofacial growth patterns may be subdivided into three components. A general component—accounting for most variation–defines variations in proportions related to size increase, known as allometry. Factors residual to and independent of size discriminate shape. Brain growth predominates in the fetal period, flattening the cranial base. This base determines the displacement of the nasomaxillary segment; growth of the orbital contents and nasal septum becomes less important as their relative size decreases.

The period of greatest displacement of the nasomaxillary segment (downward and forward "growth") is between the second and third months pc concomitant with precocious expansion of the temporal lobes of the cerebrum. In anencephaly, the absence of the brain results in nonflattening of the cranial base, allowing the facial bones to occupy anomalous positions. During the second and third months pc, the mandible first lags behind the maxilla in growth and then speeds up to regain parity.

The second component of regional variation is alveolar remodeling; the third is condylar growth. Sexual dimorphism progressively favors males over females with age, as a result of accumulating differences in size and related proportional changes in shape. Timing of the condylar growth spurt, as evident from the ramus height, produces secondary dimorphism that diminishes after adolescence.

After 4 years of age, craniofacial growth is not proportional. Neurocranial components grow relatively the least, and mandibular parts the most; the other facial components have intermediate patterns of relative growth.

## CEPHALOMETRICS

Few, if any, of the areas, points and planes that orthodontists and anthropologists use as fixed landmarks are stationary. Implanted metallic markers move during growth, by shifting with the surface to which they are attached, by being covered with new bone or, conversely, by being exposed by resorption and then freed from their site. Bone-growth markers such as metal implants, intravital staining or radioisotope labels give information about static areas for limited periods only during active growth.

Statistical analysis of serial radiographic measurements by computers provide a new tool for determining skull growth. Calculations of mean growth patterns for large defined populations establish standards that enable one to predict statistically the probable growth pattern of individual children in that population. Interceptive therapy might be undertaken on the basis of the prediction to minimize undesirable facial and dental growth patterns.

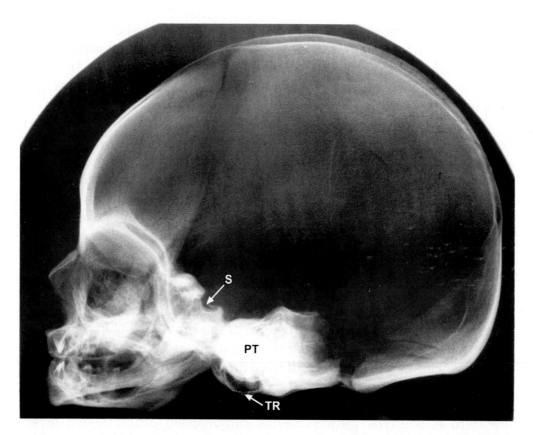

**Figure 14–5** Lateral radiograph of a neonatal skull. Slight tilting of the skull diverges superimposition of left and right sides. Calcifying tooth buds are seen in the maxillae and mandible. Note the facial and neurocranial proportions of the skull. S, Sella turcica; PT, petrous temporal bone; TR, tympanic ring.

Radiographic cephalometry is now widely used clinically for analysis of craniofacial forms; applied periodically on growing children, this provides longitudinal growth measurements (Figs. 14–5 and 14–6). Standardized positioning of the head in cephalostats allows the superimposition of serial lateral and frontal skull radiographs of an individual for the calculation of growth data. Standardized radiological landmarks and artificial planes and angles are used for cephalometric analysis; because growth changes render them unstable, great care should be exercised in their use in analysis.

Recent advances in 3-dimensional imaging software with cone-beam and digital volume computerized tomography can provide new and more accurate landmarks in cephalometric analysis of skull growth and deviations from accepted norms.

The principal radiological landmarks and their clinically recognized abbreviations (Fig. 14–7) are:

*Nasion* (N): the most depressed point of the frontonasal suture.
*Anterior nasal spine* (ANS): the most anterior point of the nasal cavity floor.
*Subspinale* (Point A): the most depressed point on the concavity between the anterior nasal spine and prosthion.
*Prosthion* (P): the most anterior point of the maxillary alveolus.
*Infradentale* (I): the most anterior point of the mandibular alveolus.

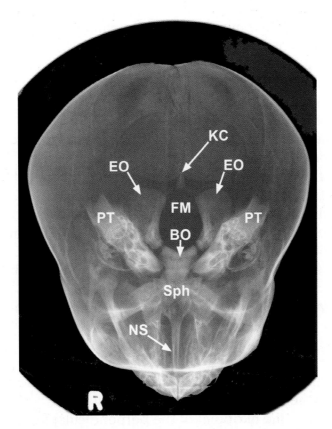

**Figure 14–6** Vertical radiograph of a neonatal skull. Calcifying tooth buds are in the superimposed maxillae and mandible. The cochlea and semicircular canals are embedded in the petrous temporal bone (PT) lateral to which are the adult-size ear ossicles in the tympanum. NS, nasal septum; Sph, body of sphenoid; BO, basioccipital; EO, exoccipital; FM, foramen magnum; KC, Kerckring's center in squamous occipital.

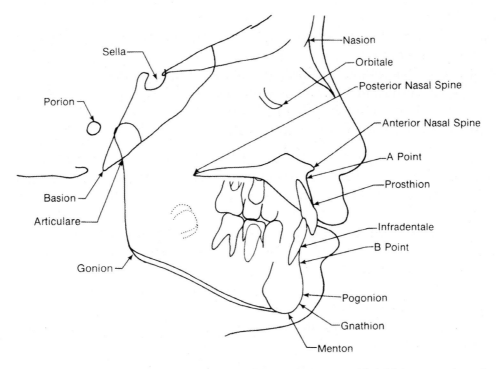

**Figure 14–7** Cephalometric tracing of lateral view x-ray of a 12-year-old child depicting the radiological landmarks used in cephalometrics. (Courtesy of Dr. K. E. Glover.)

*Supramentale* (*Point* B): the most depressed point on the concavity between infradentale and pogonion.

*Pogonion* (Pg): the most anterior point of the bony chin.

*Gnathion* (Gn): the point where the anterior and lower borders of the mandible meet.

*Menton* (M): the lowest point of the mandible.

*Gonion* (Go): the point of intersection of the mandibular base line and posterior ramus line.

*Articulare* (Ar): the point of intersection of the inferior cranial base and the posterior surface of the mandibular condyles.

*Sella* (S): the midpoint of the sella turcica (pituitary fossa).

*Basion* (Ba): the midpoint on the anterior margin of the foramen magnum (the posterior end of the midline cranial base).

*Orbitale* (O): the lowest point of the inferior border of the orbital cavity.

*Posterior nasal spine* (PNS): the most posterior midline point of the hard palate.

*Porion* (Po): the midpoint of the upper margin of the external acoustic meatus.

*Bolton point* (BP): the highest point of the curve between the occipital condyle and the lower border of the occipital bone.

*Registration point* (R): the midpoint of the perpendicular from sella to the Bolton-nasion line.

The chief planes are:

*Frankfort plane*: the line passing through porion and orbitale.

*Sella-nasion plane*: the line passing through sella and nasion (SN).

*Occlusal plane*: a line passing through the occlusal surfaces of the posterior teeth.

*Mandibular plane*: line tangent to the lower border of the mandible passing through menton.

*Palatal plane*: line joining anterior and posterior nasal spines.

*Facial plane*: vertical line joining nasion to pogonion.

*Bolton plane*: line from Bolton point to nasion.

*Y-axis* (*growth axis*): line from sella to gnathion.

Various cephalometric analyses are available for the clinical evaluation of facial form; the clinician can select the linear and angular measurements, and/or interrelationships, it is thought will provide the best assessment of the individual patient's facial disproportion. In most cases, the relationship of the various measurements, lines, planes and angles is more important than the absolute size of a specific measurement. Data derived from longitudinal growth studies are being used in attempts to develop methods that will predict growth more accurately. This will eventually benefit the clinician, who analyses facial form at the time of examination, but needs to extrapolate to predict how the face would look at a later date with or without treatment.

## SELECTED BIBLIOGRAPHY

Bildsoe H, Loebel DAF, Jones VJ. Requirements for Twist I in frontonasal and skull vault development in the mouse embryo. Dev Biol 2009; 331: 176–188.

Bettega G, Chenin M, Sadek H, et al. Three–dimensional fetal cephalometry. Cleft Palate Craniofac J 1996; 33:463–467.

Chadduck WM, Boop FA, Blankenship JB, Husain M. Teningioma and sagittal craniosynostosis in an infant: case report. Neurosurgery1992; 30:441–442.

Cohen MM Jr, McLean RE (eds). Craniosynostosis: diagnosis, evaluation and management. New York: Oxford University Press, 2000.

Connerney J, Andreeva V, Leshem Y, et al. Twist1 homodimers enhance FGF responsiveness of the cranial sututres and promote suture closure. Dev Biol 2008; 318:323–334.

Guimaraes-Ferreira J, Miguens J, Lauritzen C. Advances in craniosynostosis research and management. Adv Tech Standards Neurosurg 2004;29:23–83.

Hajihosseini MK, Duarte R, Pegrum J, et al. Evidence that Fgf10 contributes to the skeletal and visceral defects of an Apert syndrome mouse model. Dev Dyn 2009; 238:376–385.

Kanev P M. Congenital malformations of the skull and meninges. Otolaryngol Clin North Am 2007; 40:9–26.

Kolpakova-Hart E, McBratney-Owen B, Hou B, et al. Growth of cranial synchondroses and sutures requires polycystin-1. Dev Biol 2008; 321: 407–419.

Kreiborg S, Cohen MM Jr. Characteristics of the infant Apert skull and its subsequent development. J Craniofac Genet Dev Biol 1990; 10:399–410.

Lagravère MO, Major P. Proposed reference point for 3-dimensional cephalometric analysis with cone-beam computerized tomography. Am J Orthod Dentofac Orthoped 2005; 128: 657–660.

Lenton KA, Nacamuli RP, Wan DC, Helms JA, Longaker MT. Cranial suture biology. Curr Topics Dev Biol 2005; 66: 287–328.

Machin GA. Thanatophoric dysplasia in monozygotic twins discordant for cloverleaf skull: prenatal diagnosis, clinical and pathological findings [letter]. Am J Med Genet 1992; 44:842–843.

Mathijssen IM, Vaandrager JM, van der Meulen JC, et al. The role of bone centers in the pathogenesis of craniosynostosis: an embryologic approach using CT measurements in isolated craniosynostosis and Apert and Crouzon syndromes. Plast Reconst Surg 1996; 98:17–26.

Mathijssen IM, van Splunder J, Vermeij-Keers C, et al. Tracing craniosynostosis to its developmental stage through bone center displacement. J Craniofac Genet Develop Biol 1999; 19:57–63.

Opperman LA, Gakunga PT, Carlson DS. Genetic factors influencing morphogenesis and growth of sutures and synchondroses in the craniofacial complex. Semin Orthod 2005; 11:199–208.

Opperman LA, Nolen AA, Ogle RC. TGF-beta 1, TGF-beta 2, and TGF-beta 3 exhibit distinct patterns of expression during cranial suture formation and obliteration in vivo and in vitro [see comments]. J Bone Mineral Res 1997; 12:301–310.

Opperman LA, Passarelli RW, Morgan EP, Reintjes M, Ogle RC. Cranial sutures require tissue interactions with dura mater to resist osseous obliteration in vitro. J Bone Mineral Res 1995; 10:1978–1987.

Pretorius DH, Nelson TR. Prenatal visualization of cranial sutures and fontanelles with three-dimensional ultrasonography. J Ultrasound Med 1994; 13: 871–876.

Rice DP (ed), Craniofacial sutures: development, disease and treatment. Frontiers of oral biology. Vol 12. Basel: Karger, 2008.

Slater BJ, Lenton KA, Kwan MD, et al. Cranial sutures: a brief review. Plast Reconstr Surg 2008; 121:170e–178e.

Stelnicki EJ, Vanderwall K, Harrison MR, et al. The in utero correction of unilateral coronal craniosynostosis. Plast Reconst Surg 1997; 101:262–269.

Ting M-C, Wu NL, Roybal PG, et al. EphA4 as an effector of Twist 1 in the guidance of osteogenic precursor cells during calvarial bone growth in craniosynostosis. Development 2009; 136: 855–864.

Twigg SRF, Healy C, Babbs C, et al. Skeletal analysis of the Fgfr3 P244R mouse, a genetic model for the Muenke craniosynostosis syndrome. Dev Dyn 2009; 238:331–342.

Young N, Minugh-Purvis T, Shimo B, et al. Indian and sonic hedgehogs regulate synchondrosis growth plate and cranial base development and function. Dev Biol 2006; 299:272–282.

# 15 Tongue and Tonsils

## TONGUE

The tongue arises in the ventral wall of the primitive oropharynx from the inner lining of the first four pharyngeal arches. The covering oropharyngeal mucous membrane rises into the developing mouth as a swelling sac, the result of invasion by muscle tissue from the occipital somites.

During the fourth week postconception (pc), paired lateral thickenings of mesenchyme appear on the internal aspect of the first pharyngeal arches to form the *lingual swellings*. Between and behind these swellings a median eminence appears, the *tuberculum impar* (unpaired tubercle), whose caudal border is marked by a blind pit. This pit, the *foramen cecum* (Fig. 15–1), marks the site of origin of the *thyroid diverticulum*, an endodermal duct that appears during the somite period. The diverticulum migrates caudally ventral to the pharynx (see Figures 15–3, 15–5), as the *thyroglossal duct*, which bifurcates and subdivides to form the *thyroid gland*.* The gland descends to reach its definitive level caudal to the thyroid cartilage at the end of the 7th week pc. The thyroglossal duct normally disintegrates and disappears between the 5th and 10th weeks pc. The caudal attachment of the duct may persist as the pyramidal lobe of the thyroid gland.

The lingual swellings grow and fuse with each other, encompassing the tuberculum impar, to provide the ectodermally derived mucosa of the

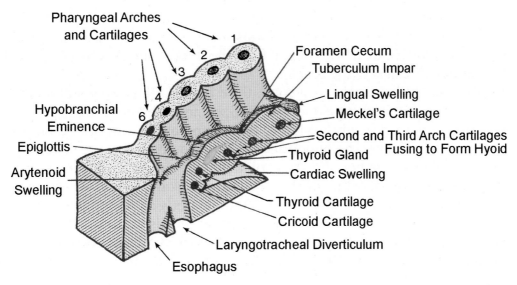

Figure 15–1  Tongue primordia arising in the ventral wall of the pharynx of a 4-week-old embryo.

---

*Thyroid tissue occasionally remains in the substance of the tongue, giving rise to a *lingual thyroid gland*.

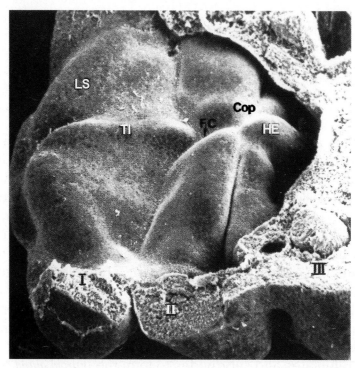

**Figure 15–2** Scanning electron micrograph of the developing tongue of a 33- to 35-day-old embryo. The pharyngeal arches (I, II, III) border the floor of the mouth The lingual swelling (LS) develops from the first pharyngeal arch, the tuberculum impar (TI) between the first and second pharyngeal arches and the hypobranchial eminence (HE) from the third pharyngeal arch. The foramen cecum (FC) is hidden between the tuberculum impar and the copula (Cop). (From Shaw, Sweeney et al. Textbook of oral biology. Philadelphia: W.B. Saunders, 1978; by permission of Drs Waterman and Meller and the publishers, W. B. Saunders.)

body (anterior two-thirds) of the tongue (Fig. 15–2).[†] Around the periphery of the fused, elevated lingual swellings there is an epithelial proliferation into the underlying mesenchyme. Degeneration of the central cells of this horseshoe-shaped lamina forms a sulcus, the *linguogingival groove*, which frees the body of the tongue from the floor of the mouth except for the midline *frenulum* of the tongue.

The ventral bases of the second, third and fourth pharyngeal arches elevate into a united, single midventral prominence known as the *copula* (a yoke). A posterior subdivision of this prominence is identified as the *hypobranchial eminence*. The endodermally derived mucosa of the second to fourth pharyngeal arches and the copula provide the covering for the root (posterior one-third) of the tongue. A V-shaped *sulcus terminalis*, whose apex is the foramen cecum, demarcates the mobile body of the tongue from its fixed root (Fig. 15–4). The line of the sulcus terminalis is marked by 8 to 12 large circumvallate papillae that develop at 2 to 5 months pc. Two different mechanisms guided by WNT11 and SHH expression patterns are respon-

---

[†]In the adult tongue, it is difficult to identify the level where the embryonic oropharyngeal membrane demarcated the transition from ectoderm to endoderm. The greater part of the mucosa of the body of the tongue is believed to be of ectodermal origin.

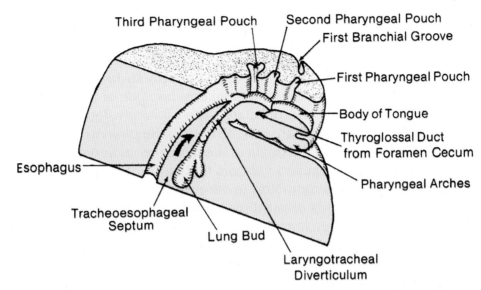

Figure 15–3 Tongue and laryngeal development in a 7-week-old embryo.

sible for circumvallate papilla formation. The mucosa of the dorsal surface of the body of the tongue develops fungiform papillae by WNT induction much earlier—at 11 weeks pc. Filiform papillae develop later, and are not complete until postnatally. At birth, the root mucosa becomes pitted by deep crypts that develop into the lingual tonsil, the completion of which is marked by lymphocytic infiltration (Fig. 15–4).

Taste buds arise by inductive interaction between epithelial cells[‡] and invading gustatory nerve cells from the chorda tympani (facial), glossopharyngeal and vagus nerves. Taste buds form in greatest concentration on the dorsal surface of the tongue and in lesser numbers on the palatoglossal arches, palate, posterior surface of the epiglottis and posterior wall of

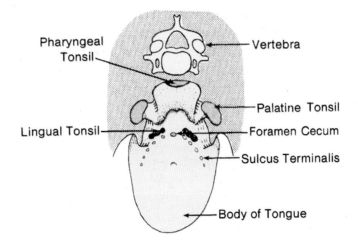

Figure 15–4 Tongue and pharynx of adult. Note the "ring" of lymphoid tissue formed by the lingual, palatine and pharyngeal tonsils.

---

[‡]Taste buds are derived from both ectodermal and endodermal epithelial cells.

the oropharynx. Gustatory cells start to form as early as the seventh week pc, but taste buds are not recognizable until 13 to 15 weeks pc, when taste perception is initiated.* Initially, only single taste buds are present in the fungiform papillae, but these multiply, possibly by branching, in later fetal life. All of the taste buds in the fungiform papillae of the tongue are present at birth, but some circumvallate taste buds develop postnatally.

The muscles of the tongue arise in the floor of the pharynx in the occipital somite region opposite the origin of the hypoglossal nerve. The earlier expression of myogenic regulatory factors (MRF4, MyoD, myogenin) in the potential tongue muscles compared to other somatic muscles reflects the earlier functional demands of suckling immediately preceding and after birth. The glossogenic muscle mass pushes forward as the *hypoglossal cord* beneath the mucous layer of the tongue, carrying the hypoglossal nerve along with it. The path of the hypoglossal nerve in the adult is explained by its embryological origins from its dorsally located brainstem origin, tracking ventrally, superficial to the main arteries and nerves, and ending under the tongue (Fig. 15–5).

The combination of diverse embryological sources of the tongue is reflected in its complex innervation. The embryological components of the tongue, while moving upward and ventrally into the mouth, retain their initially established nerve supplies. Thus, the mucosal contributions of the first pharyngeal arch (trigeminal nerve) are reflected in the lingual nerve's tactile sensory supply to the body of the tongue. The second pharyngeal arch (facial nerve) accounts for gustatory sensation from the body of the

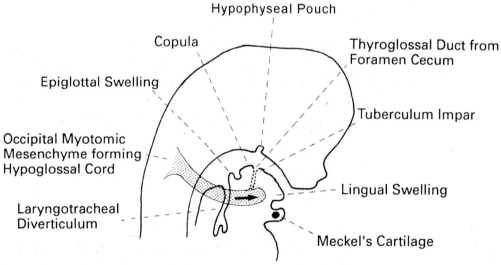

**Figure 15–5** Schematic paramedian section of 5-week-old embryo illustrating development of the ventral wall of the oropharynx, and path of migration of the occipital somite myotomes forming the tongue muscles.

*The addition of sweet saccharine to amniotic fluid induces increased swallowing; used therapeutically to reduce excess amniotic fluid (hydramnios).

tongue through the chorda tympani nerve[§§]. The third- and fourth-arch contributions are recognizable by the mixed tactile and gustatory glossopharyngeal and vagal nerve innervation of the mucosa of the root of the tongue. The palatoglossus muscle is innervated by the pharyngeal plexus, the fibers of which are derived from the third and fourth arch (glossopharyngeal and vagus) and accessory nerves. Finally, the motor innervation of all the musculature of the tongue, except palatoglossus, by the hypoglossal nerve reflects its occipital somite origin.

The tongue's rapid enlargement relative to the space in which it develops results in its occupation of the whole of the stomodeal chamber that later will divide into the mouth, oropharynx and nasopharynx. The initial partition of the stomodeal chamber, by the laterally developing palatal shelves, is delayed by the relatively enormous tongue reaching from the floor to the roof of the stomodeum. Only with later enlargement of the stomodeum does the tongue descend into the mouth chamber proper, allowing the palatal shelves to close off the mouth from the nasal fossae (see p. 50).

The entire tongue is within the mouth at birth; its posterior one-third descends into the pharynx by the age of 4 years. The tongue normally doubles in length, breadth and thickness between birth and adolescence, its anterior portion reaching near maximal size by about 8 years, while the posterior region continues to grow to reach adult size at 15 to 16 years. In early stages, its growth tends to be precocious relative to the size of the mouth, reflecting its early role in suckling. Also, the large tongue in a small mouth partly accounts for the peculiar tongue-thrusting character of the infant's early swallowing pattern, in which the tongue fills the space between the separated jaws during swallowing. The later enlargement of the mouth facilitates the conversion to the adult pattern of swallowing, in which the tongue tip lies against the palate behind the maxillary incisor teeth (see p. 201).

The hypobranchial eminence, derived from the bases of the third and fourth pharyngeal arches, forms the epiglottis, which guards the entrance to the larynx during swallowing. Cartilage differentiates within the epiglottis by the 15th week pc. The epiglottis is well developed by the 21st week, and is in full contact with the soft palate by the 23rd to 25th week. This contact may relate to fetal respiratory viability, which will enable neonates to breath while swallowing liquids during suckling.

The sites of the second and third pharyngeal arches in the adult pharynx are marked, respectively, by the anterior and posterior pillars of the fauces, between which the palatine (faucial) tonsils develop. Growth of the third and fourth pharyngeal arches, in contributing to the root of the tongue, obliterates the ventral portions of the first and second pharyngeal pouches, leaving the dorsal portions to develop into the auditory tubes and palatine tonsillar fossae, respectively (see p.76).

---

[§§]The chorda tympani nerve is considered to be a pretrematic branch of the second pharyngeal arch nerve (facial nerve) that invades first-arch territory.

## Anomalies of Development

Retention of an abnormally short lingual frenum results in *ankyloglossia* (tongue-tie), a fairly common developmental anomaly. Persistence of the thyroglossal duct may give rise to islands of aberrant thyroid tissue, cysts, fistulae or sinuses in the midline. A *lingual thyroid gland* at the site of the foramen cecum, at the junction of the body and root of the tongue, is not uncommon. Because the tongue influences the paths of eruption of the teeth, the state of its development is of considerable interest to the orthodontist.

The tongue may fail to achieve normal growth rate, resulting in an abnormally small tongue (*microglossia*) or, conversely, overdevelopment (*macroglossia*). Rarely, the tongue fails to develop (*aglossia*) or, as a result of failure of fusion of its components, it becomes forked, bifid or trifid; such clefts are part of the syndrome of *orodigitofacial dysostosis*, which also manifests as hyperplasia of the labial frenula and cleft palate. Microglossia characterizes hypodactylia and occurs in persons with cleft palate, and macroglossia typifies anencephaly, trisomy 21, CHARGE* and Beckwith-Wiedemann syndromes.

## TONSILS

The endoderm lining the second pharyngeal pouch between the tongue and soft palate invades the surrounding mesenchyme as a group of solid buds. The central parts of these buds degenerate, forming the *tonsillar crypts*. Invading lymphoid cells surround the crypts, becoming grouped as lymphoid follicles.

Lymphoid tissue invades the palatine, posterior pharyngeal (adenoids) and lingual tonsillar regions during the third to fifth month pc. These lymphoid masses encircle the oropharynx to form a ring (Waldeyer's ring) of immunodefensive tissue that grows markedly postnatally to bulge into the oropharynx (see Fig. 15–4).

The palatine tonsils arise at the site of the second pharyngeal pouch, while the pharyngeal and lingual tonsils develop in the mucosa of the posterior wall of the pharynx and the root of the tongue, respectively. Lateral extensions of the lymphoid tissue posterior to the openings of the auditory tubes form the tubal tonsils.

These disparate embryonic origins of the tonsils are reflected in differences in their cytology, growth, and involution characteristics. The tonsils are the site of migration of both B and T lymphocytes that synthesize immunoglobulins. Tonsillar growth is variable and cannot be considered to be true growth, but rather an individual response by each tonsil to the development of immunocompetence. Accordingly,

---

*C, coloboma of the eye; H, heart disease; A, atresia of choanae; R, retarded growth; G, genital hypoplasia; E, ear anomalies. CHARGE combines choanal atresia with anomalous skull base and facial defects.

the lymphoid tissue in the four tonsillar sites may not coincide in their growth and regression rates, each achieving its greatest size at a different age, and each enlarging individually in response to immunological challenges. The sizes of the tonsils are thus variable, and reflect more the state of the tonsillar immunodefense mechanisms than the person's age.

Lymphoid tissue is faster growing on the posterior nasopharyngeal wall than elsewhere, achieving its greatest size there by 5 years of age; it thereby narrows the nasopharyngeal airway at this age, with possible mouth-breathing consequences. Thereafter, lymphoid tissue diminishes until the age of 10, when it again increases slightly, briefly, and then resumes the decline in size. Normally, the nasopharynx enlarges in pre-adolescence and early adolescence owing to the concurrent accelerated growth of the bony nasopharynx and involution of the pharyngeal tonsil. Nasopharyngeal enlargement coincides with the adolescent growth spurt to meet increased metabolic demands for oxygen.

Between 8 and 12 years of age is a critical period for the eruption of permanent teeth. The muscle imbalances caused by mouth breathing and the infantile pattern of swallowing could adversely influence tooth eruption patterns and facial development. Dental malocclusion and a narrow "adenoidal facies" have been attributed to mouth breathing habits induced by exuberant pharyngeal (adenoids) and palatine tonsillar growth. Chronic allergies resulting in pharyngeal mucosal hypertrophy, nasal infections, and mechanical blockage by the conchae or deviation of the nasal septum may also lead to mouth-breathing, inducing a syndrome of respiratory obstruction characterized by a tongue-thrusting swallow and dental malocclusion.

## SELECTED BIBLIOGRAPHY

Achiron R, Ben Arie A, Gabbay U, et al.Development of the fetal tongue between 14 and 26 weeks of gestation: in utero ultrasonographic measurements. Ultrasound Obstet Gynecol 1997; 9:39–41.

Barlow LA, Northcutt RG. Analysis of the embryonic lineage of vertebrate taste buds. Chem Senses 1994; 19:715–724.

Choi G, Suh YL, Lee HM, et al. Prenatal and postnatal changes of the human tonsillar crypt epithelium. Acta Otolaryngol Suppl 1996; 523:28–33.

Emmanouil-Nikoloussi EN, Kerameos-Foroglou C. Developmental malformations of human tongue and associated syndromes (review). Bull Group Intl Rech Sci Stomatol Odontol 1992; 35:5–12.

Holibka V. High endothelial venules in the developing human palatine tonsil. Adv Otorhinolaryngol 1992; 47:54–58.

Kim J-Y, Lee M-J, Kim Y-J, et al. SHH and ROCK1 modulate the dynamic epithelial morphogenesis in circumvallate papilla development. Dev Biol 2009; 325: 273–280.

Kimes KR, Mooney MP, Siegel MI, Todhunter JS. Size and growth rate of the tongue in normal and cleft lip and palate human fetal specimens. Cleft Palate Craniofac J 1991; 28:212–216.

Mistretta CM. The role of innervation in induction and differentiation of taste organs: introduction and background. Ann N Y Acad Sci 1998; 855:1–13.

Oakley B. Taste neurons have multiple inductive roles in mammalian gustatory development. Ann NY Acad Sci 1998; 855:50–57.

Okano J, Sakai Y, Shiota K. Retinoic acid down-regulates Tbx1 expression and induces abnormal differentiation of tongue muscles in fetal mice. Dev Dyn 2008; 237:3059–3070.

Slipka J. The development and involution of tonsils. Adv Otorhinolaryngol 1992, 47:1–4.

Stone LM, Finger TE. Mosaic analysis of the embryonic origin of taste buds. Chem Senses 1994; 19:725–735.

Strek P, Litwin JA, Nowogrodzka-Zagorska M, Miodonski AJ. Microvasculature of the dorsal mucosa of human fetal tongue: a SEM study of corrosion casts. Anat Anz 1995; 177:361–366.

Temple EC, Hutchinson J, Laing DG, Jinks AL. Taste development: differential growth rates of tongue regions. Dev Brain Res 2002; 135:65–70.

Witt M, Reutter K. Embryonic and early fetal development of human taste buds: a transmission electron microscopical study. Anat Rec 1996; 246:507–523.

Witt M, Reutter K. Innervation of developing human taste buds. An immunohistochemical study. Histochem Cell Biol 1998; 109:281–291.

Witt M, Kasper M. Immunohistochemical distribution of CD44 and some of its isoforms during human taste bud development. Histochem Cell Biol 1998; 110:95–103.

Witt M, Kasper M. Distribution of cytokeratin filaments and vimentin in developing human taste buds. Anat Embryol 1999; 199:291–299.

# 16 Salivary Glands

The three major sets of salivary glands—the parotid, the submandibular and the sublingual—originate uniformly from oral epithelial buds invading the underlying mesenchyme (Fig. 16–1). All parenchymal (secretory) tissue of the glands arises from proliferation of oral epithelium, which is either ectodermal (for the major glands) or endodermal (for the lingual glands) in origin. Differentiating salivary epithelial cells express Notch 1 to 4, Jagged 1 and 2, and Delta 1. The stroma (capsule and septa) of the glands originates from mesenchyme that may be of either mesodermal or neural crest origin.

In all the salivary glands, following initial formation of the buds, the epithelial cell cord elongates to form the main duct primordium, which invades the subepithelial stroma. At the distal end of this solid mass is a terminal bulb; this is the anlage of the intralobular salivary parenchyma. Branching produces arborization and each branch terminates in one or two solid end bulbs. Branching morphogenesis involves changes in gene expression patterns, reorganization and movement of different cell types by temporal and spatial engagement of several signaling pathways. There are two morphologically distinct cell populations at the single bulb stage. An outer layer of columnar cells with organized E-cadherin junctions will form the secreting acini. The inner layer of cells forms the ductal system. The branching ductal structure is created by repetitive bifurcations, leading to the formation of new epithelial outgrowths. Elongation of the end bulbs follows, and lumina appear in their centers, transforming the end

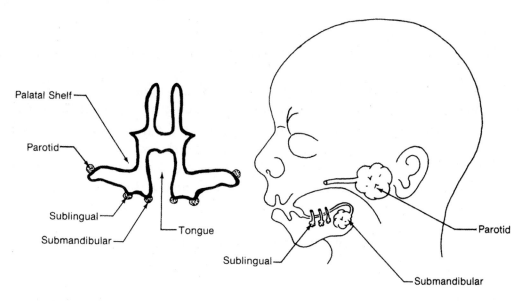

Figure 16–1 Schemata of the major salivary glands budding from the oral cavity. Their origins from the mouth are retained through their excretory ducts. Coronal sectional view through mouth (left).

bulbs into terminal tubules. These tubules join the canalizing ducts (which are forming in the epithelial cord) to the peripheral acini. Canalization results from faster mitosis of the outer layers of the cord than of the inner cell layers and is completed prior to lumen formation beginning in the terminal bulbs. Necrosis of cord cells as a mechanism of canalization has never been observed. Canalization is complete by the sixth month post-conception (pc).

The lining epithelium of the ducts, tubules and acini differentiate both morphologically and functionally. Contractile myoepithelial cells arise from neural crest ectomesenchyme to surround the acini. Myoepithelial cells differentiate at the time of onset of fetal secretory activity in the acini, and achieve their full complement coincident with completion of the adult acinar-intercalated duct pattern at 24 weeks in the submandibular and 35 weeks in the parotid gland. Interaction between epithelia, mesenchyme, nerves and blood vessels is necessary for complete functional salivary gland morphogenesis. Autonomic innervation of the parenchymal cells is a key event in salivary gland development. Sympathetic nerve stimulation is necessary for acinar differentiation while parasympathetic nerve stimulation is important for overall gland growth.

The parotid gland buds are the first to appear at the sixth week pc on the inner cheek near the angles of the mouth, and then grow back toward the ear. The maxillary and mandibular prominences merge, displacing the opening of the duct on the inside of the cheek to some distance dorsally from the corner of the mouth. In the "parotid," or ear region, the epithelial cord of cells branches between the divisions of the facial nerve and canalizes to provide the acini and ducts of the gland. The duct and acinar system is embedded in a mesenchymal stroma that is organized into lobules and the whole gland becomes encapsulated by fibrous connective tissue. The parotid gland duct, repositioned upward, traces the path of the embryonic epithelial cord in the adult. The parotid ducts are canalized at 10 weeks, the terminal buds at 16 weeks and secretions commence at 18 weeks pc.

The submandibular salivary gland buds appear late in the sixth week as a grouped series forming epithelial outgrowths on either side of the midline in the linguogingival groove of the floor of the mouth at the sites of the future papillae. An epithelial cord proliferates dorsally into the mesenchyme beneath the developing mylohyoid muscle, turning ventrally while branching and canalizing, to form the acini and duct of the submandibular gland. Differentiation of the acini starts at 12 weeks; serous secretory activity starts at 16 weeks, increases until the 28th week, and then secretion diminishes. The serous secretions during the 16th to 28th weeks contribute to the amniotic fluid and contain amylase and possibly nerve and epidermal growth factors. Growth of the submandibular gland continues postnatally with the formation of mucous acini. The mesenchymal stroma separates off the parenchymal lobules, and provides the capsule of the gland.

The sublingual glands arise in the eighth week pc as a series of about 10 epithelial buds just lateral to the submandibular gland anlagen. These branch and canalize to provide a number of ducts opening independently beneath the tongue.

A great number of smaller salivary glands arise from the oral ectodermal and endodermal epithelium, and remain as discrete acini and ducts scattered throughout the mouth. Labial salivary glands, on the inner aspect of the lips, arise during the 9th week pc and are morphologically mature by the 25th week pc.

## ANOMALIES OF DEVELOPMENT

Mutations or deletions of FGF10 or PITX2 will result in salivary gland aplasia. Failure of canalization of the buds to form ducts before acinar salivary secretion commences results in retention cysts appearing. Agenesis of the large salivary glands is rare.

## THE JUXTA-ORAL ORGAN OF CHIEVITZ

This isolated structure appears in the adult as a tiny (7- to 17-mm long) white solid strand resembling a nerve, lying ventrodorsally in the cheek between the buccotemporal fascia and the parotid duct penetration of the buccinator muscle. It arises in the embryo as an oral epithelial invasion at the corners of the mouth, developing earlier than the parotid gland anlagen. Its occurrence results from Bone Morphogenetic Protein 7 (BMP7) expression. It is closely associated with the buccal branch of the mandibular nerve that innervates it, but loses its connection with the buccal sulcus, and becomes embedded in a dense connective-tissue sheath. It may be a sensory receptor; its function is unknown.

## SELECTED BIBLIOGRAPHY

Adi MM, Chisholm DM, Waterhouse JP. Histochemical study of lectin binding in the human fetal minor salivary glands. J Oral Pathol Med 1995; 24:130–135.

Chi JG. Prenatal development of human major salivary glands. Histological and immunohistochemical characteristics with reference to adult and neoplastic salivary glands. J Korean Med Sci 1996; 11:203–216.

Chisholm DM, Adi MM. A histological, lectin and S-100 histochemical study of the developing prenatal human sublingual salivary gland. Arch Oral Biol 1995; 40:1073–1076.

D'Andrea V, Malinovsky L, Biancari F, et al. The Chievitz juxtaparotid organ. Giornale di Chirurgia 1999; 20:213–217.

Denny PC, Ball WD, Redman RS. Salivary glands: a paradigm for diversity of gland development. Crit Revue Oral Biol Medicine 1997; 8:51–75.

Espin-Ferra J, Merida-Velasco JA, Garcia-Garcia JD, et al. Relationships between the parotid gland and the facial nerve during human development. J Dent Res 1991; 70:1035–1040.

Guizetti B, Radlanski RJ. Development of the parotid gland and its closer neighboring structures in human embryos and fetuses of 19–67 mm CRL. Anat Anz 1996; 178:503–508.

Guizetti B, Radlanski RJ. Development of the submandibular gland and its closer neighboring structures in human embryos and fetuses of 19–67 mm CRL. Anat Anz 1996; 178:509–515.

Hayashi Y, Kurashima C, Takemura T, Hirokawa K. Ontogenic development of the secretory immune system in human fetal salivary glands. Pathol Immunopathol Res 1989; 8:314–320.

Ito M, Nakashima M, Yoshioka M, Imaki J. Organogenesis of the juxta-oral organ in mice. J Anat 2009; 215:452–461.

Jaskoll T, Melnick M. Submandibular gland morphogenesis: stage-specific expression of TGF-alpha/EGF, IGF, TGFβ, TNF, and IL-6 signal transduction in normal embryonic mice and the phenotypic effects of TGF-beta2, TGF-beta3 and EGF-r null mutations. Anat Rec 1999; 256:252–268.

Lee SK, Hwang JO, Chi JG, et al. Prenatal development of myoepithelial cell of human submandibular gland observed by immunohistochemistry of smooth muscle actin and rhodamine-phalloidin fluorescence. Pathol Res Pract 1993; 189:332–341.

Lourenco SV, Uyekita SH, Lima DMC, Soares FA. Developing human minor salivary glands: morphological parallel relation between the expression of TGF-beta isoforms and cytoskeletal markers of glandular maturation. Virchows Arch 2008; 452:427–434.

Lourenco SV, Camillo CMC, Buim MEC et al. Human salivary gland branching morphogenesis. Histochem Cell Biol 2007; 128:361–369.

Melnick M, Jaskoll T. Mouse submandibular gland morphogenesis: a paradigm for embryonic signal processing. Crit Rev Oral Biol Med 2000; 11:199–215.

Melnick M, Phair RD, Lapidot SA, Jaskoll T. Salivary gland branching morphogenesis: a quantitative systems analysis of the Eda/Edar/NFkB paradigm. BMC Dev Biol 2009; 9:32. doi:10.11186/147-213X-9-32.

Merida-Velasco JA, Sanchez-Montesinos I, Espin-Ferra J, et al. Development of the human submandibular salivary gland. J Dent Res 1993; 72:1227–1232.

Müller M, Jasmin JR, Monteil RA, Loubiere R. Embryology and secretory activity of labial salivary glands. J Biol Buccale 1991; 19:39–43.

Nitta M, Kume T, Nogawa H. FGF alters epithelial competence for EGF at the initiation of branching morphogenesis of mouse submandibular gland. Dev Dyn 2009; 238: 315–323.

Patel VN, Rebustini IT, Hoffman MP. Salivary gland branching morphogenesis. Differentiation 2006; 74:349–364.

Thrane PS, Rognum TO, Brandtzaeg P. Ontogenesis of the secretory immune system and innate defence factors in human parotid glands. Clin Exp Immunol 1991; 86:342–348.

Tucker AS. Salivary gland development. Seminar Cell Dev Biol 2007; 18: 237–244.

# 17 Muscle Development

Myogenesis is first manifested by the expression of myogenic regulatory factors (MRFs) that include MyoD1, MYF5, MRF-4/herculin/Myf-6, MyHCs and Myogenin (MYOG) that differentiate myofibers with contractile properties from the paraxial mesoderm. Myogenic populations arise from unsegmented head mesoderm and segmented (somitic) mesoderm. The unsegmented muscle progenitors have a prolonged and necessary interaction with neural crest cells for development, and provide the extraocular and pharyngeal arch muscles. The segmented somitic mesoderm develops the neck, tongue, laryngeal and diaphragmatic muscles.

The approximately 60 distinct skeletal muscles of the head can be categorized into the axial (neck), laryngoglossal, pharyngeal (branchial) and extraocular muscles. The axial muscles are derived from preotic somites and move the head. The laryngoglossal muscles are derived from both preotic somites and pharyngeal arch mesoderm, moving the larynx, mouth and tongue. The pharyngeal muscles attach to the mandible, maxilla and pharynx, and are responsible for mastication and swallowing. The extraocular muscles derive from the prechordal and first pharyngeal arch mesoderm and move the eye.

Craniofacial voluntary muscles develop from paraxial mesoderm that condenses rostrally as incompletely segmented *somitomeres* and segmented *somites* of the occipital and rostral cervical regions (Fig. 17–1). The myomeres of the somitomeres and the myotomes of the somites form primitive muscle cells, termed *myoblasts*; these divide and fuse to form

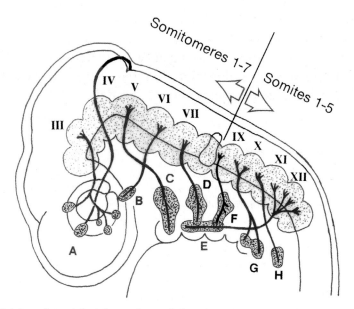

Figure 17–1 Origins of craniofacial muscles and their nerve supplies. Nerves: III, oculomotor; IV, trochlear; V3, mandibular trigeminal; VI, abducens; VII, facial; IX, glossopharyngeal; X, vagus; XI, spinal accessory; XII, hypoglossal. Muscle groups: A, ocular; B, lateral rectus (ocular); C, masticatory; D, facial; E, glossal; F, pharyngeal; G, laryngeal; H, nuchal.

multinucleated *myotubes* that cease further mitosis and thus become *myocytes* (muscle fibers). Most muscle fibers develop before birth, but increase in number and size in early infancy. Motor nerves establish contact with the myocytes, stimulating their activity and further growth by hypertrophy; failure of nerve contact or activity results in muscle atrophy.

Myogenic cells are spatially patterned by their intimately surrounding connective tissues. Muscles in the craniocervical regions derive their investing connective-tissue components from three sources: neural crest tissue provides the epimysium, perimysium and endomysium surrounding the myocytes of the extrinsic ocular, glossal and all pharyngeal-arch skeletal muscles; the connective tissues of the laryngeal muscles arising from the first and second (occipital) somites are derived from postotic lateral plate mesoderm; and the connective-tissue components of the axial cervical muscles (trapezius, sternomastoid) are of somitic origin.

The craniofacial muscles are derived from the seven somitomeres and the seven most rostral somites, gaining their cranial innervation sequentially (Table 17–1). Four extrinsic ocular muscles (superior, medial and inferior rectus and inferior oblique) derive from unsegmented paraxial head mesoderm and the first two somitomeres that arise from the prechordal plate and are supplied by the oculomotor (IIIrd cranial) nerve. The superior oblique ocular muscle arises from the third somitomere, derived from prechordal plate mesoderm and is innervated by the trochlear (IVth cranial) nerve. The fourth somitomere myomere invades the first pharyngeal arch to provide the four muscles of mastication (masseter, temporalis and medial and lateral pterygoids), the tensor tympani, tensor veli palatini, anterior belly of the digastric and mylohyoid muscles, all innervated by the trigeminal (Vth cranial) nerve. The lateral rectus ocular muscle derives from the fifth somitomere, supplied by the abducent (VIth cranial) nerve. The sixth somitomere myomere invades the second pharyngeal arch to provide the facial muscles, the stylohyoid, stapedius and posterior belly of the digastric, all supplied by the facial (VIIth cranial) nerve. The seventh somitomere forms the third pharyngeal-arch muscle, the stylopharyngeus, innervated by the glossopharyngeal (IXth cranial) nerve.

TABLE 17–1: **Craniofacial Muscle Origins**

| Mesodermal Origin | Muscles | Innervation |
| --- | --- | --- |
| Somitomeres 1, 2 | Superior, inferior and medial ocular recti; Inferior oblique of eye | Oculomotor (III) |
| Somitomere 3 | Superior oblique of eye | Trochlear (IV) |
| Somitomere 4 | 1st arch masticatory muscles | Trigeminal (V) |
| Somitomere 5 | Lateral ocular rectus | Abducens (VI) |
| Somitomere 6 | 2nd arch facial muscles | Facial (VII) |
| Somitomere 7 | 3rd arch stylopharyngeus | Glossopharyngeal (IX) |
| Somites 1, 2 | Laryngeal muscles | Vagus (X) |
| Somites 1–4 | Tongue muscles | Hypoglossal (XII) |
| Somites 3–7 | Sternomastoid, trapezius | Accessory (XI) |

The myotomes of the first four (occipital) somites invade the fourth, fifth and sixth pharyngeal arches, carrying their vagal (Xth) and spinal accessory (XIth cranial) nerves to provide the levator palatini, palatopharyngeus, palatoglossus and the extrinsic and intrinsic laryngeal muscles. The hypoglossal cord, derived from the occipital somites (1 to 4) and supplied by the hypoglossal (XIIth cranial) nerve, migrates into the tongue region to form the intrinsic and extrinsic glossal muscles and contributes to the laryngeal muscles. Myotomic derivatives of the third to seventh somites, innervated by the spinal accessory (XIth cranial) nerve, form the sternomastoid and trapezius muscles.

The mesenchyme of the pharyngeal arches gives rise to special visceral (striated) musculature innervated by special visceromotor cranial nerve fibers that are under voluntary control. The transition from the specially striated visceral muscles of the mouth and pharynx to the normal unstriated (smooth) visceral muscle of the gut takes place in the esophagus, where voluntary control of food ingestion is lost.

The mesenchyme of the first pharyngeal arch, which phylogenetically is associated with the jaws, appropriately enough gives rise primarily to the muscles of mastication and some swallowing muscles. The second-arch mesenchyme* provides the muscles of facial expression, and the mesenchyme of the third, fourth, and fifth or sixth arches merges into the palatofaucial, pharyngeal and laryngeal muscle groups (for details, see p. 67). The tongue, pharyngeal and laryngeal muscles are of somitic origin and arise from ocipital somites 1-5 (Figs. 17–2 and 17–3; see Figs. 15–5 and 17–1).

The orofacial muscles are the first to develop in the body, in keeping with the cephalocaudal sequence of fetal development. The genioglossus and geniohyoid muscles are the first premuscle masses to differentiate from occipital and cervical myotomic mesenchyme at 32 to 36 days of age. The facial premuscle masses are formed between the ages of 8 and 9 weeks, menstrual age;** and, after migration, all the facial muscles are in their final positions by 14.5 weeks. The mylohyoid muscle and the anterior belly of the digastric, which form the floor of the mouth, are the earliest of the first pharyngeal arch muscles to differentiate. The mylohyoid muscle initially attaches to the ventral border of Meckel's cartilage, but later migrates dorsally to attach to the fetal mandible.

Of the palatal muscles, the tensor veli palatini is the first to develop from the first pharyngeal arch as a mesenchymal condensation within the vertical palatal shelves at 40 days pc. Next, the levator veli palatini and palatopharyngeus, derived from the fourth pharyngeal arch, develop

---

*The hyoid arch muscles, phylogenetically associated with the gill (pharyngeal) arches that regress in mammalian development, are adapted to the new mammalian function of facial expression. Fishes and reptiles have no muscles of facial expression.

**Menstrual age is 2 weeks more than the true age (i.e., fertilization age) of the fetus. All subsequent ages mentioned in this chapter are menstrual ages.

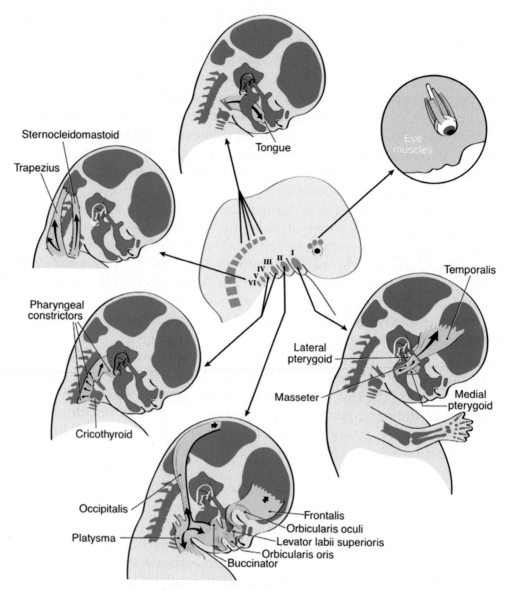

**Figure 17–2** Schematic description of the embryonic origins of (in clockwise order) the ocular, masticatory, facial, pharyngeal, neck and tongue muscles from somitomere, pharyngeal and somite sources.

simultaneously at 45 days pc. The uvular muscle develops at the time the palatal shelves fuse by mesenchymal migration from the fourth pharyngeal arch. The palatoglossus muscle, also derived from the fourth pharyngeal arch, is the last palatal muscle to differentiate.

Second-arch mesenchyme destined to form the facial musculature is not initially subdivided into distinct muscle masses. Migration of the differentiating premyoblasts and early myoblasts extends from the region of the second pharyngeal arch in sheet-like laminae. The superficial lamina spreads from a location caudal to the external acoustic meatus in all directions and around the meatus into the temporal, occipital, cervical and mandibular regions. Migration of the second-arch myoblasts into

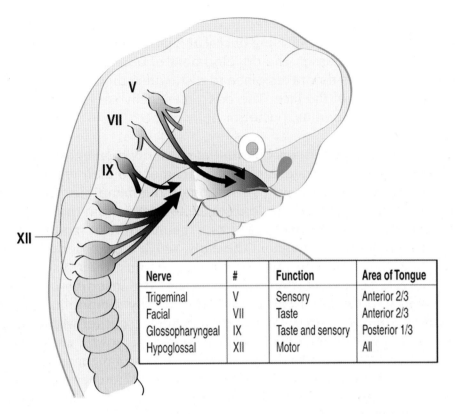

| Nerve | # | Function | Area of Tongue |
|---|---|---|---|
| Trigeminal | V | Sensory | Anterior 2/3 |
| Facial | VII | Taste | Anterior 2/3 |
| Glossopharyngeal | IX | Taste and sensory | Posterior 1/3 |
| Hypoglossal | XII | Motor | All |

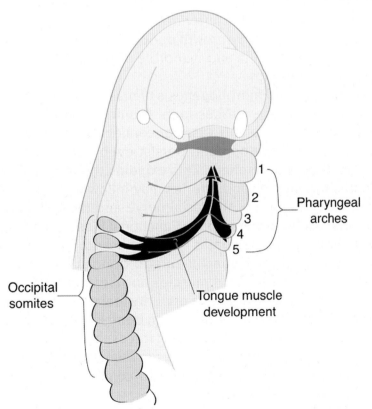

**Figure 17–3** Schematic depiction of the origin of the tongue muscles from the occipital somite myotomes. The path of their migration is traced by the path of the hypoglossal nerve, XII.

the mesenchyme of the merged maxillary and mandibular prominences provides the important suckling buccal and labial muscles. Differentiation of the premuscle masses, the development of boundaries, and the gaining of attachments now takes place to distinguish the delicate superficial mimetic muscles of the face. The deep mesenchymal lamina condenses to become the stapedius, posterior belly of the digastric, and stylohyoid muscles.

The masticatory muscles differentiate as individual entities from first-arch mesenchyme, migrate, and gain attachment to their respective sites of origin on the cranium and of insertion on the mandible. The masseter and medial pterygoid have little distance to migrate, but their growth and attachments are closely associated with the mandibular ramus, which undergoes remodeling throughout the early, active growth period. As a consequence, these muscles must continually readjust their insertions and, to a much lesser extent, their sites of origin. The insertion of the lateral pterygoid into the head and neck of the rapidly remodeling mandibular condyle requires its constant reattachment, together with elongation concomitant with spheno-occipital synchondrosal growth, which synchondrosis intervenes between the origin and insertion of the muscle. The temporalis muscle's attachment to the temporal fossa stretches a considerable distance from its site of mandibular coronoid insertion as the muscle becomes employed in mastication. Its insertion, too, has to reattach constantly to the rapidly resorbing anterior border of the ramus and coronoid process during the most active growth period. The attachments of the buccinator muscle to the maxilla and mandible also require readjustment as the alveolar processes grow.

The histogenesis and morphogenesis of muscles and nerves influence each other; as the muscle masses form, the nerve and blood supply to them differentiates. Nerve and vascular connections, established at the time of muscle-fiber development, persist even after the muscles have migrated from their site of origin. This explains the long and sometimes tortuous paths that nerves and arteries may follow in adult anatomy; the wide paths of distribution of the facial nerve and the facial artery to the mimetic facial muscles are examples. Functional muscular activities begin as soon as neurological reflex paths are established.

Muscle fibers gain their attachments to bone some time after their differentiation. The migration of muscles and ligaments relative to their bony attachments is a consequence of periosteal growth. The attachment of muscles to bones has some influence on bone formation, particularly as the muscles become functional and exert forces that invoke Wolff's Law of bone response. Hypertrophy of muscles is associated with enlargement of correlated skeletal units; muscle atrophy commonly induces a like response in the associated bones.

The earliest muscle movement is believed to be reflex in origin, not spontaneous activity. Muscular response to a stimulus first develops in the perioral region, as a result of tactile cutaneous stimuli applied to the lips, indicating that the trigeminal nerve is the first cranial nerve to become active;* the earliest movements in response to such exteroceptive stimuli have been elicited at 7.5 weeks menstrual age. Spontaneous muscle movements are believed to begin only at 9.5 weeks menstrual age. Stroking the face of the 7.5-week embryo produces a reflex bending of the head and upper trunk away from the stimulus as a total neuromuscular response. This early contralateral avoiding reaction recapitulates the phylogenetically protective reflexes of primitive creatures, replaced later by a positive ipsilateral response to a stimulus.

Stimulation of the lips of the fetus at 8.5 weeks results in incomplete but active reflex opening of the mouth in conjunction with all of the neuromuscular mechanism sufficiently mature to react at this age. From 8.5 to 9.5 weeks of age, mouth opening forms part of a total contralateral reflex response to a stimulus, with lateral head and trunk flexion and movement of the rump and all four extremities. Mouth opening without concomitant head or extremity movements can be elicited only much later, at about 15.5 weeks. Mouth closure is initially passive, but after the 11th week it is active and rapid as a result of the initiation of muscle stretch reflex activity. Swallowing begins at 12.5 weeks in association with extension reflexes; and, at 13 to 14 weeks, early activity of the facial muscles may be manifested by a sneering expression in response to eyelid stimulation—the angle of the mouth is retracted, the lateral part of the upper lip is elevated, and the nasal ala on the ipsilateral side is raised (not bilaterally, as occurs postnatally). These early motor capabilities are unrelated to emotions. The spread of facial muscle activity is portrayed by the ability of the fetus to squint and scowl at 15 weeks. Tongue movements may begin as early as 12.5 weeks, active lip movements begin at 14.5 weeks, and the gag reflex can be elicited at 18.5 weeks.

The early differentiation of the mylohyoid and digastric muscles would account for the early mouth-opening ability and may be essential to normal development. The withdrawal of the tongue from between the vertical palatal shelves (see p. 132) and the development of synovial cavities in the temporomandibular joint (see p. 163) may depend on these early mouth movements.

From 10 weeks pc onward, mouth-opening reflexes become progressively less associated with a total lateral body reflex response to a stimulus, indicating the development of inhibitory nerve pathways. However, head movements remain strongly associated with mouth movements even into the postnatal period, accounting for the "rooting reflex," whereby perioral stimulation leads to ipsilateral head rotation, which in the infant is associated with suckling. Another remnant of the total reflex response is the hand-grasp reflex when an infant suckles.

Complex suckling movements involving mouth opening, lip protrusion and tongue movements are not manifested spontaneously until 24 weeks of age, although individual components of the movement can be elicited by stimulation about the mouth much earlier. Intrauterine thumb sucking

---

*Myelinization, an indicator of nerve activity, appears first in the trigeminal nerve at 12 weeks but is not complete until the age of 1 to 2 years.

has been demonstrated as early as 18 weeks. Crying may start between the 21st and 29th weeks pc, reflecting the related muscle activities of the larynx and spasmodic "inhalation" and "exhalation" by the thoracic cage musculature. Full swallowing and suckling permitting survival occurs at only 32 to 36 weeks of fetal age. Some preliminary earlier swallowing occurs as early as 12 weeks, when the fetus literally drinks the amniotic fluid in which it is bathed.* The coordinated effective combination of suckling and swallowing is an indicator of neurological maturation that is particularly important for the survival of premature infants. Respiratory movements may be elicited by stimulus as early as 13 weeks, but spontaneous rhythmical respiration necessary for survival does not occur until much later. Increasingly complex muscle movements, producing mastication and speech, depend upon development of the appropriate reflex proprioceptive mechanisms.

The cutaneous covering of the lips of the fetus is sharply delineated from the adjacent skin and oral mucosa (Fig. 17–4). The primitive epithe-

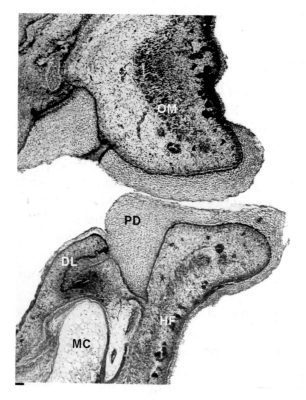

**Figure 17–4** Paramedian sagittal section of the lips of a 12-week-old fetus. Note the nature of the multilayered periderm (PD), the developing orbicularis oris muscle (OM), the dental lamina (DL) and Meckel's cartilage (MC). Hair follicles (HF) are forming in the cutaneous areas. (×56, reduced to 80% on reproduction) (Courtesy of Dr. R. R. Miethke.)

*The importance of this early swallowing is indicated by the excess amniotic fluid (hydramnios) found in the amniotic sacs of fetuses unable to swallow because of esophageal atresia. Near term, the normal fetus will swallow as much as 200 to 600 mL of amniotic fluid a day. The swallowed amniotic fluid is absorbed by the gut, whence it is carried by the fetal bloodstream to the placenta. It is then passed on to the maternal body for elimination. Interestingly, amniotic fluid is not normally inspired into the lungs of the fetus.

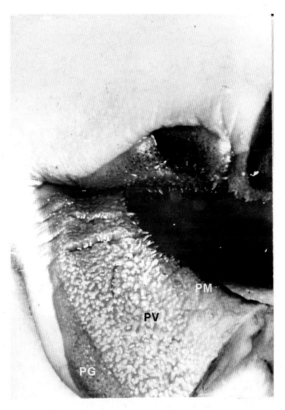

**Figure 17–5** Lips and commissure of the mouth of a 39-week-old fetus. Note in the lower lip the outermost smooth pars glabra (PG) that narrows towards the commissure. The central pars villosa (PV) is covered with fine villi. The inner vestibular zone, pars mucosa (PM), is continuous with the vestibule of the mouth. (Approximately ×4, reduced to 80% on reproduction) (Courtesy of Dr. R. R. Miethke.)

lium of the vermilion surface of the lip forms a distinctive multilayered periderm that is shed in utero. At birth, the surface of the infant's lips (Fig. 17–5) is subdivided into a central highly mobile suckling area characterized by fine villi, *pars villosa*, distinct from an outer smooth zone, *pars glabra*, and an inner vestibular zone, *pars mucosa*. The villous portion of the infant lip is adhesive—more so than the glabrous or vestibular portions; during suckling, this adhesion may result from swelling of the blood vessels in the villi, establishing an airtight seal around the nipple.

The conspicuous philtrum of the neonatal upper lip gradually loses its clarity during childhood, the central depression becoming shallower in the adult. The rare phenomenon of *double lip* (either upper or lower) results from hypertrophy of the inner pars villosa and an exaggerated boundary line demarcating it from the outer pars glabra. *Congenital fistulae* of the lower lip, usually bilateral, seldom unilateral, and occasionally median, are rare. Their occurrence may be genetically determined as an autosomal dominant trait in the Van der Woude syndrome caused by mutations in the interferon regulatory factor-6 gene (IRF6).

With use, muscles increase in size, due to hypertrophy of their individual fibers. The converse, muscle disuse, results in their atrophy. At birth, the suckling muscles of the lips (orbicularis oris) and cheeks

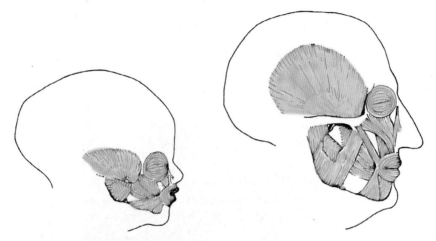

**Figure 17–6** Muscle development at birth and in adulthood. In infancy, the suckling facial muscles are relatively better developed than the mucles of mastication. In adulthood, the muscles of mastication are more strongly developed than the facial muscles. Compare the area of attachment of the temporalis muscle in the infant and adult.

(buccinators) are relatively better developed than the muscles of mastication (Fig. 17–6). Indeed, at birth, mobility of the face is limited to eyelids, the middle of the lips, and slight corrugation in the forehead and mental protuberance areas. Between birth and adulthood, the facial muscles increase fourfold and the muscles of mastication sevenfold in weight. The masseter and medial pterygoid are better developed at birth than the temporalis and lateral pterygoid muscles. The buccinator muscle is prominent in the cheek of the neonate; its powerful suckling capabilities are enhanced by a large subcutaneous adipose mass, forming a "sucking pad"** that prevents collapse of the cheeks during suckling. The tongue musculature is well developed at birth, and the tongue has a wide range of movement.

All of the complex interrelated orofacial movements of suckling, swallowing, breathing and gagging are reflex in origin rather than learned, and constitute *unconditioned congenital reflexes* necessary for survival. *Conditioned acquired reflexes* develop with maturation of the neuromuscular apparatus and are generally learned as "habits." The development of abnormal patterns of movement ("bad habits") is likely to be the result of conditioned fetal reflex activity developing out of sequence, or the omission of a specific response to a sequential triggering stimulus.

Until the primary first molars erupt, the infant swallows with jaws separated and tongue thrust forward, using predominantly the facial muscles (orbicularis oris and buccinators) innervated by the facial nerve. The pattern, known as the infantile swallow, is a nonconditioned congenital reflex. During swallowing, contrary to the action in adults, the infant's lips suck

---

**The buccal fat pad of Bichat is peculiarly loose in texture and is bounded by a connective-tissue capsule. The fat in the pad persists even in emaciation, indicating its structural and mechanical function rather than fat storage.

and make stronger movements than the tongue. After eruption of the posterior primary teeth, at 18 months of age onward, the child tends to swallow with the teeth brought together by masticatory muscle action, without a tongue thrust. This mature swallow is an acquired conditioned reflex, and is intermingled with the infantile swallow during a transition period. As the child grows older, variation in the pattern decreases as the adult swallowing pattern is increasingly adopted. The movements of the mature swallow are primarily of those muscles innervated by the trigeminal nerve, namely, the muscles of mastication and the mylohyoid. Once the facial-nerve musculature has been relieved of its swallowing duties, it is better able to perform the delicate mimetic activities of facial expression and speech that are acquired from 18 months onward.

The infant's cry is a nonconditioned reflex, which accounts for its lack of individual character and sporadic nature. Speech, on the other hand, is a conditioned reflex, which differs among individuals but is regular by virtue of the sophisticated control required.

Mastication is a conditioned reflex, learned by initially irregular and poorly coordinated chewing movements.* The proprioceptive responses of the temporomandibular joint and the periodontal ligaments of the erupting dentition establish a stabilized chewing pattern aligned to the individual's dental intercuspation.

The conversion of the infantile swallow into the mature swallow, of infantile suckling into mastication and of infantile crying into speech, are all examples of the substitution of conditioned reflexes acquired with maturation for the unconditioned congenital reflexes of the neonate. Superimposed upon these reflex movements are voluntary activities under conscious control that are acquired by learning and experience.

The maturation of normal neuromuscular reflexes and the development of a proper equilibrium of muscular forces during orofacial growth is necessary for development of normal jaw morphology and dental occlusion. Tongue movements and lip and cheek pressures guide erupting teeth into normal occlusion. The retention of the tooth-apart, tongue-thrusting infantile pattern of swallowing into childhood creates abnormal myofunctional pressures upon the teeth resulting in a characteristic "open bite" pattern of malocclusion. Muscle malfunctioning, either by their hypertonicity or hypotonicity, particularly of the orbicularis oris–buccinator-tongue complex results in dental malocclusion.† The pressures exerted by these muscles determine in part the form of the dental arches.

---

*The proprioceptive neuromuscular spindles are much sparser in the lateral pterygoid muscle than in the other masticatory muscles, accounting for its uncoordinated behavior.

†*The ornithologist is quite absurd*

*To think a swallow is a bird;*

*The swallow is a tongue-confusion,*

*That causes dental malocclusion.*

H. Bloomer (1963)

## ANOMALIES OF DEVELOPMENT

Congenital myopathic conditions affecting facial development include trismus, a condition of the failure of the mouth to open widely, often termed "lockjaw." The rare Dutch-Kentucky/Hecht-Beals syndrome prominently includes trismus arising from a point mutation in the myosin heavy chain-8 gene (MYH8) that contributes to muscle fiber contraction. Another notable rare condition is the Freeman-Sheldon syndrome that exhibit a "whistling facies" phenotype that arises from a similarly placed point mutation in the myosin heavy chain-3 gene (MYH3).

## SELECTED BIBLIOGRAPHY

Burdi AR, Spyropoulous MN. Prenatal growth patterns of the human mandible and masseter muscle complex. Am J Orthod 1978; 74:380.

Gasser RF. Development of the facial muscles in man. Am J Anat 1967; 120:357.

Humphrey T. The development of the mouth opening and related reflexes involving the oral area of human fetuses. Ala J Med Sci 1968; 5:126–157.

Humphrey T. The relation between human fetal mouth opening reflexes and closure of the palate. Am J Anat 1969; 125:317–344.

Humphrey T. Development of oral and facial motor mechanisms in human fetuses and their relation to craniofacial growth. J Dent Res 1971; 50:1428.

Mooney MP, Siegel MI, Kimes KR, et al. Development of the orbicularis oris muscle in normal and cleft lip and palate human fetuses using three-dimensional computer reconstruction. Plast Reconstr Surg 1988; 81:336.

Noden DM, Francis-West P. The differentiation and morphogenesis of craniofacial muscles. Dev Dyn 2006; 235:1194–218.

Rinon A, Lazar H, Marshall H, et al. Cranial neural crest cells regulate head muscles patterning and differentiation during vertebrate embryogenesis. Development 2007; 134: 3065–3075.

Rodriguez-Vazquez JF, Merida-Velasco JR, Arraez-Aybar LA, Jimenez-Collado J. Anatomic relationships of the orbital muscle of Müller in human fetuses. Radiol Surg Anat 1998; 20:341–344.

Rodriguez-Vazquez JF, Merida Velasco JR, Jimenez Collado J. Orbital muscle of Müller: observations on human fetuses measuring 35–150 mm. Acta Anat 1990; 139:300–303.

Shih HP, Gross MK, Kioussi C. Muscle development: forming the head and trunk muscles. Acta Histochem 2008; 110:97–108.

Trainor PA, Tam PP. Cranial paraxial mesoderm and neural crest cells of the mouse embryo: co-distribution in the craniofacial mesenchyme but distinct segregation in the branchial arches. Development 1995; 121:2569–2582.

Tzahor E. Heart and craniofacial muscle development: a new developmental theme of distinct myogenic fields. Dev Biol 2009; 327: 273–279.

Zahng L, Yoshimura Y, Hatta T, Otani H. Myogenic determination and differentiation of the mouse palatal muscle in relation to the developing mandibular nerve. J Dent Res 1999; 78:1417–1425.

# 18 Special Sense Organs

The organs of the special senses of olfaction, gustation, vision, balance and hearing are all located in the craniofacial complex. Parts of these special sense organs initially arise in a rather similar manner.* Localized areas of surface ectoderm are induced by underlying cranial nerve extensions to thicken and differentiate into distinct placodes. The subsequent fates of the olfactory, lens and otic placodes will be briefly described individually.

## NOSE

Development of the external apparatus of the nose has been considered together with the development of the face (p. 47).

The special sensory olfactory epithelium of the nose appears as the olfactory (nasal) placodes (see Figure 3–5), on the inferolateral aspects of the frontonasal prominence toward the end of the somite period. The relative "sinking" of the olfactory placodes into the depths of the olfactory pits causes the specialized sensory olfactory epithelium of each placode to be located ultimately in the lateral walls of the upper fifth of each nasal cavity. The olfactory nerve cells connect with the olfactory bulb of the brain through the cribriform plate of the ethmoid bone.

The sensory olfactory epithelium differs from the respiratory epithelium in the lower nasal cavity. Bipolar olfactory receptor cells protrude dendritic sensory cilia and axons that synapse with the brain's olfactory bulbs. The olfactory cilia become functional during the fetal period and play an important role in suckling in newborns.

### Anomalies of Development

Diminished or lack of smell, anosmia, is a phenotypic expression of mutations found in the Kallmann syndrome caused by mutation in either the KAL1 or FGFR1 genes. Absence of the nose, arhinia, is an extremely rare anomaly of facial development.

## EYE

The embryonic prechordal plate provides the precursor to the eyes by sending Sonic hedgehog (SHH) signaling and PAX6 expression, suppressing the median part of the originally continuous right and left optic fields of the neural plate. This produces bilateral retinal primordia. Failure of this prechordal plate suppression results in a single retinal primordium, and hence cyclopia.

---

*The organs of the special sense of gustation, the taste buds, discussed on p. 181, differ in this respect in their origin from the other special sense organs.

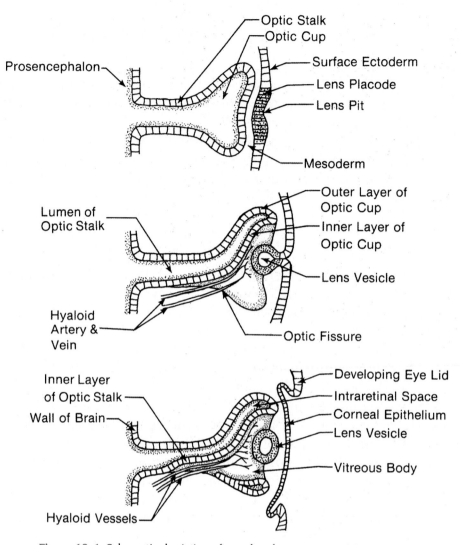

**Figure 18–1** Schematic depiction of eye development at various stages.

The eye is derived from surface ectoderm, neural ectoderm, neural crest tissue and mesoderm. The light-sensitive portion of the eye, the retina, is a direct outgrowth from the forebrain, projecting bilaterally as the *optic vesicles* which are connected to the brain by the optic stalks (Fig. 18–1). The neuroectodermal optic vesicles induce their overlying surface ectoderm to thicken. This forms the *lens placodes*, each of which invaginates in its center by the development of peripheral folds, which fuse to convert it into a closed *lens vesicle*. These vesicles sink beneath the surface ectoderm; initially hollow, they become filled with lens fibers to form the lenses. The optic vesicles also invaginate partly, to form the double-layered *optic cups*, and the optic stalks become the *optic nerves*. The outer layer of the optic cup acquires neural crest pigmentation to become the pigmented layer of the retina, and the inner layer differentiates into the light-sensitive nervous layer (Fig. 18–2).

Meningeal ectomesenchyme (of neural crest origin) surrounding the optic cups and lenses forms the *sclera* and *choroid* over the cups, the *ciliary*

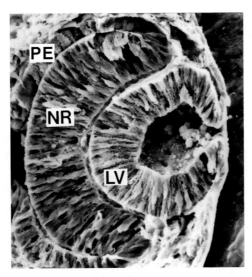

Figure 18–2  Scanning electron micrograph of a sectioned optic cup and lens vesicle of an 11-day-old mouse embryo, approximating a 36-day-old human embryo. The lens vesicle (LV) overlies the neural retina (NR) adjacent to the pigmented epithelium (PE). (Courtesy of Drs. K. K. Sulik and G. C. Schoenwolf.)

*bodies* at the margins of the cups, and the *cornea* over the lenses. Mesoderm invades the optic cups to form the *vitreous* body and the transient hyaloid artery. The extrinsic muscles of the eye are derived from the prechordal somitomeres (see p. 191).

The cutaneous ectoderm overlying the cornea forms the *conjunctiva*. Ectodermal folds develop above and below the cornea, and, with their central core of mesenchyme, form the *eyelids*. The eyelids close at the end of the eighth week and remain closed until the seventh month postconception (pc).

The eyes migrate from their initially lateral positions toward the midline of the face (p. 45), and overstimulation and undermigration produce anomalies of facial appearance (hypotelorism and hypertelorism). The visual ability of the neonate is exceedingly poor. The ability to resolve visual details is some 40 times less than that of adults, with uncoordinated movements of the eyes and no depth appreciation. Visual acuity improves to nearly adult equivalence by the end of the first year.

### Malformations

The migration of the eyes from their initial lateral location is subject to the expression of the *cyclops* gene which if perturbed will result in a manifestation of cyclopia. The SOX2 mutation or perturbation will result in anophthalmia, and the absence or perturbation of the PAX6 gene will result in aniridia.

## EAR

The three parts of the ear—external, middle and internal—arise from separate, diverse embryonic origins, reflecting the complicated phylogenetic history of the adaptation of the primitive pharyngeal arch apparatus for hearing and balance.

## The External Ear

The external ear forms around the first pharyngeal groove (see Fig. 5–1), which deepens to become the external acoustic meatus, initially located in the mandibulocervical region. The auricle develops as a series of six swellings, or hillocks, surrounding the dorsal aspect of the first pharyngeal groove. Three of the hillocks develop from the first (mandibular) pharyngeal arch, and the other three from the second (hyoid) pharyngeal arch (Figs. 18–3 and 18–4). Differential growth and fusion of the hillocks by

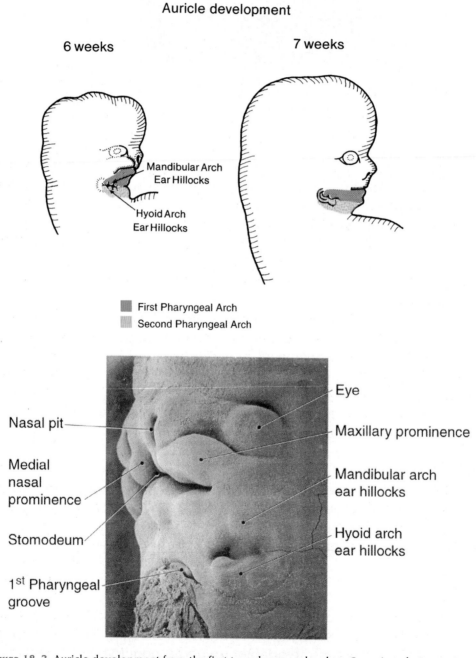

Auricle development

Figure 18–3  Auricle development from the first two pharyngeal arches. Scanning electron micrograph of a 6-week-old human embryo. (Courtesy of Dr. K. K. Sulik.)

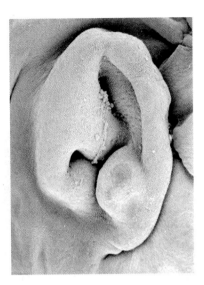

**Figure 18–4** Scanning electron micrograph of developing auricle of a human fetus at 9 weeks pc. (Courtesy of Drs. K.K. Sulik and G C. Schoenwolf.)

the end of the eighth week produces the characteristic shape of the auricle. The auricle and external acoustic meatus migrate cranially from their original cervical location, and by the fourth month pc reach their "normal" position. Elastic cartilage differentiates in the mesenchyme around the external acoustic meatus.

The tympanic ring of the temporal bone forms the boundaries of the tympanic membrane, which closes off the external acoustic meatus from the middle ear (Fig. 18–5). At birth, the external acoustic meatus is shallow; therefore, the tympanic ring and tympanic membrane are located superficially. Also, both the ring and the membrane are markedly oblique in the neonate; these structures achieve nearly adult size by birth, and thus require this orientation for their accommodation within the still fetal-sized acoustic meatus from the late fetal stage onward. Outward growth of the bony tympanic ring and cartilage of the meatus deepens the meatus during infancy and childhood, and allows adult orientation of the tympanic membrane and consequently of the ossicular chain.

### Middle Ear

The middle ear develops from the tubotympanic recess derived from the first pharyngeal pouch (p. 75). The endodermal lining of the tympanic recess comes into proximity with the ectodermal lining of the external acoustic meatus and, with a thin layer of intermediate mesoderm, forms the tympanic membrane. Expansion of the tympanic cavity surrounds and envelops the chain of three ear ossicles developing from the first and second pharyngeal arch cartilages (see Chapter 4) (Fig. 18–6). The ossicles thus appear to lie within the tympanic cavity, although in reality are outside it, surrounded by the pharyngeal endodermal membrane. The tympanic cavity achieves its nearly adult size by 37 weeks pc. Further expansion of the tympanic cavity postnatally gives rise to the mastoid air cells.

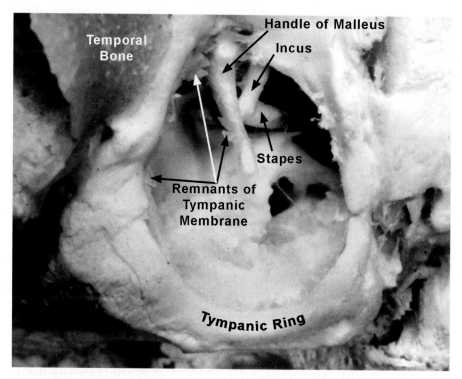

**Figure 18–5** Photograph of the tympanum in a neonatal skull. The tympanic membrane has been torn away to reveal the three ear ossicles in situ. The base of the stapes is in the fenestra vestibuli, and the fenestra cochleae is seen below it. Note the superficial location of the middle ear in the skull of the newborn, due to absence of a bony external acoustic meatus.

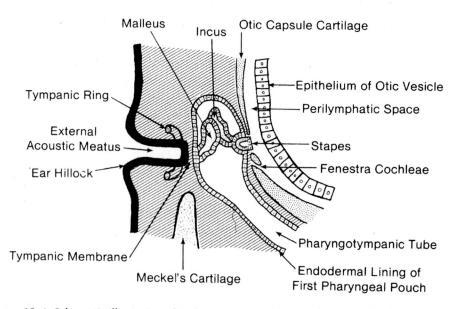

**Figure 18–6** Schematic illustration of early stage (5 week pc) of ear development. The external ear (auricle and external acoustic meatus) forms around the first pharyngeal groove. The middle ear develops from the first pharyngeal pouch and the ear ossicles from the first (malleus, incus) and second (stapes) pharyngeal arches. The internal ear develops from the otic vesicle.

The muscles attaching to the auditory tube, the tensor veli palatini and the tensor tympani, differentiate at 12 and 14 weeks pc, respectively. These muscles, with the later-developing salpingopharyngeus, function at birth to open the tube. Fluid clearance is difficult in the neonate owing to the narrow cylindrical lumen and horizontal orientation of the tube. By contrast, the adult tube is downwardly angled medially, with a funnel-shaped lumen facilitating middle ear drainage. Swallowing aids the establishment of hearing, which normally is impaired for the first 2 days after birth.

The malleus and incus* are derived from the dorsal end of the first pharyngeal arch cartilage (p. 67), the joint between them representing the primitive jaw joint (see Chapter 13). The stapes derives in part from the dorsal end of the second arch cartilage, in which three ossification centers appear. Ossification** of the ear ossicles begins in the fourth month pc and proceeds rapidly to form functional bones by the 25th week pc. These are the first bones in the body to attain their ultimate size. The cartilage of the otic capsule breaks down around the footplate of the stapes to form the oval window. Failure of this chondrolysis is a source of one form of congenital deafness.

The tensor tympani muscle, attaching to the malleus, is derived from the first pharyngeal arch and is innervated by the mandibular division of the trigeminal nerve of that arch. The stapedius muscle, attached to the stapes, is derived from the second pharyngeal arch and, accordingly, is innervated by the facial nerve of that arch.

### Inner Ear

The preplacodal ectodermal region of the inner ear that gives rise to the otic placodes is determined by a combination of low levels of bone morphogenetic protein (BMP) activity with high levels of fibroblast growth factor (FGF) *signaling* induced by the DLX family of transcription factors. The complex architecture of the inner ear semicircular canals is shaped by cross-repressive interactions between the IG superfamily protein LRIG3 and the axon guidance molecule Netrin1. The internal ear arises from the *otic placode* at 21 to 24 days pc under the influence of FGF and Spalt 4 *signaling* from the underlying paraxial mesoderm on the nonneural ectoderm adjacent to the hindbrain. This is the first sensory organ to begin development. Epitheliomesenchymal interactions between the otic placode and subjacent mesenchyme are necessary for the histogenesis and

---

* The incus arises from the separated end of Meckel's cartilage that corresponds with the pterygoquadrate cartilage of inframammalian vertebrates.

** Ossification of these bones is endochondral, but the anterior process of the malleus forms independently in membrane bone. After birth, this anterior malleolar process shrinks to less than one-third its prenatal length. Initial ossification appears at 17 weeks pc on the long process of the incus, followed by the neck of the malleus, spreading to the manubrium and head. Stapedial ossification begins at its base at the 18th week.

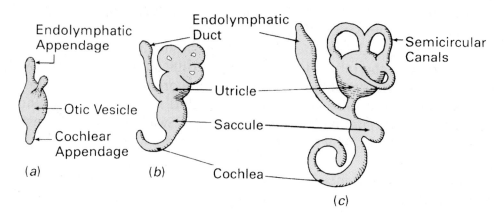

**Figure 18–7** Stages of internal ear development from the otic vesicle: (a) 5 weeks; (b) 6 weeks; (c) 7 weeks.

morphogenesis of the labyrinth of the inner ear. The vestibular and acoustic components develop under different genetic influences, accounting for variation in hearing and balancing impairments in genetic disturbances of these senses.

Invagination of the placode creates the *otic cup*, and apposition of its folded margins forms the *otic vesicle*, or *otocyst*, that sinks beneath the surface ectoderm. Subsequent complicated configurations of the otocyst give rise to the endolymphatic duct and sac, the saccule and utricle, the three semicircular canals and the cochlear duct that together form the *membranous labyrinth* (Fig. 18–7). The otocyst induces chondrogenesis in the surrounding mesenchyme to form the otic capsule. The surrounding cartilage of the otic capsule conforms to the intricate shape of the membranous labyrinth and forms the *bony labyrinth* when intramembranous ossification of the modiolus occurs. The rigidity imparted by the location of the labyrinths, deeply embedded within bone, determines a fixed orientation of the three semicircular canals on each side to each other and also to the head, allowing the development of balance and centrifugal senses. The capacity of the cochlea to respond to vibratory stimuli becomes established between 24 and 25 weeks pc.

### Anomalies of Development

Anomalies of the ear include anotia and microtia, afflicting the auricle (which is absent or reduced) and resulting in nonpatency of the external acoustic meatus (atresia). The auditory tube is hypoplastic in nearly all cases of cleft palate. A more severe facial anomaly is *synotia*, in which the ears are abnormally located ventrally in the upper part of the neck (see Fig. 3–20), almost invariably accompanied by *agnathia* (see p. 56). This association has been attributed to absence of the neural crest tissue that normally migrates into the lower anterior part of the face. Not only does the mandible fail to form, but the otocysts that form the ear occupy a position that otherwise would have been occupied by mandibular neural-crest ectomesenchyme. The presence and growth of the mandible appears to be a factor in determining the location of the ears.

# SELECTED BIBLIOGRAPHY

Abraira VE, Rio T, Tucker AF, et al. Cross-repressive interactions between Lrig3 and netrin 1 shape the architecture of the inner ear. Development 2008; 135:4091–4099.

Achiron R, Gottlieb Z, Yaron Y, et al. The development of the fetal eye: in utero ultrasonographic measurements of the vitreous and lens. Prenatal Diag 1995; 15:155–160.

Ars B. Organogenesis of the middle ear structures. J Laryngol Otol 1989; 103:16–21.

Bagger-Sjoback D. Embryology of the human endolymphatic duct and sac. ORL J Otorhino-larynol Relat Spec 1991; 53:61–67.

Barembaum M, Bronner-Fraser M. Spalt4 mediates invagination and otic placode gene expression in cranial ectoderm. Development 2007; 134: 3805–3814.

Barishak YR. Embryology of the eye and its adnexae. Dev Ophthalmol 1992; 24:1–142.

Bremond-Gignac DS, Banali K, Deplus S, et al. In utero eyeball development study by magnetic resonance imaging. Surg Radiol Anat 1997; 19:319–322.

Costa-Neves M, Rega R de M, Wanderley SS. Quantitative growth of the eye in the human fetus. Ital J Anat Embryol 1992; 97:55–59.

Declau F. Development of the human external auditory canal. Acta Otorhinolaryngol Belg 1995; 49:95–99.

Declau F, Moeneclaey L, Marquet J. Normal growth pattern of the middle ear cleft in the human fetus. J Laryngol Otol 1989; 103:461–465.

Denis D, Burguiere O, Burillon C. A biometric study of the eye, orbit, and face in 205 normal human fetuses. Invest Ophthalmol Visual Sci 1998; 39:2232–2238.

Denis D, Faure F, Volot F, et al. Ocular growth in the fetus. 2. Comparative study of the growth of the globe and the orbit and the parameters of fetal growth. Ophthalmology 1993; 207:125–132.

Denis D, Righini M, Scheiner C, et al. Ocular growth in the fetus. 1. Comparative study of axial length and biometric parameters in the fetus. Ophthalmology 1993; 207:117–124.

Dominguez-Frutos E, Vandrell V, Alvarez Y et al. Tissue-specific requirements for FGF8 during early inner ear development. Mech Dev 2009; 126:873–881.

Esterberg R, Fritz A. dlx3b/4b are required for the formation of the preplacode region and otic placode through local modulation of BMP activity. Dev Biol 2009; 325:189–199.

Fekete DM, Development of the vetebrate ear: insights from knockouts and mutants. Trends Neurosci 1999; 22:263–269.

Fini ME, Strissel KJ, West-Mays JA. Perspectives on eye development. Dev Gen 1997; 20:175–185.

Gasser RF, Shigihara S, Shimada K. Three-dimensional development of the facial nerve path through the ear region in human embryos. Ann Otorhinolaryngol 1994; 103:395–403.

Gill P, Vanhook J, Fitzsimmons J, et al. Fetal ear measurements in the prenatal detection of trisomy 21. Prenatal Diag 1994; 14:739–743.

Goldstein I, Tamir A, Zimmer EZ, Itskovitz-Eldor J. Growth of the fetal orbit and lens in normal pregnancies. Ultrasound Obstet Gynecol 1998; 12:175–179.

Jeffrey N, Spoor F. Prenatal growth and development of the modern human labyrinth. J Anat 2004; 204: 71–92.

Karmody CS, Annino DJ Jr. Embryology and anomalies of the external ear. Facial Plast Surg 1995; 11:251–256.

Kimura M, Umehara T, Udagawa J, et al. Development of olfactory epithelium in the human fetus: scanning electron microscopic observations. Congen Anom 2009; 49:102–107.

Ladher RK, Freter S, Sai X. FGF *signaling* is involved in the induction and morphogenesis of the inner ear. Dev Biol 2008; 319: 600.

Lambert PR, Dodson EE. Congenital malformations of the external auditory canal. Otol Clin North Am 1996; 29:741–760.

Miodonski AJ, Gorczyca J, Nowogrodzka-Zagorska M, et al. Microvascular system of the human fetal inner ear: a scanning electron microscopic study of corrosion casts. Scanning Microsc 1993; 7:585–594.

Moraes F, Novoa A, Jerome-Majewska LA et al. Tbx1 is required for proper neural crest migration and to stabilise spatial patterns during middle and inner ear development. Mech Dev 2005; 122:199–212.

Morsli H, Tuorto F, Choo D, et al. Otx1 and Otx2 activities are required for the normal development of the mouse inner ear. Development 1999; 126:2335–2345.

Ng M, Linthicum FH. Morphology of the developing human endolymphatic sac. Laryngscope 1998; 108:190–194.

Nishikori T, Hatta T, Kawauchi H, Otani H. Apoptosis during inner ear development in human and mouse embryos: an analysis by computer-assisted three-dimensional reconstruction. Anat Embryol 1999; 200:19–26.

Noramly S, Grainger RM. Determination of the embryonic inner ear. J Neurobiol 2002; 53:100–128.

Oguni M, Setogawa T, Matsui H, et al. Timing and sequence of the events in the development of extraocular muscles in staged human embryos: ultrastructural and histochemical study. Acta Anat 1992; 143:195–198.

Oguni M, Setogawa T, Otani H, Hatta T, Tanaka O. Development of the lens in human embryos: a histochemical and ultrastructural study. Acta Anat 1994; 149:31–38.

Peck JE. Development of hearing. Part II. Embryology. J Am Acad Audiol 1994; 5:359–365.

Piza J, Northrop C, Eavey RD. Embryonic middle ear mesenchyme disappears by redistribution. Laryngoscope 1998; 108:1378–1381.

Pujol R, Lavigne-Rebillard M, Uziel A. Development of the human cochlea. Acta Otolaryngol Suppl 1991; 482:7–12.

Rodriguez-Vazquez JF. Development of the stapes and associated structures in human embryos. J Anat 2005; 207–165–173.

Salminen M, Meyer BI, Bober E, Gruss P. Neutrin1 is required for semicircular canal formation in the mouse inner ear. Development 2000; 127:13–22.

Shimizu T, Salvador L, Hughes-Benzie R, et al. The role of reduced ear size in the prenatal detection of chromosomal abnormalities. Prenatal Diag 1997; 17:545–549.

Sohmer H, Freeman S. Functional development of auditory sensitivity in the fetus and neonate. J Basic Clin Physiol Pharmacol 1995; 6:95–108.

Torres M, Giraldez F. The development of the vertebrate inner ear. Mech Dev 1998; 71:5–21.

Ulatowska-Blaszyk K, Bruska M. The cochlear ganglion in human embryos of developmental stages 18 to 19. Folia Morphol (Warsz) 1999; 58:29–35.

Vazquez E, San Jose I, Naves J, et al. P75 and Trk oncoproteins expression is developmentally regulated in the inner ear of human embryos. Int J Dev Biol 1996; 1:77S–78S.

# 19 Development of the Dentition (Odontogenesis)

Teeth developed in primitive fishes from the adaptation of placoid scales overlying their jaws to form dermal denticles into multiple rows of teeth. By contrast, mammals have single-rowed dentitions. This phylogenetic dermal origin of teeth is reflected in the embryonic development of human teeth, which, although they develop submerged beneath the oral gingival epithelium, originate in part from ectodermal tissue. Teeth are derived from two of the primary germ layers, ectoderm and mesoderm, with a neural crest contribution. The enamel of teeth is derived from oral ectoderm, and neural crest tissue provides material for the dentine, pulp and cementum. The periodontium is of both neural crest and mesodermal origin.

Prior to any histological evidence of tooth development, the alveolar nerves have grown into the jaws; their branches form plexuses adjacent to sites of ectomesenchymal condensation, suggesting a possible neural inductive influence. Ectomesenchyme derived from the neural crest is the primary material of odontogenesis. A great number of genes are expressed in developing teeth that are associated with signaling molecules and epithelial-mesenchymal interactions. Signaling molecules from PAX9, MSX1, nerve growth factor (NGF), the Sonic hedgehog (SHH), fibroblast growth factor (FGF), bone morphogenetic protein (BMP), Distal-less (DLX) and Wingless (WNT) families regulate early stages of tooth morphogenesis. The transmission factor odd-skipped related -2 (OSR2) restricts the expression of the ectomesenchymal BMP4-MSX1 signaling pathway to the oral ectodermal region that will form the dental lamina, accounting for a single tooth row. These gene products are organizers of odontogenesis, among other structures, whose distinct dental patterns are formed by these genes and transcription factors. (Fig. 19–1, Fig. 19–2).

Inductive interaction between neural crest tissue and pharyngeal endoderm, and subsequently with oral ectoderm, is followed by proliferation of the oral ectoderm. Fibroblast growth factors and their receptors are expressed in several successive key steps in tooth formation regulated by reciprocal tissue interactions. These interactions produce the first morphologically identifiable manifestation of tooth development, the *dental lamina*. Later, the neural crest cells form the individual *dental papillae*, determining the ultimate number of teeth (Figs. 19–2 and 19–3).

Potential odontogenic tissue can be identified as early as the 28th day of development (fertilization age) as areas of ectodermal epithelial thickening on the margins of the stomodeum at the same time that the oropharyngeal membrane disintegrates. The oral epithelium thickens on the inferolateral borders of the maxillary prominences and on the superolateral borders of the mandibular arches where the two join to form

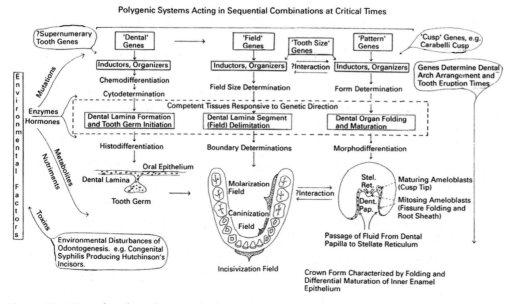

**Figure 19–1** Postulated mechanism of odontogenesis. (Copyright by Canadian Dental Association. Reprinted by permission.)

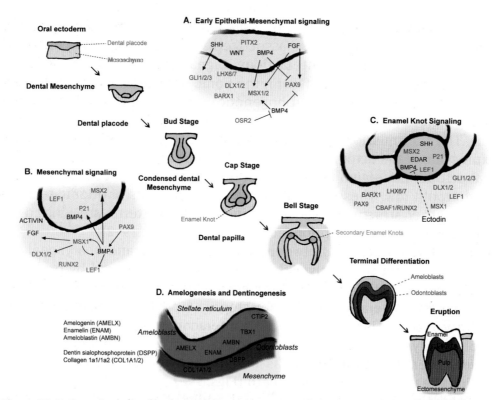

**Figure 19–2** Genetic and molecular signaling pathways in odontogenesis. (A) Patterning of the dentition is initiated by reciprocal epithelial-mesenchymal signaling in the thickening oral ectoderm by BMP and FGF cues that regulate transcription factors such as DLX and MSX family members. (B) Mesenchymal signaling induces formation of the dental papillae. (C) Differentiation of the enamel knot induces SHH expression to generate the tooth patterning signaling center. (D) Signaling factors in amelogenesis and dentinogenesis.

the lateral margins of the stomodeum. Additional, and initially separate, odontogenic epithelium arises on the 35th day of development at the inferolateral borders of the frontonasal prominence, providing four sites of origin of odontogenic epithelium for the maxillary dentition. Thus, it seems that the anterior maxillary teeth derive from the frontonasal prominence, and the posterior maxillary teeth from the maxillary prominences. The mandibular dentition also develops four initial odontogenic sites in the mandibular arches, two on each side.

The four maxillary dental laminae coalesce on the 37th day, by which age the mandibular dental laminae have fused. The upper and lower dental laminae now form continuous horseshoe-shaped plates. Local proliferations of the dental laminae are induced in a constant genetically determined sequence into the subjacent mesenchyme at locations corresponding to the dental papillae that are forming from neural crest cells. Fibroblast growth factors (FGFs) act as mitogens for the odontogenic cells, and stimulate the expression of a transcription factor, MSX1, needed for normal tooth development (Fig. 19–3). LHX6/7 specifies molar development. The positioning of teeth depends upon reiterative signaling by the expression of BMP, FGF, SHH and WNT genes and the discrete locations of competent mesenchyme responding to a continuous inductively active epithelium. The discontinuous distribution of tooth buds along the dental lamina is due to the intermittent expression of Sostdc1 (ectodin) that is an antagonist of BMP signaling in the mesenchymal induction of teeth that influence migrating neural crest cells. The *signaling* pathways mediating the epithelial-mesenchymal interactions regulate the number of teeth and molar cusp patterns. Modification of FGF, BMP and Activin signals by endogenous inhibitors, Follistatin, Sprouty and Sostdc1, antagonize these pathways involved in dental patterning, enamel and root formation. The ectodermal projections into the underlying mesenchyme form the primordia of the *enamel organs*, and, together with the dental papillae account for the subsequent submerged development of the teeth.

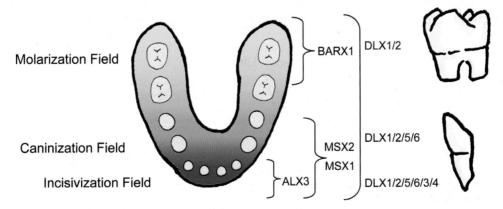

Figure 19–3 Regional gene expression patterns determining tooth shapes. Overlapping dorsal to ventral expression of DLX family members, BARX1, and MSX and ALX genes define the molar and incisor fields that pattern the dentition.

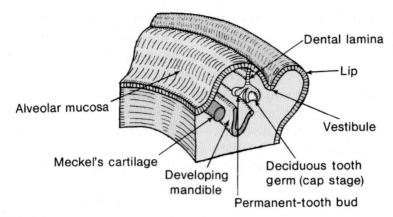

**Figure 19–3A** Schematic representation of development of the mandibular vestibular and dental laminae.

Another, and later, subjacent proliferation of the oral epithelium, the *vestibular lamina*, develops buccally and labially to the dental laminae (Fig. 19–3A). The vestibular laminae split the outer margins of the stomodeum into buccal segments that become the cheeks and lips and lingual segments in which the teeth and alveolar bone develop. A sulcus, the *vestibule* of the mouth, develops between the buccal and alveolar segments. Unsplit segments of the vestibular lamina remain as *labial frenula* (sing. *frenulum*).

Ten tooth germs, corresponding with the number of deciduous teeth, develop in each jaw. Later, the tooth germs of the permanent succedaneous teeth appear lingually to each deciduous tooth germ. The primordia of the permanent molar teeth develop from distal extensions of the dental laminae. Each tooth germ consists of an enamel organ and a dental papilla surrounded by a *dental follicle* or *sac*. The dental papilla, of neural crest origin, and dental follicle of mesodermal origin, are the anlagen of the dental pulp and part of the periodontal apparatus respectively.

Each enamel organ during its development changes from its initial small *bud* shape, enlarging by rapid mitosis of the basal cells into a *cap* shape, and later cupping into a large *bell* shape, by which shapes the three stages of enamel organ development are designated (see Fig. 19–4). Concomitant with these morphological alterations, histodifferentiation occurs within the enamel organ. Its external layer forms the *outer enamel epithelium*,

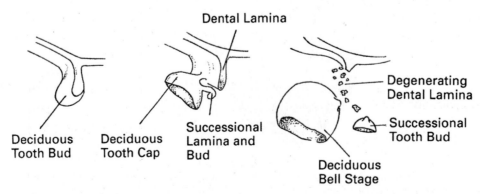

**Figure 19–4** The bud (left), cap (middle) and bell (right) stages of tooth development.

a layer of cuboidal cells subjacent to the developing follicle. The *stellate reticulum*, composed of stellate cells set in a fluid matrix, constitutes the central bulk of the early enamel organ. The indented inner layer, lining the dental papilla, forms the *inner enamel epithelium*, part of which differentiates into the transient secretory columnar *ameloblasts* that form enamel. Ameloblasts synthesize and secrete the enamel matrix proteins enamelin, amelogenin and ameloblastin that interact synergistically to provide the matrix for mineralization. The genes and signaling factors involved in amelogenesis include AMELX, AMBN, ENAM, CTIP2, KLK4, TBX1, TGF-β1, TGFβR1 and MMP20 expression (see Fig 19–2). Enamolysin (MNP20) and Kallikrein 4 (KLK4) are proteinases that degrade amelogenin, ameloblastin and enamelin during secretory and maturation phases of amelogenesis. Lining a portion of the stellate reticular surface of the inner enamel epithelium is a squamous cellular condensation, the *stratum intermedium*, that probably assists the ameloblasts in forming enamel. The inner and outer enamel epithelia form the *cervical loop*, elongating into *Hertwig's epithelial root sheath*, that, by enclosing more and more of the dental papilla, outlines the root(s) of the tooth (Figs. 19–5 and 19–6). Numerous transcription and growth factors are expressed by epithelial root sheath cells, among which are SHH, DLX2 and Patched 2. The Hertwig's epithelial root sheath participates in cementum development by differentiating into cementocytes and the epithelial rests of Malassez. The number of roots of a tooth is determined by the subdivision, or lack thereof, of the root sheath into one, two or three compartments. Delay or failure of

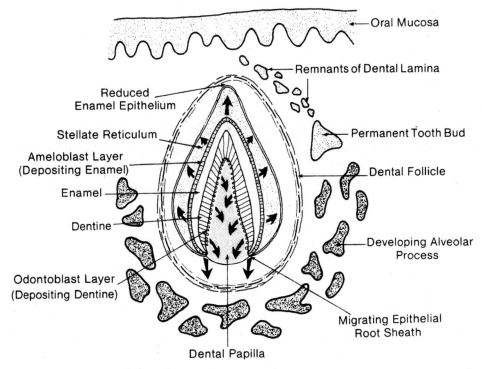

**Figure 19–5** Developing deciduous teeth showing directions of dental tissue deposition and growth.

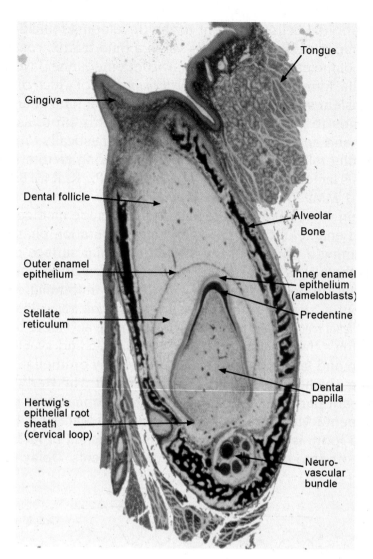

**Figure 19–6** Sectioned view of mandible revealing deciduous tooth bud, bone and neurovascular bundle. (Magnification: ×25) (Courtesy of Prof. Dr. W. Arnold.)

the epithelial root sheath to invaginate results in apical displacement of the root furcation, resulting in taurodontism. The prior presence of periodontal vessels entering the pulp creates lateral canals in the completed root canal, posing potential problems for future possible endodontic therapy.

The inner enamel epithelium interacts with the ectomesenchymal cells of the dental papilla, whose peripheral cells differentiate into *odontoblasts*. The formation of dentine by the odontoblasts precedes, and is necessary for, the induction of preameloblasts into ameloblasts to produce enamel. The inner enamel epithelium of the root sheath induces odontoblast differentiation but, lacking a stratum intermedium, fails to differentiate itself into enamel-forming ameloblasts, accounting for the absence of enamel from the roots. Cementum forms on dentine adjacent to the sites of disintegration of the outer enamel epithelium of the root sheath. The fragmentation of the root sheath, due to programmed cell death (apoptosis), leaves clusters of cells—the epithelial rests of Malassez—in the periodontal ligament. These rests are the source of potential periodontal cysts. The fibers in the initial cementum derive solely from fibers of the preexisting dental follicle that form the first principal fibers of the periodontal ligament.

The ameloblasts of the inner enamel epithelium and the adjacent odontoblasts together form a bilaminar membrane, which spreads by mitosis under genetic control that varies among the tooth germs in different areas. Different foldings of the bilaminar membrane are dictated by signaling molecules emanating from the enamel knot in the dental organ. Enamel knots are nonproliferating signaling centers regulating epithelial folding that specifies the varied shapes of incisors, canines, premolars and molars. The enamel knots are determined by expression of the p21 gene followed shortly after by SHH expression. Enamel knots identify the location of future cusps, and their spatial delineation is determined by ectodin, a secreted bone morphogenetic protein (BMP) inhibitor that suppresses ectomesenchymal proliferation, and thereby establishes the cusp tips. The confined space of the dental follicle imposes folding upon the expanding amelodentinal membrane. The ameloblasts secrete a protein matrix of amelogenins and enamelins that later mineralize as enamel rods or prisms as they retreat from the membrane. Concomitantly, the odontoblasts secrete the collagen matrix of predentine, which later calcifies into dentine (Figs. 19–5 and 19–7). Dentine deposition is a continuous process throughout life. The dental papilla differentiates into the dental pulp, the peripheral cells into odontoblasts and the remaining cells into fibroblasts. Enamel formation is restricted to the pre-eruptive phase of odontogenesis and ends with the deposition of an organic layer, the *enamel cuticle*. The enamel organ collapses after deposition of this cuticle. The inner and outer enamel epithelia together with the remains of the stratum intermedium form the *reduced enamel epithelium*, which later fuses with the overlying oral mucous membrane to initiate the pathway for eruption (Fig. 19–8).

Meanwhile, the mesenchyme surrounding the dental follicles becomes ossified, forming bony crypts in which the teeth develop, and from which they are later to erupt. An investing mesenchymal layer of the dental follicle adjacent to the cementum differentiates into the inner layer of the periodontal ligament by the development of collagen fibers. These fibers are already organized into inner, outer and intermediate layers, between cementum and bone. The periodontal ligament is the tissue through which orthodontic tooth movement is effected. Reorganization of the attachment apparatus, comprising cementum, periodontal fibers, and alveolar bone, is requisite to successful tooth movement during orthodontic treatment.

The anterior deciduous (incisor, canine and first molar) tooth germs develop first, at the sixth week of life; the second deciduous molar germs begin to appear at the seventh week. The anterior permanent (incisor, canine and premolar) tooth germs bud from the lingual side of the corresponding deciduous enamel organs, whereas the permanent molar tooth germs develop directly from backward extension of the dental lamina. The germs of the first permanent molars begin to develop at about the

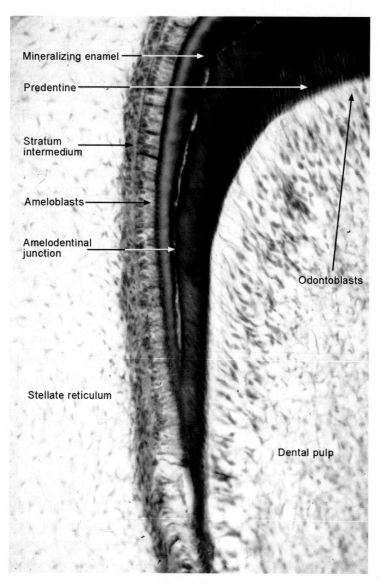

**Figure 19–7** Histological section of amelodentinal junction depicting early predentine formation in a tooth bud. (Magnification: ×125) (Courtesy of Prof. Dr. W. Arnold.)

16th week postconception (pc); those of the second and third permanent molars do not appear until after birth. Formation of most of the permanent teeth is not complete until several years after birth, and for the third molars, root formation is not complete until about 21 years. In this respect, teeth have the most prolonged chronology of development of any set of organs in the body.

## ERUPTION OF THE TEETH

The mechanisms by which teeth erupt have not been fully elucidated, and several processes have been proposed to explain the movement of teeth from their crypts into the oral cavity. The elongation of the root of a tooth during its development, and the growth of the pulp within it while the apical foramen is wide open, are likely to be sources of at least part of the eruptive force. The deposition of cementum upon the surface of the root would provide some slight eruptive movement once root formation was completed. The path of eruption ahead of the crown of a tooth would be guided by the remnants of the attachments of the dental follicle to the oral epithelium from which it originated (gubernacular cords). Blood pressure in the tissue around the root of a tooth and changes in the vascularity of the periodontal tissues have been implicated as eruptive forces.

Also, a form of "functional matrix" activity stemming from interplay between the periodontal ligament and the hard tissues has been postulated. The proliferating connective tissue of the periodontal ligament, or accumulation of periodontal tissue fluids resulting from increased vascular permeability, would tend to separate tooth and bone and thereby provide an eruptive force. This is analogous to the pathological state in which an inflamed, edematous periodontal ligament pushes a tooth out of its socket, although this may not be strictly comparable to physiological eruption.

Another theory suggests that contraction of the obliquely orientated collagen fibers of the periodontal ligament produces a "pulling" force, contrasting with most of the "pushing" forces indicated above (Fig. 19–8). The traction of the periodontal ligament has been attributed to contraction of fibroblasts: the presumed contraction of the fibroblasts of periodontal connective tissues has been likened to the contraction of scar tissue during wound healing. Contractile capabilities have been attributed to the fibroblasts (myofibroblasts) of the periodontal and cicatricial connective tissues.

An intact dental follicle is essential for eruption to occur. Cellular activity of the reduced enamel epithelium and the follicle initiates a cascade of signaling by expressing epidermal and transforming growth factors. These cytokines stimulate the follicle cells to express colony-stimulating factors, recruiting monocytes that fuse to form osteoclasts that together with the proteases from the reduced enamel epithelium resorbs overlying alveolar bone, producing an eruption pathway for the tooth. (Fig 19–8).

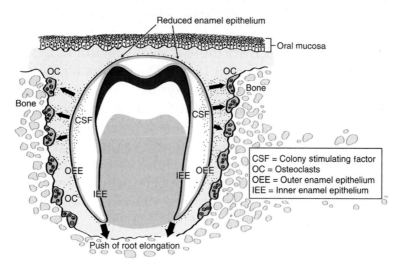

Figure 19–8 Schematic synopsis of various factors that may operate during tooth eruption.

Tooth eruption results from a combination of several factors operating concomitantly, sequentially, or sporadically during a tooth's eruption. Absence of any of the factors may be compensated for by another. Tooth eruption appears to be an intermittent rather than a continuous process* composed of alternating stages of movement and equilibrium. Individual posteruptive tooth movement, producing migration and hypereruption, is subject to local factors of mastication or tooth disuse. The net eruptive force (eruption minus resistance) of a tooth is quite small, on the order of 5 grams of pressure.

The eruption of the molar teeth is combined with their mesial drift, which ensures their contact with the anterior teeth, and their interproximal contact with one another when erupted. This tendency to mesial drift during eruption would account also for the mesial impaction of unerupted teeth, in which forward movement is greater than eruptive (upward or downward) movement. Vertical tooth eruption not only contributes to the great increase in height of the face during childhood but also compensates for loss of facial height resulting from attritional wear of the occlusal surfaces of teeth. Protrusion of the anterior teeth may contribute to a dentally prognathic facial profile.

The regular sequence of eruption of teeth suggests that it is under genetic control that programs the life cycle of the dental epithelium and follicle. There is considerable intersubject variation in ages of tooth eruption, an event highly subject to nutritional, hormonal and disease states. Disturbances of the "normal" sequence and ages of tooth eruption are contributory factors to the development of dental malocclusion, and consequently are of significance to orthodontists.

At birth the jaws contain the partly calcified crown of the 20 deciduous teeth, and the beginning of calcification of the first permanent molars (Table 19–1). Eruption of the deciduous dentition, beginning on average at 6.5 months of age, terminates at about 29 months. Dental eruption is then quiescent for nearly 4 years. At the age of 6, the jaws contain more teeth than at any other time: 48 teeth crammed between the orbits and nasal cavity and filling the body of the mandible (Fig. 19–9). Between 6 and 8 years of age, all 8 deciduous incisors are lost and 12 permanent teeth erupt. After this extreme activity there is a 2.5-year quiet period, until 10.5 years of age; then, during the next 18 months, the remaining 12 deciduous teeth are lost and 16 permanent teeth erupt.

The 6-year period of the mixed dentition, from 6 to 12 years, is the most complicated period of dental development and the one in which malocclusion is most likely to develop. A long and variable period (3 to 7 years) of quiescence follows before eruption of the four third molars completes the dentition. The third molars do not begin calcifying until the 9th year of age, and their eruption from the 16th year onward heralds the completion of dentofacial growth and development.

---

* Teeth that grow continuously, such as the incisors of rodents, erupt continuously throughout life.

TABLE 19–1: Chronology of Development and Eruption of Teeth

| Tooth | | Tooth germ completed | Calcification commences | Crown completed | Eruption in mouth | Root completed |
|---|---|---|---|---|---|---|
| Deciduous | | | | | | |
| | Incisors | | 3–4 mo pc | 2–4 mo | 6–8 mo | 1.5–2 yr |
| | Canines | 12–16 wk pc | 5 mo pc | 9 mo | 16–20 mo | 2.5–3 yr |
| | 1st molars | | 5 mo pc | 6 mo | 15–20 mo | 2–2.5 yr |
| | 2nd molars | | 6–7 mo pc | 11–12 mo | 20–30 mo | 3 yr |
| Permanent | | | | | | |
| | Central incisors | 30 wk pc | 3–4 mo | 4–5 yr | Max.: 7–9 yr | 9–10 yr |
| | | | | | Mand.: 6–8 yr | |
| | Lateral incisors | 32 wk pc | Max.: 10–12 mo | 4–5 yr | 7–9 yrs | 10–11 yr |
| | | | Mand.: 3–4 mo | | | |
| | Canines | 30 wk pc | 4–5 mo | 6–7 yr | Max.: 11–12 yr | 12–15 yr |
| | | | | | Mand.: 9–10 yr | |
| | 1st premolars | 30 wk pc | 1.5–2 yr | 5–6 yr | 10–12 yr. | 12–14 yr |
| | 2nd premolars | 31 wk pc | 2–2.5 yr | 6–7 yr | 10–12 yr | 12–14 yr |
| | 1st molars | 24 wk pc | Birth | 3–5 yr | 6–7 yr | 9–10 yr |
| | 2nd molars | 6 mo | 2.5–3 yr | 7–8 yr | 12–13 yr | 14–16 yr |
| | 3rd molars | 6 yr | 7–10 yr | 12–16 yr | 17–21 yr | 18–25 yr |

All dates postnatal, except where designated postconception (pc).

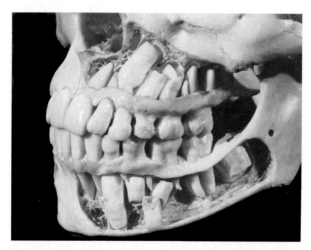

**Figure 19–9** Mixed deciduous and permanent dentitions dissected in the skull of an 8-year-old child. Note the location of the unerupted permanent teeth in the bodies of the maxilla and mandible.

All 12 permanent molars originate from identical sites in all four quadrants of the jaw. The upper molars develop within the maxillary tuberosity, three on each side, and the lower three molars of each side develop within the ascending ramus of the mandible. The first and second molars migrate forward from their sites of origin into the alveolar bone of the maxilla or mandible, from which they erupt to meet their antagonists.

Bone resorption of the anterior border of the mandibular ramus and bone deposition on the maxillary tuberosity create space for eruption of the permanent molar teeth. Failure of adequate continued bone growth of the jaws during this eruption period, for either genetic or environmental reasons, precludes space for full eruption of all the permanent teeth, resulting in maleruption, partly impacted eruption, or noneruption of the last-formed teeth.

All the teeth in the jaws are carried downward, forward and laterally as the face expands, except for the central incisors, which maintain their proximity to the median plane. The faster rate of tooth eruption is superimposed upon this slower bone movement, a combination of movements that determine dental and gnathoskeletal growth patterns. The continual tendency of the teeth to erupt and migrate means that this mechanism is constantly compensating for the attritional wear of teeth to stabilize the vertical dimension of the face. The maintenance of dental occlusion is a combination of bone remodeling and tooth eruption that reflects the neuromuscular actions of the orofacial apparatus.

## ANOMALIES OF DEVELOPMENT

Congenital absence of teeth (*anodontia*) may be total or, more frequently, partial (*hypodontia*) representing agenesis of fewer than six teeth. *Oligodontia* describes agenesis of six or more teeth, involving individual teeth that may follow a hereditary pattern, or be part of a syndrome (e.g., *ectodermal dysplasia*). Anodontia of varying degrees of severity afflict some 20%

of the population. A mutation of the PAX9 gene, located on chromosome 14, with an extra nucleotide in the gene, produces a smaller than normal PAX9 protein, leading to congenital absence of molars. Mutations of genes involved in the Ectodysplasin (EDA)–NF-kB pathway incur hypohidrotic ectodermal dysplasia that manifests oligodontia among other ectodermal defects. Transforming growth factor-alpha (TGF-$\alpha$) variants and haplotypes are associated with tooth agenesis, MSX1 and AXIN2 are involved in non-syndromic hypodontia, while SHH, PITX2, IRF6 and P63 syndromic disorders display dental agenesis. Mutations in LTBP3, the gene encoding latent TGF$\beta$-binding protein 3 results in oligodontia. Some types of teeth, for example, third molars, are frequently congenitally absent, whereas others, for example, first molars and canines, are rarely so. Anomalous forms of teeth are extremely varied.

Defects of enamel (amelogenesis imperfecta) and dentine (dentinogenesis imperfecta) may be expressions of genetic autosomal dominant disorders or sporadic environmentally determined hypoplasia or hypomineralization of the hard tissues. Teeth are particularly sensitive to deficiencies of certain vitamins and hormones, to metabolic disturbances, bacterial and viral infections and certain drugs (e.g., fluorides, tetracyclines) during their formation. These agents inflict lesions upon the forming hard tissues that are permanently retained.

## SELECTED BIBLIOGRAPHY

Arnold WH, Rezwani T, Baric I. Location and distribution of epithelial pearls and tooth buds in human fetuses with cleft lip and palate. Cleft Palate Craniofac J 1998; 35:359–365.

Bailleul-Forstier I, Molla M, Verloes A, Berdal A. The genetic basis of inherited anomalies of the teeth: Part 1: Clinical and molecular aspects of non-syndromic dental disorders. Eur J Med Genet 2008; 51:273–291.

Bailleul-Forestier I, Berdal A, Vinckier F, et al. The genetic basis of inherited anomalies of the teeth. Part 2: Syndromes with significant dental involvement. Eur J Med Genet 2008; 51:383–408.

Butler WT. Dentin matrix proteins and dentinogenesis. Conn Tiss Res 1995; 33:59–65.

Callahan N, Modesto A, Deeley K, et al. Transforming growth factor alpha (TGF A), human tooth agenesis, and evidence of segmental uniparental isodisomy. Eur J Oral Sci 2009; 117:20–26.

Chen J, Lan Y, Baek J-A, Gao Y, Jiang R. Wnt/beta-catenin signaling plays an essential role in activation of odontogenic mesenchyme during early tooth development. Dev Biol 2009; 334:174–185.

Chen S, Gluhak-Heinrich J, Wang YM et al. Runx2, Osx and Dspp in tooth development. J Dent Res 2009; 88:904–909.

Chen Y, Bei M, Woo I, et al. Msx1 controls inductive signaling in mammalian tooth morphogenesis. Development 1996; 122:3035–3044.

Chiego DJ Jr. The early distribution and possible role of nerves during odontogenesis. Int J Dev Biol; 1995; 39:191–194.

Christensen LR, Mollgard K, Kjaer I, Janas MS. Immunocytochemical demonstration of nerve growth factor receptor (NGF-R) in developing human fetal teeth. Anat Embryol 1993; 188:247–255.

Clauss F, Maniere M-C, Obry F, Waltmann E, et al. Dento-craniofacial phenotypes and underlying molecular mechanisms in hypohidrotic ectodermal dysplasia (HED): a review. J Dent Res 2008; 87:1089–1099.

Cobourne MT. The genetic control of early odontogenesis. Br J Orthod 1999; 26:21–28.

Cobourne MT. Familial human hypodontia. Br Dent J 2007; 203:203–207.

Cuisinier FJ, Steuer P, Senger B, et al. Human amelogenesis: high resolution electron microscopy of nanometer-sized particles. Cell Tiss Res 1993; 273:175–182.

Denaxa M, Sharpe PT, Pachnis V. The LIM homeodomain transcription factors Lhx6 and Lhx7 are key regulators of mammalian dentition. Dev Biol 2009; 333:324–336.

El-Sayed W, Parry DA, Shore RC et al. Mutations in the Beta Propeller WDR72 cause autosomal recessive hypomaturation amelogenesis imperfecta. Am J Hum Genet 2009; 85:699–705.

Fincham AG, Simmer JP. Amelogenin proteins of developing dental enamel. Ciba Foundation Symp 1997; 205:118–130; discussion 130–134.

Fincham AG, Moradian-Oldak J, Simmer JP. The structural biology of the developing dental enamel matrix. J Struct Biol 1999; 126:270–299.

Fraser GJ, Hulsey CD, Bloomquist RF, et al. An ancient gene network is co-opted for teeth on old and new jaws. PLos Biol 2009; 7:e1000031.

Gao Y, Li D, Han T, Sun Y, Zhang J. TGFβ1 and TGFβR1 are expressed in ameloblasts and promote MMP20 expression. Anat Rec 2009; 292:885–890.

Gibson CW. Regulation of amelogenin gene expression. Crit Rev Eukaryot Gene Expr 1999; 9:45–57.

Golonzhka O, Metzger D, Bornert J-M, et al. Ctip2/Bcl11b controls ameloblast formation during mammalian odontogenesis. Proc Natl Acad Sci 2009; 106:4278–4283.

Gorczycz J, Litwin JA, Nowogrodzka-Zagorska M, et al. Microcirculation of human fetal tooth buds: a SEM study of corrosion casts. Eur J Morphol 1994; 32:3–10.

Hatakeyama J, Fukumoto S, Nakamura N, et al. Synergistic roles of amelogenin and ameloblastin. J Dent Res 2009; 88:318–322.

Hu JC, Chun YH, Al-Hazzazi T, Simmer JP. Enamel formation and amelogenesis imperfecta. Cells Tiss Org 2007; 186:78–85.

Hu JC-C, Simmer JP. Developmental biology and genetics of dental malformations Orthod Craniofac Res 2007; 10:45–62.

Huang X, Bringas Jr P, Slankin H, Chai Y. Fate of HERS during tooth root development. Dev Biol 2009; 334:22–30.

Ikeda E, Morita R, Nakao K, et al, Tsuji T. Fully functional bioengineered tooth replacement therapy. Proc Nat Acad Sci 2009; 106:13475–13480.

Jernvall J, Thesleff I. Reiterative signaling and patterning during mammalian tooth morphogenesis. Mech Dev 2000; 92:19–29.

Kapadia H, Mues G, D'Souza R. Genes affecting tooth morphogenesis. Orthod Craniofacial Res 2007; 10:237–244.

Kassai Y, Munne P, Hotta Y, et al. Regulation of mammalian tooth cusp patterning by ectodin. Science 2005; 309:2067–2070.

Kuttunen P, Luukko K. Fgfr2b signaling integrates tooth morphogenesis and dental axon patterning. Dev Biol 2008; 319:508.

Lau EC, Slavkin HC, Snead ML. Analysis of human enamel genes: insights into genetic disorders of enamel. Cleft Palate J 1990; 27:121–130.

Limeback H. Molecular mechanisms in dental hard tissue mineralization. Curr Opin Dent 1991; 1:826–835.

Lin Y, Cheng Y-S L, Qin C, et al. FGFR2 in the dental epithelium is essential for development and maintenance of the maxillary cervical loop, a stem cell niche in mouse incisors. Dev Dyn 2009. 238:324–330.

Linde A, Goldberg M. Dentinogenesis. Crit Rev Oral Biol Med 1993; 4:679–728.

Luukko K. Neuronal cells and neurotrophins in odontogenesis. Eur J Oral Sci 1998; 1:80–93.

Maas R, Bei M. The genetic control of early tooth development. Crit Rev Oral Biol Med 1997; 8:4–39.

Mark M, Lohnes D, Mendelsohn C, et al. Roles of retinoic acid receptors and of Hox genes in the patterning of the teeth and of the jaw skeleton. Int J Dev Biol 1995; 39:111–121.

Matalova E, Fleischmannova J, Sharpe PT, Tucker AS. Tooth agenesis: from molecular genetics to molecular dentistry. J Dent Res 2008; 87:617–623.

Mitsiadis TA, Tucker AS, DeBari C, et al. A regulatory relationship between Tbx1 and FGF *signaling* during tooth morphogenesis and ameloblast lineage determination. Dev Biol 2008; 320:39–48.

Mornstad H, Staaf V, Welander U. Age estimation with the aid of tooth development: a new method based on objective measurements. Scand J Dent Res 1994; 102:137–143.

Munne PM, Tummers M, Jarvinen E, et al. Tinkering with the inductive mesenchyme: Sostdc1 uncovers the role of dental mesenchyme in limiting tooth induction. Development 2009; 136:393–402.

Nakagawa E, Itoh T, Satokata I. Odontogenic potential of post-natal oral mucosal epithelium. J Dent Res 2009; 88:219–223.

Noor A, Windpassinger C, Vitcu I, Orlic M et al. Oligodontia is caused by mutation in LTBP3, the gene encoding latent TGF-β binding protein 3. Am J Hum Genet 2009; 84:519–523.

Ohazam A, Haycraft J, Seppala M, et al. Primary cilia regulate Shh activity in the control of molar tooth number. Develop 2009; 136:897–903.

Peters H, Neubuser A, Balling R. Pax genes and organogenesis: Pax 9 meets tooth development. Eur J Oral Sci 1998; 1:38–43.

Radlanski RJ, van der linden FP, Ohnesorge I. 4D-computerized visualisation of human craniofacial skeletal growth and of the development of the dentition. Anat Anz 1999; 181:3–8.

Robinson C, Brooks SJ, Shore RC, Kirkham J. The developing enamel matrix: nature and function. Europ J Oral Sci 1998; 106(Suppl 1):282–291.

Sasaki T, Takagi M, Yanagisawa T. Structure and function of secretory ameloblasts in enamel formation. Ciba Found Symp 1997; 205:32–46.

Simmer JP, Fincham AG. Molecular mechanisms of dental enamel formation. Crit Revue Oral Biol Med 1995; 6:84–108.

Smith CE. Cellular and chemical events during enamel maturation. Crit Rev Oral Biol Med 1998; 9:128–161.

Smith CE, Wazen R, Hu Y et al. Consequences for enamel development and mineralization resulting from loss of function of ameloblastin or enamelin. Euro J Oral Sci 2009; 117:485–497.

Stockton DW, Das P, Goldenberg M, et al. Mutation of PAX9 is associated with oligodontia. Nat Genet 2000; 24:18–19.

Ten Cate AR. The role of epithelium in the development, structure and function of the tisues of tooth support. Oral Dis 1996; 2:55–62.

Ten Cate AR. The development of the periodontium—a largely ectomesenchymally derived unit. Periodontol 2000 1997; 13:9–19.

Thesleff I. Epithelial-mesenchymal signaling regulating tooth morphogenesis. J Cell Sci 2003; 116:1647–1648.

Thesleff I. The genetic basis of tooth development and dental defects. Am J Med Genet 2006; 140:2530–2535.

Thesleff I, Abert T. Tooth morphogenesis and the differentiation of ameloblasts. Ciba Found Symp 1997; 205:3–12; discussion 12–7.

Thesleff I, Sharpe P. Signalling networks regulating dental development. Mech Dev 1997; 67:111–123.

Thesleff I, Keranen S, Jernvall J. Enamel knots as signaling centers linking tooth morphogenesis and odontoblast differentiation. Adv Dent Res 2001; 15:14–18.

Thivichon-Prince B, Couble ML, Giamarchi A et al. Primary cilia of odontoblasts: possible role in molar morphogenesis. J Dent Res 2009; 88:910–915.

Tucker AS, Sharpe PT. Molecular genetics of tooth morphogenesis and patterning: the right shape in the right place. J Dent Res 1999; 78:826–834.

Tucker AS, Sharpe PT. The cutting edge of mammalian development; how the embryo makes teeth. Nat Rev Genet 2004; 5:499–508.

Tummer M, Thesleff I. The importance of signal pathway modulation in all aspects of tooth development. J Exp Zool (Mol Dev Evol) 2009; 312B:309–319

Ulm MR, Chalubinski K, Ulm C, Plockinger B, Deutinger J, Bernaschek G. Sonographic depiction of fetal tooth germs. Prenatal Diag 1995; 15:368–372.

Ulm MR, Kratochwil A, Ulm B, et al. Three-dimensional ultrasonographic imaging of fetal tooth buds for characterization of facial clefts. Early Hum Dev 1999; 55:67–75.

Wang Y, Groppe JC, Wu J, Ogawa T et al. Pathogenic mechanisms of tooth agenesis linked to paired domain mutations in human PAX9. Hum Mol Genet 2009; 18:2863–2874.

Weiss K, Stock D, Zhao Z, et al. Perspectives on genetic aspects of dental patterning. Eur J Oral Sci 1998; 106(Supl 1):55–63.

Weiss KM, Stock DW, Zhao Z. Dynamic interactions and the evolutionary genetics of dental patterning. Crit Rev Oral Biol Med 1998; 9:369–398.

Wise GE, King GJ. Mechanisms of tooth eruption and orthodontic tooth movement. J Dent Res 2008; 87:414–434.

Wright T. The molecular control of and clinical variations in root formation. Cell Tiss, Org 2007; 186:86–93.

Wright JT, Hart TC, Hart PS et al. Human and mouse enamel phenotypes resulting from mutation or altered expression of AMEL, ENAM, MMP20 and KLK4. Cells, Tiss Org 2008; 189:224–229.

Zhang Z, Lan Y, Chai Y, Jiang R. Anatagonistic actions of Msx 1 and Osr2 pattern mammalian teeth into a single row. Science 2009; 323:1232–1234.

Zeichner-David M, Diekwisch T, Fincham A, et al. Control of ameloblast differentiation. Int J Dev Biol 1995; 39:69–92.

Zhao H, Oka K, Bringas P, et al. TGF-beta type I receptor Alk5 regulates tooth initiation and mandible patterning in a type II receptor–independent manner. Dev Biol 2008; 320:19–29.

# 20 Craniofacial Disorders with Known Single Gene Mutations

## GEOFFREY A. MACHIN, MD, PhD, FRCPATH, FRCP(C).

Recent advances in the fields of molecular biology and genetic identification of developmental processes have led to an understanding where and when selected genes are activated and expressed during normal and abnormal development. Table 20–1 lists the more common disorders with known single gene mutations.

**TABLE 20–1: CRANIOFACIAL DEVELOPMENT TABLE—Disorders with Known Single Gene Mutations**

| Disorder | Mutated Gene | Malformations | Gene Function | Mutations | Comment |
|---|---|---|---|---|---|
| Oro-facial cleft lip/palate 5, OFC5 | MSX1 | Unilateral, bilateral cleft lip, palate, anodontia | Homeobox | R196P, S105X, S202X | Selective anodontia, Premolars, 1st, 3rd molars |
| OFC7 | PVRL1 | Cleft lip and/or palate-ectodermal dysplasia | Mediates entry of herpes viruses | W185X, 1 bp del 185, 1 bp del 323 | |
| OFC8, Rapp-Hodgkin, ADULT | TP73L | Ankyloblepharon, ectodermal defects, clefting | Tumor suppressor, analogous with p53 | R204W, R204Q, R279H, many others | |
| OFC10 | SUMO1 | Cleft lip, palate, primary and secondary | Posttranslational protein modification | t(2;8) with breakpoint in SUMO1 gene | Unique case |
| Popliteal pterygium syndrome, PPS; van der Woude syndrome | IRF6 | Orofacial clefts, pterygia, lip pits | Helix-turn-helix transcription factor | E92X, Q393X, R6C, many others | |
| Kallmann syndrome 2 | FGFR1 | Hypogonadism, anosmia, cleft lip or palate | Binds FGF ligand | W666R, R622X | |
| Orofaciodigital syndrome 1 | CXORF5 | Jaw, tongue clefts in region of lateral incisors | ? regulation of microtubule dynamics | S434R, 1 bp del 312G, 2 bp del 1887AT, etc | Multiorgan effects, via body situs, ciliary action; allelic with Simpson-Golabi-Behme l2 |
| Peters-plus syndrome | B3GALTL | Eye malformations, cleft lip/palate | Glycosyl-transferase | Splice site mutations | |
| Hydrolethalus syndrome 1 | HYLS1 | Hydrocephalus, polydactyly, cleft lip/palate | ? | D211G | |

| Disorder | Mutated Gene | Malformations | Gene Function | Mutations | Comment |
|---|---|---|---|---|---|
| Pallister-Hall syndrome, PHS | GLI3 | Hypothalamic hamartoma, polydactyly, imperforate anus, cleft lip/palate | Transcription factor | E543X, E1147X, 1 bp del, 2012G, and others | Allelic to Grieg cephalo-syndactyly |
| Branchiootorenal syndrome 1, BOR1 | EYA1 | Cochlear malformations, branchial fistulas, renal anomalies | Ligand for MAPK | R275X, R407Q, S454P, many more | Branchiootic 1 (BOS1) and orofacio-cervical (CFC) syndromes are allelic |
| BOR2 | SIX5 | Cervical fistulae, preauricular tags, hemifacial microsomia, renal anomalies | Interacts with EYA1 | A158T, A296R, T552M | |
| Smith-Lemli-Opitz syndrome (RSH), 1 and 2 | DHCR7 | Genital malformations, facies, cleft palate | Cholesterol synthesis | Many mutations reported | An inborn error of metabolism that causes malformations |
| Lymphedema-distichiasis syndrome | MFH1 (FOXC2) | Limb lymph-edema, double eyelash rows, cleft plate | Unknown developmental effect | Y99X, 8 bp del, NT914, many other mutations | |
| Ellis-van Creveld syndrome, EVC | EVC, EVC2 | Short-limbs, polydactyly, partial cleft upper lip, hypodontia | Unknown developmental effect | Q879X, R340X, R443Q, other mutations | EVC is allelic with Weyers acrodental dysplasia |
| Weyers acrodental dysplasia | EVC, EVC2 | Polydactyly, abnormal incisors, conical teeth | See EVC | See EVC | Allelic with EVC |
| Waardenburg syndrome 1, WS1 | PAX3 | Frontal white hair, hetero-chromia iridis dystopia canthorum, bilateral cleft lip | Transcription factor expressed in neuro-genesis, synergistic with MITF | P50L, many other mutations | |
| SC phocomelia syndrome | ESCO2 | Reduction limb malformations, cleft palate | Sister chromatid adhesion | W423X, Q202X, 1 bp ins, 750A | Allelic with Roberts syndrome |
| Fraser syndrome | FRAS1, FREM2 | Cryptophthalmos, syndactyly, renal anomalies, laryngeal stenosis, midline cleft nares and tongue | Extracellular matrix proteins | FRAS1: Q3000X, Q1266X, S1423X; FREM2: E1974K | |
| Oculodentodigital dysplasia, ODDD | GJA1 | Microphthalmia, syndactyly 4/5, small teeth, "amelogenesis imperfecta" | Connexin, gap junction channel | Y175S, S18P, G21R and many other mutations | |
| Siderius X-linked mental retardation syndrome | PHF8 | Mild mental retardation, broad nasal tip, cleft lip/palate | Transcription factor with PHF finger | R211X, 12 bp deletion exon 8/intron 8 junction | |

| Disorder | Mutated Gene | Malformations | Gene Function | Mutations | Comment |
|---|---|---|---|---|---|
| Snyder-Robinson X-linked mental retardation syndrome | SMS | Mild mental retardation, osteoporosis, cleft palate | Polyamnine synthesis | IVS4AS, G-A, +5 (splice site mutation) | |
| Stickler syndrome 1, STL1 | COL2A1 | Myopia, mitral valve prolapse, cleft palate | Type 2A collagen synthesis | R732X, R9X, P846X, others | |
| Simpson-Golabi-Behmel 2 | CXORF5 | Hydrops, renal/gastrointestinal anomalies, cleft palate | ? Regulation of microtubule dynamics | 4 bp dup exon 16 | Allelic with OFD1 |
| Cerebrofrontofacial syndrome | FLNA | Mental retardation, wide forehead, midline alveolar cleft, cleft lip/palate | Actin-binding protein | 1923C-T, splice site mutation, exon 13 | Allelic with oto palatodigital types 1, 2, Melnick-Needles syndromes |
| Arthrogryposis, distal, type 2B | TNNT3, TNN12, MYH3 | Clench fist, camptodactyly, micro stomia, cleft lip/palate | Calcium-binding muscle troponin complex; myosin heavy chain | TNN12: R174Q, R156X; TNN3: R63H; MYH3: R672H, C | |
| Solitary median maxillary central incisor (SMMCI) | SHH | Minimal manifestation of holoprosencephaly | | I111F, W128X, V332A | Allelic with HPE3 |
| Robinow syndrome | ROR2 | Frontal bossing, hypertelorism, dental crowding, midline cleft lower lip | Protein kinase | Q502X, R184C, W720X, R205X, R119X | Allelic with brachydactyly type B1 |
| Cleft palate, X-linked, CPX | TBX22 | Incomplete cleft secondary palate, ankyloglossia | T-box transcription factor | T260M, G118C, Q56X, etc | |
| Hypothyroidism, spiky hair, cleft palate | FKHL15 | Also choanal atresia, bifid epiglottis | Forkhead transcription factor | S57N, A65V | |
| Telecanthus with other anomalies, Opitz syndrome | MIDI1 | Cleft lip, larynx, hypospadias, heart defects | Transcription factor, body axis formation | E115X, L626P, Q115X | |
| Micro-ophthalmia, syndromic 2, MCOPS2 | BCL6 | Persistent primary teeth, oligodontia, cleft palate | Corepressor | P85L, R970X and others | |
| Hydrolethalus 1 | HYLS1 | CNS malformations, polydactyly, bilateral cleft lip and palate | Not known | D211G | |
| CHARGE syndrome | CHD7, SEMA3E | Coloboma, heart anomaly, choanal atresia, micro-phallus, cleft palate, ear anomalies | CHD7: expressed in ectomesenchyme SEM3E: vascular patterning | CHD7: I1028V, L1257R, Y1806X; SEM3E: S703L | |

| Disorder | Mutated Gene | Malformations | Gene Function | Mutations | Comment |
|---|---|---|---|---|---|
| Tetra-amelia, autosomal recessive | WNT3 | Amelia, lung hypoplasia, cleft lip and palate | Primary axis formation | Q83X | |
| Marshall syndrome | COL11A1 | Chondrodysplasia, facial dysmorphism, cleft palate | Minor cartilage constituent collagen | Deletions | |
| Loeys-Dietz syndrome, LDS | TGFBR1, TGBFR2 | Aortic aneurysm, cleft palate or bifid uvula | TGF beta serine/threonine kinases | TGFBR1: M318R, D400G, T200I; TGFBR2: Y336N, A355P, G357W | |
| Otospondylomegaepiphyseal dysplasia, OSMED | COL11A2 | Chondrodysplasia, sensorineural deafness, cleft palate | Minor cartilage constituent collagen | G175R, S345X | Allelic with Stickler III |
| Larsen syndrome, dominant, LRS1 | FLNB | Congenital dislocation of knees, "dish" face, cleft palate | Expressed in growth plate chondrocytes | F161C, G1586R, E227K | Allelic with atelosteogenesis I and III |
| Camptomelic dysplasia | SOX9 | Angulated bone chondrodysplasia, sex-reversed males, cleft palate | Binds to COL2A1 | T440X, K173E, H165Y | |
| Rapadilino syndrome | RECQL4 | Radial/patellar aplasia, joint dislocation, cleft palate | DNA helicase | Q1091X, W269X | Allelic with Rothmund-Thomson syndrome |
| Craniofrontonasal syndrome, CFNS | EFNB1 | Frontonasal dysplasia, bifid nasal tip, cleft palate | Ligand of ephrin-type kinase | TIIII, P54L, G151S, many others | X-linked dominant; mild in males, severe in females |
| Saethre-Chotzen syndrome, SCS | TWIST | Craniosynostosis, syndactyly, cleft palate | Transcription factor with bLHL domain | Y103X, Q119P, Y107X | |
| Atelosteogenesis type II | DTDST | Severe chondrodysplasia, small chest, cleft palate | Sulfation of proteoglycans | R279W, G255E, A715V | Allelic with diastrophic dysplasia, achondrogenesis type IIB |
| Hereditary neuralgic amyotrophy | SEPT9 | Brachial plexus neuropathy, cleft palate | Interact with cytoskeletal filaments | R88W, S93F | |
| Nail patella syndrome, NPS | LMX1B | Dysplastic nails, absent/hypoplastic patellae, cleft lip and palate | Transcription factor, interacts with PAX2 | N246K, R198X, C95F | |
| Juvenile-onset dystonia | ACTB | Rapid-onset dystonia, cleft lip and palate | Actin function | R183W | |

| Disorder | Mutated Gene | Malformations | Gene Function | Mutations | Comment |
|---|---|---|---|---|---|
| Desmosterolosis | DHCR24 | Osteosclerosis, heart anomalies, ambiguous genitalia, cleft palate | Cholesterol synthesis | K306N, Y471S, N294T and others | Same pathway as Smith-Lemli-Opitz syndrome |
| Spondyloepimetaphyseal dysplasia , Strudwick type | COL2A1 | Dwarfism, scoliosis, cleft palate | Cartilage collagen | G709C, G304C, C292V | Allelic with SED congenital, achondrogenesis/ hypochondrogenesis II, Kniest, Stickler I, spondylometaphyseal dysplasia, congenital |
| Faciogenital dysplasia | FGD1 | Joint hypermobility, "saddlebag scrotum," lower lip dimple | Interacts with actin-binding proteins | R610Q, R522H, R433L | Aarskog syndrome |
| Limb-mammary syndrome, LMS | TP63 | Severe hand/foot anomalies, unilateral mammary hypoplasia, hypodontia, cleft palate | Tumor suppressor | 2 bp del 1576TT, 2 bp del 1743AA | Allelic with Rapp-Hodgkin, ADULT, OFC8 |
| Spondylocarpotarsal synostosis syndrome | FLNB | Vertebral anomalies, carpal coalition, cleft palate | Expressed in growth plate chondrocytes | R818X, S2137X, R1607X | Allelic with LRS1, atelosteogenesis I and III |
| Kniest dysplasia | COL2A1 | Dwarfism resembling metatropic, cleft palate | Cartilage collagen | 28 bp del, 1 bp del, G103N | Allelic with SED congenital, achondrogenesis/ hypochondrogenesis II, Strudwick, Stickler I, spondylometaphyseal dysplasia, congenital |
| Treacher Collins-Franceschetti syndrome | TCOF1 | Eyelid coloboma, microtia, hypoplastic zygoma, cleft palate | Ribosome biogenesis | Q252X, Y50C, R911X | |
| Andersen cardiodysrhythmic periodic paralysis | KCNJ2 | Potassium-sensitive periodic paralysis, ventricular ectopy, dysmorphic facies, including cleft palate | Potassium channel | D71V, R218W, G300V and others | |
| Stickler syndrome, type II, STL2 | COL11A1 | Early deafness, beaded vitreous, midline clefting | Minor cartilage constituent collagen | G97V, 54 bp del | Allelic with Marshall syndrome |

| Disorder | Mutated Gene | Malformations | Gene Function | Mutations | Comment |
|---|---|---|---|---|---|
| Renpenning syndrome 1, RENS1 | PQBP1 | X-linked mental retardation, microcephaly, cleft palate | Polyglutamine binding protein | Various del and ins | |
| Mental retardation-hypotonic facies syndrome, MRXF1 | ATRX | Mental retardation, patulous lower lip, cleft palate, widely spaced, hypoplastic teeth | Helicase II | R37X, R127Q, P37X and others | Allelic with alpha-thalassemia/ mental retardation syndrome |
| Furlong syndrome, FS | TGFBR1 | Marfanoid, craniosynostosis, cleft palate | TGF beta serine/threonine kinase | S241L | Allelic with Loeys-Dietz syndrome, LDS |
| Fuhrman syndrome | WNT7A | Fibular aplasia, poly-syndactyly, cleft lip and palate | Cell signaling for cell fate | A109T | |
| Goldberg-Shprintzen megaacolon syndrome | KIAA1279 | Hirschsprung's mega-colon, microcephaly, cleft palate | Not known | E86X, R90X | |
| VACTERL with hydrocephalus, X-linked | FANCB | As per title, with branchial anomalies, cleft lip | Not known | Splice site mutation | |
| Holoprosencephaly 2, HPE2 | SIX3 | Holoprosencephaly, including midline and symmetrical cleft lip and palate | Homeobox gene, protein-protein interactions | L226V, R257P, V250A | |
| HPE3, autosomal dominant | SHH | As HPE2 | Early embryo patterning | G31R, Q100X, L105X | |
| HPE4 | TGIF | As HPE2 | Transcriptional repressor | S28C, P63R, T151A | |
| HPE5 | ZIC2 | As HPE2 | Transcription factor | Deletions, insertions | |
| HPE7 | PTCH1 | As HPE2 | Transcription suppressor | T728M, S827G, T1052M | |
| HPE9 | GLI2 | As HPE2 | Transcription factor | W113X, R151G | Allelic with SMMCI |
| Ectodermal dysplasia, anhidrotic, autosomal recessive | EDAR, EDARADD | Ectodermal dysplasia, anodontia | EDAR: transmembrane protein, interacts with EDARADD | EDAR; 18bp del EDARADD: E142K | Allelic with ED3 |
| Ectodermal dysplasia 3, ED3, autosomal dominant | EDAR | Ectodermal dysplasia, anodontia | As above | R358X | |
| Ectodermal dysplasia 1, ED1, X-linked | EDA | Ectodermal dysplasia, anodontia | ?Epithelial-mesenchymal signaling | Y61H, R96L, Q23X | Allelic with X-linked hypodontia |
| Hypodontia, X-linked | EDA | Hypodontia/anodontia without ectodermal dysplasia | ?Epithelial-mesenchymal signaling | R65G, Q358E | |

| Disorder | Mutated Gene | Malformations | Gene Function | Mutations | Comment |
|---|---|---|---|---|---|
| Incontinentia pigmenti | *IKBKG* | Variable pathology of skin, hair, teeth, including anodontia | Transcription factor | X420W, M407V, P62X | |
| Selective tooth agenesis 3, STAG3 | *PAX9* | Absent permanent molars | Transcription factor | K114X, K91E, L21P, etc | |
| Anauxetic dysplasia cartilage Hair hypoplasia | *RMRP* | Short stature, prognathism, hypodontia | Cleaves mitochondrial RNA | 14 G-A, 254 C-G | |
| Coffin-Lowry syndrome, CFS | *RPS6KA3* | Mental retardation, typical; facies, hypodontia | Activates transcription factor CREB | G75V, S227R, V82P | |
| Pyknodysostosis, PKND | *CTSK* | Skull deformity, fragile bones, persistent primary dentition | Cysteine protease | X330W, G146R, R241X | |

*Note:* The extreme variety of single gene disorders found to contain cleft lip and/or palate points to two generalizations: (1), the bilateral union of derivatives of the fronto-nasal prominence with the two maxillary processes involves many gene products acting at the right time and place; some of these gene products have many pleiotropic effects in other organ systems; (2), it remains true that the majority of cases of clefting remain "multifactorial"; however, allelism for clefting of varying degrees of severity listed in the above table identifies many candidate genes that could be screened for mutations that may predispose via less severe disturbance of gene production that need other factors in order to reach the level of actual phenotypic expression.

## SELECTED BIBLIOGRAPHY

Arnold WH, Meiselbach V. 3-D reconstruction of a human fetus with combined holoprosencephaly and cyclopia. Head Face Med 2009; 5:14, doi: 10.1186/1746–160X–5–14

Epstein CJ, Erickson RP, Wynshaw-Boris AJ. Inborn errors of development: the molecular basis of clinical disorders of morphogenesis. New York. Oxford University Press, 2004.

Hammond, P. The use of 3D face shape modelling in dysmorphology. Arch Dis Child 2007; 92:1120–1126.

Hennekam RCM, Allanson J. Gorlin's Syndromes of the Head and Neck. 5th ed. New York. Oxford University Press, 2010.

Graham JM Jr. Smith's recognizable patterns of human deformation. 3rd ed. Philadelphia: Elsevier Saunders, 2007.

Greene NDE, Stanier P, Copp AJ. Genetics of human neural tube defects. Hum Mol Genetics 2009; 18:R113–R129.

Jones KL. Smith's recognizable patterns of human malformation. 6th ed. Philadelphia: Elsevier Saunders, 2006.

Kayserili H, Uz E, Niessen C, et al. ALX4 dysfunction disrupts craniofacial and epidermal development, Hum Mol Genetics 2009; 18:4357–4366

Scheller EL, Krebsbach PH. Gene therapy: design and prospects for craniofacial regeneration. J Dent Res 2009; 88:585–596.

Stevenson RE, Hall JG (eds). Human malformations and related anomalies. 2nd ed. New York: Oxford University Press, 2006.

Twigg SRF, Versnel SL, Nurnberg G, et al. Frontorhiny, a distinctive presentation of frontonasal dysplasia caused by recessive mutations in the ALX3 homeobox gene. Am J Hum Genet 2009; 84:698–705

Wang Y, Xiao R, Yang F et al. Abnormalities in cartilage and bone development in the Apert syndrome FGFR2+/5252W mouse. Development 2005; 132: 3537–3548.

# Glossary of Selected Terms

| | |
|---|---|
| **Acalvaria** | Lacking a calvaria |
| **aCGH** | Array comparative genomic hybridization, a high-resolution comparison of a control genome versus patient's genome examined for variations (gains or losses) in genetic content |
| **Acrania** | Lacking a cranium |
| **Aglossia** | Absent tongue |
| **Agnathia** | Absent mandible |
| **Allantois** | A fetal membrane. A diverticulum of the hindgut; its blood vessels form the umbilical blood vessels |
| **Allele** | One of the alternative versions of a gene at a given locus |
| **Ameloblast** | Cell type giving rise to enamel of teeth |
| **Amelogenesis** | Process of enamel production |
| **Amnion** | A fetal membrane enveloping the fetus |
| **Anencephaly** | Absence of brain |
| **Aneuploidy** | Abnormal chromosome number. Basis of genetic defects |
| **Ankyloglossia** | Tongue-tie. Anomaly of tongue development |
| **Anlage** | Embryonic primordium of an organ |
| **Anophthalmia** | Absent eyes |
| **Anomalies** | Birth defects resulting from malformations, deformations or disruptions |
| **Anotia** | Absence of external ears |
| **Aortic arches** | Arteries encircling the embryonic pharynx in the pharyngeal arches |
| **Aplasia** | Absent development of tissue or organ |
| **Apoptosis** | Programmed cell death |
| **Atrophy** | Degeneration of a tissue or organ |
| **Autosome** | A nuclear chromosome other than sex chromosomes; 22 pairs in the human karyotype |
| **Base pair (bp)** | A pair of of complementary nucleotide bases in double-stranded DNA |
| **Bell stage** | Tooth developmental stage at which the future crown is outlined as a bell |
| **Bifid tongue** | Cleft tongue. Anomaly of development |
| **Blastocyst** | Embryonic developmental stage forming a fluid-filled cyst |
| **Blastomere** | Early cell type produced by cleavage of the zygote |
| **Bud stage** | Initial stage of tooth development, budding from the dental lamina |
| **Calvaria** | Skullcap. Roof of the neurocranium |

| | |
|---|---|
| **Cap stage** | Tooth developmental stage at which the enamel organ forms a cap over the dental papilla |
| **Caudal** | Pertaining to the tail (region) |
| **cDNA** | Complementary DNA |
| **Centromere** | Primary constriction on a chromosome where chromatids are held together |
| **Cervical loop** | Looped margin of the enamel organ outlining the future tooth root |
| **Choana** | Nasal opening |
| **Chondocranium** | Cartilaginous base of the embryonic and fetal skull |
| **Chorion** | The outermost fetal membrane, contributing to the placenta |
| **Chorionic villus sampling (CVS)** | Prenatal diagnosis at 8–10 weeks postconception |
| **Chromatids** | Two strands of chromatin, connected at the centromere, constituting a chromosome |
| **Chromosome** | The "colored body" of the nucleus of a cell composed of DNA (deoxyribonucleic acid) |
| **Chromosome spread** | Chromosomes of a dividing cell in metaphase seen under the microscope |
| **Clefts** | Defects of facial and oral development |
| **Clinical heterogeneity** | Different clinical phenotypes from mutations in the same gene |
| **Conceptus** | Products of conception. The embryo and its membranes |
| **Copula** | Component of embryonic tongue |
| **Copy number variant (CNV)** | Variation in DNA sequence by presence or absence of a DNA segment |
| **Cranial** | Pertaining to the head (region) |
| **Cyclopia** | Single eye. In reality, fused eyes |
| **Cytodifferentiation** | Specialization of structure and function of embryonic cells |
| **Deletion** | Loss of a sequence of DNA from a chromosome |
| **Deoxyribonucleic acid (DNA)** | The molecule that encodes the genes and transmits genetic information |
| **Dental lamina** | Horseshoe-shaped epithelial band giving rise to the dental buds |
| **Dental papilla** | Formative organ of dentine and the primordium of the dental pulp |
| **Dentinogenesis** | Process of dentine formation |
| **Desmocranium** | Embryonic membrane covering the brain. Precursor of the skull |
| **Diarthrosis** | Movable joint |
| **Diploid** | Double set of chromosomes (2n): 46 chromosomes in humans |
| **Disomy** | Two copies of a specific chromosome from one parent only |

| | |
|---|---|
| **Disruption** | Birth defect caused by tissue destruction |
| **Dizygotic (DZ) twins** | Twins resulting from two separately fertilized ova |
| **Dominant** | A trait phenotypically expressed in heterozygotes |
| **Dorsal** | Towards the back (posterior) |
| **Dysmorphism** | Abnormal morphological development |
| **Ectoderm** | Outermost of the three primary germ layers. Forms the nervous system, epidermis and its derivatives (hair, nails, enamel, skin glands) |
| **Ectomesenchyme** | Tissue of the neural crest |
| **Ectopic expression** | Gene expression in places where it is not normally expressed |
| **Embryo** | Portion of conceptus forming fetus prior to eighth week |
| **Enamel** | Outermost layer of the dental crown |
| **Endochondral** | Bone type formed in cartilage |
| **Endoderm** | Innermost of the three primary germ layers. Forms lining of gut and its derivatives (salivary glands, thyroid, thymus, parathyroid glands, pancreas, biliary system) |
| **Epigenetic** | Factor affecting gene function without changing genotype |
| **Euchromatin** | Genetically expressed exon component of chromatin. Contrast with heterochromatin |
| **Euploid** | Chromosome number that is the exact multiple (2n) in a haploid gamete (n) |
| **Exon** | A transcribed region of a gene present in mature messenger RNA |
| **Familial** | Any trait more common in relatives than in the general population |
| **Fertilization** | Fusion of spermatozoa and ovum to form a zygote |
| **Fetus** | The conceptus from 9 weeks until birth (40 weeks) |
| **Fetoscopy** | Technique of direct visualization of the fetus |
| **FISH** | Fluorescence in situ hybridization detection technique |
| **Fontanelle** | Membranous interbony interval in the calvaria |
| **Forebrain** | Rostral end of brain. Prosencephalon |
| **Foregut** | Rostral one-third of embryonic gut |
| **Frontonasal prominence** | Anlage of upper and middle thirds of face |
| **Gamete** | Ovum or sperm with haploid chromosome number |
| **Gene** | A hereditary unit; a sequence of chromosomal DNA producing a product |
| **Gene dosage** | The number of copies of a particular gene in the genome |

| | |
|---|---|
| **Gene map** | The characteristic arrangement of genes on the chromosomes |
| **Genetic** | Relating to genes, inheritance or ontogenesis |
| **Genome** | The complete DNA sequence of a gamete, individual, population or species |
| **Genomics** | The field of genetics studying the structure and function of the genome |
| **Genotype** | Inherited genetic constitution |
| **Germ layer** | Primary layers of ectoderm, mesoderm and endoderm |
| **Gestation** | Pregnancy |
| **Haploid** | Single set of chromosomes in normal gametes (1n) |
| **Haploinsufficiency** | Loss of function in an allele causing genetic disease |
| **Haversian bone** | Compact bone with concentric lamellae around tubular channels |
| **Hensen's node** | Precursor of primitive streak |
| **Heterochromatin** | Non-expressed intron component of chromatin |
| **Hindbrain** | Caudal part of brain |
| **Hindgut** | Caudal one-third of embryonic gut |
| **Histodifferentiation** | Specialization of tissues into various types |
| **Homozygote** | Individual or genotype with identical alleles at a given locus |
| **Hox; homeobox** | Genes with conserved DNA sequences controlling development |
| **Hyperplasia** | Abnormal increase in cell numbers |
| **Hypertrophy** | Excessive enlargement of organ or tissue |
| **Hypoplasia** | Underdevelopment of tissue or organ |
| **Incus** | (Anvil) Middle ear ossicle |
| **Inner cell mass** | Group of cells within the preimplantation embryo, giving rise to the embryo |
| **Induction** | Specific morphogenic occurrence influenced by an organizer |
| **Intramembranous** | Bone type formed in membrane |
| **Intrauterine (iu)** | Within the womb. Embryonic and fetal periods of life |
| **Intron** | Segment of a gene initially transcribed but removed from the RNA transcript |
| **Karyotype** | Chromosome constitution of an individual |
| **Leptomeninges** | Inner two layers of brain coverings. Pia mater and arachnoid |
| **Macroglossia** | Tongue enlargement |
| **Macrognathia** | Enlarged jaws, particularly the mandible |
| **Macrostomia** | Enlarged mouth, particularly the rima oris |
| **Malleus** | (Hammer) Outer ear ossicle |

| | |
|---|---|
| **Mandibular prominence** | Anlage of lower third of face |
| **Maxillary prominence** | Anlage of middle third of face |
| **Meckel's cartilage** | Skeleton of first pharyngeal arch. Precursor of mandible |
| **Medial nasal prominence** | Anlage of central part of face |
| **Mesencephalon** | Midbrain |
| **Mesoderm** | Middle layer of three primary germ layers. Forms dermis, connective tissues, bone, cartilage, vessels, etc. |
| **Microglossia** | Diminutive tongue |
| **Micrognathia** | Diminutive jaws, particularly the mandible |
| **Midbrain** | Central part of brain |
| **Midgut** | Central part of embryonic gut |
| **Monozygotic (MZ)** | Twins derived from a single zygote |
| **Morphogen** | Regional substance that diffuses to form a concentration gradient for development |
| **Morula** | Solid mass of blastomeres |
| **Mutation** | Transmissable alteration in genetic material |
| **Naris** | Nostril |
| **Nasal fin** | Transient embryonic membrane between maxillary and medial nasal prominences |
| **Neural crest** | Secondary germ cell line arising bilaterally at closure line of embryonic neural groove. Forms ectomesenchyme, the precursor of several tissue types |
| **Neural plate** | Specialized ectoderm forming neural tissue |
| **Neural tube** | Anlage of central nervous system |
| **Neurocranium** | Brain case composed of embryonic desmocranium and chondrocranium |
| **Neurulation** | Formation of neural plate and neural tube |
| **Notochord** | Midline axis of the embryo |
| **Odontoblast** | Dentine-forming cell |
| **Olfactory** | Pertaining to smell (the nose) |
| **Oocyte** | Female gamete prior to ovulation |
| **Organizer** | Agent or part causing differentiation. Induction |
| **Oronasal membrane** | Transient embryonic membrane between stomodeum and nasal cavities |
| **Oropharyngeal membrane** | Transient embryonic membrane between stomodeum and pharynx |
| **Osteoblast** | Bone-forming cell |
| **Osteoclast** | Bone-destroying cell |
| **Osteocytes** | Bone cells located in lacunae |
| **Otic** | Pertaining to the internal ear |

| | |
|---|---|
| **Ovum** | Female gamete after ovulation |
| **p arm** | In cytogenetics, the short arm of a chromosome |
| **Palate** | Structure separating mouth from nose |
| **Parenchyma** | Functional tissue of an organ |
| **Parotid** | (Alongside the ear). Largest salivary gland |
| **PCR** | Polymerase chain reaction; technique of DNA or RNA amplification |
| **Periodontal** | Around the tooth. Dental attachment apparatus |
| **Pharyngeal arches** | A series of paired arches in the embryonic neck region demarcated by pharyngeal grooves |
| **Pharyngeal grooves** | Indentations of the embryonic neck region between the pharyngeal arches. The first groove forms the external acoustic meatus |
| **Placode** | Plaque-like thickening of ectoderm |
| **Pluripotent** | Embryonic cell giving rise to multiple cell types |
| **Primitive streak** | Initial germ disk axial organizer |
| **Primordium** | First recognizable stage of development of an organ or structure |
| **Prominence** | Protrusion or swelling |
| **Prosencephalon** | Forebrain |
| **Pulp** | Innermost dental tissue |
| **q arm** | In cytogenetics, the long arm of a chromosome |
| **Rathke's pouch** | Stomodeal diverticulum. Anlage of adenohypophysis |
| **Recessive** | A trait expressed only in homozygotes or hemizygotes |
| **Reichert's cartilage** | Skeleton of second pharyngeal arch. Anlage of hyoid, styloid and stapes bones |
| **Rest** | Persistent fragment of embryonic tissue in the adult |
| **Retzius' striae** | Incremental lines of enamel deposition |
| **Rhombencephalon** | Hindbrain |
| **Rostral (beak)** | Toward cephalic end of the body |
| **RNA** | Ribonucleic acid |
| **Somite** | Segmental paired block of mesoderm. Anlage of vertebral column and segmented musculature |
| **Somitomere** | Rostral paired mass of partially segmented mesoderm. Anlage of cranial muscles |
| **Spermatozoon** | Male gamete |
| **Stapes** | (Stirrup) Inner ear ossicle |
| **Stomodeum** | Midfacial ectodermal invagination. Anlage of mouth and nose |

| **Stroma** | Supporting framework of an organ |
| **Suture** | Immovable fibrous joint in the skull |
| **Synarthrosis** | Immovable joint between bones |
| **Synchondrosis** | Cartilaginous joint |
| **Syndesmosis** | Fibrous joint between bones. A suture |
| **Syndrome** | A consistent complex of symptoms and signs |
| **Synostosis** | Bony joint |
| **Teratogen** | Agent or factor producing defective development |
| **Teratology** | Abnormal development |
| **Trimester** | The three 3-month periods of gestation |
| **Triploid** | Three copies of each chromosome in a cell |
| **Trisomy** | Extra (third) chromosome in a diploid cell $(2n + 1)$ |
| **Tuberculum** | Eminence or swelling |
| **Uterus** | The womb |
| **Ventral** | Toward the front (anterior) |
| **Vestibule** | Entrance to the oral cavity |
| **Viscerocranium** | Facial skeleton derived from the pharyngeal arches |
| **Zygote** | (Zygos = yoke) The fertilized ovum |

# Index

Page numbers followed by f and t indicate figures and tables

# The Global Loanable Funds Market

The loanable funds market is global, not national. Lenders on the supply side of the market want to earn the highest possible real interest rate and they will seek it by looking everywhere in the world. Borrowers on the demand side of the market want to pay the lowest possible real interest rate and they will seek it by looking everywhere in the world. Financial capital is mobile: it moves to the best advantage of lenders and borrowers.

## International Capital Mobility

If a US supplier of loanable funds can earn a higher interest rate in Tokyo than in New York, funds supplied in Japan will increase and funds supplied in the US will decrease – funds will flow from the US to Japan.

If a US demander of loanable funds can pay a lower interest rate in Paris than in New York, the demand for funds in France will increase and the demand for funds in the US will decrease – funds will flow from France to the US.

Because lenders are free to seek the highest real interest rate and borrowers are free to seek the lowest real interest rate, the loanable funds market is a single, integrated, global market. Funds flow into the country in which the interest rate is highest and out of the country in which the interest rate is lowest.

When funds leave the country with the lowest interest rate, a shortage of funds raises the real interest rate. When funds move into the country with the highest interest rate, a surplus of funds lowers the real interest rate. The free international mobility of financial capital pulls real interest rates around the world toward equality.

Only when the real interest rates in New York, Tokyo and Paris are equal does the incentive to move funds from one country to another stop.

Equality of real interest rates does not mean that if you calculate the average real interest rate in New York, Tokyo and Paris, you'll get the same number. To compare real interest rates, we must compare financial assets of equal risk.

Lending is risky. A loan might not be repaid. Or the price of a stock or bond might fall. Interest rates include a risk premium – the riskier the loan, other things remaining the same, the higher is the interest rate. The interest rate on a risky loan minus that on a safe loan is called the *risk premium* and the gaps between interest rates are called *interest rate spreads*.

International capital mobility brings real interest rates in all parts of the world to equality except for differences that reflect differences in risk – differences in the risk premium.

## International Borrowing and Lending

A country's loanable funds market connects with the global market through net exports. If a country's net exports are negative ($X < M$), the rest of the world supplies funds to that country and the quantity of loanable funds in that country is greater than national saving. If a country's net exports are positive ($X > M$), the country is a net supplier of funds to the rest of the world and the quantity of loanable funds in that country is less than national saving.

## Demand and Supply in the Global and National Markets

The demand for and supply of funds in the global loanable funds market determines the world equilibrium real interest rate. This interest rate makes the quantity of loanable funds demanded equal the quantity supplied in the world economy. But it does not make the quantity of funds demanded and supplied equal in each national economy. The demand for and supply of funds in a national economy determine whether the country is a lender to or a borrower from the rest of the world.

### The Global Loanable Funds Market

Figure 12.10(a) illustrates the global market. The demand for loanable funds curve, $DLF_W$, is the sum of the demands in all countries. Similarly, the supply of loanable funds curve, $SLF_W$, is the sum of the supplies in all countries. The world equilibrium real interest rate makes the quantity of funds supplied in the world as a whole equal to the quantity demanded. In this example, the equilibrium real interest rate is 5 per cent a year and the equilibrium quantity of funds is €10 trillion.

### An International Borrower

Figure 12.10(b) shows the loanable funds market in a country that borrows from the rest of the world. The country's demand for loanable funds curve, $DLF$, is part of the world demand in Figure 12.10(a). The country's supply of loanable funds curve, $SLF_D$, is part of the world supply.

**Figure 12.10** Borrowing and Lending in the Global Loanable Funds Market

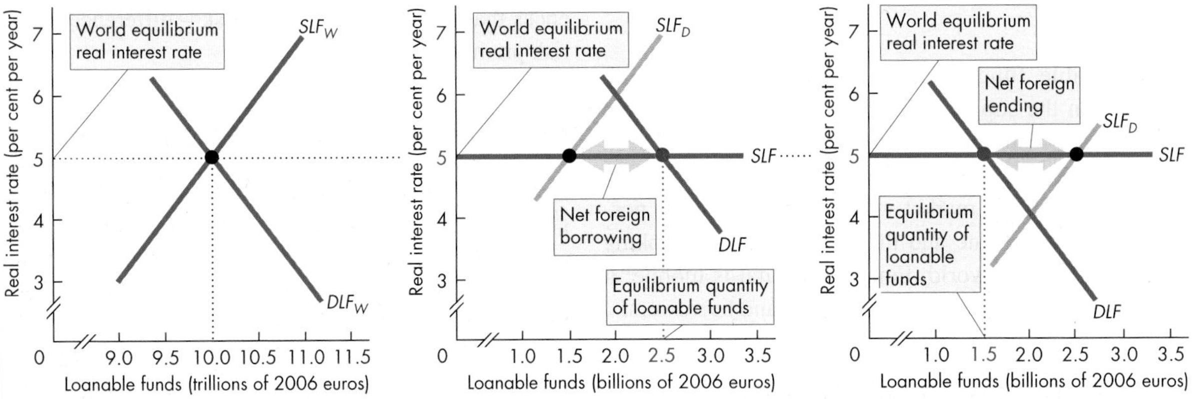

**(a) The global market**   **(b) An international borrower**   **(c) An international lender**

In the global loanable funds market in part (a), the demand for loanable funds curve, $DLF_W$, and the supply of funds curve, $SLF_W$, determine the world real interest rate. Each country can get funds at the world real interest rate and faces the (horizontal) supply curve $SLF$ in parts (b) and (c).

At the world real interest rate, borrowers in part (b) want more funds than the quantity supplied by domestic lenders ($SLF_D$). The shortage is made up by international borrowing.

At the world real interest rate, domestic lenders in part (c) want to lend more than domestic borrowers demand. The excess quantity supplied goes to foreign borrowers.

If this country were isolated from the global market, the real interest rate would be 6 per cent a year (where the $DLF$ and $SLF_D$ curves intersect). But if the country is integrated into the global economy, with an interest rate of 6 per cent a year, funds would *flood into* it. With a real interest rate of 5 per cent a year in the rest of the world, suppliers of loanable funds would seek the higher return in this country. In effect, the country faces the supply of loanable funds curve, $SLF$, which is horizontal at the world equilibrium real interest rate.

The country's demand for loanable funds and the world interest rate determine the equilibrium quantity of loanable funds – €2.5 billion in Figure 12.10(b).

## An International Lender

Figure 12.10(c) shows the situation in a country that lends to the rest of the world. As before, the country's demand for loanable funds curve, $DLF$, is part of the world demand and the country's supply of loanable funds curve, $SLF_D$, is part of the world supply in Figure 12.10(a).

If this country were isolated from the global economy, the real interest rate would be 4 per cent a year (where the $DLF$ and $SLF_D$ curves intersect). But if this country is integrated into the global economy, with an interest rate of 4 per cent a year, funds would quickly

*flow out* of it. With a real interest rate of 5 per cent a year in the rest of the world, domestic suppliers of loanable funds would seek the higher return in other countries. Again, the country faces the supply of loanable funds curve, $SLF$, which is horizontal at the world equilibrium real interest rate.

The country's demand for loanable funds and the world interest rate determine the equilibrium quantity of loanable funds – €1.5 billion in Figure 12.10(c).

## Changes in Demand and Supply

A change in the demand or supply in the global loanable funds market changes the real interest rate in the way shown in Figure 12.6 (see p. 283). The effect of a change in demand or supply in a national market depends on the size of the country. A change in demand or supply in a small country has no significant effect on global demand or supply, so it leaves the world real interest rate unchanged and changes only the country's net exports and international borrowing or lending. A change in demand or supply in a large country has a significant effect on global demand or supply, so it changes the world real interest rate as well as the country's net exports and international borrowing or lending. Every country feels some of the effect of a large country's change in demand or supply.

# Greenspan's Interest Rate Puzzle

The real interest rate paid by big corporations in the US fell from 5.5 per cent a year in 2001 to 2.5 per cent a year in 2005. Alan Greenspan, then the Chairman of the Federal Reserve, said he was puzzled that the real interest rate was falling at a time when the US government budget deficit was increasing.

Why did the real interest rate fall?

The answer lies in the global loanable funds market. Rapid economic growth in Asia and Europe brought a large increase in global saving, which in turn increased the global supply of loanable funds. The supply of loanable funds increased because Asian and European saving increased strongly.

The US government budget deficit increased the US and global demand for loanable funds. But this increase was very small compared to the increase in the global supply of loanable funds.

The result of a large increase in supply and a small increase in demand was a fall in the world equilibrium real interest rate and an increase in the equilibrium quantity of loanable funds.

Figure 1 illustrates these events. The supply of loanable funds increased from $SLF_{01}$ in 2001 to $SLF_{05}$ in 2005. (In the figure, we ignore the change in the global demand for loanable funds because it was small relative to the increase in supply.)

With the increase in supply, the real interest rate fell from 5.5 per cent to 2.5 per cent a year and the quantity of loanable funds increased.

In the US, borrowing from the rest of the world increased to finance the increased government budget deficit.

The interest rate puzzle illustrates the important fact that the loanable funds market is a global market, not a national market.

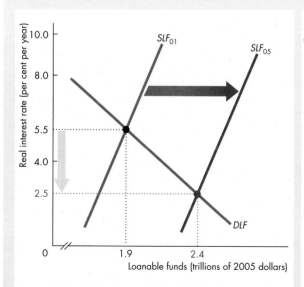

**Figure 1   The Global Loanable Funds Market**

## Review Quiz

1   Why do loanable funds flow among countries?
2   What determines the demand for and supply of loanable funds in an individual economy?
3   What happens if a country has a shortage of loanable funds at the world real interest rate?
4   What happens if a country has a surplus of loanable funds at the world real interest rate?
5   How is a government budget deficit financed in an open economy?

You can work these questions in Study Plan 12.4 and get instant feedback.

To complete your study of financial markets, take a look at *Reading Between the Lines* on pp. 290–291 and see how you can use the model of the loanable funds market to understand the events in the EU financial market crisis of 2010.

# Reading Between the Lines

# Budget Deficits in Europe

The Financial Times, 25 October 2010

## Eurozone Nations are Prepared to Slash Spending

#### Daniel Pimlott

The UK is far from alone within Europe in moving rapidly to curtail government borrowing. Greece, Ireland, Spain and Portugal are already committed to swinging the axe; all are still struggling to escape recession.

The coalition's deficit policies are almost as radical as those pursued by some of Britain's struggling neighbours in the EU, in spite of much more favourable borrowing conditions for the UK.

The Greek deficit was more than 15 per cent of GDP in 2009, in Spain it was 11.2 per cent and 9.4 per cent in Portugal. This year Ireland's is set to hit a staggering 32 per cent if the costs of its bank bail-out are factored in.

By comparison, Britain's deficit was 11 per cent of GDP in the last financial year.

If all goes to plan, Greece and Ireland should bring their deficits below the 3 per cent limit set in the Maastricht Treaty by 2014, Spain by 2013 and Portugal by 2012. Britain appears a relative laggard, dropping below the 3 per cent threshold only in 2014–15. . . .

Greece is cutting public sector salaries and pensions by 15 to 20 per cent, Portugal has warned of pay cuts of up to 10 per cent and Ireland and Spain have also pared back pay and reduced pension costs. Ireland and Portugal have both cut child benefits and other programmes.

In Britain, public sector pay freezes will last for two years, and there will be an average rise in pension contributions of about 3 percentage points; the benefits bill will be cut by about 10 per cent. . . .

## The Essence of the Story

◆ Many governments are cutting spending to reduce their budget deficits.

◆ The UK is facing severe cuts in government spending although the government faces more favourable borrowing conditions than some other EU countries.

◆ Greece, Ireland, Spain and Portugal are projected to bring their budgets down to 3 per cent of GDP in the period 2012–2014.

◆ The UK is not expected to bring the budget deficit down to below 3 per cent of GDP until 2014–2015.

# Economic Analysis

- A budget deficit increases the demand for loanable funds and, other things being equal, raises the real rate of interest, which raises the cost of government borrowing.

- Governments in some countries face a cost of borrowing that makes their budget unsustainable.

- A high cost of borrowing means that a government uses its budget to pay higher interest charges, which diverts resources from public services.

- A cut in public services can put political pressure on governments to default on their debt. When this happens, default risk rises, and this brings a decrease in the supply of loanable funds, which raises the real interest rate (and cost of borrowing) even further.

- Figure 1 illustrates this effect of a budget deficit. The deficit increases the demand for loanable funds and shifts the $DLF$ curve rightward and the increase in default risk decreases the supply of loanable funds, which shifts the $SLF$ curve leftward. The real interest rate rises.

- Figure 2 shows the sources of increased default risk: the government deficits and debts as percentages of GDP for the UK, Ireland, Spain, Portugal and Greece in 2009–2010.

- Figure 3 shows the interest rate spreads on the five governments' bonds relative to German government bond rate, which is considered to have a low (zero) risk of default.

- The global loanable funds market puts a high risk premium on Greece's debt.

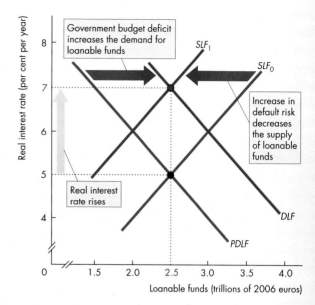

Figure 1  **The market for loanable funds**

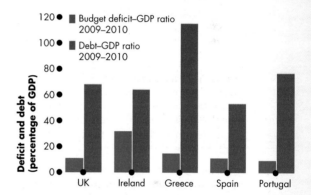

Figure 2  **Budget deficits and debts**

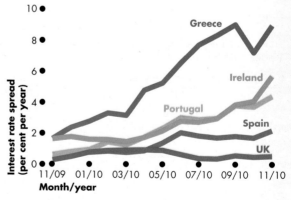

Figure 3  **Bond interest rate spreads**

# SUMMARY

## Key Points

### Financial Institutions and Financial Markets (pp. 274–278)

◆ Capital (*physical capital*) is a real productive resource; financial capital is the funds used to buy capital.

◆ Gross investment increases the quantity of capital and depreciation decreases it. Saving increases wealth.

◆ The markets for financial capital are the markets for loans, bonds and stocks.

◆ Financial institutions ensure that borrowers and lenders can always find someone with whom to trade.

Working Problems 1 to 5 will give you a better understanding of financial institutions and markets.

### The Loanable Funds Market (pp. 278–284)

◆ Investment in capital is financed by household saving, a government budget surplus and funds from the rest of the world.

◆ The quantity of loanable funds demanded depends negatively on the real interest rate and the demand for loanable funds changes when profit expectations change.

◆ The quantity of loanable funds supplied depends positively on the real interest rate and the supply of loanable funds changes when disposable income, expected future income, wealth and default risk change.

◆ Equilibrium in the loanable funds market determines the real interest rate and quantity of funds.

Working Problems 6 to 9 will give you a better understanding of the loanable funds market.

### Government in the Loanable Funds Market (pp. 285–286)

◆ A government budget surplus increases the supply of loanable funds, lowers the real interest rate and increases investment and the equilibrium quantity of loanable funds.

◆ A government budget deficit increases the demand for loanable funds, raises the real interest rate and increases the equilibrium quantity of loanable funds, but decreases investment in a crowding-out effect.

◆ The Ricardo–Barro effect is the response of rational taxpayers to a budget deficit: private saving increases to finance the budget deficit. The real interest rate remains constant and the crowding-out effect is avoided.

Working Problems 10 to 15 will give you a better understanding of government in the loanable funds market.

### The Global Loanable Funds Market (pp. 287–289)

◆ The loanable funds market is a global market.

◆ The equilibrium real interest rate is determined in the global loanable funds market and national demand and supply determine the quantity of international borrowing or lending.

Working Problems 16 to 18 will give you a better understanding of the global loanable funds market.

## Key Terms

Bond, 275
Bond market, 275
Crowding-out effect, 286
Demand for loanable funds, 280
Financial capital, 274
Financial institution, 276
Gross investment, 274
Loanable funds market, 278
Mortgage, 275
Mortgage-backed security, 276
National saving, 279
Net investment, 274
Net taxes, 278
Net worth, 277
Nominal interest rate, 279
Real interest rate, 279
Saving, 274
Stock, 276
Stock market, 276
Supply of loanable funds, 281
Wealth, 274

## STUDY PLAN PROBLEMS AND APPLICATIONS

myeconlab   You can work Problems 1 to 18 in MyEconLab Chapter 12 Study Plan and get instant feedback.

## Financial Institutions and Financial Markets (Study Plan 12.1)

Use the following information to work Problems 1 and 2.

Michael is an Internet service provider. On 31 December 2009, he bought an existing business with servers and a building worth €400,000. During his first year of operation, his business grew and he bought new servers for €500,000. The market value of some of his older servers fell by €100,000.

**1** What was Michael's gross investment, depreciation, and net investment during 2010?

**2** What is the value of Michael's capital at the end of 2010?

**3** Lori is a student who teaches golf at the weekend and in a year earns €20,000 after paying her taxes. At the beginning of 2010, Lori owned €1,000 worth of books, CDs, and golf clubs and she had €5,000 in a savings account at the bank. During 2010, the interest on her savings account was €300 and she spent a total of €15,300 on consumption goods and services. There was no change in the market values of her books, CDs and golf clubs.

   **a** How much did Lori save in 2010?

   **b** What was her wealth at the end of 2010?

**4** In a speech at the CFA Society of Nebraska in February 2007, William Poole, former Chairman of the St Louis Federal Reserve Bank said:

Over most of the post-Second World War period, the personal saving rate averaged about 6 per cent, with some higher years from the mid-1970s to mid-1980s.

   The negative trend in the saving rate started in the mid-1990s, about the same time the stock market boom started. Thus it is hard to dismiss the hypothesis that the decline in the measured saving rate in the late 1990s reflected the response of consumption to large capital gains from corporate equity stock.

   Evidence from panel data of households also supports the conclusion that the decline in the personal saving rate since 1984 is largely a consequence of capital gains on corporate equities.

   **a** Is the purchase of corporate equities part of household consumption or saving? Explain your answer.

   **b** Equities reap a capital gain in the same way that houses reap a capital gain. Does this mean that the purchase of equities is investment? If not, explain why it is not.

**5 G-20 Leaders Look to Shake off Lingering Economic Troubles**

The G-20 aims to take stock of the economic recovery. One achievement of the G-20 in Pittsburgh could be a deal to require that financial institutions hold more capital.

Source: *USA Today*, 24 September 2009

What are the financial institutions that the G-20 might require to hold more capital? What exactly is the 'capital' referred to in the news clip? How might the requirement to hold more capital make financial institutions safer?

## The Loanable Funds Markets (Study Plan 12.2)

Use the following information to work Problems 6 and 7.

First Call plc is a mobile phone company. It plans to build an assembly plant that costs £10 million if the real interest rate is 6 per cent a year. If the real interest rate is 5 per cent a year, First Call will build a larger plant that costs £12 million. And if the real interest rate is 7 per cent a year, First Call will build a smaller plant that costs £8 million.

**6** Draw a graph of First Call's demand for loanable funds curve.

**7** First Call expects its profit from the sale of mobile phones to double next year. If other things remain the same, explain how this increase in expected profit influences First Call's demand for loanable funds.

**8** Draw a graph to illustrate how an increase in the supply of loanable funds and a decrease in the demand for loanable funds can lower the real interest rate and leave the equilibrium quantity of loanable funds unchanged.

**9** Use the information in Problem 4.

   **a** US household income has grown considerably since 1984. Has US saving been on a downward trend because Americans feel wealthier?

   **b** Explain why households preferred to buy corporate equities rather than bonds.

## Government in the Loanable Funds Market (Study Plan 12.3)

Use the following table to work Problems 10 to 12.

The table shows an economy's demand for loanable funds and the supply of loanable funds schedules, when the government's budget is balanced.

| Real interest rate (per cent per year) | Loanable funds demanded | Loanable funds supplied |
|:---:|:---:|:---:|
| | (billions of 2006 euros) | |
| 4 | 850 | 550 |
| 5 | 800 | 600 |
| 6 | 750 | 650 |
| 7 | 700 | 700 |
| 8 | 650 | 750 |
| 9 | 600 | 800 |
| 10 | 550 | 850 |

**10** Suppose that the government has a budget surplus of €100 billion. What are the real interest rate, the quantity of investment, and the quantity of private saving? Is there any crowding out in this situation?

**11** Suppose that the government has a budget deficit of €100 billion. What are the real interest rate, the quantity of investment, and the quantity of private saving? Is there any crowding out in this situation?

**12** Suppose that the government has a budget deficit of €100 billion and the Ricardo–Barro effect occurs. What are the real interest rate and the quantity of investment?

Use the table in Problem 10 to work Problems 13 to 15.

Suppose that the quantity of loanable funds demanded increases by €100 billion at each real interest rate and the quantity of loanable funds supplied increases by €200 billion at each interest rate.

**13** If the government budget is balanced, what are the real interest rate, the quantity of loanable funds, investment, and private saving? Does any crowding out occur?

**14** If the government budget becomes a deficit of €100 billion, what are the real interest rate, the quantity of loanable funds, investment, and private saving? Does any crowding out occur?

**15** If the government wants to stimulate investment and increase it to €900 billion, what must it do?

## The Global Loanable Funds Market (Study Plan 12.4)

Use the following information to work Problems 16 and 17.

**Global Saving Glut and US Current Account**
Remarks by Ben Bernanke (when a governor of the Federal Reserve) on 10 March 2005:

The US economy appears to be performing well: output growth has returned to healthy levels, the labor market is firming, and inflation appears to be under control. But, one aspect of US economic performance still evokes concern: the nation's large and growing current account deficit (negative net exports). Most forecasters expect the nation's current account imbalance to decline slowly at best, implying a continued need for foreign credit and a concomitant decline in the US net foreign asset position.

**16** Why is the US, with the world's largest economy, borrowing heavily on international capital markets – rather than lending, as would seem more natural?

**17 a** What implications do the US current account deficit (negative net exports) and our reliance on foreign credit have for economic performance in the US?

**b** What policies, if any, should be used to address this situation?

**18 IMF Says It Battled Crisis Well**

The International Monetary Fund (IMF) reported that it acted effectively in combating the global recession. Since September 2008, the IMF made $163 billion available to developing countries. While the IMF urged developed countries and China to run deficits to stimulate their economies, the IMF required developing countries with large deficits to cut spending and not increase spending.

Source: *The Wall Street Journal*, 29 September 2009

**a** Explain how increased government budget deficits change the loanable funds market.

**b** Would the global recession have been less severe had the IMF made larger loans to developing countries?

# ADDITIONAL PROBLEMS AND APPLICATIONS

  You can work these problems in MyEconLab if assigned by your lecturer.

## Financial Institutions and Financial Markets

**19** On 1 January 2009, Terry's Towing Service owned 4 tow trucks valued at €300,000. During 2009, Terry's bought 2 new trucks for a total of €180,000. At the end of 2009, the market value of all of the firm's trucks was €400,000. What was Terry's gross investment? Calculate Terry's depreciation and net investment.

Use the following information to work Problems 20 and 21.

The Office for National Statistics reported that the UK capital stock was £4689.2 billion at the end of 2007, £4816.8 billion at the end of 2008, and £4908.6 billion at the end of 2009. Depreciation in 2008 was £105 billion, and gross investment during 2009 was £197 billion (all in 2006 pounds).

**20** Calculate UK net investment and gross investment during 2008.

**21** Calculate UK depreciation and net investment during 2009.

**22** Annie runs a fitness centre. On 31 December 2009, she bought an existing business with exercise equipment and a building worth €300,000. During 2010, business improved and she bought some new equipment for €50,000. At the end of 2010, her equipment and buildings were worth €325,000. Calculate Annie's gross investment, depreciation and net investment during 2010.

**23** Karrie is a golf pro, and after she paid taxes, her income from golf and interest from financial assets was €1,500,000 in 2010. At the beginning of 2010, she owned €900,000 worth of financial assets. At the end of 2010, Karrie's financial assets were worth €1,900,000.

  **a** How much did Karrie save during 2010?

  **b** How much did she spend on consumption goods and services?

## The Loanable Funds Markets

Use the following information to work Problems 24 and 25.

In 2010, the Lee family had disposable income of £80,000, wealth of £140,000, and an expected future income of £80,000 a year. At a real interest rate of 4 per cent a year, the Lee family saves £15,000 a year; at a real interest rate of 6 per cent a year, they save £20,000 a year; and at a real interest rate of 8 per cent, they save £25,000 a year.

**24** Draw a graph of the Lee family's supply of loanable funds curve.

**25** In 2011, suppose that the stock market crashes and the default risk increases. Explain how this increase in default risk influences the Lee family's supply of loanable funds curve.

**26** Draw a graph to illustrate the effect of an increase in the demand for loanable funds and an even larger increase in the supply of loanable funds on the real interest rate and the equilibrium quantity of loanable funds.

**27** **Greenspan's Conundrum Spells Confusion for Us All**

In January 2005, the interest rate on bonds was 4 per cent a year and it was expected to rise to 5 per cent a year by the end of 2005. As the rate rose to 4.3 per cent a year during February, most commentators focused, not on why the interest rate rose, but on why it was so low before. Explanations of this 'conundrum' included that unusual buying and expectations for an economic slowdown were keeping the interest rate low.

*Source: Financial Times, 26 February 2005*

  **a** Explain how 'unusual buying' might lead to a low real interest rate.

  **b** Explain how investors' 'expectations for an economic slowdown' might lead to a lower real interest rate.

## Government in the Loanable Funds Market

Use the following news clip to work Problems 28 and 29.

**India's Economy Hits the Wall**

At the start of 2008, India had an annual growth of 9 per cent, huge consumer demand, and increasing foreign investment. But by July 2008, India had 11.4 per cent a year inflation, large government deficits, and rising interest rates. Economic growth is expected to fall to 7 per cent a year by the end of 2008. A Goldman Sachs report suggests that India needs to lower the government's deficit, raise educational achievement, control inflation and liberalize its financial markets.

*Source: Business Week, 1 July 2008*

**28** If the Indian government reduces its deficit and returns to a balanced budget, how will the demand or supply of loanable funds in India change?

29   With economic growth forecasted to slow, future incomes are expected to fall. If other things remain the same, how will the demand or supply of loanable funds in India change?

30   **Federal Deficit Surges to $1.38 trillion in August**

US House Republican Leader John Boehner of Ohio asks: when will the White House tackle these jaw-dropping deficits that pile more and more debt on future generations while it massively increases federal spending?

Source: *USA Today*, 11 September 2009

Explain the effect of the federal deficit and the mounting debt on US economic growth.

## The Global Loanable Funds Market

31   **The Global Savings Glut and Its Consequences**

Several developing countries are running large current account surpluses (representing an excess of savings over investment) and rapid growth has led to high saving rates as people save a large fraction of additional income. In India, the saving rate has risen from 23 per cent a decade ago to 33 per cent today. China's saving rate is 55 per cent. The glut of saving in Asia is being put into US bonds. When a poor country buys US bonds, it is in effect lending to the US.

Source: The Cato Institute, 8 June 2007

a   Graphically illustrate and explain the impact of the 'glut of savings' on the real interest rate and the quantity of loanable funds.

b   How do the high saving rates in Asia influence investment in the US?

Use the following information to work Problems 32 to 35.

Most economists agree that the problems we are witnessing today developed over a long period of time. For more than a decade, a massive amount of money flowed into the US from

investors abroad because the US is an attractive and secure place to do business. This large influx of money to US financial institutions – along with low interest rates – made it easier for Americans to get credit. These developments allowed more families to borrow money for cars and homes and college tuition – some for the first time. They allowed more entrepreneurs to get loans to start new businesses and create jobs.

President George W. Bush, *Address to the Nation*,
24 September 2008

32   Explain why, for more than a decade, a massive amount of money flowed into the US. Compare and contrast your explanation with that of the President.

33   Provide a graphical analysis of the reasons why the interest rate was low.

34   Funds have been flowing into the US since the early 1980s. Why might they have created problems in 2008 but not earlier?

35   Could the US stop funds from flowing in from other countries? How?

## Economics in the News

36   After you have studied *Reading Between the Lines* on pp. 290–291 answer the following questions.

a   Why are governments in the Eurozone and the UK taking actions aimed at cutting their budget deficits?

b   In what ways might it be argued that the UK has a less acute budget problem than Ireland, Greece, Spain and Portugal?

c   Why are borrowing costs for Greece, Ireland, Spain and Portugal so high compared to those for the UK and Germany?

d   Draw a graph of the loanable funds market for Greece to illustrate your answer to part (c).

## CHAPTER
# 13

# Money and Banking

**After studying this chapter you will be able to:**

◆ Define money and describe its functions

◆ Explain what banks are and do

◆ Describe the functions of a central bank

◆ Explain how the banking system creates money

◆ Explain how the demand for and supply of money determine the nominal interest rate

◆ Explain how the quantity of money influences the price level and the inflation rate

When you want to buy something, you use coins, notes, write a cheque, or present a debit or credit card. Are all these things money? When you deposit some coins or notes in the bank, is it still money? What happens when the bank lends your money to someone else? How can you still get it back if it's been lent out? Why does the amount of money in the economy matter? How does it affect the interest rate? You can find the answers in this chapter. And in *Reading Between the Lines* at the end of the chapter, you can see how the quantity of money changed in the Eurozone in 2010.

## ◆ What Is Money?

What do cowrie shells, wampum, whales' teeth, tobacco, cattle and pennies have in common? The answer is that all of them are (or have been) forms of money. **Money** is any commodity or token that is generally acceptable as a means of payment. A **means of payment** is a method of settling a debt. When a payment has been made there is no remaining obligation between the parties to a transaction. So what cowrie shells, wampum, whales' teeth, cattle and pennies have in common is that they have served (or still do serve) as the means of payment. But money has three other functions:

◆ A medium of exchange

◆ A unit of account

◆ A store of value

## Medium of Exchange

A *medium of exchange* is an object that is generally accepted in exchange for goods and services. Money acts as such a medium. Without money, it would be necessary to exchange goods and services directly for other goods and services – an exchange called *barter*. Barter requires a double coincidence of wants, a situation that rarely occurs. For example, if you want a pizza, you might offer a CD in exchange for it. But you must find someone who is selling pizza and who wants your CD.

A medium of exchange overcomes the need for a double coincidence of wants. And money acts as a medium of exchange because people with something to sell will always accept money in exchange for it. But money isn't the only medium of exchange. You can buy with a credit card. But a credit card isn't money. It doesn't make a final payment and the debt it creates must eventually be settled by using money.

## Unit of Account

A *unit of account* is an agreed measure for stating the prices of goods and services. To get the most out of your budget you have to work out, among other things, whether seeing one more film is worth the price you have to pay, not in pounds and pence, but in terms of the number of ice creams, beers or cups of tea that you have to give up. It's easy to do such calculations when all these goods have prices in terms of pounds and pence (see Table 13.1). If the price of a cinema ticket is £4 and

a pint of beer in the Students' Union costs £1, you know straight away that seeing one more film costs you 4 pints of beer. If the price of a cup of tea is 50 pence, one more cinema ticket costs 8 cups of tea. You need only one calculation to work out the opportunity cost of any pair of goods and services.

But imagine how troublesome it would be if your local cinema posted its price as 4 pints of beer; and if the Students' Union announced that the price of a pint of beer was 2 ice creams; and if the corner shop posted the price of an ice cream as 1 cup of tea; and if the café priced a cup of tea as 5 rolls of mints!

Now how much running around and calculating do you have to do to work out how much that film is going to cost you in terms of the beer, ice cream, tea or mints that you must give up to see it? You get the answer for beer from the sign posted at the cinema, but for all the other goods you're going to have to visit many different shops to establish the prices you need to work out the opportunity costs you face.

Cover up the column labelled 'price in money units' in Table 13.1 and see how hard it is to work out the number of local telephone calls it costs to see one film.

It is much simpler for everyone to express their prices in terms of pounds and pence.

---

### Table 13.1

### The Unit of Account Function of Money Simplifies Price Comparisons

| Good | Price in money units | Price in units of another good |
|---|---|---|
| Cinema ticket | £4.00 each | 4 pints of beer |
| Beer | £1.00 per pint | 2 ice creams |
| Ice cream | £0.50 per cone | 1 cup of tea |
| Tea | £0.50 per cup | 5 rolls of mints |
| Mints | £0.10 per roll | 1 local phone call |

*Money as a unit of account.* The price of a cinema ticket is £4 and the price of a cup of tea is 50 pence, so a cinema ticket costs 8 cups of tea (£4.00/£0.50 = 8).

*No unit of account.* You go to a cinema and learn that the price of a ticket is 4 pints of beer. You go to a café and learn that a cup of tea costs 5 rolls of mints. But how many rolls of mints does it cost you to see a film? To answer that question, you go to the Students' Union bar and find that a pint of beer costs 2 ice creams. Now you head for the ice cream shop, where an ice cream costs 1 cup of tea. Now you get out your pocket calculator: 1 cinema ticket costs 4 pints of beer, or 8 ice creams, or 8 cups of tea, or 40 rolls of mints!

Sometimes we use a unit of account that is not money. An example is the European Currency Unit that preceded the euro. Also, the euro existed as a unit of account before it became money – a means of payment – on 1 January 2002.

## Store of Value

Money is a *store of value* in the sense that it can be held and exchanged later for goods and services. If money were not a store of value, it could not serve as a means of payment.

Money is not alone in acting as a store of value. A physical object such as a house, a car, a work of art or a computer can act as a store of value. The most reliable and useful stores of value are items that have a stable value. The more stable the value of a commodity or token, the better it can act as a store of value and the more useful it is as money. No store of value has a completely stable value. The value of a house, a car or a work of art fluctuates over time. The value of the commodities and tokens that are used as money also fluctuate over time. And when there is inflation, their values persistently fall.

Because inflation brings a falling value of money, a low inflation rate is needed to make money as useful as possible as a store of value.

## Money in the UK Today

In the UK today, money consists of:

◆ Currency
◆ Deposits at banks and building societies

### Currency

The notes and coins held by individuals and businesses are known as **currency**. These notes and coins are money because the government declares them to be so. The Royal Mint maintains the inventory of coins in circulation and the Bank of England issues notes. (In Scotland and Northern Ireland, private banks also issue notes, but they must hold £1 of Bank of England notes for every £1 they issue.)

### Deposits at Banks and Building Societies

Deposits at banks and building societies are also money. This type of money is an accounting entry in an electronic database in the banks' and building societies' computers. They are money because they can be converted instantly into currency and because they are used directly to settle debts. In fact, deposits are the main means of settling debts in modern societies. The owner of a deposit transfers ownership to another person simply by writing a cheque – an instruction to a bank – that tells the bank to change its database, debiting the account of one depositor and crediting the account of another.

### The Official UK Measure of Money

The official measure of money in the UK today is known as M4. **M4** consists of currency held by the public plus bank deposits and building society deposits. M4 does *not* include currency held by banks and building societies and it does *not* include currency or bank deposits owned by the UK government. Figure 13.1 shows the components that make up M4.

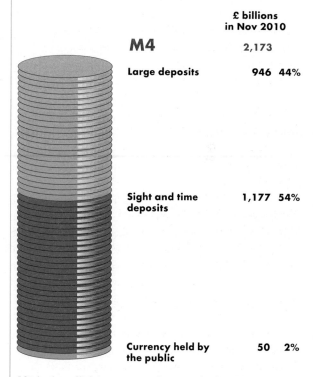

**Figure 13.1**   The Official UK Measure of Money

|  | £ billions in Nov 2010 |  |
|---|---|---|
| **M4** | 2,173 | |
| Large deposits | 946 | 44% |
| Sight and time deposits | 1,177 | 54% |
| Currency held by the public | 50 | 2% |

M4 is the official measure of money in the UK. It is the sum of currency held by the public, bank deposits and building society deposits. Currency represents only 2 per cent of the money in the UK economy.

Source of data: Bank of England.

 myeconlab Animation

## Are All the Components of M4 Really Money?

Money is the means of payment. So the test of whether something is money is whether it serves as a means of payment. Currency passes the test.

Deposits are divided into two types: sight deposits and time deposits. A *sight deposit* (sometimes called a chequeable deposit) can be transferred from one person to another by writing a cheque or using a debit card. So a sight deposit is clearly money. A *time deposit* is a deposit that has a fixed term to maturity. Although not usually a chequeable deposit, technological advances in the banking industry have made it easy to switch funds from a time deposit to a sight deposit. Because of the ease with which funds in a time deposit can be switched into a sight deposit, time deposits are included in the definition of money.

## Cheques, Debit Cards and Credit Cards Are Not Money

The funds you've got in the bank are your money. When you write a cheque, you are telling your bank to move some funds from your account to the account of the person to whom you've given the cheque. Writing a cheque doesn't create more money. The money existed before you wrote the cheque. When your cheque is paid, the money is still there but it moves from you to the person to whom you wrote the cheque.

Using a debit card is just like writing a cheque except that the transaction takes place in an instant. The funds are electronically transferred from your account to that of the person you are paying the moment your card is read.

A credit card is just an ID card, but one that lets you take a loan at the instant you buy something. When you sign a credit card sales slip, you are saying: "I agree to pay for these goods when the credit card company bills me." Once you get your statement from the credit card company, you must make the minimum payment due (or clear your balance). To make that payment you need money – currency or a bank deposit. So although you use a credit card when you buy something, the credit card is not the *means of payment* and it is not money. The currency or the bank deposit that you use is money.

We've seen that the main component of money is deposits at banks and building societies. These institutions play a crucial role in our economic life and we're now going to examine that role.

## Money in the Eurozone

The official Eurozone measure of money is called M3, but the items included in the Eurozone M3 are very similar to those in M4 in the UK. Figure 1 shows the numbers. The most interesting feature of euro money is the large amount of currency held by the public, 8 per cent of the total, compared with 2 per cent in the UK. Think about the reasons for this huge difference!

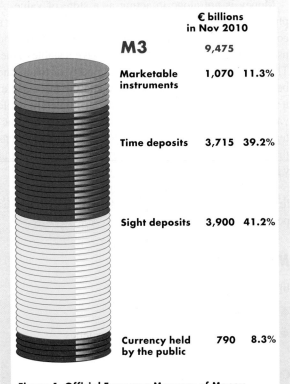

|  | € billions in Nov 2010 |  |
|---|---|---|
| **M3** | 9,475 | |
| Marketable instruments | 1,070 | 11.3% |
| Time deposits | 3,715 | 39.2% |
| Sight deposits | 3,900 | 41.2% |
| Currency held by the public | 790 | 8.3% |

**Figure 1   Official Eurozone Measure of Money**

Source of data: European Central Bank.

### Review Quiz

1   What makes something money? What functions does money perform? Why do you think Polo mints don't serve as money?
2   What are the largest components of money in the UK and in the Eurozone today?
3   Are all the components of M4 really money?
4   Why are cheques, debit cards and credit cards not money?

You can work these questions in Study Plan 13.1 and get instant feedback.

**Monetary Financial Institutions**

A **monetary financial institution** is a financial firm that takes deposits from households and firms. These deposits are components of M4. You will learn what these institutions are, what they do, the economic benefits they bring, how they are regulated and how they have innovated to create new financial products.

## Types of Monetary Financial Institutions

The deposits of two types of financial firms make up the UK's money. They are

◆ Commercial banks
◆ Building societies

### Commercial Banks

A *commercial bank* is a private firm, licensed by the Bank of England under the Banking Act 1987 to take deposits and make loans.

UK commercial banks are very large and five firms dominate the banking markets: Barclays, HSBC, Lloyds Banking Group, Royal Bank of Scotland Group and Standard Chartered. The assets of the largest commercial banks exceed £2 trillion.

These very large firms offer a wide range of banking services and have extensive international operations. The deposits of commercial banks represent the bulk of the deposits in the M4 definition of money.

### Building Societies

A *building society* is a private firm licensed under the Building Societies Act 1986 to accept deposits and make loans mostly to mortgage borrowers.

Building societies are much smaller than commercial banks and most of them serve their local communities. The largest, Nationwide, has assets of £150 billion. Size falls steeply with the assets of the next largest, Britannia, at £32 billion and the third largest, Yorkshire at £16 billion.

Unlike a bank, a building society is owned by its depositors, obtains its funds in the form of savings accounts and keeps its reserves not at the Bank of England but as a deposit in a commercial bank.

The combined deposits of the largest 50 building societies in November 2010 were £290 billion.

## What Monetary Financial Institutions Do

Monetary financial institutions provide services such as cheque clearing, account management, credit cards and Internet banking, all of which provide an income from service fees. But they earn most of their income by using the funds they receive from depositors to make loans and to buy securities that earn a higher interest rate than that paid to depositors. In this activity, they must perform a balancing act, weighing return against risk. To see this balancing act, we'll focus on the commercial banks.

A commercial bank puts the funds it receives from depositors and other funds that it borrows into four types of assets:

1  A bank's **reserves** are notes and coins in the bank's vault or in a deposit account at the Bank of England. (We'll study the Bank of England later in this chapter.) These funds are used to meet depositors' currency withdrawals and to make payments to other banks. In normal times, a bank keeps about 1 per cent of deposits as reserves.

2  *Liquid assets* are overnight loans to other banks and institutions, UK government Treasury bills and commercial bills. These assets are the banks' first line of defence if they need reserves. Liquid assets can be sold and instantly converted into reserves with virtually no risk of loss. Because they have a low risk, they earn a low interest rate.

   The interest rate on overnight loans is closely linked to the interest rate set by the Bank of England as its main policy interest rate (see p. 305).

3  *Investment securities* are UK government bonds and other bonds such as mortgage-backed securities. These assets can be sold and converted into reserves but at prices that fluctuate, so they are riskier than liquid assets and have a higher interest rate.

4  *Loans and advances* are funds committed for an agreed-upon period of time to corporations to finance investment and to households to finance the purchase of homes, cars and other durable goods. The outstanding balances on credit card accounts are also bank loans. Loans are a bank's riskiest and highest-earning assets: they can't be converted into reserves until they are due to be repaid, and some borrowers default and never repay.

Table 13.2 provides a snapshot of the sources and uses of funds of all the monetary financial institutions in the UK in November 2010.

## Economic Benefits Provided by Monetary Financial Institutions

You've seen that a monetary financial institution earns part of its profit because it pays a lower interest rate on deposits than it earns on loans. What benefits do these institutions provide that make this outcome occur? Monetary financial institutions provide four benefits:

◆ Create liquidity
◆ Pool risk
◆ Lower the cost of borrowing
◆ Lower the cost of monitoring borrowers

### Create Liquidity

Monetary financial institutions create liquidity by *borrowing short and lending long* – taking deposits and standing ready to repay them on short notice or on demand and making loan commitments that run for terms of many years.

### Pool Risk

A loan might not be repaid – a default. If you lend to one person who defaults, you lose the entire amount loaned. If you lend to 1,000 people (through a bank) and one person defaults, you lose almost nothing. Monetary financial institutions pool risk.

### Lower the Cost of Borrowing

Imagine there are no monetary financial institutions and a firm is looking for £1 million to buy a new factory. It hunts around for several dozen people from whom to borrow the funds. Monetary financial institutions lower the cost of this search. The firm gets its £1 million from a single institution that gets deposits from a large number of people but spreads the cost of this activity over many borrowers.

### Lower the Cost of Monitoring Borrowers

By monitoring borrowers, a lender can encourage good decisions that prevent defaults. But this activity is costly. Imagine how costly it would be if each household that lent money to a firm incurred the costs of monitoring that firm directly. Monetary financial institutions can perform this task at a much lower cost.

## How Monetary Financial Institutions Are Regulated

The collapse of a large bank would have damaging effects on the entire financial system and economy. Regulation seeks to lower the risk of collapse and lessen the damage if it occurs.

To lower the risk of bank failure, commercial banks are required to hold levels of reserves and owners' capital that equal or surpass ratios laid down by regulation.

The **required reserve ratio** is the minimum percentage of deposits that a bank is required to hold in reserves. This minimum is designed to ensure that a bank does not run out of cash. The *required capital ratio* is the minimum percentage of assets that must be financed by the bank's owners. This ratio is designed to ensure that a bank's assets will never be worth less than its deposits.

A new Banking Act of 2009 seeks to lessen the damage if failure occurs. It gives powers to the so-called *Tripartite Authorities* (HM Treasury, the Financial Services Authority and the Bank of England) to intervene in a distressed bank or building society to reduce the effects of failure on overall economic stability.

---

**Table 13.2**

Monetary Financial Institutions: Sources and Uses of Funds

| | Funds (billions of pounds) | Percentage of deposits |
|---|---|---|
| **Total funds** | 3,759 | 132 |
| ***Sources*** | | |
| Deposits | 2,837 | 100 |
| Borrowing | 520 | 18 |
| Own capital and other sources | 402 | 14 |
| ***Uses*** | | |
| Reserves | 158 | 6 |
| Liquid assets | 336 | 12 |
| Investment securities* | 669 | 24 |
| Loans and advances | 2,596 | 92 |

Commercial banks get most of their funds from depositors and use most of them to make loans and advances. In normal times banks hold about 1 per cent of deposits as reserves but in 2010 they held an unusually large 6 per cent as reserves.

Source of data: The Bank of England. The data are for November, 2010. *Investment securities includes other assets.

## Northern Rock and the Sub-prime Loans Crisis

Northern Rock plc is a UK bank that was taken into public ownership at the height of the financial crisis caused by the problems created by US sub-prime loans.

Formerly a building society that converted to a bank in 1997, Northern Rock continued to specialize in mortgage lending. During the 2000s the bank expanded its deposits and borrowing from £22 billion in 2000 to £109 billion in 2007. Its profit rose from £149 million in 1997 to a peak of £557 million in 2006.

Northern Rock's business model was 'originate' and 'distribute'. The bank borrowed on the interbank loans market and used the funds to make mortgage loans to its customers (originate). By 2006, some of its lending was in the form of sub-prime (high-risk) mortgages. It then created mortgage-backed securities, which it sold on the global capital market (distribute).

The interest the bank received on its mortgage loans was paid to the holders of the mortgage-backed securities and the funds raised by selling these securities were used to pay back lenders in the interbank loans market.

This part of Northern Rock's business was kept separate from its normal banking business and no required capital ratio applied to it, so the bank was able to expand its borrowing and lending without having to use any of its own funds.

Figure 1 shows how the bank's balance sheet expanded and the bank's growing dependence on borrowing (the red bars) rather than on customers' deposits (the blue bars).

When the sub-prime loans crisis hit the world economy, Northern Rock was unable to raise funds in the interbank market, and as customers queued to withdraw their deposits, the bank faced a liquidity crisis. In February 2008 the bank was taken into public ownership.

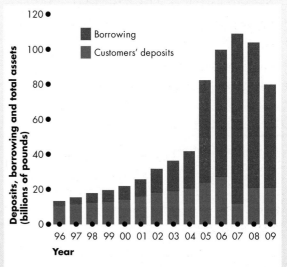

**Figure 1  Northern Rock's Spectacular Rise and Fall**

Source of data: Bureau van dijk Bankscope.

## Financial Innovation

In the pursuit of larger profit, banks and building societies are constantly seeking ways to improve their products in a process called financial innovation. The major financial innovations included the introduction of credit cards, debit cards, automatic teller machines, interest-bearing sight deposits and automatic transfers between sight and time deposits. These innovations occurred because the development of computing power lowered the cost of calculations and record keeping.

During the 2000s, when interest rates were low and banks were flush with funds, sub-prime mortgages were developed in the US. To avoid the risk of carrying these mortgages, mortgage-backed securities were developed. The original lending institution sold these securities, lowered their own exposure to risk and obtained funds to make more loans. The model of originating mortgage

loans and selling them as mortgage-backed securities to other financial institutions was copied by a number of UK banks – the most notorious being Northern Rock.

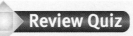
**Review Quiz**

1   What is a monetary financial institution?
2   What are the main economic functions of a monetary financial institution?
3   What are the four types of assets held by banks?
4   How do monetary financial institutions create liquidity, pool risk, and lower borrowing costs?

You can work these questions in Study Plan 13.2 and get instant feedback.

You now know what money is. Your next task is to learn about central banking and the ways in which a central bank can influence the quantity of money.

## ◈ Central Banking

A central bank is a public authority that provides banking services to governments and commercial banks, supervises and regulates financial institutions and markets and conducts monetary policy. *Monetary policy* is the attempt to control inflation, moderate the business cycle and provide the foundation for sustained economic growth by influencing the quantity of money, interest rates and the exchange rate. We study monetary policy in Chapter 16. Our aim in this chapter is to learn about the role of a central bank in the process of creating and influencing the quantity of money and the interest rate. We'll briefly describe two central banks:

◆ The European Central Bank
◆ The Bank of England

## The European Central Bank

The **European Central Bank (ECB)** is the central bank of the Eurozone – the members of the European Union that use the euro as their currency. The ECB was established on 1 June 1998.

National central banks, the largest of which are the Banque de France, Deutsche Bundesbank and Banca d'Italia, provide banking services to their governments and commercial banks and supervise and regulate their national financial institutions and markets. The Executive Board of the ECB together with the governors of the national central banks of the Eurozone constitute the Governing Council, which is the highest decision-making body in the ECB. Through this membership of the Governing Council, national central banks play a role in setting Eurozone monetary policy.

## The Bank of England

The **Bank of England** is the central bank of the UK. It was established by Parliament in 1694 in a deal between a syndicate of wealthy individuals and the government of King William and Queen Mary. The syndicate lent the government £1.2 million in return for the right to issue bank notes. And so the Bank of England notes we use today were born.

The Bank of England was first formally recognized as the central bank with the passage of the Bank of England Act of 1946, which took the Bank into public ownership.

For the next 50 years, the Bank of England was under the firm day-to-day control of the Treasury (the government) and its role was simply to implement the government's decisions. But in 1997, a major change occurred and the Bank was given independence to determine monetary policy, subject to objectives set by the government. The centrepiece of the new arrangement, which remains in place today, was the creation of the Monetary Policy Committee.

### Monetary Policy Committee

The Bank of England's **Monetary Policy Committee (MPC)** formulates the UK's monetary policy. Its members are the Governor and two Deputy Governors of the Bank, two members appointed by the Governor of the Bank after consultation with the Chancellor of the Exchequer and four members appointed by the Chancellor of the Exchequer. The persons appointed by the Chancellor must have 'knowledge or experience which is likely to be relevant to the Committee's functions' – which in practice means that they are academic economists.

To appreciate the monetary policy tools available to a central bank, we must first learn about its financial structure, summarized in its balance sheet. We'll focus here on the Bank of England but the principles apply to all central banks.

## The Bank of England's Balance Sheet

The Bank of England influences the economy through the size and composition of it balance sheet – the assets that it owns and the liabilities that it owes.

### The Bank's Assets

The Bank of England has two main assets:

1 UK government securities
2 Loans to monetary financial institutions

The Bank holds UK government securities – Treasury bills and longer-term government bonds – that it buys in the bond market. When the Bank buys or sells bonds, it participates in the *loanable funds market* (see pp. 278–283).

The Bank makes loans to monetary financial institutions. These loans are made using *repurchase agreements*. Under a repurchase agreement – called a **repo** – a commercial bank sells a government bond to the Bank of England and simultaneously agrees to *repurchase* it (buy it back) usually two weeks later. In normal times, this item is small but during the global financial crisis, the Bank provided loans on an unprecedented scale.

## The Bank's Liabilities

The Bank has two liabilities:

1  Notes in circulation
2  Deposits of commercial banks

Bank of England notes are the £5, £10, £20 and £50 notes that we use in our cash transactions. Some of these notes are part of *currency* – a component of the M4 definition of money (see p. 299). And some of them are in the tills and vaults of the commercial banks – part of the banks' reserves.

The Bank of England's other liability is the deposits of commercial banks, which are part of these institutions' reserves.

## The Monetary Base

The Bank of England's liabilities plus the coins issued by the Royal Mint make up the **monetary base**. Coins are part of the monetary base but do not appear in the Bank of England balance sheet because the Royal Mint, which issues coins, is a branch of the government and not a part of the Bank of England.

The Bank's assets are the sources of the monetary base. They are also called the backing for the monetary base. The Bank's liabilities are the uses of the monetary base as currency held by the public and bank reserves (notes and coins in the bank's vault or in a deposit account at the Bank of England). Table 13.3 provides a snapshot of the sources and uses of the monetary base in December 2010.

We'll next look at the Bank's tool kit.

---

### Table 13.3

### The Sources and Uses of the Monetary Base

| Sources (billions of pounds) | | Uses (billions of pounds) | |
|---|---|---|---|
| Government bonds | 14 | Notes held by the public | 53 |
| Loans to banks | 181 | Bank reserves | 142 |
| **Monetary base** | **195** | **Monetary base** | **195** |

Source of data: Bank of England. The data are for 15 December 2010.

---

# The Bank of England's Policy Tools

The Bank of England has four policy tools to influence the quantity of money and the interest rate. They are:

◆  Bank Rate
◆  Open market operations
◆  Lender of last resort
◆  Required reserve ratio

## Bank Rate

**Bank Rate** is the interest rate that the Bank of England charges on secured overnight loans to commercial banks. It is the official policy interest rate to which many other interest rates are linked. Among them are the interest rate that the Bank pays to commercial banks on their reserve deposits and the interest rates the commercial banks pay on deposits and charge on loans.

## Open Market Operations

An **open market operation** is the purchase or sale of securities by the central bank in the *loanable funds market*. The term 'open market' refers to commercial banks and the general public but not the government. The Bank of England does not transact with the government.

When the Bank buys government bonds, it pays for them with newly created bank reserves. When the Bank sells government bonds, the Bank is paid with reserves held by the commercial banks. So open market operations directly influence the reserves of banks. By changing the quantity of bank reserves, the Bank of England changes the amount of bank lending, which influences the quantity of money and the economy more broadly.

### An Open Market Purchase

To see how an open market operation changes bank reserves, suppose the Bank of England buys £100 million of government securities from HSBC. When the Bank of England makes this transaction, two things happen:

1  HSBC has £100 million less securities, and the Bank has £100 million more securities.

2  The Bank places £100 million in HSBC's deposit account at the Bank of England (bank reserves in Table 13.3) to pay for the securities.

Figure 13.2 shows the effects of these actions on the balance sheets of the Bank and HSBC. Ownership of the securities passes from HSBC to the Bank of England, so

**Figure 13.2** The Bank of England Buys Securities in the Open Market

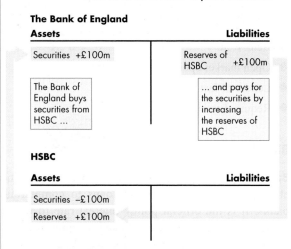

When the Bank of England buys securities in the open market, it increases bank reserves. The Bank of England's assets and liabilities increase and the selling bank's reserves increase and securities decrease.

myeconlab Animation

HSBC's assets decrease by £100 million and the Bank's assets increase by £100 million, as shown by the blue arrow running from HSBC to the Bank. The Bank pays for the securities by placing £100 million in HSBC's reserve account at the Bank, as shown by the green arrow running from the Bank to HSBC. The Bank's assets and liabilities increase by £100 million. HSBC's total assets are unchanged: it sold securities to increase its reserves.

**An Open Market Sale**

If the Bank of England sells £100 million of government securities to HSBC in the open market:

1  HSBC has £100 million more securities, and the Bank has £100 million less securities.

2  HSBC pays for the securities by using £100 million of its reserve deposit at the Bank.

You can follow the effects of these actions by reversing the arrows and the plus and minus signs in Figure 13.2. Ownership of the securities passes from the Bank to HSBC, so the Bank's assets decrease by £100 million and HSBC's assets increase by £100 million. HSBC uses £100 million of its reserves to pay for the securities. Both the Bank's assets and liabilities decrease by £100 million. HSBC's total assets are unchanged: it has used reserves to buy securities.

**ECONOMICS IN ACTION**

## The Bank of England's Balance Sheet Explodes

The Bank of England's balance sheet underwent some remarkable changes during the financial crisis of 2007–2008 and the recession that the crisis triggered.

The figure shows the effects of these changes on the size and composition of the monetary base by comparing the situation in December 2010 with that before the financial crisis began in January 2007.

In 2007, a normal year, the monetary base was £58 billion and more than half of the base was currency. But between 2007 and 2010 the Bank made huge repo loans to commercial banks that more than tripled the monetary base to £194 billion. Almost all of this increase was composed of bank reserves, which increased from £20 billion in 2007 to a staggering £142 billion in 2010.

Left unchecked, this huge volume of reserves would eventually be loaned by the banks and create an explosion in the quantity of money.

When, and how quickly, to unwind the large increase in the monetary base and bank reserves is a source of much disagreement and debate.

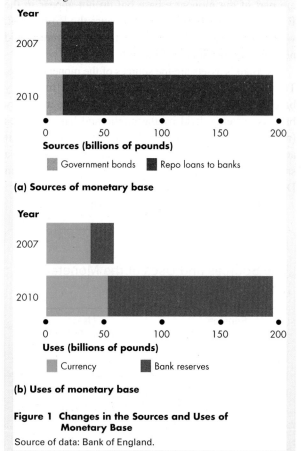

(a) Sources of monetary base

(b) Uses of monetary base

**Figure 1  Changes in the Sources and Uses of Monetary Base**

Source of data: Bank of England.

## Lender of Last Resort

The Bank of England is the **lender of last resort**, which means that if all the banks are short of reserves, they can borrow from the central bank. Normally, last-resort loans are made overnight and secured with a repurchase agreement (a *repo*).

In recent years the Bank of England has lent on repurchase agreements for longer periods and boosted the reserves of the commercial banks massively. This form of injection of reserves is called **quantitative easing**. The reserves made available by quantitative easing are indicated in Table 13.3 as 'Loans to banks'.

In September 2007 the Bank of England made a large last-resort loan facility available to the bank Northern Rock when it was unable to obtain funds from the wholesale interbank market.

## Required Reserve Ratio

The *required reserve ratio* (the minimum percentage of deposits that a bank is required to hold as reserves) can be varied to make banks hold more reserves. The Bank of England doesn't vary this percentage very often. But some central banks (the People's Bank of China is one) frequently use this tool and it is available to the Bank of England if it should choose to use it.

### Review Quiz

1  What is a central bank?
2  What are the central banks of the Eurozone and the UK and what functions do they perform?
3  What are the main items in the balance sheet of a central bank?
4  What is the monetary base and how does it relate to the items in the Bank of England's balance sheet?
5  What are a central bank's policy tools?
6  How does an open market operation change the monetary base?
7  What is quantitative easing and how does it change the monetary base?

You can work these questions in Study Plan 13.3 and get instant feedback.     myeconlab

Next, we're going to see how the banking system – the commercial banks and the Bank of England – creates money and how the quantity of money changes when the Bank of England changes the monetary base.

## ◆ How Banks Create Money

Banks* create money. But this doesn't mean that they have smoke-filled back rooms in which counterfeiters are busily working. Remember that most money is in the form of deposits, not currency. What banks create is deposits and they do so by making loans.

## Creating Deposits by Making Loans

The easiest way to see that banks create deposits is to think about what happens when Helen fills up her car with petrol at a BP service station and pays using her Visa credit card issued by Barclays. When Helen keys in her PIN, she takes a loan from Barclays and obligates herself to repay the loan at a later date. The electronic transfer of funds from Helen's Barclays Visa account to BP's bank is instantaneous. Barclays credits BP's bank account with the value of the sale (less the commission).

You can see that these transactions have created a bank deposit and a loan. Helen has increased the size of her loan (her credit card balance), and BP has increased the size of its bank deposit (minus the bank's commission). And because deposits are money, this transaction has created money.

If Helen and BP use the same bank, no further transactions take place. But the outcome is essentially the same when two banks are involved. If BP's bank is the Royal Bank of Scotland, then Barclays uses its reserves to pay the Royal Bank.

Barclays still has an increase in loans but now it has a decrease in its reserves at the Bank of England; the Royal Bank of Scotland has an increase in its reserves at the Bank of England and an increase in deposits.

The banking system as a whole has an increase in loans and deposits and no change in reserves.

You know that the interest rate that banks pay on deposits is much less than what they receive on loans. So creating deposits by making loans is a profitable business. What keeps this business in check?

The quantity of loans and deposits that the banking system can create is limited by three factors:

◆ The monetary base

◆ Desired reserves

◆ Desired currency holding

---

* In this section, we'll use the term banks to refer to commercial banks and building societies – the monetary financial institutions whose deposits are money.

## The Monetary Base

You've seen that the *monetary base* is the sum of Bank of England notes and banks' deposits at the Bank of England – the Bank of England's liabilities – plus coins issued by the Royal Mint. The size of the monetary base limits the total quantity of money that the banking system can create because banks have a desired level of reserves, households and firms have a desired level of currency holding and both of these desired holdings of the monetary base depend on the quantity of deposits.

## Desired Reserves

A bank's *desired reserves* – the reserves that it *plans* to hold – contrast with its *required reserves*, which is the minimum quantity of reserves that a bank must hold.

The quantity of desired reserves depends on the level of deposits and is determined by the **desired reserve ratio** – the ratio of reserves to deposits that the banks plan to hold. The desired reserve ratio exceeds the required reserve ratio by an amount that the banks determine to be prudent on the basis of their daily requirements and in the light of the current situation.

## Desired Currency Holding

The ratio of money held as currency to money held as bank deposits depends on how households and firms choose to make payments: whether they plan to use currency or debit cards and cheques. These plans change slowly so the desired ratio of currency to deposits also changes slowly. If bank deposits increase, desired currency holding also increases. For this reason, when banks make loans that increase deposits, some currency leaves the banks – the banking system leaks reserves. We call the leakage of reserves into currency the *currency drain* and we call the ratio of currency to deposits the **currency drain ratio**.

We've sketched the way that a loan creates a deposit and described the three factors that limit the amount of loans and deposits that can be created. We're now going to examine the money creation process more closely and discover a money multiplier.

## The Money Creation Process

The money creation process begins with an increase in the monetary base, which occurs if the Bank of England buys securities. The Bank pays for the securities it buys with newly created bank reserves.

When the Bank of England buys securities from a bank, the bank's reserves increase but its deposits don't change. So the bank has excess reserves. A bank's **excess reserves** are its actual reserves minus its desired reserves.

When a bank has excess reserves, it makes loans and creates deposits and money in a process like the one we described on the previous page when Helen buys petrol with her credit card.

When the entire banking system has excess reserves, total loans and deposits increase. One bank can make a loan and get rid of excess reserves. But the banking system as a whole can't get rid of excess reserves so easily. When the banks make loans and create deposits, the extra deposits lower excess reserves for two reasons:

1. The increase in deposits increases desired reserves.
2. A currency drain decreases total reserves.

But excess reserves don't completely disappear, so the banks lend some more and the process repeats.

As the process of making loans and increasing deposits repeats, desired reserves increase, total reserves decrease through the currency drain and eventually, enough new deposits have been created to use all the new monetary base.

Figure 13.3 summarizes one round in the process we've just described. The sequence, which repeats until excess reserves are eliminated, has the following eight steps:

1. Banks have excess reserves.
2. Banks lend excess reserves.
3. The quantity of money increases.
4. New money is used to make payments.
5. Some of the new money remains on deposit.
6. Some of the new money is a *currency drain*.
7. Desired reserves increase because deposits have increased.
8. Excess reserves decrease.

If the Bank of England sells securities, then banks have negative excess reserves – they are short of reserves. When the banks are short of reserves, loans and deposits decrease and the process we've described above works in a downward direction until desired reserves plus desired currency holdings have decreased by an amount equal to the decrease in monetary base.

A money multiplier determines the change in the quantity of money that results from a change in the monetary base.

**Figure 13.3**   How the Banking System Creates Money by Making Loans

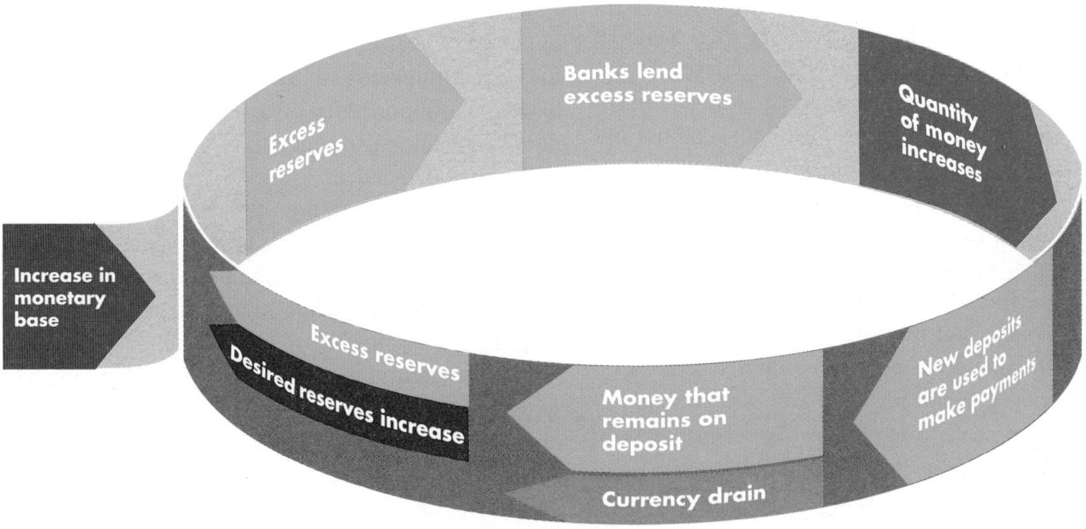

The Bank of England increases the monetary base, which increases bank reserves and creates excess reserves. Banks lend the excess reserves, new bank deposits are created and the quantity of money increases. New money is used to make payments. Some of the new money remains on deposit at banks and some leaves the banks in a currency drain. The increase in bank deposits increases banks' desired reserves. But the banks still have excess reserves, though less than before. The process repeats until excess reserves have been eliminated.

**myeconlab** Animation

## The Money Multiplier

The **money multiplier** is the ratio of the change in the quantity of money to the change in monetary base. For example, if a £1 million increase in the monetary base increases the quantity of money by £2.5 million, then the money multiplier is 2.5.

The smaller the banks' desired reserve ratio and the smaller the currency drain ratio, the larger is the money multiplier. (See the Mathematical Note on pp. 318–319 for details on the money multiplier.)

### Review Quiz

1    How do banks create money?
2    What factors limit the quantity of money that the banking system can create?
3    A bank manager tells you that she doesn't create money. She just lends the money that people deposit in the bank. Explain to her why she's wrong.

You can work these questions in Study Plan 13.4 and get instant feedback.     **myeconlab**

### ECONOMICS IN ACTION

## The Variable Money Multiplier

We can measure the money multiplier, other things remaining the same, as the ratio of the quantity of money to the monetary base.

In the UK in 2007, the monetary base (in round numbers) was £60 billion and M4 was £1,500 billion, so M4 was 25 times the monetary base. The money multiplier was 25: a £1 million change in the monetary base would bring a £25 million change in M4.

The situation in 2010 was very different from that in 2007. In 2010, the monetary base was £200 billion and M4 was £2,200 billion, so M4 was only 11 times the monetary base. The money multiplier was 11: a £1 million change in the monetary base would bring an £11 million change in M4.

What happened to make the money multiplier fall so much? The answer is a global financial crisis and a very large increase in the commercial banks' desired reserve ratio. The currency drain ratio actually increased slightly.

**The Money Market**

There is no limit to the amount of money we would like to *receive* in payment for our labour or as interest on our savings. But there is a limit to how big an inventory of money we would like to *hold* and neither spend nor use to buy assets that generate an income. The *quantity of money demanded* is the inventory of money that people plan to hold on any given day. It is the quantity of money in our wallets and in our deposit accounts at banks. The quantity of money held must equal the quantity supplied, and the forces that bring about this equality in the money market have powerful effects on the economy, as you will see in the rest of this chapter.

But first, we need to explain what determines the amount of money that people plan to hold.

## The Influences on Money Holding

The quantity of money that people choose to hold depends on four main factors. They are:

◆ The price level

◆ The *nominal* interest rate

◆ Real GDP

◆ Financial innovation

Let's look at each of them.

### The Price Level

The quantity of money measured in pounds is *nominal money*. The quantity of nominal money demanded is proportional to the price level, other things remaining the same: if the price level rises by 10 per cent, people hold 10 per cent more nominal money. If you hold £20 to buy your weekly movies and coffee, you will increase your money holding to £22 if the prices of movies and coffee – and your wage rate – increase by 10 per cent.

The quantity of money measured in constant pounds (for example, in 2006 pounds) is real money. *Real money* is equal to nominal money divided by the price level and is the quantity of money measured in terms of what it will buy.

In the above example, when the price level rises by 10 per cent and you increase your money holding by 10 per cent, your real money holding is constant. Your £22 at the new price level buys the same quantity of goods and is the same quantity of real money as your £20 at the original price level. *The quantity of real money demanded is independent of the price level.*

### The *Nominal* Interest Rate

A fundamental principle of economics is that as the opportunity cost of something increases, people try to find substitutes for it. Money is no exception. The higher the opportunity cost of holding money, other things remaining the same, the smaller is the quantity of real money demanded.

The interest rate is the opportunity cost of holding money. To see why, recall that the opportunity cost of any activity is the value of the best alternative forgone. The alternative to holding money is holding a savings bond or a Treasury bill that earns interest. By holding money instead, you forgo the interest that you otherwise would have received. This forgone interest is the opportunity cost of holding money.

Money loses value because of inflation. Shouldn't the inflation rate be part of the cost of holding money? It is. Other things remaining the same, the higher the expected inflation rate, the higher is the interest rate and so the higher is the opportunity cost of holding money.

### Real GDP

The quantity of money that households and firms plan to hold depends on the amount they spend, and the quantity of money demanded in the economy as a whole depends on aggregate expenditure – real GDP.

Again, suppose that you hold an average of £50 to finance your weekly purchases of goods. Now imagine that the prices of these goods and of all other goods remain constant, but that your income increases. As a consequence, you now spend more and you also keep a larger amount of money on hand to finance your higher volume of expenditure.

### Financial Innovation

Technological change and the arrival of new financial products – called *financial innovation* – change the quantity of money held. The major financial innovations are the widespread use of:

1   Interest-bearing sight deposits

2   Automatic transfers between sight and time deposits

3   Automatic teller machines

4   Credit cards and debit cards

These innovations have occurred because of the development of computing power that has lowered the cost of calculations and record keeping.

## The Demand for Money Curve

We summarize the effects of the influences on money holding by using the demand for money curve. The **demand for money** is the relationship between the quantity of real money demanded and the interest rate – the opportunity cost of holding money – all other influences on the amount of money that people wish to hold remaining the same.

Figure 13.4 shows a demand for money curve, *MD*. When the interest rate rises, everything else remaining the same, the opportunity cost of holding money rises and the quantity of money demanded decreases – there is a movement along the demand for money curve. Similarly, when the interest rate falls, the opportunity cost of holding money falls and the quantity of money demanded increases – there is a downward movement along the demand for money curve.

When any influence on the amount of money that people plan to hold changes, there is a change in the demand for money and the demand for money curve shifts. Let's look at these shifts.

## Shifts in the Demand for Money Curve

A change in real GDP or a financial innovation changes the demand for money and shifts the demand for money curve.

Figure 13.5 illustrates the changes in the demand for money. A decrease in real GDP decreases the demand for money and shifts the demand for money curve leftward from $MD_0$ to $MD_1$. An increase in real GDP has the opposite effect: it increases the demand for money and shifts the demand for money curve rightward from $MD_0$ to $MD_2$.

The influence of financial innovation on the demand for money curve is more complicated. Financial innovation decreases the demand for currency and might increase the demand for some types of deposits and decrease the demand for others. But generally financial innovation decreases the demand for money.

Changes in real GDP and financial innovation have brought large shifts in the UK demand for money curve.

**Figure 13.4**   The Demand for Money

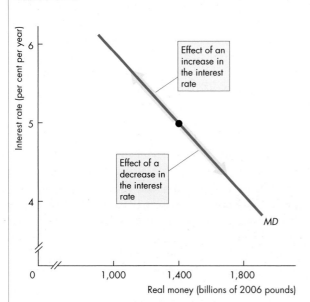

The demand for money curve, *MD*, shows the relationship between the quantity of real money that people plan to hold and the interest rate, other things remaining the same. The interest rate is the opportunity cost of holding money. A change in the interest rate leads to a movement along the demand for money curve.

myeconlab  Animation

**Figure 13.5**   Changes in the Demand for Money

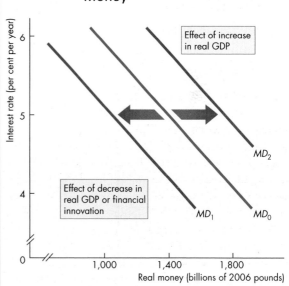

A decrease in real GDP decreases the demand for money and shifts the demand curve leftward from $MD_0$ to $MD_1$. An increase in real GDP increases the demand for money and shifts the demand curve rightward from $MD_0$ to $MD_2$. Financial innovation can either increase or decrease the demand for money depending on the specific innovation.

myeconlab  Animation

## Money Market Equilibrium

You now know what determines the demand for money, and you've seen how the banking system creates money. Let's now see how the money market reaches equilibrium.

Money market equilibrium occurs when the quantity of money demanded equals the quantity of money supplied. The adjustments that occur to bring money market equilibrium are fundamentally different in the short run and the long run.

### Short-run Equilibrium

The quantity of money supplied is determined by the actions of the banks and the Bank of England. A change in the quantity of money brings a change in the interest rate.

In Figure 13.6, the Bank uses open market operations to make the quantity of real money supplied £1,400 billion and the supply of money curve *MS*. With the demand for money curve *MD*, the equilibrium interest rate is 5 per cent a year.

### Figure 13.6 Money Market Equilibrium

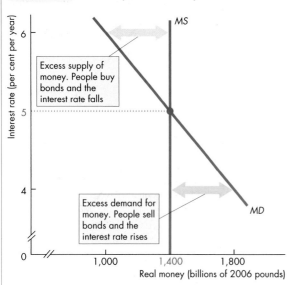

Money market equilibrium occurs when the quantity of money demanded equals the quantity supplied. In the short run, real GDP determines the demand for money curve, *MD*, and the Bank of England determines the quantity of real money supplied and the supply of money curve, *MS*. The interest rate adjusts to achieve equilibrium, here 5 per cent a year.

myeconlab Animation

If the interest rate were 4 per cent a year, people would want to hold more money than is available. They would sell bonds, bid down their price and the interest rate would rise. If the interest rate were 6 per cent a year, people would want to hold less money than is available. They would buy bonds, bid up their price and the interest rate would fall.

### The Short-run Effect of a Change in the Supply of Money

Starting from a short-run equilibrium, if the Bank of England increases the quantity of money, people find themselves holding more money than the quantity demanded. With a surplus of money holding, people enter the loanable funds market and buy bonds. The increase in demand for bonds raises the price of a bond and lowers the interest rate (refresh your memory by looking at p. 278).

If the Bank of England decreases the quantity of money, people find themselves holding less money than the quantity demanded. They enter the loanable funds market and sell bonds. The increase in the supply of bonds lowers the price of a bond and raises the interest rate.

Figure 13.7 illustrates the effects of the changes in the quantity of money that we've just described. When the supply of money curve shifts rightward from $MS_0$ to $MS_1$, the interest rate falls to 4 per cent a year; when the supply of money curve shifts leftward to $MS_2$, the interest rate rises to 6 per cent a year.

### Long-run Equilibrium

You've just seen how the nominal interest rate is determined in the money market at the level that makes the quantity of money demanded equal the quantity supplied. You learned in Chapter 12 (on p. 282) that the real interest rate is determined in the loanable funds market at the level that makes the quantity of loanable funds demanded equal the quantity of loanable funds supplied. You also learned in Chapter 12 (on p. 279) that the real interest rate equals the nominal interest rate minus the inflation rate.

When the inflation rate equals the expected (or forecast) inflation rate and when real GDP equals potential GDP, the money market, the loanable funds market, the goods market and the labour market are in long-run equilibrium – the economy is in long-run equilibrium.

If in long-run equilibrium, the quantity of money increases, eventually a new long-run equilibrium is

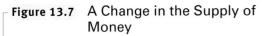
**Figure 13.7**   A Change in the Supply of Money

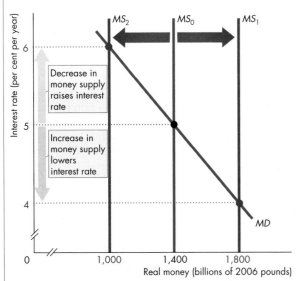

An increase in the supply of money shifts the supply of money curve from $MS_0$ to $MS_1$ and the interest rate falls. A decrease in the supply of money shifts the supply of money curve from $MS_0$ to $MS_2$ and the interest rate rises.

 Animation ───────────────────◆

reached in which nothing real has changed. Real GDP, employment, the real quantity of money and the real interest rate all return to their original levels. But something does change: the price level. The price level rises by the same percentage as the rise in the quantity of money. Why does this outcome occur in the long run?

The reason is that real GDP and employment are determined by the demand for labour, the supply of labour and the productivity of labour – by real forces that limit production; and the real interest rate is determined by the demand for and supply of (real) loanable funds – the real forces described in Chapter 12 (pp. 280–282). The only variable that is free to respond to a change in the supply of money in the long run is the price level. The price level adjusts to make the quantity of real money supplied equal to the quantity demanded.

So when the nominal quantity of money changes, in the long run the price level changes by a percentage equal to the percentage change in the quantity of nominal money. In the long run, the change in the price level is proportional to the change in the quantity of money.

## The Transition from the Short Run to the Long Run

How does the economy move from the first short-run response to an increase in the quantity of money to the long-run response?

The adjustment process is lengthy and complex. Here, we'll only provide a sketch of the process. A more thorough account must wait until you get to Chapter 14.

We start out in long-run equilibrium and the Bank of England increases the quantity of money by 10 per cent. There is an excess demand for money and the nominal interest rate falls (just like you saw in Figure 13.6). The real interest rate falls too.

With a lower real interest rate, people want to borrow and spend more. Firms want to borrow to invest and households want to borrow to invest in bigger homes or to buy more consumer goods.

The increase in the demand for goods cannot be met by an increase in supply because the economy is already at full employment. So there is a general shortage of all kinds of goods and services, which makes the price level rise. As the price level rises, the real quantity of money decreases. The decrease in the quantity of real money raises the nominal interest rate and the real interest rate. As the interest rate rises, spending plans are cut back, and eventually, the original full-employment equilibrium is restored. At the new long-run equilibrium, the price level has risen by 10 per cent and nothing real has changed.

◆ **Review Quiz**

1   What are the main influences on the quantity of real money that people and businesses plan to hold?
2   Show the effects of a change in the nominal interest rate and a change in real GDP using the demand for money curve.
3   How is money market equilibrium determined in the short run?
4   How does a change in the supply of money change the interest rate in the short run?
5   How does a change in the supply of money change the interest rate in the long run?

You can work these questions in Study Plan 13.5 and get instant feedback.

We explore the long-run link between money and the price level on the next two pages, where we study the quantity theory of money.

## The Quantity Theory of Money

In the long run, the price level adjusts to make the quantity of real money demanded equal the quantity supplied. A special theory of the price level and inflation – the quantity theory of money – explains this long-run adjustment of the price level.

The **quantity theory of money** is the proposition that in the long run, an increase in the quantity of money brings an equal percentage increase in the price level. To explain the quantity theory of money, we first need to define the velocity of circulation.

The **velocity of circulation** is the average number of times a pound of money is used annually to buy the goods and services that make up GDP. But GDP equals the price level ($P$) multiplied by real GDP ($Y$). That is:

$$GDP = PY$$

Call the quantity of money $M$. The velocity of circulation, $V$, is determined by the equation:

$$V = PY/M$$

For example, if GDP is £1,000 billion ($PY = £1,000$ billion) and the quantity of money is £250 billion, then the velocity of circulation is 4.

From the definition of the velocity of circulation, the *equation of exchange* tells us how $M$, $V$, $P$ and $Y$ are connected. This equation is:

$$MV = PY$$

Given the definition of the velocity of circulation, the equation of exchange is always true – it is true by definition. It becomes the quantity theory of money if the quantity of money does not influence the velocity of circulation or real GDP. In this case, the equation of exchange tells us that the price level in the long run is determined by the quantity of money. That is:

$$P = M(V/Y)$$

where $(V/Y)$ is independent of $M$. So a change in $M$ brings a proportional change in $P$.

We can also express the equation of exchange in growth rates,[1] in which form it states that:

$$\text{Money growth rate} + \text{Rate of velocity change} = \text{Inflation rate} + \text{Real GDP growth rate}$$

Solving this equation for the inflation rate gives:

$$\text{Inflation rate} = \text{Money growth rate} + \text{Rate of velocity change} - \text{Real GDP growth rate}$$

## Does the Quantity Theory Work?

On average, as predicted by the quantity theory of money, the inflation rate fluctuates in line with fluctuations in the money growth rate plus the velocity growth rate minus the real GDP growth rate. Figure 1 shows the relationship between money growth (M4 definition) and inflation in the UK. You can see a clear relationship between the two variables.

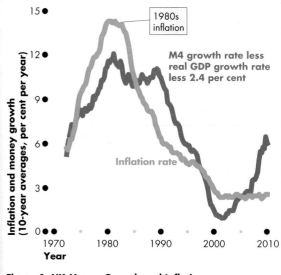

**Figure 1  UK Money Growth and Inflation**

Source of data: Bank of England.

In the long run, the rate of velocity change is not influenced by the money growth rate. More strongly, in the long run, the rate of velocity change is approximately zero. With this assumption, the inflation rate in the long run is determined as

---

[1] To obtain this equation, begin with

$$MV = PY$$

and then changes in these variables are related by the equation

$$\Delta MV + M\Delta V = \Delta PY + P\Delta Y$$

Divide this equation by the equation of exchange to obtain

$$\Delta M/M + \Delta V/V = \Delta P/P + \Delta Y/Y$$

The term $\Delta M/M$ is the money growth rate, $\Delta V/V$ is the rate of velocity change, $\Delta P/P$ is the inflation rate and $\Delta Y/Y$ is the real GDP growth rate.

Over the period since 1973, velocity has steadily decreased at an average annual rate of 2.5 per cent and we have subtracted that constant from the growth rate of M4 minus the growth rate of real GDP. These data are 10-year averages to reflect the long-run nature of the quantity theory.

International data also support the quantity theory. Figure 2 shows a scatter diagram of the inflation rate and the money growth rate in 134 countries and Figure 3 shows the inflation rate and money growth rate in countries with inflation rates below 20 per cent a year. You can see

a general tendency for money growth and inflation to be correlated, but the quantity theory (the red line) does not predict inflation precisely.

The correlation between money growth and inflation isn't perfect, and the correlation does *not* tell us that money growth *causes* inflation.

Money growth might cause inflation; inflation might cause money growth; or some third variable might cause both inflation and money growth. Other evidence does confirm, though, that *causation runs from money growth to inflation*.

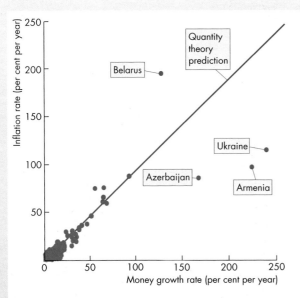

**Figure 2  134 Countries: 1990–2005**

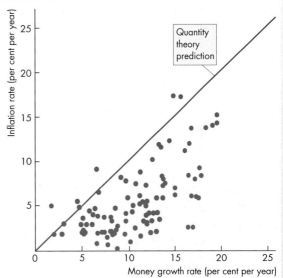

**Figure 3  Lower-inflation Countries: 1990–2005**

Sources of data: International Financial Statistics Yearbook, 2008 and International Monetary Fund, World Economic Outlook, October, 2008.

$$\text{Inflation rate} = \text{Money growth rate} - \text{Real GDP growth rate}$$

In the long run, fluctuations in the money growth rate minus the real GDP growth rate bring equal fluctuations in the inflation rate.

Also, in the long run, with the economy at full employment, real GDP equals potential GDP, so the real GDP growth rate equals the potential GDP growth rate. This growth rate might be influenced by inflation, but the influence is most likely small and the quantity theory assumes that it is zero. So the real GDP growth rate is given and doesn't change when the money growth rate changes – inflation is correlated with money growth.

## Review Quiz

1  What is the quantity theory of money?
2  How is the velocity of circulation calculated?
3  What is the equation of exchange?
4  Does the quantity theory accurately predict the effects of money growth on inflation?

You can work these questions in Study Plan 13.6 and get instant feedback.

You now know what money is, how the banks create it and how the quantity of money influences the nominal interest rate in the short run and the price level in the long run. *Reading Between the Lines* on pp. 316–317 looks at the actions taken by the ECB to increase the quantity of money and lower interest rates.

# Reading Between the Lines

# ECB Conducts Expansionary Monetary Policy

The Financial Times, 8 November 2010

## ECB Forced to Act as Crisis Fears Rise

Ralph Atkins, David Oakley and Peter Wise

The European Central Bank has been forced to intervene in government bond markets for the first time in almost a month, as financial markets fret that the escalating Eurozone crisis is moving into a new and more dangerous phase.

The ECB said it spent €711m buying government debt last week, [but that] almost certainly understated significantly the scale of its actions. . . .

Bond yields in the so called Eurozone 'peripheral' economies rose to record levels on Monday. . . .

Irish 10-year bond yields rose to 7.75 per cent, the highest since the launch of the euro, while Portuguese yields increased to 6.67 per cent, close to a level the government has indicated as being the limit of what Lisbon can sustain.

Its latest intervention pointed to mounting ECB concern, but last week's bond purchases were still small in comparison with the €64bn spent since May. . . .

The ECB has so far refused to embark on asset purchases on the scale seen at the US Federal Reserve, which last week announced it was pumping $600bn into the financial system. Jean Claude Trichet, [ECB] president, has said the ECB programme was aimed simply at ensuring the correct functioning of markets.

Axel Weber, Germany's Bundesbank president, has voiced public opposition to even the current programme, which he fears is creating inflation risks. Last month, Mr Weber called for the programme to be phased out. . . .

## The Essence of the Story

◆ The ECB conducted a €711 million open market purchase of government bonds in the first week of November 2010.

◆ The move was prompted by a sharp rise in the interest rate on Ireland's and Portugal's government bonds arising from concerns that these countries might default on their debt.

◆ The ECB injected €64 billion of monetary base during 2010 and the German central bank warned that the increase in the quantity of money brought the risk of a rise in the inflation rate.

◆ The ECB bond purchases are much smaller than those of the US Federal Reserve.

# Economic Analysis

- The ECB conducted a €711 million open market purchase of government bonds in the first week of November 2010.

- As Figure 1 shows, this purchase was tiny compared with the €65 billion accumulated purchases of bonds since May 2010.

- Bond purchases are open market operations that increase the monetary base. Bond sales decrease the monetary base.

- From May to November 2010, the Eurozone monetary base increased by €27 billion, an increase of 3.5 per cent.

- During the same seven months, the Eurozone quantity of M3 money increased by €146 billion, an increase of 1.6 per cent.

- Figure 2 shows the *changes* in the monetary base and M3 from May to November 2010. The €27 billion increase in the monetary base brought a €146 billion increase in M3 money: a money multiplier of 5.4.

- In 2010, the *level* of M3 was €9,452 billion and the *level* of the monetary base was €786 billion: a money multiplier of 12.

- The multiplier effect of a *change* in the monetary base was smaller than the ratio of the *level* of M3 to the monetary base because the banks desired reserve ratios increased.

- Figure 3 shows that the Eurozone M3 multiplier fell from 12.2 in April to less than 12 in November.

- Banks have a larger desired reserve ratio because the global financial crisis made them less willing to lend to each other.

- As long as the banks hold the additional monetary base as reserves, the inflation risk noted by the German central bank is small.

- If inflation does appear on the horizon, the ECB can sell bonds and decrease the monetary base to prevent the quantity of M3 from growing too quickly.

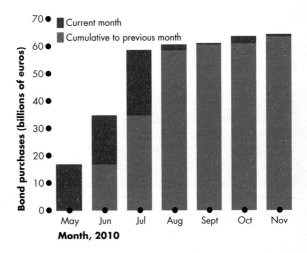

Figure 1  ECB bond purchases in 2010: May to November

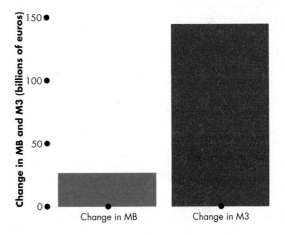

Figure 2  Changes in monetary base and M3: May to November 2010

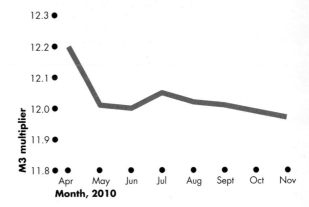

Figure 3  The M3 money multiplier in 2010

# The Money Multiplier

This note explains the basic maths of the money multiplier and shows how the value of the multiplier depends on the banks' desired reserve ratio and the currency drain ratio.

To make the process of money creation concrete, we work through an example for a banking system in which each bank has a desired reserve ratio of 10 per cent of deposits and the currency drain ratio is 50 per cent of deposits. (Although these ratios are larger than the ones in the UK economy, they make the process end more quickly and enable you to see more clearly the principles at work.)

Figure 1 keeps track of the numbers. Before the process begins, all the banks have no excess reserves. Then the monetary base increases by £100,000 and one bank has excess reserves of this amount.

The bank lends the £100,000 of excess reserves. When this loan is made, new money increases by £100,000.

Some of the new money will be held as currency and some as deposits. With a currency drain ratio of 50 per cent of deposits, one-third of the new money will be held as currency and two-thirds will be held as deposits. That is, £33,333 drains out of the banks as currency and £66,667 remains in the banks as deposits. The increase in the quantity of money of £100,000 equals the increase in deposits plus the increase in currency holdings.

The increased bank deposits of £66,667 generate an increase in desired reserves of 10 per cent of that amount, which is £6,667. Actual reserves have increased by the same amount as the increase in deposits: £66,667. So the banks now have excess reserves of £60,000.

The process we've just described repeats but begins with excess reserves of £60,000. The figure shows the next two rounds. At the end of the process, the quantity of money has increased by a multiple of the increase in the monetary base. In this case, the increase is £250,000, which is 2.5 times the increase in the monetary base.

The sequence in the figure shows the first stages of the process that finally reaches the total shown in the final row of the 'money' column.

To calculate what happens at the later stages in the process and the final increase in the quantity of money,

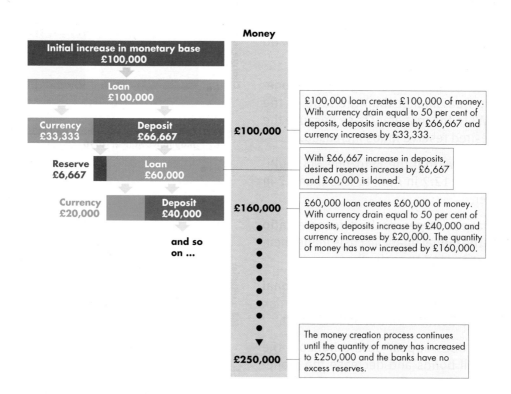

**Figure 1 The money creation process**

look closely at the numbers in the figure. The initial increase in reserves is £100,000 (call it $A$). At each stage, the loan is 60 per cent (0.6) of the previous loan and the quantity of money increases by 0.6 of the previous increase. Call that proportion $L$ ($L = 0.6$). We can write down the complete sequence for the increase in the quantity of money as:

$$A + AL + AL^2 + AL^3 + AL^4 + AL^5 + \ldots$$

Remember, $L$ is a fraction, so at each stage in this sequence, the amount of new loans and new money gets smaller. The total value of loans made and money created at the end of the process is the sum of the sequence,[1] which is:

$$A/(1 - L)$$

If we use the numbers from the example, the total increase in the quantity of money is:

£100,000 + 60,000 + 36,000 + . . .

$$= £100,000 \, (1 + 0.6 + 0.36 + \ldots)$$

$$= £100,000 \, (1 + 0.6 + 0.6^2 + \ldots)$$

$$= £100,000 \times 1/(1 - 0.6)$$

$$= £100,000 \times 1/(0.4)$$

$$= £100,000 \times 2.5$$

$$= £250,000$$

The magnitude of the money multiplier depends on the banks' desired reserve ratio and the currency drain ratio. Let's explore this relationship.

The money multiplier is the ratio of money to the monetary base. Call the money multiplier $mm$, the quantity of money $M$, and the monetary base $MB$. Then:

$$mm = M/MB$$

Next recall that money, $M$, is the sum of deposits and currency. Call deposits $D$ and currency $C$. Then:

$$M = D + C$$

Finally, recall that the monetary base, $MB$, is the sum of banks' reserves and currency. Call banks' reserves $R$. Then:

$$MB = R + C$$

Use the equations for $M$ and $MB$ in the $mm$ equation to give:

$$mm = M/MB = (D + C)/(R + C)$$

Now divide all the variables on the right-hand side of the equation by $D$ to give:

$$mm = M/MB = (1 + C/D)/(R/D + C/D)$$

In this equation, $C/D$ is the *currency drain ratio* and $R/D$ is the banks' reserve ratio. If we use the values of the example on the previous page, $C/D = 0.5$ and $R/D = 0.1$, and:

$$mm = (1 + 0.5)/(0.1 + 0.5)$$

$$= 1.5/0.6 = 2.5$$

## The UK Money Multiplier

The money multiplier in the UK can be found by using the formula above along with the values of $C/D$ and $R/D$ in the UK economy.

Using the M4 definition of money to measure deposits, $D$, the numbers for December 2010 are:

$$C = £50 \text{ billion}$$

$$R = £150 \text{ billion}$$

$$MB = £200 \text{ billion}$$

$$D = £2,150 \text{ billion}$$

$$C/D = 0.023$$

$$R/D = 0.070$$

So

$$mm = (1 + 0.023)/(0.023 + 0.070) = 11$$

---

[1] The sequence of values is called a convergent geometric series. To find the sum of a series such as this, begin by calling the sum $S$. Then write the sum as

$$S = A + AL + AL^2 + AL^3 + AL^4 + AL^5 + \ldots$$

Multiply by $L$ to get

$$LS = AL + AL^2 + AL^3 + AL^4 + AL^5 + AL^6 + \ldots$$

and then subtract the second equation from the first to get

$$S(1 - L) = A$$

or

$$S = A/(1 - L)$$

## SUMMARY

## Key Points

### What is Money? (pp. 298–300)

◆ Money is the means of payment and it functions as a medium of exchange, unit of account and store of value.

◆ M4 – currency held by the public and bank and building society deposits – is the main measure of money in the UK today.

Working Problems 1 to 4 will give you a better understanding of what money is.

### Monetary Financial Institutions (pp. 301–303)

◆ Commercial banks and building societies are monetary financial institutions: their liabilities are money.

◆ Monetary financial institutions create liquidity, minimize the cost of borrowing, minimize the cost of monitoring borrowers and pool risk.

Working Problems 5 and 6 will give you a better understanding of monetary financial institutions.

### Central Banking (pp. 304–307)

◆ A central bank is a public authority that provides banking services to banks and governments and manages the nation's financial system.

◆ The liabilities of the central bank are bank notes and bank reserves. These items plus coins are the monetary base.

Working Problems 7 to 9 will give you a better understanding of central banks.

### How Banks Create Money (pp. 307–309)

◆ Banks create money by making loans.

◆ The total quantity of money that can be created is limited by the monetary base, the banks' desired reserve ratio and the currency drain ratio.

Working Problems 10 to 14 will give you a better understanding of how banks create money.

### The Money Market (pp. 310–313)

◆ The quantity of money demanded is the amount of money that people plan to hold.

◆ The quantity of real money equals the quantity of nominal money divided by the price level.

◆ The quantity of real money demanded depends on the nominal interest rate, real GDP and financial innovation.

◆ The nominal interest rate makes the quantity of money demanded equal the quantity supplied.

◆ When the quantity of money increases, the nominal interest rate falls (the short-run effect).

◆ In the long run, when the quantity of money increases, the price level rises and the nominal interest rate returns to its initial level.

Working Problems 15 and 16 will give you a better understanding of the money market.

### The Quantity Theory of Money (pp. 314–315)

◆ The quantity theory of money is the proposition that money growth and inflation move up and down together in the long run.

Working Problem 17 will give you a better understanding of the quantity theory of money.

## Key Terms

Bank of England, 304
Bank Rate, 305
Currency, 299
Currency drain ratio, 308
Demand for money, 311
Desired reserve ratio, 308
European Central Bank (ECB), 304
Excess reserves, 308
Lender of last resort, 307
M4, 299
Means of payment, 298
Monetary base, 305
Monetary financial institution, 301
Monetary Policy Committee (MPC), 304
Money, 298
Money multiplier, 309
Open market operation, 305
Quantitative easing, 307
Quantity theory of money, 314
Repo, 304
Required reserve ratio, 302
Reserves, 301
Velocity of circulation, 314

# STUDY PLAN PROBLEMS AND APPLICATIONS

**myeconlab**  You can work Problems 1 to 19 in MyEconLab Chapter 13 Study Plan and get instant feedback.

## What is Money? (Study Plan 13.1)

**1**  In the UK today, money includes which of the following items?

   **a**  Bank of England bank notes in Barclay's cash machines

   **b**  Your bank debit card

   **c**  Coins inside a vending machine

   **d**  A £10 bank note in your wallet

   **e**  The cheque you've just written to pay for your rent

   **f**  The loan you took out last August to pay for your university fees

**2**  Suppose that in June, currency held by individuals and businesses was £400 billion; sight deposits were £4,800 billion; time deposits were £2,000 billion; M4 was £9,000 billion. What is the other item that makes up M4 and what is its value?

**3**  Suppose that in July, the public held £1,500 billion in currency, £5,000 billion in bank deposits and £7,000 billion in building societies. Banks held £10,000 billion in currency and building societies held £2,000 billion in currency. Calculate M4.

**4**  **One More Thing Cell Phones Could Do: Replace Wallets**

Soon you'll be able to pull out your cell phone and wave it over a scanner to make a payment. The convenience of whipping out your phone as a payment mechanism is driving the transition.

   Source: *USA Today*, 21 November 2007

If people can use their cell phones to make payments, will currency disappear? How will the components of M4 change?

## Monetary Financial Institutions

(Study Plan 13.2)

Use the following news clip to work Problems 5 and 6.

**Basel Committee Unveils Bank Capital Buffer Plan**

Regulators want banks to hold a 'counter-cyclical capital buffer' – a required capital ratio that fluctuates with the state of the economy. The idea is to strengthen the global banking industry by putting the brakes on lending when a bubble emerges and provide a cushion to protect the banks from falling into financial difficulty.

   Source: *Financial Times*, 17 July 2010

**5**  Explain a bank's 'balancing act' and how the required capital ratio makes bank failure less likely.

**6**  During the time of an emerging credit bubble, why might it be beneficial for the banks to be required to have a larger capital ratio?

## Central Banking (Study Plan 13.3)

**7**  Suppose that at the end of December 2009, the monetary base was €700 billion, euro bank notes were €650 billion, and banks' reserves at the ECB were €20 billion. Calculate the quantity of coins.

**8**  **Fast Growth in 'Broad' Money**

The Bank of England's quantitative easing programme may be having an increasing effect. Holdings of M4 'broad' money were up from 6.2 per cent in the three months to April. The Bank of England pumped £200bn in newly created cash into the economy between February 2009 and early 2010.

   Source: *Financial Times*, 30 June 2010

What are the Bank of England's policy tools and which policy tool did it use when it 'pumped £200bn in newly created cash into the economy'?

**9**  The Bank of England sells £20 million of securities to HSBC. Enter the transactions that take place to show the changes in the following balance sheets.

**Bank of England**

| Assets (millions) | Liabilities (millions) |
| --- | --- |
|  |  |

**HSBC**

| Assets (millions) | Liabilities (millions) |
| --- | --- |
|  |  |

## How Banks Create Money (Study Plan 13.4)

**10**   The commercial banks in Zap have

Reserves €250 million

Loans €1,000 million

Deposits €2,000 million

Total assets €2,500 million

If the banks hold no excess reserves, calculate their desired reserve ratio.

Use the following information to work Problems 11 and 12.

In the economy of Nocoin, banks have deposits of €300 billion. Their reserves are €15 billion, two-thirds of which is in deposits with the central bank. Households and businesses hold €30 billion in bank notes. There are no coins!

**11**   Calculate the monetary base and the quantity of money.

**12**   Calculate the banks' desired reserve ratio and the currency drain ratio (as percentages).

Use the following news clip to work Problems 13 and 14.

**Banks Drop on Higher Reserve Requirement**

China's central bank will raise its reserve ratio requirement by a percentage point to a record 17.5 per cent, stepping up a battle to contain lending growth. Banks' ratio of excess reserves to deposits was 2 per cent. Every half-point increase in the required reserve ratio cuts banks' profits by 1.5 per cent.

Source: *People's Daily Online*, 11 June 2008

**13**   Explain how increasing the required reserve ratio influences the banks' money creation process.

**14**   Why might a higher required reserve ratio decrease bank profits?

## The Money Market (Study Plan 13.5)

**15**   The spreadsheet provides information about the demand for and supply of money in Minland. Column A is the nominal interest rate, $r$. Columns B and C show the quantity of money demanded at two different levels of real GDP: $Y_0$ is £10 billion and $Y_1$ is £20 billion. The quantity

|   | A | B | C |
|---|---|---|---|
| 1 | $r$ | $Y_0$ | $Y_1$ |
| 2 | 7 | 1.0 | 1.5 |
| 3 | 6 | 1.5 | 2.0 |
| 4 | 5 | 2.0 | 2.5 |
| 5 | 4 | 2.5 | 3.0 |
| 6 | 3 | 3.0 | 3.5 |
| 7 | 2 | 3.5 | 4.0 |
| 8 | 1 | 4.0 | 4.5 |

of money supplied is £3 billion. Initially, real GDP is £20 billion. What happens in Minland if the interest rate:

**a**   Exceeds 4 per cent a year.

**b**   Is less than 4 per cent a year.

**16**   The figure shows the demand for money curve.

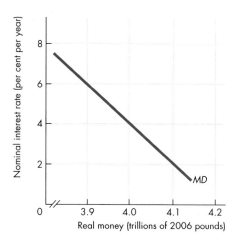

If the central bank decreases the quantity of real money supplied from £4 trillion to £3.9 trillion, explain how the price of a bond will change.

## The Quantity Theory of Money

(Study Plan 13.6)

**17**   Quantecon is a country in which the quantity theory of money operates. In year 1, the economy is at full employment and real GDP is £400 million, the price level is 200, and the velocity of circulation is 20. In year 2, the quantity of money increases by 20 per cent. Calculate the quantity of money, the price level, real GDP, and the velocity of circulation in year 2.

## Mathematical Note (Study Plan 13.MN)

**18**   In Problem 11, the banks have no excess reserves. Suppose that the Bank of Nocoin, the central bank, increases bank reserves by €0.5 billion.

**a**   What happens to the quantity of money?

**b**   Explain why the change in the quantity of money is not equal to the change in the monetary base.

**c**   Calculate the money multiplier.

**19**   In Problem 11, the banks have no excess reserves. Suppose that the Bank of Nocoin, the central bank, decreases bank reserves by €0.5 billion.

**a**   Calculate the money multiplier.

**b**   What happens to the quantity of money, deposits and currency?

**myeconlab**  You can work these problems in MyEconLab if assigned by your lecturer.

## What is Money?

**20**  Sara withdraws £1,000 from her savings account at the Lucky Building Society, keeps £50 in cash, and deposits the balance in her chequing account at HSBC. What is the immediate change in currency and in M4?

**21**  Rapid inflation in Brazil in the early 1990s caused the cruzeiro to lose its ability to function as money. Which of the following commodities would most likely have taken the place of the cruzeiro in the Brazilian economy? Explain why.

**a**  Tractor parts

**b**  Packs of cigarettes

**c**  Loaves of bread

**d**  Impressionist paintings

**22  From Paper-Clip to House, in 14 Trades**

A 26-year-old Montreal man appears to have succeeded in his quest to barter a single, red paperclip all the way up to a house. It took almost a year and 14 trades.

Source: CBC News, 7 July 2006

Is barter a means of payment? Is it just as efficient as money when trading on e-Bay? Explain.

## Monetary Financial Institutions

Use the following news clip to work Problems 23 and 24.

**The War on Moral Hazard Begins at Home**

Northern Rock was a narrow bank, with only retail customers, and Northern Rock failed; Lehman Brothers was a pure investment bank, but Lehman too failed. The issues in financial reform are to do with the behaviour of businesses, not the structure of their industry. Wrong. The point of structural reform of the banking system is not to prevent banks from failing. It is to allow them to fail without imposing large costs on taxpayers, their customers and the global economy.

Source: *Financial Times*, 26 January 2011

**23**  Explain why attempts by banks to maximize profits can sometimes lead to bank failures.

**24**  Explain the effects of higher required capital ratios, higher required reserve ratios and restrictions on the types of investments banks are permitted to make. What types of structural reforms might allow banks to fail without imposing large costs on taxpayers and bank customers?

## Central Banking

**25**  Explain the distinction between a central bank and a commercial bank.

**26**  If the Bank of England makes an open market sale of £1 million of securities to a bank, what initial changes occur in the economy?

**27**  Set out the transactions that the Bank of England undertakes to increase the quantity of money.

**28**  Describe the Bank of England's assets and liabilities. What is the monetary base and how does it relate to the Bank of England's balance sheet?

**29  Eurozone Banks Reluctant to Return ECB's Funds**

The European Central Bank (ECB) injected €73.5 billion into the region's banks to combat the Irish debt crisis by buying government bonds. The banks are reluctant to return these funds and offered the ECB just over €60 billion. They want to keep the extra liquidity.

Source: *Financial Times*, 29 December 2010

What is the rationale behind the ECB injecting funds into the region's banks and why might the banks be reluctant to repay the funds?

## How Banks Create Money

**30**  Banks in New Transylvania have a desired reserve ratio of 10 per cent and no excess reserves. The currency drain ratio is 50 per cent. Then the central bank increases the monetary base by €1,200 billion.

**a**  How much do the banks lend in the first round of the money creation process?

**b**  How much of the initial amount lent flows back to the banking system as new deposits?

**c**  How much of the initial amount lent does not return to the banks but is held as currency?

**d**  Why does a second round of lending occur?

## The Money Market

**31** Explain the change in the nominal interest rate in the short run if

  **a** Real GDP increases.

  **b** The money supply increases.

  **c** The price level rises.

**32** In Minland in Problem 15, the interest rate is 4 per cent a year. Suppose that real GDP decreases to $10 billion and the quantity of money supplied remains unchanged. Do people buy bonds or sell bonds? Explain how the interest rate changes.

## The Quantity Theory of Money

**33** The table provides some data for the US in the first decade following the Civil War.

| Item | 1869 | 1879 |
| --- | --- | --- |
| Quantity of money | $1.3 billion | $1.7 billion |
| Real GDP (1929 dollars) | $7.4 billion | Z |
| Price level (1929 = 100) | X | 54 |
| Velocity of circulation | 4.50 | 4.61 |

Source of data: Milton Friedman and Anna J. Schwartz, *A Monetary History of the United States 1867–1960*

  **a** Calculate the value of X in 1869.

  **b** Calculate the value of Z in 1879.

  **c** Are the data consistent with the quantity theory of money? Explain your answer.

## Mathematical Note

**34** In the UK, the currency drain ratio is 0.38 of deposits and the reserve ratio is 0.002. In Australia, the quantity of money is $150 billion, the currency drain ratio is 33 per cent of deposits, and the reserve ratio is 8 per cent.

  **a** Calculate the UK money multiplier.

  **b** Calculate the monetary base in Australia.

## Economics in the News

**35** After you have studied *Reading Between the Lines* on pp. 316–317 answer the following questions.

  **a** By how much did the monetary base of the Eurozone increase between May 2010 and November 2010?

  **b** How did the ECB increase the monetary base?

  **c** How did the increase in the monetary base increase M3?

  **d** Was the percentage increase in the money base the same as that predicted by the money multiplier?

  **e** Why did M3 not grow by a larger percentage than the monetary base?

  **f** If when the monetary base increased, the banks had not increased their excess reserves, what does the quantity theory predict would have happened to the inflation rate?

**36** **US Federal Reserve at Odds with ECB over Value of Policy Tool**

Many central banks use monetary aggregates as a guide to policy decision, but Bernanke [Ben Bernanke, Chairman of the US Federal Reserve] believes US reliance on monetary aggregates would be unwise because the empirical relationship between US money growth, inflation and output growth is unstable. Bernanke said that the Federal Reserve had 'philosophical' and economic differences with the European Central Bank and the Bank of England regarding the role of money and that debate between institutions is healthy. 'Unfortunately, forecast errors for money growth are often significant', reducing their effectiveness as a tool for policy, Bernanke said. 'There are differences between the US and Europe in terms of the stability of money demand', Bernanke said. Ultimately, the risk of bad policy arising from a devoted following of money growth led the Federal Reserve to downgrade the importance of money measures.

Source: *International Herald Tribune*, 10 November 2006

  **a** Explain how the debate surrounding the quantity theory of money could make monetary aggregates a less useful tool for policy makers.

  **b** What do Bernanke's statements reveal about his stance on the accuracy of the quantity theory of money?

# Aggregate Supply and Aggregate Demand

**After studying this chapter you will be able to:**

◆ Explain what determines aggregate supply

◆ Explain what determines aggregate demand

◆ Explain how real GDP and the price level are determined and what brings economic growth, inflation and the business cycle

◆ Describe the main schools of thought in macroeconomics

The pace at which production grows and prices rise is uneven. Sometimes our economy is expanding and sometimes production and jobs shrink.

This chapter explains a model – the aggregate supply–aggregate demand model or *AS–AD* model – that represents the consensus view of macroeconomists about the forces that make our economy expand, that bring inflation and that cause business cycle fluctuations.

In *Reading Between the Lines* at the end of the chapter, we use the *AS–AD* model to interpret the course of real GDP and the price level in the German economy in 2010.

## Aggregate Supply

The purpose of the aggregate supply–aggregate demand model that you study in this chapter is to explain how real GDP and the price level are determined and how they interact. The model uses similar ideas to those that you encountered in Chapter 3 when you learned how the quantity and price in a competitive market are determined. But the *aggregate* supply–*aggregate* demand model (*AS–AD* model) isn't just an application of the competitive market model. Some differences arise because the *AS–AD* model is a model of an imaginary market for the total of all the final goods and services. The quantity in this 'market' is real GDP and the price is the price level measured by the GDP deflator.

One thing that the *AS–AD* model shares with the competitive market model is that both distinguish between *supply* and the *quantity supplied*. We begin by explaining what we mean by the quantity of real GDP supplied.

## Quantity Supplied and Supply

The *quantity of real GDP supplied* is the total quantity of goods and services, valued in constant base year (2006) pounds, that firms plan to produce during a given period. This quantity depends on the quantity of labour employed, the quantity of physical and human capital and the state of technology.

At any given time, the quantity of capital and the state of technology are fixed. They depend on decisions that were made in the past. The population is also fixed. But the quantity of labour is not fixed. It depends on decisions made by households and firms about the supply of and demand for labour.

The labour market can be in any one of three states: at full employment, above full employment, or below full employment. At full employment, the quantity of real GDP supplied is *potential GDP*, which depends on the full-employment quantity of labour. Over the business cycle, employment fluctuates around full employment and the quantity of real GDP supplied fluctuates around potential GDP.

## Aggregate Supply Time Frames

*Aggregate supply* is the relationship between the quantity of real GDP supplied and the price level. This relationship is different in the long run than in the short run and to study aggregate supply, we distinguish between two time frames:

◆ Long-run aggregate supply
◆ Short-run aggregate supply

## Long-run Aggregate Supply

**Long-run aggregate supply** is the relationship between the quantity of real GDP supplied and the price level when the money wage rate changes in step with the price level to maintain full employment. The quantity of real GDP supplied at full employment equals potential GDP and this quantity is the same regardless of the price level.

The *long-run aggregate supply curve* in Figure 14.1 illustrates long-run aggregate supply as the vertical line at potential GDP labelled *LAS*. Along the long-run aggregate supply curve, as the price level changes, the money wage rate also changes so the real wage rate remains at the full-employment equilibrium level and real GDP remains at potential GDP. The long-run aggregate supply curve is always vertical and is always located at potential GDP.

The long-run aggregate supply curve is vertical because potential GDP is independent of the price level. The reason for this independence is that a movement along the *LAS* curve is accompanied by a change in two sets of prices: the prices of goods and services – the price level – and the prices of the factors of production, most notably, the money wage rate. A 10 per cent increase in the prices of goods and services is matched by a 10 per cent increase in the money wage rate. Because the price level and the money wage rate change by the same percentage, the real wage rate remains unchanged at its full-employment equilibrium level. So when the price level changes and the real wage rate remains constant, employment remains constant and real GDP remains constant at potential GDP.

### Production at a Pepsi Plant

You can see more clearly why real GDP is unchanged when all prices change by the same percentage by thinking about production decisions at a Pepsi bottling plant. How does the quantity of Pepsi supplied change if the price of Pepsi changes and the wage rate of the workers and prices of all the other resources used vary by the same percentage? The answer is that the quantity supplied doesn't change. The firm produces the quantity that maximizes profit. That quantity depends on the price of Pepsi relative to the cost of producing it. With no change in price relative to cost, production doesn't change.

# Short-run Aggregate Supply

**Short-run aggregate supply** is the relationship between the quantity of real GDP supplied and the price level when the money wage rate, the prices of other resources and potential GDP remain constant. Figure 14.1 illustrates this relationship as the short-run aggregate supply curve *SAS* and the short-run aggregate supply schedule. Each point on the *SAS* curve corresponds to a row of the short-run aggregate supply schedule. For example, point *A* on the *SAS* curve and row *A* of the schedule tell us that if the price level is 100, the quantity of real GDP supplied is £1,200 billion. In the short run, a rise in the price level brings an increase in the quantity of real GDP supplied. The short-run aggregate supply curve slopes upward.

With a given money wage rate, there is one price level at which the real wage rate is at its full-employment equilibrium level. At this price level, the quantity of real GDP supplied equals potential GDP and the *SAS* curve intersects the *LAS* curve. In this example, that price level is 110. If the price level rises above 110, the quantity of real GDP supplied increases along the *SAS* curve and exceeds potential GDP; if the price level falls below 110, the quantity of real GDP supplied decreases along the *SAS* curve and is less than potential GDP.

## Back at the Pepsi Plant

You can see why the short-run aggregate supply curve slopes upward by returning to the Pepsi bottling plant. If production increases, marginal cost rises and if production decreases, marginal cost falls (see Chapter 2, p. 33).

If the price of Pepsi rises with no change in the money wage rate and other costs, Pepsi can increase profit by increasing production. Pepsi is in business to maximize its profit, so it increases production.

Similarly, if the price of Pepsi falls while the money wage rate and other costs remain constant, Pepsi can avoid a loss by decreasing production. The lower price weakens the incentive to produce, so Pepsi decreases production.

## And for the Economy

What's true for Pepsi bottlers is true for the producers of all goods and services. When all prices rise, the *price level* rises. If the price level rises and the money wage rate and other factor prices remain constant, all firms increase production and the quantity of real GDP supplied increases. A fall in the price level has the opposite effect and decreases the quantity of real GDP supplied.

**Figure 14.1**  Long-run and Short-run Aggregate Supply

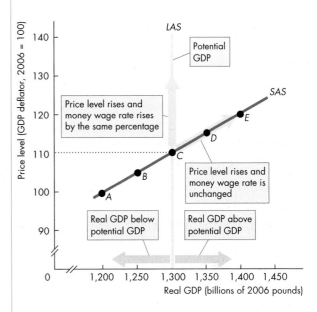

| | Price level (GDP deflator) | Real GDP (billions of 2006 pounds) |
|---|---|---|
| *A* | 100 | 1,200 |
| *B* | 105 | 1,250 |
| *C* | 110 | 1,300 |
| *D* | 115 | 1,350 |
| *E* | 120 | 1,400 |

In the long run, the quantity of real GDP supplied is potential GDP and the *LAS* curve is vertical at potential GDP. In the short run, the quantity of real GDP supplied increases if the price level rises, while all other influences on supply plans remain the same.

The short-run aggregate supply curve, *SAS*, slopes upward. The short-run aggregate supply curve is based on the aggregate supply schedule in the table. Each point *A* to *E* on the curve corresponds to the row in the table identified by the same letter.

When the price level is 110, real GDP equals potential GDP (£1,300 billion). If the price level is greater than 110, real GDP exceeds potential GDP; if the price level is below 110, real GDP is less than potential GDP.

# Changes in Aggregate Supply

A change in the price level brings a change in the quantity of real GDP supplied, which is illustrated by a movement along the short-run aggregate supply curve. It does not change aggregate supply. Aggregate supply changes when an influence on production plans other than the price level changes. These other influences are changes in potential GDP and changes in the money wage rate. Let's begin by looking at a change in potential GDP.

## Changes in Potential GDP

An increase in potential GDP increases both long-run aggregate supply and short-run aggregate supply. Figure 14.2 shows these effects.

Initially, the long-run aggregate supply curve is $LAS_0$ and the short-run aggregate supply curve is $SAS_0$. If potential GDP increases to £1,400 billion, long-run aggregate supply increases and the long-run aggregate supply curve shifts rightward to $LAS_1$. Short-run aggregate supply also increases, and the short-run aggregate supply curve shifts rightward to $SAS_1$. The two supply curves shift by the same amount only if the full-employment price level remains constant, which we will assume to be the case.

Potential GDP can increase for any of three reasons:

◆ An increase in the full-employment quantity of labour

◆ An increase in the quantity of capital

◆ An advance in technology

Let's look at these influences on potential GDP and the aggregate supply curves.

## An Increase in the Full-employment Quantity of Labour

A Pepsi bottling plant that employs 100 workers bottles more Pepsi than an otherwise identical plant that employs 10 workers. The same is true for the economy as a whole. The larger the quantity of labour employed, the greater is real GDP.

Over time, real GDP increases because the labour force increases. But (with constant capital and technology) *potential* GDP increases only if the full-employment quantity of labour increases. Fluctuations in employment over the business cycle bring fluctuations in real GDP. But these changes in real GDP are fluctuations around potential GDP and long-run aggregate supply.

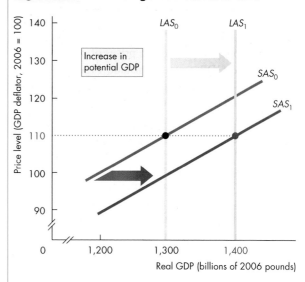

**Figure 14.2   A Change in Potential GDP**

An increase in potential GDP increases both long-run aggregate supply and short-run aggregate supply. The long-run aggregate supply curve shifts rightward from $LAS_0$ to $LAS_1$ and the short-run aggregate supply curve shifts from $SAS_0$ to $SAS_1$.

> **myeconlab** Animation

### An Increase in the Quantity of Capital

A Pepsi bottling plant that has two production lines has more capital and produces more output than an otherwise identical plant that has one production line. For the economy, the larger the quantity of capital, the more productive is the workforce and the greater is its potential GDP. Potential GDP per person in capital-rich EU economies is vastly greater than that in capital-poor China and Russia.

Capital includes *human capital*. One bottling plant is managed by an economics graduate with an MBA and has a workforce with an average of 10 years of experience. This plant produces a much larger output than an otherwise identical plant that is managed by someone with no business training or experience and that has a young workforce that is new to bottling. The first plant has a greater amount of human capital than the second. For the economy as a whole, the larger the quantity of *human capital* – the skills that people have acquired in school and through on-the-job-training – the greater is potential GDP.

### An Advance in Technology

A Pepsi bottling plant that has pre-computer age machines produces less than one that uses the latest robot technology. Technological change enables firms to produce more from any given amount of inputs. So even with fixed quantities of labour and capital, improvements in technology increase potential GDP.

Technological advances are by far the most important source of increased production over the past two centuries. Because of technological advances, one farmer in the UK today can feed 100 people and one auto worker can produce almost 14 cars and lorries in a year.

Let's now look at the effects of changes in the money wage rate and other resource prices.

### Changes in the Money Wage Rate and Other Resource Prices

When the money wage rate or the money prices of other resources (such as the price of oil) change, short-run aggregate supply changes but long-run aggregate supply does not change.

Figure 14.3 shows the effect on aggregate supply of an increase in the money wage rate. Initially, the short-run aggregate supply curve is $SAS_0$. A rise in the money wage rate *decreases* short-run aggregate supply and shifts the short-run aggregate supply curve leftward to $SAS_2$.

The money wage rate (and other resource prices) affect short-run aggregate supply because they influence firms' costs. The higher the money wage rate, the higher are firms' costs and the smaller is the quantity that firms are willing to supply at each price level. So an increase in the money wage rate decreases short-run aggregate supply.

A change in the money wage rate does not change long-run aggregate supply because on the *LAS* curve, a change in the money wage rate is accompanied by an equal percentage change in the price level. With no change in *relative* prices, firms have no incentive to change production and real GDP remains constant at potential GDP. With no change in potential GDP, the long-run aggregate supply curve remains at *LAS*.

### What Makes the Money Wage Rate Change?

The money wage rate can change for two reasons: departures from full employment and expectations about inflation. Unemployment above the natural rate puts downward pressure on the money wage rate, and unemployment below the natural rate puts upward pressure on the money wage rate. An expected increase in

**Figure 14.3  A Change in the Money Wage Rate**

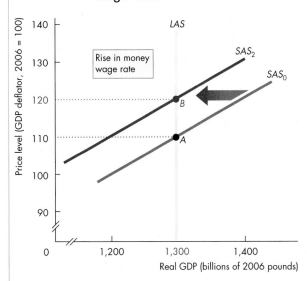

A rise in the money wage rate decreases short-run aggregate supply and shifts the short-run aggregate supply curve leftward from $SAS_0$ to $SAS_2$. A rise in the money wage rate does not change potential GDP, so the long-run aggregate supply curve does not shift.

 Animation

the inflation rate makes the money wage rate rise faster, and an expected decrease in the inflation rate slows the rate at which the money wage rate rises.

### Review Quiz

1  If the price level and the money wage rate rise by the same percentage, what happens to the quantity of real GDP supplied? Along which aggregate supply curve does the economy move?
2  If the price level rises and the money wage rate remains constant, what happens to the quantity of real GDP supplied? Along which aggregate supply curve does the economy move?
3  If potential GDP increases, what happens to aggregate supply? Is there a shift of or a movement along the *LAS* curve? Does the *SAS* curve shift or is there a movement along the *SAS* curve?
4  If the money wage rate rises and potential GDP remains the same, does the *LAS* curve or the *SAS* curve shift or is there a movement along the *LAS* curve or the *SAS* curve?

You can work these questions in Study Plan 14.1 and get instant feedback.

## Aggregate Demand

The quantity of real GDP demanded is the sum of real consumption expenditure ($C$), investment ($I$), government expenditure ($G$) and exports ($X$) minus imports ($M$). That is:

$$Y = C + I + G + X - M$$

The *quantity of real GDP demanded* is the total amount of final goods and services produced in the UK that people, businesses, governments and foreigners plan to buy.

These buying plans depend on many factors. The four main ones are:

1  The price level
2  Expectations
3  Fiscal policy and monetary policy
4  The world economy

We first focus on the relationship between the quantity of real GDP demanded and the price level. To study this relationship, we keep all other influences on buying plans the same and ask: How does the quantity of real GDP demanded vary as the price level varies?

## The Aggregate Demand Curve

Other things remaining the same, the higher the price level, the smaller is the quantity of real GDP demanded. This relationship between the quantity of real GDP demanded and the price level is called **aggregate demand**. Aggregate demand is described by an aggregate demand schedule and an aggregate demand curve.

Figure 14.4 shows an aggregate demand curve ($AD$) and an aggregate demand schedule. Each point on the $AD$ curve corresponds to a row of the schedule. For example, point $C'$ on the $AD$ curve and row $C'$ of the schedule tell us that if the price level is 110, the quantity of real GDP demanded is £1,300 billion.

The aggregate demand curve slopes downward for two reasons:

◆  Wealth effect
◆  Substitution effects

### Wealth Effect

When the price level rises but other things remain the same, *real* wealth decreases. Real wealth is the amount

**Figure 14.4**  Aggregate Demand

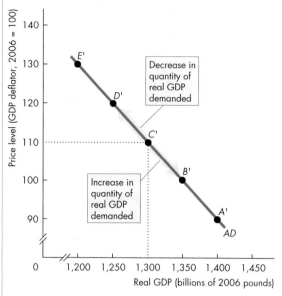

| | Price level (GDP deflator) | Real GDP (billions of 2006 pounds) |
|---|---|---|
| $A'$ | 90 | 1,400 |
| $B'$ | 100 | 1,350 |
| $C'$ | 110 | 1,300 |
| $D'$ | 120 | 1,250 |
| $E'$ | 130 | 1,200 |

The aggregate demand curve ($AD$) shows the relationship between the quantity of real GDP demanded and the price level. The aggregate demand curve is based on the aggregate demand schedule in the table. Each point $A'$ to $E'$ on the curve corresponds to the row in the table identified by the same letter. For example, when the price level is 110, the quantity of real GDP demanded is £1,300 billion, shown by point $C'$ in the figure.

A change in the price level with all other influences on aggregate buying plans remaining the same brings a change in the quantity of real GDP demanded and a movement along the $AD$ curve.

 Animation

of money in the bank, bonds, shares and other assets that people own, measured not in pounds but in terms of the goods and services that this money, bonds and shares will buy.

People save and hold money, bonds, shares and other assets for many reasons. One reason is to build up funds for education expenses. Another reason is to build up enough funds to meet possible medical or other big bills. But the biggest reason is to build up enough funds to provide a retirement income.

If the price level rises, real wealth decreases. People then try to restore their wealth. To do so, they must increase saving and, equivalently, decrease current consumption. Such a decrease in consumption is a decrease in aggregate demand.

### Maria's Wealth Effect

You can see how the wealth effect works by thinking about Maria's buying plans. Maria lives in Moscow, Russia. She has worked hard all summer and saved 20,000 rubles (the ruble is the currency of Russia), which she plans to spend attending graduate school when she has finished her economics degree. So Maria's wealth is 20,000 rubles. Maria has a part-time job, and her income from this job pays her current expenses. The price level in Russia rises by 100 per cent, and now Maria needs 40,000 rubles to buy what 20,000 rubles once bought. To try to make up some of the fall in value of her savings, Maria saves even more and cuts her current spending to the bare minimum.

### Substitution Effects

When the price level rises and other things remain the same, interest rates rise. The reason is related to the wealth effect that you've just studied. A rise in the price level decreases the real value of the money in people's pockets and bank accounts. With a smaller amount of real money around, banks can get a higher interest rate on loans. But faced with higher interest rates, people and businesses delay plans to buy new capital and consumer durable goods and cut back on spending.

This substitution effect involves changing the timing of capital consumer durable goods purchases and is called an *intertemporal* substitution effect – a substitution across time. Saving increases to increase future consumption.

To see this intertemporal substitution effect more clearly, think about your own plan to buy a new computer. At an interest rate of 5 per cent a year, you might borrow £1,000 and buy the new machine you've been researching. But at an interest rate of 10 per cent a year, you might decide that the payments would be too high. You don't abandon your plan to buy the computer, but you decide to delay your purchase.

A second substitution effect works through international prices. When the UK price level rises and other things remain the same, UK-made goods and services become more expensive relative to foreign-made goods and services. This change in *relative prices* encourages people to spend less on UK-made items and more on foreign-made items. For example, if the UK price level rises relative to the price level in France, fewer Vauxhall Astras are sold in France and more Renaults are sold in the UK. Exports from the UK decrease, imports into the UK increase and the quantity of UK real GDP demanded decreases.

### Maria's Substitution Effects

In Moscow, Maria makes some substitutions. She was planning to trade in her old motor scooter and get a new one. But with a higher price level and faced with higher interest rates, she decides to make her old scooter last one more year. Also, with the prices of Russian goods sharply increasing, Maria substitutes a low-cost dress made in Malaysia for the Russian-made dress she had originally planned to buy.

### Changes in the Quantity of Real GDP Demanded

When the price level rises and other things remain the same, the quantity of real GDP demanded decreases – a movement up along the *AD* curve as shown by the arrow in Figure 14.4. When the price level falls and other things remain the same, the quantity of real GDP demanded increases – a movement down along the *AD* curve.

We've now seen how the quantity of real GDP demanded changes when the price level changes. How do other influences on buying plans affect aggregate demand?

## Changes in Aggregate Demand

A change in any factor that influences buying plans other than the price level brings a change in aggregate demand. The main factors are:

◆ Expectations

◆ Fiscal policy and monetary policy

◆ The world economy

### Expectations

An increase in expected future disposable income, other things remaining the same, increases the amount of consumption goods (especially items such as cars) that people plan to buy today and increases aggregate demand today.

An increase in the expected future inflation rate increases aggregate demand today because people decide to buy more goods and services at today's relatively lower prices. An increase in expected future profit increases the investment that firms plan to undertake today and increases aggregate demand today.

## Fiscal Policy and Monetary Policy

The government's attempt to influence the economy by setting and changing taxes, making transfer payments and purchasing goods and services is called **fiscal policy**. A tax cut or an increase in transfer payments – for example, unemployment benefits or welfare payments – increases aggregate demand. Both of these influences operate by increasing households' *disposable* income. **Disposable income** is aggregate income minus taxes plus transfer payments. The greater the disposable income, the greater is the quantity of consumption goods and services that households plan to buy and the greater is aggregate demand.

Government expenditure on goods and services is one component of aggregate demand. So if the government spends more on hospitals, schools and motorways, aggregate demand increases.

**Monetary policy** consists of changes in interest rates and in the quantity of money in the economy. The quantity of money in the UK is determined by the Bank of England and the banks (in a process described in Chapter 13). An increase in the quantity of money increases aggregate demand.

To see why money affects aggregate demand, imagine that the Bank of England borrows the army's helicopters, loads them with millions of new £5 notes and sprinkles these notes like confetti across the nation. People gather the newly available money and plan to spend some of it. So the quantity of goods and services demanded increases. But people don't plan to spend all the new money. They save some of it and lend it to others through the banks. The interest rate falls, and with a lower interest rate, people plan to buy more consumer durables and firms plan to increase their investment.

## The World Economy

Aggregate demand in each individual country is influenced by events in the world economy. The two main influences are changes in the foreign exchange rate and changes in world income. The *foreign exchange rate* is the amount of a foreign currency that you can

## ECONOMICS IN ACTION

### Fiscal Policy to Fight Recession

In 2008, as recession deepened, the world's two largest economies embarked on a massive fiscal stimulus. The US Congress cut taxes by $300 billion and increased government expenditure by $540 billion, totalling 6 per cent of US GDP. In China, government spending was increased by $200 billion or 5 per cent of GDP. The UK stimulus was 1.5 per cent of GDP.

The idea of these fiscal measures was to stimulate business investment and consumption expenditure and increase aggregate demand.

### Monetary Policy to Fight Recession

In October 2008 and the months that followed, the central banks of the major Western economies, the US Federal Reserve, the European Central Bank, the Bank of Canada and the Bank of England, together cut their interest rates and took other measures to ease credit and encourage banks and other financial institutions to increase their lending.

Like the accompanying fiscal stimulus packages, the idea of these interest rate cuts and easier credit was to stimulate business investment and consumption expenditure and increase aggregate demand.

0.20%

**Ben Bernanke**
**Federal Reserve**

1.75%

**Jean-Claude Trichet**
**ECB**

0.50%

**Mervyn King**
**Bank of England**

0.25%

**Mark Carney**
**Bank of Canada**

buy with a unit of domestic currency. Other things remaining the same, a rise in a country's foreign exchange rate decreases aggregate demand.

To see how the UK's foreign exchange rate influences aggregate demand in the UK, suppose that £1 is worth €1.10. A pair of Gucci shoes made in Italy costs €220 and an equivalent pair of Church's shoes made in England costs £190. In pounds, the Gucci shoes cost £200, so people around the world buy the cheaper Church's shoes from the UK.

Now suppose the exchange rate rises to €1.40 per pound. The Gucci shoes now cost £157.14 and are cheaper than the Church's shoes. People switch from Church's to Gucci shoes. As they make this switch, UK exports decrease, UK imports increase and aggregate demand in the UK decreases.

An increase in foreign income increases UK exports and increases UK aggregate demand – the aggregate demand for UK-produced goods and services. For example, an increase in income in the US, Japan and Germany increases the American, Japanese and German consumers' and producers' planned expenditures on UK-produced consumption goods and capital goods.

## Shifts of the Aggregate Demand Curve

When aggregate demand changes, the aggregate demand curve shifts. Figure 14.5 shows two changes in aggregate demand and summarizes the factors that bring about such changes.

Aggregate demand increases and the aggregate demand curve shifts rightward from $AD_0$ to $AD_1$ when expected future disposable income, inflation or profit increases; government expenditure on goods and services increases; taxes are cut; transfer payments increase; the quantity of money increases and interest rates fall; the foreign exchange rate falls; or foreign income increases.

Aggregate demand decreases and the aggregate demand curve shifts leftward from $AD_0$ to $AD_2$ when expected future disposable income, inflation or profit decreases; government expenditure on goods and services decreases; taxes increase; transfer payments decrease; the quantity of money decreases and interest rates rise; the foreign exchange rate rises; or foreign income decreases.

**Figure 14.5**   Changes in Aggregate Demand

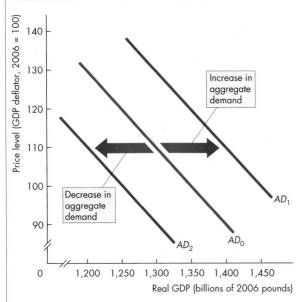

**Aggregate demand**

*Decreases if*:

- Expected future disposable income, inflation or profit decreases

- Fiscal policy decreases government expenditure on goods and services, increases taxes or decreases transfer payments

- Monetary policy increases interest rates and decreases the quantity of money

- The foreign exchange rate increases or foreign income decreases

*Increases if*:

- Expected future disposable income, inflation or profit increases

- Fiscal policy increases government expenditure on goods and services, decreases taxes or increases transfer payments

- Monetary policy decreases interest rates and increases the quantity of money

- The foreign exchange rate decreases or foreign income increases

 Animation ————————◆

### Review Quiz

1   What does the aggregate demand curve show? What factors change and what factors remain the same when there is a movement along the aggregate demand curve?
2   Why does the aggregate demand curve slope downward?
3   How do changes in expectations, fiscal policy, monetary policy and the world economy change aggregate demand and the aggregate demand curve?

You can work these questions in Study Plan 14.2 and get instant feedback.

## Explaining Macroeconomic Trends and Fluctuations

The purpose of the *AS–AD* model is to explain changes in real GDP and the price level. The model's main purpose is to explain business cycle fluctuations in these variables. But the model also aids our understanding of economic growth and inflation trends. We begin by combining aggregate supply and aggregate demand to determine real GDP and the price level in equilibrium. Just as there are two time frames for aggregate supply, there are two time frames for macroeconomic equilibrium: a long-run equilibrium and a short-run equilibrium. We'll first look at short-run equilibrium.

## Short-run Macroeconomic Equilibrium

The aggregate demand curve tells us the quantity of real GDP demanded at each price level, and the short-run aggregate supply curve tells us the quantity of real GDP supplied at each price level. **Short-run macroeconomic equilibrium** occurs when the quantity of real GDP demanded equals the short-run quantity of real GDP supplied at the point of intersection of the *AD* curve and the *SAS* curve. Figure 14.6 illustrates such an equilibrium at a price level of 110 and real GDP of £1,300 billion (point *C* and *C'*).

To see why this position is the equilibrium, think about what happens if the price level is something other than 110. Suppose, for example, that the price level is 120 and that real GDP is £1,400 billion (at point *E* on the *SAS* curve). The quantity of real GDP demanded is less than £1,400 billion, so firms are unable to sell all their output. Unwanted inventories (stocks) pile up, and firms cut both production and prices. Production and prices are cut until firms can sell all their output. This situation occurs only when real GDP is £1,300 billion and the price level is 110.

Now suppose that the price level is 100 and real GDP is £1,200 billion (at point *A* on the *SAS* curve). The quantity of real GDP demanded exceeds £1,200 billion, so firms are unable to meet demand for their output. Inventories (stocks of finished but unsold items) decrease and customers clamour for more goods and services than firms are producing. So firms increase production and raise prices. Production and prices increase until firms can meet demand. This situation occurs only when real GDP is £1,300 billion and the price level is 110.

**Figure 14.6** Short-run Macroeconomic Equilibrium

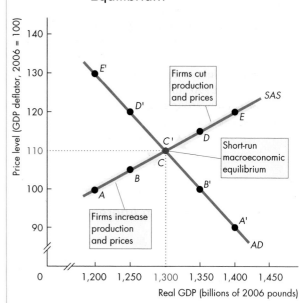

Short-run macroeconomic equilibrium occurs when real GDP demanded equals real GDP supplied – at the intersection of the aggregate demand curve (*AD*) and the short-run aggregate supply curve (*SAS*).

 Animation

In short-run macroeconomic equilibrium, the money wage rate is fixed. It does not adjust to bring full employment. So in the short run, real GDP can be greater than or less than potential GDP. But in the long run, the money wage rate does adjust and real GDP moves towards potential GDP. Let's look at the long-run equilibrium and see how we get there.

## Long-run Macroeconomic Equilibrium

**Long-run macroeconomic equilibrium** occurs when real GDP equals potential GDP – equivalently, when the economy is on its *LAS* curve.

When the economy is away from long-run equilibrium, the money wage rate adjusts. If the money wage rate is too high, short-run equilibrium is below potential GDP and the unemployment rate is above the natural rate. With an excess supply of labour, the money wage rate falls. If the money wage rate is too low, short-run equilibrium is above potential GDP and the unemployment rate is below the natural rate. With an excess demand for labour, the money wage rate rises.

Figure 14.7 shows the long-run equilibrium and how it comes about. If the short-run aggregate supply curve is $SAS_1$, the money wage rate is too high to achieve full employment. A fall in the money wage rate shifts the $SAS$ curve to $SAS^*$ and brings full employment. If the short-run aggregate supply curve is $SAS_2$, the money wage rate is too low to achieve full employment. Now, a rise in the money wage rate shifts the $SAS$ curve to $SAS^*$ and brings full employment.

In long-run equilibrium, potential GDP determines real GDP and potential GDP and aggregate demand together determine the price level. The money wage rate adjusts to put the $SAS$ curve through the long-run equilibrium point.

Let's now see how the $AS–AD$ model helps us to understand economic growth and inflation.

## Economic Growth and Inflation in the *AS–AD* Model

Economic growth results from a growing labour force and increasing labour productivity, which together make potential GDP grow. Inflation results from a growing quantity of money that outpaces the growth of potential GDP (Chapter 13, pp. 314–315).

The $AS–AD$ model explains and illustrates economic growth and inflation. It explains economic growth as increasing long-run aggregate supply and it explains inflation as a persistent increase in aggregate demand at a faster pace than that of the increase in potential GDP.

> ### ECONOMICS IN ACTION

## UK Economic Growth and Inflation

The figure is a scatter diagram of UK real GDP and the price level. The graph has the same axes as those of the $AS–AD$ model. Each dot represents a year between 1960 and 2010. The red dots are recession years. The pattern formed by the dots shows the combination of economic growth and inflation. Economic growth was fastest during the 1960s; inflation was fastest during the 1970s.

The $AS–AD$ model interprets each dot as being at the intersection of the $SAS$ and $AD$ curves.

### Figure 14.7 Long-run Macroeconomic Equilibrium

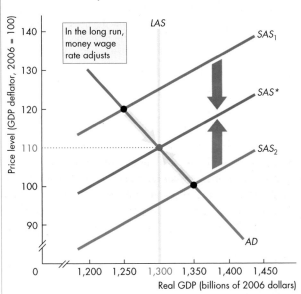

In long-run macroeconomic equilibrium, real GDP equals potential GDP. So long-run equilibrium occurs where the aggregate demand curve *AD* intersects the long-run aggregate supply curve *LAS*. In the long run, aggregate demand determines the price level and has no effect on real GDP. The money wage rate adjusts in the long run, so the *SAS* curve intersects the *LAS* curve at the long-run equilibrium price level.

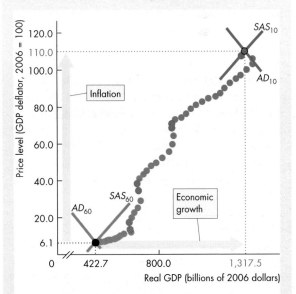

**Figure 1  The Path of Real GDP and the Price Level**

Source of data: Office for National Statistics

Figure 14.8 illustrates this explanation in terms of the shifting *LAS*, *SAS* and *AD* curves.

When the *LAS* curve shifts rightward from $LAS_0$ to $LAS_1$, potential GDP grows from £1,300 billion to £1,400 billion and in long-run equilibrium, real GDP also grows to £1,400 billion.

When the *AD* curve shifts rightward from $AD_0$ to $AD_1$, which is a growth of aggregate demand that outpaces the growth of potential GDP, the price level rises from 110 to 120.

If aggregate demand were to increase at the same pace as long-run aggregate supply, real GDP would grow with no inflation.

Our economy experiences periods of growth and inflation, like those shown in Figure 14.8, but it does not experience steady growth and steady inflation. Real GDP fluctuates around potential GDP in a business cycle. When we study the business cycle, we ignore economic growth and focus on the fluctuations around the trend. By doing so, we see the business cycle more clearly. Let's now see how the *AS–AD* model explains the business cycle.

## The Business Cycle in the *AS–AD* Model

The business cycle occurs because aggregate demand and short-run aggregate supply fluctuate but the money wage rate does not adjust quickly enough to keep real GDP at potential GDP. Figure 14.9 shows three types of short-run equilibrium.

Figure 14.9(a) shows an above full-employment equilibrium. An **above full-employment equilibrium** is an equilibrium in which real GDP exceeds potential GDP. The gap between real GDP and potential GDP is the **output gap**. When real GDP exceeds potential GDP, the output gap is called an **inflationary gap**.

The above full-employment equilibrium shown in Figure 14.9(a) occurs where the aggregate demand curve $AD_0$ intersects the short-run aggregate supply

---

ECONOMICS IN ACTION

### The UK Business Cycle

The UK economy had an inflationary gap in 2004 (at *A* in the figure), full employment in 2008 (at *B*) and a recessionary gap in 2009 (at *C*). The fluctuating output gap in the figure is the real-world version of Figure 14.9(d) and is generated by fluctuations in aggregate demand and short-run aggregate supply.

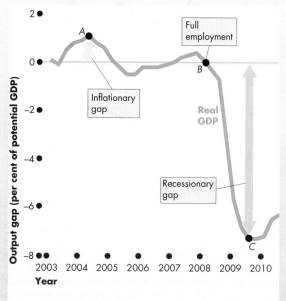

**Figure 1  The UK Output Gap**

Source of data: Office for National Statistics.

---

**Figure 14.8**  Economic Growth and Inflation

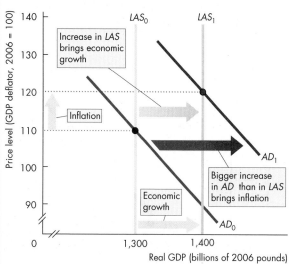

Economic growth is the persistent increase in potential GDP. Economic growth is shown as an ongoing rightward shift of the *LAS* curve. Inflation is the persistent rise in the price level. Inflation occurs when aggregate demand increases by more than the increase in long-run aggregate supply.

myeconlab Animation

curve $SAS_0$ at a real GDP of £1,320 billion. There is an inflationary gap of £20 billion.

Figure 14.9(b) is an example of **full-employment equilibrium**, in which real GDP equals potential GDP. In this example, the equilibrium occurs where the aggregate demand curve $AD_1$ intersects the short-run aggregate supply curve $SAS_1$ at an actual and potential GDP of £1,300 billion.

In part (c), there is a below full-employment equilibrium. A **below full-employment equilibrium** is an equilibrium in which potential GDP exceeds real GDP. When potential GDP exceeds real GDP, the output gap is called a **recessionary gap**.

The below full-employment equilibrium shown in Figure 14.9(c) occurs where the aggregate demand curve $AD_2$ intersects the short-run aggregate supply curve $SAS_2$ at a real GDP of £1,280 billion with a recessionary gap of £20 billion.

The economy moves from one type of macroeconomic equilibrium to another as a result of fluctuations in aggregate demand and in short-run aggregate supply. These fluctuations produce fluctuations in real GDP. Figure 14.9(d) shows how real GDP fluctuates around potential GDP.

Let's now look at some of the sources of these fluctuations around potential GDP.

**Figure 14.9    The Business Cycle**

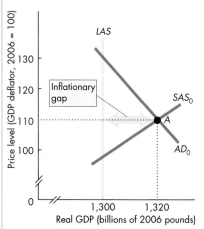

**(a) Above full-employment equilibrium**

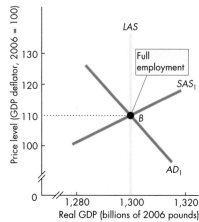

**(b) Full-employment equilibrium**

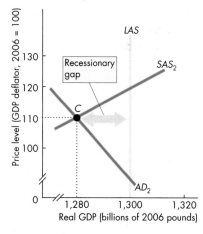

**(c) Below full-employment equilibrium**

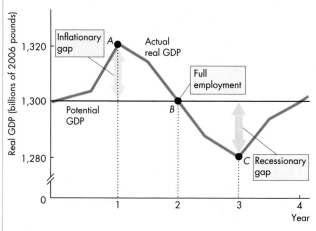

**(d) Fluctuations in real GDP**

Part (a) shows an above full-employment equilibrium in year 1, part (b) shows full-employment equilibrium in year 2 and part (c) shows a below full-employment equilibrium in year 3. Part (d) shows how real GDP fluctuates around potential GDP in a business cycle.

In year 1, an inflationary gap exists and the economy is at point *A*, in parts (a) and (d). In year 2, the economy is in full-employment equilibrium and the economy is at point *B* in parts (b) and (d). In year 3, a recessionary gap exists and the economy is at point *C* in parts (c) and (d).

## Fluctuations in Aggregate Demand

One reason real GDP fluctuates around potential GDP is that aggregate demand fluctuates. Let's see what happens when aggregate demand increases.

Figure 14.10(a) shows an economy at full employment. The aggregate demand curve is $AD_0$, the short-run aggregate supply curve is $SAS_0$ and the long-run aggregate supply curve is $LAS$. Real GDP equals potential GDP at £1,300 billion and the price level is 110.

Now suppose that the world economy expands and that the demand for UK-made goods increases in Japan, Canada and the US. The increase in UK exports increases aggregate demand and the aggregate demand curve shifts rightward from $AD_0$ to $AD_1$ in Figure 14.10(a).

Faced with an increase in demand, firms increase production and raise prices. Real GDP increases to £1,350 billion and the price level rises to 115. The economy is now in an above full-employment equilibrium.

Real GDP exceeds potential GDP and there is an inflationary gap.

The increase in aggregate demand has increased the prices of all goods and services. Faced with higher prices, firms have increased their output rates. At this stage, prices of goods and services have increased but the money wage rate has not changed. (Recall that as we move along a short-run aggregate supply curve, the money wage rate is constant.)

Because the price level has increased and the money wage rate is unchanged, workers have experienced a fall in the buying power of their wages and firms' profits have increased. In these circumstances, workers demand higher wages and firms, anxious to maintain their employment and output levels, meet those demands. If firms do not raise the money wage rate, they will either lose workers or have to hire less productive ones.

As the money wage rate rises, the short-run aggregate supply curve begins to shift leftward. In Figure 14.10(b),

**Figure 14.10**    An Increase in Aggregate Demand

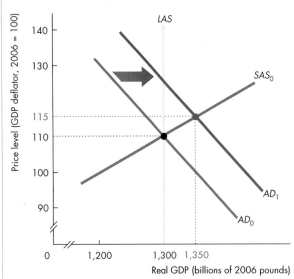

**(a) Short-run effect**

An increase in aggregate demand shifts the aggregate demand curve from $AD_0$ to $AD_1$. In the short run (part a), real GDP increases from £1,300 billion to £1,350 billion and the price level rises from 110 to 115. The economy has moved up along the $SAS$ curve. In this situation, an inflationary gap exists.

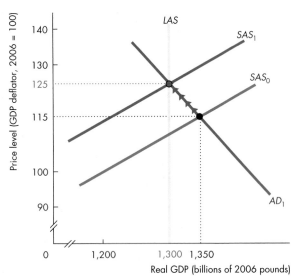

**(b) Long-run effect**

In the long run (part b), with an inflationary gap, the money wage rate starts to rise. The short-run aggregate supply curve starts to shift leftward from $SAS_0$ to $SAS_1$. As the $SAS$ curve shifts leftward, it intersects the aggregate demand curve $AD_1$ at higher price levels and real GDP decreases. Eventually, the price level rises to 125 and real GDP decreases to £1,300 billion – potential GDP.

the short-run aggregate supply curve shifts from $SAS_0$ towards $SAS_1$. The rise in the money wage rate and the shift in the $SAS$ curve produce a sequence of new equilibrium positions. Along the adjustment path, real GDP decreases and the price level rises. The economy moves up along its aggregate demand curve as the arrow heads show.

Eventually, the money wage rate rises by the same percentage as the price level. At this time, the aggregate demand curve $AD_1$ intersects $SAS_1$ at a new long-run equilibrium. The price level has risen to 125, and real GDP is back where it started, at potential GDP.

A decrease in aggregate demand has similar but opposite effects to those of an increase in aggregate demand. That is, a decrease in aggregate demand shifts the aggregate demand curve leftward. Real GDP decreases to less than potential GDP and a recessionary gap emerges. Firms cut prices. The lower price level increases the purchasing power of wages and increases firms' costs relative to their output prices because the money wage rate remains unchanged. Eventually, the money wage rate falls and the short-run aggregate supply curve shifts rightward. But the money wage rate changes slowly, so real GDP slowly returns to potential GDP and the price level falls slowly.

Let's now work out how real GDP and the price level change when aggregate supply changes.

## Fluctuations in Aggregate Supply

Fluctuations in short-run aggregate supply can bring fluctuations in real GDP around potential GDP. Suppose that initially, real GDP equals potential GDP. Then there is a large but temporary rise in the price of oil. What happens to real GDP and the price level?

Figure 14.11 answers this question. The aggregate demand curve is $AD_0$, the short-run aggregate supply curve is $SAS_0$ and the long-run aggregate supply curve is $LAS$. Equilibrium real GDP is £1,300 billion, which equals potential GDP, and the price level is 110. Then the price of oil rises. Faced with higher energy and transportation costs, firms decrease production. Short-run aggregate supply decreases and the short-run aggregate supply curve shifts leftward to $SAS_1$. The price level rises to 120 and real GDP decreases to £1,250 billion.

Because real GDP decreases, the economy experiences recession. Because the price level increases, the economy experiences inflation. A combination of recession and inflation, called **stagflation**, actually occurred in the UK in the mid-1970s.

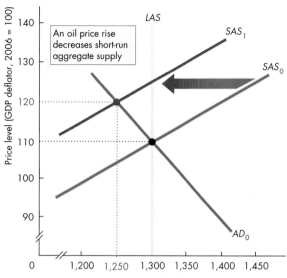

**Figure 14.11**   A Decrease in Aggregate Supply

An oil price rise decreases short-run aggregate supply

An increase in the price of oil decreases short-run aggregate supply and shifts the short-run aggregate supply curve leftward from $SAS_0$ to $SAS_1$. Real GDP decreases from £1,300 billion to £1,250 billion, and the price level increases from 110 to 120. The economy experiences both recession and inflation – a situation known as stagflation.

myeconlab  Animation

### Review Quiz

1  Does economic growth result from increases in aggregate demand, short-run aggregate supply or long-run aggregate supply?
2  Does inflation result from increases in aggregate demand, short-run aggregate supply or long-run aggregate supply?
3  Describe the three types of short-run macro-economic equilibrium.
4  How do fluctuations in aggregate demand and short-run aggregate supply bring fluctuations in real GDP around potential GDP?

You can work these questions in Study Plan 14.3 and get instant feedback.

We can use the $AS$–$AD$ model to explain and illustrate the views of the alternative schools of thought in macroeconomics. That is your next task.

## Macroeconomic Schools of Thought

Macroeconomics is an active field of research and much remains to be learned about the forces that make our economy grow, bring inflation and generate business cycles. There is a greater degree of consensus and certainty about economic growth and inflation trends – the longer-term changes in real GDP and the price level – than there is about the business cycle – the short-term fluctuations in these variables. Here, we'll look only at differences of view about short-term fluctuations.

The *AS–AD* model that you've studied in this chapter provides a good foundation for understanding the range of views that macroeconomists hold about this topic. But what you will learn here is just a first glimpse at the scientific controversy and debate. We'll return to these issues at various later points in the text and deepen your appreciation of the alternative views.

Classification usually requires simplification. And classifying macroeconomists is no exception to this general rule. The classification that we'll use here is simple, but it is not misleading. We identify three macroeconomic schools of thought and examine the views of each group in turn. We examine:

◆ The classical view
◆ The Keynesian view
◆ The monetarist view

## The Classical View

A **classical** macroeconomist believes that the economy is self-regulating and that it is always at full employment. The term 'classical' derives from the name of the founding school of economics that includes Adam Smith, David Ricardo and John Stuart Mill.

A **new classical** view is that business cycle fluctuations are the efficient responses of a well-functioning market economy that is bombarded by shocks that arise from the uneven pace of technological change.

The classical view can be understood in terms of beliefs about aggregate demand and aggregate supply.

### Aggregate Demand Fluctuations

In the classical view, technological change is the most significant influence on both aggregate demand and aggregate supply. For this reason, classical macroeconomists don't use the *AS–AD* framework. But their

views can be interpreted in this framework. A technological change that increases the productivity of capital brings an increase in aggregate demand because firms increase their expenditure on new plant and equipment. A technological change that lengthens the useful life of existing capital decreases the demand for new capital, which decreases aggregate demand.

### Aggregate Supply Response

In the classical view, the money wage rate that lies behind the short-run aggregate supply curve is instantly and completely flexible. The money wage rate adjusts so quickly to maintain equilibrium in the labour market that real GDP always adjusts to equal potential GDP.

Potential GDP itself fluctuates for the same reasons that aggregate demand fluctuates: technological change. When the pace of technological change is rapid, potential GDP increases quickly and so does real GDP. When the pace of technological change slows, so does the growth rate of potential GDP.

### Classical Policy

The classical view of policy emphasizes the potential for taxes to stunt incentives and create inefficiency. By minimizing the disincentive effects that taxes have, employment, investment and technological advance are at their efficient levels and the economy expands at an appropriate and rapid pace.

## The Keynesian View

A **Keynesian** macroeconomist believes that left alone, the economy would rarely operate at full employment and that to achieve and maintain full employment, active help from fiscal policy and monetary policy is required. The term 'Keynesian' derives from the name of one of the twentieth century's most famous economists, John Maynard Keynes.

The Keynesian view is based on beliefs about the forces that determine aggregate demand and short-run aggregate supply.

### Aggregate Demand Fluctuations

In the Keynesian view, *expectations* are the most significant influence on aggregate demand. And expectations are based on herd instinct or, what Keynes himself called 'animal spirits'. A wave of pessimism about future profit prospects can lead to a fall in aggregate demand and plunge the economy into recession.

### Aggregate Supply Response

In the Keynesian view, the money wage rate that lies behind the short-run aggregate supply curve is extremely sticky downward. Basically, the money wage rate doesn't fall. So if there is a recessionary gap, there is no automatic mechanism for getting rid of it. If it were to happen, a fall in the money wage rate would increase short-run aggregate supply and restore full employment. But the money wage rate doesn't fall, so the economy remains stuck in recession.

A modern version of the Keynesian view known as the **new Keynesian** view holds that not only is the money wage rate sticky but that prices of goods and services are also sticky. With a sticky price level, the short-run aggregate supply curve is horizontal at a fixed price level.

### Policy Response Needed

The Keynesian view calls for fiscal policy and monetary policy to actively offset the changes in aggregate demand that bring recession. By stimulating aggregate demand in a recession, full employment can be restored.

## The Monetarist View

A **monetarist** is a macroeconomist who believes that the economy is self-regulating and that it will normally operate at full employment, provided that monetary policy is not erratic and that the pace of money growth is kept steady. The term 'monetarist' was coined by an outstanding twentieth century economist, Karl Brunner, to describe his own and Milton Friedman's views.

The monetarist view can be interpreted in terms of beliefs about the forces that determine aggregate demand and short-run aggregate supply.

### Aggregate Demand Fluctuations

In the monetarist view, the *quantity of money* is the most significant influence on aggregate demand. And the quantity of money is determined by the Bank of England. If the Bank of England keeps money growing at a steady pace, aggregate demand fluctuations will be minimized and the economy will operate close to full employment. But if the Bank of England decreases the quantity of money or even just slows its growth rate too

abruptly, the economy will go into recession. In the monetarist view, all recessions result from inappropriate monetary policy.

### Aggregate Supply Response

The monetarist view of short-run aggregate supply is the same as the Keynesian view – the money wage rate is sticky. If the economy is in recession, it will take an unnecessarily long time for it to return unaided to full employment.

### Monetarist Policy

The monetarist view of policy is the same as the classical view on fiscal policy. Taxes should be kept low to avoid disincentive effects that decrease potential GDP. Provided that the quantity of money is kept on a steady growth path, no active stabilization is needed to offset changes in aggregate demand.

## The Way Ahead

You are now ready to start using the aggregate supply–aggregate demand model to better understand macroeconomic performance and policy. In the next chapter, you will learn how changes in aggregate supply and aggregate demand bring economic growth, inflation and fluctuations in economic activity. Then, in the final chapter, you will see how fiscal policy and monetary policy can be used to achieve faster growth, stable prices and a smoother cycle.

### Review Quiz

1   What are the defining features of classical macroeconomics and what policies do classical macroeconomists recommend?
2   What are the defining features of Keynesian macroeconomics and what policies do Keynesian macroeconomists recommend?
3   What are the defining features of monetarist macroeconomics and what policies do monetarist macroeconomists recommend?

You can work these questions in Study Plan 14.4 and get instant feedback.

To complete your study of the *AS–AD* model, take a look at the German economy in 2009–2010 through the eyes of this model in *Reading Between the Lines* on pp. 342–343.

# Reading Between the Lines

# Aggregate Supply and Aggregate Demand in Action

The Financial Times, 12 January 2011

## Domestic Demand Spurs Growth in Germany

Ralph Atkins and Quentin Peel

Germany last year experienced its most dramatic economic turn round since the country's reunification. Gross domestic product expanded 3.6 per cent compared with the previous year – at least partly reversing a 4.7 per cent contraction in 2009, the federal statistical office in Wiesbaden reported on Wednesday.

The improvement in Europe's largest economy, led by a rebound in investment spending after its worst recession since the Second World War, provided welcome news for Eurozone policymakers – and also strengthened Germans' convictions that their focus on fiscal discipline is justified.

A surge in imports and modest pick-up in consumer spending, as well as the investment splurge, were cited by economists as evidence that domestic demand was increasingly driving growth – boosting the prospects that Germany's revival will have a knock-on effect in the Eurozone.

But despite Berlin's proclaimed fiscal prudence, the full effects of tightening measures implemented by Berlin have yet to be felt. Government spending rose 2.2 per cent last year, while the public sector deficit rose to 3.5 per cent of GDP.

Germany was . . . better placed than most European economies to benefit last year from rapid growth in countries such as China. . . . Hopes that the export and investment-led growth of 2010 will spark a rebound in consumer spending this year are based on the unexpectedly strong improvement in Germany's labour market.

Nevertheless, the composition of growth in 2010 left some observers sceptical about the speed with which Germany's export dependency is waning. Held back by weak car sales, consumer spending rose just 0.5 per cent last year. The proportion of their disposable incomes that Germans saved also rose.

## The Essence of the Story

- During 2010 real GDP in Germany grew by 3.6 per cent.

- The rapid growth of GDP was led by growth in investment and exports.

- Consumer spending increased by only 0.5 per cent as Germans saved more.

- Germany is heavily dependent on exports for growth in demand.

# Economic Analysis

- The quantity of real GDP demanded is the sum of real consumption, $C$, investment, $I$, government expenditure, $G$, and net exports, $X - M$:

$$Y = C + I + G + X - M$$

- The large increase in Germany's real GDP in 2010 resulted from an increase in aggregate demand that came mainly from investment and exports.

- Figure 1 shows the growth rates of consumption, investment and exports from the third quarter of 2008 to the fourth quarter of 2010.

- Figure 1 shows that the fluctuations in investment and exports are much larger than those in consumption. (The growth rate of real GDP is not shown but it lies between the three curves in the figure.)

- The rapid growth in Germany's exports, particularly those of engineering goods, resulted from a large increase in demand from China and other rapidly expanding economies in East Asia.

- A depreciation of the euro against the Chinese yuan and the US dollar also helped to boost Germany's exports.

- Germany's rapid real GDP growth decreased its recessionary gap.

- We estimate Germany's recessionary gap at the end of 2010 at 1 per cent of potential GDP.

- Figure 2 shows Germany's aggregate demand and aggregate supply curves in 2009 and 2010.

- The long-run aggregate supply curve is *LAS* and the short-run aggregate supply curve is *SAS*.

- In 2009, the aggregate demand curve was $AD_0$. Real GDP was €2,170 billion (in 2000 prices) and the price level was 109.

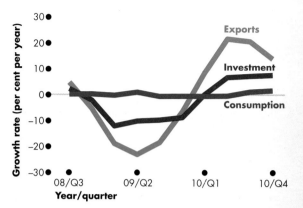

**Figure 1  Growth of Germany's consumption, investment and exports**

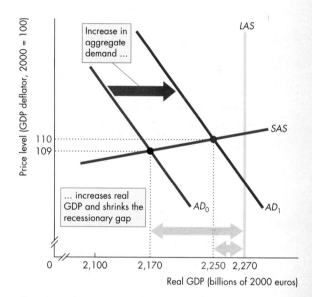

**Figure 2  Germany's aggregate demand and aggregate supply**

- In 2010, aggregate demand increased and the $AD$ curve shifted rightward to $AD_1$. Real GDP increased to €2,250 billion and the recessionary gap closed to 1 per cent of potential GDP.

- The news article implies that Germany relies too much on exports and not enough on domestic consumption.

- That view is not correct. Germany has a comparative advantage in many engineering production activities, and Germany and its trading partners gain from international trade.

◢ **SUMMARY**

## Key Points

### Aggregate Supply (pp. 326–329)

◆ In the long run, the quantity of real GDP supplied is potential GDP.

◆ In the short run, a rise in the price level increases the quantity of real GDP supplied.

◆ A change in potential GDP changes both long-run and short-run aggregate supply. A change in the money wage rate or other resource prices changes only short-run aggregate supply.

Working Problems 1 to 3 will give you a better understanding of aggregate supply.

### Aggregate Demand (pp. 330–333)

◆ A rise in the price level decreases the quantity of real GDP demanded because of wealth and substitution effects.

◆ Changes in expectations, fiscal policy, monetary policy and the world economy change aggregate demand.

Working Problems 4 to 7 will give you a better understanding of aggregate demand.

### Explaining Macroeconomic Trends and Fluctuations (pp. 334–339)

◆ Aggregate demand and short-run aggregate supply determine real GDP and the price level.

◆ In the long run, real GDP equals potential GDP and aggregate demand determines the price level.

◆ Economic growth occurs because potential GDP increases and inflation occurs because aggregate demand grows more quickly than potential GDP.

◆ Business cycles occur because aggregate demand and aggregate supply fluctuate.

Working Problems 8 to 16 will give you a better understanding of macroeconomic trends and fluctuations

## Macroeconomic Schools of Thought (pp. 340–341)

◆ Classical economists believe that the economy is self-regulating and always at full employment.

◆ Keynesian economists believe that full employment can be achieved only with active policy.

◆ Monetarist economists believe that recessions result from inappropriate monetary policy.

Working Problems 17 to 19 will give you a better understanding of macroeconomic schools of thought.

## Key Terms

Above full-employment equilibrium, 336
Aggregate demand, 330
Below full-employment equilibrium, 337
Classical, 340
Disposable income, 332
Fiscal policy, 332
Full-employment equilibrium, 337
Inflationary gap, 336
Keynesian, 340
Long-run aggregate supply, 326
Long-run macroeconomic equilibrium, 334
Monetarist, 341
Monetary policy, 332
New classical, 340
New Keynesian, 341
Output gap, 336
Recessionary gap, 337
Short-run aggregate supply, 327
Short-run macroeconomic equilibrium, 334
Stagflation, 339

# STUDY PLAN PROBLEMS AND APPLICATIONS

myeconlab   You can work Problems 1 to 19 in MyEconLab Chapter 14 Study Plan and get instant feedback.

## Aggregate Supply (Study Plan 14.1)

**1** Explain the influence of each of the following events on the quantity of real GDP supplied and aggregate supply in India and use a graph to illustrate.

- ◆ UK firms move their call handling, IT and data functions to India.
- ◆ Petrol prices rise.
- ◆ Wal-Mart and Starbucks open in India.
- ◆ Universities in India increase the number of engineering graduates.
- ◆ The money wage rate rises.
- ◆ The price level in India increases.

**2 Wages Could Hit Steepest Plunge in 18 Years**

A bad economy is starting to drag down wages for millions of workers. The average weekly wage has fallen 1.4% this year through September. Colorado will become the first state to lower its minimum wage since the federal minimum wage law was passed in 1938, when the state cuts its rate by 4 cents an hour.

Source: *USA Today*, 16 October 2009

Explain how the fall in the average weekly wage and the minimum wage will influence aggregate supply.

**3** Chinese Premier Wen Jiabao has warned Japan that its companies operating in China should raise pay for their workers. Explain how a rise in wages in China will influence the quantity of real GDP supplied and aggregate supply in China.

## Aggregate Demand (Study Plan 14.2)

**4** South Africa trades with the UK. Explain the effect of each of the following events on South Africa's aggregate demand.

- ◆ The government of South Africa cuts income taxes.
- ◆ The UK experiences strong economic growth.
- ◆ South Africa sets new environmental standards that require power utilities to upgrade their production facilities.

**5** The Bank of England cuts the quantity of money and all other things remain the same. Explain the effect of the cut in the quantity of money on aggregate demand in the short run.

**6** Kenya trades with the UK. Explain the effect of each of the following events on the quantity of real GDP demanded and aggregate demand in Kenya.

- ◆ The UK goes into a recession.
- ◆ The price level in Kenya rises.
- ◆ Kenya increases the quantity of money.

**7 Durable Goods Orders Surge in May, New Home Sales Dip**

The US government announced that demand for durable goods rose 1.8 per cent, while sales of new homes dropped 0.6 per cent in May. US companies suffered a sharp drop in exports as other countries struggle with recession.

Source: *USA Today*, 24 June 2009

Explain how the items in the news clip influence US aggregate demand.

## Explaining Macroeconomic Trends and Fluctuations (Study Plan 14.3)

Use the following graph to work Problems 8 to 10.

Initially, the short-run aggregate supply curve is $SAS_0$ and the aggregate demand curve is $AD_0$.

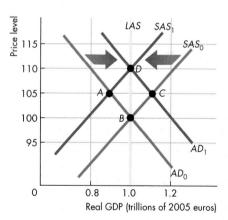

**8** Some events change aggregate demand from $AD_0$ to $AD_1$. Describe two events that could have created this change in aggregate demand. What is the equilibrium after aggregate demand changed? If potential GDP is €1 trillion, the economy is at what type of macroeconomic equilibrium?

**9** Some events change aggregate supply from $SAS_0$ to $SAS_1$. Describe two events that could have created this change in aggregate supply. What is the equilibrium after aggregate supply changed? If potential GDP is €1 trillion, does the economy have an inflationary gap, a recessionary gap or no output gap?

**10** Some events change aggregate demand from $AD_0$ to $AD_1$ and aggregate supply from $SAS_0$ to $SAS_1$. What is the new macroeconomic equilibrium?

Use the following data to work Problems 11 to 13.

The following events have occurred in UK history:

◆ A deep recession hits the world economy.

◆ The world oil price rises sharply.

◆ UK businesses expect future profits to fall.

**11** Explain for each event whether it changes short-run aggregate supply, long-run aggregate supply, aggregate demand or some combination of them.

**12** Explain the separate effects of each event on UK real GDP and the price level, starting from a position of long-run equilibrium.

**13** Explain the combined effects of these events on UK real GDP and the price level, starting from a position of long-run equilibrium.

Use the following data to work Problems 14 and 15.

The table shows the aggregate demand and short-run aggregate supply schedules of Mainland, a country in which potential GDP is €1,050 billion.

| Price level | Real GDP demanded | Real GDP supplied in the short run |
|---|---|---|
| | (billions of 2005 euros) | |
| 100 | 1,150 | 1,050 |
| 110 | 1,100 | 1,100 |
| 120 | 1,050 | 1,150 |
| 130 | 1,000 | 1,200 |
| 140 | 950 | 1,250 |
| 150 | 900 | 1,300 |
| 160 | 850 | 1,350 |

**14** What is the short-run macroeconomic equilibrium real GDP and price level?

**15** Does the country have an inflationary gap or a recessionary gap and what is its magnitude?

**16** **Geithner Urges Action on Economy**

The US Treasury Secretary Timothy Geithner is reported as having said that the US can no longer rely on consumer spending to be the growth engine of recovery from recession. The government needs to sow the seeds for business investment and exports. 'We can't go back to a situation where we're depending on a near short-term boost in consumption to carry us forward,' he said.

Source: *The Wall Street Journal*,
12 September 2010

**a** Explain the effects of an increase in consumer spending on the short-run macroeconomic equilibrium.

**b** Explain the effects of an increase in business investment on the short-run macroeconomic equilibrium.

**c** Explain the effects of an increase in exports on the short-run macroeconomic equilibrium.

## Macroeconomic Schools of Thought

(Study Plan 14.4)

**17** Describe what a classical macroeconomist, a Keynesian, and a monetarist would want to do in response to each of the events listed in Problem 11.

**18** **Adding Up the Cost of Obama's Agenda**

When campaigning, Barack Obama has made a long list of promises for new federal programmes costing tens of billions of dollars. Obama has said he would strengthen the nation's bridges and dams ($6 billion a year), extend health insurance to more people (part of a $65-billion-a-year health plan), develop cleaner energy sources ($15 billion a year), curb home foreclosures ($10 billion in one-time spending) and add $18 billion a year to education spending. In total a $50-billion plan to stimulate the economy through increased government spending. A different blueprint offered by McCain proposes relatively little new spending and tax cuts as a more effective means of solving problems.

Source: *Los Angeles Times*, 8 July 2008

**a** Based upon this news clip, explain what macroeconomic school of thought Barack Obama most likely follows.

**b** Based upon this news clip, explain what macroeconomic school of thought John McCain most likely follows.

**19** Based upon the news clip in Problem 16, explain what macroeconomic school of thought US Treasury Secretary Timothy Geithner most likely follows.

**ADDITIONAL PROBLEMS AND APPLICATIONS**

 You can work these problems in MyEconLab if assigned by your lecturer.

## Aggregate Supply

**20** Explain for each event whether it changes the quantity of real GDP supplied, short-run aggregate supply, long-run aggregate supply or a combination of them.

- ◆ UK car producers switch to a new technology that raises productivity.
- ◆ Toyota and Honda build additional plants in the UK.
- ◆ The prices of car parts imported from China rise.
- ◆ Workers in UK car plants agree to a cut in the money wage rate.
- ◆ The UK price level rises.

## Aggregate Demand

**21** Explain for each event whether it changes the quantity of real GDP demanded or aggregate demand.

- ◆ UK car producers switch to a new technology that raises productivity.
- ◆ Toyota and Honda build new plants in Wales.
- ◆ The prices of car parts imported from China rise.
- ◆ Workers in UK car plants agree to a lower money wage rate.
- ◆ The UK price level rises.

**22 Inventories Surge**

The US Commerce Department reported that wholesale inventories rose 1.3 per cent in July, the best performance since July 2008. A major driver of the economy since late last year has been the restocking of depleted store shelves.

Source: Associated Press, 13 September 2010

Explain how a surge in inventories influences current aggregate demand.

**23 Low Spending Is Taking Toll on Economy**

The US Commerce Department reported that the economy continued to stagnate during the first three months of the year, with a sharp pullback in consumer spending the primary factor at play. Consumer spending fell for a broad range of goods and services, including cars, auto parts, furniture, food and recreation, reflecting a growing inclination toward thrift.

Source: *The New York Times*, 1 May 2008

Explain how a fall in consumer expenditure influences the quantity of real GDP demanded and aggregate demand.

## Explaining Macroeconomic Trends and Fluctuations

Use the following information to work Problems 24 to 26.

The following events have occurred in UK history:

- ◆ The world economy goes into an expansion.
- ◆ UK businesses expect future profits to rise.
- ◆ The government increases its expenditure on goods and services in a time of war or increased international tension.

**24** Explain for each event whether it changes short-run aggregate supply, long-run aggregate supply, aggregate demand or some combination of them.

**25** Explain the separate effects of each event on UK real GDP and the price level, starting from a position of long-run equilibrium.

**26** Explain the combined effects of these events on UK real GDP and the price level, starting from a position of long-run equilibrium.

Use the following data to work Problems 27 and 28.

In Japan, potential GDP is 600 trillion yen and the table shows the aggregate demand and short-run aggregate supply schedules.

| Price level | Real GDP demanded | Real GDP supplied in the short run |
|---|---|---|
| | (billions of 2005 yen) | |
| 75 | 600 | 400 |
| 85 | 550 | 450 |
| 95 | 500 | 500 |
| 105 | 450 | 550 |
| 115 | 400 | 600 |
| 125 | 350 | 650 |
| 135 | 300 | 700 |

**27 a** Draw a graph of the aggregate demand curve and the short-run aggregate supply curve.

**b** What is the short-run equilibrium real GDP and price level?

**28** Does Japan have an inflationary gap or a recessionary gap and what is its magnitude?

Use the following information to work Problems 29 to 31.

**Spending by Women Jumps**

The magazine *Women of China* reported that Chinese women in big cities spent 63% of their income on consumer goods last year, up from a meager 26% in 2007. Clothing accounted for the biggest chunk of that spending, at nearly 30%, followed by digital products such as mobile phones and cameras (11%) and travel (10%). Chinese consumption as a whole grew faster than the overall economy in the first half of the year and is expected to reach 42% of GDP by 2020, up from the current 36%.

Source: *The Wall Street Journal*, 27 August 2010

29  Explain the effect of a rise in consumption expenditure on real GDP and the price level in the short run.

30  If the economy had been operating at a full-employment equilibrium,

   a  Describe the macroeconomic equilibrium after the rise in consumer spending.

   b  Explain and draw a graph to illustrate how the economy can adjust in the long run to restore a full-employment equilibrium.

31  Why do changes in consumer spending play a large role in the business cycle?

32  **It's Pinching Everyone**

   The current inflationary process is a global phenomenon, but emerging and developing countries have been growing significantly faster than the rest of the world. Because there is no reason to believe that world production will rise miraculously at least in the immediate future, many people expect that prices will keep on rising. These expectations in turn exacerbate the inflationary process. Households buy more of non-perishable goods than they need for their immediate consumption because they expect prices to go up even further. What is worse is that traders withhold stocks from the market in the hope of being able to sell these at higher prices later on. In other words, expectations of higher prices become self-fulfilling.

   Source: *The Times of India*, 24 June 2008

   Explain and draw a graph to illustrate how inflation and inflation expectations 'become self-fulfilling'.

## Macroeconomic Schools of Thought

33  **Should Congress Pass a New Stimulus Bill? No, Cut Taxes and Curb Spending Instead**

   The first stimulus was not too meager, but it was the wrong policy prescription. Anybody who studies economic history would know that government spending doesn't produce long-term, sustainable growth, and jobs. The only sure way to perk up the job market is to cut taxes permanently and rein in public spending and excessive regulation.

   Source: sgvtribune.com, 11 September 2010

   Economists from which macroeconomic school of thought would recommend a second spending stimulus and which a permanent tax cut?

## Economics in the News

34  After you have studied *Reading Between the Lines* on pp. 342–343, answer the following questions.

   a  Describe the growth of the German economy during 2010.

   b  Did Germany have a recessionary gap, an inflationary gap or full employment at the end of 2010?

   c  Use the *AS–AD* model to illustrate the German economy during 2010.

   d  Suppose that aggregate demand continues to expand rapidly through 2011 and that the ECB does not act strongly enough to dampen the expansion. Use the *AS–AD* model to illustrate the state of the German economy at the end of 2011. Indicate whether there is full employment, a recessionary gap or an inflationary gap.

   e  Suppose that aggregate demand continues to expand rapidly through 2011 but that the ECB acts strongly enough to halt the expansion. Use the *AS–AD* model to illustrate the state of the economy at the end of 2011. Indicate whether there is full employment, a recessionary gap or an inflationary gap.

# CHAPTER 15

# Growth, Inflation and Cycles

## After studying this chapter you will be able to:

- ◆ Define economic growth and explain the implications of sustained growth
- ◆ Describe the economic growth trends in the UK and other countries and regions
- ◆ Explain the sources of economic growth
- ◆ Explain how demand-pull and cost-push forces bring cycles in inflation and output
- ◆ Explain the main theories of the business cycle

In China, real GDP doubles in seven years. In the UK, it doubles every 25 years or so. Why? What makes an economic miracle like the one we see in China?

In 2011, both inflation and unemployment in the UK have risen and real GDP growth has fallen. We want rapid income growth, low unemployment and low inflation, but can we have all three at the same time? Or do we face a trade-off among them?

You'll see that we face a trade-off in the short run but not in the long run. At the end of the chapter, in *Reading Between the Lines*, you will see how China is handling this short-run trade-off between growth and inflation.

## The Basics of Economic Growth

**Economic growth** is a sustained expansion of production possibilities measured as the increase in real GDP over a given period.

Even slow economic growth maintained over many centuries brings great wealth. That is the story of human economic growth up to the Industrial Revolution that began around 1760.

Rapid economic growth maintained over only a small number of years can transform a poor nation into a rich one. That has been the story of Hong Kong, South Korea and Taiwan, and it is the story of China, India and some other Asian economies today.

The absence of growth can condemn a nation to devastating poverty. Such has been the fate of Sierra Leone, Somalia, Zambia and much of the rest of Africa.

The goal of this chapter is to help you to understand why some economies expand rapidly and why others stagnate. We'll begin by learning how to calculate the economic growth rate and by discovering the magic of sustained growth.

## Calculating Growth Rates

We express the **economic growth rate** as the annual percentage change of real GDP. To calculate this growth rate, we use the formula:

$$\text{Real GDP growth rate} = \frac{\text{Real GDP in current year} - \text{Real GDP in previous year}}{\text{Real GDP in previous year}} \times 100$$

For example, if real GDP in the current year is £1,320 billion and if real GDP in the previous year was £1,200 billion, then the economic growth rate is 10 per cent.

The growth rate of real GDP tells us how rapidly the *total* economy is expanding. This measure is useful for telling us about potential changes in the balance of economic power among nations. But it does not tell us about changes in the standard of living.

The standard of living depends on **real GDP per person** (also called *per capita* real GDP), which is real GDP divided by the population. So the contribution of real GDP growth to the change in the standard of living depends on the growth rate of real GDP per person. We use the above formula to calculate this growth rate, replacing real GDP with real GDP per person.

Suppose, for example, that in the current year, when real GDP is £1,320 billion, the population is 60.6

million. Then real GDP per person is £1,320 billion divided by 60.6 million, which equals £21,782. And suppose that in the previous year, when real GDP was £1,200 billion, the population was 60 million. Then real GDP per person in that year was £1,200 billion divided by 60 million, which equals £20,000. Use these two real GDP per person values with the growth formula above to calculate the growth rate of real GDP per person. That is,

$$\text{Real GDP per person growth rate} = \frac{£21,782 - £20,000}{£20,000} \times 100 = 8.9 \text{ per cent}$$

The growth rate of real GDP per person can also be calculated (approximately) by subtracting the population growth rate from the real GDP growth rate. In the example you've just worked through, the growth rate of real GDP is 10 per cent. The population changes from 60 million to 60.6 million, so the population growth rate is 1 per cent. The growth rate of real GDP per person is approximately equal to 10 per cent minus 1 per cent, which equals 9 per cent.

Real GDP per person grows only if real GDP grows *faster* than the population grows. If the growth rate of the population exceeds the growth of real GDP, real GDP per person falls.

## The Magic of Sustained Growth

Sustained growth of real GDP per person can transform a poor society into a wealthy one. The reason is that economic growth is like compound interest.

### Compound Interest

Suppose that you put £100 in the bank and earn 5 per cent a year interest on it. After one year, you have £105. If you leave that £105 in the bank for another year, you earn 5 per cent interest on the original £100 and on the £5 interest that you earned last year. You are now earning interest on interest! The next year, things get even better. Then you earn 5 per cent on the original £100 and on the interest earned in the first year and the second year. You are even earning interest on the interest that you earned on the interest of the first year.

Your money in the bank is growing at a rate of 5 per cent a year. Before too many years have passed, your initial deposit of £100 will have grown to £200. But after how many years?

The answer is provided by a formula called the **Rule of 70**, which states that the number of years it takes for

**Figure 15.1**   The Rule of 70

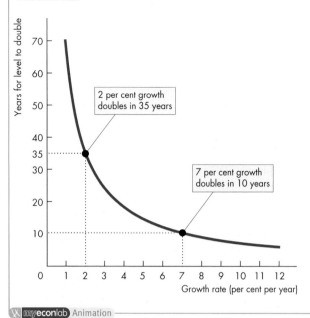

| Growth rate (per cent per year) | Years for level to double |
|:---:|:---:|
| 1 | 70.0 |
| 2 | 35.0 |
| 3 | 23.3 |
| 4 | 17.5 |
| 5 | 14.0 |
| 6 | 11.7 |
| 7 | 10.0 |
| 8 | 8.8 |
| 9 | 7.8 |
| 10 | 7.0 |
| 11 | 6.4 |
| 12 | 5.8 |

The number of years it takes for the level of a variable to double is approximately 70 divided by the annual percentage growth rate.

myeconlab Animation

the level of any variable to double is approximately 70 divided by the annual percentage growth rate of the variable. Using the Rule of 70, you can now calculate how many years it takes your £100 to become £200. With your money growing at 5 per cent per year, it will double in 70 divided by 5, which is 14 years.

## Applying the Rule of 70

The Rule of 70 applies to any variable, so it applies to real GDP per person. Figure 15.1 shows the doubling time for growth rates of 1 per cent per year to 12 per cent per year.

You can see that real GDP per person doubles in 70 years (70 divided by 1) – an average human life span – if the growth rate is 1 per cent a year. It doubles in 35 years if the growth rate is 2 per cent a year and in just 10 years if the growth rate is 7 per cent a year.

We can use the Rule of 70 to answer other questions about economic growth. For example, in 2000, US real GDP per person was approximately 8 times that of China. China's recent growth rate of real GDP per person was 7 per cent a year. If this growth rate were maintained, how long would it take China's real GDP per person to reach that of the US in 2000?

The answer, provided by the Rule of 70, is 30 years. China's real GDP per person doubles in 10 (70 divided by 7) years. It doubles again to 4 times its current level in another 10 years. And it doubles yet again to 8 times its current level in another 10 years. So after 30 years of growth at 7 per cent a year, China's real GDP per person will be 8 times its current level and equal that of the US in 2000. Of course, after 30 years, US real GDP per person would have increased, so China would still not have caught up to the US.

### Review Quiz

1   What is economic growth and how do we calculate its rate?
2   What is the relationship between the growth rate of real GDP and the growth rate of real GDP per person?
3   Use the Rule of 70 to calculate the growth rate that leads to a doubling of real GDP per person in 20 years.

You can work these questions in Study Plan 15.1 and get instant feedback.

You now know the basics of economic growth. Let's next review the trends in economic growth in the UK and around the world.

## Economic Growth Trends

You've seen the power of economic growth to increase incomes. At a 1 per cent growth rate, it takes a human life span to double the standard of living. But at a 7 per cent growth rate, the standard of living doubles every decade. How fast is our economy growing? How fast are other economies growing? Are poor countries catching up to rich ones, or do the gaps between the rich and poor persist or even widen? Let's answer these questions.

## Growth in the UK Economy

Figure 15.2 shows real GDP per person in the UK for the 100 years from 1910 to 2010. The red line is the path of real GDP and the black line is potential GDP. The trend in potential GDP per person tells us about economic growth. Fluctuations around potential GDP tell us about the business cycle.

Some extraordinary events dominate the first 50 years in this graph: two World Wars and two periods, the 1920s and the 1930s, of extreme recession and depression. The recession of 2008–2009 is clearly visible in the graph as a serious event, but it is not on the scale of severity of those interwar depressions.

For the century as a whole, the average growth rate was 1.6 per cent a year, which represents a doubling of real GDP per person every 44 years.

But the economic growth rate has varied. During the years to 1950, it was 1.2 per cent per year – too slow to double real GDP per person in the 50-year period. In the 50 years to 2010, the growth rate was 2.1 per cent per year – doubling the level in 33 years.

Growth was most rapid during the 1960s at 2.2 per cent per year and the 1980s at 2.8 per cent per year.

A major goal of this chapter is to explain why our economy grows and why the long-term growth rate varies. Another goal is to explain variations in the economic growth rate across countries. Let's look at some facts about other countries' growth rates.

**Figure 15.2** One Hundred Years of Economic Growth in the UK

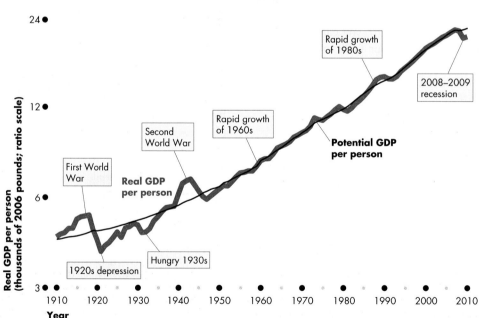

During the 100 years from 1910 to 2010, real GDP per person in the UK grew by 1.6 per cent a year, on average. The growth rate was slower during the first 50 years, at 1.2 per cent (58 years to double) than in the second 50 years at 2.1 per cent (33 years to double). Growth was fastest during the 1960s and the 1980s.

Sources of data: Charles Feinstein, *National Income Expenditure and Output of the United Kingdom 1855–1965*, Cambridge, Cambridge University Press, 1972; Office for National Statistics.

myeconlab Animation

## Real GDP Growth in the World Economy

Figure 15.3 shows real GDP per person in the US and in other countries between 1960 and 2010. Part (a) looks at the seven richest countries – known as the G7 nations. Among these nations, the US has the highest real GDP per person. In 2010, Canada had the second-highest real GDP per person, ahead of Japan and France, Germany, Italy and the UK (collectively the Europe Big 4).

During the 50 years shown here, the gaps between the US, Canada and the Europe Big 4 have been almost constant. But starting from a long way below, Japan grew fastest. It caught up to Europe in 1982 and to Canada in 1990, but during the 1990s, Japan's economy stagnated.

Many other countries are growing more slowly than, and falling further behind, the US. Figure 15.3(b) looks at some of these countries.

In Central and South America, real GDP per person was 28 per cent of the US level in 1960 and reached 30 per cent of the US level by 1980, but then growth slowed and by 2010, real GDP per person in these countries was 23 per cent of the US level.

In Eastern Europe, real GDP per person has grown more slowly than anywhere except Africa, and fell from 32 per cent of the US level in 1980 to 19 per cent in 2003 and then increased again to 22 per cent in 2010.

Real GDP per person in Africa, the world's poorest continent, fell from 10 per cent of the US level in 1960 to 5 per cent in 2007 and then increased slightly to 6 per cent in 2010.

**Figure 15.3**   Economic Growth Around the World: Catch-up or Not?

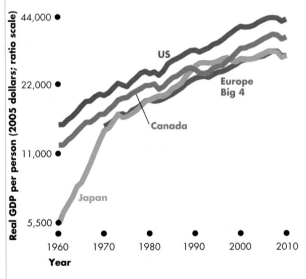

**(a) Catch-up?**

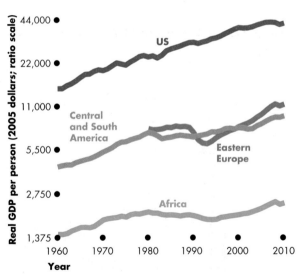

**(b) No catch-up?**

Real GDP per person has grown throughout the world. Among the rich industrial countries in part (a), real GDP per person has grown slightly faster in the US than in Canada and the four big countries of Europe (France, Germany, Italy, and the UK). Japan had the fastest growth rate before 1973 but then growth slowed and Japan's economy stagnated during the 1990s.

Among a wider range of countries shown in part (b), growth rates have been lower than that of the US. The gaps between the real GDP per person in the US and in these countries have widened. The gaps between the real GDP per person in the US and Africa and in the US and Eastern Europe have widened.

Sources of data: (1960–2007) Alan Heston, Robert Summers and Bettina Aten, Penn World Table Version 6.3, Center for International Comparisons at the University of Pennsylvania (CICUP), August 2009; and (2008–2010) International Monetary Fund, World Economic Outlook, April 2010.

myeconlab Animation

### ECONOMICS IN ACTION

## Fast Trains on the Same Track

Four Asian economies, Hong Kong, Korea, Singapore and China, have experienced spectacular growth, which you can see in Figure 1. During the 1960s, real GDP per person in these economies ranged from 3 to 28 per cent of that in the US. But by 2010, real GDP per person in Singapore and Hong Kong had surpassed that of the US.

The figure also shows that China is catching up rapidly but from a long way behind. China's real GDP per person increased from 3 per cent of the US level in 1960 to 26 per cent in 2010.

The Asian economies shown here are like fast trains running on the same track at similar speeds and with a roughly constant gap between them. Singapore and Hong Kong are hooked together as the lead train, which runs about 20 years in front of Korea and about 34 years in front of China.

Real GDP per person in Korea in 2010 was similar to that in Hong Kong in 1988, and real GDP in China in 2010 was similar to that of Hong Kong in 1976. Between 1976 and 2010, Hong Kong transformed itself from a poor developing economy into one of the richest economies in the world.

The rest of China is now doing what Hong Kong has done. China has a population 200 times that of Hong Kong and more than 4 times that of the US. So if China continues its rapid growth, the world economy will change dramatically.

As these fast-growing Asian economies catch up with the US, we can expect their growth rates to slow. But it will be surprising if China's growth rate slows much before it has closed the gap on the US.

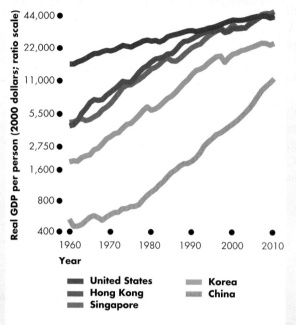

**Figure 1 Closing the Gap**

Sources of data: (1960–2007) Alan Heston, Robert Summers, and Bettina Aten, Penn World Table Version 6.3, Center for International Comparisons at the University of Pennsylvania (CICUP), August 2009; and (2008–2010) International Monetary Fund, *World Economic Outlook*, April 2010.

Even modest differences in economic growth rates sustained over a number of years bring enormous differences in the standard of living. So the facts about economic growth in the UK and around the world raise some big questions.

What are the preconditions for economic growth and what sustains it? How can we identify the sources of economic growth and measure the contribution that each source makes? What can we do to increase the sustainable rate of economic growth?

We're now going to address these questions. We start by seeing how potential GDP is determined and what makes it grow. You will see that labour productivity growth is the key to rising living standards and go on to explore the sources of this growth.

### Review Quiz

1 What has been the average growth rate in the UK over the past 100 years? In which period was growth most rapid and in which was it slowest?

2 Describe the gaps between the levels of real GDP per person in the US and other countries. For which countries are the gaps narrowing? For which countries are the gaps widening? For which countries are the gaps remaining unchanged?

3 Compare the growth rates and levels of real GDP per person in Hong Kong, Singapore, South Korea, China and the US. How far is China behind the other Asian economies?

You can work these questions in Study Plan 15.2 and get instant feedback.

# ◇ Why Real GDP Grows

Economic growth occurs when real GDP increases. But a one-shot rise in real GDP or a recovery from recession isn't economic growth. Economic growth is a sustained, year-after-year increase in potential GDP.

What makes real GDP grow? The answer is labour productivity growth. **Labour productivity** is the quantity of real GDP produced by an hour of labour. Labour must grow if real GDP per person is to grow. So what makes labour productivity grow?

## Labour Productivity Growth

The fundamental precondition for labour productivity growth is the *incentive* system created by firms, markets, property rights and money. These four social institutions are the same as those described in Chapter 2 (see pp. 41–42) that enable people to gain by specializing and trading.

It was the presence of secure intellectual property rights in Britain in the middle 1700s that got the Industrial Revolution going (see *Economics in Action* on p. 356). And it is their absence in some parts of Africa today that is keeping labour productivity stagnant.

With the preconditions for labour productivity growth in place, three things influence its pace:

◆ Physical capital growth

◆ Human capital growth

◆ Technological advances

## Physical Capital Growth

As the amount of capital per worker increases, labour productivity increases. Production processes that use hand tools can create beautiful objects, but production methods that use large amounts of capital per worker are much more productive. The accumulation of capital on farms, in textile factories, in iron foundries and steel mills, in coal mines, on building sites, in chemical plants, in car plants, in banks and insurance companies and in shopping malls has added incredibly to our labour productivity.

## Human Capital Growth

Human capital – the accumulated skill and knowledge of human beings – is the fundamental source of labour productivity growth. Human capital grows when a new discovery is made and it grows as more and more people learn how to use past discoveries.

The development of one of the most basic human skills – writing – was the source of some of the earliest major gains in productivity. The ability to keep written records made it possible to reap ever-larger gains from specialization and trade.

Later, the development of mathematics laid the foundation for the eventual extension of knowledge about physical forces and chemical and biological processes. This base of scientific knowledge was the foundation for the technological advances of the Industrial Revolution and of today's Information Revolution.

But a lot of human capital that is extremely productive is much more humble. It takes the form of millions of individuals learning and becoming remarkably more productive by repetitively doing simple production tasks.

One much-studied example of this type of human capital growth occurred in the Second World War. With no change in physical capital, thousands of workers and managers in US shipyards learned from experience and accumulated human capital that more than doubled their productivity in less than two years.

## Technological Advances

The accumulation of physical capital and human capital has made a large contribution to labour productivity growth. But technological change – the discovery and the application of new technologies – has made an even greater contribution.

Labour is many times more productive today than it was a hundred years ago but not because we have more steam engines and more horse-drawn carriages per person. Rather, it is because we have transport equipment that uses technologies that were unknown a hundred years ago and that are more productive than the old technologies were.

To reap the benefits of technological change, capital must increase. Some of the most powerful and far-reaching fundamental technologies are embodied in human capital – for example, language, writing and mathematics.

But most technologies are embodied in physical capital. For example, to reap the benefits of the internal combustion engine, millions of horse-drawn carriages had to be replaced with cars; and to reap the benefits of digital music, millions of Discmans had to be replaced by iPods and giant server farms had to be built to operate iTunes and other online shops.

## Intellectual Property Rights Propel Economic Growth

In 1760, when the states that 16 years later would become the United States of America were developing agricultural economies, England was on the cusp of an economic revolution, the Industrial Revolution.

For 70 dazzling years, technological advances in the use of steam power, the manufacture of cotton, wool, iron and steel, and in transport, accompanied by massive capital investment associated with these technologies, transformed the economy of England. Incomes rose and brought an explosion in an increasingly urbanized population.

By 1825, advances in steam technology had reached a level of sophistication that enabled Robert Stephenson to build the world's first steam-powered rail engine (the Rocket pictured here) and the birth of the world's first railroad.

Why did the Industrial Revolution happen? Why did it start in 1760? And why in England?

Economic historians say that intellectual property rights – England's patent system – provide the answer.

England's patent system began with the Statute of Monopolies of 1624, which gave inventors a monopoly to use their idea for a term of 14 years. For about 100 years, the system was used to reward friends of the royal court

rather than true inventors. But from around 1720 onward, the system started to work well. To be granted a 14-year monopoly, an inventor only had to pay the required £100 fee (about £14,000 in today's money) and register his or her invention. The inventor was not required to describe the invention in too much detail, so registering and getting a patent didn't mean sharing the invention with competitors.

This patent system, which is in all essentials the same as today's, aligned the self-interest of entrepreneurial inventors with the social interest and unleashed a flood of inventions, the most transformative of which was steam power and, by 1825, the steam locomotive.

## Policies for Achieving Faster Growth

Growth theory supported by empirical evidence tells us that to achieve faster economic growth, we must increase the growth rate of physical capital, the pace of technological advance, or the growth rate of human capital and openness to international trade.

The main suggestions for achieving these objectives are:

◆ Stimulate saving

◆ Enforce intellectual property rights

◆ Improve the quality of education

◆ Encourage international trade

Saving finances investment, so stimulating saving increases economic growth. Tax incentives can increase saving and economists claim that a consumption tax does a better job than an income tax and provides the best saving incentive.

By funding basic education and by ensuring high standards in basic skills such as language, mathematics and science, governments can contribute to a nation's growth potential.

Trade, not aid, stimulates economic growth. It works by extracting the available gains from specialization and trade. The fastest-growing nations are those most open to trade.

### ◆ Review Quiz

1 What are the preconditions for labour productivity growth?
2 What are the three influences on the pace of labour productivity growth?
3 What are the five suggestions for stimulating labour productivity growth?

You can work these questions in Study Plan 15.3 and get instant feedback.

## Inflation Cycles

In the long run, inflation is a monetary phenomenon. It occurs if the quantity of money grows faster than potential GDP. But in the short run, many factors can start an inflation, and real GDP and the price level interact. To study these interactions, we distinguish between two sources of inflation:

◆ Demand-pull inflation
◆ Cost-push inflation

## Demand-pull Inflation

An inflation that results from an initial increase in aggregate demand is called **demand-pull inflation**. Demand-pull inflation can be kicked off by any of the factors that change aggregate demand. Examples are a cut in the interest rate, an increase in the quantity of money, an increase in government expenditure, a tax cut, an increase in exports, or an increase in investment stimulated by an increase in expected future profits.

### Initial Effect of an Increase in Aggregate Demand

Suppose that last year the price level was 110 and both real GDP and potential GDP were £1,300 billion. Figure 15.4(a) illustrates this situation. The aggregate demand curve is $AD_0$, the short-run aggregate supply curve is $SAS_0$ and the long-run aggregate supply curve is $LAS$.

Now aggregate demand increases and the aggregate demand curve shifts rightward to $AD_1$. Such a situation arises if, for example, the Bank of England lowers the interest rate or UK exports increase.

With no change in potential GDP and with no change in the money wage rate, the long-run aggregate supply curve and the short-run aggregate supply curve remain at $LAS$ and $SAS_0$, respectively.

The price level rises to 113 and real GDP increases above potential GDP to £1,350 billion. The economy experiences a 2.7 per cent rise in the price level (a price level of 113 compared with 110 in the previous year) and a rapid expansion of real GDP. Unemployment falls below its natural rate. The next step in the unfolding story is a rise in the money wage rate.

**Figure 15.4**   A Demand-pull Rise in the Price Level

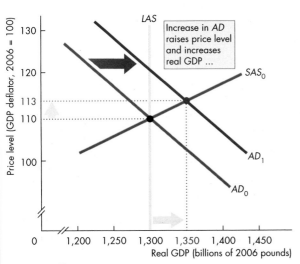

**(a) Initial effect**

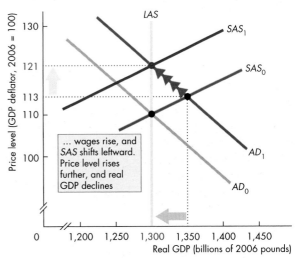

**(b) The money wage adjusts**

In part (a), the aggregate demand curve is $AD_0$, the short-run aggregate supply curve is $SAS_0$ and the long-run aggregate supply curve is $LAS$. The price level is 110 and real GDP is £1,300 billion, which equals potential GDP. Aggregate demand increases to $AD_1$. The price level rises to 113 and real GDP increases to £1,350 billion.

In part (b), starting from an above full-employment equilibrium, the money wage rate begins to rise and the short-run aggregate supply curve shifts leftward towards $SAS_1$. The price level rises further and real GDP returns to potential GDP.

## Money Wage Response

Real GDP cannot remain above potential GDP for ever. With unemployment below its natural rate, there is a shortage of labour. In this situation, the money wage rate begins to rise. As the money wage rate rises, short-run aggregate supply starts to decrease and the *SAS* curve starts to shift leftward. The price level rises further and real GDP begins to decrease.

With no further change in aggregate demand – the aggregate demand curve remains at $AD_1$ – this process comes to an end when the short-run aggregate supply curve has shifted to $SAS_1$ in Figure 15.4(b). At this time, the price level has increased to 121 and real GDP has returned to potential GDP of £1,300 billion, the level from which it started.

## A Demand-pull Inflation Process

The events that we've just studied bring *a one-time rise in the price level*, not inflation. For inflation to occur, aggregate demand must persistently increase.

The only way in which aggregate demand can persistently increase is if the quantity of money persistently increases. Suppose the government has a budget deficit that it finances by selling bonds. Also suppose that the Bank of England buys these bonds. When the Bank of England buys bonds, it creates more money. If the Bank of England responds continually to the budget deficit, aggregate demand increases year after year. The aggregate demand curve keeps shifting rightward. This persistent increase in aggregate demand puts continual upward pressure on the price level. The economy now experiences demand-pull inflation.

Figure 15.5 illustrates the process of demand-pull inflation. The starting point is the same as that shown in Figure 15.4. The aggregate demand curve is $AD_0$ and the short-run aggregate supply curve is $SAS_0$. Real GDP is £1,300 billion and the price level is 110. Aggregate demand increases, shifting the aggregate demand curve to $AD_1$. Real GDP increases to £1,350 billion and the price level rises to 113. The economy is at an above full-employment equilibrium. There is a shortage of labour and the money wage rate rises. The short-run aggregate supply curve shifts leftward to $SAS_1$. The price level rises to 121 and real GDP returns to potential GDP.

But the Bank of England increases the quantity of money again and aggregate demand continues to increase. The aggregate demand curve shifts rightward to $AD_2$. The price level rises further to 125 and real GDP again exceeds potential GDP at £1,350 billion. Yet

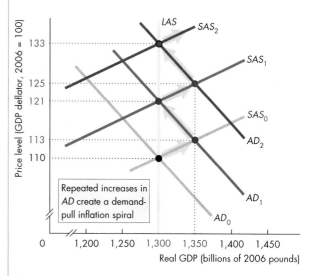

**Figure 15.5** A Demand-pull Inflation Spiral

Repeated increases in *AD* create a demand-pull inflation spiral

Each time the quantity of money increases, aggregate demand increases and the aggregate demand curve shifts rightward from $AD_0$ to $AD_1$ to $AD_2$ and so on.

Each time real GDP goes above potential GDP, the money wage rate rises and the short-run aggregate supply curve shifts leftward from $SAS_0$ to $SAS_1$ to $SAS_2$ and so on.

The price level rises from 110 to 113, 121, 125, 133 and so on. There is a perpetual demand-pull inflation. Real GDP fluctuates between £1,300 billion and £1,350 billion.

again, the money wage rate rises and decreases short-run aggregate supply. The *SAS* curve shifts to $SAS_2$ and the price level rises further to 133. As the quantity of money continues to grow, aggregate demand increases and the price level rises in an ongoing demand-pull inflation process.

## Demand-pull Inflation in Liverpool

You may better understand the inflation process that we've just described by considering what is going on in an individual part of the economy, such as a Liverpool soft drinks factory.

### Initial Increase in Demand

Initially, when aggregate demand increases, the demand for soft drinks increases and the price of soft drinks rises. Faced with a higher price, the soft drinks factory works overtime and increases production. Conditions are good for workers in Liverpool and the soft drinks factory finds it hard to hang on to its best people. To do so it has to offer higher money wages. As money wages increase, so do the soft drinks factory's costs.

### Aggregate Demand

What happens next depends on what happens to aggregate demand. If aggregate demand remains unchanged, the firm's costs are increasing but the price of soft drinks is not increasing as quickly as the factory's costs. Production is scaled back. Eventually, the money wage rate and costs increase by the same percentage as the price of soft drinks. In real terms, the soft drinks factory is in the same situation as it was initially – before the increase in aggregate demand. The soft drinks factory produces the same quantity of soft drinks and employs the same amount of labour as before the increase in aggregate demand.

But if aggregate demand continues to increase, so does the demand for soft drinks and the price of soft drink rises at the same rate as the money wage rate. The soft drinks factory continues to operate above full employment and there is a persistent shortage of labour. Prices and wages chase each other upward in an unending spiral.

### Demand-pull Inflation in the UK

A demand-pull inflation like the one you've just studied occurred in the UK during the 1970s.

In 1972–1973, the government pursued an expansionary monetary and fiscal policy: its goal was to lower the unemployment rate and boost the rate of economic growth. The aggregate demand curve shifted rightward, the price level increased quickly and real GDP moved above potential GDP. The money wage rate started to rise more quickly and the short-run aggregate supply curve shifted leftward.

The Bank of England responded with a further increase in the growth rate of the quantity of money. Aggregate demand increased even more quickly and a demand-pull inflation spiral unfolded.

By the mid-1970s, the inflation rate had reached more than 20 per cent a year. Contrary to the government's goal, the growth rate of real GDP didn't increase and the unemployment rate didn't decrease. On the contrary, the late 1970s were years of extremely high unemployment and slow real GDP growth.

You've seen how demand-pull inflation arises. Let's now see how an aggregate supply shock brings cost-push inflation.

## Cost-push Inflation

An inflation that is kicked off by an increase in costs is called **cost-push inflation**. The two main sources of increases in costs are:

1  An increase in the money wage rate

2  An increase in the money prices of raw materials

At a given price level, the higher the cost of production, the smaller is the amount that firms are willing to produce. So if the money wage rate rises or if the prices of raw materials (for example, oil) rise, firms decrease their supply of goods and services. Aggregate supply decreases, and the short-run aggregate supply curve shifts leftward.[1]

Let's trace the effects of such a decrease in short-run aggregate supply on the price level and real GDP.

### Initial Effect of a Decrease in Aggregate Supply

Suppose that last year the price level was 110 and real GDP was £1,300 billion. Potential real GDP was also £1,300 billion. Figure 15.6(a) illustrates this situation. The aggregate demand curve was $AD_0$, the short-run aggregate supply curve was $SAS_0$ and the long-run aggregate supply curve was $LAS$.

Now the world's oil producers form a price-fixing organization that strengthens their market power and increases the relative price of oil. They raise the price of oil, and this action decreases short-run aggregate supply. The short-run aggregate supply curve shifts leftward to $SAS_1$. The price level rises to 117 and real GDP decreases to £1,250 billion. The economy is at a below full-employment equilibrium and there is a recessionary gap.

The event that we've just described is a *one-time rise in the price level*. It is not inflation. In fact, a supply shock on its own cannot cause inflation. Something more must happen to enable a one-time supply shock, which causes a one-time rise in the price level, to be converted into a process of ongoing inflation. The quantity of money must persistently increase. Sometimes it does increase, as you will now see.

---

[1] Some cost-push forces, such as an increase in the price of oil accompanied by a decrease in the availability of oil, can also decrease long-run aggregate supply. We'll ignore such effects here and examine cost-push factors that change only short-run aggregate supply.

**Figure 15.6** A Cost-push Rise in the Price Level

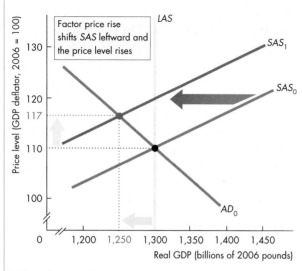

**(a) Initial cost push**

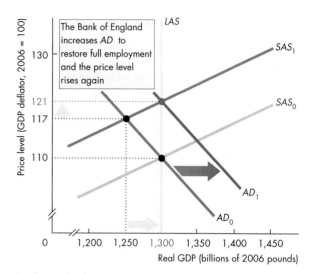

**(b) The Bank of England responds**

Initially, the aggregate demand curve is $AD_0$, the short-run aggregate supply curve is $SAS_0$ and the long-run aggregate supply curve is *LAS*. A decrease in aggregate supply shifts the short-run aggregate supply curve to $SAS_1$. The price level rises to 117 and real GDP decreases to £1,250 billion. The economy experiences a one-time rise in the price level.

In part (b), if the Bank of England responds by lowering the interest rate and increasing aggregate demand to restore full employment, the aggregate demand curve shifts rightward to $AD_1$. The economy returns to full employment, but the price level rises further to 121.

myeconlab Animation

## Aggregate Demand Response

When real GDP decreases, unemployment rises above its natural rate. In such a situation, there is often an outcry of concern and a call for action to restore full employment. Suppose that the Bank of England cuts the interest rate and increases the quantity of money. Aggregate demand increases. In Figure 15.6(b), the aggregate demand curve shifts rightward to $AD_1$ and full employment is restored. But the price level rises further to 121.

## A Cost-push Inflation Process

The oil producers now see the prices of everything they buy increasing, so oil producers increase the price of oil again to restore its new high relative price. Figure 15.7 continues the story. The short-run aggregate supply curve now shifts to $SAS_2$. The price level rises and real GDP decreases.

The price level rises further, to 129, and real GDP decreases to £1,250 billion. Unemployment increases above its natural rate.

If the Bank of England responds yet again with an increase in the quantity of money, aggregate demand increases and the aggregate demand curve shifts to $AD_2$. The price level rises even higher – to 133 – and full employment is again restored. A cost-push inflation spiral results. The combination of a rising price level and falling real GDP is called **stagflation**.

You can see that the Bank of England has a dilemma. If it does not respond when producers raise the oil price, the economy remains below full employment. If it lowers the interest rate and increases the quantity of money to restore full employment, it invites another oil price hike that will call forth yet a further increase in the quantity of money.

If the Bank of England responds to each oil price hike by increasing the quantity of money, inflation will rage along at a rate decided by oil producers. But if the Bank of England keeps the lid on money growth, the economy remains below full employment.

**Figure 15.7** A Cost-push Inflation Spiral

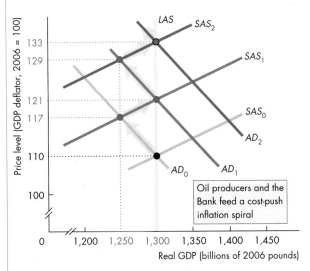

When a cost increase (for example, an increase in the world oil price) decreases short-run aggregate supply from $SAS_0$ to $SAS_1$, the price level rises to 117 and real GDP decreases to £1,250 billion. The central bank responds with an increase in the quantity of money that shifts the aggregate demand curve from $AD_0$ to $AD_1$. The price level rises again to 121 and real GDP returns to £1,300 billion. A further cost increase occurs, which shifts the short-run aggregate supply curve again, this time to $SAS_2$. Real GDP decreases again and the price level now rises to 129. The central bank responds again and the cost-push inflation spiral continues.

myeconlab Animation ————————————◆

## Cost-push Inflation in Liverpool

What is going on in the Liverpool soft drinks factory when the economy is experiencing cost-push inflation?

When the oil price increases, the costs of producing soft drinks rise. These higher costs decrease the supply of soft drinks, increase the price and decrease the quantity produced. The factory lays off some workers.

This situation persists until either the Bank of England increases aggregate demand or the price of oil falls. If the Bank increases aggregate demand, the demand for soft drinks increases and so does the price. The higher price brings higher profits and the factory increases its production. It rehires the laid-off workers.

## Cost-push Inflation in the UK

A cost-push inflation like the one you've just studied occurred in the UK during the 1970s. In 1974 the Organization of the Petroleum Exporting Countries

(OPEC) raised the price of oil fourfold. The higher oil price decreased aggregate supply, which caused the price level to rise more quickly and real GDP to shrink. The Bank of England then faced a dilemma: would it increase the quantity of money and accommodate the cost-push forces or would it keep aggregate demand growth in check by limiting money growth?

In 1975, 1976 and 1977, the Bank of England repeatedly allowed the quantity of money to grow and inflation proceeded rapidly. In 1979 and 1980, OPEC was again able to push oil prices higher. On that occasion, the Bank of England decided not to respond to the oil price hike with an increase in the quantity of money. The result was a recession but also, eventually, a fall in inflation.

## Expected Inflation

If inflation is expected, the fluctuations in real GDP that accompany demand-pull and cost-push inflation that you've just studied don't occur. Instead, inflation proceeds as it does in the long run, with real GDP equal to potential GDP and unemployment at its natural rate. Figure 15.8 explains why.

Suppose that last year the aggregate demand curve was $AD_0$, the aggregate supply curve was $SAS_0$ and the long-run aggregate supply curve was $LAS$. The price level was 110 and real GDP was £1,300 billion, which is also potential GDP.

To keep things as simple as possible, suppose that potential GDP does not change, so the $LAS$ curve does not shift. Also suppose that aggregate demand *is expected to increase* to $AD_1$.

In anticipation of this increase in aggregate demand, the money wage rate rises and the short-run aggregate supply curve shifts leftward. If the money wage rate rises by the same percentage as the price level is expected to rise, the short-run aggregate supply curve for next year is $SAS_1$.

If aggregate demand turns out to be the same as expected, the aggregate demand curve is $AD_1$. The short-run aggregate supply curve, $SAS_1$, and $AD_1$ determine the actual price level at 121. Between last year and this year, the price level increased from 110 to 121 and the economy experienced an inflation rate equal to that expected. If this inflation is ongoing, aggregate demand increases (as expected) in the following year and the aggregate demand curve shifts to $AD_2$. The money wage rate rises to reflect the expected inflation and the short-run aggregate supply curve shifts to $SAS_2$. The price level rises, as expected, to 133.

**Figure 15.8** Expected Inflation

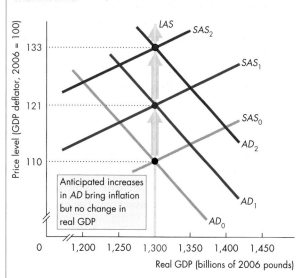

Potential real GDP is £1,300 billion. Last year, the aggregate demand curve was $AD_0$ and the short-run aggregate supply curve was $SAS_0$. The actual price level was the same as the expected price level: 110.

This year, aggregate demand is expected to increase to $AD_1$. The expectation of the price level changes from 110 to 121. As a result, the money wage rate rises and the short-run aggregate supply curve shifts to $SAS_1$.

If aggregate demand actually increases as expected, the actual aggregate demand curve $AD_1$ is the same as the expected aggregate demand curve. Real GDP is £1,300 billion and the actual price level is 121. The inflation is correctly expected.

Next year, the process continues with aggregate demand increasing as expected to $AD_2$ and the money wage rate rising to shift the short-run aggregate supply curve to $SAS_2$. Again, real GDP remains at £1,300 billion and the price level rises, as expected, to 133.

myeconlab Animation

What caused this inflation? The immediate answer is that because people expected inflation, the money wage rate increased and the price level increased. But the expectation was correct. Aggregate demand was expected to increase and it did increase. It is the actual and expected increase in aggregate demand that caused the inflation.

An expected inflation at full employment is exactly the process that the quantity theory of money predicts. To review the quantity theory of money, see Chapter 13, pp. 314–315.

This broader account of the inflation process and its short-run effects show why the quantity theory of money doesn't explain the fluctuations in inflation. The economy follows the course described in Figure 15.8, but as predicted by the quantity theory, only if aggregate demand growth is forecasted correctly.

## Forecasting Inflation

To anticipate inflation, people must forecast it. Some economists who work for macroeconomic forecasting agencies, banks, insurance companies, trades unions and large companies specialize in inflation forecasting. The best forecast available is one that is based on all the relevant information and is called a **rational expectation**. A rational expectation is not necessarily a correct forecast. It is simply the best forecast with the information available. It will often turn out to be wrong, but no other forecast that could have been made with the information available could do better.

## Inflation and the Business Cycle

When the inflation forecast is correct, the economy operates at full employment. If aggregate demand grows faster than expected, real GDP rises above potential GDP, the inflation rate exceeds its expected rate and the economy behaves like it does in a demand-pull inflation. If aggregate demand grows more slowly than expected, real GDP falls below potential GDP and the inflation rate slows.

Let's now take a closer and more systematic look at the business cycle and the theories about what causes cycles in economic activity.

### Review Quiz

1   How does demand-pull inflation begin?
2   What must happen to create a demand-pull inflation spiral?
3   How does cost-push inflation begin?
4   What must happen to create a cost-push inflation spiral?
5   What is stagflation and why does cost-push inflation cause stagflation?
6   How does expected inflation occur?
7   How do the price level and real GDP change if the forecast of inflation is incorrect?

You can work these questions in Study Plan 15.4 and get instant feedback.

## The Business Cycle

The business cycle is easy to describe but hard to explain and business cycle theory remains unsettled and a source of controversy. We'll look at two approaches to understanding the business cycle:

◆ Mainstream business cycle theory

◆ Real business cycle theory

## Mainstream Business Cycle Theory

The mainstream business cycle theory is that potential GDP grows at a steady rate while aggregate demand grows at a fluctuating rate. Because the money wage rate is sticky, if aggregate demand grows faster than potential GDP, real GDP moves above potential GDP and an inflationary gap emerges. And if aggregate demand grows more slowly than potential GDP, real GDP moves below potential GDP and a recessionary gap emerges. If aggregate demand decreases, real GDP also decreases in a recession.

Figure 15.9 illustrates this business cycle theory. Initially, actual and potential GDP are £1,000 billion. The long-run aggregate supply curve is $LAS_0$, the aggregate demand curve is $AD_0$ and the price level is 100. The economy is at full employment at point $A$.

An expansion occurs when potential GDP increases and the $LAS$ curve shifts rightward to $LAS_1$. During an expansion, aggregate demand also increases, and usually by more than potential GDP, so the price level rises. Assume that in the current expansion, the price level is expected to rise to 110 and the money wage rate has been set based on that expectation. The short-run aggregate supply curve is $SAS_1$.

If aggregate demand increases to $AD_1$, real GDP increases to £1,300 billion, the new level of potential GDP, and the price level rises, as expected, to 110. The economy remains at full employment but now at point $B$.

If aggregate demand increases more slowly to $AD_2$, real GDP grows by less than potential GDP and the economy moves to point $C$, with real GDP at £1,250 billion and the price level at 107. Real GDP growth is slower and inflation is lower than expected.

If aggregate demand increases more quickly to $AD_3$, real GDP grows by more than potential GDP and the economy moves to point $D$, with real GDP at £1,350 billion and the price level at 113. Real GDP growth is faster and inflation is higher than expected.

Growth, inflation and the business cycle arise from the relentless increases in potential GDP, faster (on average) increases in aggregate demand and fluctuations in the pace of aggregate demand growth.

**Figure 15.9**    The Mainstream Business Cycle Theory

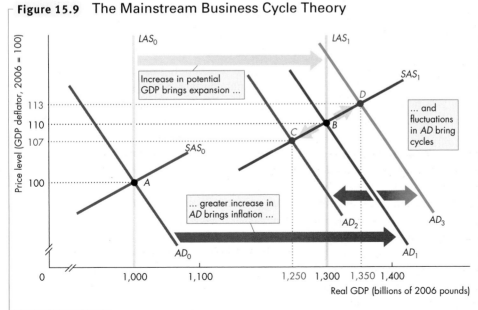

In a business cycle expansion, potential GDP increases and the *LAS* curve shifts rightward from *LAS*₀ to *LAS*₁. A greater than expected increase in aggregate demand brings inflation.

If the aggregate demand curve shifts to *AD*₁, the economy remains at full employment. If the aggregate demand curve shifts to *AD*₂, a recessionary gap arises. If the aggregate demand curve shifts to *AD*₃, an inflationary gap arises.

This mainstream theory comes in a number of special forms that differ regarding the source of fluctuations in aggregate demand growth and the source of money wage stickiness.

### Keynesian Cycle Theory

In *Keynesian* cycle theory, fluctuations in investment driven by fluctuations in business confidence – summarized by the phrase 'animal spirits' – are the main source of fluctuations in aggregate demand.

### Monetarist Cycle Theory

In *monetarist* cycle theory, fluctuations in both investment and consumption expenditure, driven by fluctuations in the growth rate of the quantity of money, are the main source of fluctuations in aggregate demand.

Both the Keynesian and monetarist cycle theories simply assume that the money wage rate is rigid and don't explain that rigidity.

Two newer theories seek to explain money wage rate rigidity and to be more careful about working out its consequences.

### New Classical Cycle Theory

In *new classical* cycle theory, the rational expectation of the price level, which is determined by potential GDP and expected aggregate demand, determines the money wage rate and the position of the *SAS* curve. In this theory, only unexpected fluctuations in aggregate demand bring fluctuations in real GDP around potential GDP.

### New Keynesian Cycle Theory

The *new Keynesian* cycle theory emphasizes the fact that today's money wage rates were negotiated at many past dates, which means that past rational expectations of the current price level influence the money wage rate and the position of the *SAS* curve. In this theory, both unexpected and currently expected fluctuations in aggregate demand bring fluctuations in real GDP around potential GDP.

The mainstream cycle theories don't rule out the possibility that occasionally an aggregate supply shock might occur. An oil price rise, a widespread drought, a major hurricane, or another natural disaster could, for example, bring a recession. But supply shocks are not the normal source of fluctuations in the mainstream theories. In contrast, real business cycle theory puts supply shocks at centre stage.

## Real Business Cycle Theory

The newest theory of the business cycle, known as **real business cycle theory** (or RBC theory), regards random fluctuations in productivity as the main source of economic fluctuations. These productivity fluctuations are assumed to result mainly from fluctuations in the pace of technological change, but they might also have other sources, such as international disturbances, climate fluctuations, or natural disasters. The origins of RBC theory can be traced to the rational expectations revolution set off by Robert E. Lucas, Jr., but the first demonstrations of the power of this theory were given by Edward Prescott and Finn Kydland and by John Long and Charles Plosser. Today, RBC theory is part of a broad research agenda called dynamic general equilibrium analysis, and hundreds of young macroeconomists do research on this topic.

We'll explore RBC theory by looking first at its impulse and then at the mechanism that converts that impulse into a cycle in real GDP.

### The RBC Impulse

The impulse in RBC theory is the growth rate of productivity that results from technological change. RBC theorists believe this impulse to be generated mainly by the process of research and development that leads to the creation and use of new technologies.

To isolate the RBC theory impulse, economists measure the change in the combined productivity of capital and labour. Figure 15.10 shows the RBC impulse for the UK from 1971 to 2010. You can see that fluctuations in productivity growth are closely correlated with real GDP fluctuations.

The pace of technological change and productivity growth is not constant. Sometimes productivity growth speeds up, sometimes it slows and occasionally it even *falls* – labour and capital become less productive, on average. A period of rapid productivity growth brings a business cycle expansion, and a slowdown or fall in productivity triggers a recession (as it did in 2009).

It is easy to understand why technological change brings productivity growth. But how does technological change decrease productivity? All technological change eventually increases productivity. But if, initially, technological change makes a sufficient amount of existing capital – especially human capital – obsolete, productivity can temporarily fall. At such a time, more jobs are destroyed than created and more businesses fail than start up.

**Figure 15.10**    The Real Business Cycle Impulse

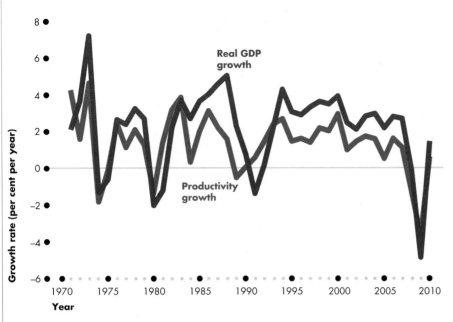

The real business cycle impulse is fluctuations in the growth rate of productivity that are caused by changes in technology.

Productivity fluctuations are correlated with real GDP fluctuations and most recessions are associated with a slowdown in productivity growth. The 2008–2009 recession is a clear example.

Sources of data: Office for National Statistics; and the authors' calculations.

myeconlab  Animation

## The RBC Mechanism

Two effects follow from a change in productivity that sparks an expansion or a contraction:

1   Investment demand changes
2   The demand for labour changes

Technological change makes some existing capital obsolete and temporarily decreases productivity. Firms expect the future profits to fall and see their labour productivity falling. With lower profit expectations, they cut back their purchases of new capital, and with lower labour productivity, they plan to lay off some workers. So the initial effect of a temporary fall in productivity is a decrease in investment demand and a decrease in the demand for labour.

According to RBC theory, the quantity of labour supplied responds to the change in demand and a cyclical rise in the real wage rate. People decide when to work by doing a cost–benefit calculation. They compare the return from working in the current period with the expected return from working in a later period. You make such a comparison when you decide to increase your study hours during the few days before an important exam. Close to the exam, the return to studying is greater than the return when the exam is a long time

away. So during the term, you take time off for the movies and other leisure pursuits, but at exam time, you study every evening and weekend.

The forces that drive the business cycle in RBC theory are the same as those that generate economic growth: technological change and the response to it.

### Review Quiz

1   Explain the mainstream theory of the business cycle.
2   What are the four special forms of the mainstream theory of the business cycle and how do they differ?
3   According to RBC theory, what is the source of the business cycle? What is the role of fluctuations in the rate of technological change?

You can work these questions in Study Plan 15.5 and get instant feedback.

You can complete your study of growth, inflation and economic fluctuations in *Reading Between the Lines* on pp. 366–367, which looks at inflationary pressures in China and the tough trade-off faced by that fast-changing economy.

# Reading Between the Lines

# China's Inflation–Growth Trade-off

The Financial Times, 21 November 2010

## China's Twilight Economy Piles Pressure on Inflation Fight

FT

James Kynge

China has lambasted the US for its decision to launch another $600bn in monetary easing, fearing that this round of 'quantitative easing' may feed the flood of money rushing into mainland China from overseas. But while capital inflows are a problem for Beijing, there should be no doubt that China's swelling money supply and resurgent inflation are primarily 'Made in China'.

Bank lending . . . is looking increasingly likely to bust through the government's solemnly decreed 2010 target. . . . But more worrying . . . are the inflationary pressures springing from a subterranean world of informal finance. Although the size of China's underground financial system is uncertain, it is unlikely to be modest. . . .

Thus the total assets contained within China's twilight economy may well be in excess of Rmb6,000bn.

If this number is added to the 2010 official lending target of Rmb7,500bn, then it becomes clear that China's 2009 record lending splurge was no 'one-off' and may well be exceeded by this year's level.

It is pressures caused by such ballooning money supply, coupled with various structural influences inherent in the take-off of China's rural economy, that are the prime causes of inflation.

China knows that it cannot bring discipline to its huge, unregulated underground economy without sacrificing growth, and yet unless it grapples with the root causes of money supply, it may fail to tame inflation.

## The Essence of the Story

◆ China's inflation rose throughout 2010.

◆ China criticizes the US for its policy of 'quantitative easing', which is flooding the world economy with money.

◆ Some of this money has gone to China and increased aggregate demand.

◆ Most of the increase in money in China comes from China's banks and its large informal banking system.

# Economic Analysis

◆ China's inflation rate during 2010 was on an upward trend as you can see in Figure 1.

◆ Figure 2 shows the main source of the increase in inflation: a money growth rate that vastly exceeds the growth rate of real GDP.

◆ You can see in Figure 2 that the inflation rate and real GDP growth rate fluctuate in sympathy with the fluctuations in money growth but with a time lag.

◆ The news article notes that in addition to the growth of money there is a large growth in credit in the informal parts of China's economy.

◆ China is experiencing both demand-pull and cost-push inflation forces.

◆ Figure 3 illustrates these forces by showing what has been happening to China's aggregate demand and aggregate supply.

◆ In 2008, aggregate demand was $AD_{08}$ and short-run aggregate supply was $SAS_{08}$. Real GDP was ¥26 trillion (in 2005 prices) and the price level was 120 (2005 = 100).

◆ In 2010, potential GDP was ¥31 trillion and the long-run aggregate supply curve was $LAS_{10}$.

◆ Between 2008 and 2010, the quantity of money increased, credit grew and a global expansion increased the demand for China's exports. Aggregate demand increased and the $AD$ curve shifted rightward to $AD_{10}$.

◆ Commodity prices and the money wage rate increased, which decreased short-run aggregate supply and the $SAS$ curve shifted leftward to $SAS_{10}$.

◆ To slow inflation, China must slow the money growth rate.

◆ This action will slow the rate of increase of aggregate demand and will temporarily slow the growth rate of real GDP.

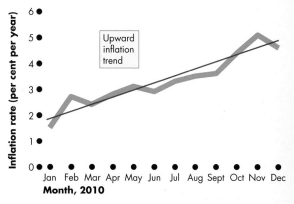

Figure 1  China's inflation in 2010

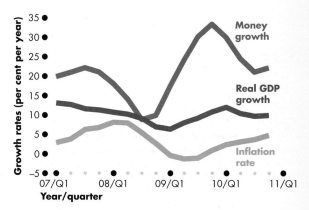

Figure 2  Money growth, real GDP growth and inflation

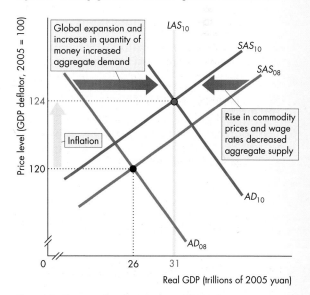

Figure 3  Changes in aggregate supply and aggregate demand

## SUMMARY

## Key Points

### The Basics of Economic Growth
(pp. 350–351)

◆ Economic growth is the sustained expansion of production possibilities and is measured as the annual percentage growth rate of real GDP.

◆ The Rule of 70 tells us the number of years in which real GDP doubles – 70 divided by the annual percentage growth rate.

Working Problems 1 to 5 will give you a better understanding of the basics of economic growth.

### Economic Growth Trends (pp. 352–354)

◆ Real GDP per person in the UK has grown at an average rate of 1.6 per cent per year. Growth was more rapid during the 1960s and the 1980s.

◆ The gap in real GDP per person between the US and Central and South America has persisted. The gaps between the US and Hong Kong, Korea and China have narrowed. The gaps between the US and Africa and Central Europe have widened.

Working Problem 6 will give you a better understanding of economic growth trends.

### Why Real GDP Grows (pp. 355–356)

◆ Labour productivity growth makes real GDP per person and the standard of living grow.

◆ Labour productivity growth requires an incentive system created by firms, markets, property rights and money.

◆ The sources of labour productivity growth are growth of physical capital and human capital and advances in technology.

◆ Policies for achieving faster growth include stimulating saving and research and development, encouraging international trade and improving the quality of education.

Working Problems 7 and 8 will give you a better understanding of why labour productivity grows.

### Inflation Cycles (pp. 357–362)

◆ Demand-pull inflation is triggered by an increase in aggregate demand and fuelled by ongoing money growth. Real GDP cycles above full employment.

◆ Cost-push inflation is triggered by an increase in the money wage rate or raw material prices and is fuelled by ongoing money growth. Real GDP cycles below full employment in a stagflation.

◆ When the forecast of inflation is correct, real GDP remains at potential GDP.

Working Problems 9 to 19 will give you a better understanding of inflation cycles.

### The Business Cycle (pp. 363–365)

◆ The mainstream business cycle theory explains the business cycle as fluctuations of real GDP around potential GDP and as arising from a steady expansion of potential GDP combined with an expansion of aggregate demand at a fluctuating rate.

◆ Real business cycle theory explains the business cycle as fluctuations of potential GDP, which arise from fluctuations in the influence of technological change on productivity growth.

Working Problem 20 will give you a better understanding of the business cycle.

## Key Terms

Cost-push inflation, 359
Demand-pull inflation, 357
Economic growth, 350
Economic growth rate, 350
Labour productivity, 355
Rational expectation, 362
Real business cycle theory, 364
Real GDP per person, 350
Rule of 70, 350
Stagflation, 360

# STUDY PLAN PROBLEMS AND APPLICATIONS

myeconlab   You can work Problems 1 to 20 in MyEconLab Chapter 15 Study Plan and get instant feedback.

## The Basics of Economic Growth
(Study Plan 15.1)

**1** Brazil's real GDP was 1,360 trillion reais in 2009 and 1,434 trillion reais in 2010. Brazil's population was 191.5 million in 2009 and 193.3 million in 2010. Calculate:

  **a** The economic growth rate.

  **b** The growth rate of real GDP per person.

  **c** The approximate number of years it takes for real GDP per person in Brazil to double if the 2010 economic growth rate and population growth rate are maintained.

**2** Japan's real GDP was 525 trillion yen in 2009 and 535 trillion yen in 2010. Japan's population was 127.6 million in 2009 and 127.5 million in 2010. Calculate:

  **a** The economic growth rate.

  **b** The growth rate of real GDP per person.

  **c** The approximate number of years it takes for real GDP per person in Japan to double if the real GDP economic growth rate returns to 3 per cent a year and the population growth rate is maintained.

Use the following data to work Problems 3 and 4.

China's real GDP per person was 9,280 yuan in 2009 and 10,110 yuan in 2010. India's real GDP per person was 30,880 rupees in 2009 and 32,160 rupees in 2010.

**3** By maintaining their current growth rates, which country will double its 2010 standard of living first?

**4** The population of China is growing at 1 per cent a year and the population of India is growing at 1.4 per cent a year. Calculate the growth rate of real GDP in each country.

**5** **China's Economy Picks Up Speed**

China's trend growth rate of real GDP per person was 2.2 per cent a year before 1980 and 8.7 per cent a year after 1980. In the year to August 2009, China's output increased by 11.3 per cent.

        Source: World Economic Outlook and
        FT.com, 14 September 2009

  **a** Distinguish between a rise in China's economic growth rate and a temporary cyclical expansion.

  **b** How long, at the current growth rate, will it take for China to double its real GDP per person?

## Economic Growth Trends (Study Plan 15.2)

**6** China was the largest economy for centuries because everyone had the same type of economy – subsistence – and so the country with the most people would be economically biggest. Then the Industrial Revolution sent the West on a more prosperous path. Now the world is returning to a common economy, this time technology- and information-based, so once again population triumphs.

  **a** Why was China the world's largest economy until 1890?

  **b** Why did the US surpass China in 1890 to become the world's largest economy?

## Why Real GDP Grows (Study Plan 15.3)

**7** **Labour Productivity on the Rise**

During the year ended June 2009, US non-farm sector output fell 5.5 per cent as labour productivity increased 1.9 per cent – the largest increase since 2003. But in the manufacturing sector, output fell 9.8 per cent as labour productivity increased by 4.9 per cent – the largest increase since the first quarter of 2005.

        Source: bls.gov/news.release, 11 August 2009

In both sectors, output fell while labour productivity increased. Did the quantity of labour (aggregate hours) increase or decrease? In which sector was the change in the quantity of labour larger?

**8** List and explain the factors that make labour productivity grow and suggest reasons that might explain why China has faster labour productivity growth than the UK and the UK has faster labour productivity growth than South Sudan.

## Inflation Cycles (Study Plan 15.4)

**9** **Pakistan: Is it Cost-Push Inflation?**

With CPI already spiking 11.8 per cent for the first ten months of the fiscal year, the average CPI inflation for the same period last year stood at 22.35 per cent. Some economists insist the current bout of inflationary pressures is spawned by increasing prices of fuel, food, raw materials, transportation, construction materials, elimination of energy subsidies, etc as indicated by the spike in the wholesale price index (WPI), which rose 21.99 per cent in April from a year earlier.

        Source: *Daily the Pak Banker*, 22 May 2010

Explain what type of inflation Pakistan is experiencing.

Use the following figure to work Problems 10 to 13. In each question, the economy starts out on the curves labelled $AD_0$ and $SAS_0$.

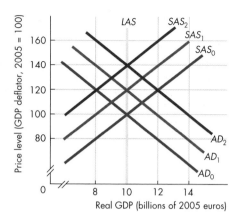

**10** Some events occur and the economy experiences a demand-pull inflation.

  **a** List the events that might cause a demand-pull inflation.

  **b** Describe the initial effects of a demand-pull inflation.

  **c** Describe what happens as a demand-pull inflation spiral proceeds.

**11** Some events occur and the economy experiences a cost-push inflation.

  **a** List the events that might cause a cost-push inflation.

  **b** Describe the initial effects of a cost-push inflation.

  **c** Describe what happens as a cost-push inflation spiral proceeds.

**12** Some events occur and the economy is expected to experience inflation.

  **a** List the events that might cause an expected inflation.

  **b** Describe the initial effects of an expected inflation.

  **c** Describe what happens as an expected inflation proceeds.

**13** Suppose that people expect deflation (a falling price level), but aggregate demand remains at $AD_0$.

  **a** What happens to the short-run and long-run aggregate supply curves? (Draw new curves if you need to.)

  **b** Describe the initial effects of an expected deflation.

  **c** Describe what happens as it becomes obvious to everyone that the expected deflation is not going to occur.

Use the following news clip to work Problems 14 to 16.

**Money's Too Loose to Mention**

UK inflation at 3.7 per cent is above target and above forecasts. This inflation can't be blamed on temporary factors such as a rise in commodity prices or a tax increase, although these events did occur and will make inflation worse before it gets better. Rather, embedded inflation and inflation expectations seem to be rising and the UK now has higher inflation than any other developed economy.

Source: *The Financial Times*, 19 January 2011

**14** Does the news clip describe a situation in which the UK is experiencing demand-pull inflation, cost-push inflation, or an expected inflation spiral? Explain.

**15** Draw a graph to illustrate the effects of the temporary factors noted in the news clip.

**16** Draw a graph to illustrate and explain how the UK might be experiencing an expected inflation spiral.

Use the following news clip to work Problems 17 to 19.

**Tight Money Won't Slay Food, Energy Inflation**

It's important to differentiate between a general increase in prices – a situation in which aggregate demand exceeds their aggregate supply – and a relative price shock. For example, a specific shock to energy prices can become generalized if producers are able to pass on the higher costs. So far, global competition has made that difficult for companies, while higher input costs have largely been neutralized by rising labour productivity. Since 2003, US core inflation has averaged less than 2 per cent a year. History also suggests the US central bank's gamble that slowing growth will shackle core inflation is a winning wager. The risk is that if US consumers don't believe price increases will slow, growing inflation expectations may become self-fulfilling.

Source: Bloomberg, 9 May 2008

**17** **a** Explain the two types of inflation described in this news clip.

  **b** Explain why 'rising labour productivity' can neutralize the effect on inflation of 'higher input costs'.

**18** Explain how 'slowing growth' can reduce inflationary pressure.

**19** Draw a graph to illustrate and explain how 'growing inflation expectations may become self-fulfilling'.

## The Business Cycle (Study Plan 15.5)

**20** **Debate on Causes of Joblessness Grows**

What is the cause of the high unemployment rate? One side says more government spending can reduce joblessness. The other says it's a structural problem – people who can't move to take new jobs because they are tied down to burdensome mortgages or firms that can't find workers with the requisite skills to fill job openings.

Source: *The Wall Street Journal*, 4 September 2010

Which business cycle theory would say that the rise in unemployment is cyclical? Which would say it is an increase in the natural rate? Why?

ADDITIONAL PROBLEMS AND APPLICATIONS

mreconlab  You can work these problems in MyEconLab if assigned by your lecturer.

## The Basics of Economic Growth

**21**  If in 2012 China's real GDP is growing at 9 per cent a year, its population is growing at 1 per cent a year, and these growth rates continue, in what year will China's real GDP per person be twice what it is in 2012?

**22**  South Africa's real GDP was 1,782 billion rand in 2009 and 1,835 billion rand in 2010. South Africa's population was 49.3 million in 2009 and 49.9 million in 2010. Calculate:

**a**  The economic growth rate.

**b**  The growth rate of real GDP per person.

**c**  The approximate number of years it takes for real GDP per person in South Africa to double if the 2010 economic growth rate and population growth rate are maintained.

**23**  Turkey's real GDP was 97.1 billion Turkish lira in 2009 and 104.7 billion Turkish lira in 2010. Turkey's population was 70.5 million in 2009 and 71.4 million in 2010. Calculate:

**a**  The economic growth rate.

**b**  The growth rate of real GDP per person.

**c**  The approximate number of years it takes for real GDP per person in Turkey to double if economic growth returns to its average since 2009 of 3.6 per cent a year and is maintained.

## Economic Growth Trends

**24**  **The New World Order**

While gross domestic product growth is cooling a bit in emerging market economies, the results are still tremendous compared with the US and much of Western Europe. The emerging market economies posted a 6.7 per cent jump in real GDP in 2008, down from 7.5 per cent in 2007. The advanced economies grew an estimated 1.6 per cent in 2008. The difference in growth rates represents the largest spread between emerging market economies and advanced economies in the 37-year history of the survey.

Source: *Fortune*, 14 July 2008

Do growth rates over the past few decades indicate that gaps in real GDP per person around the world are shrinking, growing or staying the same? Explain.

## Why Real GDP Grows

**25**  **India's Economy Hits the Wall**

Just six months ago, India was looking good. Annual growth was 9 per cent, consumer demand was huge, and foreign investment was growing. But now most economic forecasts expect growth to slow to 7 per cent – a big drop for a country that needs to accelerate growth. India needs urgently to upgrade its infrastructure and education and healthcare facilities. Agriculture is unproductive and needs better technology. The legal system needs to be strengthened with more judges and courtrooms.

Source: *Business Week*, 1 July 2008

Explain five potential sources for faster economic growth in India suggested in this news clip.

## Inflation Cycles

Use the following news clip to work Problems 26 and 27.

**Bernanke Sees No Repeat of '70s-Style Inflation**

There is little indication today that a 1970s-style cost-push spiral is about to begin. Then, as now, a serious oil price shock occurred, but today's economy is more flexible in responding to difficulties, Bernanke said. [Ben Bernanke, Chairman of the US Federal Reserve] Also, today the US Federal Reserve monitors inflation expectations. If people believe inflation will keep going up, they will change their behaviour in ways that aggravate inflation – thus, a self-fulfilling prophecy. In the 1970s, people demanded (and received) higher wages in anticipation of rapidly rising prices; hence, the cost-push spiral began. The inflation rate has averaged about 3.5 per cent over the past four quarters. That is 'significantly higher' than the Federal Reserve would like but much lower than the double-digit inflation rates of the mid-1970s and 1980, said Bernanke.

Source: *USA Today*, 4 June 2008

**26**  Draw a graph to illustrate and explain the inflation spiral that the US experienced in the 1970s.

**27**  **a**  Explain the role that inflation expectations play in creating a self-fulfilling prophecy.

**b**  Explain Bernanke's predictions about the impact of the 2008 oil price shock as compared to the 1970s shock.

## The Business Cycle

Use the following information to work Problems 28 to 30.

Suppose that the business cycle in the UK is best described by RBC theory and that a new technology increases productivity.

**28** Draw a graph to show the effect of the new technology in the market for loanable funds.

**29** Draw a graph to show the effect of the new technology in the labour market.

**30** Explain the when-to-work decision when technology advances.

**31** **Real Wages Fail to Match a Rise in Productivity**

For most of the last century, wages and productivity – the key measure of the economy's efficiency – have risen together, increasing rapidly through the 1950s and 1960s and far more slowly in the 1970s and 1980s. But in recent years, the productivity gains have continued while the pay increases have not kept up.

Source: *The New York Times*, 28 August 2006

Explain the relationship between wages and productivity in this news clip in terms of real business cycle theory.

## Economics in the News

**32** After you have studied *Reading Between the Lines* on pp. 366–367 answer the following questions.

   **a** Given the money growth rate in China, why isn't real GDP growing at a faster pace?

   **b** If the money growth rate in China remains at the levels of 2010, what do you expect to happen to inflation in 2011 and 2012?

   **c** Use the *AS–AD* model to describe the inflationary process in China.

   **d** What policies would you recommend to the Chinese government to reduce inflation? Explain why.

**33** **Make Way for India – The Next China**

China grows at around 9 per cent a year, but its one-child policy will start to reduce the size of China's working population within the next 10 years. India, by contrast, will have an increasing working population for another generation at least.

Source: *The Independent*, 1 March 2006

**a** Given the expected population changes, do you think China or India will have the greater economic growth rate? Why?

**b** Would China's growth rate remain at 9 per cent a year without the restriction on its population growth rate?

**c** India's population growth rate is 1.6 per cent a year, and in 2005 its economic growth rate was 8 per cent a year. China's population growth rate is 0.6 per cent a year and in 2005 its economic growth rate was 9 per cent a year. In what year will real GDP per person double in each country?

**34** **Germany Leads Slowdown in Eurozone**

The pace of German economic growth has weakened 'markedly', but the reason is the weaker global prospects. Although German policymakers worry about the country's exposure to a fall in demand for its export goods, evidence is growing that the recovery is broadening with real wage rates rising and unemployment falling, which will lead into stronger consumer spending.

Source: *The Financial Times*, 23 September 2010

**a** How does 'exposure to a fall in demand for its export goods' influence Germany's aggregate demand, aggregate supply, unemployment and inflation?

**b** Use the *AS–AD* model to illustrate your answer to part (a).

**c** What do you think the news clip means by 'the recovery is broadening with real wage rates rising and unemployment falling, which will lead into stronger consumer spending'?

**d** Use the *AS–AD* model to illustrate your answer to part (d).

## Data Graphing

**35** Use the Data Grapher to create a graph of the growth rate of real GDP per person in the UK, Canada, Germany and the US.

   **a** Which country had the fastest growth of real GDP per person since 1980 and which had the slowest?

   **b** In which country has real GDP per person fluctuated most?

# Fiscal Policy and Monetary Policy

### After studying this chapter you will be able to:

◆ Describe the UK government's recent budgets

◆ Explain the effects of fiscal policy on output and employment

◆ Describe the objectives and framework of UK monetary policy

◆ Explain how the Bank of England influences interest rates

◆ Explain the transmission channels through which the Bank of England influences inflation and real GDP

Every spring, the Chancellor of the Exchequer presents his budget. In 2010, UK governments (central and local) spent 47 pence of every pound earned and had a budget deficit of £149 billion. How does the budget influence the economy? Can the government create jobs and stimulate economic growth?

Every month, six eminent economists join the Governor and Deputy Governors of the Bank of England to decide whether to change the interest rate. How do the Bank of England's interest rate decisions influence jobs, growth and inflation?

This chapter answers these questions. And *Reading Between the Lines* at the end of the chapter looks at the Bank of England's dilemma at the beginning of 2011.

**Government Budgets**

A government's **budget** is an annual statement of projected outlays and receipts during the next year together with the laws and regulations that will support those outlays and receipts. The finance minister – the Chancellor of the Exchequer in the UK – presents the budget to Parliament in what is often a piece of political theatre and always a major media event.

A government's budget has three major purposes:

1   To state the scale and allocation of the government's outlays and its plans to finance its activities

2   To stabilize the economy

3   To encourage the economy's long-term growth and balanced regional development

Before the Second World War, the budget had only the first of these goals – to plan and finance the business of government.

But during the late 1940s and early 1950s, the budget began to assume its second purpose – stabilization of the economy.

In more recent years, the budget has assumed its third goal of helping to secure faster sustained economic growth and to seek balance across regions.

Today, the budget is the tool used by a government in pursuit of its fiscal policy. **Fiscal policy** is a government's use of its budget to achieve macroeconomic objectives such as full employment, sustained economic growth and price-level stability. It is the fiscal policy aspects of the budget that we focus on in this chapter.

Government budgets differ in size and detail, but they all have the same components. Here, we'll illustrate a government budget by looking at the UK.

## Highlights of the UK Budget in 2010

Table 16.1 shows the main items in the UK government's budget. The numbers are projections for the fiscal year beginning in April 2010. The three main items in the budget are:

◆   Receipts

◆   Outlays

◆   Budget balance

### Table 16.1

### The Government Budget in 2010/11

| Item | | Projections (billions of pounds) |
|---|---|---|
| **Receipts** | | **531** |
| Taxes on income and wealth | | 189 |
| Taxes on expenditure | | 186 |
| National Insurance contributions | | 97 |
| Other receipts and royalties | | 59 |
| **Outlays** | | **695** |
| Expenditure on goods and services | | 388 |
| *Health* | 107 | |
| *Education* | 59 | |
| *Law and order* | 22 | |
| *Defence* | 46 | |
| *Other* | 154 | |
| Transfer payments | | 265 |
| Debt interest | | 42 |
| **Budget balance (surplus +/deficit – )** | | **–164** |

Source of data: HM Treasury, Budget 2010.

### Receipts

Receipts come from four sources:

1   Taxes on income and wealth

2   Taxes on expenditure

3   National Insurance contributions

4   Other receipts and royalties

The largest source is *taxes on income and wealth*, which were projected to be £189 billion in 2010/11. These are the taxes paid by individuals on their incomes and wealth and the taxes paid by businesses on their profits.

The second largest source is *taxes on expenditure*, which in 2010/11 were projected at £186 billion. These taxes include VAT and special duties and taxes on gambling, alcoholic drinks, petrol, luxury items and imported goods.

Third in size are *National Insurance contributions*, projected to be £97 billion in 2010/11. This item comes from contributions paid by workers and employers to fund the welfare and healthcare programmes.

Fourth in size are *other receipts and royalties*. This item includes oil royalties, stamp duties, car taxes, miscellaneous rents, dividends from abroad and profits from nationalized industries.

## Outlays

Outlays are classified in three broad categories:

1  Expenditure on goods and services
2  Transfer payments
3  Debt interest

*Expenditure on goods and services* is by far the largest item at £388 billion in 2010/11.

Table 16.1 lists some of the larger components of these expenditures. Healthcare (expenditure on the National Health Service) took £107 billion and education took another £59 billion. The provision of law and order and defence, the two traditional roles of government, took only £68 billion between them.

*Transfer payments* – £265 billion in 2010/11 – are payments to individuals, businesses, other levels of government and the rest of the world. These payments include National Insurance benefits, healthcare benefits, unemployment benefits, welfare supplements, grants to local authorities and aid to developing countries.

*Debt interest*, which in 2010/11 is projected to be £42 billion, is the interest on the government debt minus interest received by the government on its own investments.

The bottom line of the government budget is the balance – the surplus or deficit.

## Budget Balance

The government's budget balance is equal to its receipts minus its outlays. That is:

$$\text{Budget balance} = \text{Receipts} - \text{Outlays}$$

If receipts exceed outlays, the government has a **budget surplus**. If outlays exceed receipts, the government has a **budget deficit**. If receipts equal outlays, the government has a **balanced budget**. In fiscal year 2010/11, with projected outlays of £695 billion and receipts of £531 billion, the projected government deficit is £164 billion.

How typical is the budget of 2010/11? Let's look at its recent history.

## The Budget in Historical Perspective

Figure 16.1 shows the government's receipts, outlays and budget balance since 1970/71. The data are expressed as percentages of GDP, so you may think of the numbers as telling you how many pence of each pound that we earn the government gets and spends.

Figure 16.1 shows at a glance that the current deficit is one of the largest but that deficits are not new. Why does the government have such a large deficit? Let's answer this question by looking at receipts and outlays in a bit more detail.

**Figure 16.1**   UK Government Receipts, Outlays and Budget Balance

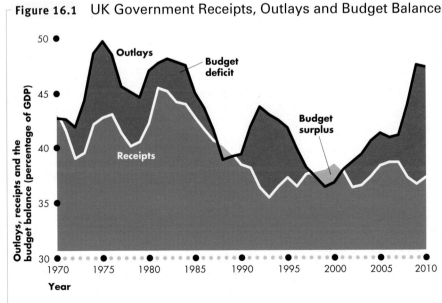

The figure records the UK government's receipts, outlays and budget deficit as percentages of GDP.

During the 1970s, the budget deficit became large and persisted well into the 1980s. A budget surplus appeared briefly in 1988, but income tax cuts and an increase in outlays turned the budget into a deficit again by 1990.

The budget returned to surplus at the end of the 1990s and in 2000, but for the rest of the 2000s a large and growing deficit emerged.

Source of data: HM Treasury, *Budget 2010*.

myeconlab Animation

## Receipts

Figure 16.2 shows the components of receipts received by the government as a percentage of GDP, from 1988 to 2010. Government receipts as a percentage of GDP decreased sharply from 1988 to 1993. This decrease occurred because the 1990–1992 recession decreased tax receipts. Firms' profits fell, which lowered the taxes on business profits, and as the unemployment rate increased, the receipts from personal income taxes decreased.

Receipts trended upward from 1994 to 2000 as the economy settled into a long boom. They then settled to a plateau as the economy grew at a steady rate.

Receipts reached a peak in 2007 and then fell as the global recession took hold.

## Outlays

Figure 16.3 shows the components of government outlays as percentages of GDP, between 1988 and 2010. Like receipts, outlays fluctuate over the business cycle. But unlike receipts, outlays have trended upwards. And the main source of increase is expenditure on goods and services, up from 20 per cent of GDP in 1990 to 27 per cent in 2010. Transfer payments have increased too, from 15 per cent of GDP in 1990 to 18 per cent in 2010.

Interest payment on government debt is a small component of government outlays. The amount of interest paid depends on the amount of debt. In recent decades the ratio of debt to GDP fell so interest payments fell too. But in 2010 government debt jumped to become a large percentage of GDP and interest payments increased sharply.

## Deficit, Debt and Capital

**Government debt** is the total amount of borrowing by the government. It is the sum of past deficits minus the sum of past surpluses plus payments to buy assets minus receipts from the sale of assets.

A budget deficit or the purchase of assets increases government debt and a budget surplus or the sale of state-owned assets reduces government debt.

Figure 16.4 shows the history of UK government debt from 1975 to 2010. In 1975, the debt–GDP ratio was just under 60 per cent. The debt–GDP ratio fell during the next 15 years and fell especially sharply during the 1980s as the government sold off state-owned assets such as British Rail and British Telecom. The debt increased spectacularly during 2009 and 2010 when the budget went into deficit and the government bought a large public stake in two troubled banks: the RBS and Lloyds.

**Figure 16.2** UK Government Receipts

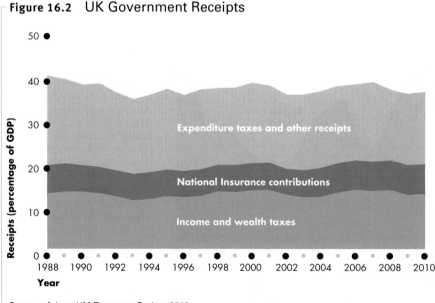

The figure shows the three components of government receipts: income and wealth taxes (including taxes on business profits), National Insurance contributions and expenditure taxes (including VAT).

Receipts from income and wealth fell during the recession of the early 1990s and 2008–2009.

Receipts increased during the expansion years from 1994 to 2001 and from 2003 to 2007.

Source of data: HM Treasury, *Budget 2010.*

myeconlab Animation

**Figure 16.3**   UK Government Outlays

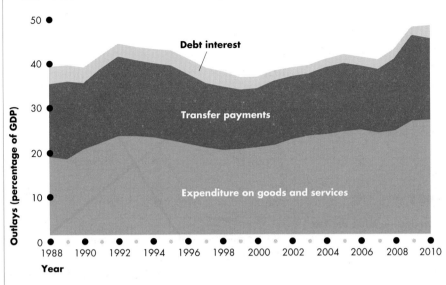

The figure shows three components of government outlays: expenditure on goods and services, transfer payments and debt interest.

Expenditure on goods and services has trended upward.

Transfer payments have also trended upward, but they are dominated by their cyclical changes.

Debt interest fell from 1996 to 2009 but then jumped in 2010.

Source of data: HM Treasury, *Budget 2010*.

Animation

**Figure 16.4**   UK Government Debt

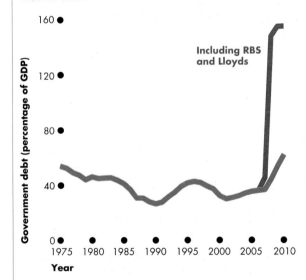

In 1975, UK government debt was 59 per cent of GDP. During the 1970s and 1980s, the government reduced its debt by selling state assets such as British Rail and British Telecom. Government debt rose sharply after the 1990–1992 recession and fell from 1997 to 2002. In 2008–2010, a large budget deficit and the part-nationalization of two banks, RBS and Lloyds, increased government debt astronomically.

Source of data: HM Treasury, *Budget 2010*.

Animation

Like individual and business debt, government debt is incurred to buy assets. Governments own public assets such as roads, bridges, schools and universities, public libraries and defence equipment. But the value of UK government assets is only £400 billion, which falls well short of its total debt.

 **Review Quiz**

1   What are the functions of a government's budget?
2   What are the goals of fiscal policy?
3   Describe the main sources of receipts and outlays in the budget of the UK government.
4   Under what circumstances does a government have a budget surplus?
5   Explain the connection between a government's budget deficit and its debt.

You can work these questions in Study Plan 16.1 and get instant feedback.

Now that you know what the main components of the government's budget are, it is time to study the *effects* of fiscal policy.

## The Effects of Fiscal Policy

Taxes, government expenditures and the government budget balance influence economic performance in a number of ways. We're going to focus on three of them:

◆ The effects of taxes on the incentives to work, invest and save

◆ The effects of taxes and government expenditure on aggregate demand

◆ Intergenerational effects

## Incentive Effects of Taxes

A tax on a transaction drives a wedge – called the **tax wedge** – between the price paid by buyers and the price received by sellers and decreases the quantity traded. (Refresh your memory of this proposition by checking Chapter 5, pp. 111–116).

We'll look at two taxes, that on labour income and on interest income from capital.

### The Effects of the Income Tax on Employment

A tax on wage income weakens the incentive to work and drives a wedge between the take-home wage of workers and the cost of labour to firms. The result is a smaller quantity of labour and a lower real GDP.

Figure 16.5 illustrates an economy-wide labour market. The demand for labour curve is *LD*, and the supply of labour curve is *LS*. With no income tax, the labour market is in equilibrium at a real wage rate of £15 an hour and 50 billion hours of labour a year employed. The economy is at full employment.

An income tax has no effect on the demand for labour, which remains at *LD*. The reason is that the quantity of labour that firms plan to employ depends only on how productive labour is and what labour costs: its real wage rate.

But an income tax changes the supply of labour. The reason is that for each pound of before-tax earnings, workers must pay the government an amount determined by the income tax code. So workers look at the after-tax wage rate when they decide how much labour to supply.

An income tax shifts the supply curve leftward to *LS* + *tax*. The vertical distance between the *LS* curve and the *LS* + *tax* curve measures the amount of income tax. With the smaller supply of labour, the before-tax wage rate rises to £17.50 an hour but the after-tax wage rate falls to £10 an hour.

**Figure 16.5** The Effects of the Income Tax on Employment

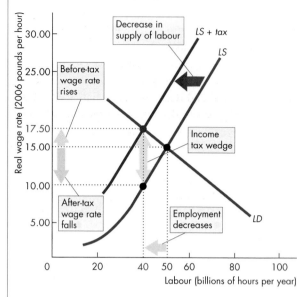

With no income tax, the real wage rate is £15 an hour and employment is 50 billion hours. An income tax shifts the supply of labour curve leftward to *LS* + *tax*. The before-tax wage rate rises to £17.50 an hour, the after-tax wage rate falls to £10 an hour, and the quantity of labour employed decreases to 40 billion hours. With less labour employed, real GDP decreases.

myeconlab Animation ◆

The new equilibrium quantity of labour employed is 40 billion hours a year – less than in the no-tax case. Because employment decreases, so does real GDP.

### Taxes on Expenditure and the Tax Wedge

The tax wedge that we've just considered is only a part of the wedge that affects labour's supply decisions. Taxes on consumption expenditure add to the wedge. The reason is that a tax on consumption raises the prices paid for consumption goods and services and is equivalent to a cut in the real wage rate.

The incentive to supply labour depends on the quantity of goods and services that an hour of labour can buy. The higher the taxes on goods and services and the lower the after-tax wage rate, the less is the incentive to supply labour. If the income tax rate is 25 per cent and the tax rate on consumption expenditure is 10 per cent, a pound earned buys only 65 pence worth of goods and services. The tax wedge is 35 per cent.

## Taxes and the Incentive to Save and Invest

A tax on interest income weakens the incentive to save and drives a wedge between the after-tax interest rate earned by savers and the interest rate paid by firms. These effects are analogous to those of a tax on labour income. But they are more serious for two reasons.

First, a tax on labour income decreases the quantity of labour employed and decreases potential GDP, while a tax on capital income decreases the quantity of saving and investment and slows the growth rate of real GDP.

Second, the true tax rate on interest income is much higher than that on labour income because of the way in which inflation and taxes on interest income interact.

The interest rate that influences investment and saving plans is the *real after-tax interest rate*. The real after-tax interest rate subtracts the income tax rate paid on interest income from the real interest rate. But the taxes depend on the nominal interest rate, not the real interest rate. So the higher the inflation rate, the higher is the true tax rate on interest income. Here is an example. Suppose the real interest rate is 4 per cent a year and the tax rate is 40 per cent.

If there is no inflation, the nominal interest rate equals the real interest rate. The tax on 4 per cent interest is 1.6 per cent (40 per cent of 4 per cent), so the real after-tax interest rate is 4 per cent minus 1.6 per cent, which equals 2.4 per cent.

If the inflation rate is 6 per cent a year, the nominal interest rate is 10 per cent. The tax on 10 per cent interest is 4 per cent (40 per cent of 10 per cent), so the real after-tax interest rate is 4 per cent minus 4 per cent, which equals zero. The true tax rate in this case is not 40 per cent but 100 per cent!

## Effect of Income Tax on Saving and Investment

In Figure 16.6, initially there are no taxes. Also, the government has a balanced budget. The demand for loanable funds curve, which is also the investment demand curve, is *DLF*. The supply of loanable funds curve, which is also the saving supply curve, is *SLF*. The interest rate is 3 per cent a year, and the quantity of funds borrowed and lent is £200 billion a year.

A tax on interest income has no effect on the demand for loanable funds. The quantity of investment and borrowing that firms plan to undertake depends only on how productive capital is and what it costs – its real interest rate. But a tax on interest income weakens the incentive to save and lend and decreases the supply of loanable funds. For each pound of before-tax interest,

ECONOMICS IN ACTION

# Some Real World Tax Wedges

Edward C. Prescott of Arizona State University, who shared the 2004 Nobel Prize for Economic Science, has estimated the tax wedges for a number of countries, among them the US, the UK and France.

## The US Tax Wedge

The US tax wedge is a combination of 13 per cent tax on consumption and 32 per cent tax on incomes. The income tax component of the US tax wedge includes social security taxes and is the marginal tax rate – the tax rate paid on the marginal dollar earned.

## France's Tax Wedge

Prescott estimates that in France, taxes on consumption are 33 per cent and taxes on incomes are 49 per cent.

## The UK Tax Wedge

The estimates for the UK fall between those for the US and France. The figure shows these components of the tax wedges in the three countries.

## Does the Tax Wedge Matter?

According to Prescott's estimates, the tax wedge has a powerful effect on employment and potential GDP. Potential GDP in France is 14 per cent below that of the US (per person), and the entire difference can be attributed to the difference in the tax wedge in the two countries.

Potential GDP in the UK is 41 per cent below that of the US (per person), and about a third of the difference arises from the different tax wedges. (The rest is due to different productivities.)

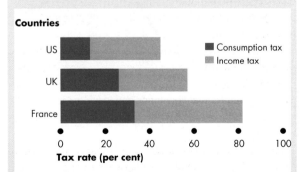

Figure 1  Three Tax Wedges

Source of data: Edward C. Prescott, *American Economic Review*, 2003.

savers must pay the government an amount determined by the tax code. So savers look at the after-tax real interest rate when they decide how much to save.

When a tax is imposed, saving decreases and the supply of loanable funds curve shifts leftward to *SLF + tax*. The amount of tax payable is measured by the vertical distance between the *SLF* curve and the *SLF + tax* curve. With this smaller supply of loanable funds, the interest rate rises to 4 per cent a year but the after-tax interest rate falls to 1 per cent a year. A tax wedge is driven between the interest rate and the after-tax interest rate, and the equilibrium quantity of loanable funds decreases. Saving and investment also decrease.

You now know how income taxes influence employment, saving, investment and real GDP through their incentive effects. Next we look at the effects of both taxes and spending on aggregate demand.

**Figure 16.6** The Effects of a Tax on Capital Income

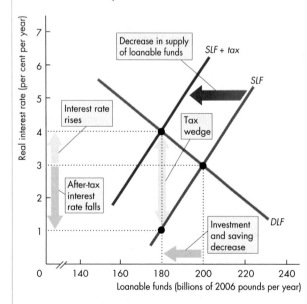

The demand for loanable funds and investment demand curve is *DLF*, and the supply of loanable funds and saving supply curve is *SLF*. With no income tax, the real interest rate is 3 per cent a year and investment is £200 billion. An income tax shifts the supply curve leftward to *SLF + tax*. The interest rate rises to 4 per cent a year, the after-tax interest rate falls to 1 per cent a year, and investment decreases to £180 billion. With less investment, the real GDP growth rate decreases.

ⓧ myeconlab Animation ━━━━━━━━━━━━━◆

# Fiscal Policy and Aggregate Demand

The 2008–2009 recession brought Keynesian macroeconomic ideas back into fashion and put a spotlight on **fiscal stimulus** – the use of fiscal policy to increase employment and real GDP.

A fiscal policy action that is triggered by the state of the economy with no action by government is called **automatic fiscal policy**. A fiscal policy action initiated by government is called **discretionary fiscal policy**. It requires a change in a spending or tax law.

Whether automatic or discretionary, an increase in government expenditure or a decrease in taxes can stimulate production and jobs. An increase in expenditure on goods and services directly increases aggregate expenditure. An increase in payments such as unemployment benefits increases disposable income and consumption expenditure. Lower taxes also strengthen the incentives to work, save and invest.

## Automatic Fiscal Policy

Tax receipts and means-tested spending change automatically in response to the state of the economy.

The tax laws define the tax *rates* that people must pay. So the amount paid in taxes depends on incomes, which in turn depend on GDP. When real GDP increases in a business cycle expansion, incomes rise, so tax receipts rise. When real GDP decreases in a recession, incomes fall, so tax receipts fall.

Similarly, government programmes pay benefits to qualified people and businesses that depend on the economic state of recipients. When the economy expands, unemployment falls, the number of people experiencing economic hardship decreases, so means-tested spending decreases. When the economy is in a recession, unemployment is high and the number of people experiencing economic hardship increases, so means-tested spending on unemployment benefits increases.

Because government receipts fall and outlays increase in a recession, the budget provides automatic stimulus that helps to shrink the recessionary gap. Similarly, because receipts rise and outlays decrease in a boom, the budget provides automatic restraint to shrink an inflationary gap.

The government budget balance that arises from the business cycle is called the **cyclical surplus or deficit**. The budget balance that would occur if the economy were at full employment is called the **structural surplus or deficit**. In 2010, the UK budget deficit was £131 billion, almost £100 billion of which was structural.

## Discretionary Fiscal Stimulus

An increase in government expenditure has a direct effect on aggregate demand. A tax cut influences aggregate demand by increasing disposable income and consumption expenditure. Both forms of fiscal stimulus have multiplier effects.

Let's look at the two main fiscal policy multipliers: the government expenditure and tax multipliers.

The **government expenditure multiplier** is the quantitative effect of a change in government expenditure on real GDP. Because government expenditure is a component of aggregate expenditure, an increase in government spending increases aggregate expenditure and real GDP. But does a £1 billion increase in government expenditure increase real GDP by £1 billion, or more than £1 billion, or less than £1 billion?

When an increase in government expenditure increases real GDP, incomes rise and the higher incomes bring an increase in consumption expenditure. If this were the only consequence of increased government expenditure, the government expenditure multiplier would be greater than 1.

But an increase in government expenditure increases government borrowing (or decreases government lending if there is a budget surplus) and raises the real interest rate. With a higher cost of borrowing, investment decreases, which partly offsets the increase in government spending. If this were the only consequence of increased government expenditure, the multiplier would be less than 1.

The actual multiplier depends on which of the above effects is stronger and the consensus is that the crowding-out effect is strong enough to make the government expenditure multiplier less than 1.

The **tax multiplier** is the quantitative effect of a change in taxes on real GDP. The demand-side effects of a tax cut are likely to be smaller than an equivalent increase in government expenditure. The reason is that a tax cut influences aggregate demand by increasing disposable income, only part of which gets spent. So the initial injection of expenditure from a £1 billion tax cut is less than £1 billion.

A tax cut has similar crowding-out consequences to a spending increase. A tax cut increases government borrowing (or decreases government lending), raises the real interest rate and cuts investment.

The tax multiplier effect on aggregate demand depends on these two opposing effects and is probably quite small.

Figure 16.7 shows how fiscal stimulus is supposed to work if it is perfectly executed and has its desired effects.

Potential GDP is £1,400 billion and real GDP is below potential at £1,300 billion, so the economy has a recessionary gap of £100 billion.

To restore full employment, the government passes a fiscal stimulus package. An increase in government expenditure and a tax cut increase aggregate expenditure by $\Delta E$. If this were the only change in spending plans, the $AD$ curve would shift rightward to become the curve labelled $AD_0 + \Delta E$ in Figure 16.7. But if fiscal stimulus sets off a multiplier process that increases consumption expenditure and does not crowd out much investment expenditure, aggregate demand increases further and the $AD$ curve shifts to $AD_1$.

With no change in the price level, the economy would move from point $A$ to point $B$ on $AD_1$. But the increase in aggregate demand brings a rise in the price level along the upward-sloping $SAS$ curve and the economy moves to point $C$.

At point $C$, the economy returns to full employment and the recessionary gap is eliminated.

**Figure 16.7    Expansionary Fiscal Policy**

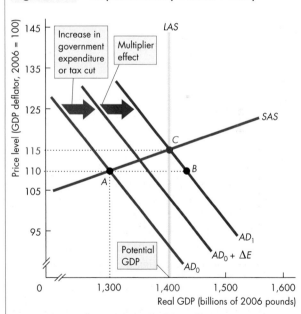

Potential GDP is £1,400 billion, real GDP is £1,300 billion, and there is a £100 billion recessionary gap. An increase in government expenditure and a tax cut increase aggregate expenditure by $\Delta E$. The multiplier increases consumption expenditure and doesn't crowd out investment, the $AD$ curve shifts rightward to $AD_1$. The price level rises to 115, real GDP increases to £1,400 billion and the recessionary gap is eliminated.

myeconlab Animation

## Magnitude and Timing of Stimulus

Economists have diverging views about the size of the government expenditure and tax multipliers (see *Economics in Action* opposite). This fact makes it impossible for the government to determine the amount of stimulus needed to close a given output gap. Further, the actual output gap is not known and can only be estimated with error. For these two reasons, discretionary fiscal policy is risky.

Also, discretionary fiscal stimulus actions are seriously hampered by three time lags: a recognition lag, a legislation lag and an impact lag. Even if the magnitude of stimulus could be right, getting the timing wrong could end up with larger rather than smaller fluctuations in employment and output.

## Intergenerational Effects

You've seen that most of the UK budget deficit is structural. It will be present even when full employment returns unless the government takes some actions to reduce the deficit.

Is a structural budget deficit a burden on future generations? If it is, how will the burden be borne? And is the budget deficit the only burden on future generations? What about the deficit in the state pension fund? Does it matter who owns the bonds that the government sells to finance its deficit? What about the bonds owned by foreigners? Won't repaying those bonds impose a bigger burden than repaying bonds owned by UK residents?

To answer questions like these, we use a tool called **generational accounting** – an accounting system that measures the lifetime tax burden and benefits of each generation.

Income taxes and National Insurance contributions are paid by people who have jobs. Pensions are paid to people after they retire. Healthcare benefits are also provided on a larger scale to older retired people. So to compare taxes and benefits, we must compare the value of taxes paid by people during their working years with the benefits received in their retirement years. To compare the value of an amount of money at one date with that at a later date, we use the concept of present value. A **present value** is an amount of money that, if invested today, will grow to equal a given future amount when the interest that it earns is taken into account. We can compare pounds paid today with pounds received in 2030 or any other future year by using present values.

By using present values, we can assess the magnitude of the government's **fiscal imbalance**, the present value of its debts in state pensions and other benefits.

### ECONOMICS IN ACTION

## How Big Are the Fiscal Stimulus Multipliers?

When the US government cut taxes by $300 billion and increased government expenditure by almost $500 billion, by how much did aggregate expenditure and real GDP change? How big were the fiscal policy multipliers? Was the government expenditure multiplier larger than the tax multiplier? These questions are about the multiplier effects on *equilibrium real GDP*, not just on aggregate demand.

President Obama's economic adviser, Christina Romer, a University of California, Berkeley, professor, expected the multiplier to be about 1.5. She was expecting the spending increase of $500 billion to go a long way towards closing the $1 trillion output gap in 2010.

Robert Barro, a professor at Harvard University, says this multiplier number is not in line with previous experience. Based on his calculations, an additional $500 billion of government spending would increase aggregate expenditure by only $250 billion because it would lower private spending in a crowding-out effect by $250 billion – the multiplier is 0.5.

Patrick Minford, a professor at Cardiff University, says that the government expenditure multiplier on real GDP is even smaller and is 0.35. He arrives at this number based on 30 years of research on the UK economy. Harald Uhlig, a professor at the University of Chicago, agrees with Minford's assessment of the multiplier and says this number also applies to the US.

If Minford and Uhlig are correct, a $500 billion increase in government spending increases aggregate expenditure by between $150 billion and $200 billion.

Using generational accounting and present values, economists have studied the situation facing governments arising from their pension and healthcare obligations, and they have found some time bombs!

On the assumption of strict control of government spending, economists estimate that the UK fiscal imbalance is 20 per cent of GDP. This figure is large but not an impossible one for the government to plan for. A more recent estimate is much less optimistic. Four economists at Freiburg University estimate that the UK fiscal imbalance is a staggering 510 per cent of GDP. If this figure is correct, when added to the government's market debt in 2010, the total debt obligation of the UK government is 575 per cent of GDP – or £8.3 trillion (in 2010 prices).

There is greater agreement about tax multipliers. Because tax cuts strengthen the incentive to work, save and invest, they increase aggregate supply as well as aggregate demand.

The tax multipliers get bigger as more time elapses. Harald Uhlig says that after one year, the tax multiplier is 0.5, so the $300 billion tax cut would increase real GDP by about $150 billion by early 2010. But with two years to respond, real GDP would be $600 billion higher – a multiplier of 2. And after three years, the tax multiplier builds up to more than 6. Patrick Minford's research on the UK economy supports the findings of Uhlig.

The implications of the work of Barro, Uhlig and Minford are that tax cuts are a powerful way to stimulate real GDP and employment but spending increases are not effective.

Christina Romer agrees that the economy hasn't performed in line with a multiplier of 1.5 but says other factors deteriorated and without the fiscal stimulus, the outcome would have been even worse.

Christina Romer 1.5

Robert Barro 0.5

Patrick Minford 0.35

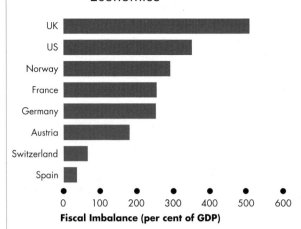

**Figure 16.8**    Fiscal Imbalances in Eight Economies

Fiscal Imbalance (per cent of GDP)

Fiscal imbalance is an enormous problem for many countries. On current tax and benefit rates, the UK government has a true debt of more than 5 years' GDP. The US government isn't far behind at almost 4 years' GDP. Even Norway and Germany, normally considered to have sound fiscal policies, owe almost 3 years' GDP to future citizens. Spain is at the other extreme with a fiscal imbalance of only a few months' GDP.

Source of data: Christian Hagist, Stefan Moog, Bernd Raffelhüschen and Johannes Vatter, 'Public Debt and Demography – An International Comparison Using Generational Accounting', Cesifo DICE Report 4 2009.

myeconlab Animation

division of the fiscal imbalance between the current and future generations, assuming that the current generation will enjoy the existing levels of taxes and benefits.

The optimistic estimate is that people born in 1972 (aged 25 in 1997) will pay 65 per cent more in taxes over their lifetime than those born in 1997.

Figure 16.8 shows the Freiburg economists' estimates of international fiscal imbalances for eight countries. The UK has the largest fiscal imbalance but the US, France and Germany also have sizeable fiscal imbalances.

Fiscal imbalance is an enormous obligation for many countries and it points to a catastrophic future and can only be corrected with some combination of a rise in income taxes or National Insurance contributions, a cut in government discretionary spending, a cut in unemployment and other welfare state benefits, or a rise in the state pension age.

A fiscal imbalance must eventually be corrected and when it is, people either pay higher taxes or receive lower benefits. The concept of generational imbalance tells us who will pay. **Generational imbalance** is the

### Review Quiz

1   How does an income tax influence employment?
2   How does an income tax influence investment and saving and why are income taxes on capital income more powerful than those on labour income?
3   What is the distinction between automatic and discretionary fiscal policy?
4   What is the distinction between the cyclical and structural budget balance?
5   How can government use discretionary fiscal policy to stimulate the economy and what are the dangers in using it?
6   What is generational fiscal imbalance and why is it a problem?

You can work these questions in Study Plan 16.2 and get instant feedback.

## ◈ Monetary Policy Objectives and Framework

A nation's monetary policy objectives and the framework for setting and achieving them stem from the relationship between the central bank and government. Monetary policy making involves two activities:

1   Setting the policy objectives

2   Achieving the policy objectives

In a few countries, the central bank sets the objectives and decides how to achieve them. And in some countries, the government makes all the monetary policy decisions and tells the central bank what actions to take. But in most countries, including the UK, the government sets the monetary policy objectives and the central bank decides how to achieve them.

Here, we'll describe the objectives of UK monetary policy and the framework and assignment of responsibility for achieving those objectives.

## Monetary Policy Objectives

The objectives of monetary policy are ultimately political and are determined by government. But they are pursued by the actions of the central bank. The Bank of England Act of 1998 sets out the objectives of UK monetary policy.

### Bank of England Act 1998

The 1998 Bank of England Act sets out the Bank's monetary policy objectives as being:

(a)   to maintain price stability, and

(b)   subject to that, to support the economic policy of Her Majesty's Government, including its objectives for growth and employment.[1]

The Act also requires the Chancellor of the Exchequer to specify annually in writing:

(a)   what price stability is to be taken to consist of, and

(b)   what the economic policy of Her Majesty's Government is to be taken to be.[2]

One of the most important innovations in the 1998 Act is its establishment of the Monetary Policy Committee or MPC, an independent group of six experts who with the governor and two deputy governors make the monetary policy decisions. (See Chapter 13, p. 304 for more details on the composition of the MPC.)

## Remit for the Monetary Policy Committee

The Chancellor renews and if necessary modifies the remit for the Monetary Policy Committee at roughly annual intervals. This remit is stated in two parts corresponding to the two monetary policy objectives.

### Price Stability Objective

The first part of the remit for the Monetary Policy Committee is an operational definition of 'price stability'. Since the beginning of 2004, this objective has been specified as a target inflation rate of 2 per cent a year as measured by the 12-month increase in the Consumer Prices Index (CPI).

Although the inflation target is renewed annually, the intention is that inflation be locked in at a low and stable rate over the long term. To achieve long-term price stability, deviations from the inflation target in either direction that exceed 1 percentage point require the Governor of the Bank to write an open letter to the Chancellor explaining why the target has been missed and what steps will be taken to bring the inflation rate back to its target. And for every three months that the inflation rate misses its target by more than 1 percentage point, a further explanation must be provided.

### Government Economic Policy Objectives

The government's economic policy objectives as they relate to monetary policy are to achieve high and stable levels of economic growth and employment.

Price stability is the key goal and a major contributor to achieving the other goals of government economic policy. Price stability provides the best available environment for households and firms to make the saving and investment decisions that bring economic growth. So price stability encourages the maximum sustainable growth rate of potential GDP.

But in the short run, the Bank of England faces a trade-off between inflation and economic growth and employment. Taking an action that is designed to lower the inflation rate and achieve stable prices might mean slowing the economic growth rate and lowering employment.

---

[1]  Bank of England Act (1998) section 11.
[2]  Bank of England Act (1998) section 12.

In both the primary objective of price stability and the goal of high and stable growth and employment, monetary policy in the UK is similar to that in the rest of the EU (see *Economics in Action* on p. 386) and to many other inflation targeting countries.

## Actual Inflation and the Inflation Target

Figure 16.9 compares the CPI measure of inflation and the target of 2 per cent a year since the beginning of 2004. January 2004 was the date the Bank of England was charged by the Chancellor of the Exchequer to switch from a target of 2.5 per cent a year inflation measured by the Retail Prices Index less mortgage interest payments (RPIX) to a target of 2 per cent a year measured by the Consumer Prices Index (CPI). Between January 2004 and January 2011, the average rate of increase of the CPI was just above the target at 2.4 per cent a year.

The Bank of England was successful in keeping inflation within the target range of 1 per cent to 3 per cent a year for three years from the beginning of 2004. But during those years, the inflation rate moved from the bottom to the top of the target range. Inflation burst through the upper limit of the target range in March 2007. This event triggered an open letter from the Governor to the Chancellor as required by the Chancellor's remit for the Monetary Policy Committee. The 3 per cent a year upper bound was breached again from May 2008 to February 2009 and throughout 2010.

### Rationale for an Inflation Target

Two main benefits flow from adopting an inflation target. The first is that the purpose of the Bank of England's policy actions are more clearly understood by financial market traders. A clearer understanding leads to fewer surprises and mistakes on the part of savers and investors.

The second benefit is that the target provides an anchor for expectations about future inflation. Firmly held expectations of low inflation make the short-run trade-off between inflation and economic growth and employment as favourable as possible. Also, firmly held (and correct) inflation expectations help individuals and firms to make better economic decisions, which in turn help to achieve a more efficient allocation of resources and a more stable economic growth rate.

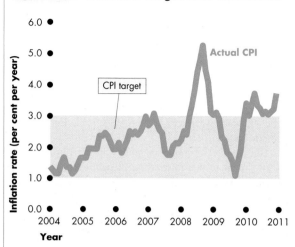

**Figure 16.9**   Inflation Target and Outcomes

The MPC's inflation target is a range of 1 per cent to 3 per cent a year. Inflation was inside the target from 2004 until March 2007. From May 2008 to February 2009 and throughout 2010, inflation has been above the 3 per cent a year upper limit.

Source of data: Office for National Statistics.

myeconlab   Animation

### Controversy About Inflation Targeting

Not everyone agrees that inflation targeting brings benefits. Critics argue that by focusing on inflation, the Bank of England sometimes permits the unemployment rate or real GDP growth rate to suffer.

The fear of these critics is that if the inflation rate begins to edge upward towards and perhaps beyond a full percentage point above target, the Bank of England might rein in aggregate demand and push the economy into recession. At the same time, the Bank might end up permitting the pound to rise on the foreign exchange market and making exports suffer.

One response of supporters of inflation targeting is that by keeping inflation low and stable, monetary policy makes its maximum possible contribution towards achieving full employment and sustained economic growth.

Another response is 'look at the growth and unemployment record'. From May 1997 when the Bank of England was made operationally independent and given the goal of price stability, until 2008, the UK economy was free from recession and had falling unemployment. Only when the entire global economy was reeling from the financial crisis did UK real GDP fall and unemployment begin to rise.

## Monetary Policy in the Eurozone

The Eurozone is the 17 member states of the EU that use the euro as their currency. The European Central Bank (ECB), which was established in 1998, is the Eurozone's central bank.

The conduct of monetary policy in the Eurozone is very similar to that in the UK. In fact, today there has been a convergence of views on how monetary policy should be conducted and the central banks of most industrial countries pursue monetary policy using similar objectives, tools and decision-making frameworks.

The objectives of Eurozone monetary policy are laid out in Article 105 of the Treaty Establishing the European Community (the Treaty of Rome), which assigns overriding importance to price stability as the ECB's monetary policy goal. The Treaty also requires the ECB to support broader Community economic policies, which means supporting policies aimed at achieving sustained growth and high employment.

The ECB's Governing Council has defined price stability as 'a year-on-year increase in the Harmonised Index of Consumer Prices (HICP) for the euro area of . . . below, but close to, 2 per cent a year over the medium term.'

Like the Bank of England and most other central banks, the ECB recognizes 'that ensuring price stability is the most important contribution that monetary policy can make to achieve a favourable economic environment and a high level of employment'. In other words, price stability is the goal of monetary policy *because it contributes to the achievement of other economic objectives.*

### Review Quiz

1  What are the objectives of monetary policy?
2  What is the rationale for setting an inflation target?
3  What is the Bank of England's record in achieving the inflation target?

You can work these questions in Study Plan 16.3 and get instant feedback.

You now know the objective of monetary policy and the Bank of England's record in achieving it. You're now going to see how the Bank conducts monetary policy.

## The Conduct of Monetary Policy

How does the Bank of England conduct its monetary policy? This question has two parts:

◆  What is the monetary policy instrument?
◆  How does the Bank make its monetary policy decisions?

## The Monetary Policy Instrument

A **monetary policy instrument** is a variable that a central bank can directly control or closely target. The Bank of England must choose between two possible instruments: the monetary base or an interest rate.

The Bank's choice of monetary policy instrument is an interest rate. The Bank sets Bank Rate (also known as the Bank of England Base Rate), which is linked to the interest rate that banks earn on reserves and pay on borrowed reserves. The Bank then trades in the repo market to make the **repo rate** – the interest rate in the repo market – equal to Bank Rate. Banks can borrow and lend reserves in the repo market. A bank that is short of reserves and a bank that has excess reserves can use a repo to move the reserves from one bank to the other. The Bank of England also trades in the repo market.

Figure 16.10 shows the Bank Rate since January 2004. Bank Rate is normally changed in steps of a quarter of a percentage point.[3] The rate reached a peak of 5.75 per cent a year in 2007 and then fell in rapid succession in much greater steps than a quarter of a per cent to a low of 0.5 per cent a year in April 2009. The sharp fall in the Bank Rate was a coordinated attempt by the central banks of the developed world to deal with the credit crunch and the global financial crisis.

Between 2004 and 2007, Bank Rate was on a rising trend. The reason is that the inflation rate had moved up from below target to above target and by 2007 the inflation rate was pushing against the upper limit of a 3 per cent a year rate of increase of the CPI.

Since 2007, the Bank Rate has been lowered, first in short steps and then in rapid steps as the full scale of the economic crisis became apparent. During 2010, the inflation rate has been above the upper bound of 3 per cent a year but the interest rate has remained at the historically low level of 0.5 per cent a year.

---

[3] When you read about interest changes in the press, you might encounter the term 25 basis points. A basis point is 100th of 1 per cent, so 25 basis points is 0.25 percentage points.

## Figure 16.10    Bank Rate

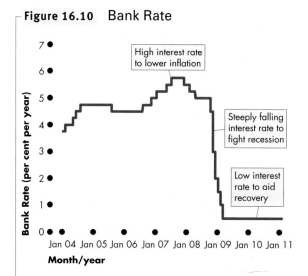

The Bank of England sets Bank Rate and then takes actions to ensure that the banking system is supplied with its desired level of reserves. When the inflation rate is above 2 per cent a year and the Bank wants to avoid going above target, it raises Bank Rate. When the inflation rate is below 2 per cent a year and the Bank wants to avoid going below target, it lowers Bank Rate.

Source of data: Bank of England.

myeconlab Animation

## Figure 16.11    The Market for Bank Reserves

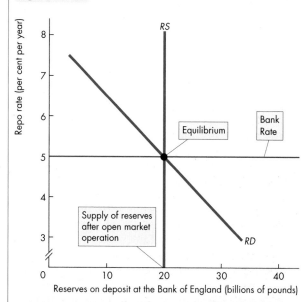

The demand curve for reserves is *RD*. The quantity of reserves demanded decreases as the repo rate rises because the repo rate is the opportunity cost of holding reserves. The supply curve of reserves is *RS*. The Bank of England uses open market operations to make the supply of reserves equal the quantity of reserves demanded (£20 billion in this case) at a repo rate equal to Bank Rate (5 per cent a year in this case).

myeconlab Animation

Having decided the appropriate level for Bank Rate, how does the Bank of England move the repo rate to its target level? The answer is by using open market operations (see Chapter 13, pp. 305–307) to adjust the quantity of monetary base.

To see how an open market operation changes the repo rate, we need to examine the repo market. The higher the repo rate, the greater is the quantity of overnight loans supplied on repurchase agreements and the smaller is the quantity of overnight loans demanded in the repo market. The equilibrium repo rate balances the quantities demanded and supplied.

An equivalent way of looking at the forces that determine the repo rate is to consider the demand for and supply of bank reserves. Banks hold reserves to meet their desired reserve ratio so that they can always make payments. But reserves are costly to hold. The alternative to holding reserves is to lend them in the repo market and earn the repo rate. The higher the repo rate, the higher is the opportunity cost of holding reserves and the greater is the incentive for banks to economize on the quantity of reserves held.

So the quantity of reserves demanded by banks depends on the repo rate. The higher the repo rate, other things remaining the same, the smaller is the quantity of reserves demanded.

Figure 16.11 illustrates the demand for bank reserves. The *x*-axis measures the quantity of reserves that banks hold on deposit at the Bank of England, and the *y*-axis measures the repo rate. The demand for reserves is the curve labelled *RD*.

The Bank's open market operations determine the supply of reserves shown by the supply curve *RS*. To decrease reserves, the Bank conducts an open market sale. To increase reserves, the Bank conducts an open market purchase.

Equilibrium in the market for bank reserves determines the repo rate where the quantity of reserves demanded by the commercial banks equals the quantity of reserves supplied by the Bank of England. By using open market operations, the Bank adjusts the supply of reserves to keep the repo rate equal to Bank Rate.

Next, we see how the Bank makes its policy decision.

## ECONOMICS IN ACTION

### Bank of England Decision Making

The MPC meets monthly to set the Bank Rate and throughout the month the committee gets an extensive briefing by the economists of the Bank of England where all the available industry, national and international data on economic performance, financial markets and inflation expectations are reviewed, discussed and weighed in a careful deliberative process.

The MPC meeting lasts two days and on the second day members explain their views as to what they think are the important factors in the economy and what they think the interest rate decision should be.

The Governor of the Bank then puts to the meeting the decision that he thinks will command a majority. Any member in a minority is asked to record what the interest rate should be and justify that decision formally in the minutes.

The interest rate decision is announced at 12 noon on the second day of the deliberations. After announcing a Bank Rate decision, the Bank engages in public communication to explain the reasons for the MPC's decision. The Bank of England's communication exercise is extremely thorough and includes a detailed and carefully researched *Inflation Report* and press conference with the Governor.

The Governor's press conference is recorded and a video placed on the Bank's website. (Take a look!)

### The Bank of England's Decision-making Strategy

The Bank of England (along with most other central banks) follows a process that uses an *inflation targeting rule*. To implement its inflation targeting rule, the Bank must gather and process a large amount of information about the economy, the way it responds to shocks and the way it responds to policy. The Bank must then process all this data and come to a judgement about the best level at which to set Bank Rate.

The process begins with an exercise that uses a model of the UK economy that you can think of as a sophisticated version of the *AS–AD* model (see Chapter 14). The Bank's economists provide the MPC with a variety of forecasts and scenarios running two years into the future. Crucially the inflation rate is forecasted with probabilities assigned to each scenario so that the MPC is aware of the uncertainty and risks that surround any particular forecast.

### Review Quiz

1   What is the Bank of England's monetary policy instrument?
2   What is the main influence on the MPC's interest rate decision?
3   What happens when the Bank of England buys or sells securities in the open market?
4   How is the repo rate determined?

You can work these questions in Study Plan 16.4 and get instant feedback.

## Monetary Policy Transmission

You've seen that the Bank of England's goal is to keep the price level stable (keep the CPI inflation rate at 2 per cent a year) and to achieve maximum growth and employment (keep the output gap close to zero). And you've seen how the Bank can use its power to set Bank Rate at its desired level. We're now going to trace the events that follow a change in Bank Rate and see how those events lead to the ultimate policy goal. We'll begin with a quick overview of the transmission process and then look at each step a bit more closely.

### Overview

When the Bank of England lowers Bank Rate, other short-term interest rates and the exchange rate also fall. The quantity of money and the supply of loanable funds increase. The long-term real interest rate falls. The lower real interest rate increases consumption expenditure and investment. And the lower exchange rate makes UK exports cheaper and imports more costly. So net exports increase. Easier bank loans reinforce the effect of lower interest rates on aggregate expenditure. Aggregate demand increases, which increases real GDP and the price level relative to what they would have been. Real GDP growth and inflation speed up.

When the Bank raises Bank Rate, the sequence of events that we've just reviewed plays out but the effects are in the opposite directions.

Figure 16.12 provides a schematic summary of these ripple effects for both a cut (on the left) and a rise (on the right) in Bank Rate.

The ripple effects summarized in Figure 16.12 stretch out over a period of between one and two years but the time lags involved and the strength of each of the effects are never quite the same and are unpredictable.

The interest rate and exchange rate effects are immediate. They occur on the same day that the MPC announces its decision. Sometimes they even anticipate the decision. The effects on money and bank loans follow in a few weeks and run for a few months. Real long-term interest rates change quickly and often in anticipation of the short-term rate changes. Spending plans change and real GDP growth changes after about one year. And the inflation rate changes between one year and two years after the change in Bank Rate. But these time lags are especially hard to predict and can be longer or shorter.

We're going to look at each stage in the transmission process, starting with the interest rate effects.

**Figure 16.12**    The Ripple Effects of a Change in Bank Rate

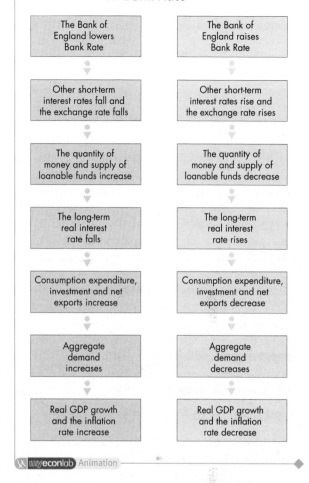

ⓜ myeconlab Animation

### Short-term Interest Rates and the Exchange Rate

As soon as the MPC announces a change in Bank Rate, other short-term interest rates change. An open-market operation changes bank reserves and the repo rate immediately moves in line with Bank Rate.

Other short-term interest rates such as those paid by the UK government on 3-month Treasury bills and by large companies on 3-month commercial bills move closely with the repo rate.

The exchange rate responds to changes in the interest rate in the UK relative to the interest rates in other countries – called *the UK interest rate differential*.

When the Bank of England raises Bank Rate, the UK interest rate differential rises and, other things remaining the same, the pound appreciates. And when the Bank lowers Bank Rate, the UK interest rate differential falls and, other things remaining the same, the pound depreciates.

## Money and Bank Loans

The quantity of money and bank loans change when the Bank of England changes Bank Rate. A rise in Bank Rate decreases the quantity of money and bank loans and a fall in Bank Rate increases the quantity of money and bank loans. These changes occur for two reasons: the quantity of money supplied by the banking system changes and the quantity of money demanded by households and firms changes.

You've seen that the Bank changes the quantity of bank reserves to keep the repo rate equal to Bank Rate. A change in the quantity of bank reserves changes the monetary base, which in turn changes the quantity of deposits and loans that the banking system can create. A rise in Bank Rate decreases reserves and decreases the quantity of deposits and bank loans created; and a fall in Bank Rate increases reserves and increases the quantity of deposits and bank loans created.

The quantity of money created by the banking system must be held by households and firms. The change in the interest rate changes the quantity of money demanded. A fall in the interest rate increases the quantity of money demanded and a rise in the interest rate decreases the quantity of money demanded.

## The Long-term Real Interest Rate

Demand and supply in the market for loanable funds determine the long-term real interest rate, which equals the long-term nominal interest rate minus the expected inflation rate. The long-term real interest rate influences expenditure decisions.

In the long run, demand and supply in the loanable funds market depend only on real forces – on saving and investment decisions. But in the short run, when the price level is not fully flexible, the supply of loanable funds is influenced by the supply of bank loans. Changes in Bank Rate change the supply of bank loans, which changes the supply of loanable funds and changes the interest rate in the loanable funds market.

A fall in Bank Rate that increases the supply of bank loans increases the supply of loanable funds and lowers the equilibrium real interest rate. A rise in Bank Rate that decreases the supply of bank loans decreases the supply of loanable funds and raises the equilibrium real interest rate.

These changes in the real interest rate, along with the change in the quantity of money and loans, change expenditure plans.

## Expenditure Plans

The ripple effects that follow a change in Bank Rate change three components of aggregate expenditure:

◆ Consumption expenditure
◆ Investment
◆ Net exports

### Consumption Expenditure

Other things remaining the same, the lower the real interest rate, the greater is the amount of consumption expenditure and the smaller is the amount of saving.

### Investment

Other things remaining the same, the lower the real interest rate, the greater is the amount of investment.

### Net Exports

Other things remaining the same, the lower the interest rate, the lower is the exchange rate and the greater are exports and the smaller are imports.

So eventually, a cut in Bank Rate increases aggregate expenditure and a rise in Bank Rate curtails aggregate expenditure. These changes in aggregate expenditure plans change aggregate demand, real GDP and the price level.

## Aggregate Demand, Real GDP and the Price Level

After a long and variable time lag, and going through the process we've just described, a rise in Bank Rate decreases aggregate demand. Similarly, a fall in Bank Rate increases aggregate demand.

These changes in aggregate demand change real GDP and the price level in the way that you studied in Chapter 14, pp. 334–339.

The Bank of England raises Bank Rate when it wants to remove an inflationary gap and lowers Bank Rate when it sees a recessionary gap. To refresh your memory on these gaps, look at Figure 14.9 on p. 337 and to see how an increase in aggregate demand changes real GDP and the price level, look back at Figure 14.10 on p. 338.

Sometimes the normal monetary policy actions that we've described aren't enough and the bank must take the extraordinary measures that we'll now examine.

# Extraordinary Monetary Stimulus

During the financial crisis and recession of 2008–2009 and its aftermath, the Bank of England took two sets of extraordinary policy actions:

◆ Deep interest rate cuts
◆ Quantitative easing

## Deep Interest Rate Cuts

The Bank of England's first and natural response to the 2007 financial crisis was to lower Bank Rate. It acted slowly at first but by March 2009, Bank Rate had been lowered to an extraordinary 0.5 per cent per year.

## Quantitative Easing

The Bank of England launched a programme of quantitative easing in March 2009. **Quantitative easing (QE)** occurs when the Bank of England creates an increase in the monetary base by buying government bonds and high grade corporate bonds in the open market. The sellers of these bonds might be commercial banks but they are also pension funds and insurance companies. The Bank set aside £200 billion for QE purchases.

QE is a type of *open market operation*. In normal times, the Bank of England performs open market operations by buying repurchase agreements, *repos*, and UK Treasury bills. These open market operations supply the quantity of reserves that enable the Bank of England to keep the repo rate close to Bank Rate.

With the large interest rate cuts after October 2008, open market purchases were used on a massive scale to keep the banks well supplied with reserves. The banks' holdings of securities fell and their reserves increased.

The Bank of England's QE open market operations take place in the market for loanable funds. With short-term interest rates as low as they can go, the goal of QE is to increase the monetary base and lower long-term interest rates.

The idea is that QE would make the banks flush with excess reserves, which they would lend to firms and households. The quantity of money would increase and asset prices would rise. With easier access to credit and greater wealth from higher asset prices, consumption expenditure and investment would increase aggregate demand and real GDP would grow more quickly.

Did QE succeed in achieving its goals? The final verdict is not yet in but a first look at the effects of QE is not encouraging.

QE did not lower long-term interest rates (although it might have prevented them from rising) and it did not bring a large increase in bank lending and the quantity of money.

Interest rates on long-term bonds had fallen from around 5 per cent in mid-2008 to around 3.25 per cent in March 2009 when QE began. From March 2009 to end 2010, interest rates on long-term bonds had no visible trend or change.

The commercial banks reserves swelled but rather than increasing loans to firms and households, the banks sat on their excess reserves. Consumers used any spare cash to pay off debt (repay loans to the banks).

The overall outcome is that the monetary base has risen but the quantity of money has not. The growth of the M4 definition of money and the money multiplier fell dramatically during 2009. And both M4 and the money multiplier remained low during 2010.

Supporters of QE say that without it the recession would be even worse and if there is a fault it is that the Bank of England has been too timid and should have employed QE on a larger scale.

The goal of these massive and unusual injections of reserves into the commercial banks was designed to ensure that the banks didn't fail. Failure would have had a ripple effect (a tsunami effect is perhaps a better metaphor) through the entire national and global financial system and would have brought an enormous crash in the quantity of money (bank deposits) in the UK economy.

### Review Quiz

1 Describe the channels by which monetary policy ripples through the economy and explain how each channel operates.
2 How do the Bank of England's actions change interest rates and the exchange rate?
3 How do the Bank of England's actions change the quantity of money and loans?
4 How do the Bank of England's actions influence real GDP and the price level (and inflation rate)?
5 What were the extraordinary policy actions taken by the Bank of England in response to the global financial crisis? Did they work?

You can work these questions in Study Plan 16.5 and get instant feedback.

To complete your study of macroeconomic policy, look at the Bank of England's dilemma in 2011 in *Reading Between the Lines* on pp. 392–393.

# Reading Between the Lines

# Monetary Policy Dilemma

The Financial Times, 1 February 2011

## Conflicting Data Paint Picture of Two-speed Economy

Norma Cohen

Conflicting data have presented a picture of a two-speed economy that is likely to sharpen the dilemma the Bank of England's policy setters face at their monthly meeting next week.

Output from the UK manufacturing sector surged to a record high in January according to a closely watched survey, with readings for new orders showing a particularly sharp rise. Offsetting that positive finding were new data showing that lending to businesses and households was very weak in December, coupled with news that the National House price survey showed a 0.1 per cent decline in January from a month earlier. . . .

The Markit/CIPS survey for the purchasing managers' index rose to 62 in January from 58.7 in December, the highest reading since the survey was created in 1992.

Underscoring the growth message – given the historical link between expansion and rising prices – the survey also flashed a danger signal on inflation. Input prices – the cost of goods the manufacturers need to assemble their products – registered their highest reading on record. Markit, which compiles the index said average purchase prices had risen at the steepest pace in the survey's history. . . .

In any case, offsetting the strong message from the manufacturing survey, were new data from the Bank showing that lending to private non-financial companies contracted again in December, that approvals for loans to buy homes fell to a 21 month low and that a key measure of money supply is contracting. . . .

Over all, the data suggest very sluggish lending to the household sector. The rate at which total net lending to households is growing, looked at over the previous six month or 12 month periods, is the slowest since the Bank began keeping records in 1988. On these measures net lending is expanding at rates of 0.4 and 0.7 per cent.

## The Essence of the Story

- A survey of purchasing managers in the manufacturing sector indicates a fast recovering UK economy.

- Bank lending to businesses is weak and new mortgage loans and house prices have fallen.

- Other data suggest a build up of inflationary pressure with input prices rising rapidly.

- With conflicting information about different parts of the economy, the recovery remains fragile.

# Economic Analysis

- The UK economy is sending conflicting signals that make it difficult to read the true strength of the recovery.

- Figure 1 shows the strong expansion of manufacturing output throughout 2010. This signal suggests a strong recovery.

- Inflationary pressure has been building up with input prices of the production industries rising at double-digit rates and CPI inflation is above the upper bound of the inflation target (see Figure 16.9, p. 385).

- Inflation expectations are also increasing. Figure 2 shows that inflation is expected to hit 4 per cent a year in 2011 and to be close to 3 per cent per year in five years.

- Both the manufacturing output and inflation data suggest a strong recovery that requires a a rise in Bank Rate and a reversal of quantitative easing (QE) to bring the inflation rate back into the target range.

- Other indicators point in the opposite direction. Figure 3 shows the rate of growth of bank lending to businesses and households, which fell throughout 2010.

- The dilemma for the Bank of England is whether it should raise Bank Rate to choke off rising inflation expectations or keep Bank Rate low and anticipate that a weakening recovery will remove the inflationary pressures.

- If the recovery really is fragile, raising Bank Rate might stop the recovery and send the economy into a double dip recession.

- If the recovery really is strong, not raising Bank Rate risks a permanent rise in the expected inflation rate, which will be costly to lower in the future.

- Making the wrong decision will increase the volatility of real GDP growth and inflation and delay the recovery. The outcome could be higher inflation or lower real GDP growth.

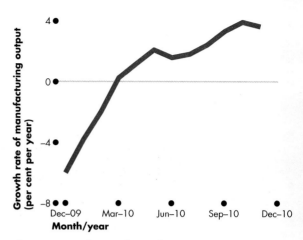

Figure 1  Growth rate of manufacturing output

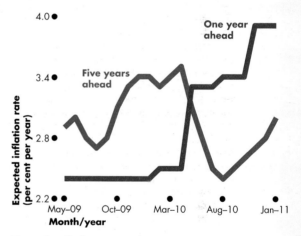

Figure 2  Inflation expectations

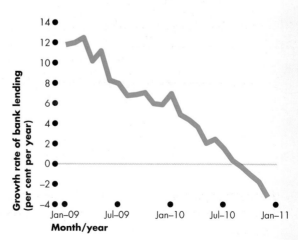

Figure 3  Growth of bank lending

**SUMMARY**

## Key Points

### Government Budgets (pp. 374–377)

◆ The government budget finances the activities of the government and is used to conduct fiscal policy.

◆ Government receipts come from taxes on income and wealth, taxes on expenditure and National Insurance contributions.

◆ When government outlays exceed receipts, the government has a budget deficit.

Working Problems 1 to 3 will give you a better understanding of government budgets.

### The Effects of Fiscal Policy

(pp. 378–383)

◆ Taxes weaken the incentive to work, save and invest and decrease employment and real GDP.

◆ Fiscal policy can be automatic or discretionary.

◆ Automatic fiscal policy might stimulate demand in recession and restrain demand in a boom.

◆ Discretionary fiscal policy has multiplier effects of uncertain magnitude.

◆ Generational accounting estimates what future generations will pay to the current generation.

Working Problems 4 to 14 will give you a better understanding of the effects of fiscal policy.

### Monetary Policy Objectives and Framework (pp. 384–386)

◆ The Bank of England Act 1998 requires the Bank to achieve stable prices and high and stable economic growth and employment.

◆ Since 2004, the Bank has been required to achieve a CPI inflation rate of 2 per cent a year.

Working Problems 15 to 17 will give you a better understanding of monetary policy objectives and framework.

### The Conduct of Monetary Policy

(pp. 386–388)

◆ Bank Rate is the monetary policy instrument.

◆ The Monetary Policy Committee (MPC) sets Bank Rate monthly.

◆ The Bank keeps the repo rate close to Bank Rate by using open market operations.

Working Problems 18 to 20 will give you a better understanding of the conduct of monetary policy.

### Monetary Policy Transmission

(pp. 389–391)

◆ A change in Bank Rate changes other interest rates, the exchange rate, the quantity of money and loans, aggregate demand and eventually real GDP and the price level.

◆ The Bank of England responded to the financial crisis with deep interest rate cuts, and quantitative easing.

Working Problems 21 to 27 will give you a better understanding of monetary policy transmission.

## Key Terms

Automatic fiscal policy, 380
Balanced budget, 375
Budget, 374
Budget deficit, 375
Budget surplus, 375
Cyclical surplus or deficit, 380
Discretionary fiscal policy, 380
Fiscal imbalance, 382
Fiscal policy, 374
Fiscal stimulus, 380
Generational accounting, 382
Generational imbalance, 383
Government debt, 376
Government expenditure multiplier, 381
Monetary policy instrument, 386
Present value, 382
Quantitative easing (QE), 391
Repo rate, 386
Structural surplus or deficit, 380
Tax multiplier, 381
Tax wedge, 378

## STUDY PLAN PROBLEMS AND APPLICATIONS

myeconlab  You can work Problems 1 to 27 in MyEconLab Chapter 16 Study Plan and get instant feedback.

## Government Budgets (Study Plan 16.1)

Use the following news clip to work Problems 1 and 2.

**The Budget**

George Osborne says he has little option but to push on with the harshest public spending cuts in living memory because a reversal would alarm the bond markets and plunge Britain into 'financial turmoil'. Responding to growing clamour for him to explore a 'plan B' for recovery, the Chancellor insisted that there would be no weakening of the government's resolve in implementing austerity measures.

Source: *The Financial Times*, 30 January 2011

1   What is the UK government's plan for fiscal policy in the budget 2010?

2   What would be a 'plan B' for the government to adopt?

3   At the end of 2008, the government of China's debt was ¥4,700 billion. (¥ is yuan, the currency of China.) In 2009, the government spent ¥6,000 billion and ended the year with a debt of ¥5,300 billion. How much did the government receive in tax revenue in 2009? How can you tell?

## The Effects of Fiscal Policy (Study Plan 16.2)

4   The government is considering raising the tax rate on labour income and asks you to report on the supply-side effects of such an action. Answer the following questions using appropriate graphs. You are being asked about *directions* of change, not exact magnitudes. What will happen to

a   The equilibrium level of employment and why?

b   Real GDP?

5   What fiscal policy might increase investment and speed economic growth? Explain how the policy would work.

6   Suppose that instead of taxing *nominal* capital income, the government taxed real capital income. Use appropriate graphs to explain and illustrate the effect that this change would have on

a   The tax rate on capital income.

b   Investment and the real interest rate.

7   The economy is in a recession, and the recessionary gap is large.

a   Describe the discretionary and automatic fiscal policy actions that might occur.

b   Describe a discretionary fiscal stimulus package that would not increase the budget deficit.

c   Explain the risks of discretionary fiscal policy in this situation.

Use the following news clip to work Problems 8 to 9.

**Obama's Economic Recovery Plan**

If the president is serious about focusing on jobs, a good start would be to freeze all tax rates and cut federal spending back to where it was before all the recent bailouts and stimulus spending.

Source: *USA Today*, 9 September 2010

8   What would be the effect on the budget deficit and real GDP of freezing tax rates and cutting government spending?

9   What would be the effect on jobs of freezing tax rates and cutting government spending?

10   The economy is in a recession, the recessionary gap is large, and there is a budget deficit.

a   Do we know whether the budget deficit is structural or cyclical? Explain your answer.

b   Do we know whether automatic stabilizers are increasing or decreasing the output gap? Explain your answer.

c   If a discretionary increase in government expenditure occurs, what happens to the structural deficit or surplus? Explain.

11   The research of economists Patrick Minford and Harald Uhlig suggests that tax cuts to stimulate the economy would pay for themselves in the long run.

a   Explain what is meant by tax cuts paying for themselves. What does this statement imply about the tax multiplier?

b   Why would tax cuts not pay for themselves?

12   What would have a larger effect on aggregate demand: $150 billion worth of tax rebates or $150 billion worth of government spending?

13   Explain whether a stimulus package centred around a one-time consumer tax rebate is likely to have a small or a large supply-side effect.

14   The Office for Budget Responsibility projects that, under current policies, public debt will reach 233 per cent of GDP in 30 years and nearly 500 per cent in 50 years.

a   What is a fiscal imbalance? How might the government reduce the fiscal imbalance?

b   How would your answer to part (a) influence the generational imbalance?

## Monetary Policy Objectives and Framework (Study Plan 16.3)

**15** 'Monetary policy is too important to be left to the MPC. The government should be responsible for it.' How is responsibility for monetary policy allocated among the MPC, Parliament, and the government?

**16** **Mervyn King Gives Warning over UK Public Deficit**

Mervyn King says the government must cut the public deficit.

Source: *BBC*, 20 January 2010

**a** Does the Governor of the Bank of England have either authority or responsibility for the UK government budget deficit?

**b** How might a government budget deficit complicate the Bank's monetary policy? [Hint: Think about the effects of a deficit on interest rates.]

**c** How might the Bank's monetary policy complicate Parliament's deficit cutting? [Hint: Think about the effects of monetary policy on interest rates.]

**17** **Inflation: Surging Fuel Costs Push CPI to 3.4 per cent**

At 3.4 per cent, consumer price inflation (CPI) is now way above the Bank of England's government-set target of 2 per cent, the highest since January and one of the steepest rates in Europe.

Source: *The Guardian*, 20 April 2010

**a** What does this news clip imply about the MPC's interest rate decisions?

**b** How can the 3.4 per cent inflation rate be reconciled with the Bank of England's obligations under the 1998 Bank of England Act?

## The Conduct of Monetary Policy

(Study Plan 16.4)

**18** How does the Bank of England hit its repo rate target? Illustrate your answer with an appropriate graph.

Use the following news clip to work Problems 19 and 20.

**Bank of England's Trade-off**

When the Bank of England's MPC meets on Thursday, it will be shaping up for its first three-way vote, amid an intensifying debate on the trade-off between apparent signs of inflation and indications that the economy is sinking into stagnation.

Source: *The Financial Times*, 6 October 2010

**19** Explain the dilemma faced by the Bank of England in October 2010.

**20** **a** Why might the MPC have decided to cut Bank Rate in the months following the October 2010 meeting?

**b** Why might the MPC have decided to raise Bank Rate in the months following the October 2010 meeting?

## Monetary Policy Transmission

(Study Plan 16.5)

**21** What are the roles of Bank Rate and the long-term interest rate in the monetary policy transmission process?

**22** **a** Is it the long-term nominal interest rate or the long-term real interest rate that influences spending decisions? Explain why.

**b** How does the market determine the long-term nominal interest rate and why doesn't it move as much as the short-term rates?

Use the following news clip to work Problems 23 and 24.

**The Pound's Sharp Fall**

Masahiro Sakane, chairman of Komatsu, the Japanese maker of construction and mining equipment, says the company's plant in north-east England will benefit from the pound's sharp fall against the euro.

Source: *The Financial Times*, 5 March 2010

**23** How does a lower sterling exchange rate influence monetary policy transmission?

**24** Would a fall in the exchange rate mainly influence unemployment or inflation?

Use the following news clip to work Problems 25 to 27.

**Shrinking Economy Shock**

The UK economy shrank in the final quarter of 2010, a shock contraction that casts doubt on the strength of growth in the industrialized world and the wisdom of early fiscal tightening.

Source: *The Financial Times*, 25 January 2011

**25** If real GDP continues to shrink, what would most likely happen to the output gap and unemployment in 2011?

**26** **a** What actions that the Bank of England had taken in 2009 and 2010 would you expect to influence UK real GDP growth in 2011? Explain how those policy actions would transmit to real GDP.

**b** Draw a graph of aggregate demand and aggregate supply to illustrate your answer to part (a).

**27** What further actions might the Bank of England take in 2011 to influence the real GDP growth rate in 2011?

# Government Budgets

**28** UK public sector net debt as a percentage of GDP in 2009/10 was 154.7 but excluding 'financial interventions' by the Bank of England, the net debt was 53.6 per cent of GDP.

Explain what accounts for this big difference in the two figures. What did the UK government do in 2008 to inflate the budget deficit and increase the debt–GDP ratio?

# The Effects of Fiscal Policy

Use the following information to work Problems 29 and 30.

Suppose that in the UK, investment is £160 billion, saving is £140 billion, government expenditure on goods and services is £150 billion, exports are £200 billion and imports are £250 billion.

**29** What is the amount of tax revenue? What is the government budget balance?

**30** **a** Is the government's budget exerting a positive or negative impact on investment?

**b** What fiscal policy action might increase investment and speed economic growth? Explain how the policy action would work.

Use the following news clip to work Problems 31 and 32.

Sir Richard Lambert, the outgoing head of the CBI, accused the government of failing to articulate a clear vision for economic growth. Commenting on the 50 per cent tax rate, he said that business investment in the UK will suffer if high paid individuals drifted elsewhere for tax reasons.

Source: *The Financial Times*, 25 January 2011

**31** Why has the UK government raised the top rate of tax to 50 per cent?

**32** What are the possible long-term consequences of such a tax rise on the supply side of the economy, for tax revenues and the budget deficit?

Use the following news clip to work Problems 33 and 34.

**Tax Hikes for Top Earners**

750,000 more people will start to pay the 40% rate of tax as a result of forthcoming tax rises. However, 500,000 people will no longer be paying income tax because the point at which income tax starts to be paid will rise. The government has

made the tax changes revenue neutral. The main gainers from the tax changes are lone parents and low income households.

Source: BBC, 31 January 2011

**33** Explain the potential effects of the tax changes on aggregate demand.

**34** Explain the potential effects of the tax changes on wages and employment.

**35** The economy is in a boom and the inflationary gap is large.

**a** Describe the discretionary and automatic fiscal policy actions that might occur.

**b** Describe a discretionary fiscal restraint package that could be used that would not produce serious negative supply-side effects.

**c** Explain the risks of discretionary fiscal policy in this situation.

**36** The economy is growing slowly, the inflationary gap is large, and there is a budget deficit.

**a** Do we know whether the budget deficit is structural or cyclical? Explain your answer.

**b** Do we know whether automatic stabilizers are increasing or decreasing aggregate demand? Explain your answer.

**c** If a discretionary decrease in government expenditure occurs, what happens to the structural budget balance? Explain your answer.

Use the following news clip to work Problems 37 to 39.

**Juicing the Economy Will Come at a Cost**

The $150-billion stimulus plan will bump up the deficit, but not necessarily dollar for dollar. Here's why: if the stimulus works, the increased economic activity will generate federal tax revenue. But it isn't clear what the cost to the economy will be if a stimulus package comes too late – a real concern since legislation could get bogged down by politics.

Source: CNN, 23 January 2008

**37** Explain why $150 billion of stimulus won't increase the budget deficit by $150 billion.

**38** Is the budget deficit arising from the action described in the news clip structural or cyclical or a combination of the two? Explain.

**39** Why might the stimulus package come 'too late'? What are the potential consequences of the stimulus package coming 'too late'?

## Monetary Policy Objectives and Framework

**40** The deep 2008–2009 recession and the overshoot of inflation above the upper bound of the target suggests that the inflation target should be raised. Do you agree? Why or why not?

**41** The European Central Bank (ECB) targets the Eurozone inflation rate to make it remain below but close to 2 per cent a year. To pursue this goal, the ECB sets the official ECB interest rate but pays close attention to the growth rate of the quantity of money.

   **a** Compare and contrast the policy objectives of the ECB and the Bank of England.

   **b** Compare and contrast the policy strategies of the ECB and the Bank of England.

## The Conduct of Monetary Policy

**42** Looking at Bank Rate since 2000, identify periods during which, with the benefit of hindsight, the rate might have been kept too low. Identify periods during which it might have been too high.

**43** Explain the dilemma that rising inflation and weakening growth poses for the Bank of England.

**44** Why might the Bank of England decide to lower interest rates when inflation is rising and growth is weakening?

**45** Why might the Bank of England decide to raise interest rates when inflation is rising and growth is weakening?

## Monetary Policy Transmission

Use the following information to work problems 46 to 48.

From 2008 to 2010 the rate of interest on UK 10-year maturity bonds fell from 4.6 per cent a year to 3.6 per cent a year. During the same period, the Bank Rate fell from 4.7 per cent a year to 0.5 per cent a year.

**46** What role does the long-term real interest rate play in the monetary policy transmission process?

**47** How does the Bank Rate influence the long-term real interest rate?

**48** What do you think happened to inflation expectations between 2008 and 2010 and why?

Use the following information to work problems 49 and 50.

Financial markets predict a 95 per cent or more certainty that rates will rise by a quarter of a percentage point in June, October and January over 2011 and 2012, leaping from 0.5 per cent to 1.25 per cent.

Source: *The Financial Times*, 24 January 2011

**49** How do expectations of the future of the interest rate influence the exchange rate?

**50** How does monetary policy influence the exchange rate?

**51** Between August 2007 when the global financial crisis started and April 2008, Bank Rate was cut from 5.75 per cent to 5 per cent. Only when the shockwaves intensified in October 2008 did the Bank of England respond with extraordinary rate cuts, dropping Bank Rate to 0.5 per cent by March 2009.

   **a** Why was the Bank of England so timid in its initial interest rate cuts in the first year of the global financial crisis?

   **b** How would you expect the massive rate cuts between October 2008 and March 2009 to influence real GDP and the inflation rate in 2009, 2010 and 2011? Describe the transmission mechanisms and the time lags.

## Economics in the News

**52** After you have studied *Reading Between the Lines* on pp. 392–393 answer the following questions.

   **a** Why does the Bank of England face a dilemma in setting monetary policy?

   **b** What would be the short-term and long-term consequences of delaying a rise in the interest rate if inflation turned out to remain above the upper bound of the target throughout 2011?

   **c** What would be the short-term and long-term consequences of raising interest rates immediately if the UK economy was weak during 2011?

   **d** What is the role of expectations in determining what the Bank of England monetary policy should be in the current period?

**53** The governor of the Bank of England Mervyn King said that inflation could reach 5 per cent a year within a few months and that this was of more concern than the surprise drop in GDP in the fourth quarter of 2010.

Source: *The Daily Telegraph*, 15 February 2011

   **a** What was the Bank of England's monetary policy throughout 2010?

   **b** Given the Governor's comments, what would you expect the Bank of England's monetary policy to be in 2011?

# Glossary

**Above full-employment equilibrium**
A macroeconomic equilibrium in which real GDP exceeds potential GDP. (p. 336)

**Absolute advantage** A person who is more productive than others has an absolute advantage. (p. 38)

**Aggregate demand** The relationship between the quantity of real GDP demanded and the price level. (p. 330)

**Allocative efficiency** A situation in which goods and services are produced at the lowest possible cost and in quantities that provide the greatest benefit. We cannot produce more of any good without giving up some of another good that we *value more highly*. (p. 33)

**Automatic fiscal policy** A fiscal policy action that is triggered by the state of the economy with no action by the government. (p. 380)

**Average cost pricing rule** A rule that sets price to cover cost including normal profit, which means setting the price equal to average total cost. (p. 192)

**Average fixed cost** Total fixed cost per unit of output. (p. 136)

**Average product** The average product of a factor of production. It equals total product divided by the quantity of the resource employed. (p. 131)

**Average total cost** Total cost per unit of output. (p. 136)

**Average variable cost** Total variable cost per unit of output. (p. 136)

**Balanced budget** A government budget in which revenues and expenditures are equal. (p. 375)

**Bank of England** The central bank of the UK. (p. 304)

**Bank Rate** The Bank of England's official interest rate. The interest rate that the Bank of England charges on secured overnight loans to the commercial banks. (p. 305)

**Barrier to entry** A legal or natural constraint that protects a firm from potential competitors. (p. 178)

**Below full-employment equilibrium**
A macroeconomic equilibrium in which potential GDP exceeds real GDP. (p. 337)

**Benefit** The benefit of something is the gain or pleasure that it brings and is determined by preferences. (p. 8)

**Big trade-off** A trade-off between equity and efficiency. (p. 95)

**Black market** An illegal trading arrangement in which the price exceeds the legally imposed price ceiling. (p. 106)

**Bond** A promise to make specified payments on specified dates. (p. 275)

**Bond market** The market in which bonds issued by firms and governments are traded. (p. 275)

**Budget** An annual statement of the government's projected outlays and receipts during the next year together with the laws and regulations that support those outlays and receipts. (p. 374)

**Budget deficit** A government's budget balance that is negative – outlays exceed receipts. (p. 375)

**Budget surplus** A government's budget balance that is positive – receipts exceed outlays. (p. 375)

**Business cycle** The periodic but irregular up-and-down movement of total production and other measures of economic activity. (p. 235)

**Capital** The tools, equipment, buildings, and other constructions that businesses now use to produce goods and services. (p. 4)

**Capital accumulation** The growth of capital resources. (p. 36)

**Capture theory** A theory of regulation that states that the regulation is in the self-interest of producers. (p. 191)

**Cartel** A group of firms that has entered into a collusive agreement to limit output and increase prices and profits. (p. 213)

***Ceteris paribus*** Other things being equal – all other relevant things remaining the same. (p. 22)

**Chain volume measure** A measure that uses the prices of two adjacent years to calculate the real GDP growth rate. (p. 244)

**Change in demand** A change in buyers' plans that occurs when some influence on those plans other than the price of the good changes. It is illustrated by a shift of the demand curve. (p. 54)

**Change in supply** A change in sellers' plans that occurs when some influence on those plans other than the price of the good changes. It is illustrated by a shift of the supply curve. (p. 59)

**Change in the quantity demanded**
A change in buyers' plans that occurs when the price of a good changes but all other influences on buyers' plans remain unchanged. It is illustrated by a movement along the demand curve. (p. 57)

**Change in the quantity supplied** A change in sellers' plans that occurs when the price of a good changes but all other influences on sellers' plans remain unchanged. It is illustrated by a movement along the supply curve. (p. 61)

**Classical** Describes a macroeconomist who believes that the economy is self-regulating and that it is always at full employment. (p. 340)

**Collusive agreement** An agreement between two (or more) producers to restrict output, raise the price, and increase profits. (p. 216)

**Command system** A method of organizing production that uses a managerial hierarchy. (pp. 84, 203)

**Comparative advantage** A person or country has a comparative advantage in an activity if that person or country can perform the activity at a lower opportunity cost than anyone else or any other country. (p. 38)

**Competitive market** A market that has many buyers and many sellers, so no single buyer or seller can influence the price. (p. 52)

**Complement** A good that is used in conjunction with another good. (p. 55)

**Constant returns to scale** Features of a firm's technology that lead to constant long-run average cost as output increases. When constant returns to scale are present, the *LRAC* curve is horizontal. (p. 142)

**Consumer Prices Index (CPI)** An index that measures the average of the prices paid by consumers for a fixed 'basket' of consumer goods and services. (p. 261)

**Consumer surplus** The value of a good minus the price paid for it, summed over the quantity bought. (p. 87)

**Consumption expenditure** The total payment for consumer goods and services. (p. 229)

**Cooperative equilibrium** The outcome of a game in which the players make and share the monopoly profit. (p. 217)

**Cost-push inflation** An inflation that results from an initial increase in costs. (p. 359)

**Crowding-out effect** The tendency for the government budget deficit to raise the real interest rate and *decrease* investment. (p. 286)

**Currency** The notes and coins held by households and firms. (p. 299)

**Currency drain ratio** The ratio of currency to deposits. (p. 308)

**Cycle** A tendency for a variable to alternate between upward and downward movements. (p. 243)

**Cyclical surplus or deficit** The actual budget balance minus the structural surplus or deficit. (p. 380)

**Cyclical unemployment** The fluctuations in unemployment over the business cycle. (p. 257)

**Deadweight loss** A measure of inefficiency. It is equal to the decrease in consumer surplus and producer surplus that results from an inefficient level of production. (p. 91)

**Deflation** A process in which the price level falls – a negative inflation. (p. 260)

**Demand** The relationship between the quantity of a good that consumers plan to buy and the price of the good when all other influences on buyers' plans remain the same. It is described by a demand schedule and illustrated by a demand curve. (p. 53)

**Demand curve** A curve that shows the relationship between the quantity demanded of a good and its price when all other influences on consumers' planned purchases remain the same. (p. 54)

**Demand for loanable funds** The relationship between the quantity of loanable funds demanded and the real interest rate when all other influences on borrowing plans remain the same. (p. 280)

**Demand for money** The relationship between the quantity of real money demanded and the interest rate – the opportunity cost of holding money – when all other influences on the amount of money that people plan to hold remain the same. (p. 311)

**Demand-pull inflation** An inflation that results from an initial increase in aggregate demand. (p. 357)

**Depreciation** The decrease in the value of a firm's capital that results from wear and tear and obsolescence. (p. 230)

**Desired reserve ratio** The ratio of the reserves to deposits that banks consider prudent to hold. (p. 308)

**Diminishing marginal returns** The tendency for the marginal product of an additional unit of a factor of production to be less than the marginal product of the previous unit of the factor. (p. 133)

**Direct relationship** A relationship between two variables that move in the same direction. (p. 16)

**Discouraged workers** People who are available and willing to work but have stopped actively looking for jobs because they believe that no jobs are available. (p. 255)

**Discretionary fiscal policy** A fiscal policy action that is initiated by the government (Chancellor of the Exchequer in the UK). (p. 380)

**Diseconomies of scale** Features of a firm's technology that lead to rising long-run average cost as output increases. (p. 142)

**Disposable income** Aggregate income minus taxes plus transfer payments. (p. 332)

**Dominant-strategy equilibrium** An equilibrium in which the best strategy of each player is to cheat *regardless of the strategy of the other player.* (p. 215)

**Duopoly** A market structure in which two producers of a good or service compete. (p. 212)

**Economic activity rate** The percentage of the working-age population who are economically active. (p. 255)

**Economically active** The people who have a job or are willing and able to take a job. (p. 253)

**Economically inactive** The people who do not want a job. (p. 253)

**Economic growth** The expansion of production possibilities that results from capital accumulation and technological change. (pp. 36, 350)

**Economic growth rate** The annual percentage change in real GDP. (p. 350)

**Economic model** A description of some aspect of the economic world that includes only those features of the world that are needed for the purpose at hand. (p. 10)

**Economic profit** A firm's total revenue minus its total cost. (p. 152)

**Economic rent** Any surplus – consumer surplus, producer surplus or economic profit. It is also the income received by the owner of a factor of production over and above the amount required to induce that owner to offer the factor for use. (p. 186)

**Economics** The social science that studies the *choices* that individuals, businesses, governments, and entire societies make and how they cope with *scarcity* and the *incentives* that influence and reconcile those choices. (p. 2)

**Economies of scale** Features of a firm's technology that lead to a falling long-run average cost as output increases. (pp. 142)

**Efficiency** A situation in which the available resources are used to produce goods and services at the lowest possible cost and in quantities that give the greatest value or benefit. (p. 5)

**Efficient scale** The quantity at which average total cost is a minimum – the quantity at the bottom of the U-shaped *ATC* curve. (p. 206)

**Elastic demand** Demand with a price elasticity greater than 1; other things remaining the same, the percentage change in the quantity demanded exceeds the percentage change in price. (p. 80)

**Elasticity of supply** The responsiveness of the quantity supplied of a good to a change in its price, other things remaining the same. (p. 81)

**Employment rate** The percentage of people of working age who have jobs. (p. 254)

**Entrepreneurship** The human resource that organizes the other three factors of production: labour, land, and capital. (p. 4)

**Equilibrium price** The price at which the quantity demanded equals the quantity supplied. (p. 62)

**Equilibrium quantity** The quantity bought and sold at the equilibrium price. (p. 62)

**European Central Bank (ECB)** The central bank of the Eurozone – the members of the EU that use the euro as their currency. (p. 304)

**Excess capacity** A firm has excess capacity if it produces below its efficient scale. (p. 206)

**Excess reserves** A bank's actual reserves minus its desired reserves. (p. 308)

**Expansion** A business cycle phase between a trough and a peak – the phase in which real GDP increases. (p. 235)

**Exports** The goods and services that we sell to people in other countries. (pp. 230)

**External diseconomies** Factors outside the control of a firm that raise the firm's costs as the industry produces a larger output. (p. 165)

**External economies** Factors beyond the control of a firm that lower the firm's costs as the industry produces a larger output. (p. 165)

**Factors of production** The productive resources that businesses use to produce goods and services. (p. 3)

**Final good** An item that is bought by its final user during the specified time period. (p. 228)

**Financial capital** The funds that firms use to buy physical capital. (p. 274)

**Financial institution** A firm that operates on both sides of the market for financial capital. It is a borrower in one market and a lender in another. (p. 276)

**Firm** An economic unit that hires factors of production and organizes those factors to produce and sell goods and services. (p. 41)

**Fiscal imbalance** The present value of the government's commitments to pay benefits minus the present value of its tax revenues. (p. 382)

**Fiscal policy** The government's attempt to influence the economy by setting and changing taxes, making transfer payments, and purchasing goods and services. (pp. 332, 374)

**Fiscal stimulus** The use of fiscal policy to increase production and employment. (p. 380)

**Frictional unemployment** The unemployment that arises from normal labour turnover – from people entering and leaving the workforce and from the ongoing creation and destruction of jobs. (p. 257)

**Full employment** A situation in which the unemployment rate equals the natural unemployment rate. At full employment, there is no cyclical unemployment – all unemployment is frictional and structural. (p. 257)

**Full-employment equilibrium** A macroeconomic equilibrium in which real GDP equals potential GDP. (p. 337)

**Game theory** A tool that economists use to analyse strategic behaviour – behaviour that takes into account the expected behaviour of others and the recognition of mutual interdependence. (p. 214)

**GDP deflator** One measure of the price level, which is an index of the prices of all the goods and services in GDP. It is calculated as nominal GDP divided by real GDP, multiplied by 100. (p. 264)

**Generational accounting** An accounting system that measures the lifetime tax burden and benefits of each generation. (p. 382)

**Generational imbalance** The division of the fiscal imbalance between the current and future generations, assuming that the current generation will enjoy the existing levels of taxes and benefits. (p. 383)

**Goods and services** The objects that people value and produce to satisfy their wants. (p. 3)

**Government debt** The total amount of borrowing by the government. It equals the sum of past budget deficits minus the sum of past budget surpluses minus plus payments to buy assets minus receipts from the sale of assets. (p. 376)

**Government expenditure** Goods and services bought by the government. (p. 230)

**Government expenditure multiplier** The magnification effect of a change in government expenditure on goods and services on equilibrium expenditure and real GDP. (p. 381)

**Gross domestic product (GDP)** The market value of all the final goods and services produced within a country during a given time period – usually a year. (p. 228)

**Gross investment** The total amount spent on purchases of new capital and on replacing depreciated capital. (pp. 230, 274)

**Human capital** The knowledge and skill that people obtain from education, on-the-job training, and work experience. (p. 3)

**Hyperinflation** An inflation rate that exceeds 50 per cent a month. (p. 260)

**Imports** The goods and services that we buy from people in other countries. (p. 230)

**Incentive** A reward that encourages an action or a penalty that discourages one. (p. 2)

**Inelastic demand** A demand with a price elasticity between 0 and 1; the percentage change in the quantity demanded is less than the percentage change in price. (p. 80)

**Inferior good** A good for which demand decreases as income increases. (p. 56)

**Inflation** A process in which the price level is rising and money is losing value. (p. 260)

**Inflationary gap** The amount by which real GDP exceeds potential GDP. (p. 336)

**Inflation rate** The annual percentage change in the price level. (p. 263)

**Interest** The income that capital earns. (p. 4)

**Intermediate good** An item that is produced by one firm, bought by another firm and used as a component of a final good or service. (p. 228)

**Inverse relationship** A relationship between variables that move in opposite directions. (p. 17)

**Investment** The purchase of new plant, equipment, and buildings and additions to inventories. (p. 229)

**Keynesian** Describes a macroeconomist who believes that left alone, the economy would rarely operate at full employment and that to achieve and maintain full employment, active help from fiscal policy and monetary policy is required. (p. 340)

**Labour** The work time and work effort that people devote to producing goods and services. (p. 3)

**Labour productivity** The quantity of real GDP produced per hour of labour. (p. 355)

**Land** The gifts of nature that we use to produce goods and services. (p. 3)

**Law of demand** Other things remaining the same, the higher the price of a good, the smaller is the quantity demanded; the lower the price of a good, the larger is the quantity demanded. (p. 53)

**Law of diminishing returns** As a firm uses more of a variable input, with a given quantity of other inputs (fixed inputs), the marginal product of the variable input eventually diminishes. (p. 133)

**Law of supply** Other things remaining the same, the higher the price of a good, the greater is the quantity supplied; the lower the price of a good, the smaller is the quantity supplied. (p. 58)

**Legal monopoly** A market structure in which there is one firm and entry is restricted by the granting of a monopoly franchise, government licence, patent or copyright. (p. 178)

**Lender of last resort** If all UK banks are short of reserves they can borrow from the Bank of England – the Bank of England is the lender of last resort in the UK. (p. 307)

**Linear relationship** A relationship between two variables that is illustrated by a straight line. (p. 16)

**Loanable funds market** The aggregate of all the individual markets in which households, firms, governments, banks and other financial institutions borrow and lend. (p. 278)

**Long run** A period of time in which the quantities of all factors of production can be varied. (p. 130)

**Long-run aggregate supply** The relationship between the quantity of real GDP supplied and the price level when the money wage rate changes in step with the price level to maintain full employment; real GDP equals potential GDP. (p. 326)

**Long-run average cost curve** The relationship between the lowest attainable average total cost and output when both capital and labour are varied. (p. 141)

**Long-run market supply curve** A curve that shows how the quantity supplied in a market varies as the market price varies after all the possible adjustments have been made, including changes in each firm's plant and the number of firms in the market. (p. 165)

**Long-run macroeconomic equilibrium** A situation that occurs when real GDP equals potential GDP – the economy is on its long-run aggregate supply curve. (p. 334)

**M4** A measure of money that consists of currency held by the public plus bank deposits and building society deposits. (p. 299)

**Macroeconomics** The study of the performance of the national economy and the global economy. (p. 2)

**Margin** When a choice is changed by a small amount or by a little at a time, the choice is made at the margin. (p. 9)

**Marginal benefit** The benefit that a person receives from consuming one more unit of a good or service. It is measured as the maximum amount that a person is willing to pay for one more unit of the good or service. (pp. 9, 34)

**Marginal benefit curve** A curve that shows the relationship between the marginal benefit of a good and the quantity of that good consumed. (p. 34)

**Marginal cost** The *opportunity cost* of producing one more unit of a good or service. It is the best alternative forgone. It is calculated as the increase in total cost divided by the increase in output. (pp. 9, 33, 136)

**Marginal cost pricing rule** A rule that sets the price of a good or service equal to the marginal cost of producing it. (p. 191)

**Marginal product** The increase in total product that results from a one-unit increase in the variable input, with all other inputs remaining the same. It is calculated as the increase in total product divided by the increase in the variable input employed, when the quantities of all other inputs are constant. (p. 131)

**Marginal revenue** The change in total revenue that results from a one-unit increase in the quantity sold. It is calculated as the change in total revenue divided by the change in quantity sold. (p. 152)

**Market** Any arrangement that enables buyers and sellers to get information and to do business with each other. (p. 42)

**Market failure** A state in which the market does not allocate resources efficiently. (p. 91)

**Markup** The amount by which the firm's price exceeds its marginal cost. (p. 207)

**Means of payment** A method of settling a debt. (p. 298)

**Microeconomics** The study of the choices that individuals and businesses make, the way those choices interact in markets and the influence governments exert on them. (p. 2)

**Minimum efficient scale** The smallest quantity of output at which the long-run average cost curve reaches its lowest level. (p. 143)

**Minimum wage** A regulation that makes the hiring of labour below a specified wage rate illegal. The lowest wage rate at which a firm may legally hire labour. (p. 109)

**Monetarist** A macroeconomist who believes that the economy is self-regulating and that it will normally operate at full employment, provided that monetary policy is not erratic and that the pace of money growth is kept steady. (p. 341)

**Monetary base** The sum of the liabilities of the Bank of England plus coins issued by the Royal Mint. (p. 305)

**Monetary financial institution** A financial firm that takes deposits from households and firms. (p. 301)

**Monetary policy** The central bank conducts a nation's monetary policy by changing interest rates and adjusting the quantity of money. (p. 332)

**Monetary Policy Committee (MPC)** The committee in the Bank of England that has the responsibility for formulating monetary policy. (p. 304)

**Monetary policy instrument** A variable that the central bank can directly control or closely target. (p. 386)

**Money** Any commodity or token that is generally acceptable as a means of payment. (pp. 42, 298)

**Money multiplier** The ratio of the change in the quantity of money to the change in monetary base. (p. 309)

**Money price** The number of pounds or euros that must be given up in exchange for a good or service. (p. 52)

**Monopolistic competition** A market structure in which a large number of firms compete by making similar but slightly different products and compete on product quality, price, and marketing and are free to enter and exit the industry. (p. 202)

**Monopoly** A market structure in which there is one firm, which produces a good or service that has no close substitute and in which the firm is protected from competition by a barrier preventing the entry of new firms. (p. 178)

**Mortgage** A legal contract that gives ownership of a home to the lender in the event that the borrower fails to meet the agreed loan payments (repayments and interest). (p. 275)

**Mortgage-backed security** A type of bond that entitles its holder to the income from a package of mortgages. (p. 276)

**Nash equilibrium** The outcome of a game that occurs when player A takes the best possible action given the action of player B and player B takes the best possible action given the action of player A. (p. 215)

**National saving** The sum of private saving (saving by households and businesses) and government saving (budget surplus). (p. 279)

**Natural monopoly** A market in which economies of scale enable one firm to supply the entire market at the lowest possible cost. (p. 178)

**Natural unemployment rate** Natural unemployment as a percentage of the labour force. The unemployment rate when the economy is at full employment – all unemployment is frictional and structural. (p. 257)

**Negative relationship** A relationship between variables that move in opposite directions. (p. 17)

**Net exports** The value of exports minus the value of imports. (p. 230)

**Net investment** Net increase in the capital stock – gross investment minus depreciation. (pp. 230, 274)

**Net taxes** Taxes paid to governments minus cash payments received from governments. (p. 278)

**Net worth** The market value of what a financial institutions has lent minus the market value of what it has borrowed. (p. 277)

**New classical** Describes a macroeconomist who holds the view that business cycle fluctuations are the efficient responses of a well-functioning market economy bombarded by shocks that arise from the uneven pace of technological change. (p. 340)

**New Keynesian** A Keynesian who holds the view that not only is the money wage rate sticky but that prices of goods and services are also sticky. (p. 341)

**Nominal GDP** The value of the final goods and services produced in a given year valued at the prices that prevailed in that same year. It is a more precise name for GDP. (p. 233)

**Nominal interest rate**  The number of pounds (or euros) that a unit of capital earns. (p. 279)

**Normal good**  A good for which demand increases as income increases. (p. 56)

**Normal profit**  The return that an entrepreneur receives. (p. 152)

**Oligopoly**  A market structure in which a small number of firms compete and natural or legal barriers prevent the entry of new firms. (p. 212)

**Open market operation**  The purchase or sale of government bonds by the central bank in the loanable funds market. (p. 305)

**Opportunity cost**  The highest-valued alternative that we give up to get something. (pp. 8, 31)

**Output gap**  Real GDP minus potential GDP. (pp. 258, 336)

**Payoff matrix**  A table that shows the payoffs for every possible action by each player for every possible action by each other player. (p. 214)

**Perfect competition**  A market in which there are many firms each selling an identical product; there are many buyers; there are no restrictions on entry into the industry; firms in the industry have no advantage over potential new entrants; and firms and buyers are well informed about the price of each firm's product. (p. 152)

**Perfectly elastic demand**  Demand with an infinite price elasticity; the quantity demanded changes by an infinitely large percentage in response to a tiny price change. (p. 80)

**Perfectly inelastic demand**  Demand with a price elasticity of zero; the quantity demanded remains constant when the price changes. (p. 80)

**Perfect price discrimination**  Price discrimination that extracts the entire consumer surplus. (p. 189)

**Positive relationship**  A relationship between two variables that move in the same direction. (p. 16)

**Potential GDP**  The quantity of real GDP at full employment – when all the economy's labour, capital, land and entrepreneurial ability are fully employed. (p. 234)

**Preferences**  A description of a person's likes and dislikes and the intensity of those feelings. (pp. 8, 34)

**Present value**  The amount of money that, if invested today, will grow to be as large as a given future amount when the interest that it will earn is taken into account. (p. 382)

**Price cap**  A government regulation that sets the maximum price that may legally be charged. (p. 106)

**Price cap regulation**  A regulation that specifies the highest price that the firm is permitted to set. (p. 193)

**Price ceiling**  A government regulation that sets the maximum price that may legally be charged. (p. 106)

**Price discrimination**  The practice of selling different units of a good or service for different prices or of charging one customer different prices for different quantities bought. (p. 179)

**Price elasticity of demand**  A units-free measure of the responsiveness of the quantity demanded of a good to a change in its price, when all other influences on buyers' plans remain the same. (p. 79)

**Price floor**  A regulation that makes it illegal to charge a price lower than a specified level. (p. 109)

**Price level**  The average level of prices. (p. 260)

**Price support**  A government guaranteed minimum price of a good. (p. 119)

**Price taker**  A firm that cannot influence the price of the good or service it produces. (p. 152)

**Producer surplus**  The price received for a good minus its minimum supply-price (or marginal cost) summed over the quantity sold. (p. 89)

**Product differentiation**  Making a product slightly different from the product of a competing firm. (p. 203)

**Production efficiency**  A situation in which the economy cannot produce more of one good without producing less of some other good. (p. 31)

**Production possibilities frontier**  The boundary between the combinations of goods and services that can be produced and the combinations that cannot. (p. 30)

**Production quota**  An upper limit to the quantity of a good that may be produced in a specified period. (p. 117)

**Production subsidy**  A payment made by the government to a producer for each unit produced. (p. 118)

**Profit**  The income earned by entrepreneurship. (p. 4)

**Property rights**  Legally established titles to the ownership, use and disposal of anything that people value, and which are enforceable in the courts. (p. 42)

**Quantitative easing (QE)**  Lending on repurchase agreements to inject reserves into commercial banks. (pp. 307, 391)

**Quantity demanded**  The amount of a good or service that consumers plan to buy during a given time period at a particular price. (p. 53)

**Quantity supplied**  The amount of a good or service that producers plan to sell during a given time period at a particular price. (p. 58)

**Quantity theory of money**  The proposition that in the long run, an increase in the quantity of money brings an equal percentage increase in the price level. (p. 314)

**Rate of return regulation**  A regulation that requires the firm to justify its price by showing that the price enables it to earn a specified target per cent return on its capital. (p. 192)

**Rational choice**  A choice that compares costs and benefits and achieves the greatest benefit over cost for the person making the choice. (p. 8)

**Rational expectation**  The most accurate forecast possible – a forecast that uses all the available relevant information. (p. 362)

**Real business cycle theory** A theory that regards random fluctuations in productivity as the main source of economic fluctuations. (p. 364)

**Real GDP** The value of final goods and services produced in a given year when valued at the prices of a reference base year. (p. 233)

**Real GDP per person** Real GDP divided by the population. (pp. 234, 350)

**Real interest rate** The quantity of goods and services that a unit of capital earns. It is the nominal interest rate adjusted for inflation and is approximately equal to the nominal interest rate minus the inflation rate. (p. 279)

**Recession** A business cycle phase in which real GDP decreases for at least two successive quarters. (p. 235)

**Recessionary gap** The amount by which potential GDP exceeds real GDP. (p. 337)

**Reference base period** The period in which the CPI or RPI is defined to be 100. (p. 261)

**Regulation** Rules administered by a government agency to influence prices, quantities, entry and other aspects of economic activity in a firm or industry. (p. 191)

**Relative price** The ratio of the price of one good or service to the price of another good or service. A relative price is an opportunity cost. (p. 52)

**Rent** The income that land earns. (p. 4)

**Rent ceiling** A regulation that makes it illegal to charge a rent higher than a specified level. (p. 106)

**Rent seeking** The pursuit of wealth – any attempt to capture a consumer surplus, a producer surplus, or an economic profit. (p. 186)

**Repo** A repurchase agreement in which a commercial bank sells a government bond to the Bank of England and simultaneously agrees to *repurchase* it (buy it back) usually two weeks later. (p. 304)

**Repo rate** The interest rate in the repo market. (p. 386)

**Required reserve ratio** The ratio of reserves to deposits that banks are required, by regulation, to hold. (p. 302)

**Reserves** Cash in a bank's vault plus its deposit at the central bank. (p. 301)

**Retail Prices Index (RPI)** An index that measures the average of the prices paid by consumers for a fixed 'basket' of consumer goods and services. (p. 261)

**Rule of 70** A rule that states that the number of years it takes for the level of a variable to double is approximately 70 divided by the annual percentage growth rate of the variable. (p. 350)

**Saving** The amount of income that households have left after they have paid their taxes and bought their consumption goods and services. (p. 274)

**Scarcity** Our inability to satisfy all our wants. (p. 2)

**Scatter diagram** A diagram that plots the value of one economic variable against the value of another for a number of different values of each variable. (p. 14)

**Search activity** The time spent looking for someone with whom to do business. (p. 106)

**Self-interest** The choices that you think are the best for you. (p. 5)

**Short run** The period of time in which the quantity of at least one factor of production is fixed and the quantities of the other factors can be varied. The fixed factor is usually capital – that is, the firm has a given plant size. (p. 130)

**Short-run aggregate supply** The relationship between the quantity of real GDP supplied and the price level when the money wage rate, the prices of other factors of production and potential GDP remain constant. (p. 327)

**Short-run market supply curve** A curve that shows how the quantity supplied in a market varies as the market price varies when the each firm's plant and the number of firms remain the same. (p. 158)

**Short-run macroeconomic equilibrium** A situation that occurs when the quantity of real GDP demanded equals the short-run quantity of real GDP supplied – at the point of intersection of the *AD* curve and the *SAS* curve. (p. 334)

**Shutdown point** The output and price at which the firm just covers its total variable cost. In the short run, the firm is indifferent between producing the profit-maximizing output and shutting down temporarily. (p. 156)

**Signal** An action taken by an informed person (or firm) to send a message to uninformed people or an action taken outside a market that conveys information that can be used by that market. (p. 210)

**Single-price monopoly** A monopoly that must sell each unit of its output for the same price to all its customers. (p. 179)

**Slope** The change in the value of the variable measured on the *y*-axis divided by the change in the value of the variable measured on the *x*-axis. (p. 20)

**Social interest** Choices that are the best for society as a whole. (p. 5)

**Social interest theory** A theory that politicians supply the regulation that achieves an efficient allocation of resources. (p. 191)

**Stagflation** The combination of inflation and recession. (pp. 339, 360)

**Stock** A certificate of ownership and claim to the firm's profits. (p. 276)

**Stock market** A financial market in which shares of stocks of corporations are traded. (p. 276)

**Strategies** All the possible actions of each player in a game. (p. 214)

**Structural surplus or deficit** The budget balance that would occur if the economy were at full employment and real GDP were equal to potential GDP. (p. 380)

**Structural unemployment** The unemployment that arises when changes in technology or international competition change the skills needed to perform jobs or change the locations of jobs. (p. 257)

**Substitute**  A good that can be used in place of another good. (p. 55)

**Sunk cost**  The past expenditure on a plant that has no resale value. (p. 130)

**Supply**  The relationship between the quantity of a good that producers plan to sell and the price of the good when all other influences on sellers' plans remain the same. It is described by a supply schedule and illustrated by a supply curve. (p. 58)

**Supply curve**  A curve that shows the relationship between the quantity supplied and the price of a good when all other influences on producers' planned sales remain the same. (p. 58)

**Supply of loanable funds**  The relationship between the quantity of loanable funds supplied and the real interest rate when all other influences on lending plans remain the same. (p. 281)

**Symmetry principle**  A requirement that people in similar situations be treated similarly. (p. 96)

**Tax incidence**  The division of the burden of a tax between the buyer and the seller. (p. 111)

**Tax multiplier**  The quantitative effect of a change in taxes on real GDP. (p. 381)

**Tax wedge**  The gap between the before-tax and after-tax wage rates. (p. 378)

**Technological change**  The development of new goods and better ways of producing goods and services. (p. 36)

**Time-series graph**  A graph that measures time (for example, months or years) on the $x$-axis and the variable or variables in which we are interested on the $y$-axis. (p. 242)

**Total cost**  The cost of all the factors of production that a firm uses. (p. 135)

**Total fixed cost**  The cost of the firm's fixed inputs. (p. 135)

**Total product**  The maximum output that a given quantity of factors of production can produce. (p. 131)

**Total revenue**  The value of a firm's sales. It is calculated as the price of the good multiplied by the quantity sold. (p. 152)

**Total surplus**  The sum of consumer surplus and producer surplus. (p. 90)

**Total variable cost**  The cost of all the firm's variable inputs. (p. 135)

**Trade-off**  An exchange – giving up one thing to get something else. (p. 8)

**Transactions costs**  The costs that arise from finding someone with whom to do business, of reaching an agreement about the price and other aspects of the exchange, and of ensuring that the terms of the agreement are fulfilled. The opportunity costs of conducting a transaction. (p. 93)

**Trend**  The general tendency for a variable to move in one direction. (p. 243)

**Unemployment rate**  The percentage of the people in the labour force who are unemployed. (p. 254)

**Unit elastic demand**  Demand with a price elasticity of 1; the percentage change in the quantity demanded equals the percentage change in price. (p. 80)

**Utilitarianism**  A principle that states that we should strive to achieve 'the greatest happiness for the greatest number of people'. (p. 94)

**Velocity of circulation**  The average number of times a pound (or euro) of money is used annually to buy the goods and services that make up GDP. (p. 314)

**Wages**  The income that labour earns. (p. 4)

**Wealth**  The market value of all the things that people own. (p. 274)

**Workforce**  The sum of the people who are employed and who are unemployed. (p. 253)

**Working-age population**  The total number of men aged 16 to 64 and women aged 16 to 59 who are not in prison, hospital or some other form of institutional care. (p. 253)

# Index

Note: key terms and pages on which they are defined appear in **bold**.

# Publisher's Acknowledgements

We are grateful to the following for permission to reproduce copyright material:

## Text

Extract on page 44 after Crop Switch Worsens Global Food Price Crisis, *The Guardian*, 05/04/2008 (Vidal, J.), Copyright Guardian News & Media Ltd 2008; Extract on page 98 after Volcano Cloud Hangs Over European Economy, *The Associated Press*, 19/04/2010 (Odula, T.); Extract on page 122 after Government Support to Farmers Rises Slightly in OECD Countries, *OECD News Release*, 01/07/2010, OECD (2010), Government support to farmers rises slightly in OECD countries, News Release 01/07/2010, http://www.oecd.org/agriculture/policies; Extract on page 170 after Kenyan Tea Growers say Strike has Little Impact, *reuters.com, 10/22/2010 Issue*, 22/10/2010 (Denge, M.); Extract on page 194 after Google under Investigation for Alleged Breach of EU Competition Rule, *The Telegraph*, 24/02/2010 (Ahmed, K.), copyright © Telegraph Media Group Limited; Extract on page 220 adapted from The Tablet Computer Has Gone Mainstream, *The Telegraph online*, 21/10/2010 (Beaumont, C.), copyright © Telegraph Media Group Limited.

## The Financial Times

Extract on page 70 from Coffee Surges on Poor Colombian Harvests, *The Financial Times*, 30/07/2010 (Blas, J.); Extract on page 240 from Employers Fear Recovery is in Peril from Spending Cuts, *The Financial Times*, 06/10/2010 (Pimlotte, D.); Extract on page 266 adapted from Measuring up with a Tale of Two Indices, *The Financial Times*, 14/09/2010 (Giles, C.); Extract on page 290 after Eurozone Nations are Prepared to Slash Spending, *The Financial Times*, 25/10/2010 (Pimlott, D.); Extract on page 316 after ECB Forced to Act as Crisis Fears Rise, *The Financial Times*, 08/11/2010 (Atkins, R., Oakley, D. and Wise, P.); Extract on page 342 adapted from Domestic Demand Spurs Growth in Germany, *The Financial Times*, 12/01/2011 (Atkins, R. and Peel, Q.); Extract on page 366 adapted from China's Twilight Economy Piles Pressure on Inflation Fight, *The Financial Times*, 21/11/2010 (Kynge, J.); Extract on page 392 after Conflicting Data Paint Picture of Two-speed Economy, *The Financial Times*, 01/02/2011 (Cohen, N.).

## Cartoons

Cartoon on page 2 from Frank Modell/The New Yorker Collection/www.cartoonbank.com; Cartoon on page 91 from Mike Twohy/The New Yorker Collection/www.cartoonbank.com; Cartoon on page 190 from *Voodoo Economics*, Chronicle Books (William Hamilton 1992) p. 3.

## Photographs

(Key: b-bottom; c-centre; l-left; r-right; t-top)

**airbus.com:** Airbus S.A.S 2010 41; **Alamy Images:** ACE STOCK LIMITED 236l, Adrian Sherratt 237l, Alex Segre 227, Caro 236r, Catchlight Visual Services 237r, Charles Polidano / Touch The Skies 129, China Images 349, David Hancock 177, David Levenson 325, Imagestate Media Partners Limited – Impact Photos 163r, Jeff Morgan 02 1, Johnny Greig 251, Juice Images 151, Mark Fagelson 161, Picture Contact BV 99, Picturebank 83, Simon James 297, sportsphotographer.eu 201, vario images GmbH & Co.KG 143; **Corbis:** Dave Reede / All Canada Photos 29; **Fotolia.com:** Chadaeva Tolkunay 65, Sabine 6l, terex 163l; **Getty Images:** Alexey SAZONOV / AFP 67, Andy Wong / AFP / Getty Images 373, BEN STANSALL / AFP 7, Bloomberg 277t, 383, Bloomberg 277t, 383, Christopher Furlong 105, Fox Photos 252, Kevork Djansezian 51, Rama Lakshmi / TWP 5, Torn Williams 383t; **John Tamblyn:** Prelims; **Patrick Minford:** 383b; **Pearson Education Ltd:** Photodisc. Photolink 6r; **Press Association Images:** Charles Dharapak 332l, Christian Lutz 332tr, J. Scott Applewhite 332tc, Johnny Green / PA Archive 273, 332bc, The Canadian Press, Sean Kilpatrick 332br; **Reuters:** Jason Reed 277b, Kevin Lamarque 289; **Robert Barro, Harvard University:** 383c; **Science & Society Picture Library:** National Railway Museum 356.

In some instances we have been unable to trace the owners of copyright material, and we would appreciate any information that would enable us to do so.